KT-195-618

High-Performance Training for Sports

David Joyce
Daniel Lewindon

Editors

NORWICH CITY COLLEGE

Stock No.	253 861		
Class	613.711 JOY		
Cat.	NH	Proc	3WL

Human Kinetics

253 861

Library of Congress Cataloging-in-Publication Data

High-performance training for sports / David Joyce, Daniel Lewindon, editors.
   pages cm.
 Includes bibliographical references and index.
1. Sports--Physiological aspects. 2. Physical education and training. I. Joyce, David, 1976-
RC1235.H54 2014
613.7'11--dc23

              2013042014

ISBN-10: 1-4504-4482-2 (print)
ISBN-13: 978-1-4504-4482-8 (print)

Copyright © 2014 by David Joyce and Dan Lewindon

All rights reserved. Except for use in a review, the reproduction or utilization of this work in any form or by any electronic, mechanical, or other means, now known or hereafter invented, including xerography, photocopying, and recording, and in any information storage and retrieval system, is forbidden without the written permission of the publisher.

This publication is written and published to provide accurate and authoritative information relevant to the subject matter presented. It is published and sold with the understanding that the author and publisher are not engaged in rendering legal, medical, or other professional services by reason of their authorship or publication of this work. If medical or other expert assistance is required, the services of a competent professional person should be sought.

The web addresses cited in this text were current as of February 2014, unless otherwise noted.

Associate Acquisitions Editor: Chris Wright
Developmental Editor: Cynthia McEntire
Managing Editor: Elizabeth Evans
Copyeditor: Ann Prisland
Indexer: Nan N. Badgett
Permissions Manager: Martha Gullo
Cover Designer: Jonathan Kay
Photograph (cover): Image Source / Aurora Photos
Photographs (interior): © Human Kinetics, unless otherwise noted
Photo Asset Manager: Laura Fitch
Visual Production Assistant: Joyce Brumfield
Photo Production Manager: Jason Allen
Art Manager: Kelly Hendren
Associate Art Manager: Alan L. Wilborn
Illustrations: © Human Kinetics, unless otherwise noted
Printer: Premier Print Group

We thank Rugby WA in Floreat, Western Australia, and Edith Cowan University in Joondalup, Western Australia, for assistance in providing the location for the photo shoot for this book.

Human Kinetics books are available at special discounts for bulk purchase. Special editions or book excerpts can also be created to specification. For details, contact the Special Sales Manager at Human Kinetics.

Printed in the United States of America   10 9 8 7 6 5 4 3 2

Website: www.HumanKinetics.com

United States: Human Kinetics
P.O. Box 5076, Champaign, IL 61825-5076
800-747-4457
e-mail: humank@hkusa.com

Canada: Human Kinetics
475 Devonshire Road Unit 100, Windsor, ON N8Y 2L5
800-465-7301 (in Canada only)
e-mail: info@hkcanada.com

Europe: Human Kinetics
107 Bradford Road, Stanningley, Leeds LS28 6AT, United Kingdom
+44 (0) 113 255 5665
e-mail: hk@hkeurope.com

Australia: Human Kinetics
57A Price Avenue, Lower Mitcham, South Australia 5062
08 8372 0999
e-mail: info@hkaustralia.com

New Zealand: Human Kinetics
P.O. Box 80, Torrens Park, South Australia 5062
0800 222 062
e-mail: info@hknewzealand.com

E5891

High-Performance Training for Sports

Contents

Foreword

Mark Verstegen
President and Founder, EXOS, TeamEXOS.com

I am truly excited for the publication of *High-Performance Training for Sports*. Rarely does a globally-respected group of diverse professionals come together to contribute to a singular work like this book. It is a daunting task to take such talented contributors who each posses such depth and breadth of subject-matter expertise to play such a defined role within the total scope of the work. The closest analogy in the athletic world is probably when you create a national team of stars who must align to the greater good of the country, their coaches and their teammates. We all know the winning formula usually has to do with the quality of the people and culture that comprise their leadership. This book is a shining example of that.

David Joyce and Daniel Lewindon are exceptional people, practitioners and visionary leaders who had the courage to bring these globally-respected subject-matter experts together as one team for the benefit of all the interrelated fields that help athletes and teams achieve their goals. This is what we do every day at EXOS (formerly Athletes' Performance and Core Performance), as well. We work together to upgrade lives by designing and delivering health and performance game plans.

High-Performance Training for Sports brings the invaluable and rich global perspective of best practices from the leaders who are working hard to research and apply this knowledge and experience on a daily basis. The contributors are to be commended for their openness and passion in creating such powerful work for all to benefit.

Much insightful information is presented for our application. Yes, each situation and each athlete is unique and you must take into account the existing culture, athlete mix, goals, priorities, resources, teammates, facilities and role you play within the organization. But you can readily find ways to use the rich knowledge in this book. Here's a recommendation: At the end of each chapter hand-write three actionable points of implementation into your current situation. Then try them out and see how they upgrade your system and benefit your athletes.

What those of us in this profession love most about what we do is directly helping others achieve what is important to them. And with this comes an incredible responsibility to make sure we are leaving no ethical stone unturned to help them realize their dreams.

We should all thank the winning team of *High-Performance Training for Sports* for reinforcing what we currently know and extending our knowledge in an approachable way, allowing us to start applying the information on our next Monday. Moreover, we should embrace the winning, collaborative culture that made this book possible. For it is that eagerness to share our expertise and knowledge across professional fields that will ensure a strong future for our respective professions and advance us further toward our collective goal of proactive health through human performance.

Introduction:
Understanding Modern Athletes

David Joyce
Western Force Rugby, Australia and Edith Cowan University, Australia

Daniel Lewindon
Rugby Football Union, UK

There is a vast difference between elite athletes of today compared to those from previous generations. The rules and objectives of the sports may be similar, but the processes undertaken to be the best in the world are markedly different. Sacrifices have always been made to be number one, but the increasing significance and popularity of sport on the world stage has meant becoming an athlete is a career choice that requires total attention and commitment, forsaking all others.

No single athlete is an island, however. Whilst an Olympic gold medal may be awarded to an individual athlete, it actually is a symbol of the success of the team and the process that has supported that individual. The slogan painted on the wall of the dining hall at the London Olympics in 2012 claiming "none of us is as good as all of us" is a poignant reminder of the necessary teamwork behind the scenes required for sport honours.

For many years, the world of business has led the way in terms of strategic thinking, process management and contingency planning, not to mention best-practice team structures. This has spawned a strong philosophical basis with respect to world-class practice. Currently, there is a growing awareness of the lessons to be learned from business that can be applied to the sport world.

Sport success requires long-term planning, stability and commitment from CEO to masseur, all with a singular vision of improving performance. In this way, high-performance sport is no longer a goal attainable for the committed amateur. It is a goal that needs careful and considered planning.

The top athletes of today have all been carefully nurtured since they were adolescents, or in some cases, since they were children. They have been identified as genetically gifted and sufficiently talented and then groomed and progressively exposed to a training and competitive environment aimed at building a top adult performer.

Over the last decade, much has changed in the field of athletic preparation. New technology development and ever-advancing physiological research has meant that what was considered cutting edge 10 years ago is now considered old and outdated. The high-performance landscape now would be virtually unrecognizable to someone witnessing it from the turn of the century.

Determinants of Sport Success

To be an elite sportperson requires a combination of technical and tactical skill, physical capacities and vast reserves of psychological and emotional strength. Sport cultures around the world place different values on these components. For example, Asian sport success is based on a blueprint of technical superiority, and the training culture in Asia builds vast reserves of mental resilience. The Western Hemispheric model of success is often (but not always) predicated by physiological superiority. These approaches are not dichotomous, of course, but reflect more a difference in emphasis.

It is our opinion that the ideal model is a combination of the two hemispheres, one in which physical, technical and tactical skills are developed, a structure of psychological strength is emphasised and all this is developed within an organisational culture that is uncompromising in its pursuit of excellence.

Aims of Performance Training

Every sport requires careful, precise execution of skills. Even a sport that is largely the domain of physiological prowess, such as track cycling, requires immense skill to avoid the energy leaks that dissipate the power generated by the athlete.

The aim of performance training is twofold:

1. Develop the physiological reserves to be able to perform the tasks of the sport to a higher level and with less decay over time than opponents. Put simply, athletes aim to take opponents to a red zone more often than the opponents can handle. This red zone can be more skill orientated, such as in table tennis or fencing; it can be more mentally orientated, such as in golf; it can be more physically orientated, such as in cycling; or it can be a combination of all these domains. In fact, a strong argument can be made that success in most sports requires asserting red-zone superiority in all these domains.

2. Be robust enough to withstand the technical and tactical training without getting injured.

Developing Athleticism to Support Technical Skill

The aim of athletic training should be to enable the individual to tolerate training loads and therefore maximise his or her exposure to technical and tactical coaching. This is evident in a sport such as diving but can also be applied to sports such as swimming and rowing, in which it can be argued that the difference between first and fourth is unlikely to be due to physical fitness but instead to technical proficiency and mental resiliency.

What is clear, however, is that without this physical base, an athlete's ability to tolerate the thousands of hours of training required for technical expertise is dramatically compromised.

Seeing the Wood, Not Just the Trees

Given the unprecedented rise in both the profile and riches in elite sport, it is natural that there is increasing importance placed on every area that contributes to sport performance. It is no longer enough to look at improving a single area and expecting across-the-board improvements.

Let's use cross country running as an example. It is easy to think that the point of difference is aerobic capacity. If we compare the difference between a world-class performer and a club runner, we will undoubtedly see a difference in aerobic fitness level. The difference between first and eighth in the world championships, though, is unlikely to be the size of the aerobic engine. It is more likely to be differences in strength, movement efficiency or tactical ability. We can see, therefore, that if we want to really enhance performance, we need to look across many areas. This is even more critical in team sport in which there are greater numbers of moving parts that will determine the outcome.

Significantly financed organisations may have the ability to employ experts in all areas of performance, but the reality for most coaches is that this is simply not possible. As such, an appreciation and understanding of a wide variety of contributors to sport success is needed. The aim of this book is to facilitate this objective.

High-Performance Programme

The environment that surrounds the athlete or team will vary considerably according to the financial resources available. Irrespective of this, though, it is important for every organisation to have a clear vision of what a good environment looks like, which extends to facilities, equipment and staff.

In many instances, we find that the programme is king. By this, we mean that the training is planned but inflexible. The athlete is then expected to be shoehorned into the programme; there is little individualisation. This approach is attractive in that it requires less work and can be replicated year after year. This philosophy is flawed, however, because it relies on the premise that all athletes have the same needs, and the belief that the state of athletes is consistent over time.

We can see clearly that this is not the case. Indeed, this point is articulately explained in almost every chapter in this text, but is specifically covered in chapters 1 and 6. Athletes are not clones, and their responses to training and competition vary from day to day, week to week, month to month and season to season. Of course, this is not even factoring in the other stresses—financial, relational, educational—that all athletes are subject to. If the programme is king, we disregard all these variables, and as a consequence, it will largely be down to chance if our programmes are perfectly appropriate for each athlete at that particular time.

Bespoke Programming

With this in mind, then, the ideal model is unquestionably one in which the athlete is placed at the centre, and appropriate bespoke programmes are installed according to the athlete's needs.

Take, for example, a basketball team. Likely within this group there will be vast differences in athletic capacities, training and injury histories, weaknesses and asymmetries, to mention but a few variables. The athlete-centred approach examines the relative needs of each individual and then programmes appropriately to take each athlete on a journey.

This is particularly important when the group's age and training profile is disparate. Older athletes may not need the same in-season load as younger athletes. Likewise, it is folly to subject a developing athlete who has just broken into the senior squad to the same training load as a seasoned veteran, who has a body adapted over the years to the rigors of training. The programme-is-king approach fails to discriminate.

This bespoke approach often does take some explaining to the playing group, though, especially to those athletes who are accustomed to everyone sharing the pain in training. Some players in team sport do not like being given days off, because in their own minds, they feel as though they are letting down their teammates. Alternatively, hackles can be raised within the playing group if a member is seen to be treated differently.

The way to get around this is to explain to the group as a whole the philosophy of athlete-centred programming and how this may mean that not everyone will be doing the same thing at the same time. Some will be resting when others are working hard. This is nothing personal; it is just that bespoke training is the best way to ensure the group is optimally prepared for competition.

This approach is labour intensive, however; it essentially means that the athletic performance coaches have to design and deliver separate programmes to each member of the team. This is not as insurmountable as it seems, though, because inevitably common threads will run through the team at any given time. As a result, the individual tailoring comes from modifications to the theme with specific work-ons factored into each programme to ensure that athletic or injury risk factors are addressed.

Interdisciplinary Work

In order for this athlete-centred approach to become a reality, the organisation should embrace a framework of interdisciplinary work. This differs from the multidisciplinary environment often spouted as being the ideal. Multidisciplinary structures involve many professions (fitness, medical, coaching, psychology, nutrition, and so on) working independently of each other while providing input to the athlete or team.

Interdisciplinary structures, however, embrace a philosophy of collaborative problem solving and input into an athlete's programme. This distinction seems down to semantics, but in reality it is much more significant a mind shift. Instead of having a framework consisting of multiple silos in which each profession works independently, interdisciplinary structures essentially work together as one, embracing the fact that on occasion, a certain member of the managerial staff will have a greater role than the others due to the particular problem being faced.

Culture of Success

Establishing this framework of an open, challenging and supportive interdisciplinary team is vital, but it will be effective only if a culture of success is driven by all stakeholders, including executives, coaches, athletic performance staff and athletes or players. In order for this culture to be established, it is vital that all stakeholders share the same collective vision, one in which the motivation to win and be successful as a group overrides any one individual's desire for personal glory. Fame and adulation often follow success, but these trappings should not be the motivation, or at some stage creep will occur within the culture, and the power of the group will diminish. Often the desire to go the extra yard in the final minute is not born out of physical superiority but rather comes from a deep-seated desire to succeed for your teammates.

Within successful teams, culture is held in extremely high regard and at its most successful if driven by the playing group themselves, who set the standards in training intensity and quality and apply those expectations to everyone in the group. Furthermore, in our experience, these personal and professional standards extend beyond the training field into an athlete's everyday life. The significance of this quality cannot be overemphasised.

Mental Resilience

The characteristic that all truly world-class athletes have in common is a fierce desire to be the best and to do whatever it takes to get there. Sport at this level demands more than most people are willing to give. It requires a dedication and a tolerance of self-inflicted pain and sacrifice that is so great that it would disturb most people. The absolute elite all have an inner switch that allows them to keep going when all else have given in. This can be a difficult and even frightening concept to understand. It is, however, the reality of high-performance sport, and to truly excel requires this dedication. We must acknowledge, though, that unfortunately this competitive desire can be so strong that it forces people into unethical or illegal territories, which is why we will always need the boundaries to be vigilantly patrolled.

There is now a burgeoning recognition that mental toughness is one of the primary determinants of sport success. For many years, we have attempted to identify athletic talent on the basis of anthropometric or physiological qualities, which has been successful up to a point. Although there are many mentally tough people who never made it due to a lack of physical attributes, what is certain is the fact that every world-class performer has an inner belief and psychological robustness that can overcome any physical shortcomings.

It is beyond the scope of this book to discuss performance psychology in the depth that it deserves, but it would be remiss not to acknowledge the pivotal role mental resilience plays in sport success. In fact, many professional organisations now profile and scrutinise young athletes for this quality before signing them.

It is clear that high performance is about having a composite of physical, technical and mental attributes that, when combined, create an athlete capable of repeatedly displaying superior physical prowess and executing skills under the most extreme of pressures. This book is aimed at enabling the coach to develop the physical aspects of high performance.

Vital to remember at this point, though, is that it is folly to assume that these three areas are separate. All things being equal, it is the athlete who holds an inner belief that he or she is better prepared physically who will likely have the resilience to overcome opponents when it comes down to the crunch. Likewise, the capacity to display technical excellence without decay in the final moments of competition is largely contingent on the existence of an impressive athletic base. No single aspect of high performance exists as an island, and improvements in one domain are likely to enhance performance as a whole.

Challenges Faced by the Modern Athlete

The quest to be the best athlete in a given sport does not rest solely on an individual's ability to train hard. In days past, all but the top athletes needed employment outside of sport in order to put food on the table. They had to source their own medical care, nutritional supplements, equipment and the like. These days, being a sportperson is an occupation in the same way that being an accountant, plumber or nurse is. The most recognisable athletes all comfortably subsist on the backs of their sport exploits and do not have to worry about researching the best supplements or rehabilitation programmes, let alone buying their own training shoes.

Therefore, it is easy to think that modern athletes have nothing to preoccupy their minds other than their sport. Certainly, this is the aim of many sport directors who want to remove any extraneous preoccupations from their athletes. Undoubtedly, this has enabled our current stars to reach heights of athletic performance never before seen, but this comes at its own cost as well.

Current athletes are not under less pressure than past athletes, just different pressure. Arguably, expectations placed on our young sportpeople are greater than ever. Not only are they expected to perform well in competition, but they are also pressed by the media and public into being role models, which is a huge burden. Our current generation is faced with new challenges such as social media and the access the public now has to them over this platform. Athletes are subject to the whims of popular opinion, and it takes a strong will to be able to ignore them.

Undoubtedly, today's athletes have the world open to them, but if all athletes have to think about is the sport, and they concentrate all their attention into it, when things are not going well, there often is no outlet. Our physiological response to stress has not changed in thousands of years, which is why we must embrace a holistic model of care for athletes, one that recognises that training is not the only stress placed on them.

Understanding Context

It is the aim of this text to provide the reader with a deep understanding of the physical training of athletes. However, this does not in itself guarantee transference into sport success. There is a need to understand the context within which this knowledge can be applied. Successful application also requires a deep appreciation of the sport itself and the individual athletes. Each person will respond differently to training due to differences in genetics, personality, training and injury history, outside influences and beliefs.

This is why it is so important to understand the context and environment in which we operate. Much of the success of any programme will depend on how well the concepts are communicated in the given environment. The world's best programme on paper will have no purchase and therefore no effect if it is not communicated well.

Vision of This Text

With so much riding on the physical preparation of athletes, there is a need for best practices to be communicated among those working in high performance around the world. Innovations in the field of sport and exercise science in the last decade have meant that many of the publications on the shelves today contain information that needs updating. This resource not only provides this update but also presents the information in a new way. The concepts that are advanced in this text will provide an intimate insight into the world of high performance.

The topics covered in this book present cutting-edge performance science in a manner that allows the information to be of immediate and practical relevance. It is hoped that the information presented will stimulate discussions and facilitate a change in practice to one that is an accurate representation of what is truly considered to be high performance.

Experts

The task of maximising human performance involves the pursuit of excellence in a number of areas. This book is the result of a collaboration of people who are recognised as world leaders in each domain of athletic performance, all writing about their own specific areas of expertise. They explain what best practice is in their fields and bring to life what the research says about their fields. In this way, some of the world's best people are effectively distilling the research and methods of world-class practice and providing the reader with the best ways to *apply* the science.

These authors have been selected according to three criteria:

1. Their experience, record and worldwide reputation within their specific branch of applied athletic performance
2. Their ability to apply the latest research in a practical and pragmatic manner
3. Their ability to communicate best-practice principles in such a way that they are immediately understandable and applicable to the reader

This book is the product of the collaboration of world leaders in high-performance sport for disseminating not just the science behind world-class athletic performance, but more importantly, the *application* of this science in the real world. Our vision is for this book to be a manual that is immediately applicable to any athlete, coach or support professional involved in activities in which physical performance is paramount. This focus is not limited to traditional sports, with military and industrial athletes also requiring elite physical preparation.

How to Best Use This Book

Textbooks are not usually designed to be read from first page to last, and this is no exception. We have, however, structured the contents in such a way that there is a narrative and consistency of themes that run throughout.

The first section deals with the fundamental processes involved in developing athletes who are resilient to injury. The second section then discusses key athletic capacities and how to develop them. Few sports use just one athletic domain, however, and it is the skilful combining of all the attributes of performance that is discussed in the third section.

We expect that each chapter will provide the reader with immediate practical knowledge. The aim is to provide enough practical examples to allow the coach to take it to his or her place of work and use the information contained within straightaway. Each chapter is rich in detail as well, though, and covers topics in a depth that will reward repeat reading.

Today, most people are time poor, and the prospect of trawling through the vast mountain of scientific research for best-practice principles is insurmountable. This publication seeks to provide athletes, practitioners, coaches and scientists with a reputable source of valid, up-to-date and practical information that is not only usable after the first read, but also includes enough detail that further in-depth review of the chapters will be rewarded. The text contains enough *ready-to-use* information and programmes that the reader could potentially take the book with him or her and use it as a basis for a training session. Moreover, it also provides a sound discussion of the thought processes behind these programmes so that readers will be able to understand how to modify and progress the programmes should the need become apparent.

The breadth of topics covered by the world-class contributors means that the book provides a comprehensive resource for the athlete or coach seeking the latest in sport conditioning principles and programmes. It does not seek to be a book of recipes. It is this dissemination of wisdom that is invaluable not just to athletes or students, but to anyone working in the field who strives to maximise outcomes in terms of sport-specific performance.

After reading each chapter, the reader not only will understand the latest thinking about the topic discussed, but will also understand how to apply this knowledge in an integrated way, drawing on the expertise of leaders across multiple disciplines

As we asserted previously, no single element of sport performance exists as an island, and in some instances, a particular issue is covered in multiple chapters. For example, the topic of fatigue is covered in both the monitoring and recovery chapters (chapters 6 and 24, respectively). The book has been deliberately designed this way to demonstrate the linkages that need to be made among multiple areas in order to excel in sport. We suggest, therefore, that in order to get the most out of the publication, the reader chooses his or her own adventure and exploits these deliberate crossovers.

These crossovers further demonstrate the need for interdisciplinary work within the performance framework. It becomes evident that retraining the injured rower, for example, needs to take into account strength, aerobic fitness, cross-training, training-load monitoring and recovery. This book, therefore, has relevancy for sport and fitness coaches as well as for medical and rehabilitation personnel such as doctors, physiotherapists and athletic trainers.

PART

I

Building Robust
Athletes

Andrew Cowie/Colorsport/Icon SMI

CHAPTER 1

Evaluating Athletic Capacities

Mike McGuigan, PhD, CSCS*D
Sports Performance Research Institute New Zealand, AUT University

A critical component in preparing athletes for high performance is evaluating their physical capacities. Practitioners have two key goals in the business of training athletes:

1. Improve their physical, technical, and psychological abilities to help them reach the highest possible levels of performance.
2. Develop a precisely controlled training programme to assure that maximal performance is attained at the right moment of the competitive season, that is, at each point of a major competition.

Underlying these objectives is building a robust athlete; to do this effectively, we need to determine the physical capacities of our athletes. Without this critical information it is difficult to design effective training programmes. The aim of this chapter is to provide an understanding of the athletic testing process as well as methods to determine the most appropriate tests to use that will produce a full, accurate picture of the strengths and weaknesses of an athlete. It will also demonstrate the most effective ways of presenting the results so that a strategic approach to athletic enhancement can be developed and communicated to all stakeholders.

Understanding the Needs of the Sport and Team

Coaches and scientists have long been interested in assessing the capacities of athletes. For example, exercise physiologist A.V. Hill measured the acceleration of sprinters in 1927 using large wire coils set up at intervals alongside a track while the athletes wore a magnet.[1] A number of tests are available to the practitioner to assess the physical qualities of athletes. When one is designing a testing battery for athletes, it is important to conduct a thorough needs analysis of the sport and individual requirements to determine which tests are most appropriate.

Like training, assessment of physical capacities must be specific, so it is important to avoid implementing tests just for the sake of testing. The data that are generated need to be meaningful and used to affect athletic performance in some manner. Tests that are used need to be examined critically and not chosen solely because they have been used previously or because the equipment and expertise are available. There is clearly a high level of importance in analysing both sport-specific and athlete-specific physiological data in order to begin the strategic approach to individualised training programme design. Figure 1.1 shows a proposed

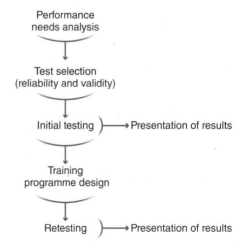

Figure 1.1 Test-retest cycle of physical capacity assessment. A critical aspect is the effective ongoing assessment and presentation of results to quantify training progress and assess training effectiveness.

approach that can be used for selecting and using tests for assessment of physical capacities.

There are a number of reasons for assessing the physical capacities of athletes. These can include

1. providing objective information on the effect of the training programmes,
2. assessing the impact of a specific intervention strategy,
3. assisting with the process of making informed decisions regarding programme manipulation,
4. maximising athlete and coach understanding about the needs of the sport,
5. effectively using data from new technologies, and
6. adding to the growing body of elite athlete preparation research.

Understanding the specific needs of the sport has implications for designing position-specific training programmes with regard to conditioning, strength, power, agility and speed development. Within a sport itself (e.g., netball, football, rugby union), there may be significant differences among positions. Prescribing training programmes and exercises based on the demands of each position may help prepare athletes for the specific demands of their match roles and facilitate optimal performance. This needs analysis process should involve performance analyses of athletes during match play, along with selecting appropriate tests of physical capacity. Doing so should assist with developing individualised training programmes to meet the specific demands of the sport.

Selecting Appropriate Tests of Physical Competence

It is critical that practitioners select appropriate tests for assessing the physical competence of their athletes. Two vital considerations in developing assessment protocols for measuring athlete capacities are validity and reliability. These components often are discussed interchangeably but are separate factors that need to be considered when selecting a testing battery for athletes.

A laboratory or field-based test that measures exercise performance capacity must be both reliable and valid and sensitive to small changes in an athlete's fitness level. Several factors need to be

Wisdom

Validity refers to whether the specific test measures what it is supposed to measure. Validity is important for distinguishing *among* athletes and is often assessed by comparing practical test scores to criterion test scores.

Reliability refers to how repeatable the performance is. This is optimally assessed with repeated trial and is important for tracking performance *within* athletes.

considered related to the preparation and execution of data collection to help ensure that accurate measurements are recorded. These include

1. the training and assessment of testers;
2. sufficient numbers of testing assistants to conduct the testing efficiently;
3. thoughtful preparation of data entry sheets or computer spreadsheets;
4. availability of precise and calibrated equipment;
5. efficient design of the testing environment;
6. the structure of the testing session, including the order the tests are conducted in;
7. familiarisation of testing procedures for the athletes, including clear instructions and demonstrations on how to perform the tests; and
8. assurance that athletes give maximal effort during the testing.

A key component of the testing process is preparation for the testing sessions, which will go a long way to ensuring both valid and reliable testing protocols. Performing some pilot testing of the protocols should also be considered.

Reliability

The reliability of the tests is often considered the most important factor because it affects the precision of assessment of athletes, patients, clients and study participants. For example, when dealing in elite sport, the margin of gains in performance and the difference between achieving success and not are so small that knowing a performance test is reliable is critical. When performing measurements of any physical capacity, it is therefore vitally important to establish whether the method is reliable.

There are a number of methods that are available to the practitioner that can be used to measure reliability. These methods include correlations, typical error of measurement and change in the mean.

Correlations

The most common form of reliability is retest reliability, which refers to the reproducibility of a variable measured more than once. A common example where this might be useful is when performing a one-repetition maximum (1RM) test. We want to ensure that when we test an athlete on day 1 that we would get the same result on day 2. A retest correlation is a common method to measure reliability. A correlation of 1.00 refers to a perfect relationship between variables, and 0.00 represents no relationship whatsoever. Pearson correlation coefficients or intraclass correlation coefficients (ICC) are both used for quantifying retest reliability. However, the ICC is a more appropriate measure of retest reliability, particularly for repeat tests greater than two, which ideally is what should be used to establish retest reliability. Spreadsheets are available online that can be used to calculate reliability measures.[2]

Typical Error of Measurement

Typical error of measurement is a more useful method for assessing changes in performance of an athlete because it provides a direct measure of the amount of error associated with the test. Measurement error refers to variation in a measure from any source (e.g., technical, biological). An important type of typical error is the coefficient of variation (CV), which refers to the typical error expressed as a percentage of the athlete's mean score. This can be useful for representing reliability of performance tests. We can use this approach to calculate typical error for all the tests that are used in an assessment battery and then make sound conclusions about whether the changes seen in response to a training programme are meaningful or not.

Let's say, for example, that vertical jump testing is performed on three separate days (more than two repeat tests is always better!) and the following results are obtained: day 1, 65 centimetres; day 2, 66 centimetres; day 3, 68.5 centimetres. The difference scores are 1 centimetre and 2.5 centimetres, and the standard deviation of these difference scores is 1.06. The typical error is then calculated as standard deviation of difference scores / square root of 2, or 1.06 / root2 = 0.75. This should be calculated based on results from multiple athletes.

The spreadsheet available online can be used to calculate this measure and also allows for calculation of this within-subject variation as a %CV.[2]

Change in the Mean

The simple change in the mean is another measure of reliability.[3] This change consists of two components: random change and systematic change. Random change in the mean is due to sampling error whereas the systematic change is the non-random change in the value between trials (e.g., athlete motivation). A simple way to calculate is to do a paired t-test between the pairs of trials. A t-test is a statistical test that allows a comparison between two means. A paired t-test can be used when comparing groups of athletes who have been tested more than once (i.e., repeat testing). This test can be performed using Excel or commercially available statistics programmes. It is important to choose or design tests with small learning effects or allow the athletes plenty of familiarisation trials to reduce any learning effects.

The question is often asked what the acceptable reliability of a test is. Although there are no preset standards for acceptable reliability measures, it is often suggested that ICC values above 0.75 may be considered reliable, and this index should be at least 0.90 for most clinical applications. Some scientists have arbitrarily chosen an analytical goal of 10 per cent or below for the CV, but the merits of this value are a source of conjecture. This value would appear to be quite a liberal interpretation, and the coach should be encouraged to use tests with extremely high reliability where possible. An important concept to remember is that high reliability is a prerequisite for monitoring small but clinically important changes in an individual and for quantifying such effects in controlled trials with samples of reasonable size. We need to know if the tests are good enough to detect any changes in the results of the athletic tests that we have chosen to implement. If reliability is insufficiently high, we may never know the true status of the athlete or the effect of training programmes.

Validity

Validity is also extremely important as it deals with the fundamental question of whether the test is really assessing what it purports to measure. Validity also deals with the issue of how well the test relates to competition performance of the athlete. As is the case with determining reliability, we can also use an online spreadsheet to calculate validity.[4] An unusual aspect of research on performance enhancement is that researchers have rarely investigated the effect of various interventions on performance in actual competitive events.[3] The traditional approach has been to use performance in laboratory or field tests that simulates the event. This is no doubt due to logistical reasons such as recruitment of participants and the ability to measure variables that underlie or explain the effects of treatments that might help or hinder performance.

Unfortunately, the relationship between performance in tests and performance in competition has not been explored adequately, so it is uncertain how a change in performance in a test translates into a change in performance in an event. Regardless of the reliability of a test, the practitioner needs to be satisfied that improvements that may be measured in the test will be reproduced in the event. In the past, researchers have addressed this problem by performing a validity study in which performance of a group of athletes in the test is correlated either with their performance in the event or with current personal best performances.[5]

Wisdom

Using laboratory or performance tests that satisfy the most important criteria, that 'changes in the test results are directly related to changes in competitive performance',[4] is vitally important.

Integrating Results With Injury Screening and Injury-Rehabilitation Testing

Testing does not form just the first rung of the training ladder, however. Key parts of any training programme are injury prevention and injury rehabilitation. Testing is just as important in these domains in order to

1. avoid guesswork when determining progress and efficacy of interventions; and
2. facilitate communication among all members of the performance, medical and coaching teams.

It is now common for high-performance programmes to have a multidisciplinary approach to athlete preparation, with professionals such as physiotherapists, strength and conditioning coaches and performance analysts working together. The existing research makes a strong case for high levels of integration of fitness-testing data with injury and medical screening. Although much more research on these approaches is needed, in addition to clearer validation and assessment of the various commercially available screening tools, some interesting preliminary data show the effectiveness of this approach. Anecdotal reports of high-performance programmes with highly integrated approaches to injury prevention are also promising. One study investigated the effects of an interdisciplinary approach to athlete preparation on injury rates and performance in collegiate

---

CASE STUDY

A 28-year-old international women's field hockey representative with a history of knee injuries was preparing for the 2012 Olympic Games. The player was unable to undertake all field sessions and suffered significant knee pain with dynamic resistance training exercises. After case management discussions among the physiotherapist, strength and conditioning coach and sport scientist, it was decided to implement an isometric assessment and training protocol in an attempt to increase muscular strength and rate of force development in the lead-up (final 8 weeks) to the Olympic Games. The test selected was the isometric squat, which has excellent reliability for force measures (CV ≤ 2 per cent). Regular weekly assessment using force-plate technology provided objective data on force production and rate of force development. The data were collected during training sessions and used to adjust the training and rehabilitation intervention with weekly meetings held among the various support staff. This approach also was an effective way of incorporating the testing into training and providing an additional monitoring tool for coaching staff (see chapter 6).

baseball players.⁶ There was an overall decrease in injury rates and increased performance over a 5-year period, which was attributed to collaborative efforts among sport coaches, sports medicine and sport science departments. For this approach to be successful, close communication among all parties is critical. Accordingly, it is vital that the tests employed are understood by the entire performance team, that the results yielded provide information of real value in assessing the status of the athlete and that this information is communicated effectively.

Determination of Priorities for Intervention

An important part of the process of athlete assessment is determining the priorities for intervention. After the testing is complete, one of the key considerations is what capacities need to be targeted by the training programme. A fundamental question is often this: Is it important to focus on weaknesses,

continue to develop strengths or try to do a combination of both? For example, figure 1.2 shows the results of strength and power testing for a hypothetical athlete. Based on these testing data, it can be seen that the athlete is relatively poor on force-related capacities such as maximal strength and loaded jumping. Assuming performance in the sport was contingent on high levels of force production, it could therefore be concluded that the athlete would benefit from a subsequent training programme that has a greater strength-development emphasis. Such an approach is critical when individualising training programmes to ensure time and effort are allocated most effectively. Within this context, we also need to consider the impact that training certain capacities will have on other physical capacities. Frequent retesting of these physical qualities will assist with this process and provide the practitioner with regular feedback on the effect of the programme and specific interventions. These concepts will be explored further in subsequent chapters.

Figure 1.2 Strength and power profile for athlete. The zero indicates that the athlete has reached the required standard for that particular test.

Calculating the Worthwhile Change Value of a Test Performance

Another key consideration, and one that is directly related to the reliability and validity of a test, is what is a worthwhile change in a test performance? Worthwhile change refers to the ability of a test to detect the smallest practically important change.

The smallest worthwhile change can be calculated as

0.5% CV or 0.2 × between-athlete standard deviation.[5]

Consideration also needs to be given to understanding what degree of change is required to be practically important both for the individual and for the group when dealing with athletes. When using this concept, the practitioner will need to make an assessment of the magnitude of change and consider the noise associated with the test. This will depend on the type of athlete population that is being tested and the type of test being used.

The concept of identifying the smallest worthwhile change in athlete performance is an important one as it goes to the heart of what the practitioner is trying to achieve in athlete preparation. By determining the worthwhile change of performance, it is possible to calculate the amount of enhancement that is required for an athlete to improve his or her medal chances.[5] This calculation also has large implications for team sport athletes as it goes some way to determining whether the change that has been seen in a particular test is worthwhile and can therefore greatly assist with the interpretation of test results.

For example, when testing athletes, it can be useful to determine the smallest worthwhile enhancement of evenly matched competitors. This approach has been investigated using a number of athlete populations;[7] it involves calculating the value of the CV for elite athletes in the particular event. This research suggests that practitioners want to be confident about measuring half this value when testing an elite athlete or studying factors affecting performance with subelite athletes. By using this approach, practitioners can calculate the worthwhile change for the tests being used that are specific to the athlete groups they are working with. Some examples of the CVs from published and unpublished studies of series of competitions are shown in table 1.1. It should be noted that CVs for individual tests are best

Table 1.1 Typical Coefficient of Variations (CV) for Different Events

Event	CV
Running and hurdling events up to 1,500 m	0.8%
Running up to 10 km and steeplechase	1.1%
Cross country (subelite)	1.5%
Half marathon (subelite)	2.5%
Marathon (subelite)	3.0%
High jump	1.7%
Pole vault, long jump	2.3%
Discus, javelin, shot put	2.5%
Mountain biking	2.4%
Swimming (various distances)	1.4%
Cycling 1-40 km	1.3%
Rowing	0.6%-1.4%
Weightlifting: snatch	2.7%
Weightlifting: clean and jerk	2.3%

Data from W. Hopkins et al., 2009, "Progressive statistics for studies in sports medicine and exercise science," *Medicine & Science in Sports & Exercise* 41(1): 3-12; M. McGuigan and M. Kane, 2004, "Reliability of performance of elite Olympic weightlifters," *Journal of Strength and Conditioning Research* 18(3): 650-653; A. Stewart and W. Hopkins, 2000, "Consistency of swimming performance within and between competitions," *Medicine & Science in Sports & Exercise* 32(5): 997-1001; and T.B. Smith and W.G. Hopkins, 2011, "Variability and predictability of finals times of elite rowers," *Medicine & Science in Sports & Exercise* 43(11): 2155-2160.

calculated using the athletes the coach is working with and not by relying on published results from other laboratories or programmes.

Interpreting the Significance of Changes in Test Results

Along with selecting the most appropriate tests for assessment of physical capacity, it is also important to interpret the data that have been generated. A wide range of methods is available to assist with this interpretation. When it comes to interpretation of changes in test results, the practitioner should not be concerned with statistical significance for practical programming purposes due to reasons such as the small sample sizes often dealt with in sport environments in addition to the small but important performance changes. Different approaches can be used to assist with test-result interpretation, including likelihood of practically important change, effect sizes, per cent difference, Z scores and modified Z scores.

We assess team athletes with fitness tests, but there is no clear relationship between fitness-test performance and team performance.[5] So this poses the problem of how to decide on the smallest worthwhile change or difference in fitness test performance. The solution is to use nontraditional approaches such as the standardised change or difference. This measure is also known as Cohen's effect size, a measure useful in meta-analyses to assess magnitude of differences or changes in the mean in different studies.[7] With this method, the practitioner expresses the difference, or change in the mean, as a fraction of the between-subject standard deviation (change in mean / standard deviation of prescore).[3] This is a similar measure to a Z score. Again, there are no clear guidelines as to what constitutes a smallest worthwhile difference or change with this measure, but some research suggests this would be 0.20.[3] For example, a value of 0.20 would be equivalent to moving from the 80th to the 85th percentile. For performance tests of athletes from individual sports, it has been suggested to calculate half the event-to-event variation in a top athlete's competitive performance. When dealing with fitness tests for team sports, a general guideline is approximately 0.20 of the between-athlete standard deviation.[5] Table 1.2 shows a suggested scale for classifying both effect sizes (calculated as difference in the means) and correlation coefficients.

For example, let's say we are interested in calculating the smallest worthwhile change for relative peak power on a countermovement jump test. Ten athletes complete the testing and get scores of 65, 63, 56, 62, 64, 58, 49, 66, 62, and 45 watts/kilogram. The between-athlete standard deviation is 7.03

watts/kilogram. The smallest worthwhile change for this test is calculated to be $7.03 \times 0.2 = 1.41$ watts/kilogram. We know, therefore, that on a repeat test after a period of training, we would be seeking an improvement of >1.41 watts/kilogram to consider the intervention successful. It is important to work out these scores of smallest worthwhile changes using the same (or a similar) population of athletes being tested, in addition to using as many athletes as possible, in order for outlying scores not to have too great an effect on the overall score.

Presenting the Results for Maximal Impact

The various approaches discussed in this chapter need to be married with a strategic approach to the presentation of the results to coaches. It is not enough to have developed a reliable and valid testing battery, collected data and determined whether the changes are worthwhile or not. If the information is not presented to the coach or athletes in a way that makes sense to them, then the ability of that information to make a difference to the performance of the athlete will be reduced. To assist with interpretation of the results, we need to make an assessment about magnitude of the change, taking into account the reliability of the test.

Presenting the results in a way the coach and athlete will understand can be done in a number of ways and by using a combination of methods. A good first step is to graph the results in some way. Typically, numbers by themselves are not particularly helpful or well understood by coaches and athletes. By graphing data we may be able to identify trends in the results or visualise large changes in physical capacities. Some examples of these methods and how they can be used are provided here.

- Use the simple *per cent change*. For example, the athlete has changed by +2.5 per cent since the last test. This can also be reported along with the noise of the test (expressed as typical error) and the smallest worthwhile change.

- Use *likely limits* for the true value. The simplest approach for reporting likely limits is the observed change plus or minus the typical error.[5] For example: the athlete has changed by +2.5 per cent since the last test, and so the smallest worthwhile change is 1.0 per cent. With such information, the results can be interpreted using terms such as possibly

Table 1.2 Classification Scale for Effect Size Scores and Correlation Coefficients

Descriptor	Effect size	Correlation coefficient
Trivial	0.0	0.0
Small	0.2	0.1
Moderate	0.6	0.3
Large	1.2	0.5
Very large	2.0	0.7
Nearly perfect	4.0	0.9
Perfect	Infinite	1.0

Data from W. Hopkins et al., 2009, "Progressive statistics for studies in sports medicine and exercise science," *Medicine & Science in Sports & Exercise* 41(1): 3-12.

harmful, likely substantially positive, unclear but likely to be beneficial and so on.[3]

• Use *Z scores* by calculating the athlete's score: average score / standard deviation. Figures and graphs are often good ways to present data to coaches and athletes. A visual image can demonstrate to the coach and athlete where the athlete's performance lies within in the group. Graphing the Z scores using radar plots provides a pictorial representation of the athlete's strengths and weaknesses relative to the group and therefore can be a useful tool for prescribing specific training to target those weaknesses. Figure 1.3 shows an example of a radar plot of Z scores.

This approach can be particularly useful for one-off testing. However, an important part of the testing process is retesting and comparing to previous results. A problem can arise with this approach in testing squads when athletes may not be available due to injury. With small sample sizes, a particularly strong (or weak) score by an athlete in a specific test may result in significant changes in means or standard deviations. An alternative approach can be to use modified Z scores, where benchmark means and standard deviations are determined for the various tests. These benchmarks can be determined by the practitioner (e.g., it may be decided that the benchmark, or target, for relative countermovement jump power is 60 W/kg). These benchmarks are typically developed based

on a number of sources, including published literature on a similar population, previous testing data with that population or coach feedback. Once these benchmarks are developed, the Z scores can be calculated as follows:

Z score = (athlete's score – benchmark score) / standard deviation.

Figure 1.4 shows an example of Z scores for an athlete measured over time using this approach.

• Standard difference score is a Z score on the change in performance score (posttest – pretest), where individual difference scores are subtracted from the mean difference score and divided by the standard deviation of the difference scores.[8] An advantage of this approach is it allows the practitioner to visualise the individuals exhibiting large changes in performance.

• Numerous other methods can be used to present data. For example, some individuals may find Z scores confusing, so an alternative such as a standard ten (STEN) score could be used as it reports results from 1 to 10. These can be calculated from Z scores or the original testing data. To calculate STEN scores use either approach:

STEN = (Z score × 2) + 5.5

or

STEN = [(test result – mean test result) / standard deviation] × 2 + 5.5

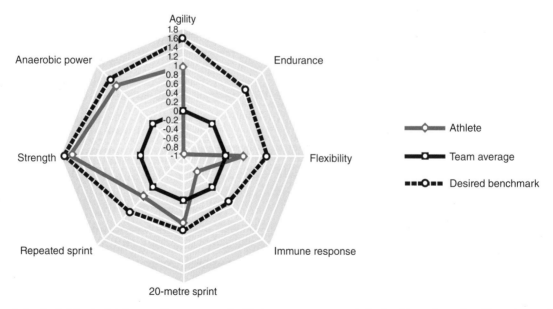

Figure 1.3 Individual athlete results compared with team average and desired benchmarks. Note that as it is an average of Z scores, the team average will always come out to zero using the traditional calculation.

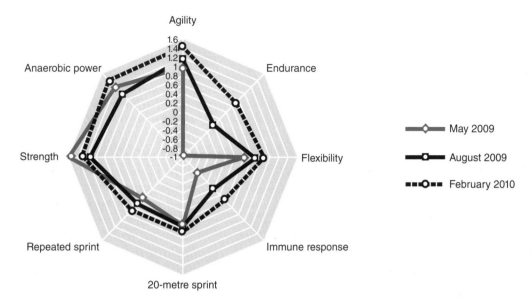

Figure 1.4 Monitoring an individual athlete over time.

Another key part of the reporting process is the time taken to give these results to coaches and athletes. This needs to be done as quickly as possible so that coaches have time to implement changes in training programmes to have an impact and correct any identified weaknesses. Just as poor presentation of testing data can limit the potential for improving athletes' training results, taking excessive time to deliver the information to the key stakeholders has a negative impact. Practitioners should aim to provide testing reports that are meaningful and timely and that provide specific recommendations for the coach and athletes.

Wisdom

Under normal circumstances the presentation of testing results to coaches should be within 72 hours of the testing being completed.

From Data to Performance

An important measure in training programmes is the amount of transfer of training to sport performances. For example, resistance training has been shown to improve strength, power and speed in a number of athletic populations. In addition to improving these physical qualities, resistance training also has significant benefits for athletes in terms of increasing muscle size and decreasing risk of injury. However, the ultimate goal of athlete preparation is maximising performance during competition. Therefore, training also needs to be looked at within the context of whether it provides significant benefits to match performance, particularly when considering team sports. There is actually limited evidence in the scientific literature showing strong relationships between training such as resistance exercise and a motor performance such as agility. These are important factors to consider when designing testing batteries for sports and measuring transfer of physical capacity to sport performance.

The use of training programmes designed to increase underlying physical qualities in elite athletes in an attempt to improve athletic performance is commonplace. There is a large body of literature that shows that physical training can increase a number of performance markers across a wide array of sports. For example, explosive strength training has been shown to increase sprinting speed and vertical jump ability in soccer players,[9] and high-load resistance training has been shown to improve acceleration and throwing velocity in elite handball players.[10] These are common findings across a wide range of team sports. However, the question that remains unanswered in many sports is this: To what extent do these physical capacities and their development contribute to success in terms of improved match performance? There are also issues concerning the extent of transfer that occurs from training to these measures of performance. This is a critical consideration for the practitioner as this ultimately determines what physical capacities need to be assessed.

There is some evidence that modes of training can improve other, more specific motor abilities such as agility. However, this research is less compelling with mixed findings on the potential benefits on measures such as change in direction speed.[11] One of the challenges with this area of research is that there is no clear agreement on which types of measures best reflect these types of capacities. It could be that straight-line sprinting and planned changes of direction are unlikely to represent the specific cognitive and physical demands of a team sport such as soccer and rugby.[11] Reactive agility tests involving reacting cues such as audio, visual or kinesthetic signals could be more specific. In addition, studies that have used short training periods have had limited success with improving speed and agility.[12] These issues could help explain why the results of training studies concerning motor abilities have been mixed. The mixed results also demonstrate the need to keep abreast of research developments and to continually look to ensure that the testing battery employed provides a valid insight into sport performance.

Studies also have demonstrated positive transfer of specific training on sport-specific skills such as bat velocity in baseball[13] and kicking velocity.[14] One study demonstrated that 10 weeks of explosive resistance training using bench press throws improved throwing speed and base running speed in baseball players.[15] Ballistic training has also been shown to improve kicking speed and force in martial artists.[16] These results highlight the importance of exercise specificity and the impact it can have on the adaptations seen in sport-specific tasks.

However, the research is not conclusive, with some studies showing improvements in strength and power without concurrent changes in more specific sport skills. A limited body of research exists on the transfer of physical capacities such as strength and power to motor performance. It would appear that this transfer occurs but is quite minimal with large increases in muscular strength resulting in only minor changes in motor performance. The concept of lag time has been proposed as a possible explanation.[17] This refers to the time it takes for an athlete to learn how to use his or her increased strength and power.[17] This concept has some support from the longitudinal studies in elite athletes with large improvements shown in strength and power, particularly at the early stages of an athlete's career.[18, 19] Studies also have shown that improvements in speed and agility are smaller and tend to occur later in an athlete's career.[19]

Researchers have attempted to account for differences in playing ability by using objective skill criteria.[20] The results of this study demonstrated that skill characteristics but not physiological or anthropometric characteristics differentiated between successful and less successful Rugby League players. However, all physiological and anthropometric characteristics were related to playing ability. Another study investigated the relationship between U.S. football-playing ability (as determined by coaches) and selected physiological measures.[21] Of all the measures conducted in the athletes, the strongest predictor of playing ability was vertical jump performance. Another study using several levels of Rugby Union players showed that higher-level athletes produced greater absolute and relative strength and power outputs than did less skilled athletes.[18] These studies further highlight the issue of identifying measures that are most critical to performance. Only when this is done effectively is it possible to assess the impact of training programmes on athlete performance.

Sprinting is a critical factor in most team sport performance, and strength training has been shown to improve speed. Sprint ability has been shown to be linked to making a team in the National Football League (NFL) but only for the running back position.[22] For other physical performance tests such as agility, bench press, and vertical and horizontal jumps, the relationships were low. This result again highlights the importance of selecting tests that accurately reflect on-field performance and taking into consideration sport- and also position-specific differences and requirements. Clearly, more research is needed to determine key sport-performance variables and how those variables can be influenced by training.

The use of conditioning programmes designed to increase underlying physical qualities in elite athletes in an attempt to improve athletic performance is also commonplace. Although the extent to which qualities of strength and power are important to sport performance may vary depending on the activity, the associations between these qualities and performance have been well documented in the literature. For example, research has shown that club-head speed is related to a golfer's handicap, and that golfers with lower handicaps are able to generate higher club-head speeds.[23] There is also an increasing number of training studies with high-performance athletes that are attempting to address questions concerning the role of training programmes for improving athlete performance.

Notwithstanding the difficulties with conducting research in elite athletes, there is clearly a need for more well-controlled research studies in this population. Alternative approaches could be considered by researchers to answer some of these questions. It has been suggested that research design and conclusions from interventions in elite athletes often miss benefits to individual athletes because the group means show no statistically significant difference with training or experimental interventions. This approach is also useful when sufficient participant numbers are not possible, which is often the case in research conducted with elite athletes. Single–case study research design in elite sport could potentially provide the ability to detect positive intervention outcomes in individual athletes and continue to allow for the athlete's training and performance to be optimised.[24]

As has been discussed, the concept of transfer can be difficult to quantify, but Zatsiorsky and Kraemer[25] have suggested a formula where transfer can be expressed as being a function of the following:

transfer = gain in performance / gain in trained exercise

For example, if 8 weeks of strength training using the squat exercise increases 1RM 21 per cent, increases vertical jump 21 per cent and increases 40-metre sprint performance by 2.3 per cent, these results show that the training has excellent transference to vertical jump performance but considerably less to sprint performance. What has proved to be more difficult to quantify for some sports is how much strength training transfers to performance. An emerging area of research, and one that has the potential to have a significant impact on athlete preparation, is establishing the connection between physical capacity, fitness and actual match performance. This research may help determine the most appropriate tests of physical capacity for individual sports and athletes.

Summary

A number of tests are available to assess athletes. Assessment of physical capacities must be specific, so practitioners should avoid implementing tests just for the sake of testing. It is also important to critically examine what tests are used and not choose tests solely because they have been used previously or because the equipment and expertise are available. In addition to having reliable and valid tests, it is critical to understand and recognise why each test is included and whether it is appropriate, for example, to assess an underlying physical quality or predict performance. Practitioners are encouraged to follow a systematic and evidence-based process to identify the test or tests used to assess physical capacities.

Practitioners must consider a number of critical factors when determining the physical capacities of their athletes. It is important to find the smallest worthwhile change or difference that would be measured in the test. Measure such changes in athletes with a well-designed and well-chosen test that is specific to the sport and individual. Confidence in the results of the test being used can be improved greatly by doing multiple trials. The practitioner should also clearly understand what quality is being assessed. Always use tests that have highest reliability; to improve reliability, always adhere to strict, consistent protocols.

While the test itself is critical, the presentation of the testing results to the coach and athlete is perhaps even more critical. Practitioners are encouraged to consider methods of presentation that will be meaningful and always think about how the data can be used to affect athlete performance. A fundamental question to consider is if the assessment is not achieving a specific goal, then it should be removed from the battery being used to assess physical capacities.

CHAPTER 2

Developing Younger Athletes

Rhodri S. Lloyd, PhD, ASCC, CSCS*D, and Jon L. Oliver, PhD
Cardiff School of Sport, Cardiff Metropolitan University, Cardiff, UK

Scientific research clearly tells us that young athletes can enhance physical performance and reduce injury risk when exposed to appropriate training. However, it is imperative that this training stimulus is part of an appropriately structured, holistic training programme, delivered by suitably qualified personnel.

Younger athletes are a unique population, routinely exposed to sport-specific training and extensive competitive schedules at a time when they are experiencing a wide range of physical, physiological and psychological changes as a result of growth and maturation. Inappropriate training prescription or poor pedagogical approaches could actually reduce training adaptations or, in some cases, lead to injury or reductions in welfare and well-being.

Consequently, it is imperative that we understand the fundamentals of paediatric exercise science to ensure that training prescription is at all times suitable for the unique demands of young athletes. This chapter will attempt to bridge the gap between the science and application of training young athletes by

- examining the effects of growth and maturation on physical performance and exploring how these should drive long-term athletic development programmes;

- identifying rationales and methods of developing athletic motor skills, strength and power, speed, flexibility, endurance and agility in young athletes; and

- exploring confounding issues when designing training plans for young athletes.

Influence of Growth and Maturation on Physical Performance

Youth is a global term, which includes both children (approximately 2-10 and 2-11 yrs in females and males, respectively) and adolescents (approximately 11-19 yrs in girls and 12-19 yrs in males). Adolescence is a more difficult stage of development to define in terms of chronological age due to different maturation rates among children of the same age. *Growth* refers to a quantifiable change in body composition, body size or dimensions of specific regions of the body, whereas *maturation* refers to the highly variable timing and tempo of progressive change within the human body from childhood to adulthood; in addition to growth, maturation influences overall physical performance capabilities.[1]

Classic paediatric data show that physical performance indices in youth improve in a nonlinear fashion as a result of growth and maturation.[2] This in itself provides a challenge to the coach working with a young athlete. Any performance adaptation needs to be large enough to inspire confidence that change has occurred due to the programme implemented, and not solely as a result of the growth and maturation processes. During childhood, such changes in performance primarily can be attributed to nervous system development and cerebral maturation.[3] Specifically, improvements in motor unit recruitment, firing frequency, synchronisation and neural myelination are all deemed to enhance neuromuscular performance.[4] During this stage of development, existing motor-control programmes are subconsciously refined and reinforced, which enables young athletes to perform coordinated skills with greater efficiency. This naturally occurring refinement of motor control programming is a key reason for childhood to be viewed as the best time to develop correct movement patterns, athletic motor skills and inter- and intramuscular coordination.

Once the child reaches the onset of puberty, both males (12-14 yrs) and females (11-13 yrs) experience what is referred to as the adolescent growth spurt, a phase of physical development during which growth hormone and sex hormone concentrations are significantly increased.[5] It is during this phase of development that further nervous system maturation and adaptation in muscle mass, body composition and other structural parameters change, leading to natural adaptations in physical components such as speed, strength, aerobic endurance and muscular power.[6-9]

Wisdom

Appreciation and understanding of growth and maturation are essential in order to ensure that training is based on the needs of the individual as opposed to a blanket approach based simply on chronological age.

Chronological and Biological Age

Literature has clearly demonstrated that individuals of the same chronological age can differ markedly with respect to biological age,[10] sometimes by as much as 4 or 5 years. The relative mismatch and wide variation in biological age among children of the same chronological age emphasises the obvious limitations in using chronological age as a basis for exercise prescription for youth.

Since biological age will provide a more accurate reflection of the stage of development of the young athlete, it is recommended that coaches longitudinally track (approximately every 3-6 months) basic somatic measures, which can be used to predict biological age. For example, Mirwald and colleagues[11] developed a regression equation that can predict how far in years an individual is from peak height velocity (PHV) to within a standard error of approximately 6 months. Measures of stature, body mass and leg length are entered into the female equation (equation 1) or male equation (equation 2), which will estimate years from PHV at any given time for the young athlete.

Training Age

Although biological age is a better guide than chronological age, coaches also should be aware of the training age of the athlete. *Training age* refers to the number of years an athlete has been in appropriately designed formalised training.[12] Exercise selection and progression largely will be driven by technical competency, but coaches also should take into account the biological age and training age of their athletes. Two case studies will depict the relative importance of both biological age (case study 1) and training age (case study 2).

Case Study 1

Two 14-year-old rugby players enter an age-grade rugby team. Both are somewhat light for their respective positions and in need of gaining additional body mass. Basic somatic measures determine player A to be 2 years pre-PHV and therefore a late maturer and player B to be 1 year post-PHV and therefore an early maturer.

Despite being the same age chronologically, the internal environments of these two players differ markedly. Player A is still to experience the adolescent growth spurt and the concomitant changes in hormonal profiling that aid muscle mass development. Consequently, irrespective of the fact that player A needs to gain body mass, coaches would be better served prescribing training

Maturity offset = −16.364 + 0.0002309 × leg length and sitting height interaction + 0.006277 × age and sitting height interaction + 0.179 x leg by height ratio + 0.0009428 × age and weight interaction

(equation 1)

Maturity offset = −29.769 + 0.0003007 × leg length and sitting height interaction − 0.01177 × age and leg length interaction + 0.01639 x age and sitting height interaction + 0.445 × leg by height ratio

(equation 2)

programmes geared towards strength and motor skill development. An emphasis on motor skill development is especially important due to the disruption in motor-control programmes that can sometimes eventuate as a result of the adolescent growth spurt, a concept referred to as adolescent awkwardness.

Player B, deemed 1 year post-PHV, would be more aligned with peak weight velocity (PWV), a period during which body mass naturally increases as a result of the surge in sex hormone concentrations. Testosterone, the predominant sex hormone in males, promotes protein synthesis; ultimately, this would be a favourable time to prescribe muscle-building (hypertrophy) training programmes to realise the main goal of the player's athletic development.

Case Study 2

A strength and conditioning coach is assigned two 11-year-old female hockey players to her development programme. Player A has a training age of 3 years and can demonstrate technical competency in a range of motor skills. Player B has a training age of zero, has never been involved in formalised training and cannot demonstrate satisfactory levels of competency in fundamental movement patterns.

Although player B would be prescribed a training programme geared towards improving basic movement skills and base levels of muscular strength, player A could be prescribed more advanced training methods, for example weight-lifting progressions (e.g., clean and jerk, snatch) and advanced plyometrics.

These two vignettes demonstrate the realities of working with young athletes, especially within a squad environment. Irrespective of chronological or biological age, young athletes must be trained according to their training age. For example, a mature, 16-year-old female with a very low training age would still need to master basic, primal motor skills before being exposed

---

Wisdom

Basing individualised training programmes primarily on technical competency is vital. Consideration also needs to be given to training age and biological age of the young athlete.

---

to more advanced forms of training irrespective of her chronological age. The two cases also highlight the need for a long-term approach to the physical development of children and adolescents, a concept that has received a great deal of attention recently.[12]

Long-Term Athletic Development Modelling

Despite the fact that children of the same chronological age can vary markedly in biological age, early concepts into development models of talented youth were in fact based on chronological classifications. In order to address the interaction between maturation and training, Balyi and Hamilton[13] developed the long-term athlete development model, which has been adopted by many sport-governing bodies. However, researchers and practitioners have recently questioned this model due to the distinct lack of empirical evidence to support its concepts of windows of opportunity[14] and to the fact that its selection of just five physical qualities is somewhat limited.[12]

More recently, the youth physical development (YPD) model has been proposed, which provides practitioners with a more holistic overview of youth exercise prescription.[12] The YPD model acknowledges that all fitness qualities are trainable at all stages of development for both males (figure 2.1a) and females (figure 2.1b), however, coaches should prioritise certain training foci at different times. For a combination of performance-enhancing, injury-preventing and general health–promoting benefits, muscular strength and motor skill development are central to the model at all stages of development.

Developing Motor Skill Competency in the Young Athlete

Fundamental movement skills (FMS) are the building blocks for more advanced, sport-specific movement patterns. Broad categories of FMS include locomotive, manipulative and stabilising skills, and it is these that appear as hallmarks of common FMS programmes and testing

YOUTH PHYSICAL DEVELOPMENT (YPD) MODEL FOR MALES																				
CHRONOLOGICAL AGE (YEARS)	2	3	4	5	6	7	8	9	10	11	12	13	14	15	16	17	18	19	20	21+

AGE PERIODS	EARLY CHILDHOOD	MIDDLE CHILDHOOD	ADOLESCENCE	ADULTHOOD	
GROWTH RATE	RAPID GROWTH ⟷ STEADY GROWTH ⟷ ADOLESCENT SPURT ⟷ DECLINE IN GROWTH RATE				
MATURATIONAL STATUS	YEARS PRE-PHV ⟵ PHV ⟶ YEARS POST-PHV				
TRAINING ADAPTATION	PREDOMINANTLY NEURAL (AGE-RELATED) ⟷ COMBINATION OF NEURAL AND HORMONAL (MATURITY-RELATED)				
PHYSICAL QUALITIES	FMS	FMS	FMS	FMS	
	SSS	SSS	SSS	SSS	
	Mobility	Mobility	Mobility		
	Agility	Agility	Agility	Agility	
	Speed	Speed	Speed	Speed	
	Power	Power	Power	Power	
	Strength	Strength	Strength	Strength	
	Hypertrophy	Hypertrophy	Hypertrophy	Hypertrophy	
	Endurance & MC	Endurance & MC	Endurance & MC	Endurance & MC	
TRAINING STRUCTURE	UNSTRUCTURED	LOW STRUCTURE	MODERATE STRUCTURE	HIGH STRUCTURE	VERY HIGH STRUCTURE

Figure 2.1*a* The youth physical development (YPD) model for males. (Note: Font size refers to importance; light-shaded boxes refer to preadolescent periods of adaptation; dark-shaded boxes refer to adolescent periods of adaptation; PHV = peak height velocity; FMS = fundamental movement skills; SSS = sport-specific skills; MC = metabolic conditioning).

Reprinted, by permission, from R.S. Lloyd and J.L. Oliver, 2012, "The Youth Physical Development model: A new approach to long-term athletic development," *Strength and Conditioning Journal* 34(3): 61-72.

protocols.[15] The YPD model suggests that motor skill development should initially focus on FMS mastery, with less focus placed on sport-specific skills (SSS). This is to reduce the risk of sport specialisation in the young athlete, which has previously been linked to increased injury risk and prevalence of musculoskeletal pain.[16] However, while we acknowledge that FMS are core skills that coaches should look to develop in an attempt to make well-rounded young athletes, it is suggested that in order to make the transition to elite-level sport more successful, certain athletic motor skill competencies (AMSC) should also be central to any motor skill development programme.[17] An overview of the skills that comprise AMSC is provided in figure 2.2.

The AMSC comprise key independent movement patterns that will feature in most advanced training movements commonly used by elite-level athletes. However, it is recognised that in order to develop motor skill competency in young athletes, the training environment should be safe, fun and full of varied stimuli. For example, a child athlete with a training age of zero would not be exposed to advanced training methods such as weightlifting or advanced plyometrics as soon as he or she starts the training journey. In such a situation, the challenge to the coach would be to develop those composite AMSC required for successful performance of advanced exercises masked within an engaging, age-appropriate training environment.

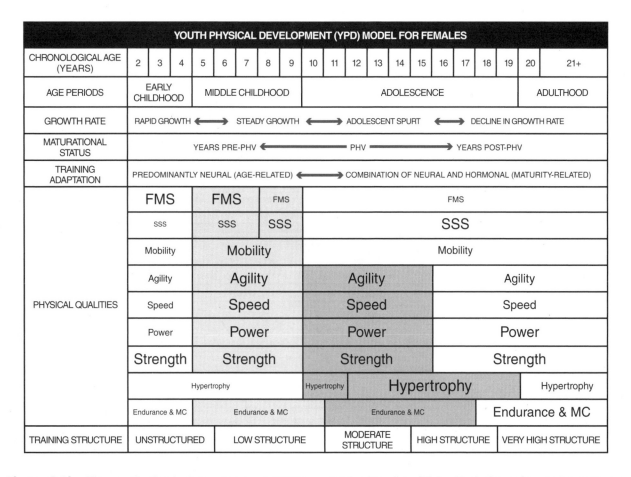

Figure 2.1b The youth physical development (YPD) model for females. (Note: Font size refers to importance; light-shaded boxes refer to preadolescent periods of adaptation; dark-shaded boxes refer to adolescent periods of adaptation; PHV = peak height velocity; FMS = fundamental movement skills; SSS = sport-specific skills; MC = metabolic conditioning).

Reprinted, by permission, from R.S. Lloyd and J.L. Oliver, 2012, "The Youth Physical Development model: A new approach to long-term athletic development," *Strength and Conditioning Journal* 34(3): 61-72.

Therefore, instead of simply instructing the child to perform cleans or snatches, the coach may prescribe fun-based warm-up activities (e.g., use of bunny hops or similar animal shapes [figure 2.3, *a-c*]), body-weight management exercises (e.g., shoulder stand to stand [figure 2.4, *a-c*]) or low-load resistance-training exercises using basic equipment (e.g., band-resisted overhead squat [figure 2.5, *a-c*]).

None of these movements provides substantial external load to the athlete and therefore enables competency and control in such AMSC as lower-body bilateral competency, antirotation and upper-body pulling to remain the primary training focus. Naturally, as the technical competency of the young athlete increases, the load and complexity of prescribed training would reflect the increased training age.

Despite the child conceivably progressing to more advanced training methods and placing a greater emphasis on other fitness qualities such as strength, speed and power, it is recommended that motor skill development continues to form a key part of any athletic development programme for athletes of any age. Such a strategic approach has previously been documented for the long-term development of weightlifting, agility, speed and plyometrics in young athletes.[18-21]

As the young athlete becomes more athletically competent, motor skill development typically will become more about motor skill maintenance and take up less time within an overall training session.

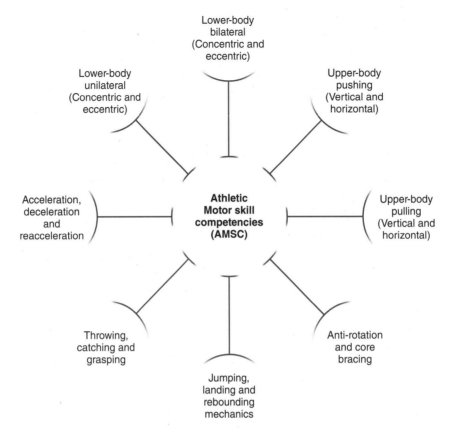

Figure 2.2 Components of athletic motor skill competencies (AMSC).

Reprinted, by permission, from J.F. Moody, F. Naclerio, P. Green, and R.S. Lloyd, 2013, Motor skill development in youths. In *Strength and conditioning for young athletes: Science and application,* edited by R.S. Lloyd and J.L. Oliver (Oxon: Routledge), fig. 4.2 on p. 53.

For example, 70 per cent of the total training session of a prepubertal child with a training age of zero may be devoted to developing basic motor skills; for an adolescent athlete approaching the start of adulthood, this proportion of time may be reduced to 10 to 15 per cent of the total training time. This training focus transition is evident in the sample strength and conditioning sessions shown in table 2.1 for an 8-year-old, prepubertal boy with a training age of zero years and in tables 2.2 and 2.3 for a 17-year-old, postpubertal male with a training age of 8 years.

Developing Strength and Power in the Young Athlete

The development of strength and power in youth has previously been a source of great debate, yet despite earlier misconceptions there is now a wealth of evidence supporting the use of resistance training by both children and adolescents.[22, 23] Conceivably, if a child is ready to engage in sport activities, then he or she is ready to participate in resistance training. Although there is no minimum age requirement for a child to start resistance training, the child must be sufficiently mature to understand instructions and be able to choose to participate. In our experience, and on the proviso that appropriate exercise prescription, developmentally appropriate pedagogy and qualified supervision are stressed, then children can safely and effectively engage in resistance training from the age of 5 or 6 years.

Training-induced gains in muscular strength and power during childhood are not typically a result of structural changes at a muscle-fibre level, but are instead usually driven by improvements in both inter- and intramuscular coordination. Consequently, it is not uncommon for a child to become stronger and more powerful without any noticeable change in body composition. Irrespective of the lack of structural adaptation, the relative gains in muscular strength during childhood can actually be greater than those experienced during adolescence.[24]

Figure 2.3 Bunny hops: (*a*) starting position; (*b*) reach to floor; (*c*) kick heels up and back, supporting body weight on hands. Return to start position.

Figure 2.4 Shoulder stand to stand: (*a*) shoulder stand; (*b*) roll down spine to sitting position; (*c*) stand up.

Figure 2.5 Low-load band-resisted overhead squat: (*a*) starting position with band secured under feet and in both hands; (*b*) squat; (*c*) return to starting position.

Table 2.1 Sample Whole-Body Strength and Conditioning Session for 8-Year-Old, Prepubertal Boy With Training Age of Zero Years

Exercise	Key movement pattern developed	Volume (sets × reps)	Intensity (%1RM)	Rest (min)
WARM-UP (FMS)				
Foam roller complex	Whole-body myofascial release therapy	2 × 10 each site	NA	1
Goblet squat	Thoracic extension and hip mobilisation	2 × 8	Body weight	1
Split squat	Lower-body unilateral and gluteal activation	2 × 6 each leg	Body weight	1
Low-box jump	Jumping, landing and rebounding mechanics	2 × 6	Body weight	1
Scapula push-up	Scapula retraction	2 × 8	Body weight	1
Monster band push-press	Upper-body pushing (vertical)	2 × 8	Light band	1
Monster band pull-down	Upper-body pulling (vertical)	2 × 8	Light band	1
Plank variations	Antirotation and core bracing	2 × 30 sec	Body weight	1
MAIN (RESISTANCE)				
Overhead squat	Lower-body bilateral	3 × 6	Wooden dowel or junior barbell	2
Elevated press-up	Upper-body pushing (horizontal)	3 × 8	Body weight	2
TRX supine pull-up	Upper-body pulling (horizontal)	3 × 8	Body weight	2
AUXILIARY EXERCISES				
Stretching complex	NA	2 × 20 sec	NA	1

Table 2.2 Sample Strength and Conditioning Lower-Body Session for 17-Year-Old, Postpubertal Male With Training Age of 8 Years

Exercise	Key movement pattern developed	Volume sets × reps)	Intensity (%1RM)	Rest (min)
WARM-UP (FMS)				
Foam roller complex	Lower-body myofascial release therapy	2 × 10 each site	NA	1
Miniband walk	Gluteal activation	2 × 10 each leg	NA	1
Clam shell	Gluteal activation	2 × 8 each leg	NA	1
Drop jump (30 cm)	Jumping, landing and rebounding mechanics	3 × 3	Body weight	1 or 2
MAIN (RESISTANCE)				
Snatch	Lower-body bilateral (concentric)	3 × 3	85	2 or 3
Overhead squat	Lower-body bilateral (eccentric and concentric)	4 × 5	85	2 or 3
Barbell step-up	Lower-body unilateral	3 × 5 each leg	85	2 or 3
AUXILIARY EXERCISES				
Romanian deadlift	Lower-body bilateral (eccentric)	3 × 5	85	2 or 3

Table 2.3 Sample Strength and Conditioning Upper-Body Session for 17-Year-Old, Postpuberal Male With Training Age of 8 Years

Exercise	Key movement pattern developed	Volume (sets × reps)	Intensity (%1RM)	Rest (min)
WARM-UP (FMS)				
Foam roller complex	Upper-body myofascial release therapy	2 × 10 each site	NA	1
Y, T, W, Ls	Scapula retraction	5 × 1	NA	1
Sitting T-spine rotation	Thoracic spine mobilisation	3 × 4 each side	NA	1
MAIN (RESISTANCE)				
Bench pull	Upper-body pulling (horizontal)	4 × 5	85	2 or 3
Dumbbell bench press	Upper-body pushing (horizontal)	4 × 5	85	2 or 3
Wide grip pull-up	Upper-body pulling (vertical)	3 × 6	80	2 or 3
Snatch press	Upper-body pushing (vertical)	3 × 6	80	2 or 3
AUXILIARY EXERCISES				
Barbell rollout	Antirotation and core bracing	3 × 8	80	2 or 3

Given the strong evidence supporting the use of resistance training throughout all stages of maturation in terms of performance enhancement and injury prevention, resistance training is one of the cornerstones of long-term youth physical development strategies.[12] Similar to the development of motor skill competency, early exposure to resistance training will increase the likelihood of the young player making a successful transition from junior ranks to elite-level sport.

Certainly, for those young athletes involved in sports requiring high levels of power, recent research has suggested that long-term changes in

Wisdom

Owing to the close associations between muscular strength and a range of athletic qualities, prioritising strength development and motor skill development within youth-based strength and conditioning programmes that typically have numerous additional commitments within a given training block is recommended.

muscular power rely heavily on changes in maximal strength levels.[25] However, it would appear that the performance benefits of resistance training are multifactorial in nature with a range of physical performance characteristics, including upper-body muscular strength and endurance, lower-body power and cardiorespiratory endurance, responding favourably to a short-term integrative neuro-muscular training programme.[26]

Adding weight to this argument, we now know that measures of muscular strength and power can be significantly enhanced when children are exposed to a variety of forms of resistance training, including manual resistance, machine weights, plyometric training, resistance bands and medicine balls and free-weight exercises.[22]

During childhood, strength increases in a linear fashion for both girls and boys. However, sex-related differences in muscular strength are more evident as children enter adulthood, with males consistently outperforming females. As the child enters puberty, his or her markedly different hormonal environment will lead to natural gains in muscle mass, and consequently, levels of muscular strength and power will increase.[3] At the onset of PWV, and on the proviso that the adolescent athlete has a satisfactory training age and requisite technical competency, this will be an ideal opportunity to expose the athlete to hypertrophy-based training.[12]

Increased muscle cross-sectional area (mCSA) has previously been associated with increased force-producing capacities in junior weightlifters;[27] therefore, it would make sense that training strategies geared towards preferential hypertrophy development are prescribed in order to take advantage of the increased anabolic state during mid- to late-adolescence. It is worth noting that although girls may not be able to experience increases in muscle mass of the same magnitude as boys (due to reduced levels of testosterone), they should still be able to achieve a minor degree of hypertrophy from increases in circulating levels of and sensitivity to insulin, insulin-like growth factor and growth hormone.

Aside from the performance enhancement benefits of resistance training in developing both health- and skill-related components of fitness, research indicates that the training modality is equally effective in reducing the risk of injury in young athletes. Recent data suggest that approximately 50 per cent of injuries within youth sports could have been avoided with appropriate preparatory conditioning, inclusive of resistance training.[28, 29]

Wisdom

Even though there are many mechanisms of injury, and the elimination of all injuries is unrealistic, young athletes should engage regularly in year-round resistance training to reduce their chances of injury, especially those overuse in nature. This is an important notion for the coach to consider, as many of those working with young athletes may have to alleviate fears of parents, sport coaches or the athletes themselves at the start of a formalised strength and conditioning programme.

Similar to developing motor skills, when programming for muscular strength and power for young athletes, the primary consideration of the strength and conditioning coach should be training age and technical competency. For example, resistance for a young, inexperienced athlete can be provided in the form of body-weight exercises and exercises that use basic resistance training equipment. However, for young athletes who can demonstrate competent movement patterns, more advanced training strategies such as weightlifting (snatch, clean and jerk and their derivatives) and other multimuscle, multijoint exercises (squat, deadlift, press and pull) can be used to great effect. Earlier research showed that with appropriate coaching and supervision, 70 young male and female weightlifters age 7 to 16 years were able to make significant improvements in strength and power, without a single injury, over a 12-month period.[30]

Wisdom

Irrespective of the resistance-training mode, the complexity, volume, intensity or frequency of training should never be increased at the expense of technical competency.

Developing Speed, Agility and Flexibility in the Young Athlete

Speed and agility are fundamental components of sport and therefore should be key elements within the training programmes of young athletes. They are also common forms of locomotion that are routinely viewed as components of FMS development in children. Irrespective of this, there is a general lack of both developmental and applied research on either of these performance variables. However, childhood represents a unique opportunity to develop gross motor patterns owing to the neural plasticity associated with this stage of development. Therefore, it would appear logical to suggest that the coach should look to develop relevant techniques for accelerating, decelerating, sprinting, changing direction and cutting within technical running drills.

However, in addition to developing technical competency for speed and agility performance, the ability to develop greater forces quickly in the shortest ground-contact times possible is crucial for effective performance, even in young athletes. Additionally, adequate levels of muscular strength are deemed critical in order to safely and effectively absorb the ground-reaction forces often encountered during maximal sprint performance, and in particular during unanticipated cutting manoeuvres.[31] Therefore, in addition to the necessary motor skill development, strength and power training—with its capacity to generate force and reduce injury risk—should still be viewed as a key component of any youth-based speed and agility programme.

Developing Speed

Speed can be considered the product of stride frequency and stride length. Stride frequency may actually be reduced during the transition from childhood to adulthood, but this reduction is more than compensated for by concomitant increases in stride length, resulting in a net increase in speed with maturation. Increases in stride length are partly explained by increases in lower-limb length, facilitating an increase in the distance covered while in contact with the ground. However, with 95 per cent of adult leg length attained by age 12, a greater amount of the gain in stride length will be due to a greater distance being covered during the aerial phase of the stride. This is likely due to maturational influences improving the ability to rapidly generate large amounts of force against the ground. Consequently, a strength and conditioning coach may aim to further facilitate natural gains in force-generating capacity and stride length with appropriate training during adolescence.

It has been suggested that a reduced ground-contact period during sprinting is the primary determinant of increased sprint speed in adults,[32] although ground-contact times, which reflect the rate of muscular contraction, do not naturally improve throughout childhood and adolescence. When the athlete can reduce the ground-contact time during sprinting, the strength and conditioning coach should be confident that this reflects a training adaptation rather than a natural maturational process.

Although evidence shows that speed is trainable throughout childhood and adolescence, athletes at various stages of development respond more favourably to certain forms of training.[33] Prepubertal children respond more favourably to plyometric and sprint training (which rely heavily on high levels of neural activation), whereas adolescent athletes benefit most from a combination of strength and plyometric training (which may suggest that at this stage of development adaptations are both neural and structural in nature). These findings support the notion that sprint speed is trainable at all stages of development. However, the responsiveness to training methods may reflect the source of naturally occurring adaptation associated with both childhood and adolescence.

When prescribing plyometric drills to develop power and sprinting ability in young athletes, it is imperative to introduce this training mode gradually, owing to the high demands placed on the neuromuscular system during plyometric actions. Additionally, a gradual, progressive approach will help ensure that the training emphasis remains on movement quality (e.g., postural alignment and stability). Competent athletes can then start to focus more on training for shorter ground-contact times, recruiting larger numbers of motor units and greater use of the stretch reflex.

Wisdom

Research suggests that to develop sprint performance, prepubertal children respond well to plyometric and sprint training whereas adolescents are best served by a combination of strength and plyometric training.

Practically, inexperienced children and adolescents should perform low-intensity plyometric exercises that focus on developing sound movement mechanics. Exercise prescription for this category of child is somewhat limited by the imagination of a coach, but an element of fun and challenge will need to be maintained. However, youths with an experienced training age and high levels of motor competency can regularly include higher-intensity plyometric activities such as drop jumping or multiple bounding. We previously developed a plyometric-development model that illustrates how an inexperienced child can transition from relatively unstructured, fun-based training with minimal eccentric loading to a highly structured, sport-specific level of plyometric training with much higher eccentric loadings.[21]

Developing Agility

There are two main attributes for successful agility performance: change-of-direction speed (CODS) and cognitive function (see chapter 13). Prepubescence is an opportune time to develop motor skill patterns, muscular strength and running speed, owing to the neural plasticity associated with this stage of development.[12] Additionally, this stage of development will also serve as an ideal opportunity to enhance overall cognitive capacity and decision-making processes due to the strengthening and pruning of synaptic pathways.[34, 35]

Agility is a complex fitness component to measure, owing to the number of components influencing its performance. Combining this with the fact that little is known about how each component develops throughout childhood and adolescence means that it is somewhat difficult to identify optimal training approaches for either the child or adolescent athlete.

We have, however, proposed an agility-training model that recommends primary training foci for each stage of development.[19] The model acknowledges that irrespective of maturation, FMS training, change-of-direction speed training and reactive agility training should all be featured in the athletic programmes of all young athletes. However, we also suggest that each stage of development should have a primary training focus that is commensurate with the growth and maturational processes taking place at each stage of development. The adapted agility-training model displayed in figure 2.6 is based on the notion that an athlete has entered formalised training during childhood.

Developing Endurance

Owing to the high volumes of sport-specific training and competition that are routinely completed by

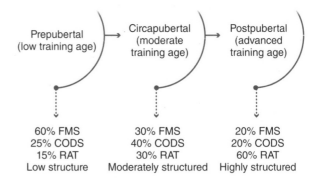

Primary agility training emphasis for different athletic populations
(suggested % session training time)

Prepubertal (low training age)	Circapubertal (moderate training age)	Postpubertal (advanced training age)
60% FMS	30% FMS	20% FMS
25% CODS	40% CODS	20% CODS
15% RAT	30% RAT	60% RAT
Low structure	Moderately structured	Highly structured

Figure 2.6 Primary agility-training focus for prepubertal, circapubertal and postpubertal young athletes.

Adapted, by permission, from R.S. Lloyd, P. Read, J.L. Oliver, R.W. Meyers, S. Nimphius, and I. Jeffreys, 2013, "Considerations for the development of agility during childhood and adolescence," *Strength and Conditioning Journal* 35(3): 2-11.

young athletes, it could be argued that developing endurance should be a low priority in most youth athletic-training programmes. Further, based on the fact that most sports do not require exceptional levels of endurance and that endurance remains trainable into adulthood, it is proposed that at no stage during childhood or adolescence should endurance be viewed as a primary training goal.[12]

Wisdom

In addition to speed and agility development, young athletes need to be allowed to develop musculoskeletal systems that are sufficiently robust to tolerate the repetitive impact forces commonly experienced during aerobic or anaerobic endurance activity.

Interestingly, recent research reported that higher levels of aerobic capacity in children were associated with greater risk of skeletal fracture, especially in children with lower levels of muscular strength.[36] Additionally, evidence has demonstrated that an integrated neuromuscular training programme focusing on motor skill and muscular strength development can actually elicit positive changes in 1.6 kilometre run performance.[26] The authors of this research cited the notion that children are nonmetabolic specialists, and therefore training adaptations are not necessarily specific to the demands of the activity.[26]

Should the coach decide that specific endurance training outside technical or tactical sessions is warranted, research clearly shows that prepubertal children can make significant gains in aerobic power after a high-intensity interval training protocol.[37] Especially in the case of inexperienced prepubertal children, any training session loosely designed to indirectly enhance endurance should be of high intensity and interval in nature to more closely resemble the activity patterns commonly seen in free playtime and to provide some level of overload. When working with children and young adolescents, trainers need to be highly proactive and sensitive to short-term fluctuations in endurance performance, especially during various stages of development.

Developing Flexibility

Flexibility is recognised as a key physical performance quality in young athletes. The importance of flexibility is sport specific. For example, aesthetic sports such as gymnastics are, to a certain degree, scored on extreme body positions, but other sports such as baseball or golf require large ranges of motion (ROM) to increase the distance over which force is applied (impulse). Irrespective of the requirements of the sport, it should be recognised that an athlete must be able to demonstrate appropriate levels of strength through the range of motion typically used for his or her sport. Despite its relative importance for sport performance, flexibility is a largely underresearched area of study within paediatrics. From the available literature, researchers have suggested that prepubescence is a key time frame in which to develop flexibility, with the age bracket of 6 to 11 years proposed as a sensitive period for morphological changes.[12, 38, 39]

Physiologically, the increased pliability and reduced musculotendinous stiffness (both passive and active) of muscle tissue associated with this stage of development may enable greater ROM to be attained. Evidence also suggests that levels of flexibility tend to plateau or even decrease at around the time of the adolescent growth spurt and into adulthood,[38] which may suggest that maintaining previously acquired levels of flexibility should be the training focus for later stages of development.

Owing to the low impact of flexibility training, young athletes can perform flexibility training from twice weekly to daily, depending on the demands of the sport. If the coach or athlete is looking to develop chronic changes in ROM, it is recommended that stretches be held for 10 to 30 seconds. This recommendation is different from short-duration, preactivity mobility exercises that athletes routinely perform, during which the main goal is an acute change in muscular elasticity and ROM. Irrespective of the training mode selected, coaches must pay close attention to postural integrity and alignment while athletes stretch.

Should Young Athletes Specialise Early?

Designing training programmes for single-sport athletes would require a phase of physical preparation prior to the onset of the competitive phase. However, for those athletes involved in multiple sports that may overlap, we need to ensure preparation phases are built into each competitive season. Central to this philosophy is the need to ensure that the child has sufficient time to rest and recover and to enable normal growth and maturation processes to occur. Additionally, the preparation phases should be viewed as an opportunity to regain or improve on precompetition levels of fitness that would typically have plateaued or decreased as a result of the demands of the competitive season. This approach is essential for reducing the likelihood youth athletes experiencing nonfunctional overreaching or overtraining, which can lead to performance decrements and reductions in overall health and well-being. Previous research showed that nonfunctional overreaching or overtraining occurred in approximately 30 per cent of young athletic population across a breadth of different sports.[40]

Early sport specialisation refers to when children focus on a single sport and complete year-round specific training at a young age. Risks associated with early specialisation include social isolation, burnout and overuse injuries,[41] all of which make a long-term approach to youth physical development somewhat challenging. Certain sports such as gymnastics lend themselves more to earlier specialisation than others; for most sports, however, specialisation should be delayed until adolescence to ensure the child athlete is exposed to a breadth of training environments that develop fundamental motor skills before training focuses on sport-specific skills. Unfortunately, more sports are trying to promote earlier specialisation, and consequently, many strength and conditioning coaches working with young athletes will have to deal with the additional risks of overtraining and overuse injuries.

Summary

Owing to the complex nature of growth and maturation, strength and conditioning provision for young athletes requires an appreciation and understanding of paediatric exercise science. This chapter has reviewed key principles governing successful long-term athletic development programmes, and in doing so has highlighted the following messages:

• Training age should be the main variable that determines training programme design. However, biological age must also be considered to ensure training programmes are as effective as possible.

• Youth-based strength and conditioning programmes should aim to develop a range of health- and skill-related fitness components. However, programmes should centre on developing muscular strength levels and motor skill proficiency.

• In order to develop speed a coach may focus on increasing the rate and magnitude of force applied during the ground-contact period while also aiming to reduce that period. These objectives represent qualities that do and do not naturally develop with maturation, respectively.

• Prepubescence is an ideal stage of development to learn motor skill patterns and force-producing capacities required for agility performance.

• Flexibility training is an important part of any youth physical development programme, but coaches should remember that an athlete must be able to produce strength through the range of motion typically used for his or her sport.

• Attention must be given to the overall physical and psychosocial demands placed on the young athlete, especially on those who are involved in multiple sports. It is imperative that strength and conditioning is not simply viewed as an add-on to the overall training programme but rather is seen as an essential and definitive component in its own right.

CHAPTER 3

Enhancing Movement Efficiency

Craig Ranson, PhD
Cardiff Metropolitan University, UK, and Welsh Rugby Union

David Joyce
Western Force Rugby, Australia and Edith Cowan University, Perth, Australia

The sport world is littered with individuals who have impressive physical attributes, such as a huge anaerobic capacity or formidable lower-body strength. Some have become world champions. Others have never made the leap to stardom because, despite these qualities, the poor postures and movement strategies they adopt compromise their ability to apply force efficiently and repeatedly. Essentially, they leak energy, making the metabolic cost of performing at high intensities or over long durations expensive and performance limiting.

Athletes don't just need to be strong; they also need to be efficient. This concept applies to power-based sports as well as to endurance sports. Inefficient movement is metabolically costly, which means that onset of fatigue will be quicker, and subsequent performance decay will be larger. It is easy to see this in swimming. An inefficient swimmer who has a costly technique will become fatigued after just a few laps of a pool, whereas a similarly conditioned swimmer using an efficient stroke can continue at high pace, lap after lap.

Although other significant variables—such as technical and tactical awareness, mental and emotional resiliency, dedication and professionalism—interact to determine sport success, it is the aim of this chapter is to discuss the impact of human movement efficiency on performance. This discussion seeks to provide strategies for assessment and optimisation of motion competencies that can be used by coaches, therapists and athletes.

Attaining Movement Efficiency

Sport commentators often describe athletes as being efficient performers. When the word *efficiency* is pared back to its physical roots, it describes the output relative to the cost of the input. Therefore, an inefficient mover is one whose output, whether it is during running, cycling, rowing or swimming, is less than his or her input. The two critical variables to consider when assessing movement efficiency are the force generated and the force applied. These are not always the same, and if inequalities exist, so does inefficiency.

Effective Force Generation

Sport provides a graphic demonstration of physics in action. Within athletic pursuits, force is applied to the ground (such as during running, jumping and skating), to water (such as during swimming and rowing), to an object (such as a shot-put or bicycle) or to another person (such as through a martial arts kick or when a footballer has to fend off an opponent). Clearly, it is an advantage to be able to generate greater forces, and yet it is not always the case that the athlete with the greatest strength emerges the victor. This observation extends from sports traditionally regarded as power sports, such as weightlifting and track cycling, to endurance sports, such as marathon running or triathlon, as well as to team sports, such as soccer and handball.

Successful performances in many sports rely on the generation of muscular power. In most cases, it is not just a one-off powerful movement that is required because sport success is often contingent on multiple efforts. Therefore, *enduring* power production is sought, with sport events able to be considered as combinations of hundreds, if not thousands, of demonstrations of Newtonian physics. Minimising the decay in this power expression between the first repetitions (e.g., a single effort like a high jump or paddle stroke or, more broadly, a sprint or boxing round) and the last is often the difference between winning and losing. It is the ability to apply or overcome resistance that lies at the heart of this quest.

The generation of power comes at a metabolic cost, which is why runners cannot maintain sprint pace for an entire marathon. The body's ability to provide the fuel for these working muscles depends on a quality broadly termed *fitness*, a concept that can encompass many variables. In this context fitness is generally used to describe the ability of the metabolic (cardiovascular and cardiopulmonary) systems to supply working muscles with an adequate supply of energy. Increasing the capacity of this system to perform these duties is the focus of chapters 14 and 16.

Wisdom

The role of a metabolic system is analogous to the locomotive engine on a steam train. It fuels the body's ability to generate force. The greater the force required to be generated, the harder the engine is required to work.

Effective Force Application

Although important, the amount of force that can be generated is not the only consideration, and this brings us to the second variable: force application. The force generated may be quite different to the amount of force that can be successfully applied. An easy way to conceptualise this is by thinking of trying to drive a bent nail into a plank of wood. Irrespective of the size of the hammer (or, indeed, the strength of the person holding it), the nail will not enter the wood with the precision or energy cost-effectiveness of a straight nail. Thus, the force generated onto the head of the nail is quite different to the force transferred to the wood. This is an example of an *energy leak*. When a leak is present, less force or speed can be generated, or the metabolic cost of its generation is inflated.

Athletes often are perceived as being unfit if they labour around the field of play, whether that be an athletic track, a swimming pool, a football pitch, a skating rink or a basketball court. Perhaps they *are* unfit (the locomotive is not able to continually power the train), but a bigger problem may be their ability to transfer force efficiently. Attempting to improve fitness may be effective in an untrained person, but highly trained athletes have much smaller windows for fitness gains. Improving the ability to run around the playing field or move through the water may instead rely on plugging energy leaks.

A mind shift may be required in those people who assume, for example, that the yo-yo intermittent recovery test (or other field tests purported to examine fitness) is an evaluation of aerobic capacity. In actual fact, any such test is nothing more than an assessment of an individual's ability to run repeated shuttles. Unquestionably, the ultimate failure point occurs when energy reserves are depleted such that the athlete is unable to complete a particular repetition in the required time. However, this does not necessarily mean that the factor that discriminates between athletes when completing this test is cardiovascular power.

Imagine you have to water your plants and that if you fill your 5-litre watering can, you will have just enough to do the 5-minute job. Imagine now, that you fill your can but you discover it has a number of holes in the side and is leaking 200 millilitres a minute. You will be left short. Is this because the watering can was not big enough or because it leaked? Seal the leaks, and the watering can would be big enough.

The same applies to the repeated shuttles example. If the athlete's running mechanics were suboptimal, or if turning technique was poor, irrespective of metabolic capacity, the athlete would be spending energy reserves at a much greater rate than a more efficient counterpart. This is the same as the watering-can example. The limiter, therefore, may not be the size of the aerobic bank but the body's spending habits.

In this instance, if a training programme addresses the identified energy leaks—the physical and technical deficits—and the athlete becomes a more efficient runner, less energy would be spent per stride. This means that either the number of strides taken can be greater, or the force applied per stride can be higher. It would be tempting to think any improvements in a follow-up repeated running test were due to improvements in aerobic fitness, but in fact, the athlete may not be any fitter, just spending energy more wisely. The watering can is no bigger; it just no longer leaks.

This same theory also accounts for the world-class performances that can be witnessed in paddling sports such as swimming, rowing and kayaking. Less physically gifted athletes can still reach great heights in rowing if they are so technically sound that they do not leak energy through unwanted body or paddle motions. Every stroke is effective and efficient. Conversely, an athlete with terrific physical capacities may still not row fast if his or her technique is such that the rower cannot apply force efficiently through the oar onto the water. These are people coaches describe as muscling through the water, which is energy expensive. Often, these athletes are found to be unable to transfer performances on the rowing ergometer to the regatta courses, where technical prowess is critical.

Wisdom

Efficient movement is the desirable outcome from mechanical and metabolic standpoints. It is not being suggested that efficiency is sought at the expense of optimal athlete conditioning or fitness. However, movement efficiency is the structure upon which strength and cardiovascular fitness are built.

Swimming provides an interesting context in which to analyse movement efficiency. Many people think that the aim is to push the arm through the water as fast as possible, but this is incorrect. Instead, efficient swimmers grab hold of the water and use it as an anchor to propel the body forward, using both lift and drag to best advantage. As the swimmer's hand enters the water, it attempts to push back onto still water. The problem is that water begins to move and becomes more elusive to push against. The swimmer, therefore, aims to find calm water to push against, which is one reason why an expert swimmer's hand and upper limb move in a curved path during the pull phase of the stroke. When the aim is to create propulsion in water, the odds are stacked against performers when it comes to force application; for that reason, although strength is important, efficiency in applying that strength is of greater concern.

Swimming is not just about maximising propulsion, however. It is also about minimising the negative effects of drag. Each type of drag has an exponential effect on propulsive force, and athletes must work to minimise forms of drag. For swimming, strategies that can be employed include wearing tight swimsuits and removing hair. Maintaining arrow-like, streamlined body shapes also reduce the effects of profile and wave drag. Therefore, it is not the strongest swimmer who will be the fastest, but rather the one most skillful at applying force to a moving platform whilst simultaneously minimising drag.

Wisdom

In swimming, the person who is technically skilled in maximising propulsive forces and minimising drag forces will be efficient and fast. In some sports, therefore, efficiency is determined not just by the force applied but by the external forces that are minimised. This concept also applies to sports such as cycling, downhill skiing, bob skeleton and rowing.

Achieving Movement Efficiency

The body is designed for efficient movement. Joints and bones are well structured to be able to deal with the positions demanded of them as well as the forces transferred through them. Much, then, depends on how the active (force-producing) components function. Not only do they control the position of the joints, but they also control the amount of applied force. With this in mind, this section will focus on musculo-tendinous efficiency.

Musculo-Tendinous Function in Optimising Athletic Movement

Muscles and tendons interact to be both the drivers and limiters of human movement. They produce the energy that is transferred to the skeleton so that joints can initiate or resist motion. However, the way we are traditionally taught about muscle and tendon action is not necessarily an accurate reflection of reality. A deeper understanding of these concepts is fundamental to understanding and enhancing movement efficiency.

Isometric Muscular Actions Are Essential for Powerful Motion

It may seem oxymoronic but, in most cases, joint movement is made possible by tendon excursion as opposed to changes in muscle length. The muscle–tendon unit is formed by the respective series and parallel coupling of muscle tissue with elastic tendon and fascial elements. These elastic components transfer muscular energy to the skeleton. The combination of elastic and contractile elements within muscle–tendon units can create confusion as to the type of muscular action that is occurring. For example, although there may be net lengthening of a muscle–tendon unit as it elongates under load (usually termed *eccentric*), often it is only the elastic elements that stretch whilst the muscular elements act isometrically or even contract slightly.[1]

Think of an elastic band attached to a weight. Overall, the entire system may lengthen as we pull on the band, but it is only allowed to do so because it is held securely at the top by the weight. This is a similar situation to that found in the body. Although the entire muscle–tendon complex may lengthen, often it is the muscle component that provides the steady anchor, allowing the elastic nature of the tendons to accommodate to the changing joint positions associated with movement. These isometric muscular actions during musculotendinous elongation are especially prevalent in bi-articular muscles, those producing fast and powerful sport movements, such as the biceps and triceps brachii during hitting and throwing and the hamstrings and gastrocnemius during sprinting.

Despite a considerable amount of training and rehabilitation literature devoted to the benefits of eccentric (sometimes termed *negative*) muscular work, true eccentric muscular actions during fast, high-force sport activities are simply not possible for three primary reasons. First, the energy cost and heat production of fascicular lengthening and shortening during concentric–eccentric muscular actions would make repeating more than just a few movement cycles unsustainable. Second, the required changeover from fascicular lengthening to shortening (eccentric to concentric) would not be fast or powerful enough to facilitate high-velocity motion. Third, if muscular elements were lengthening during eccentric muscular-action phases, tension would effectively be reduced in the elastic components, significantly reducing their spring-like properties and power-production potential.

Instead, the job of the muscle when joints are rotating at high velocity is to create and maintain tension in the spring-like elastic elements so that energy stored in the tendons and fascia is optimally transferred to the skeleton.[1] An example of this is the hamstring during the second half of the swing phase of fast running. The classic theory is that the hamstring first acts eccentrically to decelerate extension of the knee before reversing to act concentrically to extend the hip as the lower limb retracts towards the ground. Given that the hip and knee joints might be rotating at several hundred degrees per second, it is much more likely that the first job of the muscular elements is to contract slightly in order to take up slack in the hamstring that results from the extreme knee-flexion position early in the swing phase. Taking up this muscle slack and tensioning the hamstring tendons by then maintaining an isometric muscular action as the knee extends in late swing will create a forceful elastic recoil, facilitating powerful retraction of the lower limb before the initial foot contact.

The bottom line is that much of the lengthening that is apparent with so-called eccentric exercises, such as Nordic hamstring curls, is actually occurring in the noncontractile (tendon and fascial) tissue whilst the actual muscle action is mostly isometric. Nordic curls have been shown to be useful in preventing and rehabilitating hamstring injuries.[2] However, Nordics can cause painful delayed-onset muscle soreness (DOMS) and are extremely difficult to do into outer-range knee extension. Maximal isometric hamstring–loading exercises can be used to strengthen the hamstring musculotendinous unit without significant DOMS and arguably use a more appropriate muscular action and lower-limb position. Examples of these include the single-leg hamstring bridge in the extended-knee position (figure 3.1) and the single-leg isometric hip extension in the glute–ham machine (figure 3.2). Both can be loaded to induce maximal isometric hamstring recruitment in a similar position and range (midstance) to where maximal hamstring force is produced during high-speed running.

By training these muscles in this fashion, the athlete uses the body's own intrinsic efficiency system, one in which the muscle is working as a stable anchor point for the more efficient tendon to stretch and recoil.

Figure 3.1 Single-leg hamstring bridge with a lower-limb position that reflects the midstance phase of fast running.

Figure 3.2 Single-leg isometric hip extension with a lower-limb position that reflects the midstance phase of fast running.

Muscles Are Only Powerful in a Narrow-Length Range

Another important principle to apply when targeting energy leaks is the need to use the most productive muscle lengths. Although versatile in being able to act in a variety of modes over a wide range of motion, maximal force production is possible only when musculotendinous units are at or near their optimal length. An example length–tension curve is illustrated in figure 3.3. Note that isolated muscle force capability is greatest in the midrange;

however, the influence of creating tension in the passive (tendon and fascial) components allows force production to be maintained in outer-range (lengthened) positions.

If the amount of force that can be produced by a muscle–tendon unit depends on this length–tension relationship, the most efficient and effective sport movements will occur when as many of the key muscle groups involved in the movement as possible are acting within their most favourable length-tension ranges. Mechanisms for activating and training movement patterns that maximise optimal length–tension advantages are introduced in the following section.

Motor Patterning for Efficient Athletic Movement

For any give movement task, countless combinations of joint motions and muscular actions can be used. As a rule, the body will always seek to take the path of least resistance when it comes to movement because this is the most metabolically efficient. An example is that someone with a restriction in ankle dorsiflexion will tend to roll into excessive pronation or even rotate externally from the hip in order to propel the body forward during locomotion. The way the body organises itself to meet a functional end is quite extraordinary, but what is most metabolically efficient in the short term will not necessarily be the most mechanically efficient.

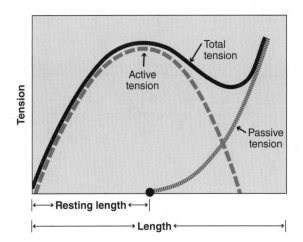

Figure 3.3 Typical length–tension curves for a musculotendinous unit. The active tension is provided by contracting the muscular elements, and the passive tension is provided by stretching the tendofascial elements.

This adaptability is both a blessing and a curse. Coaches, therapists and athletes can become somewhat paralysed by choice and do not always choose the correct or most efficient motor pattern to complete a given task. This is the degrees-of-freedom problem and something that needs to be overcome in order to organise movement patterns to be as efficient and effective as possible.

To do so, the body tends to default to the adoption of characteristic postures and movement patterns that often are difficult to change (see explanation of attractors in chapter 9). These postures or movement patterns generally fall into the category of being efficient (such as having a vertical thigh position at the point of toe-off in the running cycle) or inefficient (such as having an extended thigh posture at toe-off). Although athletes will tend to use one or the other (mild thigh extension at toe-off is rarely seen), they can flip between the two patterns or revert to the less efficient mode when fatigued or under pressure.

The reason the vertical thigh position (neutral hip flexion and extension) during toe-off is more efficient than an extended thigh position is two-fold. First, if the thigh is extended, the hip flexor muscles will be elongated, which is a suboptimal position for producing tension (figure 3.3). Therefore, hip-flexion power during forward swing will be compromised. Second, the range of flexion the hip will have to traverse during forward swing will be longer. Because the ability to recover the swing limb quickly is a major determinant of running speed, having a longer, weaker forward swing will be inefficient and slow.

An attractor that facilitates optimal length–tension postures of the hip and pelvic muscles in a number of sport activities is the lock position of the pelvis.[3] This position is attained during the phase of motion during which the standing, lower-limb forces are highest, for example, the midstance position during running, the backswing of baseball hitting (figure 3.4a) or the tennis forehand (figure 3.4b) and the cocking phase of throwing (figure 3.4c). It involves a posture of the free (nonstance) side of the pelvis being slightly elevated and internally rotated. This posture places the majority of the trunk and femur muscles attaching to the stance side of the pelvis in their optimum length–tension range (near midrange) so that energy can be most effectively transferred from the ground through the trunk to the upper limb (in the case of upper-limb activities) and from the hip to the knee to the ankle (in the case of lower-limb activities).

Another benefit of the lock position is that it takes advantage of the primitive extension reflex whereby hip flexion off the non-weight-bearing

Figure 3.4 Sport examples of the lock pelvic position: (*a*) during the backswing of baseball hitting; (*b*) just before the impact of a tennis forehand; (*c*) during the transition between the windup and acceleration phases of baseball pitching.

limb produces a powerful reflexive hip, knee and ankle triple extension on the opposite-stance side. The hip flexion associated with the lock pelvic position, therefore, can reflexively augment power production in the stance limb (figure 3.5).

The antithesis of the lock pelvic position is one in which the free side of the pelvis is dropped during the midstance phase of running (figure 3.6; stance-side hip and pelvic musculature is placed in an adverse length-tension position). Sometimes known as the Trendelenburg sign, it places the stance-side lateral pelvic musculature (gluteus maximus, tensor fasciae latae and the attaching iliotibial tract, along with the smaller abductors gluteus medius and gluteus minimus) in an unfavourable, lengthened position. Force transfer through the pelvis is thereby limited.

An easy way to think about the pelvic lock position is to picture a crane on a building site. In order to be able to lift heavy construction bins, the crane needs to be stable at its base; otherwise, the system will break down. The body operates in a similar way, which is why athletes need to be strong and efficient in achieving and securing the locked pelvic position.

This lock position is a critical attractor in efficient force acceptance and force transfer. Should this mechanism fail due to muscular weakness or a faulty motor pattern, the body is forced to work harder to attain the functional goals being requested by the brain (or coach!). If the body has to work harder, it will consume vastly more energy reserves, and performance endurance will be compromised.

An assessment of the strength and holding capacity of the lateral hip muscles should be a part of every athletic programme. These muscles help maintain a strong pelvic lock position, crucial for force transference to both the upper and lower limbs. The ability to hold a lateral support (plank) posture (figure 3.7) is one method of assessing the capacity of the lateral pillar musculature.

Wisdom

The fact that the pelvic lock position in midstance is so critical to the striking and throwing sports where the upper limb is (seemingly) dominant demonstrates our contention that the shoulders start at the feet. Pelvic motion and strength also are critical to performance and healthy shoulder function in swimmers. Without an efficient kick produced by the hips, the upper limbs are required to pick up the slack, something that can lead to slow times and sore shoulders.

Figure 3.5 The pelvic lock position during the mid-support phase of a high jump take-off.

Figure 3.6 Dropped swing-leg side of the pelvis.

Figure 3.7 Lateral or side-plank position.

Lock Position Training Drills

A common energy leak during many running-based sport activities is excessive trunk motion, particularly rotation. An arm swing that goes across the body or a foot plant that crosses the midline is a manifestation of excessive rotation. Such overrotation of the trunk and pelvis needs to be counteracted by opposite rotations of either the upper or lower limbs. Energy that should be used for propelling the body forward is leaked into the compensatory rotational movements. Faulty movement patterns or insufficient trunk strength can both be factors in this error.

Drills that can be used to quickly and effectively improve trunk-muscle recruitment involve running with the arms stretched overhead. Bilateral overhead arm positions cause a reflexive co-contraction of the trunk musculature on the pelvis. This promotes stiffness of the lower trunk and pelvis, further augmenting potential for energy transfer and reducing unwanted rotational or lateral motion of the trunk and pelvis. Infants have undeveloped trunk strength and coordination and when learning to walk and run will naturally adopt this attractor overhead-arm position in order to access this reflex, which stiffens and stabilises the trunk. Running with a stick held as high as possible overhead (figure 3.8) will also harness this reflex and can have immediate positive effects on subsequent running technique.

For the lock-position walking drill (figure 3.9), the athlete begins with both arms reaching high overhead, holding a broomstick in both hands. Walking or skipping forward, the athlete pushes the stance-side arm upward whilst obtaining lock position, elevation of the pelvis on the swing side, hip flexion to approximately 80 degrees and maximal knee flexion and dorsiflexion. Elbows remain straight. Simultaneously, the athlete forcefully plantar-flexes the stance ankle.

Movement Control Versus Movement Freedom

Some athletes do not suffer from the problem of too much movement during athletic function. These individuals move in block-like patterns due to *too much* muscle activity and hence demand too much of their energy systems. Co-contractions around joints are helpful to stabilise motion segments but are

Figure 3.8 Overhead-stick runs stimulate co-contraction of all trunk muscles and reduce unwanted trunk motion.

Figure 3.9 Lock-position walking drill.

energy-thirsty, so this block-like motion is another example of mechanical (and therefore metabolic) inefficiency.

This is an important point to make because sometimes seeking to control movement results in rigidity around joints. Movement efficiency is about being adept at exploring movement throughout the range of motion (ROM) and being strong and stable. Often, training programmes are uniplanar and neglect combination movements. Drills that encourage athletes to explore somewhat unfamiliar motions are helpful in allowing participants to cope with a larger scope of movement demands within training or competition.

Having a broader window of acceptance and an ability to explore new movements and dissociate components of movements can be achieved by including novel drills into warm-ups or dedicated movement-efficiency sessions. Drills designed to this end may include

- hula hoop,
- overhead squat,
- Turkish get-up,
- lumbo-pelvic dissociation in lying, sitting and standing positions with variations in thoracic, hip and knee postures,
- gymnastic-type activities such as rolling and jumping and
- monkey bars with long crossover swings.

Alternatives to normal technical training such as yoga, martial arts, salsa dancing and indoor rock climbing can also be helpful in this pursuit, especially when trying to develop strength and coordination in different ROM.

Identifying and Remedying Common Energy Leaks

This section provides examples and potential remedies for common energy leaks that occur during fundamental sport activities such as running, throwing and swimming.

Running

Running is the core physical skill of many of the world's most popular sports. Therefore, it is surprising that running skill training is often neglected in programmes that prepare for running sports. Examples of adverse running mechanics that result in significant energy leaks have been provided in the previous sections. Table 3.1 lists these along with other common faults and provides examples of assessment techniques that might be used to correct them. A more detailed description of one major running energy leak, excessive braking force due to contacting the ground too far in front of the centre of mass, and a corrective drill are presented in the next section.

Overcoming a Running Technique That Has Excessive Braking Forces

Fast, efficient running is characterised by a short ground-contact time and lower-limb positioning that produces optimal horizontal and vertical propulsion forces. Normally, the foot position at initial contact should be just in front of the runner's centre of mass. Unwanted braking forces can occur if initial contact is too far in front of the centre of mass. This not only produces a backward-directed braking ground-reaction force, but it effectively increases the ground-contact time. The result either will be slower running or more energy required to maintain the same speed.

A drill that can be used to correct this error and minimise braking is overstride barefoot running at a fast pace (see table 3.1). The athlete's feet should be bare as opposed to shod with a minimalist or barefoot-type running shoe,[4] and therefore the surface needs to be safe, not too hard or abrasive. Firm grass is ideal. Tarmac, synthetic or dirt tracks should be avoided. Asking the athlete to overstride whilst running barefoot (figure 3.10) will automatically cause him or her to fully retract the swing leg before contacting the ground: Contacting too far in front will be uncomfortable on a bare foot.

This is an example of an implicit coaching technique that uses drills to improve movement patterns. It relies on the individual's ability to self-organise or problem solve the best way to achieve the goal of a drill and is more effective than the ineffective, yet highly prevalent, explicit coaching method that relies on instructing athletes how to move. With the lower-limb segments rotating several hundred degrees per second in fast running, it is unlikely the athlete would improve if instructed to 'pull the front leg back hard so that it

Table 3.1 Technique Criteria, Testing and Sample Exercises for Efficient, Fast Running

Plane	Phase	Optimal (attractor)	Energy leak	Test/Assessment	Drill/Exercise
Sagittal	Midstance to toe-off	Neutral anterior-posterior pelvic tilt	Anterior pelvic tilt	45° double-leg lower	Overhead-stick run
		Vertical thigh (neutral hip extension)	Extended hip and thigh		Hurdle split jump
		Plantar flexion at toe-off	Neutral ankle at toe-off	Single-leg calf raise (bent and straight knee)	Single-leg clean to low box
	Forward swing	Maximal knee flexion	Submaximal knee flexion	Sagittal high-speed video	Uphill or stair run
		Ankle dorsiflexion	Plantar flexion		Lock walking and skipping drills
	Forward swing to reversal	Hip and thigh flexion to just below horizontal	Low hip and thigh flexion angle		Falling start acceleration
					Uphill or ramp run
	Backward swing to initial contact	Initial contact just in front of centre of mass	Initial contact too far in front of centre of mass (insufficient swing-leg retraction)		Overstride barefoot running on grass
	Initial contact to mid-stance	Active plantar flexion	Dorsiflexed ankle	Single-leg calf-raise capacity (bent & straight knee)	Active plantar-flexion jump
Frontal	Initial contact to midstance	Elevated swing-leg side of pelvis	Dropped swing-leg side of pelvis	Side plank in lock position, 30 sec hold	Lock walking and skipping drills
Axial	Midstance to toe-off	Minimal trunk rotation	Excessive trunk rotation	Front plank, 30 sec, opposite arm and leg lifted	Acceleration holding ball

Figure 3.10 Overstride barefoot running drill.

lands just in front of your body; then don't let your hip extend past the line of your body before you lift the foot off!'

Throwing

Many sports incorporate a throwing-type motion. Examples include baseball (pitching and fielding), cricket (fielding), javelin, tennis (serving), volleyball (spiking) and water polo (passing and shooting). When aiming to improve throwing power and accuracy, coaches often focus on upper-limb technique, strengthening and conditioning. However, kinetic studies have shown that those who display good technique generate the majority of their force from the large musculature of the lower trunk, pelvis and legs.[5] Table 3.2 summarises the optimal and common leak positions that occur during a throwing motion.

A key element of the preparation phase of many throwing motions is attaining a trunk and shoulder alignment that is side-on to the target.

Table 3.2 Optimal and Common Energy Leak Positions During Throwing Action

Phase	Optimal (attractor)	Energy leak	Drill/Exercise
Preparation	Side-on trunk alignment	Front-on trunk alignment	Two hands on ball before cocking
	Weight shift to back foot	Weight stays on front foot	
Cocking	Scaption glenohumeral joint alignment	Excessive horizontal extension	Turn head, keeping ball in sight
	<90° shoulder abduction	<90° shoulder abduction	Take hand high during cocking
Acceleration	110°-130° shoulder external rotation	Excessive shoulder external rotation	Internal rotation strength and stiffness exercises
	Long stride	Short stride	Drive off back foot
Follow-through	Weight moving towards target	Weight moving across target	Reach towards target

This allows weight transfer to the back leg and potentiates maximal power contribution potential of the trunk and lower limbs. To demonstrate how important this is, have players try to throw from a seated or kneeling position or whilst standing front-on to the target and starting with their weight on the front feet. Throwing velocity and distance will be significantly limited.

An excellent implicit training drill involves encouraging players in throwing sports such as cricket to keep two hands on the ball in the pre-cocking phase. Baseball automatically facilitates this skill as the ball is first held in the gloved, nondominant hand and then transferred to the throwing-arm hand, during which time the trunk has to rotate to a powerful side-on position as the weight shifts to the back foot.

Excessive external rotation of the throwing shoulder during the late-cocking and acceleration phase is also a common energy leak. Again, the powerful shoulder internal rotators will be unfavourably elongated and will have a greater range of internal rotation and shoulder flexion to traverse before ball release.

Swimming

Swimming is a sport in which movement efficiency is vital in order to maximise propulsion whilst at the same time minimise the negative effects of drag. In sprints, the ability to forcefully push off the blocks and turns is one of the most critical determinants of a successful performance. In fact, over one-third of the distance covered in a 100-metre freestyle race is generated from the start and turn. With this in mind, it is critical that the swimmer does not leak energy in these tasks, so avoiding a countermovement on the blocks is

important. Isometric pretension and then concentric explosion is important. This movement can be cued by teaching the athlete to take up the slack in the back, buttock, posterior thigh and calf muscles when the starter calls, 'Set'. The athlete then counterrotates the hips to lock the pelvis and optimise power transfer to the shoulder girdle and upper limbs. When the pistol fires, the swimmer can then dive in, aiming his or her head at the opposite end.

Many drills are aimed at reducing the effects of drag; these are readily found in texts dedicated to swimming. Following are some suggestions for the athlete:

- Imagine swimming downhill. Push the chest towards the bottom of pool. This will lift the legs and hips.

- Imagine swimming in a narrow tunnel. This reduces unwanted drag and wasteful trunk lateral flexion.

- Always swim with the gaze directed at the pool surface directly underneath, not 2 metres in front. This will help reduce wave drag.

There is a separate but important consideration with respect to movement competency in swimmers and indeed any other sportsperson who engages in cross-training. Swimming tends to be an activity that people specialise in from a young age, and swimmers often lack a more rounded support in land-based movement competencies. This helps explain why swimmers are often poor runners or inefficient performers in the gym. With this in mind, care needs to be taken when swimmers engage in technical lifting and jumping drills. High-impact activities, including running, are often risky in this population.

Summary

The capacity to generate and sustain force is a critical and in many ways a defining feature of sport success. The ability to achieve these goals, however, is contingent on an ability to organise the body so that movement is efficient. Inefficient motion is metabolically costly and may limit performance in the short term, for example, through reduced jump height or throw distance. In the long term, the athlete may be unable to physiologically support inefficient motion, as is the case in those with poor running, cycling, rowing or skiing technique. Moreover, inefficient movement predisposes injury to a specific inefficient segment (such as reduced ankle motion leading to ankle injury) or anywhere along the kinetic chain (such as poor pelvic and hip control, leading to shoulder dysfunction in throwers).

Therefore, technical excellence should be considered not just from a sport-skill perspective but also from a movement-competency perspective. Adding resistance, speed or volume should be considered only if movement efficiency is maintained. Training should be approached from a standpoint of taking athletes to their technical and movement-competency threshold.

CHAPTER 4

Stabilising and Strengthening the Core

Andy Barr
New York Knickerbockers, United States

Daniel Lewindon
Rugby Football Union, UK

Core stability is a term that has exploded into medical and sport consciousness in the last 20 years and now has an established place in most athlete development, injury prevention and rehabilitation programs. Although our understanding and belief systems regarding the core have evolved significantly over the last 50 years, this development has also resulted in many differing philosophies, priorities and definitions across continents and between cultures and professions.

Historically, medical circles have investigated and prioritised the effects of pain and pathology on specific spinal muscular structures, function and neuromuscular patterning and the effects of poor posture and movement strategies on injury risk. Conversely, strength and conditioning researchers have focused on the development of maximal trunk strength and optimal mechanics to deliver the best platform for athletic function. Inevitably, over time both groups have generated best-practice models and created their own languages and terminology. It is also worth considering that in the last few years, the health and fitness industry, armed with an ever-expanding advertising culture, has attempted to influence our understanding of core training by packaging and branding exercises and equipment with the aim of delivering the aesthetic and perceived performance improvements that the public needs. This has all resulted in a lack of clarity in concepts and communication between professionals and with athletes, and a potential disconnect between medical and performance circles regarding the best methods of delivering appropriate stability programs to athletes.

The aims of this chapter are to bring together some established concepts and evidence-based practices to deliver a pragmatic solution to stability development and maintenance. As such it will

- provide an understanding of the structure and function of the core that is equally applicable to both medical and performance spheres and demystifies some of the terminology in circulation;
- present a best-practice model of core assessment critical to understanding athlete limitations;
- discuss and demonstrate a program of progressive core development needed to build physical robustness and maximise performance; and
- discuss a strategic approach to integrating the delivery of core stability training both before and during the competitive season.

What Is the Core?

To fully understand both the assessment and training of the core we need to appreciate what we are dealing with. Previous research and publications have described and characterised the core by region, tissue structure and action. Before generating a worthwhile definition to guide our training strategies, it is worth exploring what the core is a little further and reviewing the current evidence for the efficacy of core training.

Characterising the Core by Region

In purely anatomical terms, the core might be expected to refer to the trunk (i.e., the lumbar spine and pelvis) as the central portion of the body, and this is certainly most practitioners' understanding when they hear this phrase. However, this is a constrained definition in terms of stability training; many professionals have extended the definition to include aspects of hip, thoracic, scapula and even cervical spine awareness, control and strength.[1] Since muscles originating in the lumbar spine extend directly to the thoracic and cervical spine and through connective tissue to the skull, fingertips and toes, this understanding reinforces that an abs-only approach is far too limited in its perspective.

A better solution, therefore, might be to upgrade the term *core stability* to *postural control*. This concept begins with the trunk (including the pelvis) but also gives consideration to ensuring awareness, appropriate control and dissociative qualities are demonstrable throughout the spine, scapula–thoracic articulation and hips in all three planes of motion. This ensures that task quality remains a priority to the athlete and practitioner in all training. For clarity and consistency within this chapter, however, we will continue to use the term *core stability* to refer to this system.

Wisdom

The core is a term that captures the whole spine and proximal peripheral joints; it also considers movement competency and control throughout the chain.

Characterising the Core by Its Components

The core system has a number of passive and active components that contribute to its function.[2] The *passive system* is composed of the vertebral bodies, joints and their corresponding capsuloligamentous restraints. In the spine, passive restraints contribute little to the stability needed for normal function, with approximately 10 kg quoted as the compressive force required for the spine to buckle in the absence of soft tissues.[2] However, passive restraints do convey a significant amount of sensory information to the central nervous system (CNS) via mechanoreceptors, which in turn will have a bearing on the modulation of muscle tone, activation and patterning.

A well-grooved sensory (afferent) pathway is vital in core stability training. In addition to the information sent from the passive structures, the body's internal monitoring system also receives input from the active components (muscles and tendons) and the visual and vestibular systems (inner ear). Time permitting, this information is then assimilated and interpreted by the higher centres (premotor cortex in the brain), allowing the musculoskeletal system to deliver a dose-appropriate action plan or motor pattern to maintain stability or generate motion.

Therefore, a significant consideration in stability training should be directed towards developing and optimising spinal proprioception and appropriate neuromuscular patterning in sport and life-relevant situations. Doing so will maximise the dynamic correspondence of training to function and result in a better long-term carryover.

Pain (or even a history of pain) has the potential to affect the quality of information received by the control centres of the brain and the brain's interpretation of events. This has been shown to result in rapid changes to neighbouring tissue structure[3, 4] (i.e., tissue closest to the spine) and forms the basis of the literature that has demonstrated alterations in the timing and sensitivity of recruitment of the core muscles in those with a history of back and neck pain.

It is often argued that habitual poor posture will dampen passive tissue sensory information, altering resting muscle tone and length and potentially predisposing individuals to injury. From a mechanical perspective studies of posture have shown a significant increase in posterior spinal disc loading when sitting in a flexed position and disproportionate loading through specific spinal joints with certain posture types.[5-7] Sustained tension to collagenous tissue will result in changes to its inherent stiffness over time;[8, 9] by extension, sloppy posture, where the body rests on its passive restraints with little active contribution, has the potential to expose the system to creep and injury. Good posture and postural control need to be reinforced in all core stability training.

Wisdom

The core needs to be trained in good posture and have relevance to the desired movement patterns undertaken in sport wherever possible.

The *active system* is composed of multiple layers of contractile muscle and noncontractile tendon and fascial connective tissue, which envelop the spine like a multilayered barrel in a series of interconnected slings. These layers are commonly subdivided into three distinct groups: local (deep) stabilisers, global (superficial) stabilisers and global movers (figure 4.1, *a-c*).

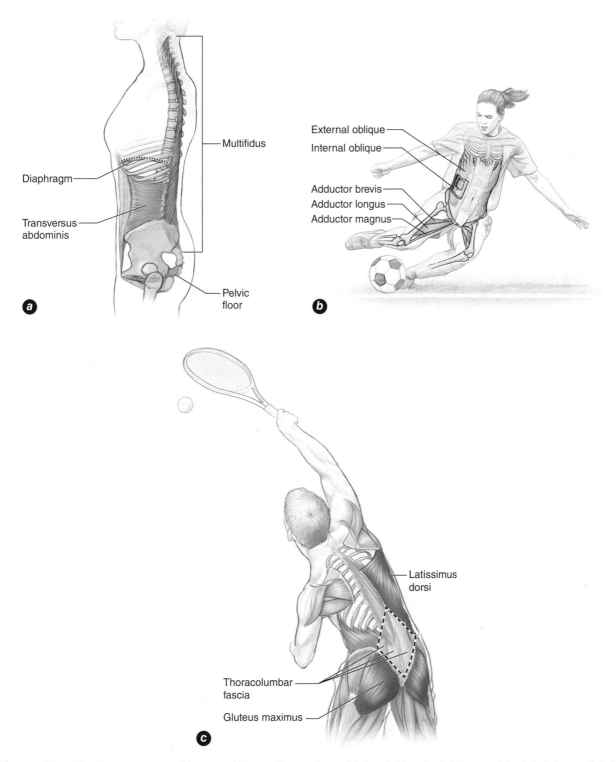

Figure 4.1 The three groups of layers of the active system: (*a*) local (deep) stabilisers; (*b*) global (superficial) stabilisers; (*c*) global movers.

Various researchers have tried to identify key muscles in core stability, often with conflicting results.[10-21] This research has included significant attention to the importance of the deeper muscles surrounding the spine, including the transverse abdominis and multifidus, and their role in preparing the trunk for limb motion. However, it is now widely accepted that no one muscle holds the key to effective spinal stability.

Much like the passive system, the smaller muscles (local stabilisers) are richly innervated with mechanoreceptors and convey a significant amount of positional information to the CNS. These muscles will fire in anticipation of motion, creating a degree of protective stiffness to counteract the expected load. They cannot generate the same forces as the more superficial muscles, being hampered by both tissue size and moment arm. (The total force exerted by the muscle depends in part on its distance from the centre of joint motion; the farther away, the greater force it can apply.) Larger, global stability muscles are also needed to stabilise the spine, particularly against greater loads.

Thus, we should consider a layered but interdependent system that reacts to the level of stability required.[1, 21] What is critical here is that a well-conditioned core system must be able to react to both low- and high-load challenges to stability, using an appropriate level of effort.

Wisdom

Local stabilisers (deep core): the muscles closest to the spine; the main monosegmental muscles that contribute a limited amount to mechanical control but convey significant sensory information and generate some preparatory stiffness.

Global stabilisers (superficial core): larger multisegmental muscles that envelop the trunk in a series of interconnected slings and resist trunk motion under load, speed and limb motion.

Global movers: large multisegmental muscles. As the name would suggest, these muscles are perhaps more suited to generating joint motion.

Table 4.1 provides examples of the specific core muscles in each category and introduces the function and dysfunction of these muscles.

Table 4.1   Core Muscles: Function and Dysfunction

Layer	Category	Function	Dysfunction	Muscle examples
Deep	Local (deep core) stabilisers	Sensory feedback of posture and movement Compression of spine, pelvis and hip joints to prevent excessive translation	Activation timing delay and reduced sensitivity to recruitment under low-threshold circumstances in the presence of pain	Transversus abdominis, segmental multifidus, diaphragm, pelvic floor, psoas major
Middle	Global (superficial core) stabilisers	Direction-related control of motion, especially in the transverse plane Dominant in postural control and alignment Most effective at decelerating motion, especially rotational motion (the brakes and the steering) in low- and high-load situations	Activation timing delay and reduced sensitivity to recruitment under low-threshold circumstances in the presence of pain Elongation and inhibition to activation in shortened or inner ranges of motion Weakened under high-load circumstances	Internal oblique, external oblique, superficial multifidus, medial quadratus lumborum, gluteus medius, deep medial gluteus maximus, proximal adductors
Superficial	Global (core) movers	Direction-specific motion Most effective muscles for generating and accelerating joint motion Trunk stabilisation in high-load sagittal plane circumstances	Increased sensitivity to low-load activation (become dominant and overactive in postural control) More tonic in recruitment and become shorter in length	Rectus abdominis, erector spinae, quadratus lumborum, latissimus dorsi, superficial lateral gluteus maximus, adductor longus, adductor magnus, tensor fasciae latae

Characterising the Core by Its Action

Effective stability requires resistance to unwanted motion and the control of necessary motion in all three movement planes.

Resistance to unwanted motion is certainly a key factor in terms of performance (see chapter 3) and injury prevention when high forces are involved and should form the basis of all high-load trunk strength training. By definition this philosophy prohibits repetitive spinal motion under load as a strategy for developing core qualities. Instead practitioners should ensure that the trunk provides a stable platform under duress for effective limb movement and force production.

Repetitive trunk movement strengthening is not only functionally inappropriate, but also has the potential to alter both muscle structure (fibre length and orientation) and neuromuscular properties.[22] Traditional sit-up exercises also create significant compressive spinal loads, which will result in unwanted and unnecessary stress to lumbar intervertebral disc mechanics.[23]

The development of inertia, however, is an incomplete description of core action as there are times both athletically and in normal life when spine motion is desirable. In these instances (e.g., a tennis serve), spinal motion must be controlled in terms of range, speed and quality to minimise unwanted or asymmetrical loads.

Spinal muscles must have the capacity to stabilise the spine against forces of varying significance and speed, but also in a metabolically efficient manner. Overactivity through bracing or total rigidity in low-force activities will unnecessarily sap the system of energy, validating a dose-appropriate response to stability and a need to consider muscle timing and patterning. Similarly, the spine must have the endurance required to do its job; this is an important consideration in developing training programs.

Wisdom

The core needs to provide the dose-appropriate platform to stabilise and modulate posture in low- and high-load situations to allow force to be delivered efficiently by the upper and lower limbs.

Assessment of Core and Postural Stability

The previous section identified two separate but linked concepts that should be assessed with athletes:

1. Low load: posture, stability, movement quality, endurance and dissociation
2. High load: posture, strength, endurance and dissociation

Test Selection

No single test will accurately measure stability in all its forms. Accordingly, any new assessment process ideally could begin with a thorough needs analysis of the individual and his or her sport. This should include consideration of habitual postures, movements, weight-room requirements and the specific functional activities that occur in the sport in order to determine how well the athlete's system can cope with the demands or circumstances he or she is exposed to when playing, training and living.

Over the past three decades, a large number of tests and testing protocols have been developed to try to gauge stability in both the athlete and layperson. It is not practical or appropriate to list all potential tests and test combinations that could be used to assess core function. What is critical, however, is that whatever tests are used consider the key factors outlined earlier. The testing process should

- assess stability (and, where appropriate, controlled motion) in all three planes,
- assess the efficiency of the athlete to stabilise in a manner appropriate to the stimulus,
- be as functionally relevant as possible,
- include facilitation of all of the sensory systems, and
- appropriately test the capacity of the system.

Postural Awareness and the Neutral Zone

Before considering common tests that can be used to assess low- and high-load stability, it is worth clarifying the athlete's starting position. It is common for athletes with and without a history of back pain to have a poor awareness of good posture.

It is crucial that postural awareness is targeted and reinforced in all assessment and training drills to optimise sensory input into the system and minimise unwanted stresses. Often termed the *neutral zone*, good posture can be found in the lumbar spine simply by maximally extending and flexing the lumbar spine until the midpoint is found. Some practitioners choose to measure control in supine and prone positions with the use of a pressure biofeedback unit (PBU) or sphygmomanometer. The PBU is placed in lumbar lordosis and inflated, and it gives a visual clue of pressure change during exercises. Good alignment should also be achieved and maintained at the thoracic and cervical spine.

Wisdom

An athlete's ability to maintain the neutral zone when the system is challenged is an indication of the athlete's level of stability and control. If the spine cannot be kept in the neutral zone when challenged at either end of the load spectrum, this indicates a lack of control.

Having correct posture and habitual movement awareness in all activities may provide the greatest protection against injury. All strength and conditioning programs present opportunities to groove optimal neuromuscular patterns under the influence of fatigue and external load to ensure maximal efficiency is achieved and sustained. One of the primary roles of the spine is to create a stable platform to enable maximal force production. Therefore, correct posture should be reinforced in all lifting and athletic movements.

There is a strong argument here that spinal health and stability as well as optimal trunk function begin with educating the athlete regarding the importance of optimising posture and movement awareness throughout daily life. Such awareness can then be reinforced in the gym environment through ensuring that perfect form is maintained in all motions to minimise unnecessary spinal loading. Doing so represents a meaningful addition to the athlete's training plan without increasing activity volume or load.

Low-Load Assessment of Core Stability

Low-load stability can be considered the platform for the development of core strength and endurance. The focus here is to assess not only isolated muscle endurance, but also athlete awareness of a neutral spine and its maintenance by virtue of functional body-weight and limb-weight movements. This should progress from single-direction stability to multiplanar control.

In terms of standards of proficiency, the athlete should be able to demonstrate effective spinal control with repeated upper- and lower-limb motion. An anecdotal repetition number of 30 is often used since it represents an activity time of more than 60 seconds, which might be considered a reasonable test of type I (slow-twitch, nonfatiguing) muscle-fibre tissue qualities.

Wisdom

Even when athletes have significant trunk strength, this does not mean they can protect themselves against unpredictable, low-force movements. This problem is related to the timing and coordination of activation, not purely to strength. Athletes also need to be efficient with their trunk movements; therefore, bracing and excessive effort to repeat the movement should not be used.

SAMPLE TESTS

The following tests involve fundamental movement strategies that are important in both athletic movements and activities of daily living. By no means is this an all-encompassing list, but it provides a platform for the development of a testing battery. For each test consider where in the chain the movement breaks down and the direction in which this occurs. Based on the principles of stability, this test should not be confined to the lower back; consider the entire chain. For example, in a squat the athlete might show good control of the lower back throughout range of motion (ROM) but may demonstrate loss of frontal-plane control through the knee (e.g., the knee may drift towards the midline as opposed to staying centred over the toes). This would be considered a loss of hip control in the frontal and axial planes.

Waiter's Bow

Direction of control
Sagittal

Instruction
Stand with the spine in neutral starting position, arms across chest, and knees soft. Bend forward from the hips only (figure 4.2, *a-b*), without a loss of spine control. A helpful coaching cue here is to "keep the chest up".

Figure 4.2 Waiter's bow: *(a)* starting position; *(b)* bow.

Squat

Direction of control
Sagittal

Instruction
Stand with the spine in neutral starting position, arms across chest. Squat by bending the knees (figure 4.3, *a-b*) whilst maintaining spine and hip control.

Figure 4.3 Squat: *(a)* starting position; *(b)* squat.

Standing Hip Flexion

Direction of control
Sagittal and frontal

Instruction
From a neutral starting posture and arms across chest, flex the hip to 90 degrees (figure 4.4) without a loss of control. Perform with both legs. (The evaluator should assess the athlete from both the front and the side.)

Figure 4.4 Standing hip flexion.

Single-Leg Balance and Catch

Direction of control
Triplaner

Instruction
Stand with the spine in neutral starting position with knees soft. Lift one leg and balance on the standing leg. Catch a ball thrown by a partner (figure 4.5) and pass it back 30 times, maintaining balance on one leg. Switch legs.

Figure 4.5 Single-leg balance and catch.

Single-Leg Hip Rotation

Direction of control
Triplanar

Instruction
Stand with the spine in neutral starting position, arms across chest, knees soft. Lift one leg forward to 90 degrees hip flexion and 90 degrees knee flexion. Rotate the flexed leg outward through the full ROM (figure 4.6, a-b) without a loss of control of the standing leg or spine. Repeat with the other leg.

Figure 4.6 Single-leg hip rotation: *(a)* stand on one leg; *(b)* rotate the flexed leg out through a full range of motion.

Single-Leg Balance With Trunk Rotation

Direction of control
Triplanar

Instruction
Stand with the spine in a neutral-zone starting position, arms across chest, knees soft. Lift one leg forward to 90 degrees hip flexion and 90 degrees knee flexion. Rotate the trunk fully to one side without a loss of control of the standing leg or spine (figure 4.7). Repeat with the other leg.

Figure 4.7 Single-leg balance with trunk rotation.

Supine Hip Flexion

Direction of control
Sagittal

Instruction
Lie on the back with knees bent and feet flat. Flex one hip to 90 degrees. Lower and extend the leg until it is parallel to the floor (figure 4.8, *a-b*). Return to the starting position and repeat with the opposite leg. Keep breathing. (The evaluator should ensure no bracing or loss of spinal position occurs during the movement.)

 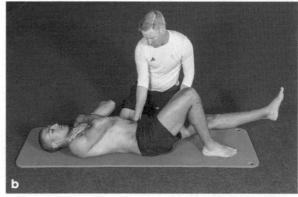

Figure 4.8 Supine hip flexion: *(a)* starting position with one hip flexed to 90 degrees; *(b)* lower leg extended until parallel to floor.

SUPINE

Bent-Knee Fall Out

Direction of control
Axial

Instruction
Lie on the back with knees bent and feet flat. Slowly and under control rotate one knee out to the side (figure 4.9) through a full ROM. Return to the starting position and repeat with the opposite leg. Keep breathing. (The evaluator should ensure no excessive bracing or loss of spinal control occurs during the movement.)

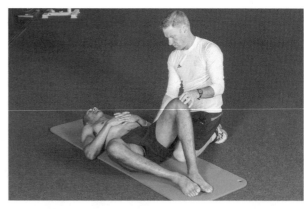

Figure 4.9 Bent-knee fall out.

Side-Lying Clam

Direction of control
Axial

Instruction
Lie on one side with hips and knees flexed to 90 degrees (figure 4.10a). Slowly rotate the top hip externally through a full ROM (figure 4.10b). Repeat with the other leg. Keep breathing. (The evaluator should ensure no excessive bracing or loss of spinal control occurs.)

Figure 4.10 Side-lying clam: *(a)* starting position; *(b)* rotate top hip.

High-Load Assessment of Core Stability

This section discusses the assessment of appropriate resistance to spinal motion to maximise the ability of the limbs to generate limb speed and force for athletic movements. The tests chosen should assess

- core-strength endurance (e.g., maximal isometric holds),
- core control during high-load and explosive movements, and
- core control during high-load, asymmetrical movements.

There is a wide scope for an individual or sport-specific approach within this framework.

In the sagittal and axial planes, assessment of core control and dissociation could be achieved with analysis of high-load resistance exercises (e.g., squat, deadlift, step-up, lunge) and high-speed video analysis of running, jumping and landing qualities, supplemented with a simple front-plank hold.

In the frontal and axial planes, asymmetrical tests including the super-yoke walk and suitcase carry (see figure 4.11) have been demonstrated to

Figure 4.11 Suitcase carry.

significantly tax frontal plane stabilisers.[24, 25] By extension, therefore, variations of heavy barbell step-ups (with or without asymmetrical perturbation) and single-arm dumbbell step-ups will also achieve a similar co-contracted state of the quadratus lumborum and lower-limb stabilisers and effectively assess core stability and dissociation in these planes. These drills can then be supplemented with side-plank endurance holds and side-plank to front-plank transition.

When possible, standards of proficiency should be based on normative data of the specific population. Validation of tests also should be achieved by comparing the athlete's competency against sport-relevant movements (e.g., comparison of a side-plank hold with frontal-plane control at initial contact in running gait; see chapter 3).

SAMPLE TESTS

In keeping with our definition of the core, we must look to build resilience in the three movement planes. Close observation of form is critical to ensure optimal trunk strength is developed; volume and load must be carefully considered as the compressive and torsional moments about the spine are much higher with these exercises.

Front Plank

Direction of control
Sagittal

Instruction
Lie on the floor with hands directly under shoulders and toes on floor. Push up until arms are extended (figure 4.12). Find a neutral-zone starting position. Hold this static position—hands directly under shoulders and a straight line from head down spine to feet—until loss of control is observed.

This test can be progressed to include a single-leg hip extension or a single-arm elevation.

Figure 4.12 Front plank.

OFF FEET

Side Plank

Direction of control
Frontal

Instruction
Lie on one side on the floor, legs stacked, lower elbow directly under the shoulder. Lift into plank position (figure 4.13) and find a neutral-zone starting position. Hold this static position—elbow directly under shoulder, body in a straight line from head down to feet—until loss of control is observed. Switch sides and repeat.

Figure 4.13 Side plank.

Transition Plank

Direction of control
Triplanar

Instruction
Start in a side-plank position, elbow directly under the shoulder, body in a straight line from head to feet. Find a neutral-zone starting position. Transition into a front plank by pivoting about the shoulder (figure 4.14, *a-c*) without any loss of linkage within the spine or between spine and hip. Switch sides and repeat.

Figure 4.14 Transition plank: (*a*) begin in side-plank position; (*b*) pivot; (*c*) end in front-plank position.

OFF FEET

Leg Press

Direction of control

Sagittal

Instruction

Start in a neutral-zone position in a leg-press machine. Back is pressed against the back pad and feet are about shoulder-width apart and flat against the platform. Knees and hips are bent at 90-degree angles. Move the weight by pressing the feet against the platform and straightening the knees (figure 4.15, *a-b*); do not lock the knees. Perform 10 repetitions at 75 per cent 1RM.

Figure 4.15 Leg press: *(a)* starting position; *(b)* press.

Bench Press

Direction of control

Sagittal

Instruction

Lie on a weight bench with feet flat on the floor. Grip the barbell with a normal, overhand grip. Start with the spine in a neutral zone position. Lower the barbell to just above the chest, then push the weight up (figure 4.16, *a-b*). Perform 10 repetitions at 75 per cent 1RM.

Figure 4.16 Bench press: *(a)* starting position; *(b)* press.

ON FEET

Woodchopper

Direction of control
Triplanar

Instruction
Stand with hands at chest height to the side of a cable machine with a high handle. (The machine should be loaded with 30% of the athlete's body weight.) Grip the high handle with both hands on one side (figure 4.17a). Start in a neutral-zone position. Rotate the trunk to bring the hands down and to the other side, ending with the handle near the far hip (figure 4.17b). Repeat to the other side. (The evaluator should look for a loss of lumbar spine control.)

Figure 4.17 Woodchopper: (a) stand in neutral-zone starting position; (b) bring hands down and to the other side.

Hop-and-Stick Square

Direction of control
Triplanar

Instruction
Mark a 4 × 4 foot square on the floor (figure 4.18). Stand on one foot in front of the first square and find a neutral-zone starting position. Hop forward into each square, sticking to each corner. (The evaluator should observe spinal posture, noting any loss of control centrally or at the hip and lower limb.) Repeat on the other side.

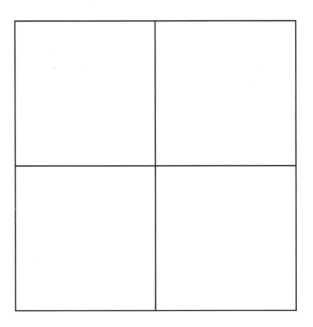

Figure 4.18 Hop-and-stick square.

Deadlift

Direction of control
Sagittal

Instruction
Load the barbell with 75 per cent 1RM. Stand behind barbell with feet hip-width apart. Squat and grip the bar. Lift the bar by extending hips and knees (figure 4.19, *a-b*). (The evaluator should watch the athlete for any loss of lumbar spine control.)

Figure 4.19 Deadlift: (*a*) starting position; (*b*) lift.

ON FEET

Delivering a Core Programme

Once the athlete's priorities have been accurately determined, the core program needs to be integrated into his or her schedule to ensure that the maximum benefits are realised. This can present a challenge as the demands on athletes will already be high, and often their weeks will already be full.

Consideration should be given to the aims of supplementary core drills within the overall context of the training cycle to ensure that not only do they reflect the sport-specific needs of the athlete, but also that the physiological (and psychological) volume and load are not excessive. Doing so requires interdisciplinary understanding and clear communication lines to ensure a cohesive, target-based strategy is introduced.

Group Training or Individual Supervision?

One of the more significant conundrums facing the practitioner working in a team is whether to deliver core training to a group or individually. Some athletes do not have the self-discipline or attention span to work without direct supervision or in a group setting; inevitably, though, if time is at a premium, a group session is a consideration.

It would be prudent to consider the cognitive demand of the exercises and technical proficiency of the athlete. When complex movement patterns or new movement skills are being introduced, it would be appropriate for sessions to be conducted individually. Once the skill has become automatic, however, there is much to be said for the use of group settings, wherein athletes can compete against each other, much the same as in all aspects of strength and conditioning.

Target-Based Approach

All athletes respond well to a targeted approach to athletic training. Consideration should be given to progressive loading that provides clear exit criteria for each level attained. The use of league tables and standards of proficiency are good methods to maximise compliance within team sport. Medical models that do not apply this approach tend to fail once the novelty of new training has worn off because the athlete will not see the goal or have a defined exit.

Timing

The timing of the program within the athlete's training day depends on the aims of the program, the underlying health of the athlete and the practicalities of the working environment. Timing decisions can be subdivided into the following.

A Rowing Perspective on Core Stabilisation and Strength Development

Alex Wolf
Head of Strength and Conditioning,
English Institute of Sport,
Great Britain Rowing

Rowing is a full-body activity. Whether on a rowing ergometer or in a boat, a rower initiates the movement by applying force through the foot stretcher; this force needs to be transferred through the entire body to the oar handle during the drive phase. The trunk has two purposes during the rowing stroke:

1. to act as a buttress against segmental spinal deformation as high forces are transferred from the legs across to the upper body, and

2. to contribute directly to power output by the generation and amplification of muscular force.

Therefore, the trunk has a complex role in providing stability as well as generating power in order to contribute to the force through the oars. This results in a unique challenge in assessing the function of the trunk for these specific tasks.

Accordingly, the rower will be assessed at multiple levels to determine where limiting factors lie:

- Low-load muscular activation and endurance are assessed by our physiotherapists.

- Trunk-muscle isometric endurance is assessed using capacity assessments such as prone extension and side-plank holds. The benchmarks we use can be seen in the table.

- Trunk-muscle rate of force development (RFD) during flexion and extension is measured with an isokinetic dynamometer. RFD during flexion and extension tasks is a critical competency since it deals with the trunk's ability to rapidly develop the forces necessary to buttress the spine against high external forces.

Core Control Screening

Our stability screening uses eight tests.

1. Single-arm lift from all fours (low load). Assume a position on all fours. Slowly lift one arm (elbow straight) to its fully flexed position (horizontal).

Return to starting position. Repeat with the other arm.

2. Single-leg extension from all fours (low load). Assume a position on all fours. Slowly lift one leg (knee straight) to its fully extended position (horizontal). Return to starting position. Repeat with the other leg.

3. Single-arm, opposite-leg lift from all fours (superman) (low load). Assume a position on all fours. Simultaneously slowly lift one arm, elbow straight, to its fully flexed position, and the opposite leg, knee straight, to its fully extended position as in tests 1 and 2. Return to the starting position. Repeat with the opposite arm and leg.

4. Double-leg lift and lower (high load). In crook lying (i.e., lie on the side with legs bent) with pressure biofeedback unit (PBU) set at 40mmHg and spine in neutral, lift both feet from the floor (hip flexion to 90 degrees) and return to the floor. Maintain PBU at 40mmHg throughout.

5. Double-leg lift and extend (high load). In crook lying (i.e., lie on the side with legs bent) with pressure biofeedback unit (PBU) set at 40mm Hg, lift both feet from the floor (hip flexion to 90 degrees). Extend hips and knees to 45 degrees. Reverse the movement to return to the floor. Maintain the PBU at 40 mmHg throughout.

6. Seated Wunda chair bilateral heel press (high load). Sit high on the Wunda chair (maximal load, levers connected). Lightly press hands on chair to engage lats; then press bar to floor with heels.

7. Reformer double-leg drive from all fours (high load). Set springs at 1 white and 1 blue. Put hands on bar and kneel on carriage on all fours. Slowly slide platform away to full hip extension whilst maintaining spinal alignment.

8. Reformer scooter (high load). Begin with one foot on rebook step and one foot on reformer (starter

Alex Wolf is head of strength and conditioning for the English Institute of Sport. He has been the lead strength and conditioning coach for Great Britain rowing for the last five years. He has worked with many Olympic, Paralympic, and professional athletes and sport teams including track and field, rugby union and football. He holds a Bsc in human biology and sport science, and MSc in biomechanics and recently completed the IOC postgraduate diploma in sport nutrition.

Capacity Assessment Benchmarks

	Prone extension (sec)	Double-leg hold (sec)	Lateral trunk (sec)
Elite level	≥150	≥150	≥150
Required level	≥120	≥120	≥120
Meaningful change	15	15	15

block) with knee not in contact with the carriage. Slowly slide carriage away to full hip extension and drop into slight lunge. Slowly return to starting position.

Trunk Isokinetic Dynamometry

For the trunk isokinetic dynamometry, the athlete is strapped into the trunk flexion–extension attachment with the knees and hips locked into place. A cushioned strap is placed across the chest; this is the point against which the athlete pulls or pushes. Neutral standing posture is found before the active movement range is set from −10 degrees to +80 degrees.

The athlete performs 5 maximal efforts of flexion and extension at 30 degrees and 90 degrees per second. The peak torque and angle of peak torque are measured. Peak torque should occur within the first 10 to 15 degrees of movement, which demonstrates an ability to create a stiffened spinal column against a high torque.

Athletes are assessed on the magnitude and the rate of torque. Athletes who are able to produce their highest torque in the first 10 to 15 degrees but have a low magnitude will be prescribed a high-force trunk-training programme. An athlete who has a high torque magnitude but produces it after the 10- to 15-degree limit is given a reactive high-force (stiffness) trunk-training programme. Those who produce a low magnitude after the threshold angle are prescribed both high-force and reactive high-force training.

Athletes are at greatest risk when they are unable to produce a high-force stiffness quality to protect the spine. This is further exacerbated when the torque produced is lower than the threshold.

Programme Development

Once we have this assessment data, we use it to prescribe individual, bespoke trunk-training programmes. The amount of data we collect is extensive, but data are useless unless they provide information. We need to have an understanding of what is good enough, that is, what the benchmarks are that the rower should reach in order to reduce injury risk and enhance performance. Thankfully, we have collected vast amounts of data over the years, and so now we can compare any individual to what world-class performers have demonstrated over a long time. We have these benchmarks for capacity, strength and RFD assessments.

The benchmarks are set as gold standards, and any results below these standards drive the bespoke programming for the rower. The rowers have continuous dosages of local segmental stability training throughout the week to supplement the higher loading requirements. Generally, this is because many rowers have previously suffered from lower-back pain or injury, and this type of work has proven to help rowers return to close to normal local stability functioning alongside the higher-loading training

To keep rowers engaged with the trunk-training programme, we provide targets to achieve throughout the season. More emphasis is given to capacity-based work in the winter, and higher-force training is emphasised closer to competition. The key training philosophy is train the adaptation and not the exercise. Once the strength and conditioning team know what adaptation is required, the exercise is selected that best supports this adaptation. For instance if extension capacity is the prime adaptation focus, then loaded back extensions, good mornings or Romanian deadlifts could be prescribed using tempo with a time-under-tension (TUT) goal of 30 to 60 seconds of work.

Capacity exercises can also be grouped to establish 5 to 8 minutes of TUT. By changing the loading by trunk quadrants (anterior, posterior left and right and lateral) every 30 seconds, the rower will not only develop capacity for the whole trunk but also target the weaker quadrants as identified from the assessments. Multiple exercises can be used to challenge that quadrant. For instance lateral trunk can be challenged with side planks, lateral holds of blocks or unilateral loading such as farmer's walks or overhead carries.

By having effective assessments and programming tools and understanding the primary adaptation an athlete is trying to overload, strength and conditioning staff can write bespoke programmes that can be updated to keep the athletes engaged. By setting specific boundaries, athletes have also been able to effectively write their own programmes.

Pretraining Core Stability

Introducing drills before a training session, whether field- or gym-based, will provide the opportunity to selectively activate primary core groups and rehearse optimal movement patterns to prepare the system for the subsequent training session.

Within-Training Core Stability

Many core programs are sandwiched within a dedicated weight session to provide an active recovery from primary lifts. This approach breaks up core development into small, manageable chunks and also serves to minimise overall time spent in the gym.

Posttraining Core Stability

There is a strong physiological argument for the use of posttraining core-endurance drills. Core muscles should be resistant to fatigue and be able to repeat efforts with no loss of control. As we know, the majority of injuries occur when an athlete is fatigued; therefore, this approach will tax the neuromuscular system in a relatively protected environment. In a healthy athlete this approach may represent the best way to integrate core training into a program to maximise injury prevention.

Strength Training

Strength training is a vital aspect of core development and should be included wherever medically safe to do so. The body prefers to make maximal efforts in the sagittal plane, which explains the high levels of core-muscle activation during heavy squats and deadlifts when compared to traditional core exercises such as the front plank.[23-25] We should not fixate just on the sagittal plane, though, because athletes need to be secure in the transverse and coronal planes as well. These muscles are not best suited to maximal efforts but need to be slightly more endurance focused. Endurance is the more subtle strength component and is often best trained using asymmetrical training, particularly when many sport movements are submaximal and have an asymmetrical component.

Case Study

Background: Right-footed professional soccer player playing central midfield with no history of lower-back pain.

Sport demands: A game of soccer is 90 minutes long. A player may cover a distance of around 10 kilometers during a game, so there is an endurance component combined with multiple explosive actions. The game involves significant amounts of deceleration and change of direction, and movements such as cutting, twisting and turning are common. The sport also involves jumping and repeated kicking, which expose the trunk to asymmetrical loading patterns. Therefore, high forces are frequently generated in the transverse and frontal planes of motion; as a result, it is essential that the core can consistently deal with challenges in these planes of motion.

Positional demands: Midfielders are exposed to the most movements in the transverse plane. The player needs to interact with players in front, behind and on both sides throughout the game, so he or she is constantly turning.

All of these aspects should be considered when testing and training the soccer player's core stability. Based on this information the most appropriate tests would be those that capture the endurance and alignment-control aspect of playing soccer and the control of high-load movements in the transverse and coronal (frontal) planes. Therefore, testing and training should relate both to the low- and high-load categories.

The assessment of this athlete is shown in table 4.2.

Assessment Interpretation

Both low- and high-load tests indicate poor control and strength of the left leg in the stance phase in both the frontal plane and the axial (transverse) plane. Specifically, this result was due to a lack of left lateral hip stability and strength.

Table 4.3 lists examples of exercises and progressions for the previously noted core–stability control issues.

Table 4.2 Assessment of Professional Soccer Midfielder

Testing category	Demonstrations of poor control
Low load	• Right-leg standing hip flexion: loss of frontal plane control about hip. • Right-leg single-leg hip rotation: loss of frontal plane control about hip. • Right-leg balance and minisquat: poor axial plane control of left lower limb.
High load	• Side plank (left = 30 sec; right = 2 min) • Left-leg hop-and-stick square: loss of frontal plane control about hip landing; axial (transverse) plane collapse of left knee. • High-speed analysis of 45-degree left-to-right cutting motion in sprinting evasion: loss of frontal plane control about hip landing; axial plane collapse of left knee.

Table 4.3 Sample Drills and Progressions to Address Core-Control Weaknesses in a Soccer Player

Load	Drill	Sets	Repetitions	Rest
Low load (posttraining under fatigue)	Side-lying clam	3	60 sec	30 sec
	Forward lean with hands on wall and hip flexion control	3	60 sec	30 sec
	Forward lean with hands on wall and hip flexion and rotation control	3	60 sec	30 sec
High load (inclusion in strength and conditioning program)	Single-arm dumbbell step-up (weight in right hand)	5	8	90 sec
	Lateral hop-and-stick square (ensure vertical alignment on landing)	5	8	90 sec

Summary

Stabilising and strengthening the core should form part of any training program, but this goes beyond simple abdominal crunches and requires consideration of the spine and shoulder–hip complex in three planes and in low- and high-load conditions. Fundamentally, the program must be functionally relevant to the athlete and his or her specific requirements, emphasise movement quality and control in its delivery and demonstrate progression and variation to keep the athlete interested and motivated. Ideally, the principles should transcend isolated training and become a key consideration in all training systems.

CHAPTER 5

Optimising Flexibility

Sue Falsone
Los Angeles Dodgers and EXOS (formerly Athletes' Performance), United States

'You are too tight. You need to stretch more!' Most athletes have heard this from a coach at one time or other. The pursuit of flexibility has been a key aim of performance training since people began exercising. Around the world, flexibility is measured in preparticipation physical screenings and used as a key performance and injury-risk measure. Yet how flexibility relates to performance and injury prevention remains inconclusive. The literature is confusing, and many studies directly contradict each other's findings. Coaches and clinicians who need to evaluate programming with a critical eye to maximise training effects in a minimal amount of time are led to this question: Does flexibility training have a place in programming?

The answer most certainly is yes, and the intricacies of where and how flexibility training is used are explored in this chapter. Empirical evidence and scientific data are evaluated to assist the reader in determining the best use of flexibility training for athletes. Tissues that affect flexibility are targeted by specific techniques, all of which

are discussed in the following pages. By the end of this chapter, readers should have the knowledge needed to create an efficient, effective flexibility program for their athletes.

Definitions

First, let's define some terms that will be used throughout this chapter.

Flexibility reflects an absolute gross range of motion (ROM) of a joint, including capsule and soft tissue surrounding that joint or a group of joints.

Instability is the abnormal movement of a joint that will not allow it to support normal load.

Stiffness refers to the tension per unit of change in length, whereas a muscle that is *short* actually has a loss of sarcomeres in series. Let's use the common exercise band as an example. There can be two lengths of a band, one *shorter* than the other (figure 5.1). Alternatively, there can be 3 feet of two colors of band, one thin and the other thick (figure 5.2). The thick band is *stiffer* than the thin band.

Figure 5.1 Two exercise bands of different lengths.

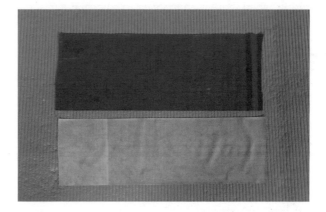

Figure 5.2 Two exercise bands of the same length, but one is thicker than the other. The thicker band is stiffer than the thinner band.

Hypermobility is an increase in the normal movement of a joint. Many people are generally hypermobile (often called double jointed), but this is not necessarily a bad thing. In many sports—gymnastics, diving, swimming—it is a competitive advantage to be hypermobile. It is possible for a joint to be hypermobile but still be stable because there is adequate control of this motion. Therefore, instability essentially refers to an inability to control this ROM and is labeled pathological as a consequence.

Hypomobility is the decrease in normal movement of a joint and is often, but not always, pathological in nature. Pain often results in adaptive mechanisms to limit motion, initially in the form of guarding. If persistent, this guarding can result in structural changes of the joint capsule, leading to a more permanent loss of joint-capsule motion if not properly addressed.

Finally, when talking about stretching and flexibility, we have to understand the properties of muscle and tendon. Muscles and tendons are *viscoelastic*, that is, they demonstrate properties of both viscous and elastic material. A *viscous material* is like honey; it resists strain and shear in a linear fashion. An *elastic material* is like a rubber band; it returns back to its original shape once the force is removed. Muscle initially will go back to its original shape; however, over time it will begin to deform based on the force placed on it.

Wisdom

Hypermobility is not necessarily pathological. It is possible for a joint to be hypermobile but still have adequate control of the motion. Instability of a joint results when there is an inability to control the motion available; this condition is pathological.

Factors Contributing to Flexibility

Flexibility is a broad term characterising a given amount of motion somewhere in the body. Many factors contribute to overall flexibility, including joint capsule, ligaments, muscle, tendon, neural structures, fascia and the interactions among all of these structures.

Joint Mobility

Joint mobility is a large contributing factor to flexibility. It depends mainly on the integrity of the joint capsule and the ligaments that are the thickenings of the capsule. A joint capsule surrounds a synovial joint and is made up of two layers, with the inner layer being a synovial membrane. It is important to note that capsule mobility will adapt based on the athlete's activity and is often a necessary change in order for the athlete to participate successfully in his or her sport. For example, the anterior shoulder capsule on the dominant side of any overhead athlete, such as a tennis player, will be more mobile compared to the nonthrowing side in order for that athlete to achieve the necessary external rotation needed to serve the ball.

Muscle Length and Tone

Muscle is a contractile tissue that contributes to flexibility. Consider the sarcomeres of muscles. Sarcomeres are made of proteins called actin and myosin that slide past each other during a muscle contraction. Through various chemical reactions, these proteins bind to each other, causing contraction and relaxation of a muscle. Optimal muscle contraction ultimately depends on the length–tension relationship of the muscle and muscle cells, including the sarcomeres. The overlap of these protein filaments in a shortened or lengthened position is less efficient than when in midrange. Static stretching before powerful movements has been shown to result in decreased power output,[1-4] making static stretching less than advantageous to perform before activity.

Neural Mobility

Neural tissue (nerves and their surrounding connective tissue) is continuous from head to feet and contributes to total motion of the trunk and limbs. A limitation in one area can limit motion in another. In a relaxed state, neural tissue lies slightly coiled. As the trunk and limbs move, the nerves accommodate this movement by first unfurling their corrugations and then sliding in their nerve beds. Only once the slack has been taken out of the system are neural tissues then required to stretch; this is an undesirable outcome and is only seen if nervous tissue is caught in adhesions or limited by something like an intervertebral disc herniation.

Consider a straight-leg-raise test. If an intervertebral disc is protruding and compresses the nerve root, that nerve is compromised. As the clinician straightens the patient's leg, the patient may experience tension, pain or altered sensations into the leg or back. This pain is often due to irritation of the nerve. In order to limit further stress, the hamstrings often spasm, which in conjunction with the associated pain accounts for the limitation found in this test. Such a situation requires a full assessment; referral to a medical professional is recommended.

Fascial Mobility

Fascia is a tissue that has been of interest in recent literature and clinical practice. Fascial tissue is congruent within all tissue in the body. It is the glue within that holds all other tissues together. Fascia is made of adjacent layers of wavelike collagen fibers, intertwined with elastic fibers and layered with adipose tissue.[5] The composition of collagen and elastic fibers makes fascia resistant to traction, yet at the same time adaptable to stretching. This seems counterintuitive. As early as the turn of the twentieth century it was reported that fascia is extremely pliable yet resistant and almost inextensible.[5-8] It is this rare physiological make-up that makes fascia, its role in flexibility and its techniques to stretch it, so interesting. Fascia may also have a proprioceptive role and may help modulate muscle tone.[6, 7, 9, 10]

Key Issues in Flexibility Training

Flexibility training is somewhat of a contentious issue in the academic and practical fields. It is a topic that tends to divide people into two camps with respect to its utility; much of the division is because some of the studies that have been published seem to contradict each other. Nevertheless, there are certainly consistencies in the research. It's worthwhile examining these consistencies when answering some of the most commonly asked questions regarding flexibility.

Is Flexibility Advantageous or Detrimental to Performance?

Flexibility provides a window of pain-free movement. But does increasing flexibility, or increasing that window of pain-free movement, actually enhance performance? The research says no, and in fact it suggests that too much flexibility may limit performance and increase the risk of injury. Stretching beyond that which is necessary for sport movement could actually be detrimental to performance.[11] It is difficult to draw definite conclusions from the research, though, because study design and quality vary so wildly. Common differences include the use of a cardiovascular warm-up, the presence or absence of control groups and even the measurement of flexibility used. These methodological flaws make conclusive statements about what flexibility does or does not do to performance difficult at best.

Shrier[12] reviewed 23 studies on the acute effects of flexibility on performance. Twenty-two of these studies showed no benefit for isometric force, isokinetic torque or jumping height. Four of these articles specifically looked at running speed as well. Of these articles, one article found that stretching improved running speed, one article found that stretching was detrimental to running speed and two studies were inconclusive. The research does not make a good case for using stretching to enhance athletic performance.

Nine studies in this review looked at the effects of regular stretching over time, not immediately before performance. These studies used a variety of subjects, including men, women, children, elite athletes and recreational athletes, and looked at variables, including isometric force production and velocity of contraction. Seven of these studies found benefits with regular stretching, two found no effects and none found detrimental effects on performance. This suggests that regular stretching over time will increase isometric force production and velocity of contraction, even though acutely the exact opposite occurs.

Looking at basic physiology may give us the best answers to the question of whether stretching enhances performance. Consider the sliding filament theory of muscle contraction. Actin slides across myosin, grabbing hold of it to create a muscular contraction. When a muscle stretches out, those actin fibers get far apart from each other, making it less efficient to grab the myosin filaments, thus decreasing the muscle's ability to contract. Decreasing a muscle's ability to contract acutely decreases strength and power and has an immediate negative impact on performance.

Should Flexibility Training Be Static or Dynamic?

Comparing static stretching to dynamic stretching has shown large differences in outcomes in the literature. McMillian and colleagues[3] studied 30 military personnel and measured a 5-step jump, an underhanded medicine ball throw and a t-test agility test. Subjects were divided into three groups: no warm-up, a static warm-up and a dynamic warm-up. The dynamic warm-up group showed moderate performance enhancement for power and agility drills when compared to the groups using static stretching and no warm-up. Dynamic stretching, therefore, has a clear advantage over static stretching when looking at performance tests of power and agility.[1, 13-15]

From a clinical standpoint, we know that a certain amount of flexibility is required for each sport and, more specifically, for each position of that sport. Depending on the activity, the amount of flexibility required varies from joint to joint and from athlete to athlete. A golfer must have a certain amount of dissociation between the upper and lower quarters in order to create ROM large enough to summate the forces in the swing to drive the ball. This relative increase in ROM is needed for proper sport performance. Therefore, if this relative increase in motion does not exist, performance will be negatively affected. However, this adaptive change in ROM happens over time, not acutely just before performance. It is a specific adaptation to imposed demands over the course of years and thousands of repetitions.

Does Inflexibility Contribute to Injury Risk?

In just about every sport in the world, across all levels from amateur to professional, team warm-ups can be observed, including types of stretching, to prepare for practice or competition. The relatively accepted practical theory is that stretching as part of a warm-up before athletic activity can assist in preparing the body for sport as well as reduce the chance of injury in the upcoming activity.

However, research is inconclusive regarding the use of routine stretching and its relationship to injury or injury prevention. In fact, several studies have shown that increasing ROM beyond that which is needed for sport may actually contribute to injury by creating relative hypermobility and potential joint instability.[16] Variations in study design make it difficult to conclusively determine independent effects of stretching on prevention of injury. A recent meta-analysis demonstrated no significant relationship between stretching and injury incidence. This large, systematic review was unable to determine any relationship between stretching and injury, either positively or negatively. These findings were in agreement with a similar systematic review, wherein the authors concluded that no definitive conclusions could be drawn as to the value of stretching for reducing the risk of exercise-related injury.[17]

Basic science studies show that acute periods of stretching decrease viscoelastic properties of muscle and tendon,[7, 8] which can work for and against athletes from an immediate performance and injury standpoint.[12] Decreasing the viscoelastic properties of a muscle will result in a decrease in stiffness of the tissues, resulting in less energy needed to move the limb. This energy savings might translate into decreased fatigue, which could theoretically improve performance. However, reducing the inherent stiffness of the musculotendinous unit might decrease its performance, particularly in explosive, high-load movements in which elastic energy and spring stiffness are primary qualities.

This information is in regards to acute stretching. The long-term results of consistent stretching would appear to be different. Long-term stretching does not seem to permanently alter the viscoelastic

Wisdom

Static stretching can have a negative effect on immediate performance. However, long-term benefits of stretching over time are well documented, making a clinical case to perform static, passive stretching at the end of the day, on an off day, after performance or as a phase during off-season training.

properties of the musculotendinous unit; rather, it actually increases the stretch tolerance of a muscle. Stretch-induced hypertrophy, an increase in muscular-force production and an increase in force velocity have been shown in multiple studies across gender, age and athletic levels.[12]

Asymmetries in Flexibility: Does It Matter?

Research is divided when it comes to asymmetries in flexibility, let alone how these relate to athletic performance. One of the best examples is with overhead athletes (e.g., baseball, tennis) and the amount of internal rotation they have in their dominant shoulders. This is termed *glehohumeral internal rotation deficit* (GIRD). GIRD is defined as shoulder ROM deficit, where the dominant shoulder lacks 20 degrees of internal rotation compared to that of the nondominant shoulder. However, some researchers and clinicians consider GIRD a necessary adaptation to the throwing motion. This asymmetry is not only present but necessary to succeed at that position in the sport. They argue that the total arc of motion (adding the amount of external rotation to the amount of internal rotation) gives a better representation of limb symmetry and caution against simply stretching internal rotation to gain more motion, as that may be actually causing hypermobility and potential instability at the joint.[18]

Asymmetrical hip ROM has been shown to be associated with risk of lumbar spine and sacroiliac joint dysfunction as well as anterior knee pain.[19, 20] Recent clinical findings and studies are shedding light on femoral bony adaptations that may be leading to such asymmetries. The discovery of cam lesions and pincer lesions in the hip (extra bone that grows either at the neck of the femur or rim of the acetabulum) may be a leading cause of athletes experiencing pain. However, if these lesions are bony, flexibility training will not change the ROM; in fact, flexibility training may be forcing two bones together into end ranges that have adapted bony growth, causing impingement, inflammation and pain at the hip.

The functional movement screen (FMS) has shown some promise as a predictor of injury risk in certain cases.[21, 22] Although using this screen may give us reason to continue to look at asymmetries and the role they play in injury and injury prediction, the FMS does not address mobility versus stability issues on an individual basis. Furthermore, stability issues may look like a mobility issue at first glance until further examination is performed. It is not clear if injury correlation has more to do with stability or mobility findings. More research is needed in this area to accurately discuss the role of asymmetries in flexibility and injury prediction.

From a clinical standpoint, this topic is debated almost daily in the training room and the clinic. Does an asymmetrical athlete (e.g., golfer, thrower, hitter) need to be symmetrical? Quite frankly, we do not know. Should we try to make throwers symmetrical by increasing the external rotation on the shoulder on the nonthrowing side? Should we try to make a right-handed golfer have equal trunk rotation to the left and right, even though the golfer never has to hit the golf ball from the right-hand side of the tee? Creating symmetry in a body that needs asymmetry does not seem to make a lot sense. Yet neither does feeding into that asymmetry with programming.

Consider a cyclist or swimmer. These athletes require fairly symmetrical movements of the body. If an asymmetry is present, it seems reasonable to think that this asymmetry, whether it is in flexibility, strength or power, could become problematic by placing extra stress on a muscle or joint. Relate this to the tires on a car being out of alignment. The driver may not have issues immediately, but if he or she drives that car for extended distances, something is going to begin to wear down.

Wisdom

It is reasonable to think that athletes in those sports that require symmetrical movements need general symmetry in the body to avoid injury. On the other hand, athletes who perform asymmetrical movement patterns, such as throwing or swinging, may not need symmetrical flexibility and ROM. In fact, asymmetries are adaptive and necessary to succeed at these sports.

Methods of Optimising Flexibility

There are many types of flexibility training. For purposes of this chapter, they are divided into two categories: passive and active.

Passive Stretching

Passive techniques are possibly what first comes to mind when most people think of stretching. Low-load, prolonged static holds to a specific muscle or group of muscles can change the viscoelastic properties of the musculotendinous unit.[8]

A tendon is responsible for transferring force from the muscle to the bone. If a static, passive stretch is placed on this musculotendinous unit and the viscosity of the tissue decreases, the passive torque on the tissue also will decrease, ultimately lowering the rate of force development and delaying muscular reaction.[8] Extrapolating this concept further would make a case for having a negative effect on performance. A lower rate of force production and a delay in muscular reaction will decrease power output as well as potentially increase injury risk. This physiology provides strong reason not to use passive, low-load prolonged stretching before activity. The process of static stretching can also have a relaxing effect on the body, letting areas of high tension and high stress release. Many people find comfort and relaxation with prolonged, low-load stretching, another reason its best place within programming may be at the end of the day, when no more training or activity will occur.

Fascial stretching is another technique that could be considered passive. Fascia is intertwined around and within all tissue, making any isolative type of movement truly not isolated. The thought process of stretching movements and body lines, instead of individual muscles, has changed the concept of static stretching to its core. Using total-body stretches, including rotation, multiple angles and multiple body parts all at once, has opened the eyes of many practitioners to think more broadly about the concept of stretching.

Fascia is so intertwined within the body that it is impossible to isolate this tissue, or any tissue from another. Fascia ties everything together, and therefore, fascial stretching requires total-body movements. When considering how close the fascia of the pectoralis major is to the deltoid as well as how it originates from the apeoneurosis of the external oblique, it is easy to see that a simple stretch of external rotation of the glenohumeral joint may not be enough. Adding in some relative right-trunk rotation (figure 5.3) may stretch this entire line.

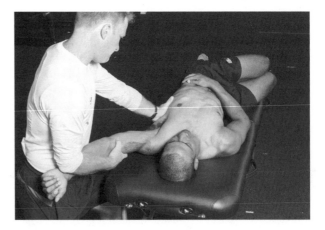

Figure 5.3 Stretching by externally rotating the glenohumeral joint with right-trunk rotation.

Active Stretching

Active (dynamic) stretching has come into favor over the last decade. All over the world, in many types of sports and disciplines, athletes move back and forth, simulating yoga-type movements, jogging or refining upcoming motor skills whilst actively stretching. This concept of movement preparation, or dynamic warm-up, is exactly that: preparing to move.

Other types of active stretching include active isolated stretching (AIS). AIS is based on two fundamental principles of human physiology. The first is Sherington's law of reciprocal inhibition, which deals with the software (neurological) side of the human system. When a muscle on one side of a joint contracts, the muscle on the opposite side receives a neurological signal to relax or release. With slow, rhythmic stretching held no longer than 2 seconds, the one muscle can be contracted, teaching it how to work in a new ROM, whilst the antagonistic muscle is ultimately lengthened. The second is Wolff's law, which has to do with the hardware (anatomical) side of the human system. All tissues are laid down in the body along the lines of stress that they are placed under. Fascial fibres are laid down along lines of stress within the body and are in conjunction with proper anatomical positioning. As we use AIS to stretch, we are laying down muscular and fascial fibers, and any present scar tissue, in a specific way that is in line with the stretching.

Another type of active stretching is resisted stretching. During resisted stretching, resistance is applied to the agonist eccentrically as it is stretched. Supposedly, this increases eccentric strength within the new ROM. This technique theoretically may be beneficial in reducing injuries, as many movement injuries happen during the deceleration phase of movement; however, this theory has not been proven through research.

Finally, muscle-activation technique (MAT) works on the contractile capabilities of a muscle. If an agonist is not firing correctly, the antagonist will get tight. When the muscle fires correctly, the tight muscle will let go, and the system will work more efficiently. The improvement in motor control leads to an overall improvement in the function of the limb, improving efficiency of the system. Other types of proprioceptive neuromuscular facilitation (PNF) techniques work off of similar principles and are well documented in neurological rehabilitation texts.

Analysing the Needs of the Sport

Analysing the flexibility needs of the athlete based on his or her sport and position is multifaceted. Using several types of analytics will help create a full picture so the needs of the athlete can be understood and a comprehensive programme can be created. Most assessments will not give all the details needed to create a program. Determining if ROM limitations are coming from joint capsule, fascia, muscle or neural limitations requires extensive, hands-on evaluation from a skilled clinician. Strength coaches and clinicians should be encouraged to work within a multidisciplinary environment, where differing expertise can be used to give a detailed assessment of each athlete and specific tissue tensions.

The simplest form of flexibility assessment could be static-position ROM using a goniometer or inclinometer. This static assessment of joint angles can provide a simple picture of ROM across a joint or several joints in a segment. Knowing general ROM norms is helpful to determine if an athlete has fundamental motion available to him or her.

Assessing dynamic flexibility becomes a bit more complicated. Multiple functional movement assessments have been developed. The functional movement screen (FMS) has been well documented from a reliability standpoint[22-24] and is widely used throughout athletic movement assessment in the United States. The FMS uses seven tests of gross movement skill, including double-leg stance, single-leg stance and tandem-stance movement. The athlete is scored on a scale of 0 to 3, with 3 indicating that the athlete can perform the movement, 2 indicating he or she can perform the movement with compensation, 1 indicating he or she cannot perform the movement patterns, and 0 indicating there is pain somewhere in the system. The FMS has been a simple way to objectify quality of movement, allowing personal trainers, strength coaches and clinicians alike to have some type of gradable scale regarding movement asymmetries.

Although the FMS does a great job looking at gross-movement patterns, it does not always provide explicit information regarding what is happening at specific links within the system. Further evaluation is necessary in order to assess where the athlete's limitations are coming from, and if they are coming from a limit in ROM or are more of an indication of lack of stability somewhere within the human system. Further clinical testing can provide more information as to whether soft tissue is limiting a movement, and which tissue type could be the limiting factor, to help tease out further implications of lack of stability within the human body that could be mimicking lack of motion.

Additional testing in the form of a clinical examination can be conducted to cover specific tissue-tension assessment in order to determine exactly which type of tissue (e.g., muscle, fascia, joint capsule limitation) or combinations of soft-tissue issues are limiting the movement.

When it comes to analysing the need of a sport or position, the use of video technologies can be extremely beneficial. These technologies allow the recording of athletic movement in real time, and then allow the clinician or coach to slow down the video, measure join angles and overlay other video for comparison in order to determine the ROM needs of the athlete. This dynamic assessment can be compared to the more static and functional movement assessments already collected to determine the athlete's missing links in flexibility.

Ultimately, there is not one true, best method for determining the flexibility needs of an athlete and the sport he or she is participating in. A compilation of multiple assessment techniques will give the professional a well-rounded picture to create a comprehensive, accurate intervention program for the athlete.

Implementing a Flexibility Programme in Sport

This chapter has discussed multiple research articles and systematic reviews, searching for the answers to the question: Does flexibility have a place in performance training programmes? If so, how and where does it fit? The research is plentiful yet answers are limited due to confounding factors in research studies and multiple variables at play when dealing with athletes of various ages, sport and activity levels.

Here is the ultimate guide, based on what is known right now, on how to use flexibility training to build a better athlete.

• Based on the literature, the acute effects of stretching show a decrease in performance measures although long-term, regular stretching has performance-enhancing effects. This conflicting research lends credibility to the need for flexibility training for the long-term health of athletes. If the majority of flexibility training is at the end of the day, after competition or practice is over, athletes can gain the long-term benefits of stretching without comprising immediate performance on the field.

• Acute effects of stretching include a decrease in the viscoelastic properties of the musculotendinous unit and small amounts of muscle damage at the lengthened range. Long-term stretching, however, does not affect the viscoelasticity of the musculotendinous unit, which lends credibility to performing flexibility training at the end of a training session or after competition or practice. The concept of decreasing viscoelasticity of the muscle and altering the length–tension relationship of the muscular spindles gives reason to perform active types of stretching, such as movement preparation and active-isolated stretching. These types of active lengthening, whilst firing agonists and antagonists, give the system the knowledge and practice to fire within the new range that has been created. Teaching the musculotendinous unit how to function in this new range increases the athlete's ability to use this new range in a safe, controlled manner.

• Muscles become short for a reason. This shortening can become a source of adaptive stability for the body. If a shortened muscle is stretched without giving stability back to the system in another way, all that has been done is take away stability from the system, albeit a compensation. Compensation is at least a learned, modified way to perform a task. If that compensation is taken away, the system is left with nothing. If this adaptive stability is taken away via flexibility training, some stability needs to be given back via strength and stability training; this provides a reason to perform more active types of stretching, allowing the agonists and antagonists to learn to work within the new range. It also makes it important to consider why something has become short. If a muscle has become short, it is reasonable to think the muscles on the opposite side of the shortened muscle have become lengthened. If this is true, there is an altered length–tension relationship of those muscles as well, causing inefficiency in firing patterns and decreased strength during movement.

It is reasonable to think that if these lengthened muscles are activated, thereby resetting the length–tension relationship of the muscular spindles, the muscles on the opposite side of the system would begin to let go. Activating the lengthened, weaker muscles versus stretching the shortened muscles is something to consider in practice. Methods such as MAT and PNF work off these principles and have been clinically shown to be effective in regaining lost ROM.

• Dynamic stretching has been shown in the research to improve immediate power and agility, as long as it is performed within 60 minutes of the activity. Use of a dynamic warm-up and dynamic flexibility training can have performance-enhancement effects when performed 60 minutes before competition or practice.

• Regular stretching produces an increase in isometric force production and velocity of contraction. The long-term benefits of stretching show performance-enhancing effects even though immediate effects are detrimental. Regular stretching after competition, practice or training can enhance performance.

Although we do know many things, there also are many things regarding flexibility training that are not yet known. Research is inconclusive,

Wisdom

The following techniques are good flexibility-gaining options to consider for the various times before and after exercise:

Before practice or competition: muscle activation techniques

Within 60 minutes of practice or competition: movement preparation and dynamic stretching

After practice or competition: static stretching

Needs further research: fascial stretching

inconsistent or confounded by complicating factors. For example, we do not yet fully understand

- the role of general flexibility on injury predication or injury prevention;
- the role of asymmetrical movement due to flexibility issues on injury risk;
- the best methods for assessing dynamic flexibility; or
- the best methods to most efficiently and effectively improve flexibility, minimise detrimental effects and maximise positive ones.

Case Study

In my work with professional baseball over several years, I have seen several instances of how flexibility can influence performance, both negatively and positively. Take, for example, one of the pitchers. He had a nonpainful throwing elbow that lacked approximately 15 degrees of extension. Nothing had happened; he had not injured himself and had never had surgery. This was an adaptive change from throwing over time. When I started working with him, I thought, *We need to increase this range of motion.*

I began working on it with ROM exercises, joint mobilisations, soft-tissue mobilisations and stretching. He gained some ROM, improving to about 7 degrees above neutral. However, his performance suffered. He began having difficulty locating his fastball. He could not locate the pitches over the plate as he once could. After much discussion and problem solving, we realised he had gained enough ROM in his elbow that it was changing his release point whilst pitching. The ball was coming out of his hand at a totally different angle. So we stopped doing all of the manual interventions. He began to stiffen up over time as he continued to pitch without being stretched.

Eventually, he began to experience some elbow pain. This required me to reevaluate his elbow. In checking his ROM, he lacked about 25 degrees of elbow extension. Now that he was in pain, I had to intervene in some way. We began working on his ROM again. Once he got to around 15 degrees short of elbow extension, he began to feel better. His pain was gone, and his performance was back to normal. After much thought, discussion with the athlete and video analysis, it dawned on me: He needed that 15-degree elbow contracture. If he improved it, his performance suffered; if it got worse, he experienced pain. The goal was no longer to restore normal motion of the joint; the goal was to maintain *his* normal motion of the joint, which was 15 degrees above neutral. The techniques used are provided in table 5.1.

Table 5.1 Therapeutic Techniques Used to Improve Elbow Extension

Manual therapy techniques*	Isolated therapeutic exercise interventions**
Proximal radioulnar joint mobilisations to promote supination	Concentric triceps strength 3 times a week with progressive intensity
Distal radioulnar joint mobilisations to promote supination	Eccentric biceps strength 3 times a week with progressive intensity
Radiocapitellar joint mobs to promote extension	Concentric and eccentric supination 3 times a week
Humeroulnar joint mobs for distraction	
Soft-tissue mobilisation with movement to triceps, biceps, and common flexor mass	

*Based on International Academy of Orthopedic Medicine–US (IAOM-US) manual therapy techniques

**In addition to individualised total-body strength program and kinetic linking exercises

Summary

Deciding where and how flexibility training fits within programming can be challenging. A combination of research-driven data and clinical experience is necessary to do what is most effective and efficient for athletes. We know that dynamic stretching before activity and static stretching after activity can provide both short- and long-term benefits for performance enhancement and injury prevention. Other techniques such as facial and resisted stretching need more evidence-based research, but they certainly have an anecdotal place within programmes. A specific needs analysis of the sport, position and individual athlete is necessary in order to implement an effective flexibility intervention.

CHAPTER 6

Monitoring the Training Response

Aaron J. Coutts, PhD
Sport and Exercise Discipline Group, Faculty of Health,
University of Technology, Sydney (UTS), Australia

Stuart Cormack, PhD
School of Exercise Science, Australian Catholic University, Melbourne, Australia

The aim of the training process is to ensure athletes are in peak condition to perform successfully during competition. However, training and performance share a complex relationship based on several factors, many of which are unique to the individual athlete and performance task. As a result, there has been an increase in the use of athlete-monitoring systems in sport, and substantial human and financial resources are now invested in this process. In fact, a significant role of coaches, sport scientists and strength and conditioning coaches is to monitor how athletes are coping with training.

To optimise the training process it is important for a coach to understand how a prescribed training dose will produce a specific physiological response, otherwise known as the dose–response relationship. Once this relationship is understood, training programs can be specifically targeted to improve an athlete's physical capacity. In order to achieve this objective, though, coaches should have careful control of the training dose provided for their athletes and use an objective measure of how their athletes respond to that training. In addition to allowing coaches to strategically design training, an effective monitoring system will help reduce illness and injury and optimise recovery.

This chapter examines methods that have been proposed for monitoring training load and fatigue in athletic environments from both theoretical and practical perspectives. A key focus is to provide interpretation of the growing amount of information in this important area so that it can be used in real-world training environments.

Understanding the Physiological Effect of Load

The key to training programme prescription is an understanding of the effect that loading places on the body. Fundamental to this is an understanding of the dose–response relationship and how it can lead to either positive or negative adaptations.

Training Dose–Response Relationship

The aim of training is to provide a stimulus that is effective in improving performance. For positive adaptations to occur, a careful balance between training dose and recovery is required.[1] After overload training, the athlete works to return to homeostasis, typically in a dose–response manner (i.e., the greater the stress, the longer the recovery period required to return to homeostasis).[2] It is during the return to homeostasis that physiological adaptations are made to ensure a similar stimulus in the future does not disrupt the individual to the same extent.[3] However, for this phenomenon (known as *supercompensation*) to occur, an adequate recovery period must follow the training stimulus (figure 6.1).

For optimal training benefits, the secondary stimulus should be imposed during the supercompensation phase. If no secondary overload is applied during this phase, the training effect may be lost as the organism returns to the pretraining homeostasis levels.[1, 3] Alternatively, if a secondary stimulus is imposed too early, additional fatigue will result, preventing a return to homeostasis. If this continues, maladaptation and diminished competitive performance will occur (see figure 6.2).

Although in theory the fatigue–recovery cycle appears simple, in reality, there are myriad complex psychophysical adaptations that occur during training that make it difficult to quantify the training load–performance response in athletes. In fact, the effect of the training dose on performance is complex. It seems that training duration and intensity are not the sole contributors to performance, and that there may not be generic relationships between training dose and performance outcomes.

Wisdom

It is likely that the relationship between training dose and performance varies between individuals and may be due to variables such as training background, genetics and psychological factors.

As a result of this understanding, it is now common that sport scientists examine the dose–response relationship (i.e., training including fitness, fatigue and performance) on a regular and individual basis to guide decisions on training content and to control training. Despite a growing body of research, there is still a relatively poor

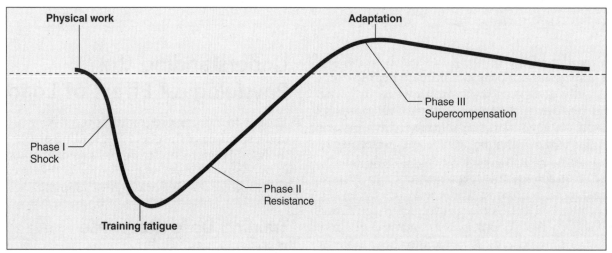

Figure 6.1 General adaptation-syndrome theory explaining response to a stressor.

Adapted from H. Selye, 1956, *The stress of life* (London: Longmans Green).

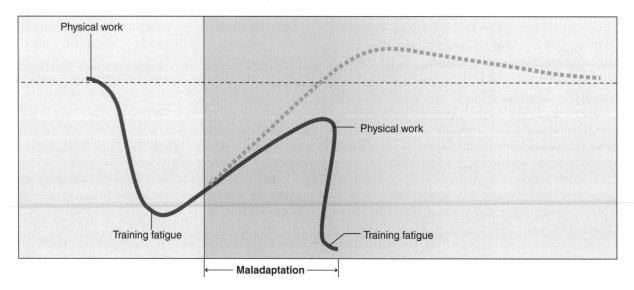

Figure 6.2 Maladaptive training due to insufficient recovery after a training dose.

understanding of the most appropriate tools that can be used to assess how individuals are coping with athletic training; continued investigation is needed.

Fatigue Continuum and Overtraining

Fatigue is a normal and desired part of the training process; its severity can be viewed as a continuum as shown in figure 6.3.[4] When the balance between stress and recovery is appropriate, athletes experience acute fatigue in response to individual training sessions and recover in a matter of hours or days. However, if intensified training continues without the required recovery period, athletes can enter a state of overreaching.[4] When athletes suffer a temporary reduction in performance as a result of overload training, they have entered a state of functional overreaching.[5] If overload training continues and unplanned fatigue persists, athletes may suffer from nonfunctional overreaching that may continue for several weeks. The final stage of the fatigue continuum is the overtraining syndrome, which is a state characterised by decrements in performance and often accompanied by psychological disturbances that remain for an extended period despite large reductions in training.[5] This state is not the result of a diagnosable illness and can be accompanied by disturbance to several physiological systems or to the athlete's psychological state.

In addition to negative performance implications, excessive training loads have been demonstrated to increase the likelihood of injury and illness in high-performing athletes.[6,7] If athletes are required to complete training and competition loads above their threshold of tolerance, they will be at high risk of illness, injury and underperformance. These increased risks further highlight the importance of closely monitoring how athletes are responding to and coping with training and competition.

Wisdom

Training is a balance between fatigue and recovery. A degree of fatigue is required; however, unplanned fatigue is undesirable. Excessive amounts of fatigue seen during periods of increased training or competition place athletes at higher risk of injury and illness.

Methods of Quantifying Load

In order to optimise the training process, it is important to be able to quantify both training load and the physiological response to this load. Numerous objective and subjective methods are available to do so, and when used appropriately, these methods can assist in guiding the training program design and implementation.

Quantifying Training

The physical training in a program is typically quantified with reference to the type, frequency, duration and intensity of each exercise session. Traditionally, training load has been described as a measure of *external load* (e.g., duration, speed and distance covered). Careful control of the external training load is important for reducing training errors. The advances in microtechnology now allow athletes to be monitored with good accuracy and in real time. Recently, technologies such as global positioning systems (GPS), accelerometers and power metres have allowed for increasingly detailed information on the external training load completed by an athlete. These advances have led to the widespread use of external measures for the quantification of training in endurance and team sport.

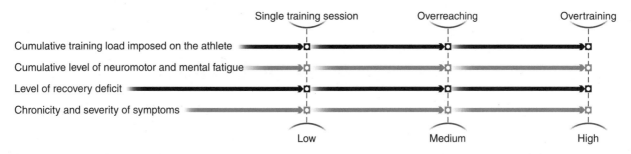

Figure 6.3 The fatigue continuum.

Accordingly, it is the relative physiological stress imposed on the athlete known as the *internal training load*, and not the external training load completed by the athlete, that determines the stimulus for adaptation.[8] The most commonly used methods for quantifying internal training load require heart rate as a measure of exercise intensity; other methods for quantifying relative training intensity include blood lactate and perception of effort.

Wisdom

Measuring external load may not accurately depict the physiological stress imposed on individual athletes because other factors such as genetic background and fitness level may play roles. Fitness outcomes are a function of multiple processes and are related to the internal (i.e., psychological and physiological) loads placed on the athletes.

Monitoring Training Loads Using Heart Rate

In order to monitor an athlete's internal training load, the intensity of each training period needs to be accurately assessed. The use of heart rate information to determine exercise intensity is based on the linear relationship between heart rate and the volume of oxygen consumed ($\dot{V}O_2$) over a wide range of steady-state submaximal workloads.[9] Due to this relationship, heart rate has become the most commonly used method for determining exercise intensity. However, it should be noted that limitations may exist with the use of heart rate to monitor exercise intensity in intermittent team sport, for heart rate may not reflect the intensity during the brief, but intense, efforts common in these sports.

Using Heart Rate Measures to Quantify the Training Impulse

The concept of the training impulse (TRIMP) has been developed as a strategy for integrating all the components of training into a single arbitrary unit suitable for a systems-model approach to training. To do this, we need heart rate information for each training session as well as knowledge of the athlete's maximal and resting heart rate values. Heart rate reserve (HRR) is calculated as maximal heart rate minus resting heart rate. A weighting factor is incorporated to emphasise the relatively greater stress of high-intensity training. This factor is calculated as the exponential of the product of average ΔHRratio and a constant (b) reflecting the generalised curve of blood lactate to exercise intensity, which is different for men and women. The TRIMP training load is calculated using the following equation:

$$\text{Training load} = D(\Delta HR\ ratio)e^{b(\Delta HR\ ratio)}$$

where D = duration of training session and b = 1.67 for females and 1.92 for males.[10]

More recently, Foster and colleagues[11] proposed an alternative approach to the TRIMP where an exercise score for each training session is calculated by multiplying the accumulated duration in each heart rate zone by a multiplier allocated to each zone (50%-60% = 1; 60%-70% = 2: 70%-80% = 3; 80%-90% = 4; 90%-100% = 5). Another possible option is to use heart rate zones that represent values below ventilatory threshold (VT), between VT and the respiratory compensation point (RCP) and above RCP,[12] representing low-, moderate- and high-intensity zones, respectively. Each method requires substantial work to determine and to monitor on a daily basis, which limits their usefulness in a team sport setting.

Limitations of Heart Rate–Based Methods

There are several limitations to using heart rate information for quantifying training load. For example, obtaining heart rate information requires a level of technological proficiency and expertise in interpreting the results. Furthermore, equipment technical failure may result in the loss of valuable information regarding a training session. Heart rate is also a relatively poor method for evaluating intensity during high-intensity exercise such as resistance, interval and plyometric training. Therefore, heart rate appears most useful for monitoring training loads in athletes undertaking endurance-based activities; different variables may be more useful for other activity modes.

Monitoring Training Loads by Rating of Perceived Exertion

An alternative method for determining exercise intensity is through an individual's perception of effort. Overall perceived exertion is an integration of information from peripheral muscles and joints that are doing the work, central cardiovascular and respiratory functions and the central nervous system.[13] Numerous scales exist for assessing perceived exertion. An early version used a 21-point scale and a later version a 15-point scale, where perceptual ratings increase linearly with power output and heart rate.[14, 15] A feature of this scale is that the difference in intensity between each score is identical; by adding zero to the score, that number can be used to denote heart rate in beats per minute. For detailed descriptions of these scales, see the 2006 work of Borg and Kaijser.[16]

To identify exertion associated with nonlinear physical responses (i.e., lactate metabolism), the category-ratio rating of perceived exertion (RPE) scale was developed. The category-ratio scale uses values ranging from 0 to 10 (CR-10) or 0 to 100 (CR-100), and values are anchored by verbal expressions to allow for individual comparisons. Furthermore, each of these verbal expressions has been placed on a ratio scale, and each carries the inherent meaning of twice the intensity of the previous value (e.g., very weak and weak). There is a high correlation between the Borg category-ratio RPE scale and both blood and muscle lactate during exercise.[17]

There does not appear to be one perfect scale for measuring perceived exertion in all situations. The Borg 15-point scale remains widely used; however, the Borg category-ratio scales may be more suited to high-intensity exercise (e.g., team sport) where fatigue is associated with nonlinear physical responses. More recently, ratings of perceived exertion have been used in conjunction with other measures in an attempt to quantify training load in athletes. The most widely used is the session-RPE (s-RPE) method.

The Session-RPE Method

Session-RPE involves multiplying training intensity using an RPE scale by training duration in minutes to create a training impulse score normally referred to as *load*.[18] The training impulse score represents the internal training load for each training session.

When determining the s-RPE, it is important that the rating refer to the entire training session. For this reason, the s-RPE should be assessed more than 10 minutes after training to reduce the likelihood of the recency effect, in which players give an s-RPE that refers to the training completed towards the end of the session rather than during the entire session.

The s-RPE method has been validated as a useful tool to estimate internal training loads at a wide range of intensities in a variety of exercise modes, including team sport. Session load (s-RPE × session duration) is the most commonly calculated metric using s-RPE values in many sport environments. Single-session values can then be summed on a daily basis and weekly load determined as the mean daily load multiplied by 7.[19] However, it is possible to calculate other variables—known as *monotony* and *strain*—that provide different and potentially valuable information.

Training monotony refers to the variation in training load during a week; it is calculated as daily mean load divided by the daily load standard deviation. Strain is the product of monotony and load.[19] When athletes undertake daily, high-volume training with few rest days, training monotony and strain are high. During such periods, athletes are at increased risk of injury and illness.[20, 21] Systematically monitoring these variables in individual athletes allow the coach to determine individual thresholds of risk for injury, illness and overreaching.

It appears that similar information on the training dose applied to individuals may be obtained using the subjective s-RPE method compared to more objective approaches.[22, 23] The added advantage of using s-RPE to assess the internal training response is that it requires nothing more than a pen, paper and clipboard, and it may provide a more valid approach during high-intensity exercise sessions (e.g., sprint, resistance and plyometric training) than heart rate methods.

Assessing an Athlete's Response to Training

Each athlete's response to training load is unique, and it would be foolish to assume a uniform reaction among athletes. Therefore, it is important to gain an insight into how each person is responding. There are a number of methods of doing so; the key ones are described in the following sections.

Assessing Training Responses With Perceptual Measures

In addition to using tools such as s-RPE to assess an athlete's acute perception of training intensity, the subjective responses of an athlete assessed through brief questionnaires may be valuable for the detection of excessive stress. These psychological assessments may be able to provide an early diagnosis of an athlete not coping with training.[20, 24-27] In particular, it has been shown that athletes who develop overreaching and overtraining often have a greater global mood disturbance and demonstrate symptoms similar to clinical depression.[4, 27] The mood-state questionnaires and the daily analysis of life demands for athletes (DALDA) are examples of psychological inventories that have been used to monitor training.

Monitoring Training Loads by Assessing Mood State

The mood-state questionnaires (i.e., POMS and BRUMS) are psychometric tools designed to assess an individual's global mood and the level of tension, depression, anger, vigour, fatigue and confusion[28, 29] (for an example see www.moodprofiling.com).

In well-trained athletes and active individuals, exercise has been shown to improve the global rating of mood state with an increase in vigour and a reduction in measures of tension, depression, anger, fatigue and confusion.[30] However, with excessive exercise the opposite has been shown to occur,[24, 27, 31, 32] suggesting that there may be a relationship between training load and mood state.

We should not rely solely on the POMS as an independent marker of fatigue and recovery because mood state is often a multifactorial response to many external stimuli. Ideally, these questionnaires should be used conjunction with other monitoring such as training-dose measures, performance tests and physiological markers. Nonetheless, the advantage of the POMS and shorter restricted-POMS questionnaires are that they are low-cost, fast-feedback monitoring tools that can be easily applied to large groups. These characteristics make them suitable for use in the team sport environment.

Daily Analyses of Life Demands for Athletes

The DALDA (table 6.1) is a questionnaire designed to assess the stress levels in athletes.[33] It consists of two main sections: part A (general stressors) and part B (stress-reaction symptoms). The DALDA provides a method by which an athlete's stress levels can be monitored daily, providing a record of the athlete's response to training loads and corresponding psychological well-being.

The strength of the DALDA is that, when plotted, the coping trends used by individual athletes are easily apparent. Through using this approach, the coach can see immediate indicators of increasing stress. The DALDA can provide useful information to be used when planning training sessions for individuals.

Other Inventories

Many other inventories exist that are suitable for assessing the well-being of an athlete. Simple wellness questionnaires have demonstrated the ability to detect changes in various perceptions of muscle soreness, fatigue and overall well-being scores in high-performance team sport athletes.[34, 35] An example of a commonly used wellness questionnaire is shown in table 6.2. Similar to the other psychometric tools mentioned in this chapter, this questionnaire is easy to apply to athletes and provides quick feedback to coaches.

Some coaches have raised concerns regarding the potential for dishonest feedback from athletes in an attempt to avoid training or perhaps hide an injury or illness. Although there is potential for this to occur, it is a rare occurrence when athletes are well educated about the purpose of these questionnaires and the need for honest feedback. In addition, the information from this type of inventory should be considered in context with other data about the status of the athlete and knowledge regarding individual personalities and reporting history.

The subjective responses to psychometric inventories can provide valuable information concerning training loads and subsequent levels of stress and may be useful in detecting early signs of overreaching. Although subjective monitoring tools are useful, there is also considerable interest in objective methods of monitoring training load and assessing fatigue status in athletes.

Wisdom

Self-reporting questionnaires can be used to identify players who may not be coping well with training. The feedback provided from these psychometric tools can be used to open dialogue with athletes and assist in directing them to appropriate support services.

Table 6.1 Daily Analyses of Life Demands for Athletes (DALDA) Questionnaire

Initials _____

Trial day _____

Date _____

Circle the correct response for this moment: A = worse than normal; B = normal; C = better than normal.

PART A							
1. Diet	A	B	C	6. Climate	A	B	C
2. Home life	A	B	C	7. Sleep	A	B	C
3. School/college/work	A	B	C	8. Recreation	A	B	C
4. Friends	A	B	C	9. Health	A	B	C
5. Sport training	A	B	C				
Total				Total			
PART B							
1. Muscle pains	A	B	C	14. Enough sleep	A	B	C
2. Techniques	A	B	C	15. Recovery between sessions	A	B	C
3. Tiredness	A	B	C	16. General weakness	A	B	C
4. Need for a rest	A	B	C	17. Interest	A	B	C
5. Supplementary work	A	B	C	18. Arguments	A	B	C
6. Boredom	A	B	C	19. Skin rashes	A	B	C
7. Recovery time	A	B	C	20. Congestion	A	B	C
8. Irritability	A	B	C	21. Training effort	A	B	C
9. Weight	A	B	C	22. Temper	A	B	C
10. Throat	A	B	C	23. Swellings	A	B	C
11. Internal	A	B	C	24. Likability	A	B	C
12. Unexplained aches	A	B	C	25. Running nose	A	B	C
13. Technique strength	A	B	C				
Total				Total			

From B.S. Rushall, 1990, "A tool for measuring stress tolerance in elite athletes," *Journal of Applied Sport Psychology* 2(1): 51-66. Reprinted by permission of Taylor & Francis Ltd.

Table 6.2 Daily Well-being Review Sheet

Name _____

Weight _____

Date _____

Present injuries _____

Sit and reach _____

	5	4	3	2	1	Score
Fatigue	Very fresh	Fresh	Normal	More tired than normal	Always tired	
Sleep quality	Very restful	Good	Difficulty falling asleep	Restless sleep	Insomnia	
General muscle soreness	Feeling great	Feeling good	Normal	Increase in soreness or tightness	Very sore	
Stress level	Very relaxed	Relaxed	Normal	Feeling stressed	Highly stressed	
Mood	Very positive mood	Generally good mood	Less interested in others and activities than usual	Snappy with teammates, family and coworkers	Highly annoyed, irritable, or down	
					Total	

Adapted, by permission, from B.D. McLean, A.J. Coutts, V. Kelly, M.R. McGuigan, and S.J. Cormack, 2010, "Neuromuscular, endocrine and perceptual fatigue responses during different length between-match microcycles in professional rugby league players," *International Journal of Sports Physiology and Performance* 5(3): 367-383.

Objective Markers of Fitness and Fatigue

Despite the plethora of tests available to assess physical performance, many are not useful for regular monitoring of fatigue status, particularly in season. There are a number of reasons for this, including their fatiguing nature, difficulties accommodating large numbers of athletes, substantial skill requirements, the need for specialised equipment (e.g., isokinetic dynamometer), limited portability (e.g., cycle ergometer) or poor test–retest reliability. As a result, other objective measures, such as neuromuscular performance tests, physiological responses to standard exercise sessions or biochemical measures taken during rest have become valuable ways to monitor athletes.

Neuromuscular Performance Tests

The assessment of neuromuscular fatigue inferred from performance tests is common in high-performance sport environments, although the validity of many of these protocols is unclear. A specific type of neuromuscular fatigue that may be of interest to those working in high-performance sport is low-frequency fatigue (LFF),[36] resulting from high-intensity, moderate-to-high force, repetitive eccentric or stretch-shortening cycle (SSC) activities.[37,38] Low-frequency fatigue has long lasting, detrimental effects on low-frequency force-generating capacity. The primary clinical method for assessing LFF is via percutaneous nerve or muscle stimulation,[39] but this laboratory-based method is impractical for regular use in athletes. As a result, single or repeated explosive activities, such as countermovement jumps (CMJ), are commonly used to assess LFF in the field.

Countermovement Jumps

The use of countermovement-jump (CMJ) protocols to assess fatigue status in high-performance sport is becoming increasingly popular because the test is easy to measure with a force plate, switch mat or linear position transducer. This technology allows the assessment of many variables including displacement, power and velocity.[40] Numerous CMJ protocols have been used for assessing athlete fatigue; however, single-repetition protocols are likely to be more efficient than multiple jumps. In most cases in the field, it is not possible to determine the source (i.e., central or peripheral) of the performance decrement.

Recent research has demonstrated the application of this approach. For example, monitoring CMJ performance over a 22-match Australian football season demonstrated that the ratio of CMJ flight time:contraction time is suppressed in the days after a match compared to 48 hours pregame and to immediate pregame values and is correlated with a measure of performance.[41] This suppression represents a state of reduced neuromuscular capacity, and these results can be used to guide the implementation of future training. Further work in elite Australian football players has shown that reductions in the ratio of flight time:contraction time negatively affect the ability to use fitness capacity and modify movement strategy.[42, 43] However, since neuromuscular fatigue is only one potential source of fatigue in athletes, it is suggested that these measures be used in conjunction with other monitoring tools mentioned in this chapter.

Wisdom

To determine the validity of any monitoring tool in high-performance sport, practitioners need to either conduct some basic in-house projects to assess potential variables or take guidance from the scientific literature. These projects can help practitioners refine assessment procedures to reduce measurement error and determine appropriate baseline values for comparison.

Physiological Markers

The use of submaximal exercise protocols may also be useful for monitoring training tolerance in both individual and team sport athletes.[44-46] For example, athletes identified as suffering performance decrements based on heart rate response to a submaximal shuttle protocol also displayed mood state and hormonal changes.[46] The following section on heart rate responses contains more information on the use of submaximal protocols for monitoring training.

Heart Rate Variability

Measurement of heart rate variability (HRV), the normal variation in beat-to-beat intervals, is gaining widespread favour throughout the sport world because it is thought to provide an insight into an individual's preparedness to train. In a healthy individual, the autonomic nervous system controls heart rate through the interaction of the sympathetic nervous system (SNS) and the parasympathetic nervous system (PNS). The SNS regulates the physiological flight-or-fight conditions such as increased heart rate and blood pressure. The PNS, on the other hand, regulates the physiological rest-and-digest conditions such as decreased heart rate and blood pressure.

The heart beats in a nonuniform fashion; this is especially the case in athletes where training can involve high heart rates and recovery is characterised by much lower heart rates. The ideal situation is one whereby the athlete has a strong sympathetic response to training and an equally powerful parasympathetic response when recovering. If scientists observe that the sympathetic system is driving the heart rate response (seen with low HRV), then they might consider decreasing training load. The opposite situation exists when the parasympathetic system is dominating, indicating that athletes are coping with the training load. However, these trends are not always observed in the field,[44] showing that HRV measures should not be used independent of other monitoring tools mentioned in this chapter.

It is thought that overtraining has a negative influence on cardiovascular autonomic control; however, the direction of shift in underlying autonomic control associated with overtraining is somewhat unclear.[47] Overreaching may be characterised by sympathetic control of heart rate, although in nonfunctional overreaching and overtraining, sympathetic control appears inhibited with an increase in parasympathetic activity.[48] Unfortunately, there is yet to be strong support from the field for using HRV to assess how team sport athletes are coping with training. This is largely due to the poor measurement error in many HRV variables when assessed outside laboratory conditions.

Heart Rate Recovery

When exercise ceases, there is a coordinated sympathetic withdrawal and parasympathetic reactivation that results in a rapid reduction in heart rate.[49] Improvements in heart rate recovery (HRR) have been associated with improvements in fitness;[44] a slower rate of recovery may be indicative of detraining[50, 51] or increased fatigue. Due to the autonomic control of HRR, there is potential for HRR to be a useful measure of autonomic nervous system status.[49] It may be capable of detecting the onset of overreaching or when athletes are not coping with the training load.[52, 53]

Biochemical Markers of Fitness and Fatigue

Hormones and other variables in blood, urine and saliva have recently been used to provide information about an athlete's adaptation to training load and thus are potentially useful for monitoring training and recovery.[54, 55]

Muscle Damage

Strenuous and unaccustomed eccentric exercise can lead to exercise-induced muscle damage (EIMD). The activity of selected enzymes and blood markers, including creatine kinase (CK), myoglobin, troponin, urea, uric acid and ammonia, have been shown to reflect muscle damage.[56-58] As a result, these measures may be useful as monitoring tools in high-performance sport.

The most commonly reported marker is CK. Typically, CK is found inside the muscle cell. However, after intense physical exercise, serum levels of CK can rise due to acute muscle damage, but this is not necessarily due to maladaptive training. Importantly, although CK measures reflect muscle damage, they do not necessarily predict performance limitations in athletes. Therefore, we recommend that CK be used to assess the short-term recovery of muscle damage from acute training or competition. This measurement is particularly useful in the early preseason adaptation phase, during periods of intensified training and in the days after competitive matches. If markers of muscle damage remain high after a reduction in training load, that may suggest delayed recovery or increased injury risk. However, the great variability in the response of these markers suggests they should be used cautiously and in conjunction with other measures.

Salivary Versus Blood Markers

Steroid hormone levels within athletes are often monitored in blood plasma, but due to the strong relationships between plasma and saliva measures and the reduced invasiveness of the collection method, saliva measures are preferred in the field.[59-61] The most common hormones monitored are cortisol and testosterone; however, the amino acids glutamine and glutamate have also shown some promise as monitoring markers.

Cortisol

Cortisol (C) is a glucocorticoid that is released from the adrenal cortex in response to physical and mental stress. It is generally considered as a catabolic marker and an objective indicator of psychobiological stress, but there are mixed reports in its suitability as a tool for monitoring athletes.[44] Elevation of salivary C is commonly reported immediately after competition; it also has been shown to be elevated during heavy training periods, such as in preseason. As a result, elevation of salivary C can be a symptom of overreaching and reflect an inability to recover between training sessions and competition.[62-64] As is always the case, training decisions should not be made on the basis of a single variable. It is always best to interpret the results in conjunction with other measures of wellness and a pragmatic interpretation of training load.

Testosterone

Testosterone (T) is a gonadal anabolic hormone that promotes muscle tissue synthesis.[65] Testosterone typically increases after short-term strenuous exercise,[66-68] but a decrease in testosterone with prolonged strenuous exercise (greater than 2 hours) has been observed.[67, 69] Testosterone response has also been reported to be extremely variable throughout a team sport season involving high-intensity contact.[62]

Although it is attractive to think that T may be a useful marker of recovery status, reflecting states of anabolism when high and catabolism when low, its high variability may limit its usefulness for monitoring in applied settings. Moreover, like other biochemical measures, these measures are relatively costly, which reduces their practical efficacy.

Testosterone-to-Cortisol Ratio

Due to the anabolic nature of T and the catabolic effects of C, the ratio between the two may reflect the body's overall anabolic–catabolic balance.[70] The T:C ratio decreases in relation to intensity and duration of physical exercise, as well as during periods of intense training or repetitive competition, and can be reversed by regenerative measures.[71] It has been suggested that a high T:C ratio reflects a state of anabolism and a state of catabolism when reduced by 30 per cent or more;[70] a low T:C ratio may indicate that an athlete is not adapting to training.

Imbalances between T and C may also be caused by psychological stress, which is why the holistic stressors of training, competition and general life need to be taken into account when assessing the demands placed on athletes.

Glutamine and Glutamate

Plasma glutamine (Gln) and glutamate (Glu) levels have been suggested to be a reliable early indicators of maladaptive training and good measures for monitoring how athletes are coping with training. Low Gln levels reported during periods of heavy training may indicate reduced immune competence and an increased risk of illness in those athletes.[72-74]

In addition to changes in glutamine and glutamate, a reduced plasma Gln:Glu ratio has been suggested as a valid global indicator of training tolerance.[74] Reductions in this ratio have been found in national-level athletes classified as overreaching;[74-76] these findings with athletes from a wide variety of sports suggest the Gln:Glu ratio could be a valuable objective monitoring tool. However, this finding is not consistent, and uncertainty exists regarding the utility of using the Gln:Glu ratio as an early indicator of athletes not coping with training.

Immune Markers

It is well accepted that exercise results in short-term compromise to the immune system; there is also a suggestion that intensified training causes depressed immune function, which makes athletes more susceptible to common illnesses.[77] Some research has shown increased illness rates in response to heightened training loads.[20] Potential markers of compromised immune status include leukocyte and cytokine concentration and salivary immunoglobulin-A secretion rate.[78] However, the capacity to use these and other markers to monitor how athletes are coping with training or check athletes for risk of impending illness is low.

Wisdom

Numerous objective markers have been proposed as useful for monitoring the fitness and fatigue response of athletes to training and competition. Unfortunately, the requirement for frequent sampling (i.e., weekly), fast determination of results, lower cost and complexity of assays coupled with the need for strict collection procedures may limit the utility of many biochemical markers.

Practical Applications and Data Presentation

Data are not helpful unless they are presented in such a manner that makes the data easily understandable. Doing so helps draw the distinction between data and information. A number of tools can be used to illustrate critical results and trends.

Validity and Reliability of Measures

The usefulness of any monitoring tool in the sport environment centres on its validity and reliability. Although these concepts are discussed in chapter 1, a brief recap is useful because these concepts lie at the heart of our ability to extract meaningful information from monitoring strategies.

Reliability refers to how repeatable a test is. A test with good reliability will produce the same result if it is performed in the same manner on another occasion. This allows confidence that any performance change is biological and not inherent error in the measurement device or test.

There are numerous types of validity, including whether the variable actually measures what it purports to. Types of validity critical to high-performance sport are construct and ecological validity: Does the measure have application in the environment in question? Is it linked to something that it theoretically should be (e.g., performance or training load)? For example, many variables can be obtained from a CMJ conducted on a force plate; however, some are not valid indicators of fatigue–recovery status because they do not have a pattern of response that makes them useful in comparison to baseline values. The variables may also not be related to training load or performance.

Baseline Values

Determining whether a variable has changed largely depends on the baseline value it is being compared with. Likely multiple baseline values can be calculated to provide points of comparison; however, a critical feature is that the calculation should allow for a meaningful comparison. For example, comparing weekly scores during a team sport competitive season should be done against a value that represents the competition phase but at the same time is fatigue free.

Comparison Points

It is best to understand and plan retesting schedules in advance; doing so will help ensure that data collection is strategic and systematic as opposed to ad-hoc. It is worthwhile planning both short- and long-term testing periods.

Acute

It is common for monitoring data to be collected on a number of timeframes. Some data, such as exercise intensity via microtechnology (i.e., GPS or accelerometers) or internal load from s-RPE are collected daily or with each session, although other data are collected weekly or even less frequently. It is arguable that the value of many monitoring tools depends on collecting data frequently and consistently.

Weekly comparisons to baseline scores are often made for biochemical, neuromuscular and match exercise-intensity data in team sport competition phases. Scores from wellness questionnaires often are collected around main training sessions throughout a week (sometimes daily) and can be averaged as weekly values. For biochemical and neuromuscular protocols, there is a specific need for high levels of consistency in pretest preparation and collection techniques.

Similarly, there is a requirement to collect weekly data at a time when the expected response is known so that changes outside that response can be highlighted. For example,

football players typically have recovered neuromuscular performance within 3 to 4 days of competition. If CMJ performance was reduced after this period, coach intervention and training manipulation would be likely. Other monitoring tools can be used less frequently. For example, psychological inventories are sometimes used monthly. In addition, values from daily or weekly monitoring tools are sometimes averaged to provide a monthly score. These measures provide athletes with feedback on chronic changes to training and competition.

Chronic

Regardless of how frequently data regarding a variable are collected, a change compared to baseline can be calculated as the isolated weekly score or perhaps as a rolling average over a period such as a month. In this case, the weekly comparison to baseline might represent acute fatigue, and the monthly average response could reflect a more chronic fatigue response. Similar analyses could also be made for various measures of fitness and fatigue to model chronic fitness and fatigue adaptations over a season.

Statistical Techniques

Although coaches are not always intimately familiar with statistical analyses of data, the selection of appropriate techniques has a major bearing on practical application. Traditional methods of statistical analysis commonly used in research often are inappropriate in practice. However, more contemporary techniques provide great insight and are extremely helpful in assisting decision making. By simply determining the change in a variable relative to its reliability value (either in absolute units or percentage) practitioners can begin to make decisions about the meaningfulness of the change. In this approach, if the change is greater than the error of the test (reliability), then coaches can be confident that the change is biological.

For example, if a valid test has an error of 3 per cent and the change between two time points is 5 per cent, then practitioners can be relatively confident that this change is worth noting. This method relies on using valid and reliable tests and collecting data consistently. Most importantly, it provides a threshold for assessing the importance of a change. More complex and stringent techniques are extensions of this approach and allow more precision regarding the magnitude of change. These techniques include calculation of the smallest worthwhile change, which represents the smallest change in a performance that can be considered important.[79]

Perhaps one of the greatest challenges is to determine what constitutes an important change in self-report inventories. Wellness questionnaires often require subjective ratings on a scale that broadly represents categories from poor to excellent. A problem with interpreting scores on these scales is the so-called automated response, in addition to the problem of the athlete who regularly reports high or low values, despite the scale often having a normal (or similar) anchor. One way around these dilemmas is to compare each response in relation to the degree to which it is above or below normal. Comparison can also be made to a value that represents what an athlete regularly reports. An example of how this has been done is to use a modification of the standard difference score.[80] On an acute level this can be represented as the following:

(Current score – Baseline score) / SD of individual baseline*

This score effectively converts the acute score to a standard deviation from the baseline. Coaches can set their own threshold to determine how many standard deviations are practically important. However, based on our experience, we recommend a threshold of $z = \geq 1.5$ as a practically effective threshold for identifying at-risk scores.

An interesting issue that arises in high-performance sport is the relative importance of inter- and intra-individual change. Although the response of an individual is critical, it is possible that a lack of change or change of a different magnitude in comparison to the group is important. For example, as part of a periodised approach, the group mean of a monitoring variable may suggest a recovered state in response to an unloading phase. In this case, although an individual's score from one point to the next may not have changed, if the group members are showing improvement, the lack of response in an individual may suggest maladaptation.

Putting It All Together and Making It Meaningful to Coaches

The ultimate value of monitoring training load and the fatigue response is when such monitoring informs decision making. For this to occur, the monitoring process needs to be part of the overall program approach. This means that data need to be collected and analysed in a coordinated, consistent manner and in a timely fashion. For example, there is little point in using a variable that cannot be analysed for 2 weeks.

Ideally, the majority of monitoring should occur as part of the normal training and competition process. The use of protocols that are particularly onerous from a time or equipment perspective or that require a specific testing session is questionable. Equally, the use of invalid or unreliable variables is not only unhelpful but can result inappropriate decisions being made.

When a mixed-methods approach is taken in conjunction with appropriate statistical analyses, coaches and support staff are able to make informed decisions regarding the training process. An example of how this might look in a high-performance setting is shown in table 6.3.

Wisdom

Despite the desire in many high-performance environments for a single number or measure that is representative of overall fatigue status, to this point such a variable has not been identified. Therefore, the prudent approach is to use a mixed-methods system in which internal and external measures of load and fatigue response are reviewed in combination with the art of coaching.

There is scientific interest in collecting and using tools to monitor and optimise the training process; however, for these tools to be useful in a practical sense, they must be meaningful to coaches. There are endless ways to present data, but coaches generally are more interested in the outcomes and recommendations than in the nuances of data collection and statistical analysis.

---

*SD = standard deviation of baseline scores (e.g., four scores collected from a preseason cup-competition phase)

Table 6.3 Sample Monitoring System for High-Performance Team Sport

Variable	Collection frequency	Statistical analysis technique	Practical value
RPE	Every session	Modified standard difference score Intra- and inter-individual comparisons	Critical
Load	Weekly	As above	Critical
Monotony	Weekly	As above	Important
Strain	Weekly	As above	Important
Wellness questionnaire	2-4 times per week	As above	Critical
Training and competition intensity	Every session	Change relative to reliability value Week-to-week and chronic variation	Very important
Psychological inventory	Weekly to monthly	As above plus psychologist interpretation	Very important
Biochemical, neuromuscular, autonomic NS markers (HRV)	Weekly	Change relative to reliability value Week-to-week and chronic variation	Important but can be expensive and require specialised equipment
Other markers (e.g., sleep)	As needed	Change relative to reliability value Week-to-week and chronic variation	Very important but rely on specific equipment and expertise

Data from E. Borg and L. Kaijser, 2006, "A comparison between three rating scales for perceived exertion and two different work tests," *Scandinavian Journal of Medicine and Science in Sports* 16(1): 57-69; F.M. Impellizzeri, E. Rampinini, and S.M. Marcora, 2005, "Physiological assessment of aerobic training in soccer," *Journal of Sports Sciences* 23(6): 583-592; B.D. McLean, A.J. Coutts, V. Kelly, M.R. McGuigan, and S.J. Cormack, 2010, "Neuromuscular, endocrine, and perceptual fatigue responses during different length between-match microcycles in professional rugby league players," *International Journal of Sports Physiology and Performance* 5(3): 367-383; and H. Selye, 1956, *The stress of life* (London: Longmans Green).

For this reason, graphical representation of data is often informative. Approaches such as the use of a traffic light system (i.e., green for good, yellow for caution, red for danger) to denote an individual athlete's status can be useful. Reporting change in percentage terms is also meaningful to most people as long as the relative change required for the information to be important is highlighted. Finally, often the most important aspect of making these types of data meaningful to coaches is to provide a qualitative inference regarding the training, competition and injury implications of specific data sets.

Summary

The emphasis on monitoring training load and fatigue in high-performance settings is likely to continue to increase. Similarly, the desire for a single tool, marker or value to represent overall fatigue status also is likely to continue, but it appears highly unlikely that one exists. Therefore, the biggest impact can be made by using a suite of valid and reliable markers analysed on multiple levels. A mixed-methods approach seems the most appropriate.

As technology continues to advance, it may be possible to accurately assess the status of discrete biological systems in the field. This enhanced precision should help to optimise individual training program manipulation. Importantly, the validity of individual variables may be somewhat environment specific. Despite a focus on objective tools, an enormous amount of data now points to the value of simple yet valuable perceptual tools such as s-RPE and psychometric inventories. A more effective use of these tools in conjunction with objective markers may hold the key to the development of effective monitoring programs.

CHAPTER 7

Retraining the Injured Athlete

Daniel Lewindon
Rugby Football Union, UK

David Joyce
Western Force Rugby, Australia and Edith Cowan University, Australia

Injury remains an all-too-frequent consequence of sport at all levels, either through trauma or the attrition associated with the constant pursuit of improved performance. Injury often results in a reduction in performance or time removed from training and competition.

Although injury can bring its own significant stresses and frustrations to the athlete, it can also present a rare opportunity to review, recondition and improve athleticism and general robustness. As seasons lengthen and competition demands increase, the windows for good-quality periods of physical improvement are narrower. Treating injury as an opportunity is often a helpful mind-set to offer to fallen athletes as coaches navigate them through a difficult and uncertain period.

This chapter discusses the strategies that should be pursued both during and in the immediate aftermath of a mid- to long-term injury (defined as 4 weeks or more). It highlights the need for an integrated approach to injury management from all support staff to ensure the best possible outcome is achieved. We discuss the management philosophy that should be adopted in terms of rehabilitation design and progression, the transition to full training and the monitoring and on-going processes required once an athlete returns to competition in order to minimise reinjury risk. Our aim is to present a philosophy of player management that is applicable to all injury scenarios and fosters an interdisciplinary approach to reconditioning the injured athlete.

Planning the Process

It is inadvisable to first start thinking about injury management after the injury has occurred. This will lead to loss of valuable time and mistakes made through inadequate preparation. It is important that the athlete has a sense of confidence in the plan of care for his or her injury and as well as in the management team, one that places the athlete at the centre of the rehabilitation model.

Interdisciplinary Approach to Athlete-Centred Rehabilitation

It is important to start by understanding who will be involved in the process. The extent of the team may vary by organisation and infrastructure, but generally speaking, it may involve any or all of the following:

- Athlete
- Coach
- Doctor or external specialists
- Physiotherapist, athletic trainer, chiropractor
- Strength and conditioning or fitness coach
- Nutritionist
- Psychologist

Sometimes all of these people will be a part of a formal team, but in many cases (especially away from professional sport) these roles will be filled by only a few individuals. The one person who does not vary, however, is the athlete. The athlete should always be at the centre of the management process. This is what we call the *performance team*, and for the team to work effectively, clarity regarding roles, responsibilities and plans needs to be achieved.

The next concept that should be understood is the importance of an interdisciplinary team, not just a multidisciplinary team. The difference may seem semantic, but it signals somewhat of a paradigm shift away from a fragmented approach involving many people, and therefore many separate opinions and outcomes, to one whereby all members of the team are unified in the plan and outcome measures. The interdisciplinary approach reinforces the concept that many aspects of rehabilitation are interrelated; as such, there will be elements of crossover in terms of input at any given time. It ensures a consistency of approach and a unity within the team and is the best way to ensure that there are no weak links in the chain or uncertainty among the management team. The philosophy of One Athlete–One Programme is vital in all mid- to long-term rehabilitation projects.

Managing the Diagnosis

Rehabilitation starts with a thorough understanding of the diagnosis and likely recovery period. Inevitably, the first question an athlete asks as soon as the injury occurs is, 'How long until I'm back competing?' The first challenge, then, is to manage the expectations of the athlete, coach and parents or other loved ones whilst providing a positive, realistic, accurate (and acceptable!) answer. In what can be an emotionally charged and initially uncertain period, this is perhaps best managed through the following cascade:

1. Ensure correct diagnosis and interdepartmental and practitioner discussion before providing narrow time lines.

2. Dissociate from the stresses and pressures applied by all concerned and your own attachment to the athlete or team.

3. Provide the athlete and coaching staff a spectrum of best- through worst-case scenarios with a thorough explanation of the processes involved in return to competition: a progressive symptom- and outcome-led rehabilitation process that will return the athlete in a better physical state.

4. Provide detailed and player-centred planning by delivering a clear, criteria-driven program to the player, which includes input from all relevant parties (including consideration of external life pressures and priorities and fundamental athletic qualities to be developed during this period).

5. Adopt and present a mindset that the injury has presented an opportunity to all concerned.

Before the athlete can mentally commit to a rehabilitation process, there needs to be a level of acceptance and a desire to move forward. Perhaps the biggest barrier is uncertainty. Uncertainty regarding the diagnosis or prognosis is a major source of anxiety in an athlete. As such, a full explanation of the injury is vital, as is a pragmatic plan for the athlete's return to play. It may take multiple explanations of an injury and the rehabilitation plan for this information to be accepted. It may come down to the athlete's learning style or even just the fact that the athlete may be in denial about the injury or what needs to happen next. It is critical to take the time to explain everything and to give the injured athlete sufficient time to ask questions. Without this effort, the athlete will find it difficult to move on and focus on the job at hand.

It is not uncommon for a contemporary athlete to request or be offered a scan for any injury. Although this procedure can provide good insight into an injured structure and the prognosis, there can be a mismatch in the functional status of the athlete versus the radiological findings.[1] Undoubtedly, we should at least consider this diagnostic technology, but only if it will change management of the injury. *Treat the man, not the scan* is an oft-quoted catch-cry. If function can be accurately proven and carefully progressed, then a successful return from injury can be accelerated. This is a powerful argument for the use of criterion-based rehabilitation, a topic that will be discussed in detail later.

Wisdom

An individual displaying anxious behaviours during rehabilitation is likely to display similar anxieties when reintegrating into competition. This often translates into a much slower rehabilitation period. Therefore, if we want to get athletes back on the field or track in as short a period as possible, we need to address these anxieties as soon as possible. A well-explained diagnosis is critical to reducing anxiety.

Thinking in Terms of Abilities, Not Disabilities

In terms of injury rehabilitation, much of the planning and delivery of rehabilitation programmes will be drawn from a thorough understanding of the lines of stress, that is, what can be pushed and what needs to be respected, for how long, and why.[2] This takes an interdisciplinary approach and represents a mindset change from a more traditional, conservative medical approach. Instead of telling the athlete what he or she cannot do, the emphasis is placed on what the athlete *can* do. This immediately ingratiates the medical team with the strength and conditioning team, coaching staff and athlete and enables a more complete use of the convalescence period.

Figure 7.1 demonstrates the understanding of an injury that is required and the key players who should form the backbone of rehabilitation planning and delivery during the injury period.

Injury as an Opportunity

No athlete wants to be injured, and so it is vital to find silver linings in what can be a somewhat cloudy sky. The best way to frame this unfortunate time in an athlete's career is that the time that it takes for an injury to heal represents an opportunity to review the athlete in his or her entirety, not simply concentrating on the injured part of the anatomy. This holistic view presents a good opportunity to improve these aspects:

- Injury-risk profile (bullet-proofing)

- Physical capacities (e.g., aerobic power, upper-body strength)
- Movement efficiency
- Psychological and emotional resiliency
- Tactical awareness

The elements of these categories are discussed in detail in other chapters of this book. The same principles can be followed to achieve outcomes with the injured athlete, although there needs to be a consideration of the lines of stress that the training will produce on a healing part. Close consultation within the interdisciplinary team of all these variables is critical to ensure the athletic needs of the individual are being met without compromising the rehabilitation objectives.

Within some environments, the sight of an injured player resting whilst the remainder of the team trains would not be well received and therefore needs to be managed with care. With this in mind, coaches should be fully informed and involved in the rehabilitation programme and have the opportunity to include stage-appropriate coaching into the schedule. This may be as simple as involving the athlete in video analysis of upcoming opponents or having the athlete participate in match-day water running, but it keeps the athlete connected with the coaches and team. It also provides the development of game understanding that may be more difficult when the athlete is fit, and so represents another opportunity.

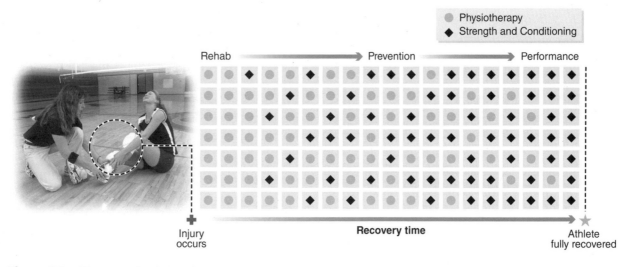

Figure 7.1 Player-centred planning process.

Delivering the Programme

Now that we understand the philosophical elements behind world-class rehabilitation, it's important that we get the delivery right. The theory will count for naught if the practice is lacking in precision and effectiveness.

Design and Delivery

All members of the performance team have critical roles to play in the planning and delivery of the rehabilitation process. A modern-day model of rehabilitation needs to be both tissue specific (incorporating physiological systems and biomechanical principles) and functional, with an emphasis on motor learning, reorganisation and sport relevance.

A rehabilitation program is invariably broken down into staged phases of escalating demand. The progamme might typically be composed of acute, low-load, moderate-load, high-load and return-to-sport sections. Ideally, there may also be some thought given to on-going prevention conditioning once the athlete has returned to sport. Whatever design or layout used, the format needs to be clear to all members of the management team and to the athlete as well; it needs to provide a clear pathway showing where the athlete is in the program and what he or she needs to achieve to move on.

Rehabilitation needs to be structured so that athletes have a series of wins. These stepping stones to success need to be arranged throughout the rehabilitation period and obviously need to be weighed up with the physical health of the healing tissues. This is where close communication between the support team and the athlete is crucial; it is vital to determine what sport-specific tasks are of particular concern to the client.

For example, after a knee injury, an athlete may be particularly concerned about sudden changes of direction whilst running. A possible rehabilitation plan could therefore progress from slow slalom runs, to tighter slalom runs, to zig-zag running, to cutting and then to reversing the direction of running. Variables can be added to this basic structure: speed, increased attention demands (e.g., using a ball), different footwear (e.g., moulded to screw-in studs) or surface demands, an opponent, unpredictable or game-relevant changes of direction, live evasion and tackling or multiopponent evasion.

Each progression would be considered only after the stepping stones have been accomplished, a key concept discussed later in this chapter.

Importance of Periodising Rehabilitation

Adaptation to an imposed demand requires both stimulus and recovery. Therefore, we must consider how to periodise rehabilitation to best ensure timely and optimal outcome.

A great deal of effort is placed into periodising training plans, but much less is placed on the formalised periodising of rehabilitation. For example, in an attempt to not load a knee injury, the athlete will be given upper-body strength programmes to do every day instead. Alternatively, an athlete who cannot yet participate in collision training in a contact sport will be assigned extra running. These are examples of lazy programme design without a strategic, long-term view of loading. It is certainly possible to overwork athletes, and it is little wonder so many athletes look stale when they come back from a long injury. With this in mind, a strategic approach to rehabilitation and training loadings should be applied from the start of the process. This is discussed in detail in chapter 18.

When planning long-term rehabilitation, start at the estimated return-to-play date (as though it was a major competition) and work backward, incorporating heavy-, medium- and low-load weeks. This will ensure all bases are covered, and the monotony of relentless rehabilitation loading does not blunt the athlete's edge.

Importance of Exit Criteria

The progression of a rehabilitation program throughout each phase should be judged on the achievement of carefully formulated, objective exit criteria, a critical aspect of rehabilitation programming. Exit criteria serve to minimise the potential for inappropriate rehabilitation sequencing, drills or volume and load, creating a clear road map of recovery for the athlete and all members of the team. Doing so requires a detailed understanding of relevant tissue loading, normal tissue function and the end game (the athlete's and any sport or position's specific requirements). Having a clear road map allows the practitioner to be more aggressive with the programme, but with the confidence that the markers set are appropriate, and therefore the risks to the athlete are minimised.

Although the sports medicine practitioner may best understand the lines of stress of the injury, all members of the team have pivotal roles to play in this process, creating an integrated programme that considers all aspects of athlete rehabilitation and performance. The key thing to note is that we should not mortgage rehabilitation outcomes based on time elapsed, but rather on achieving functional competencies. There are certain healing times that are reasonably well established (e.g., 6 weeks for an uncomplicated bone fracture, 21 days for a grade 1 hamstring strain) and can help guide prognostics. If this system is the guiding one, however, what tends to occur is that we become more fixated on the passage of time as opposed to the achievement of functional goals.

For example, we may think that a minor ankle sprain in a lacrosse player should take 10 days to heal based on physiology and established healing times. If, however, the athlete still cannot demonstrate competencies in deceleration and change of direction by this time, it is unwise to push the athlete back onto the field. It is much better to have established return-to-play criteria for the athlete to satisfy as opposed to having just crossed off days on the calendar.

This approach can be used throughout the rehabilitation period. Taking the example of the lacrosse player, let's say the player is allowed to begin drills that involve changing direction. Speed can be added once the athlete can perform the drills slowly; the athlete can perform the drills slowly once he or she can decelerate; the athlete can decelerate once he or she can run; the athlete

can run once he or she can hop; and so forth. An example of the inclusion of exit criteria in a hamstring rehabilitation programme is shown in table 7.1. Although this table an example of best practice for this particular type of injury, it is used for illustrative purposes only; the framework can be adapted to suit other types of rehabilitation programmes.

Competency-based rehabilitation also helps ensure that there is a logical flow to tissue loading. This is vital to ensure that the body is hardened to the stresses that it will be expected to face when the athlete is back training and competing fully. The achievement of milestones also helps the injured athlete chart the journey back to health and see progress, which engenders confidence both in the system and in the athlete's own body.

Special Considerations: Returning to Running

A critical consideration when returning to on-feet loading after a long period of immobilisation or reduced loading is the process of returning to running. In these cases, it is not just the injured site that needs to be considered, but rather all the other areas of the kinetic chain that may have become deconditioned. Perhaps the most obvious consideration is tendon loading. Tendons generally take 2 or 3 days to recover after periods of high load. With

Table 7.1 Exit Criteria Included in a Hamstring Rehabilitation Programme

Stage	Exit criteria	Completed
Acute	Active knee extension (seated in neutral posture): 75% range or symmetry pain-free	☐
	Pain-free gait, stairs and sit to stand	☐
	Pain-free double-leg bridge (5-sec hold) at 90-, 60- and 30-degree knee flexion	☐
Low load	Active knee extension (seated in neutral posture): 100% range or symmetry pain-free	☐
	Pain-free single-leg bridge at 30-degree knee flexion	☐
	Pain-free single-leg mid-range loading with 3 plane perturbation	☐
	2 km treadmill jog (2% incline)	☐
High load	Repeated 80% intensity linear runs with maximal acceleration and deceleration	☐
	High-intensity (sub-maximal) multi-directional running	☐
	> 80% symmetry in single-leg maximal loading and capacity texts (e.g., isokinetic knee flexion/extension, single-leg deadlift, single-leg isometric hold + prone row)	☐
Return to sport	Completion of complex agility and repeated speed under fatigue	☐
	Completion of a week of full training including repeated efforts of match intensity drills	☐
	Player, coach and performance team agreement	☐

this in mind, a suggested tendon-loading schedule over the course of a 7-day period is as follows:

Monday: Low

Tuesday: High

Wednesday: Low

Thursday: Medium

Friday: Low

Saturday: High

Sunday: Low

What is considered high load is specific to the individual. For example, a 20-minute skipping session may be low load for a boxer but high for a swimmer. Equally, it might be low load for a well-conditioned boxer but high load for a boxer who has had 2 months of reduced training after knee surgery. What is considered high load at the beginning of a retraining period should graduate to being medium and then low load over time, highlighting the need to continually monitor and adjust the retraining programme.

When considering having the athlete return to on-feet load for the first time after a particularly lengthy time off (greater than 3 months), it is useful to implement the following schedule to allow the entire kinetic chain to adapt to the increased ground-reaction forces found when running:

Week 1: 1 day on feet, 2 days off feet

Weeks 2 and 3: 1 day on feet, 1 day off feet

Weeks 4 and 5: 2 days on feet, 1 day off feet

Weeks 6 and beyond: 3 days on feet, 1 day off feet

This schedule can be accelerated somewhat if the time on the sidelines is less than 3 months. In this case we can consider the following schedule:

Week 1: 1 day on feet, 2 days off feet

Week 2: 1 day on feet, 1 day off feet

Week 3: 2 days on feet, 1 day off feet

Weeks 4 and beyond: 3 days on feet, 1 day off feet

Given these broad suggestions, it is worth reinforcing that each athlete is unique, both in terms of response to injury and also adaptive capacity within the process. Monitoring the dose response and the art of rehabilitation will play a role in the return to on-feet training.

Programme Priorities

Rehabilitation needs to be specifically tailored not only to progressively load the injured tissue but also to be functionally relevant wherever possible. Not only does this hold the interest of the athlete, but it also provides immediate clarity for why the athlete is doing particular drills. Rather than training muscles or movements, we should consider *both* in exercise selection. Here is a simple example to illustrate this point.

An athlete suffers a quadriceps strain (grade 2) and is 7 days postinjury. The athlete has a pain-free gait and is able to walk up and down stairs without discomfort.

Exercise 1: seated knee extensions under load OR

Exercise 2: forward quarter lunge plus skill plus decision-making drill

Both exercises influence the same tissue through the same range of motion and generate a similar stimulus locally. However, a forward lunge integrates the load into a familiar movement pattern, requiring a far greater sensory and motor response, thus stimulating the central and peripheral nervous systems. The additional inclusion of a decision-making skill will increase the athlete's interest and also total system demand. We are training movements but specifically targeting muscles. This principle is applicable to rehabilitation programmes for ligament and joint injury.

Proprioceptive Training

Proprioceptive training is a fundamental part of rehabilitation because injury can disrupt the body's own neuromuscular feed-forward and feedback mechanisms. Proprioception is an umbrella term used to describe the internally generated afferent information arising for peripheral areas of the body that contributes to both static and dynamic postural stability; it is made up of joint position sense, kinaesthesia (motion sense) and resistance or force sense.[3]

Functionally, this manifests as a reduction in the body's internal *dynamic defence system*. It is not something that automatically resets to normal, though, and this may be a significant reason why injuries such as ankle sprains have a high recurrence rate.[4]

Proprioceptive training must challenge the athlete in relevant ways. Standing on one leg is a good place for an athlete recovering from an ankle sprain to start; however, it is folly to assume that this will be sufficient to ensure the athlete is ready to return to the competitive environment. As the tissue-recovery process allows, the joint needs to be stressed in multiple positions, on multiple surfaces (e.g., grass, sand), against external forces (e.g., bands, weights or opponents where appropriate) and with changing cognitive-load or decision-making requirements (e.g., agility drills, catching or avoiding balls).

The timing of these proprioceptive sessions bears consideration. In the early part of a rehabilitative process, it is advisable to conduct these drills when the athlete is fresh; however, for true development of injury-saving mechanisms, repetitive and meaningful practice to groove neural pathways is required under conditions of fatigue.

Returning to Full Training and Competition

The time that surrounds the return to training and then to competition is actually the time of highest risk of reinjury. This is because the athlete will often feel better than he or she actually is, leading to a *confidence–competence mismatch*. This transition needs to be executed with skill and with a deep understanding of the loading tolerance of the injured tissue.

Returning to Training

Before being placed in the uncontrolled environment of competitive play, the athlete should be both competent and confident with competitive training. This training should replicate all facets of the demands that the player will face in competition. Depending on the characteristics of the sport, this may involve sprinting, jumping and landing, cutting, full-contact collisions, kicking, punching, catching, turning at speed, throwing, catching or diving. The athlete must demonstrate consistent proficiency in all these tasks.

Ideally, the athlete should be able to demonstrate proficiency in all aspects of training, along with stable responses to this training of a week or more, before being selected for competition. Being able to demonstrate proficiency provides information regarding the stability and endurance of the injured part; it also gives the athlete the confidence of repeated effective performance.

Taking time to demonstrate proficiency also allows time for training staff to examine the competency of the athlete and the injury under the veil of fatigue. Given that most athletic injuries occur in the latter stages of a match or competition, when the player is fatigued, it is prudent to examine this competency under relative control. The prefatigue session may or may not specifically load the injured tissue, but it must result in central fatigue and therefore disturbance to neuromuscular pathways. This can be achieved by testing key competencies immediately after a high-intensity running or cycling session. By the end stage of rehabilitation, all results should prove to the athlete and the coaching and performance team that the athlete has the physical competence and confidence required to return and thrive in the sport.

Returning to Competition

One of the more difficult problems that the performance team faces is determining when an athlete is ready to return to action after injury. The athlete can be placed under enormous pressure from the owner, coach, fans and media to get out on the track, field or floor in record time. It is vital that we remove the guesswork, because if we get it wrong, the athlete may be spending even longer on the treatment couch. Although we cannot perfectly guarantee that an injury will not recur when the player steps out onto the pitch, there are a number of factors that, if taken into consideration when determining return to competition (RTC), can help determine whether the risk of playing is acceptable.

We can divide the assessment criteria into physiological and functional categories. Physiological assessment examines the health of the athlete and the state of repair of the injury. It looks to determine the safety of the athlete. Functional assessment examines the ability of the athlete to perform the tasks demanded by the sport. This assessment seeks to determine the answers to the following questions.

Is the Athlete Fit to Play?

The foremost consideration must be the health of the athlete. In other words, is the state of the injury sufficiently healed and stable that allowing the athlete to return to action is safe? This can be a tricky minefield because it is often a grey area. If the athlete is obviously not ready, this decision usually is self-evident. It is helpful to have a clear understanding about the grounds on which this decision is to be made, so that guesswork is removed, and the decision can be communicated effectively and with authority to the coaching staff.

Pain is an obvious variable to be considered. Clearly, if the athlete is in significant distress, he or she is unlikely to be in a sound state of mind or body to perform. The absence of pain does not equal the absence of a problem; this is where assessment of the state of the injury on grounds of pain alone is always problematic. Sometimes pain (or, indeed, lack of pain) is not a good indicator of the state of repair of an injury. In some instances, the athlete may feel better than he or she actually is. For example, most people are not in pain 3 months after an anterior cruciate ligament reconstruction, yet in most instances the state of repair is not mature enough to consider a return to the playing field. To be able to answer these physiological questions with any degree of confidence, we must know healing and recovery times for the various tissues that may have been affected by the original injury. This is where a team approach with careful guidance from and communication with the medical team is critical.

Several other aspects need to be assessed, including local muscular function; ligament laxity; muscular strength, power and endurance; joint range of motion (ROM); and bony healing. The question is what is the best way to judge these parameters? Ideally, we would have an idea of what the athlete was like before the injury. We must also place a greater value on the functional use of the injured tissue rather than any one isolated muscular strength test.

Has the Athlete Returned to Baseline Measures?

The aim of rehabilitation is to return an athlete to a level of physical health and functional performance equal to or even exceeding the preinjury status. To determine whether the athlete has returned to this level, a full assessment of the injury, the kinetic chain and the entire person is required. The aim of assessing every aspect of an athlete is unrealistic, though, and is not supported by research. The field of tests that could be applied is too vast, many of which would be irrelevant to the athlete being tested. A strategic approach is required, one that relies on the gathering of intelligence as a method of sifting through all the possible things that could go wrong in order to hone in on those things that are most likely to.

The variables of interest depend on the nature of the injury and the nature of the sport. The screening tool should seek to examine the integrity of

- the injured structure;
- structures identified as commonly injured in the particular sport (e.g., the injuries seen in ice hockey are markedly different to those seen in triathlon, so it is vital to understand the sport and the risk profile associated with it); and
- structures identified as high risk according to the risk profile of the individual, based on age, past history and gender.

Commonly employed tests include isolated or multijoint ROM, localised tests of muscular strength and capacity and functional tests of kinetic chain capacity. In the case of an injury to a limb, a comparison to the noninjured side is made, but this is only appropriate when we are confident that we have a noninjured side to act as a control and when the musculoskeletal parameters in question are normally symmetrical. It is infinitely better to have a tool with which we can compare the athlete before and after injury, which provides a cogent argument for the employment of musculoskeletal screening.

Wisdom

It is only with objective measures of an athlete's musculoskeletal profile that we can be confident the athlete has completely returned to full health after an injury.

Does the Athlete Have to Be 100 Per Cent Fit?

Those working in professional sport will testify to the fact that it is often unrealistic to expect each athlete to be perfectly fit for every event or game. There is a level of acceptance that, even though the athlete may not be 100 per cent fit, he or she may be *fit enough to play*. This decision needs to be made by the medical staff in conjunction with the athlete. At all times, we must keep the athlete's best interests in mind and weigh up short-term gain versus long-term health. We need to be especially careful when we are trying to get an athlete back to competition before full recovery.

The decision about when an athlete returns to action ultimately is determined by the athlete. Members of the coaching and support teams must fully inform the athlete about his or her state of health. All athletes have the right to make up their own minds, but they should be fully informed of the risks of playing when, in our judgment, they may not be fit enough to do so. There are several reported cases of legal proceedings brought against healthcare professionals by athletes who have aggravated an injury or been permanently disabled after an early RTC when the athlete claimed he or she was not fully informed of the risks. Indeed, it may be advisable to ask the athlete sign a document stating that he or she has been fully informed of the risks of a return to play and that the athlete is playing against medical advice.

Wisdom

The question of fitness for a return to action after injury can be tricky and emotional. Our job is to get players back out on the field as quickly as possible, but moreover, to keep them there. By taking the guesswork out of the equation by being as objective and rigorous as possible, we can minimise the risk of athletes limping back into the clinic after a failed return to the pitch.

Is the Athlete Fit to Perform?

There is a significant distinction to make between the terms *fit to play* and *fit to perform*. Medical clearance to return to elite sport (fit to play) that exists in isolation without consideration of the athlete's function and overall performance status (fit to perform) is flawed and risks injury recurrence or poor performance. We must ensure that returning athletes are optimally conditioned to perform in the sport. Hence, an RTC decision must not be based solely on healing parameters but on functional ones as well.

Functional assessment of an athlete seeks to determine whether he or she will be able to perform tasks effectively and safely on the track or pitch. It is much more difficult for this to be a black-and-white assessment because so much is determined by the exact nature of the sport, the position played and the level of competition. This assessment should be carefully designed to specifically test every component of the game or event and should look to stress the injury site to

determine if it is robust enough to withstand the rigours of competition. Muscular injuries are more likely to occur when muscles are fatigued, and thus if we want to be thorough, we need to test the athlete's strength and function under fatigue.

Several tests have been validated as ways of providing objective measures of functional performance. In order to have a complete picture of an athlete's physical preparedness, we should examine recovery from a number of physiological and functional standpoints. It is impossible to provide an exhaustive list of all the tests that could be employed, and much will depend on both the injury and the demands of the sport, but table 7.2 provides some examples.

Some of the tests described in table 7.2 require equipment or technology not available to all coaches or therapists. There are other ways of determining fitness to perform. Look more at qualitative measures such as those listed in table 7.3. This list is by no means exhaustive, and there will be other factors that should be assessed, depending on the demands of the sport. The type of sport that the athlete is returning to makes a difference when assessing risk of reinjury. It may be possible to get a taekwondo fighter back to competition after a shoulder injury earlier than a rugby player, for example, due to the reduced demand on arm function in this form of martial art. This is where a knowledge of the sport is necessary, or at least, effective communication with the player or coach.

Ideally, the athlete should be able to demonstrate all the factors outlined in the fit-to-play column with none from the unfit-to-play column. Where possible, one or more members of the performance team should witness training in the competitive environment to determine proficiency in these functional tasks.

Wisdom

Inclusion of the coach in end-stage rehabilitation can be a positive move. No matter how far our scientific understanding of athletes and their sports progresses, there will always be a key role for the coach's eye when generating end-stage rehabilitation drills and testing processes and assessing training performance. It also helps to ensure that the athlete is not just physically robust, but also technically and tactically sound as well. This spread of responsibility to strengthen confidence highlights the need for a truly interdisciplinary approach to rehabilitation.

Table 7.2 Functional Outcome Measures That Can Be Used to Determine Preparedness to Compete

	Variable	Test examples	Outcome	Threshold of proficiency
Injury-specific functional test	Jumping and landing competency	Vertical jump Broad jump Three-hop distance test Crossover-hop test Star excursion balance test	Height, distance, time to stabilise, ground-reaction force (peak, total and symmetry)	Equal to preinjury status Within 10% of contralateral side
	Agility	5-0-5 Illinois RAT	Change of direction and technique	Equal to preinjury status Within 10% of matched controls
	Running capacity	MAS Yo-Yo IRT 30-15	Repeated shuttle running ability	Equal to preinjury status Within 10% of matched controls
	Speed	0-10 m 0-40 m Flying 20 m	Acceleration and top speed	Equal to preinjury status Within 10% of matched controls
Limb function tests	Double-limb muscle function	Squat Bench press Barbell shoulder press Glute–ham raise	Strength, power and fatigue index	Equal to preinjury status Within 10% of matched controls
	Single-limb muscle function	Step-up Dumbbell shoulder press	Strength, power and fatigue index	Equal to preinjury status Within 10% of contralateral side
Mechanical loading	GPS analysis	Training characteristics	Running volumes; sprinting volumes; accelerations and decelerations, including change of direction	Equivalent to competition demands
	Technical skill analysis		Speed; distance; characteristics of throw, pitch or kick	Equivalent to competition demands
Physiological testing	Response to training	Heart rate variability Session RPE	Objective and subjective responses to training load	Equal to preinjury status Within 10% of matched controls

Table 7.3 Qualitative Judgments of Preparedness to Compete

Fit to play	Unfit to play
Good balance against strong perturbations	Easily put off balance
Happy to load injured body part	Favours noninjured side
Precise stepping off line and zig-zag without losing speed	Long, loopy changes of direction
Able to rapidly accelerate, decelerate and change directions	Wary of contact or falling onto injured body part
Completion of full training (multiple sessions)	Altered biomechanics to offload injured part
Self-confidence about RTP	Long tail-off on deceleration and loss of first-step quickness on acceleration
	High centre of gravity when running and changing directions
	Mentally not ready to play or excessive anxiety

Mindset: The Psychology of Injury

It is important to accept that after a moderate-to-severe injury requiring extended time on the sideline, there is a natural grieving process that needs to be respected and worked through. Although we often think of grief as something that relates to death, it is more about loss. In sport, an injury can lead to loss of self-worth, achievement, income and even employment. Particularly in the case of a serious injury, denial, anger, bargaining and depression before acceptance may be seen. This is especially the case when culpability exists, such as when the athlete is injured by another player's recklessness. It is important to recognise that these stages are normal and not necessarily maladaptive. Also, although it is reasonable to anticipate these emotions and behaviours will peak early on after injury, they can also reemerge later in the recovery process in response to any difficulties encountered.

If the rehabilitation process is likely to be long term, consideration of personal factors (e.g., family life, holidays) and rehabilitation centre location and personnel may also become more important. Endocrine health will drive the rehabilitation process, and the role of psychological factors in recovery and performance is gaining momentum within the literature.[5] Psychological factors are explored in detail in chapter 24, but in broad terms, at a physiological level athletes are trying to maintain an anabolic status to maximise their tissue development. Hormone circulation and balance, though not cognitive, are mediated by areas of the brain and influenced by mood, so we need to ensure players are positive and upbeat throughout their recovery.

Wisdom

Any world-class rehabilitation strategy has a clear plan for returning the athlete to play and also considers additional aspects of on-field performance and life in general.

Anxiety of Returning to Competition

The prospect of returning to the sport arena after a major injury can be a frightening prospect. It involves athletes putting themselves into situations that will stress not just the site of the injury, but also the mind and central nervous system. Accordingly, the physical, mental and emotional components of the rehabilitation need to have been completed in order for a successful return to the arena to occur. If athletes are left with a sense of a lack of complete integration of all these components, a feeling that the rehabilitation is unfinished may pervade, which is likely to leave them with anxiousness regarding reinjury.

When an athlete sustains an injury, the brain places more attention on the harmed area. The brain devotes more space to the injured part because, quite rightfully, it wants to know everything that is going on around the injury zone. This can be likened to the process of increasing the numbers of security cameras trained on a known crime hot-spot. This increase in neural activity will maintain its presence whilst the brain still perceives that the threat of further injury (or reinjury) is high. These cameras do not disappear overnight or even as soon as the physiological process of healing is complete. They are still present for as long as the brain is concerned about the threat. The process of rehabilitation is complete only after the physiological process of healing is sufficiently resolved, physical performance is reinstituted and the brain is satisfied that threat levels have reduced and has turned off its cameras.

Often, an athlete will relate that the previous injury doesn't hurt any more, but it feels different or that he or she is aware of it. This sensation can be a source of annoyance and is likely due to the brain still wanting to keep tabs on the previously injured structure. Sensations that would previously have been dealt with unconsciously by the brain (like background music) are now being analysed consciously (like foreground music). More attention is placed on the injured part, even though the healing process is complete. This can become a problem when this process goes on for too long, and the security cameras never get turned off. Anxiety can result, which can be a cause of significant reductions in performance (e.g., poor skill execution, poor allocation of energy resources and decreased attention to the necessary tasks of the sport) and is said to increase the risk of actual reinjury.[6]

We often think of rehabilitation as a series of steps that physically prepare a person to return to full function by progressively loading and conditioning injured tissues to enable them to withstand stress. Although this is undoubtedly true, this definition is too reductive. Rehabilitation is a much more complicated process that has as much to do with progressively reducing the threat levels in order to turn off the internal security cameras as it does with strengthening local tissues. What is also clear is that rehabilitation is only complete when the athlete perceives it to be complete, and the fear of pain or reinjury is removed.

It is certainly not uncommon for an athlete to be able to blitz all physical tests and demonstrate excellent strength around an injured area and yet still be highly distrustful of the injury. In these situations there is an element of the rehabilitation that is not complete, and it is not enough just to wash our hands and say that our job is done. The athlete remains to be convinced within him- or herself that the rehabilitation is complete. Sometimes it may be enough for us to give the athlete permission to return to play; other times it can be a great deal trickier.

Wisdom

When returning to the competitive environment, the anxious athlete looks slow, tentative and unwilling to perform tasks at full speed. Technical and tactical applications often are less crisp, and movement often is described as being hesitant and laboured. Demotivating feelings of frustration often follow. Having an understanding that this is often the case and counselling the athlete *in advance* can be a wise move, thereby helping to set realistic expectations of both the athlete and the coaching staff.

Obviously, anxiety varies among individuals. The higher the stakes (e.g., missing a grand final or important meet, income or selection for higher honours), the more threatening the spectre of reinjury will be, and therefore the more anxious the athlete is likely to be. Another factor that may play a role is personal experience. For example, a footballer who previously came back from a hamstring injury too soon only to be reinjured and sidelined for an even lengthier period is likely to be more anxious when trying to get back the second time. Equally important is a strong level of trust between the athlete and the sport rehabilitator. Clearly, the athlete needs to be able to believe the clinician when he or she says the injury has healed and that a return to play is safe.

Summary

Injury should be packaged as an opportunity and a positive experience wherever possible. Not only will this likely improve recovery times, but it will certainly provide the opportunity to review and develop the athlete.

The rehabilitation process must be carefully constructed with functionally and physiologically appropriate exit criteria at each stage, ensuring timely, holistic and safe progressions are used. The process should include input from the whole performance team and be delivered as one bespoke plan to the athlete, demonstrating unity, a clear direction and purpose.

Rehabilitation should not be considered to be complete until the athlete has achieved all markers set, successfully returned to performance and remained symptom free for an extended period. Given that the risk of reinjury is at its highest in the first few weeks after returning to competition after an injury, monitoring the athlete's ongoing health and performance is a necessary task in ensuring that not only does the athlete return to competition, but also that he or she stays competitive.

PART

II

Developing Athletic Capacity

BPI/Image/Icon SMI

CHAPTER 8

Customizing the Warm-Up and Cool-Down

Rett Larson
Team China and EXOS (formerly Athletes' Performance), United States

In 1957, 46 male students were taken through a 5-minute warm-up and then told to throw a softball as far as they could. Weeks later, the unknowing students were brought back to the softball field and, without a warm-up, offered money to throw the ball farther than they had a week before. None of the participants was able to collect the money.[1]

It's easy to conclude from this study and countless similar ones that a proper warm-up is an ergogenic aid to athletes. Unfortunately, it's not that simple. The term *warm-up* can include any number of activities, including stretching, thermogenic exercises, calisthenics, visualisation, plyometrics, soft-tissue work and neural stimulation. These components have been studied in combinations many times, often with conclusions that are not as clear-cut as the 1960 softball study. Not only does research show that some methods used to prepare athletes for activity appear to have no effect, but some can even be detrimental to athletic performance. For this reason, it is important for coaches to understand the many options available, what works effectively in the environment and how to customise the respective components to each athlete, depending on individual needs, sport, position and training cycle.

Much like flossing teeth, warming up often is something athletes know they should be doing but don't make a habit of. This chapter explains why the warm-up should not be viewed as a separate activity that occurs before actual performance training. Instead, the chapter explains how the *integration* of a well-constructed warm-up into an athlete's training session will more effectively help develop movement proficiency, balance and core strength and reduce injury risk. The various warm-up options for creating the ideal session for athletes are broken down, thereby adding more tools to the performance-coaching toolbox. Shifting attention to the cool-down, the chapter discusses the ways elite coaches can use that time to start the regeneration process and makes the case for removing flexibility work from its usual posttraining time slot.

Benefits of a Thorough Warm-Up

There are numerous stories of athletes who were late to an event, were unable to warm-up and went on to set records. Conversely, there are published studies demonstrating an increased risk of injury when insufficiently prepared. Karpovich, for example, reported young athletes who warmed up before a 60-metre sprint had more hamstring injuries than those who did not.[2] These studies represent a minority, but they're important in setting one end of a spectrum of warm-up choices.

The truth is, if time is a factor, athletes probably will be safe with minimal warm-up. This is good news because often a full warm-up is not possible. Fortunately, most athletes do have time to integrate a warm-up into their training (and flossing before bedtime, for that matter). Those who choose not to warm up may leave athletic potential untapped as muscle imbalances go untreated, joint range of motion (ROM) fails to improve and movement mechanics continue to be limited. Failure to warm up may not directly correlate with short-term injury risk, but it almost certainly will result in an accumulation of injury risk as well as performance decrements.

The injury-reduction and performance advantages of a proper warm-up have been vetted by meta-analysis;[3] most of these advantages can be attributed to the physiological benefits of increased temperature within muscle tissue. In short, a circus contortionist is more likely to be injured than the Frankenstein on a team who cannot touch his toes if Frank is warm and the contortionist is cold. Cold soft tissue does not function as well either. The nerve impulses in frogs travel eight times more slowly than they do in humans due to frogs' lower body temperatures.[4] Therefore, coaches need to ensure that core thermogenesis is a high priority during any preparatory phase of training.

Wisdom

The warm-up may more constructively be viewed as a crucial part of the training process, rather than as a disorganised time spent before the real training begins.

Warming-up promotes many physiological effects:

- Increased muscle temperature due to fuel metabolism and the friction of sliding filaments; vasodilation improves joint ROM by decreasing the viscosity of the tissue.

- Elevated tissue temperatures enable the warm muscle to contract with more muscle fibers and at a faster rate than cold muscles are able to do. Nerve impulses and myosin ATPase activity are more rapid when body temperature is high, which decreases reaction time and may protect athletes who find themselves off balance.

- Because haemoglobin gives away more oxygen at higher temperatures, there is a greater oxygen–carbon dioxide exchange and therefore more aerobic adenosine triphosphate (ATP) available to warm muscles through increased oxygen transport efficiency.

- The venous carbon dioxide built up during the warm-up stimulates faster, deeper breathing, enhancing internal gas exchange.

- Increased blood flow to the heart and muscles charges the circulatory system.

- The hormonal system is excited.

- Increased amounts of synovial fluid in the joints decreases the viscosity of the joint capsule.

- Muscular pliability decreases muscle damage and leads to less delayed-onset muscle soreness (DOMS). Warmer muscle tissue is more pliable, so it undergoes less damage during the eccentric phase of muscle action, which most often causes DOMS-related microtrauma.

- Muscular coordination of rehearsed movements increases. The warm-up also can be a good time to reinforce important motor skills, such as agility, being trained in separate sessions (see chapter 13).

- Cardiovascular strength and work capacity increase.

- The warm-up leads to psychological increases in focus and attention whilst decreasing stress, anxiety and tension. Research has demonstrated that a warm-up decreases the fear of injury, leading to less-inhibited performance.[5]

Components of the Warm-Up

By studying both the research on warming-up and the best practices of elite coaches, we can compile a menu of warm-up activities to be chosen à la carte to create the ideal session. In the same way you wouldn't order every dish on the dinner menu, you may also elect not to use all of these components before every training session. The warm-up for an athlete who will be going for a maximal effort in the snatch during training should differ from that of an athlete who arrives for an agility session feeling tired from a bad night's sleep.

For sake of simplicity, these components have been organised into six categories: tissue quality, activation, corrective exercises, thermogenics, stretching and neural preparation. Ideally, these would be performed in the order listed, but there are no hard rules here. Time limitations, athlete weaknesses or session flow may demand that the sections be mixed together. In other instances, the coach may decide to integrate one component, such as a corrective exercise, into many of the others to address an athlete's mobility limitations.

Tissue Quality

If you've taken an anatomy class, you probably know how muscles are supposed to work, with actin proteins being ratcheted together with thick myosin filaments during voluntary muscle contraction. Unfortunately, an athlete's muscles undergo substantial stress during day-to-day training and, as a result, may not work with textbook efficiency. Indeed, many soft-tissue structures (e.g., tendons, ligaments, fascia, muscle, nerves) undergo trauma as a result of training. Before any traditional warm-up components can be addressed, it's important to make sure these elements are ready and able to work optimally. No matter how flexible a muscle might be, if the fascia surrounding it is bound tightly, that muscle won't be able to perform well. If nerve conduction or blood flow is impeded due to soft-tissue structural damage, no amount of traditional warm-up will alleviate that. Using massage techniques before training sessions can begin to repair soft-tissue damage and ready those elements for subsequent action.

Muscle

When athletes train hard, their muscles undergo microtrauma, which can create scar tissue and small knots in the muscle called *barrier trigger points*. These trigger points may impede nerve conduction and blood flow, hindering contraction speed, coordination and overall power.[6] For years, performance coaches have attempted to attack trigger points with stretching. But like a big rubber band with a knot in it, simply stretching the muscle just makes the knot tighter. Massage therapy often is used to address these issues, but this may not be practical for everyone who needs to work on muscle quality instead of muscle length. The emergence of modalities such as the foam roller and massage stick (figure 8.1, *a* and *b*) have enabled athletes to work through these trigger points using techniques like self-myofascial release (SMR), self-massage and accupressure for low cost. Using a roller to apply pressure to the sore spots in muscles enables the athlete to release the trigger points and break up the scar tissue that may inhibit performance.[7]

Soft-tissue treatments such as SMR also increase flexibility and ROM due to a process known as *autogenic inhibition*. As the foam roller applies pressure to the muscle tissue, mechanoreceptors called golgi tendon organs send a message to the brain that substantial tension is being put on the muscle, causing the brain to relax that muscle to prevent it from tearing.

The process of autogenic inhibition can be used to advantage as the athlete makes long, sweeping strokes of the roller on his or her tissue. When a sore spot is found, the athlete should pause and keep applying direct pressure to it whilst trying to relax that muscle. Slow, deep breaths help calm the nervous system and release the trigger point. If the discomfort of the acupressure is too severe, the trigger point is unlikely to be released, so the athlete must control the amount of pain felt by shifting the body to lessen the weight on the point (if using a foam roller). Athletes can spend from 30 to 60 seconds on each muscle group, depending on the quality and importance of the tissue. As the athlete's muscles develop a greater tolerance for softer modalities, harder foam rollers and smaller tools such as tennis or lacrosse balls can be used to target deeper trigger points.

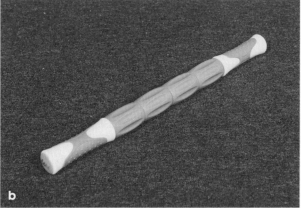

Figure 8.1 Athletes can use *(a)* rollers and *(b)* massage sticks to ease sore spots in muscles.

Spine

The spine is another area that may demand special preparation given the prevalence of back problems in sport. Much research has been done in this area in hopes of preventing career-ending injuries and keeping athletes out of pain during training.

The use of two tennis balls taped together (figure 8.2) can help floss the thoracic spine and prepare it for movement. By lying supine with the 'peanut' beneath the thoracic vertebrae, the athlete can open up the intervertebral spaces and enhance thoracic spine mobility. Greater mobility in the thoracic spine can protect the lumbar spine from unnecessary stress during trunk flexion, extension and rotation during subsequent activity.

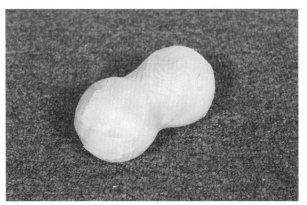

Figure 8.2 A homemade peanut made from two tennis balls taped together.

If you don't have much time to devote to spinal prep, the quadruped camel and cat motions are recommended (figure 8.3, *a* and *b*). By alternatively flexing and extending the spine the athlete primes the nervous system and reduces spinal viscosity. The athlete should take care not to make these movements stretches but instead emphasise a gentle motion between the two poses. It is also recommended that some athletes with spinal pathology exercise caution when performing these exercises first thing in the morning because their intervertebral discs are maximally hydrated for the first few hours on rising, and therefore injury risk may be increased.[8]

A third option for reducing spinal viscosity is to use a stability ball. Like the cat and camel, the action of reactively flexing and extending the spine whilst sitting on a stability ball can pump fresh fluid through the spinal tissues to nourish joint surfaces and decrease viscosity. Whilst sitting on the ball, athletes begin a series of pelvic tilts in each plane, gradually increasing the ROM and speed of the movement as they go.

The Brain and Visualisation

Since he was 7 years old, the Olympic swimmer Michael Phelps has reportedly been watching 'his videotape' every night, a mental recording of himself setting world records.[9] This visualisation technique has been employed by countless athletes who, like Phelps, are encouraged to imagine the perfect race, game or event down to the smallest detail. Such practices have been proven to enhance performance and break through training plateaus[10] but often are neglected by athletes.

Use the moments before a training session to have athletes visualise ideal movement patterns, such as executing a perfect sprint start or setting a lifting personal record. Have them imagine as much detail as possible. For those athletes whose concentration,

Figure 8.3 Spinal preparation exercises: (*a*) camel; (*b*) cat.

focus or confidence is lacking, a visualisation routine may be something to incorporate a few times throughout the warm-up. If time is short, visualisation can be combined with the tissue and spinal prep techniques previously described. For example, whilst performing thoracic spine mobilisations with the peanut, golfers can visualise themselves executing a perfect swing in slow motion.

Hormonal Stimulus

The concept of the warm-up needs to shift from simply focusing on the muscles of the body to embracing the multifactorial nature of pretraining, or competition preparation. The employment of techniques designed to manipulate hormonal responses to enhance anaerobic and force production performance is one approach to consider. When male rugby players watched video clips that were either aggressive, erotic or included training scenes, their testosterone levels and 3RM squat performance increased.[11] This indicates that hormone-boosting video montages could be integrated into precompetition warm-ups to enhance performance as well. Although hormonal responses differ among individuals, heightened testosterone levels have been seen in male athletes after they watched previous victories[12] or even held a gun.[13] Such research may have positive implications for playing video games or watching highlight footage before training.

Activation

We've all seen military movies in which a drill sergeant blows a whistle and eight cadets have to lift a boat above their heads and jog down the beach with it until they collapse. If one cadet is weaker than his or her mates, the other cadets have to work harder to compensate. Now think of your hip like that boat. When you go bounding up a flight of stairs, your brain blows a whistle that alerts all the muscles around your hip to spring into action. Some of those muscles help stabilise the joint whilst others create the movement that allows you to power upward. The problem is that sometimes the weaker muscles force the others to do more work. Even worse, some don't even hear the whistle. If this happens over a long time, an imbalance can be created around the hip that could decrease performance or lead to injury. For this reason, performing activation exercises that target the weaker stabilising muscles is essential to maximising performance.

Movement-Based Techniques

Activation exercises neurologically excite and awaken muscles. By summating muscle contractions at low levels before training or competition, the athlete can increase the rate and frequency of motor-unit recruitment. Such increases can either neutrally stimulate stabilising muscles that help bolster movement around a joint or create greater force production in muscle groups by recruiting additional motor units to do work.

Many techniques can activate muscles before training. Usually, single muscles are isolated and resisted in low-velocity movements (e.g., wall slides, quadruped hip abduction). These exercises involve progressively more movement planes and additional resistance as the muscles adapt to stress. Some of the most commonly targeted muscles during an activation session are the gluteus medius and glutueus maximus, the core and the rotator cuff. Various modalities such as elastic resistance bands (figure 8.4) and stability balls can also help stimulate greater motor-unit summation; however, as additional movement planes are integrated and become more functionally authentic, muscles will not be able to activate as completely as if they were stabilised in uniplanar isolation.

Figure 8.4 Glute resistance band walk.

Balance

Balance training has enjoyed varying degrees of popularity in the performance training community, with most elite coaches agreeing that whilst unstable surfaces can be a potent tool for stimulating muscle stabilisers to activate, too much of it in the place of closed chain lifts can hamper maximal strength.[14] For this reason, incorporating balance training into the athlete's warm-up can maximise the benefits of such exercises whilst not directly taking time away from strength training. Including balance and postural exercises (BAPS) in the warm-up allows the athlete to stimulate reactive systems and enhance proprioceptive input and kinesthetic awareness.[15] All of these combine to create greater dynamic core stability, which means that when the body is pushed out of position, it quickly finds a way back to a stable posture. Without this stability athletes run the risk of lower back or leg injury.[15]

Having an athlete stand on one leg for 30 seconds, initially with eyes open, then one eye closed, and finally both eyes closed, can be enough to engage a survival reflex that can be stimulated when the body is off balance. Similar to the fight-or-flight mechanism that engages when a person slips on a patch of ice, this reflex may release endorphins to momentarily reduce pain and activate stabiliser muscles throughout the kinetic chain. Add movement to this progression by having the athlete reach with the opposite hand to touch the outer toe of the stance leg, effectively working both the survival reflex and a series of commonly weak muscle groups.

Vibration

Increased accessibility of vibration plates has created an explosion in their use to stimulate muscle activation and enhance performance in athletes. Though the popularity of vibration training has increased, its benefits have been enjoyed throughout history. For example, in the past, sufferers of kidney stones were reportedly advised to take a drive down a bumpy road for the vibration effect.[16]

Vibration works through the tonic vibration reflex, which increases the electrical activity within the affected muscle.[17] This can enhance maximal voluntary contraction (MVC) and groove neuromuscular pathways more quickly, as well as increase motor-unit synchronisation. By stimulating the tonic vibration reflex, vibration may also recruit previously inactive motor units, resulting in enhanced development of muscular power and strength.[16]

Corrective Exercises

One of the biggest benefits of a customised warm-up is how it can be crafted to address movement restrictions in individual athletes. Of course, this is not possible without first understanding the individual's specific deficits. These need to be determined by employing a screening tool. Typical screens require the athlete to perform a series of simple movements that are common in sport to assess ROM at a joint or the athlete's ability to stabilise that joint and create clean movement.

Once the athlete has been screened, that information can be used to select exercises, stretches or soft-tissue interventions that may correct any movement deficiencies uncovered. Most corrective exercises progress their complexity linearly from basic mobility to basic stability and finally to movement-pattern retraining. Mobility exercises focus on joint ROM and tissue length and include various stretches. When a mobility problem is present, that should be the primary focus of the corrective session. Stability exercises focus on basic sequencing of movement and target postural control in different positions. Movement-pattern retraining integrates mobility and stability into specific movement patterns to reinforce coordination and timing.[18]

Anyone who has had to rehabilitate an injury knows how essential it is that prescribed corrective exercises are grooved to the point of mastery. Making such corrective and preventive exercises a part of the warm-up ensures they are not forgotten as the movement patterns improve. For the sake of flow, these correctives can be combined with the activation exercises discussed previously. In addition, the corrective exercises themselves can be helpful screens for movement problems. The best performance coaches use each phase of the warm-up to analyse athletes for imbalances and potential injury.

Thermogenics

The primary goals of a warm-up should be to keep athletes from getting injured and to prepare them to perform in training or competition. To this end, increasing tissue temperature is key. If time is short, the smart coach will skip most other warm-up activities in favor of spending more time getting muscles warm and pliable. Accordingly, it is important that athletes dress warmly in mild or cold weather. It is also important that when competing in cold weather, the time between warm-up and competition is shortened. Each athlete should be lightly sweating at the conclusion, indicating that the body's cooling system has activated and muscles are at least 1 or 2 degrees warmer.[5] A typical thermogenic session lasts 5 to 15 minutes, depending on the ambient temperature,[4] the athletes' experience level (elite athletes require more time)[5] and how many nonthermogenic exercises are mixed into it. Fatigue is the enemy here, so give athletes breaks without worrying they'll get cold; tissue temperature decreases much more slowly than it increases. The temperature of warmed muscular tissue can remain elevated for 45 to 80 minutes after warm-up if properly maintained with heat-retaining clothing.[5]

Delivering Thermogenics

When it comes to finding the most effective, engaging and stimulating way of getting athletes warm, a coach is confined only by his or her creativity. The old-school method of having athletes take two laps around the track to begin warm-up will do the trick from a tissue-warmth standpoint, but it can come at the expense of good movement. If you've ever witnessed the zombie-like jog that athletes default to in this instance, you'll understand. Most elite performance coaches instead choose to challenge their athletes with various skipping, hopping, crawling or jumping-jack progressions. These require no equipment, serve to get core temperatures up and challenge the athletes neurologically, testing concentration and enhancing focus.

Jump ropes are one of the most underutilised pieces of training equipment in the gym. They are ideal for increasing thermogenesis because they train lower-body reactive strength whilst engaging the upper body and coordination with dozens of variations. If you watch athletes closely, you should be able to gauge their nervous system readiness, timing and coordination; you may choose to extend the warm-up if the athletes can't demonstrate neuroreadiness with their ropes.[19] Jumping rope is also a self-regulating exercise, meaning the athlete cannot cheat it. If timing, core stiffness, reactivity, and fitness are not up to task, the rope will let you know.

Other modalities that can be used include agility ladders and rings, microhurdles, dot drill mats and medicine balls. When choosing drills for these modalities, start with ones that require little

coordination or elastic strength and progress to the slightly more complex drills. You are not designing an agility or movement session; rather, you're just trying to keep the athletes moving in challenging patterns that keep their heart rates up. If the difficulty of the drills becomes fatiguing, you risk compromising the effectiveness of the subsequent training session.

Adding Games

Including childhood games into even elite-athlete training sessions can be a welcome departure from the routine. If you doubt this, try introducing a game of Simon Says into the next warm-up session and watch athletes grin ear to ear as they work up a sweat. Choose games that keep athletes moving in different planes whilst not being so competitive that the athletes risk injuring themselves by going 100 percent during the first round of a game they took too seriously. The best places to look for ideas are physical education textbooks and websites. Relay races fall into this category if you can control the intensity.

Have all relays or tag-style games begin with only skipping, shuffling, crawling or jumping since those are less dynamic than running. An athlete is less likely to pull a muscle if he or she is skipping to chase down an opponent. By combining relays with activation or balance drills you can also control the intensity as desired. Three minutes of Simon Says followed by 30 seconds balancing on each leg and then doing some core bridges can be a welcome change from the usual warm-up routine.

Active and Dynamic Stretching

Sport is movement, and for that reason, the more that movement can be combined with stretching, the better. By doing so, athletes are able to rehearse basic motor patterns in a controlled environment. Compare a walking heel-to-butt quad stretch that requires single-leg balance, core stiffness and coordination with a side-lying heel-to-butt static stretch. Both stretch the quads, but the former is substantially more effective from a functional standpoint. Here are some considerations for selecting active or dynamic exercises:

- Design exercises to progress from single to multijoint. If you haven't already mobilised strategic joints during the correctives phase of the warm-up, you'll want to start with them here.

Ankles, hips and the thoracic spine are areas that typically demand individual attention.

- Choose exercises that prepare the body for that day's training session. If you'll be working on acceleration, focus on gluteal activation and thoracic spine and ankle mobility. If you're working top-speed mechanics, emphasise hip mobility, ankle stability and hamstring activation.

- Address each joint according to its function. The joints of the body are stacked in alternating order of those that should be mobile (e.g., ankles, hips, thoracic spine, shoulder, wrist) and those that need stability to avoid injury and transfer force (e.g., knees, lumbar spine, cervical spine, elbows). Mobilising the ankle will help protect the knee from unnecessary forces that might occur during vigorous changes of direction on the field. Similarly, a strong core stabilises the lumbar spine and helps transfer transverse forces from the hips and through the torso to increase throwing power.

- Start each dynamic stretch with a limited ROM and gradually increase it using greater antagonist contraction or momentum. If a muscle is forced into a new ROM too quickly, a stretch reflex can be triggered and the muscle that is trying to stretch will contract.

- Move from general exercises to those that are more specific to the sport. If the sport requires righting or tilting reflexes, such as in gymnastics, fighting, or extreme sport, incorporate devices such as stability balls into the warm-up.

- Reinforce primal movement patterns through crawling or climbing, among other movements, to help athletes in many sports.

- Encourage athletes to protect the lumbar spine by aiming to decrease the amount of bending. Eliminate exercises that create back extension, side bending or simultaneous extending and rotating.[8] Though many sports demand lumbar flexibility, it is a better idea to spend time activating and strengthening the stabilising muscles that protect against lumbar spinal hypermobility whilst focusing on hip and thoracic spine mobility. This work will likely minimise the amount of mobility demanded of the lumbar spine during competition.

- Keep an eye out for flaws or asymmetries in athletes' movements. Incorporate acceleration buildups at progressively increasing speeds and watch how speed mechanics change with increased velocity.

- Make special considerations for athletes who throw and swing. Most dynamic warm-ups focus mainly on the lower body. Emphasising scapular retraction and stabilisation throughout the warm-up is a good rule for shoulder health.

- Take advantage of the controlled environment of the warm-up to have athletes train barefoot, which will increase both ankle mobility and foot strength.

- Beware of fatigue. Include exercises that are in place, on the ground and in transit so athletes have time to recover. A good dynamic warm-up should gradually increase the athlete's work capacity and fitness levels, but it shouldn't be so intense that training suffers.

Static Stretching

The case against static stretching before training is substantial, with most research pointing toward inhibited stretch reflexes, slower reaction times, increased muscle–tendon compliance and 5 to 30 per cent decreases in strength as reasons to eliminate it from a pretraining program.[20] A recent meta-analysis of 361 research papers on the topic revealed that static stretching before activity is not associated with significant injury reductions either.[21] Moreover, from a performance standpoint, excessive stretching in general appears to be detrimental to performance in subsequent activities requiring power.[22] The problem is that traditional static stretching promotes flexibility, which is not what athletes should be trying to achieve before training or competition. Rather, they should seek to create low-viscosity compliance within the athlete's normal ROM. Here, *compliance* refers to the ability of an athlete to safely move through the natural ROM at the speeds and torque required by the sport; *flexibility* refers to increasing the normal ROM at a joint. Pretraining increases in flexibility may contribute to joint laxity or new joint angles that are not strong or stable. If an athlete's ROM needs to be improved, static stretching, proprioceptive neuromuscular facilitation (PNF), yoga and other methods can be used after or outside of training to make long-term mobility improvements.

Neural Preparation

The final component to consider during warm-up is neural preparation. *Postactivation potentiation* (PAP) is the term used to encompass any exercise that acutely enhances muscular-force output. These activities neurologically prime the pump by activating more fast-twitch motor units to either increase MVC or contraction speed.

Athletes can use tools to increase the speed of movement, for example, when a batter swings a lighter bat, runners are towed into overspeed velocities or soccer players perform quick-foot ladder drills. The nervous system learns to fire at speeds faster than normal so that during competition, faster movement becomes possible.

Alternatively, athletes can elicit PAP by resisting movements with weights or harnesses. Doing so forces muscles to contract with more force and recruit more and bigger motor units to do the required work.

High variability among athletes is one of the biggest factors to consider when including neural preparation exercises at the end of a warm-up session. As a general rule, athletes tend to get the greatest ergogenic benefit when they are resisted no more than ±10 per cent of their normal weight.[23] Any more or less has been shown to alter the mechanics of the desired movement to a point where positive carryover is not observed. Another factor to consider is the amount of time between the PAP exercise and training or competition. Research indicates that most athletes need 6 to 12 minutes of recovery time to optimise performance.[23] If there is too little time between the PAP activity and competition, fatigue may hinder performance; if there is too much, the PAP stimulus fades. Also, athletes with weight-training experience tend to benefit from PAP more than athletes of a younger training age, possibly due to a greater fatigue effect on the untrained athlete.[24]

PAP protocols are different in sports such as weightlifting or powerlifting. Athletes in these sports should use resistances that approach the goal weight for that training session. Doing this takes advantage of the staircase phenomenon, which demonstrates that a muscle contracts more forcefully after it has contracted a few times due to the active muscle requiring decreasing degrees of succeeding stimuli to elicit maximal contractions.[25] For instance, a powerlifter who is attempting a squat max might want to prepare for the maximal attempt with single repetitions of 80 per cent, 85 per cent and 90 per cent of the previous maximal weight before attempting to lift 105 per cent. The best protocols likely will be different for each lifter, though, so it's important to experiment with prelift volumes and weights.

A common method of stimulating the nervous system before training is the use of plyometrics. The jumping or throwing exercises used in this phase should to be low level since the goal is to prime the nervous system, not illicit a long-term stretch–reflex training effect. Much like the PAP exercises, plyometrics should be used to trick the neuromuscular system into producing higher firing frequencies. For this reason, quick-foot and dot drills may be more appropriate than jumping rope since the speed of the jumps is regulated by how quickly the athlete can spin the rope. Unlike the use of dot drills or quick-foot drills in the thermogenic session, their use here should be with an emphasis on speed with shorter bursts (3 sec) and more rest.

Case Study

This team warm-up example can effectively be used in running-based field sports such as soccer, rugby, football or field hockey. Note the structure and how it builds progressively to ensure the body is appropriately prepared for competition.

Tissue quality, 5 minutes: Target the muscles used to accelerate, decelerate, and rotate.

Calf: trigger point ball, 30 seconds each

Hamstrings: foam roller, 30 seconds each

Glutes: trigger point ball, 30 seconds each

Thoracic spine: peanut ball, 30 seconds

Quadriceps: foam roller, 30 seconds each

Activation, 5 minutes: Stimulate the gluteal muscles and core stabilisers.

Linear resistance walk: 30 seconds forward and backward

Single-leg balance: 30 seconds each

Lateral miniband walk: 30 seconds left and right

Single-leg balance with eyes closed intermittently: 30 seconds each

Side plank: 30 seconds each

Corrective exercise: 2 minutes. Many football players suffer from previous ankle injuries so use this time to focus on ankle mobility and stability.

> Active ankle dorsiflexion: 1 minute each. Have players line up against a wall and attempt to touch their knees to the wall whilst keeping their ankles on the ground. Have them vary the foot angle and note asymmetries between ankles.

Thermogenic and active (dynamic) stretching combined: 10 minutes.

> Jump rope two feet, forward and backward: 30 seconds each
>
> Walking knee hug: 10 metres
>
> Walking heel-to-butt quad stretch: 10 metres
>
> Jump rope lateral, jump rope hip twist: 30 seconds each
>
> Lateral lunge walking forward: 10 metres
>
> Crossover lunge walking forward: 10 metres
>
> Jump rope fast, jump rope for height: 30 seconds each
>
> Lunge forward with elbow to instep: 10 metres
>
> Thoracic spine 90-90 stretch: 1 minute
>
> Acceleration 80 per cent: 30 metres
>
> Inverted hamstring stretch: 1 minute
>
> Acceleration 90 per cent: 30 metres

Neural preparation: 2 minutes.

> Agility ladder forward run with foot-speed focus: 1 minute
>
> Agility ladder lateral run with foot-speed focus: 1 minute

Cooling Down

The period immediately after training is the most common time to begin regeneration. Traditionally this cool-down consists of 5 to 10 minutes of static stretching. Many elite training facilities have added soft-tissue treatments using foam rollers and trigger-point therapy; some even customise the tissue treatment based on athletes' movement screen results.

Other performance coaches, this author included, have gone away from this approach. Instead of using the time after a training session to work on long-term mobility through static stretching, athletes remain standing and drink a recovery shake, ensuring that this critical piece of the regeneration puzzle occurs. After drinking the shake, athletes are encouraged to use the cold-and-hot contrast baths to help flush metabolic waste from tissues. Once the baths are complete, the athletes take naps. The period directly after training becomes a time for tissue regeneration, not lengthening.

For these athletes, long-term ROM work occurs about 3 hours later once the nervous system has calmed. Athletes are taken through a stretching routine consisting of any combination of the following joint-mobility techniques.

Yoga

Many athletes benefit from the relaxation and breathing techniques of this ancient practice. It is also a good place to start a session because the slow movement progressions help warm the tissue slightly for subsequent stretching.

Soft Tissue

Since soft-tissue work is covered during a phase of warm-up, it is included here only if athletes have injuries or restrictions that could benefit from additional time doing it.

Static Stretching

The majority of time is spent with long-hold stretching, usually 30 to 60 seconds per muscle depending on the level of immobility. By holding the stretches longer, we hope to gradually see an inhibition of mechanoreceptor activity and deeper stretches. We will also use the athletes' movement-screen results to customise the routine and address any weaknesses. This template is useful to follow:

- Synchronise breathing with movement. Breathing either excites or calms the nervous system, so instead of holding stretches for an arbitrary amount of time, concentrate on slowing the breathing until the muscle relaxes.

- Gain ROM without pain. When stretches are taken to their painful end-ROM, there is a rebound effect in which the muscles tighten to avoid injury.

- Move through stretches in a logical order. Often, when stretching stops and the muscle returns to the starting position, the muscle fibers just stretched will contract. Learn to move muscles to neutral starting positions without retensing them.

- Stretch fascia, not just muscle. The thick bands of myofascia that cover muscles connect them in lines throughout the body. By thinking less about stretching individual muscles and more about elongating the fascial lines, athletes get a more accurate picture of how the body works.[26]

The spiral line of fascia crisscrosses the torso running from the skull, across the upper back to the opposite shoulder, then around the ribs to the opposite hip and down through the foot.[27] When an athlete sprints or throws a ball, he or she stretches this spiral line and gets energy from its recoil. If the fascia along this line is too taut, the mobility necessary for good sprinting or throwing mechanics can be restricted. To ease tight fascia, have athletes get into a half-kneeling hip-flexor stretch, then press forward to target the iliopsoas (figure 8.5*a*). Next, incorporate more of the spiral line by having the athletes lift the back ankle with the hand (figure 8.5*b*). Once the athletes are comfortable with that position, have them reach the free hand upward and across the body (figure 8.5*c*). Have them press forward for 10 to 20 seconds and repeat 3 to 5 times.

Proprioceptive Neuromuscular Facilitation

Studies have repeatedly shown that PNF stretching, which uses neurological reflexes to increase ROM, is an effective and time-efficient method for increasing flexibility.[28] This technique essentially tricks the stretch reflex by contracting the affected muscle repeatedly during the stretch. Through inhibitory interneurons called Renshaw cells, the stretch reflex is temporarily inhibited after the contraction, allowing for a deeper stretch. Modified PNF techniques such as contract, relax, antagonist-contract (CRAC) and contract-relax (CR) have proven especially beneficial when performed correctly.[28]

Figure 8.5 Stretching the fascia of the torso: (*a*) begin with a half-kneeling, hip-flexor stretch that targets the iliopsoas; (*b*) progress by lifting the back ankle with the opposite hand; (*c*) finally, reach the free hand up and across the body.

Total Team Warm-Up

Tony Strudwick
*Head of Fitness and Conditioning,
Manchester United Football Club*

At Manchester United, our warm-up is well planned because there are many boxes that need to be ticked before we are happy that our players are ready for kickoff. Specifically, our checklist includes

- core body temperature elevation;
- movement preparation and flexibility;
- acceleration, deceleration and change of direction;
- individual-specific preparation;
- position-specific preparation;
- skill repetition; and
- team preparation and match rehearsal.

Movement efficiency and motor competencies are important to us from an injury-prevention standpoint and a performance perspective. Accordingly, we incorporate fundamental movement skills in the warm-up. The general flow is as follows:

1. Perform movements without any regard to speed.
2. Increase the speed of the movement.
3. Do the movements under different conditions.
4. Follow with fundamental sport skills based on the movement skill.

In other words, the warm-up progresses from general mobility to football-specific drills, not forgetting vital last-minute tactical and psychological preparations. The few minutes players spend once on the pitch involve running across the pitch, integrating static and dynamic movements. This usually takes 5 minutes and involves a gradual increase in tempo. As part of the ethos of the team, this section is led by the captain.

We then go into movement-based flexibility work to increase mobility and flexibility in multiple directions. This work increases in intensity as body temperatures elevate so that players are ready for more dynamic drills.

We select from a handful of dynamic stretching drills, including the forward high-knee march, forward walking lunge, jack-knife walk, lateral lunge, backward lunge with twist, drop lunge and inverted hamstring stretches.

Stretching the hamstrings, quadriceps and groin muscles is especially important before evening matches and in cold conditions because tightness in these muscle groups increases injury risk. At Manchester United, we use a combination of static and dynamic exercises, although time spent during a static hold is no longer than 20 seconds. This pragmatic approach takes into account contemporary research and player preference of maintaining static holds. Individual choice often dictates the integration of static and dynamic movements, but this part is led by a coach with instruction and feedback. Moreover, our fitness coaches use this period to motivate and accelerate game readiness.

Dynamic exercises designed to move the body quickly form an integral component of our prematch routines. These dynamic routines emphasise progressive, whole-body, continuous movement and are typically performed in running drills that include forward and lateral moves and changes of direction. Examples of dynamic warm-up exercises include lunges, squats, hops, jumps, high knees, high kicks and leg swings. We do these to bolster the execution of rapid match-play activities such as sprinting, contesting headers and tackling, all critical for success in Premier League football.

In order to maintain the quality of skill execution, we make sure that players have adequate recovery time between repetitions. Subsequent stimulation of the aerobic systems is then performed via specific ball drills involving changes of speed and direction and specific movement patterns typical of those performed during match play.

All modes of running (e.g., forward, sideways, backward), sprinting, turning and jumping as well as intense bursts such as accelerations and decelerations are programmed into the warm-up. In addition, it is common practice at Manchester United to include position-specific preparation time. For example, central defenders work on

Tony Strudwick is head of fitness and conditioning at Manchester United FC. In the past seven seasons, he has been part of a World Club Championship, Premiership, UEFA Champions League, Carling Cup and Charity Shield winning team. He has a master's degree in physical education and sports science and earned his PhD at Liverpool John Moores University in 2006 combining headers, landing patterns, backward moves and turning to sprint. Periods are assigned to allow strikers to practice movements with a shot to goal. Goalkeepers use this time to follow a similar pattern of game preparation but work independently with the goalkeeper coach. Finally, players come together to ensure handling skills are incorporated. Strikers always work on shooting, with goalkeepers used in the final 5 minutes of the warm-up.

Football is a highly skilled game, so we add a ball to warm-up drills as appropriate. At the forefront is the need to pursue the psychological benefits of match-play rehearsal, such as passing and shooting skills. These drills are performed at the end of our warm-up so players are already warm before doing these ballistic drills and because the potentiating effect of stimulating the nervous system by means of brief, highly intense muscular efforts before competition decays after 10 to 15 minutes.

A final consideration is the timing of the warm-up so that benefits are not negated before the start of the game. Muscle and body temperature will remain elevated for some minutes after exercise is finished. We terminate the warm-up 10 minutes before the start of the match to facilitate a short recovery, give players time to change into match kit and allow for preparations and coaches' talks.

In all, our warm-up takes 20 to 25 minutes, but its content varies according to environmental conditions. For example, we reduce the intensity and duration when the weather is hot; in cold conditions we place more emphasis on elevating body temperature through a greater volume of running-based drills. The same template is used irrespective of event or opposition, although climate is taken into consideration, producing familiarity and consistency.

Substitute players could be called on at any stage, so it is vital that they are ready for action. Our substitutes warm up every 15 to 20 minutes throughout the match for approximately 5 to 10 minutes. The halftime interval also provides an excellent opportunity to raise body temperature and increase match readiness. Once again, climate plays an important role in the management of substitutes; cold winter conditions necessitate the need to extend working periods and ensure muscle temperature is optimal.

Meditation

Although not essential, having athletes meditate to end a stretching session is a popular option. Direct them to assume a supine position on the floor, close their eyes and concentrate on slowing their breathing. There are many meditation-like techniques that coaches can use to achieve maximal relaxation.

Summary

It isn't easy to find hard truths when looking at the research on how to properly prepare an athlete for training or competition. There are many ways to conduct a warm-up; the most successful coaches tend to use a variety of methods depending on the athlete's sport, imbalances, weaknesses or periodisation. The most effective components of a well-designed warm-up include those that address both the quality of the muscle tissue and its ideal functional length. The warm-up also includes exercises that activate muscle groups that are often asleep to gain greater motor-unit recruitment and stability around certain joints. Corrective exercises can be employed to address any imbalances, joint immobility or movement dysfunction discovered in an athlete.

From an injury-prevention standpoint the most important objective of the warm-up should be to increase the athlete's tissue temperature. Thermogenic activities can be easily paired with dynamic stretches to progressively challenge basic movement patterns, balance, core stiffness and coordination whilst also increasing muscle length. Finally, postactivation potentiation drills that ready the neuromuscular system for more powerful subsequent movements can be used to prime an athlete's muscles and activate more fast-twitch motor units. The ideal mix of these components should leave an athlete warm, energetic and stimulated for the activities ahead.

Traditionally, cool-down has occurred in the period immediately after training and has consisted of static stretching or soft-tissue treatments. Static stretching posttraining is of limited use. A more effective option is to use the 30 minutes after training to ensure that athletes drink a recovery beverage whilst also using cold-and-hot contrast baths to flush out metabolic waste. Long-term ROM work occurs 3 hours later, once the nervous system has calmed, and can consist of yoga, soft-tissue work, static stretching, proprioceptive neuromuscular facilitation or meditation.

CHAPTER 9

Fine-Tuning Motor Control

Frans Bosch
Fontys University of Applied Sciences, Netherlands,
and Welsh Rugby Union, UK

As our knowledge develops, more fields of research are playing a part in training theory, on the one hand making it more effective, but on the other, more complex. We now have a clearer picture of how training stimuli can lead to adaptations in the athlete, and the complexity of the interacting systems being trained is better understood than in the past. Nonetheless, we still have a great deal to learn about motor control and motor learning. Knowledge in this area has greatly expanded in recent decades, thanks especially to the dynamic systems theory. New insights have had major practical implications for coaching since biomechanical analysis can be linked to effective training exercises only if it is combined with an understanding of motor learning and control. Failing this, technique training is bound to remain a largely hit-or-miss affair.

This chapter explores a philosophy for a motor-learning approach to training with specific emphasis on straight-line and multidirectional running. The goal is to stimulate a paradigm shift and develop a template for performance professionals working with both fit and injured athletes.

Motor Control in Sport

Often, training for sport is thought of in biomechanical or physiological terms. In fact, the approach that excludes the critical component of motor control is one that is doomed to fail because it does not recognise the importance of understanding how movement is organised and executed.

Hierarchical and Decentralised Theories of Motor Control

Until the mid-1980s, knowledge of motor control was dominated by hierarchical models in which the brain was viewed as the command centre for motor control. In this model, the appropriate motor programme was enacted in response to the person's intention, which was then transmitted down to the muscles, which obediently executed the movement. Essentially, the body was seen as being totally subservient to the wishes of the brain.

The refinement of this motor-control system was introduced by schema theory, which acknowledges that movement patterns are not isolated incidents, but rather are interrelated. This provides us with the concept of movement *specificity*,[1] which means that a good level of skill in one pattern has carryover to related movement patterns. This can be seen in the way a tennis player can transfer to another hitting sport, such as golf, with relative ease. In other cases there may be little or no similarity, as can be seen in the running technique of a swimmer or cyclist because swimming and cycling have scarcely any components that are common with running. The implication for exercise design is that for transfer of learning to be maximised, specificity must be paramount. Although schema theory is an advancement from previous models, it is still unsatisfactory in explaining more open skills in which the correct execution of the movement is not determined in advance because the environment is constantly changing due to an opponent's movements, the bounce of the ball, or a change of terrain. In these instances the central command

Wisdom

Top-level athletes' complex interactions with their environment require split-second responses and flexible, highly efficient performance structures. A central command centre would fail to do this accurately, given the vast amount of information that needs to be processed and the speed with which it has to be done in sport. Complex interactions are best explained with the dynamic systems theory, which should form the basis for both the study and the coaching of athletic skills.

centre would have to process such a vast amount of external input so as to render the task impossible.[2]

Dynamic systems theory (DST) was developed in the late twentieth century to help explain these more complex interactions.[3] In DST, there is no hierarchical, top-down structuring of motor control. Instead, components are added to the movement plan at each level of the organism: some in the brain (such as the intention of the movement), some at the spinal level (such as rhythmic coordination of the movements of the extremities, as in running) and even some outside the central nervous system (e.g., the way in which muscles influence one another during co-contractions through mechanical properties such as elasticity and force–length characteristics). It can

be seen, then, that components are added to the movement everywhere at once, involving the integration of bottom-up influences (from the body to the brain) and top-down organisation of movement patterns (figure 9.1, *a* and *b*). This integration makes the way movement is controlled dependent on the situation. For instance, core-stability control in low-intensity movement can be regulated in another part of the system (by proprioceptive feedback) than high-intensity movement (by muscular properties).

Two Control Systems

Movements can be controlled in one of two ways. A person can use the working memory, that is, conscious control, for slow processes and new, ad hoc (situation-specific) movement solutions. Alternatively, a person can use the body's hard drive, or unconscious control, for movements under pressure of time and for automated movements stored in long-term memory. Growing scientific evidence suggests that the two systems operate separately.[4,5] One indicator of the strong separation of the two systems is the fact that they are linked to different, largely independent visual observation systems: Conscious control is linked to central vision (for the observation of shapes), and unconscious control is linked to peripheral vision (for the observation of movement; figure 9.2).

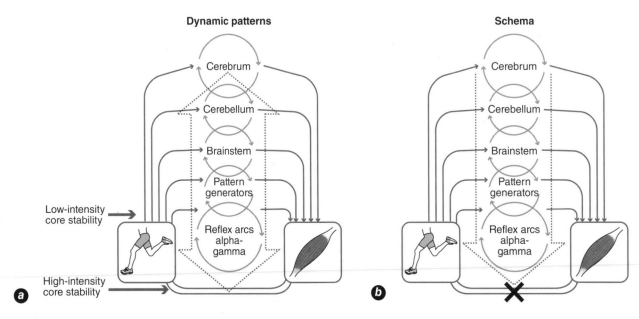

Figure 9.1 Decentralised control (*a*), with decisions being added to the movement plan at each level. The levels at which the components are added to the movement may differ greatly in low-intensity and high-intensity movements. Hierarchical organisation of control (*b*), with the command centre located in the brain and the muscles obediently executing the movement.

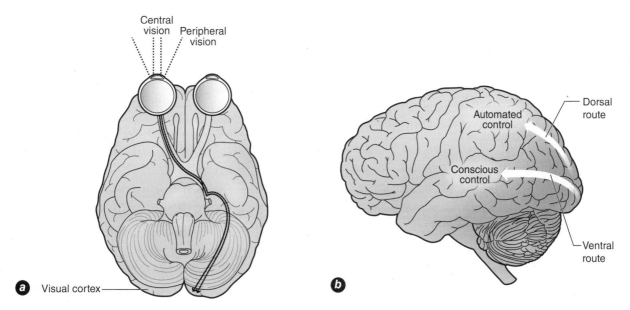

Figure 9.2 Central vision is linked to conscious control via the ventral route. Peripheral vision is linked to unconscious, automated control via the dorsal route.

Performance in sport requires the two systems to be used for the types of control they are best at. If there is sufficient time (e.g., finding the right starting position for a golf swing) or a tactical decision is needed (e.g., going up to the net more often in tennis), the working memory works best. If the movement has to be executed smoothly and under pressure of time (e.g., the actual golf swing or a crosscourt backhand in tennis), using the hard drive works best. Of course, many movements in sport require automated control, and training is therefore designed to ensure that movement patterns are efficiently stored on the hard drive. To learn and store these patterns, we need to know how the hard drive is structured (formatted). This structure enables us to find efficient performance options even under pressure of time and when interacting with an unpredictable environment.

If it is to work well, the hard drive has to be structured according to the specificity matrix (i.e., the movements that are similar and influence one another). If movements were unrelated and were simply stored as isolated incidents, we would be unable to find the right one quickly, just as a book in a library containing thousands of volumes cannot be found quickly without a retrieval system.

Combining the Theories

If hierarchical and decentralised theories of control are combined with the working memory and hard drive model, the resulting overall picture is one of two essentially separate systems. One is conscious control (figure 9.3) via the working memory, which is more or less hierarchically organised and works best when actions must be performed consciously, without pressure of time. The brain is the command centre and gives the muscles full instructions for the movement. The other is unconscious, automated control, which has a decentralised structure with components being added to the movement throughout the organism; this works best when quick action is required in a complex environment. Although the dual-control system is well accepted, the interaction between centralised and decentralised control has not, as yet, been confirmed by research. It does, however, operate well in practice.

The two systems are fundamentally different, and this has far-reaching practical implications. Movements that are constructed in the working memory cannot simply be stored on the hard drive, for their structure does not usually fit into that matrix. The result is forgotten once the training session is over. Training methods that rely heavily on the use of the working memory quickly achieve visible results: Execution improves during the training session. However, the actual learning process is invisible, with a different dynamic, and so ultimately not much is learned. In other words, not much is stored on the hard drive, and carryover is poor. However shocking this may seem to most

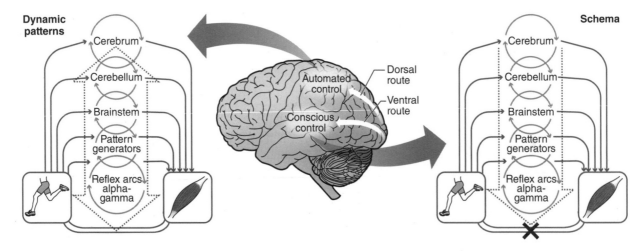

Figure 9.3 The link between automated, decentralised control and conscious, hierarchical control.

coaches, the better the practice result at the end of the training session, the less the athlete may ultimately learn. Practice results and learning results are antagonistic.

Therefore, coaching instructions that activate the working memory should be avoided. These instructions are ones that focus the learner's attention on the way the movement is executed (internal focus instructions such as 'keep your elbow bent longer', 'extend your back before you apply force', 'maintain pressure on the ball of your foot' and so on). Some 85 per cent of coaching instructions are of this kind and are unproductive. In fact, with simple movements, merely giving athletes encouragement is more effective than giving them internal-focus instructions on how to execute those movements.[6]

If too many internal-focus instructions are given during the initial stage of the learning process (also known as *knowledge of performance feedback*), the athlete not only learns how to execute a movement but also how to construct (or reconstruct) it in the working memory. In stress situations such as competition, the result may be that automated performance is suppressed (overruled), and the movement is reconstructed ad hoc in the working memory. The movement is then executed less effectively. This phenomenon is known as *choking*. The way in which instructions are given during the learning process thus may lead to choking.

Athletes who have made little or no use of the working memory during the learning process cannot resort to it in stress situations and are less likely to choke. It is far better for the athlete to use the working memory as little as possible in the first stages of learning and try to store movement patterns immediately on his or her hard drive.

Transfer of Training to Performance

Gold medals and championships are not awarded in training. The critical component is to ensure that the work done in training actually transfers across into the competitive environment. Therefore, training should be designed according to the laws of transfer.

Specificity and Transfer

To some extent automated control is structured by the specificity matrix. Specificity is also the main prerequisite for transfer of skilled practice into competition performance. In fact, solving the transfer problem is arguably the most difficult challenge faced in exercise programming. For example, it is relatively unimportant to know how a runner's strength qualities improve during strength training; what matters is how these improved qualities enhance running performance and reduce injury risk. Equally, when practising agility in a predictable environment, the point is not how finely and precisely the movements are executed in isolation, but how this execution can be used in response to an opponent's actions. To ensure optimum transfer of practice into performance, we need to know, preferably in detail, how the specificity matrix is structured; we need to know the rules whereby similarities between movements are stored on the hard drive.

In conventional training theory, such analysis of specificity has been remarkably limited. It is usually confined to seeking similarities in the outward features of movements, such as similar body postures and angular velocity in joints. The better analyses also look at similarities in muscle contractions (e.g., concentric, isometric and elastic) and recognise that similar patterns of intermuscular cooperation, especially at high levels of skill, are crucial to performance-enhancing transfer.

In addition to these fairly conventional, highly mechanical features of specificity, there are at least two others that influence transfer, disregarding similarities in energy supply:

1. *Sensory similarities.* Motor control is based on the link between sensory input and motor output. Movements that are similar in motor terms but different in sensory terms are relatively unspecific for each other. This is of particular relevance to strength training. Spatial information plays little or no role. Proprioception is often different from what it is in the competition movement because the force produced not just by machines but also by weighted bars greatly affects proprioceptive feedback. One good example of how this reduces specificity is strength training for swimmers. In swimming, gravity is effectively absent, whereas strength training depends on it. For the same reason, it is questionable how useful aqua jogging or elliptical training is to runners.

2. *Movement-result similarities.* All movement control starts with the intention of the movement, the future state it is meant to result in. In the specificity matrix, the system largely focuses on similarities in intention. This means, for example, that strength exercises with unclear intentions can hardly be linked to other types of movement. Thus the intention (goal) of a high pull is less explicitly defined than the intention of a clean (completely balanced, with the bar in the correct position at shoulder height). A high pull will produce much less transfer than a clean. Strength training includes numerous exercises (dumbbell fly, squat, lat pull and so on) with unclear intentions and thus limited transfer.

Specific training must meet five criteria:

1. Similarity in muscle action (intra- and intermuscular) to the conditions found in the sport. This can be met if the exercises are technically well executed.
2. Similarity in the external structure of the movement (motion of the limbs) to those found in the sport. This needs to be a basic guideline for training design.
3. Similarity in sensory information to what is experienced in the sport.
4. Similarity in the dominant energy system to what is used in the sport.
5. Similarity in the movement result to that which occurs in the sport. The clearer the difference between successful and nonsuccessful, the better the transfer.

Part Practice and Whole Practice for Runners

Training exercises can be divided into *part practice* and *whole practice*. In part practice, one or more components are removed from the context of the overall functional (competition) movement and practised separately, in the hope or expectation that doing so will improve the overall competition movement. In whole practice, the functional movement remains intact, and possibly simplified versions of the overall competition movement are practised. Whole practice preserves the sensory-motor features and the intention of the movement. Since specificity is present, transfer is more or less ensured, which is not the case with part practice. If training is based on part practice, the effort expended must be carefully weighed against the results achieved. In a sport-specific context, effective training depends on keeping collateral damage—stress to the system that does not enhance performance—to a minimum.

Low-speed running exercises are part practice in terms of high-speed running. Therefore, their usefulness is somewhat questionable. For instance, exercises at low horizontal speed, with high frequency of movement, are of little relevance to high-speed running since the sensory–motor conditions for maintaining correct body tension are scarcely fulfilled at low speed. In turn, high-speed running is part practice with limited transfer to agility since the sensory–motor requirements of agility (e.g., for movements in the frontal plane) are hardly a problem in straight-line running. Finally, agility in the absence of opponents is part practice in terms of competition, since the vital factor of reading your opponent is missing.

This is not to say that part practice can never be useful. Some components of a movement pattern may be so hard to improve in the context of the competition movement that they must be removed from that context in special part-practice exercises. The best way to add part-practice exercises to the overall whole-practice approach cannot be calculated from general guidelines and is an important component of the art of coaching.

The area of sport-specific training with the greatest focus on part practice is strength training. It provides no guarantee that skills will be transferred. Yet strength and coordination are so closely related that the coordinative aspects of sport-specific strength training crucially influence its effectiveness, especially for top-level athletes.

Wisdom

Strength training is coordination training with increased resistance.

For well-trained athletes, nonintegrated strength training that focuses on the quantitative scoring of so many kilograms or watts will therefore have little or no impact in terms of transfer of gains in the gym to gains in sport performance. Indeed, it can easily prove counterproductive: There is a saying that 'too much strength training slows you down'. One example of a part-practice exercise that can produce negative transfer into running performance is the double-leg squat to parallel with heavy weights. First, the coordinative aspects of the exercise bear little relation to the requirements of running at speed, given the irrelevant knee angle in a squat. Nor is the exercise of much relevance to starts and acceleration since the neural control involved in double-leg and single-leg extension is substantially different. There is little positive transfer, and the body is subjected to immense stress. In fact, the transfer often is negative since the deep squat makes the pelvis tend to rotate backward. Doing so can be technically countered only by hyperextending the lumbar spine, which eventually lengthens the

structures at the front of the spine and can lead to the well-known phenomenon of hyperlordosis. When running at speed, this lengthening of structures such as fasciae causes them to send late—and hence inadequate—signals to the abdominal muscles and the iliopsoas at the end of the stance phase (toe-off, the point at which the foot leaves the ground). This leads to loss of control over the forward rotation of the pelvis (figure 9.4), which always occurs at toe-off, and a drastic deterioration in running technique because the following pendulum is too large and round.

Figure 9.4 Significant forward rotation of the pelvis at toe-off means that the trailing knee is moved forward late (round pendulum), causing deterioration in running technique.

Wisdom

Muscle slack: Due to the dangling starting position of a muscle before the start of a contraction, the contractile elements of the muscle first have to shorten substantially before significant forces can be produced at the attachment points of the muscle.

The squat is not the only example of a strength-training exercise that can produce negative transfer into running performance. Hypertrophic effects and increased muscle slack, among others, always pose a threat to running performance.[7]

The assumption that strength training based entirely on physiology (e.g., hormonal balance, increased physiological cross-sectional area) can never do any harm in terms of skill transfer is not borne out by the facts. Sport-specific strength training should be based primarily on a cost–benefit analysis of skill transfer that is designed to minimise the drawbacks of part practice. The premise behind heavy squatting for running performance usually involves enhancing force application; however, the problem is not so much about the *amount* of force applied, but rather the speed, timing and direction of this force application. Once the athlete is strong enough, training time is much more efficiently spent developing other attributes of force production, along with technical running skills.

Dynamic Systems Theory and Running

Significant transfer between components of two movement patterns does not just depend on specificity. Another key factor is the stability of the components involved. If a component has to adapt to the environment whilst it is being executed and is highly variable, transfer will be much harder to achieve than if the component is invariable and stable. Another way to think of it is that a stable component is one that remains the same even in varying executions of a given motor pattern. It is the common feature, whereas the unstable components can change. Dynamic systems theory shows that there are always both stable and unstable components in any movement pattern. Stable components are known as *attractors* and variable components as *fluctuations* (figure 9.5).

Attractors and Fluctuations

The environment in which sport movements are performed affects the way they are executed. In the case of open skills, the adaptation to the environment is evident since the environment (e.g., the ball, the opponent, the course) is highly variable; but even in the case of closed skills, which have a

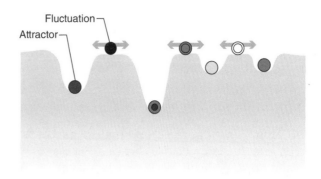

Figure 9.5 The attractor–fluctuation landscape, showing components of a movement pattern that are stable attractors (with low-energy expenditure) and components that are variable fluctuations (with high-energy expenditure). Attractors are in wells, reflecting their stability and inability to be changed. Fluctuations are free to move over the flat surfaces of the landscape, meaning they can change. The deeper the attractor well, the more robust it is.

relatively invariable environment, minor adaptations are still always required.

The quality of a movement depends not only on the athlete being able to execute its separate components properly, but also on the effectiveness of the strategy in adapting the movement to the environment. This strategy must fulfil a number of conditions. First, the adaptation should involve as few components of the movement as possible. If too many fluctuating components are involved, they cannot be controlled. This can be compared to a car. If each of the four wheels had its own steering wheel, the car could no longer be driven; it would have too many degrees of freedom. So cars are designed with just one steering wheel. The body has many degrees of freedom—all the joints with their many capabilities, and all the possible combinations of muscles that move the joints. Reducing the number of degrees of freedom is an essential part of the learning process. An effective technique includes a large number of components of movement that are not unique to a particular environment, but rather are constant and stable, with low energy expenditure—the attractors in the movement.

Second, the fluctuations that are selected must be effective in as many circumstances as possible. If adaptations can always be made using the same components of movement, the movement is easier to control than if various components have to be selected each time. What this means, for example, is that straight-line running essentially should be organised in the same way as running-based agility. For example, if during running in a football match, components have to regularly switch between being attractor and being fluctuations, control would become too difficult.

The distribution of attractors and fluctuations is self-organising (figure 9.6) and is a key part of the overall learning process. Coaches often make the mistake of applying the same strict—that is, invariable, technical—rules to fluctuation components of the movement as they do to attractor components. Doing so is counterproductive because the pursuit of perfection in every component means that the overall movement is executed less effectively. In order to give self-organisation a chance, a coach must know what components to teach with precision and what components need the freedom to vary in exercises. A coach should not correct every flaw he or she sees; rather, the coach should have a list of the essential attractors and try to help the athlete get those right.

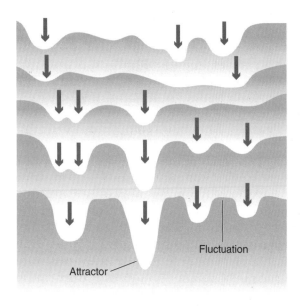

Figure 9.6 In the learning process, the initially designed attractor–fluctuation landscape (top) gradually shifts as skills increase (lower down) towards an efficient distribution of attractors and fluctuations, culminating in a distribution that ensures effective skills (bottom). As learning progresses, the depth of the wells indicates that the stable attractors are becoming more ingrained. This depth enhances the controllability of the movement even in the presence of a variable environment.

Adapted from E. Thelen, 1995, "Motor development: A new synthesis," *American Psychologist* 50(2): 79-95.

Attractors and Fluctuations in Running

Determining the distribution of attractors and fluctuations is a key part of the analysis of running movement. At present, we have to rely on theoretical modelling; however, it is evident that there are a number of attractors and fluctuations in correctly executed running and agility at speed. These can be seen in figure 9.7.

Attractors

1. Vertical movement of the head greatly depends on the stride rate, but at a given running frequency, it is constant even if the running surface is uneven and therefore it is an attractor. As the body will always organise this attractor; no coaching cue is required here.

2. The hamstrings working isometrically at their optimal length is an attractor when running. This is best improved by combining specific strength training (discussed later) with teaching good running technique.

3. In the stance phase, elastic energy must be stored and returned. This makes running economical, which means that the free side of the pelvis should be raised at push-off. In straight-line running, the free side of the pelvis should normally be higher than the stance-leg side at the point when the heel leaves the ground. This pelvic movement and the extension of the stance leg are strongly linked as reflexes to the movements of the swing leg. If the swing leg flexes explosively at the hip and knee (heel to hamstring), the stance leg will be able to extend with greater force, and the free hip will be raised. This overall pattern, known as the *extension reflex*, is a deep attractor in the running movement. Therefore, coaching cues that focus on the swing leg are critical to help ingrain this attractor.

4. In the flight phase, the leading foot should be placed from above. If the path that the foot travels towards the ground forms an angle with the line of the ground-reaction force, the next push-off will always be less effective. Correct foot placement is accompanied by the whip-from-the-hip technique: Extension of the leg is initiated at the hip, followed by knee extension and finally ankle extension from a neutral position just before foot placement. Running over slightly uneven surfaces is the most intuitive way to gain this active ankle movement

Figure 9.7 Attractors in running: (*a*) 1. vertical movement of the head, 2. hamstrings in isometric conditions; (*b*) 3. extension reflex, 4. whip from the hip, 5. no rotation at toe-off; (*c*) 6. high-knee position; 7. arm action.

before ground contact. The use of scooters will also encourage the hip-whipping attractor to develop.

5. A great deal of force must be applied early on in the push-off. This can be done only if there is no rotation forward or around the longitudinal axis to compensate for. A crucial factor is the absence of such rotation in the previous flight phase. This means there should be no residual rotation at the toe-off. A good way to coach this is to get the athlete to run without using his or her arms (e.g., holding a ball tightly with both arms to the chest), which is only possible if there is no residual rotation. There is no explicit coaching needed, just drills that allow the attractors to self-organise.

Fluctuations

6. A high-knee position is often wrongly seen as an attractor in running. Sprinters have a high-knee position, and athletes such as rugby players have a low-knee position in the swing leg.[8] Therefore, the two running patterns are fundamentally different. The knee position greatly depends on factors such as running speed and running frequency, so it is a fluctuation (see, for example, the changing knee position as running speed decreases in the course of a 400-metre race). There is little point in coaching runners for a high-knee position at submaximal speeds.

7. Arm action can vary greatly without affecting performance; it is a fluctuation used as a way to correct perturbations. There is little point in aiming for a particular elbow position or a precise direction of arm swing.

Attractors can seldom be described in terms of specific body postures and are usually organised according to more abstract principles. Attractors are manifested irrespective of the environmental context since they do not need to adapt to it. Therefore, agility has the same attractors as straight-line running. Thus, for example, the conventional idea that the feet should be kept close to the ground in a side step, with a movement similar to that of an ice hockey player, is wrong. Indeed, good players seldom execute the movement in this way. Such a side step makes inadequate use of the attractors, and their wells become shallow. Conventional ideas about agility are not usually in keeping with the conclusions of dynamic systems theory and should therefore be revised.

Attractor–Fluctuation Landscape and Exercise Variability

The need to build fluctuations (variability) into a movement pattern means that it is not enough to aim for perfect technique (e.g., the right joint angles and so on). Athletes must also be taught how to vary basic technique efficiently. This can be done only by varying the exercises.

Quite simply, there can be no attractors without fluctuations. If fluctuations prove to be effective in dealing with the environmental variations, the attractor does not need to assist with the adaptations, allowing its well to deepen.

Wisdom

If only the ideal technique is repeated and stored on the hard drive, the individual can never learn which components of the movement are suitable for adaptation to changing conditions and which ones should be used as stable components with low-energy expenditure. Therefore, exercise variety is key!

The fact that an attractor well can be deepened only by strategic choice of fluctuations has serious implications for strength training. If, for example, the squat technique is to be taught in a usable (i.e., transferable) way, it has to be varied. When heavy weights are being used, the risk of injury means that the only possible variations are in weight and repetition. In the long run, such variations are too small for an optimum learning process. Therefore, training with heavy weights (e.g., in squats, deadlifts) produces less transfer. From this we can conclude that aiming for high scores in strength training is incompatible with the laws of motor learning. This is also reflected in actual practice. As every experienced coach knows, not only do increases in strength through training eventually decline, but above a given threshold, further improvement in strength qualities ceases to have any beneficial impact on running performance. Many coaches of well-trained runners use the term *strong enough* to indicate that, beyond a given point, further improvement in strength qualities is no longer transferred into running performance. In squats, deadlifts and numerous other heavy-weight exercises, this strong enough point is reached much sooner than is commonly thought.

Variation in training is needed in order to design the attractor–fluctuation landscape. The applicability of the movement in many situations reveals whether the landscape is optimally distributed. The question that arises is how great exercise variability should be. Should exercises be varied only a little or a lot? We might conclude from the rules of specificity that the variations should not diverge too much from the required technique, for it is important to remain close to the transfer mechanisms. Yet actual practice—as well as a growing body of research—shows that plenty of variation is particularly effective. Even if the variation is so great that it intuitively seems inefficient, that still results in better learning. The reason for this is still unclear, but it may be the fact that learning does not just happen, but first has to be triggered. A stimulus is needed, and this will arise only if a movement produces an unfamiliar combination of motor output and sensory input. If only the ideal, familiar movement is repeated over and over again, the stimulus will be totally absent; unless there is enough variation, the stimulus may be inadequate.

What we have is an athlete who is sensitive to both specificity of movement and variation between movements. This variation between movements can be linked to the training law of overload. The conflicting demands of specificity and overload make the learning system somewhat conservative and ensure that movement patterns are tested from various angles before being stored in the system. The hard drive first wants to see what other patterns a movement can be linked to and where else it can be applied before it is stored in the system.

Wisdom

Attractors and fluctuations need to be trained together. After finding an effective distribution of attractors and fluctuations, the attractor wells need to be deepened through practice.

Practical Implications

What we have seen so far is this: Sport movements can be learned most effectively if the focus is on automated control. This control is decentralised for complex, high-intensity movements and should result in movement patterns that are both stable and flexible. This will happen if the attractor–fluctuation landscape is optimally designed. Attractors transfer better than fluctuations, but interaction between the two is needed throughout the learning process. Attractors must be precisely trained through specificity, and fluctuations trained through constant variation in execution (figure 9.8). Variability is needed in order to trigger learning, and more variation is required than intuition might suggest. Learning depends on specificity and variation (rather than overload), which make more or less contrary demands on the exercises and constantly vie for control, like partners in a bad marriage. All this has implications for training.

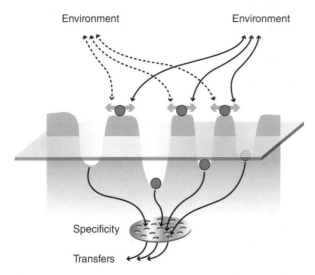

Figure 9.8 Attractors are strongly transferred to other movement patterns via the specificity matrix. Fluctuations ensure adaptation to the changing environment.

Transfer Between Running at Speed and Agility at Speed

To ensure satisfactory transfer between straight-line running at speed and agility at speed in side-steps and swerves, it is useful to focus on a number of attractors they have in common.

Absence of rotation around the longitudinal axis in the flight phase is a primary feature of running at speed and agility at speed. This skill is achieved by ceasing to apply force at the end of the push-off. In addition, there should not be any forward rotation, achieved by keeping the hips forward and having an active, dominant swing leg (i.e., bringing the free leg forward early). Absence of rotation means that the arms do not have to make compensatory movements. Since we are aiming to deepen this attractor well (and this attractor is stable between straight-line and multidirectional running), drills can be conducted, such as ensuring the athlete is carrying a ball or something similar in both hands close to the chest. Athletes with good movement technique show little decline in agility even if they are not allowed to use their arms.

An active swing leg results in swing-leg retraction before foot placement. Together with the forward action of the trailing leg, this backward movement creates a scissors motion. There should be enough time for this scissors motion—with whip from the hip and foot placement from

above—and it should be possible to execute this movement forcefully. In midstance the knee of the free leg should be ahead of the knee of the stance leg to generate a good extension reflex by raising the free side of the pelvis. The pelvic range of motion is not a good yardstick for the quality of the movement, for it greatly depends on muscle tension around the hip.

The end result should be positive running in both running at speed and agility at speed. Positive running can be measured by drawing a line through each of the athlete's thighs in a side-on video or photograph at toe-off (figure 9.9) and then bisecting the angle between the two lines. The farther forward the bisecting line points, the better the running technique.

Figure 9.9 Positive running. A line is drawn through each thigh. The angle between the two lines is then bisected. The direction of the bisecting line indicates how good the technique is.

Wisdom

For those athletes who have all these attractors refined but still have technical flaws, such as an overly extended lumbar spine that could lead to back pain or knee valgus during stance, which leads to energy leaks, it is best to focus on improving basic athletic and gymnastic competencies as opposed to trying to fix their running technique.

Transfer Between Strength Training and Running at Speed

The design of strength training for running at speed should be based on analysis of the running movement and the accompanying attractor–fluctuation landscape, using the attractor components of the movement as building blocks for the exercises. Following are some points to be considered regarding strength training for runners.

For reasons of coordination, even though recruitment and maximal force are important to running performance, overload should not be sought mainly in higher weights but rather in great variability, such as in lower but unstable weights, different surfaces, varying initial postures and so on. Variability will make strength training more interesting and less taxing.

In strength training the intention of the movement usually can be translated into the end position of the exercise. If this matches important body postures in running, there will be greater transfer. The two most important end positions are

1. the end position of the extension reflex (heel to hamstring and raised free hip), for example in single-leg cleans and step-ups; and

2. the absence of rotation at toe-off, for example in step-ups with horizontal movement and lunge variations.

How relevant to running are double-leg strength exercises? Double-leg movement leaves no scope for domination of the extension reflex, which is crucial to transfer. Actual practice shows that strength does not transfer from double-leg to single-leg patterns as a matter of course. Thus, the training programme must contain a significant proportion of single-leg exercises.

In single-leg strength exercises (e.g., step-ups, single-leg cleans) the extension reflex is enhanced by flexing the swing leg at the hip as early and as explosively as possible, with the heel moving towards the hamstring (figure 9.10).

Step-ups are suitable for training both the stance-phase attractors and the swing-phase attractors (scissors motion and foot placement from above).

Strength training for hamstrings should always take place in isometric conditions and at the optimum length for the muscle group. The pelvis should be able to rotate backward and forward during the exercise so that the body can organise itself to find the optimum length. The exercise should be designed so that the hamstrings inhibit knee extension and enhance hip extension since this function is specific for running (figure 9.11). Hamstrings that do not operate as attractors in the running movement but are required to perform variable contractions will be susceptible to injury. Although not disregarding supraspinal spinal qualities, hamstrings that do not have the necessary neuromuscular qualities or appropriate recruitment patterns are more susceptive to injury.

When dealing with a motor pattern in running, the stresses on the hamstrings are highest in high-speed running; the muscle group can deal only with those in their attractor state. This is why appropriate contraction—and hence training—of the hamstrings is the key in injury prevention.

When running at speed, large amounts of energy are transported through the body by elasticity. This energy is stored in the hamstrings of the leading leg during the lower-leg pendulum. All the muscles involved in this transport of energy must be well trained in their specialised attractor functions, for example, the abdominal muscles and hamstrings in isometric conditions for elasticity and the iliopsoas for power production.

All the muscles below the knee work in isometric conditions when running. Therefore, this muscle action is an attractor and should not be trained in varying ways, as is the case with calf raises. However, when in the attractor state, it is impossible to create an overload for running and jumping. What this means is that strength training for lower-leg muscles should be avoided altogether. A better alternative is to progress the demands on the calf musculotendinous complex by challenging the system with higher drop heights whilst maintaining short ground-contact times.

Exercises in which the stance knee is highly flexed may be relevant to starts and acceleration but are less relevant to running and agility at speed. Transfer into running at speed depends on exercises that can be initiated in an almost upright posture and require pretension to ensure good initial acceleration of resistance.

The great problem when running at speed is how to apply force as soon as possible at foot placement. The sooner force can be applied to the ground, the faster the runner is. This rate of force development greatly depends on mechanical muscular properties such as muscle slack. Strength

Figure 9.10 Strength exercise with two relevant intentions: the complete end position of the extension reflex and the absence of rotation at toe-off.

Figure 9.11 Specific strength exercise for the hamstrings: 1. Only one leg is immobilised. 2. The upper body is raised with the hamstring inhibiting knee extension and enhancing hip extension. 3. The muscle group is maintained at the same length by 4. rotating the pelvis backward and forward.

exercises should focus on developing these properties, which can be done only if the exercises are also performed with a time limit. Exercises that take only a few tenths of a second and are only effective if force is produced rapidly, such as single-leg hang cleans, are relevant here.

Wisdom

We cannot continue to assume there is a separation between the transfer of learning and other transfers such as neuromuscular qualities. Transfers in well-trained athletes are always movement specific.

Summary

It is important for the further development of training theory that the organisation and refinement of the specificity matrix, which is the basis for motor control, be more thoroughly understood so that we can gain more insight into transfer processes. The reason variability plays such a key role in learning processes, and the way in which it does so, should also be explored in more detail. Perhaps even more important, more should be done to translate the laws of motor control and motor learning into training practice.

CHAPTER 10

Using Strength Platforms for Explosive Performance

Daniel Baker, PhD
Brisbane Broncos Rugby League Football Club, Brisbane, Australia,
and School of Sport and Biomedical Science, Edith Cowan University, Perth, Australia

This chapter deals with training to generate force (i.e., strength training) for improving sports performance. The philosophies and developmental plan outlined throughout this chapter will benefit virtually every athlete, irrespective of sport or strength-training background. Although it is beyond the scope of this chapter to deal intimately with the specific needs of every sport, sample programs have been included to outline some of the progressions that need to take place in an athlete's strength-training journey.

Importance of Being Strong

The importance of strength training for improving sport performance rests on a fairly simple premise: The higher the level of resistance to overcome or resist in a sport, the greater the importance of strength required. Table 10.1 depicts 1RM data for athletes who have attained differing levels of performance in American football, Rugby League football and track and field throwing, sports in which athletes have to overcome large resistances or forces. Clearly, the athletes participating at the higher levels in these sports are stronger than their less-successful counterparts.

This differentiation is not confined just to collision football and track and field throwers, however. Higher- and lower-level rowers can be distinguished by strength levels both in absolute and relative terms;[1] it has recently been shown that 1RM chin-up strength relative to body mass is extremely highly correlated to sprint-paddling speed in competitive surfers.[2] The performance implication here is obvious when it is considered that paddling speed is critical for successful entry upon a wave, especially bigger waves.

Some sport coaches still argue, however, that strength training is not important for certain sports in which absolute strength is not manifested or in which skill appears to be more important to success. Could this be true? It has been demonstrated that 40-metre sprint times in field- and game-sport athletes are well correlated with squat and power clean strength and with loaded jump squat power relative to the athletes' body mass.[3] Increases in jump height also occur as a result of increasing strength relative to the athletes' body-mass.[4] Therefore, all athletes who need to sprint and jump, irrespective of their sport, will benefit from strength training to improve lower-body strength relative to body mass.

Not only does strength improve many sport-performance measures, but it also reduces the likelihood of injury in many athletic tasks. Athletes with injuries cannot compete optimally, so improved strength is not only important for improving pure performance measures but also for improving athletes' resilience to injury. Strength training would appear necessary for improving performance and reducing injury risk in almost every conceivable sport.

Table 10.1 Differentiation of Performance Level of Athletes From American Football, Rugby League, and Track and Field Throwing, Based on Maximal and Explosive Strength

Sport	1RM squat		1RM bench press		1RM power clean	
U.S. collegiate footballers	Division I	Division II	Division I	Division II	Division I	Division II
	192.8 ± 37.6 (n = 115)	182.5 ± 34.4 (n = 114)	144.5 ± 26.1 (n = 283)	135.2 ± 25.5 (n = 296)	123.0 ± 17.9 (n = 166)	116.5 ± 17.3 (n = 164)
Australian Rugby League	National league	State league	National league	State league	National league	State league
	175.0 ± 27.3 (n = 20)	149.6 ± 14.3 (n = 20)	141.4 ± 15.4 (n = 20)	126.1 ± 13.1 (n = 20)	124.5 ± 12.6 (n = 20)	115.0 ± 6.5 (n = 14)
Male track and field throwers	U.S. national	Collegiate	U.S. national	Collegiate	U.S. national	Collegiate
	290.3 ± 38.8 (n = 3)	266.0 ± 38.4 (n = 7)	226.8 ± 0 (n = 3)	180.8 ± 23.9 (n = 7)	186.0 ± 12.0 (n = 3)	137.7 ± 17.3 (n = 7)
Female track and field throwers	U.S. national	Collegiate	U.S. national	Collegiate	U.S. national	Collegiate
	168.8 ± 11.7 (n = 7)	84.5 ± 10.0 (n = 5)	112.8 ± 9.6 (n = 7)	61.4 ± 4.3 (n = 5)	106.5 ± 6.7 (n = 7)	79.8 ± 0 (n = 1)

Note: All data is in kilogram (kg).

Data for American football from A.C. Fry and W.J. Kraemer, 1991, "Physical performance characteristics of American collegiate football players," *Journal of Applied Sport Science Research* 5(3): 126-138. Data for rugby league from D. Baker and R.U. Newton, 2006, "Discriminative analyses of various upper body tests in professional rugby-league players," *International Journal of Sports Physiology and Performance* 1(4): 347-360; and from D. Baker and R.U. Newton, 2008, "Comparison of lower body strength, power, acceleration, speed, agility, and sprint momentum to describe and compare playing rank among professional rugby league players," *Journal of Strength and Conditioning Research* 22(1): 153-158. Data for track and fielder throwing from M.H. Stone and M.E. Stone, 1999, "General principles of strength training," UK Athletics, Strength and Conditioning Seminar, John Moores University, Liverpool, UK, September 1999.

Strength-Training Terminology

It is important that coaches, when communicating and reading research, have a certain consistency in definitions and understanding of basic terminology. To this end, these terms and definitions will be used throughout this chapter.

Strength is the ability to apply force to either overcome resistances to movement or resist unwanted movement.

Maximal strength (MS) is the ability to apply maximal levels of force or strength irrespective of time constraints.

Relative strength (RS) is the ability to apply high levels of force relative to the athlete's body mass.

Power (P) is the rate of performing work, the ability to apply force with speed (force × velocity).

Maximum power (Pmax) is the maximal power attained during the entire concentric range of movement.

Peak power is the highest power episode of force × velocity, typically for only a few milliseconds.

Explosive strength (ES) is a subquality of power but is best differentiated as the ability to overcome heavy resistances with speed. (Power is overcoming any resistance with speed, particularly medium to lighter resistances.)

Like ES, *speed strength* is a subquality of power but is best differentiated as the ability to apply lower levels of force rapidly.

Strength endurance (SE) is the ability to apply levels of force for a prolonged period without decay.

Maximal effort (ME) means training with the heaviest resistances that do not allow for the completion of any more repetitions at the conclusion of the set. Typically a set of 1 to 5 repetitions is used to develop maximal strength.

Near-maximal effort (NME) means training with heavy resistances that allow for the completion of only 1 or 2 more repetitions at the conclusion of the set. Typically a set of 1 to 6 repetitions is used.

Circa max effort means training with multiple sets of 1 or 2 repetitions with resistances around 90 per cent 1RM to develop maximal strength. This is similar to NME in concept but always uses only 1 or 2 repetitions.

Hard effort (HE) means training with heavy resistances that allow for the completion of 3 to 5 more repetitions at the conclusion of the set. Typically, a set of 1 to 8 repetitions is used to develop MS or ES.

Medium-hard effort (MHE) means training with heavy resistances that allow for the completion of more than 5 repetitions at the conclusion of the set. Typically, a set of 1 to 8 repetitions is used to develop maximal or explosive strength.

Dynamic effort (DE) means training with submaximal resistances of 40 to 75 per cent 1RM and 2 to 5 repetitions for multiple sets to develop ES and P.

Repetitive effort (RE) is the overall name given to the concept of using multiple repetitions to induce overload, typically for the training of general strength or muscle size (hypertrophy).

Heavy reps is a specific RE designation. It means to train with a heavy resistance that allows for the completion of 6 to 10 repetitions, typically 0 to 3 repetitions short of failure, to develop general strength and muscle size (myofibrillar).

High reps is a specific RE designation. It means to train with a moderate resistance that allows for the completion of 10 to 20 repetitions, typically 0 to 5 or more repetitions short of failure, to develop noncontractile hypertrophy (sarcoplasmic) or muscle conditioning.

Skill, Biomechanics and Physiology of Strength Training

Every exercise, test or display of strength or power is a distinct motor skill. Some exercises have more generality (i.e., they have aspects in common or transfer to other exercises or performance variables) although other exercises may be specific or have less transfer.[5] For example, simple strength-training exercises such as the squat, bench press and chin-up correlate well to basic sport tasks such as sprinting, jumping and paddling or to the achievement level in sports.

The manifestation of strength physiologically depends on muscle morphology factors and neural factors. The muscle morphology factors include muscle size, fibre type, pennation angles, leverage factors and so on. Neural factors include increased integrated myoelectrical activity (IEMG), motor unit synchronisation and enhanced coordination of the neural signals from contributing muscles (i.e., skill learning).[5-7]

The large initial gains in strength exhibited by novices are mainly attributed to neural and skill adaptations and would appear more pronounced in compound exercises of the lower body, such as the squat and leg press, compared to less-complex exercises. Essentially, the athlete is learning to perform the skill more effectively. The more complex the skill, the longer this process lasts and the greater the strength change that is manifested.[6, 7]

Wisdom

The neural adaptation will last longer and be more pronounced with full squats than it will with less-complex exercises such as leg extensions, especially for those athletes beginning their strength-training journey or resuming the sport after a lengthy layoff.

Every repetition can be seen as a trial for motor learning. The larger the number of trials, the greater the learning capacity. Therefore, more repetitions with resistances that are not unduly difficult to lift would appear to be the necessary prescription for novice athletes first embarking on their resistance-training journey. These resistances allow the greatest number of trials for motor skill learning; they are also the most effective for muscle hypertrophy in the initial to intermediate stages of adaptation.

The mechanisms of increasing strength through neural and morphological adaptations are theoretically easily rationalised in the early stages of training. Greater numbers of repetitions mean more trials for learning, and higher-volume loads (of a certain minimal intensity) build muscle more effectively. But it is not always the simple solution of more repetitions to learn the skill. Sometimes the skills are more complex and need a graduated learning progression.

Let's look at a few examples of learning exercises in stages that suit biomechanical and skill factors. The deadlift from the floor is a fine exercise for the development of MS and ES, but generally speaking it is far too complex to be taught to developing athletes. Typically, they lack the basic strength and body control to get into the proper starting position or maintain good mechanics during the lift.

Young athletes should develop strength in body-weight squats with soft resistances, such as sand bags and rubber bands, and use torso-bracing plank variations before learning the following deadlift progression. After the preparation provided by planks and squats, athletes should follow a top-down progression to learn the deadlift, using minimal resistance. Start at the top by lowering the barbell to just above the knee (learning the flat back or hip hinge exercise), then to just below the knee; progress to mid shin and then finally to deadlift from the floor. There will also be some progression in resistance, but the primary emphasis is on range of motion (ROM) and technique.

Wisdom

The time frame for working through skill progressions is based on technical progressions made by the athlete. Can he or she safely and with sound technique progress in ROM first and resistance second? If not, the athlete doesn't progress. This may be the case for very tall athletes. Their floor deadlifts may actually be from pins in a power rack or from blocks in order for them to be able to perform the lift with effective and safe technique.

The same top-down method of teaching and progressing exercise skills is seen with the Olympic weight-lifting exercise variations. For example, the progressions for learning the hang power clean include the

- isometric shrug,
- dynamic shrug from mid-thigh,
- power shrug from just above the knee,
- power shrug jump from just above the knee, and finally
- hang power clean.

This is a specific sequence of exercise progressions that build the skill and motor patterns of one exercise into the next (i.e., the concept of chaining and shaping smaller skills into a larger, more complex skill). The progression through this sequence can be quiet short (minutes), or it could take months, depending on when the athlete can complete each component with good mechanics.

The technically more complex Olympic weightlifting lifts can be introduced later in an athlete's lifting career. Strength can be developed easily through simple body-weight exercises that progress into simple barbell exercises, although power can be developed easily with simple jumps and throws that progress into heavier weighted jumps and throws.[8]

Wisdom

Olympic lifts will be much more effective once basic levels of strength and power have already been developed by simpler means.

Furthermore, Olympic lifts also require lower numbers of repetitions (1 to 5) to maintain velocity and avoid skill decrement. Beginners need higher numbers of repetitions to develop basic motor skills and muscle size!

Consider the following points: The mechanics of a lift will change as body size (i.e., height, mass and girth) varies across an athlete's career. The path the barbell takes through the ROM of a lift changes as the athlete gets stronger and as resistance lifted approaches 1RM. Thus, maintaining technical training and ensuring that proper biomechanics are maintained will be on-going concerns during an athlete's strength training journey, not just at the beginning.

Can an Athlete Ever Be Strong Enough?

This is a common question. The simple answer is you can't be too strong, but you can incorrectly apportion your training content in favour of increasing strength when training other avenues may prove more fruitful in improving sport performance. For example, a young shot-putter with an incline bench press 1RM of 75 kilograms throws a shot representing a resistance of about 20 per cent (7 kg shot × 2 hands = 14 kg when compared to the incline press strength). Because the athlete has a relatively low level of strength for a shot-putter, strength will increase fairly easily with dedicated training, and a commensurate increase in throwing distance should result. Over time, when the 1RM equals 150 kilograms, the resistance of the shot now represents only 10 per cent 1RM, and the shot-putter now has reduced the disadvantage that existed when he or she was less strong. But from this high level of strength, further gains become increasingly harder to attain. If the shot-putter works hard to train strength for another 5 years to attain 175-kilogram incline press 1RM, the shot now represents 8.6 per cent, or little change from the 10 per cent when the strength level was 150 kilogram.

What if the athlete had neglected throwing speed, technique and mobility work to increase strength during this time? Would the hard-fought increase in strength really yield an advantage in throwing performance if other training factors were ignored or not respected in the training regime? If the athlete had neglected throwing drills and movement speed, mobility exercises and technique work and so on just to pursue a higher 1RM score in a few lifts, then his or her performance may not have actually increased. If the shot-put performance did not improve, it would not be because the athlete was too strong, but rather because training had been imbalanced in content. If, however, the athlete had been smart and well coached, he or she would not have neglected the other aspects of training that also contribute to performance; as a result, the athlete's new strength levels could be transferred, to some degree, to throwing.

It is vital to remember that sport performance reflects a summation of factors—strength, speed, endurance, mobility, skill, tactics, mental toughness and so on—and we should not neglect others to improve just one aspect.

Another common saying is that an athlete's muscles are too strong compared to the antagonist muscles. For example, a sprinter's quadriceps are sometimes labelled too strong for the hamstrings or a swimmer's shoulder internal rotators too strong for the shoulder external rotators, scapula retractors and stabilisers. This muscular strength imbalance results primarily through usage over time in a dominant movement pattern. A better way to look at these situations is to identify the antagonists as being not strong enough to cope with the forces now generated by the dominant muscles in the competitive-movement pattern. A number of studies have shown that increasing the strength of weaker antagonist muscles actually results in increased limb-movement speed.[9] This finding also has applications in injury prevention. We should not neglect the strengthening of the agonists but rather emphasise programming towards increasing the strength of the relevant antagonist musculature.

So the question from sport athletes is not really 'Can I be too strong?' but rather 'What level of strength do I need to have to attain a high level of performance in my sport?' If that level of strength is not yet attained, continue to prioritise it. If the athlete has attained the seeming prerequisite strength levels for his or her sport, then the question is 'Will any further large gains in strength benefit performance?' If yes, again continue to prioritise strength training. If no, then maintain strength training content in proper balance with other factors, and prioritise the factors that will now lead to improved sport performance.

Athletes have many training necessities but only limited time and energy, so the coach must make judicious decisions regarding the total training content. Strength training should remain part of the total regime, but it may play a lesser role compared to endurance, skill and tactical training, as well as recovery for some athletes.

Wisdom

Are the athlete's strength levels in balance with those of the highest performers in the sport, and are the athlete's strength levels in appropriate balance within his or her body? Plan total training content according to the answers and the needs of the sport.

Analysing the Needs of the Sport and the Individual

In competitive powerlifting and Olympic weightlifting, maximal strength is the major determinant of success for competitors. Other competitive lifting sports such as strongman, kettlebell lifting and Basque stone lifting also require not only high levels of maximal strength, but also SE because the nature of these competitions is often to lift certain loads for a maximal number of repetitions or distance in specified time periods. These sports are relatively easy to analyse, but most other sports rely on a number of factors for success: strength, speed, endurance, mobility, skill, tactics, mental toughness and so on.

An analysis of strength programs shows that coaches are influenced by a number of broad philosophies such as the body-part method (influence from bodybuilding), control-and-stability method (influence from physical therapy and Pilates), body-weight training (influence from gymnastics and martial arts), energy-system or heart rate method (influence from circuit training) and strength-sport methods (influence from weightlifting, powerlifting and strongman). There are limitations to these methods, and any of these methods in isolation cannot fully develop the many strength qualities needed for sport. A better approach is to consider the movement and forces that athletes in a sport experience and prescribe training accordingly. Therefore, a movement and forces (resistance) analysis of the sport is necessary.

Analyse the sport. What are the dominant movements? What are the forces experienced? What are the best methods of training to develop the ability to apply force in these sport movements? Be sport relevant and athlete specific and give consideration to long-term athletic development.

Strength-Gain Programming for Developing Athletes

An athlete's training career can span 15 years or more, and naturally, the strength-training needs and content will vary during that time. Athletes undertake strength training to improve the following objectives or strength qualities:

- Body and limb control and joint stability
- General strength and muscle size
- Maximal strength
- Explosive strength and power
- Strength endurance

Although certain sports may require more of a certain strength quality than other strength qualities, there still exists a distinct hierarchical relationship with these objectives. With consideration to these objectives, a long-term model for resistance training, with clear pathways, objectives and content for each stage, is depicted in table 10.2 for MS and in table 10.3 for ES and P, respectively.

Wisdom

Developing athletes should have the objectives of improving body (limb) control and joint stability and then starting to develop the appropriate muscle size and general strength appropriate for the sport.

Developing athletes should begin their resistance-training journey with modified body-weight exercises performed for higher repetitions (or longer isometric holds where appropriate) such as ≥15 repetitions for 6 to 9 years of age, ≥12 for 9 to 12 years and ≥8 to 10 for 12 to 15 years. The programme should be developed around a few basic exercises, such as push-ups, pull-ups (body rows), squats, split-leg exercises (lunges, step-ups), torso stability and torso flexion and rotation exercises to improve muscle function and stability in fundamental movement patterns.[10] Table 10.4 outlines such a programme.

These basic body-weight exercises can be modified to decrease or increase the level of difficulty via the following methods:

- Alter the leverage factors.
- Alter the ROM.
- Alter the plane of movement.
- Alter the stability demands.
- Add more soft resistance to the movement.
- Use single-limb variations of these movements.[10]

Table 10.5 displays six body-weight tests, with a 0 to 5 scoring system that may be used to determine if a youth has a minimum competency in controlling and moving his or her body weight and is therefore ready to progress to more barbell-oriented training. Developing athletes should progress to heavier, barbell-oriented training only when they can display basic levels of competence in some body-weight tests.[10]

The goal of the next phase (stage 3) of training for the developing athlete, typically around the early to mid-teenage years, is to pursue general strength and muscle-size training through basic barbell exercises such as the squat; Romanian-style deadlift progressions; lunge; overhead press; bench press; bent-over row; and pull-down, pull-up or chin-up. Initially, in this phase the repetition demands remain moderate to high (e.g., 18-15 reps) to help develop not only muscle mass but also the necessary refinement of motor patterns in the basic barbell exercises that will remain the mainstay of the athlete's resistance-training career.

For ES and P training, progression through the stages runs in tandem with, but slightly behind,

Table 10.2 Long-Term Athletic Development (LTAD) Plan for Strength Development

Stage	Objective	Content
1. Introduction to body-weight strength training, pt.1	Learn to develop force not only to overcome but mainly to control the limbs and stabilise the body during basic movements through body-weight and modified body-weight exercises. Focus on technique and control.	For young athletes (6-9 yrs old), use simple exercises that allow for 15 reps or more × 1 or 2 sets. For children 9-12 yrs old, use exercises that allow for 10-15 reps × 1-3 sets. For youth 12-15 yrs old, use exercises that allow for 8-15 reps × 1-3 sets. Focus on multijoint body-weight exercises such as the squat, single-leg exercises (e.g., step-up, lunge, single-leg squat), push-up, pull-up and torso exercises. Resistance is garnered from body-weight and modified body-weight exercises and soft resistance, such as through using bands, medicine balls and sand tubes or bags.
2. Introduction to body-weight training, pt. 2	Continue to develop overcoming, control and stability force using more difficult body-weight and modified body-weight exercises.	Use more difficult variations of the stage 1 exercises that allow for only 6-12 reps × 1-4 sets. More use of soft resistance. Testing of body-weight competency will show when it is appropriate to move to the next level.
3. Introduction to barbell training for general strength and hypertrophy	Once competency of body-weight control has been developed, it is necessary or appropriate to induce a greater overload, principally from barbell training. Overload is developed mainly via squatting, deadlifting and pressing exercises. Other barbell, dumbbell, cable and body-weight exercises must also be performed to maintain strength and muscle balance, induce appropriate levels of hypertrophy and generally strengthen the musculoskeletal system as relevant to the individual and sport.	Introduction of barbell versions of basic strength exercises such as the squat, appropriate deadlift variations, bench press, overhead press using a periodised approach working from 10-12 reps (circa 60%-75% of the estimated 1RM) down to 5 or 6 reps (circa 80%-85% of the estimated 1RM) across the multiweek training cycle. Assistant strength exercises, such as single-leg exercises, other pressing variations, dumbbell exercises, pull-downs and rows, are introduced, perhaps using a slightly higher rep range (8-20 reps) to induce hypertrophy. Important body-weight exercises such as pull-ups, push-ups and torso-strength exercises continue to be performed.
4. Maximal-strength training	Maximise strength by use of even heavier resistances in the key strength exercises.	Use more doses of lower numbers of reps (1-5 reps at 80%-100% 1RM) and ME training in the key strength exercises in a traditional or wave-like periodised manner. General strength and hypertrophy continue to be developed with heavy reps (6-10 reps at 65%-85% 1RM). Add other exercises as required for the individual or sport.
5. Advanced maximal-strength training	Maximise strength by more regular use of heavier resistances in the key strength exercises plus introduce and use accommodating resistances such as bands and chains for maximal strength.	As in stage 4 but an increased use of accommodating resistances such as bands and chains for maximal strength. Greater use of specific techniques where appropriate (e.g., drop sets for hypertrophy, explosive-strength training with Olympic weightlifting lifts). Periodisation may be traditional, wave-like conjugate or modified conjugate.
6. Elite maximal-strength training	Maintain high levels of maximal strength and be able to peak maximal and explosive strength for important competitions.	As in stage 5 but more specific to the individual needs and sport or seasonal requirements. Generally less volume is needed.

Table 10.3 Long-Term Athletic Development (LTAD) Plan for Explosive Strength and Power Development

Stage	Objective	Content
1. Introduction to power training	Learn to develop force rapidly, accelerate and safely decelerate.	Paused rep body-weight jumps, hops and medicine ball throws; in-place jumps before horizontal hops.
2. Speed power training	Learn to do exercises explosively and repetitively.	Same exercises as stage 1 but with no pauses between reps. Add barbell jump squats and bench press throws when ready. Use resistances up to 20% 1RM as skill increases.
3. Ballistic power training	Increase power via increased resistance. Emphasise rapid speed of movement with heavier resistances.	Barbell jump squats and bench press throws with up to 40% 1RM. Continue to use stage 2 exercises and resistances.
4a. Power training A	Maximise power by use of even heavier resistances.	Barbell jump squats and bench press throws with 40%-60% 1RM. Continue to use stage 3 exercises and resistances.
4b. Power training B	Introduce simple power versions of weightlifting exercises.	Power shrug jumps, pulls and push presses. Emphasise speed and technique. Continue to use stage 3 exercises and resistances.
5a. Explosive strength training A	Introduce kinetically altered strength exercises that entail faster lifting speeds.	Squats, bench presses, deadlifts and others at 50%-75% 1RM with added resistance from bands and chains (10%-20% 1RM or more). Continue to use stage 4 exercises and resistances.
5b. Explosive strength training B	Introduce power clean from hang or boxes above knee.	Lighter to medium resistances (50%-85% 1RM). Emphasise speed and technique. Continue to use stage 4 exercises and resistances.
6. Heavy Olympic weightlifting	Introduce heavier weightlifting exercise versions.	Power cleans from floor, hang, or boxes; snatches; jerks; and others up 100% 1RM if athlete and sport relevant. Continue to use stage 5 exercises and resistances.

Table 10.4 Basic Body-Weight Training Program Appropriate for Teenage Athletes

Each superset (paired exercises A and B) starts every 3 minutes. The entire session takes 27 minutes plus warm-up time.

Exercise	Sets × reps
1A. Push-up variation	3 × 10-15
1B. Pull-up variation	3 × 10-15
2A. Split-leg variation	3 × 10-15 each side
2B. Squat variation	3 × 10-15
3A. Plank variation	3 × 30-60 sec
3B. Sit-up variation	3 × 10-15

From D. Baker, 2007, *Progressing the difficulty of body-weight exercises for child and youth resistance training*, DVD published by the Australian Strength and Conditioning Association, Beenleigh, Queensland, Australia.

strength levels and training experience. The reason is that developing force or strength always underpins explosive use of that force, and ES and P are highly correlated with MS.[4, 8]

Strength-Gain Programming for Intermediate Athletes

Intermediate-level athletes need to make greater improvements in MS, ES and P because once they enter the elite-athlete phase, little time may exist to drastically improve any physical parameters due to a much busier competition schedule and more time devoted to skill and tactical training.

For example, barbell variations of horizontal-pressing exercises such as incline press, narrow-grip bench press, floor bench press and various dumbbell bench press variations also start to be included alongside the bench press. A greater variety of exercise is the simplest method to avoid or break through progress plateaus that inevitably come with increased training experience.

Intense training brings with it the introduction of periodised strength training, which is the methodical cycling of training intensity and volume across time. Periodising the training stress

Table 10.5 Youth Body-Weight Testing Table

This is a rating system to assess the physical competency of youth athletes. If an athlete cannot score at least 18 points for the six tests, then he or she may not be ready to progress to heavier barbell-oriented resistance training. More body-weight and soft-resistance training may be warranted. M = male, F = female.

Exercise	5 points	4 points	3 points	2 points	1 point	0 points
Push-up	M, 35 or more F, 20 or more	M, 28-34 F, 15-19	M, 20-27 F, 10-14	M, 10-19 F, 5-9	M, 3-9 F, 1-4	M, less than 3 F, 0
Pull-up, underhand grip	M, 12 or more F, 6 or more	M, 9-11 F, 4 or 5	M, 6-8 F, 3	M, 4 or 5 F, 2	M, 1-3 F, 1	M, 0 F, 0
Full squat, number in 60 sec, with 10% body weight held on chest	M and F, 40 or more	M and F, 33-39	M and F, 26-32	M and F, 19-25	M and F, 11-18	M and F, <10
Single-leg full squat, stand on a box, average of both legs	M and F, 5 or more	M and F, 4	M and F, 3	M and F, 2	M and F, 1	M and F, 0
Front hover hold, arms straight (sec)	M and F, >121	M and F, 90-120	M and F, 60-90	M and F, 30-60	M and F, 10-30	M and F, <10
Twisting sit-up, number in 60 sec	M and F, ≥40	M and F, 33-39	M and F, 26-32	M and F, 19-25	M and F, 11-18	M and F, <10

From D. Baker, 2007, *Progressing the difficulty of body-weight exercises for child and youth resistance training*, DVD published by the Australian Strength and Conditioning Association, Beenleigh, Queensland, Australia.

is the second method employed to overcome training plateaus.

Wisdom

Strength testing is important for periodised intensity prescription; however, if athletes do not know their 1RM, the Epley formula (1RM = [weight lifted × number of reps × 0.0333] + weight lifted) has proven to be a useful method of estimating 1RM.

Although certain percentages of 1RM are traditionally used in intensity prescription, other methods based on effort are also used. These include performing sets to maximal effort (ME), near-maximal effort (NME), hard effort (HE), medium-hard effort (MHE), dynamic effort (DE) and repetitive effort (RE) (explained previously). Essentially, the coach must decide which method (% 1RM or effort prescription or both) suits his or her philosophy of training or best suits the intermediate-level athletes being trained.

Intermediates with more experience may also be exposed to kinetic variations, such as bands, chains and functional isometrics, and other more advanced techniques to help overcome plateaus in progress.

With regard to ES and P training, intermediate athletes need to ascertain their sport requirements. If they require ES to move large resistances quickly, such an opponent's body mass in collision football and grappling sports, or large implements, such as in rowing or track and field throwing, then progress must also be made in developing technique in the Olympic weightlifting exercises (e.g., snatch, clean and jerk variations). If the sport's fast-force demands are such that moving the athlete's own body mass is the main requirement, then loaded jump squats and plyometrics may become the primary method of ES and P training content rather than heavy Olympic weightlifting exercises.

Strength-Gain Programming for Elite Athletes

Generally, elite athletes have already developed the appropriate levels of MS, ES and P to successfully compete in their sports during their intermediate-athlete stage. At the elite level they are concerned with peaking or maintaining these qualities according to the nature of their competition. However, that not all elite athletes are advanced in their strength-training progressions, and an improved strength-training programme may still provide a method of further sport-performance enhancement even at the highest levels.

Although the periodisation of training is discussed in detail in chapter 18, certain elements are worth considering here. The major considerations for the elite athlete are predicated upon whether he or she is in a peaking sport (e.g., swimming, track and field), a weekly fixture sport (e.g., American football, basketball) or a tournament sport (e.g., tennis, golf, volleyball, surfing).

Elite athletes in peaking sports can have long resistance-training cycles with high workloads a few months out from competition and gradually taper the volume and increase the intensity to allow for a super-compensatory peak performance at the major competition.

However, athletes in weekly fixture sports must be concerned with competing 1 or 2 times per week for seasons of 30 weeks or more; rarely do they perform high strength-training workloads during their long season, as high workloads will have an immediate negative effect on sport performance (i.e., the weekly match). The major consideration is to maintain MS, ES and P levels as close to their preparation-period levels with a workload that minimises interference with sport performance and other important training factors such as speed, endurance, skill and tactical training. Strength training should never be neglected in weekly fixture sports, given the strong relationships between MA, ES and P and success in collision (football) sports and between lower-body relative strength and sprinting and jumping performance.

The other major considerations for elite athletes are the nature and extent of MS, ES and P adaptations consequent to many years of training. The stark reality is that large improvements are difficult for experienced strength trainers to achieve after 4 to 7 years of intense training, and small improvements in strength may actually take many years to manifest.[11, 12] Consequently, elite athletes need to consider embracing an aggressive approach to in-competition maintenance training and to consider embracing the use of alternative resistance methods such as the use of bands and chains. Even a 1 to 2 per cent improvement across the entire preparation period can be seen as worthwhile for elite athletes.

Use of Bands and Chains

The use of bands and chains to augment barbell resistance is becoming increasingly common in the strength training of athletes seeking enhanced MS, ES and P. Traditional barbell training is predicated upon the resistance that can be lifted through the weakest portion of the lift, typically undertraining the strong portions of the lift such as the lockout. Bands and chains add resistance to the top portion of lift where strength is greater. This is known as *accommodating resistance*: bands or chains that accommodate to the strength curve.

For example, heavy chains are draped over a lighter supporting chain that is itself draped over the sleeves of the barbell. When the barbell is at its lowest point of the range, the heavy chain links are furled on the floor, and their weight is not acting on the barbell. As the barbell moves upward in its range, the heavy chain links unfurl off the floor and begin to add their weight to the barbell. Therefore, at the lockout of the lift, the total resistance is equivalent to the barbell mass and the weight of the chains (see figures 10.1 and 10.2).

An alternative method to achieve accommodating resistance is through the use of one or more latex rubber bands that are anchored from below and looped over the barbell. As the barbell moves through its ROM, there is an increased stretch on the band, which in turn imparts an increasing force to the barbell. Therefore, the total resistance is equivalent to the barbell mass and stretch force exerted by the band (see figures 10.3 and 10.4).

The use of bands and chains is not a fad. Using a barbell with additional band resistance has been demonstrated to be more effective than traditional barbell training alone in improving strength and power in experienced athletes.[13] Other studies have found that supplementing a portion of the total resistance during barbell training with band or chain resistance is extremely effective during ES and P training since it allows for greater power output during the initial portion of the concentric portion of the lift.[14, 15]

Differences Between Bands and Chains

Chains have mass and can be accelerated like any weight. Bands, however, can be accelerated to a certain point where the resistance they

Figure 10.1 The bench press with added chain resistance. When the barbell is at the chest, the links of heavier chains draped over the light supporting chains are furled on the floor, and their weight is not acting on the barbell.

Figure 10.2 As the barbell moves through its range, the heavy chain links unfurl from the floor, and their weight is progressively added to that of the barbell's resistance.

Figure 10.3 The full squat performed with added band resistance. When the barbell is at the lowest position, the bands are slack and impart little or no additional resistance.

Figure 10.4 Just before lockout, the bands are imparting a large stretch resistance, which is added to the barbell resistance to garner the total resistance experienced by the athlete. This additional stretch resistance has come on gradually from just after the lowest squat position.

impart is fairly equal to the force exerted by the athlete. After this point true acceleration may not exist. In effect, bands can make a barbell exercise behave a little like a semi-isokinetic lift in certain parts of the ROM. Neither is better—both chains and bands provide accommodating resistance—but each affects the kinematics of the lifts slightly differently. When chains clear the floor, they can wobble slightly, challenging proprioceptive stability; bands can provide a little more stability since they provide an extra anchor for the barbell to the floor. All these factors need to be taken into account if the coach decides to integrate the use of bands and chains into the strength program.

Studies have shown that for the use of bands and chains to render a significant adaptation in strength and power, they must exert a force equivalent to at least 10 per cent 1RM during the lift.[15] It has been posited that forces equivalent to 15 to 20 per cent may be more effective because it is argued that this level of force causes a postactivation potentiation (PAP) effect within the repetition.[16] What this intrarepetition PAP means is, for example, if an athlete takes a barbell loaded with 85 per cent 1RM barbell mass plus 15 per cent in chains or bands from the rack for bench pressing, the muscular system senses that it requires the neural drive to lift the entire 100 per cent 1RM. However, when the barbell is lowered to the bottom of the range, the chain or band resistance deloads, and the resistance is now equivalent to 85 per cent. There is surplus neural drive to lift this resistance, resulting in an explosive initiation of the lift.

Determining Resistance With Bands and Chains

The exact resistance that bands may exert during a lift may be determined by setting up an empty barbell with the bands attached and placing the barbell on a digital scale that itself has been placed on boxes so that it is at the same height as will occur during the lift. Merely subtract the barbell mass from the digital scale reading to determine the amount of force the bands are exerting at that point in the range.

When trying to determine the barbell resistance to use for strength training with bands or chains, the process is fairly simple. The exact band or chain resistance is determined for the bottom and top portion of a lift, and the sum of these two figures is averaged. For example, if an athlete wanted to train at a 5RM-level with bands and the standard (nonband) 5RM is 100 kilograms, the athlete has to subtract the average band resistance from the 100 kilograms. So if the bands exert zero resistance at the bottom and 22.5 kilograms at the lockout, the average of these figures is 11.25 kilograms. The athlete needs to reduce the barbell from 100 kilograms to either 90 or 87.5 kilograms. Table 10.6 details the range of resistances that the most popular sizes of bands and chains provide.

Table 10.7 outlines the last 8 weeks of a preparation-period cycle for increasing 1RM bench press strength in elite field-sport athletes. Note the integration of bands and chains into the cycle and how resistance is varied throughout the range. When bands and chains are used,

Table 10.6 Resistance Garnered by Various Sizes of Bands and Chains

Chain-link diameter	Kg/m	2 × 1.5 m lengths
8 mm	1.35-1.5 kg	4.0-4.5 kg
10 mm	2.1-2.3 kg	6.5-7.0 kg
13 mm	3.8-4.0 kg	11.5-12.0 kg
16 mm	5.5-5.7 kg	16.5-17.1 kg
1m band	4.5 mm thick	5 mm thick
#1 = 12.7 mm wide	Up to 12.5 kg/band	Up to 15 kg/band
#2 = 20.6 mm wide	Up to 20 kg/band	Up to 23 kg/band
#3 = 28.6 mm wide	Up to 30 kg/band	Up to 35 kg/band
#4 = 44.4 mm wide	Up to 50 kg/band	Up to 60 kg/band

From D. Baker, 2010, *How to use bands and chains*, DVD published by Dan Baker, www.danbakerstrength.com.

the resistance can be analysed as being the minimum (bottom of range), maximal (top of range) and mean resistance. So whilst the mean resistance during weeks 2 to 4 toggles between 85 and 92 per cent 1RM, the lockout resistance that the athletes experience is close to 100 per cent every week!

The basic prescription for using bands and chains is the following:

MS: Use 70 to 90 per cent 1RM plus 10 to 25 per cent band or chain resistance × 1 to 5 reps, ME or NME.

ES: Use 50 to 70 per cent 1RM plus 10 to 25 per cent band or chain resistance × 2 to 5 reps.

Adding bands and chains to the barbell should be reserved for experienced intermediate- and elite-level athletes who have solid lifting technique. Introducing bands and chains into the training program should occur according to the progression models outlined in tables 10.2 and 10.3. Furthermore, some basic linear periodised strength programming (tables 10.8 and 10.9) should also precede the introduction of any advanced training strategy such as accommodating-resistance modalities. Athletes should also know their 5RM and 3RM (and therefore have an estimate of 1RM if it is not known) before starting to use bands or chains, so that calculations of training weights can be made, using either the effort method or the percentage 1RM method.

Wisdom

It is better to use jumps, throws, plyometrics and so on for the development of power. Save bands and chains for maximal effort and explosive strength.

Table 10.7 Sample Integration of Band and Chain Resistance Into the Bench Press Undulating Periodised Maximal Strength Cycle of an Elite Field-Sport Athlete

For weeks 2 to 7, 3 training sets (excluding lighter warm-up sets) are performed in an ascending manner, working up to a ME set of either 5RM or 3RM with either additional band resistance (weeks 2 and 3), additional chain resistance (weeks 4 and 5) or standard barbell resistance (weeks 6 and 7). The resistance can be viewed as the barbell portion (for the bottom of the lift) and band and chain portion to garner a total resistance at lockout. The mean resistance is also monitored to observe progression.

	Week 1	Week 2	Week 3	Week 4	Week 5	Week 6	Week 7	Week 8
Sets × reps	3 × 10 at 67%	3 × 5 + #2 band >5RM	3 × 3 + #2 band >3RM	3 × 5 + chains >5RM	3 × 3 + chains >3RM	3 × 5 >5RM	3 × 3 >3RM	Test new 1RM
Barbell mass kg and % 1RM*	96.2 kg 66.9%	110.4 kg 76.8%	118.6 kg 82.5%	113.6 kg 79.1%	122.1 kg 85.0%	128.8 kg 89.6%	135.4 kg 94.2%	145.4 kg 101.2%
Top resistance and % 1RM	96.2 kg 66.9%	132.9 kg 92.5%	141.1 kg 98.2%	131.1 kg 91.2%	139.6 kg 97.1%	128.8 kg 89.6%	135.4 kg 94.2%	
Mean resistance and % 1RM	96.2 kg 66.9%	121.7 kg 83.7%	129.9 kg 89.3%	122.4 kg 84.1%	130.9 kg 90.0%	128.8 kg 89.6%	135.4 kg 94.2%	

*Of previous 1RM of 143.8 kg.

Table 10.8 Methods of Intensity Progression Using Linear Progression Across an 8-Week Period

Classification	Week 1	Week 2	Week 3	Week 4	Week 5	Week 6	Week 7	Week 8
Basic 1	3 × 12-15	3 × 12-15	3 × 10-12	3 × 10-12	3 × 8-10	3 × 8-10	3 × 6-8	3 × 6-8
Basic progression 2	3 × 10-12	3 × 10-12	3 × 8-10	3 × 8-10	3 × 6-8	3 × 6-8	3 × 4-6	3 × 4-6*
Intermediate 1	3 × 10 at 63%	3 × 10 at 67%	3 × 8 at 71%	3 × 8 at 75%	3 × 6 at 79%	3 × 6 at 83%	3 × 5 at 85%	3 × 5* at 87%
Intermediate progression 2 (block)	3 × 10 at 63%	3 × 10 at 67%	3 × 10 at 71%	3 × 5 at 79%	3 × 5 at 83%	3 × 5 at 87%	3 × 3 at 91%	3 × 3* at 93%

*Use maximal effort, do as many reps as possible on the last set and recalculate 1RM from this ME set. Actual 1RM testing can take place in week 9 if desired.

Tables 10.9 Wave-Like Progression Across an 8-Week Period

	STRENGTH (HYPERTROPHY) EXERCISES							
Classification	Week 1	Week 2	Week 3	Week 4	Week 5	Week 6	Week 7	Week 8
Advanced 1 Key MS	3 × 8 at 70%	8-6-5 at 70%-75%-80%	6-5-3* at 72%-80%-88%	5-3-2* at 80%-88%-92%	3 × 8 at 70%	8-6-5 at 70%-75%-80%	6-5-3* at 74%-82%-90%	5-3-2* at 82%-90%-94%
Advanced 2 Key MS	3 × 8 at 70%	5-5-5 at 70%-75%-80%	3-3-3* at 72%-80%-88%	2-2-2* at 80%-88%-92%	3 × 8 at 70%	5-5-5 at 70%-75%-80%	3-3-3* at 74%-82%-90%	2-2-2* at 82%-90%-94%
Assistance strength	3 ×10 at 65%	3 × 8 at 72.5%	3 × 6* at 80%	2 × 5* at 85%	3 × 10 at 65%	3 × 8 at 72.5%	3 × 6* at 80%	2 × 5* at 85%
Muscle size	3 × 12-16	3 × 12-16	3 × 8-10	3 × 8-10	3 × 10-12	3 × 10-12	3 × 6-8	3 × 6-8
	ES AND P EXERCISES							
Classification	Week 1	Week 2	Week 3	Week 4	Week 5	Week 6	Week 7	Week 8
Power, jump squats and bench throws	3 × 5 at 40%-60% of relevant MS training weight	3 × 5 at 40%-60% of relevant MS training weight	3 × 4 at 40%-60% of MS training weight	3 × 3 at 40%-60% of MS training weight	3 × 5 at 40%-60% of relevant MS training weight	3 × 5 at 40%-60% of relevant MS training weight	3 × 4 at 40%-60% of MS training weight	3 × 3 at 40%-60% of MS training weight
Key ES	3 × 8 at 55%	3 × 6 at 60%	3 × 5 at 65%	3 × 4 at 70%	3 × 7 at 60%	3 × 5 at 65%	3 × 4 at 70%	3 × 3 at 75%
Key Olympic weightlifting	3 × 5 at 70%	5-5-5 at 70%-75%-80%	3-3-3* at 72%-80%-88%	2-2-2* at 80%-88%-92%	3 × 5 at 70%	5-5-5 at 70%-75%-80%	3-3-3* at 74%-82%-90%	2-2-2* at 82%-90%-94%

*Use maximal effort, do as many reps as possible on the last set and recalculate 1RM from this ME set.

Programming Templates

Even with all the theoretical knowledge of training, a coach still needs to write an effective programme that is sport relevant and athlete specific or appropriate. An easy way to conceptualise such a programme is to have basic templates from which to develop sport-relevant and athlete-appropriate programs.

Exercise-Category Templates

Exercises can be chosen from category templates such as MS, ES, P or general exercise categories for strength and muscle size. Sometimes it is the reps, sets, per cent 1RM and rest period that determine the effects and therefore the category of an exercise. For other situations the biomechanical nature of the exercise determines its classification. For example, bench press performed for 3 sets × 3 repetitions at 90 per cent 1RM, 3 sets × 3 repetitions at 70 per cent 1RM and 3 sets × 10 repetitions at 70 per cent 1RM would designate this exercise for the development of MS, ES and general strength or size, respectively. However Olympic weightlifting

exercises are always ES exercises, and jumps and throws are always P exercises. Having a number of effective exercises in each exercise category to choose from and rotate in and out of a program when appropriate makes programming simpler.

Strength-Day and Power-Day Templates

A simple method of programming is to design a training day directed towards MS and muscle-size training (also known as ME day) and another day emphasising ES and P (also known as DE day). This is a simple template to follow, where exercise variations can be selected from the exercise categories, slotted in or out and coupled with the appropriate sets, reps and per cent 1RM. This programme approach is shown in table 10.10.

Exercise-Order Templates

A simple template for developing programs is to create agonist–antagonist pairs for most exercises, known as the A and B system, with a set of each exercise pair to be completed within a specified

Tables 10.10 Two-Day-Per-Week Preparation Programme for Intermediate or Amateur Collision-Football Sport Athlete Using a Subtle Linear Progression Across 8 Weeks

The first day emphasises maximal strength and hypertrophy whilst the second day emphasises explosive strength and power. These differences are achieved through exercise selection and the prescription of sets × repetitions × intensity. All exercises start on a 4-minute turnaround.

Exercise	DAY 1: MAXIMAL STRENGTH AND HYPERTROPHY							
	Week 1	Week 2	Week 3	Week 4	Week 5	Week 6	Week 7	Week 8
1a. Bench press	3 × 10 at 63%	3 × 10 at 67%	3 × 8 at 71%	3 × 8 at 75%	3 × 6 at 79%	3 × 6 at 83%	3 × 5 at 85%	3 × 5* at 87%
1b. Bent row	3 × 10 at 63%	3 × 10 at 67%	3 × 8 at 71%	3 × 8 at 75%	3 × 6 at 79%	3 × 6 at 83%	3 × 5 at 85%	3 × 5* at 87%
2a. Military press	3 × 10 at 63%	3 × 10 at 67%	3 × 8 at 71%	3 × 8 at 75%	3 × 6 at 79%	3 × 6 at 83%	3 × 5 at 85%	3 × 5* at 87%
2b. Chin-up	3 × 10 at 63%	3 × 10 at 67%	3 × 8 at 71%	3 × 8 at 75%	3 × 6 at 79%	3 × 6 at 83%	3 × 5 at 85%	3 × 5* at 87%
3. Romanian deadlift (RDL)	3 × 10 at 63%	3 × 10 at 67%	3 × 8 at 71%	3 × 8 at 75%	3 × 6 at 79%	3 × 6 at 83%	3 × 5 at 85%	3 × 5* at 87%
4. Squat	3 × 10 at 63%	3 × 10 at 67%	3 × 8 at 71%	3 × 8 at 75%	3 × 6 at 79%	3 × 6 at 83%	3 × 5 at 85%	3 × 5* at 87%
Exercise	DAY 2: EXPLOSIVE STRENGTH AND POWER							
	Week 1	Week 2	Week 3	Week 4	Week 5	Week 6	Week 7	Week 8
1a. Narrow-grip bench press	3 × 8 at 55%	3 × 8 at 57%	3 × 7 at 59%	3 × 7 at 61%	3 × 6 at 63%	3 × 6 at 65%	3 × 5 at 67%	3 × 5 at 69%
1b. Bench throw	3 × 6 at 30%	3 × 6 at 30%	3 × 5 at 32%	3 × 5 at 32%	3 × 4 at 34%	3 × 4 at 36%	3 × 3 at 38%	3 × 3 at 40%
2a. Push press	3 × 6 at 70%	3 × 6 at 72%	3 × 5 at 76%	3 × 5 at 78%	3 × 4 at 82%	3 × 4 at 84%	3 × 3 at 88%	3 × 3* at 90%
2b. Power shrug jump	3 × 6 at 70%	3 × 6 at 72%	3 × 5 at 76%	3 × 5 at 78%	3 × 4 at 82%	3 × 4 at 84%	3 × 3 at 88%	3 × 3* at 90%
3. Jump squat	3 × 6 at 30%	3 × 6 at 30%	3 × 5 at 32%	3 × 5 at 32%	3 × 4 at 34%	3 × 4 at 36%	3 × 3 at 38%	3 × 3 at 40%
4. Front squat	3 × 6 at 70%	3 × 6 at 72%	3 × 5 at 76%	3 × 5 at 78%	3 × 4 at 82%	3 × 4 at 84%	3 × 3 at 88%	3 × 3* at 90%

*Use maximal effort, do as many reps as possible on the last set and recalculate 1RM from this ME set.

time, such as 2, 3 or 4 minutes. The rationale for this template is that it facilitates programming balance (not excessive agonist training), promotes better recovery within the workout and maximises available time efficiently.

The same method of alternating roughly opposite movements can be seen in the intermediate program in table 10.11. Here, the upper-body movements are paired but not the heavy lower-body movements. It is difficult to effectively pair opposite movements for these key compound lower-body lifts because they essentially use all the lower-body muscles. Accordingly, when training these lifts for MS, rarely are they used in a paired A and B system.

In the paired A and B system, it is also common not to train the key upper-body MS exercises for athletes with more strength-training experience. Note in table 10.11 the bench press performed for MS is trained by itself, but other upper-body exercises are still paired as agonist–antagonist grouping.

ES and P training can be trained in agonist–antagonist pairing (e.g., alternating sets of cleans and sets of jerks) or in agonist heavy–light pairings (known as contrasting-resistance complex training). In this latter example, ES box squats and narrow-grip bench presses are alternated with light-resistance jump squats and bench throws, respectively (see table 10.12).

Table 10.11 Sample Programme Template for a Single Training Session Emphasising Upper-Body Strength and Hypertrophy

Warm-up 1 (3 min)	Mobility	Thoracic spine and hip drills, foam rolling
Warm-up 2 (6 min)	Functional ROM exercises, mobility with stability and resistance	Choose 6 bodyweight, kettlebell or band exercises × 12 reps each; attain full ROM
Maximal strength ME (4 × 4 min = 16 min)	1. Bench press	Warm-up sets: 60 kg/5 reps, 80 kg/3 reps, 100 kg/1 rep; do all 3 sets in 4 min Training sets (75%-80%-85% 1RM × 5 reps); 112.5 kg/5 reps, 120 kg/5 reps, 127.5 kg/5 reps
Heavy reps (3 × 4 min = 12 min)	2a. Incline dumbbell press 2b. Pendlay row	37.5 kg, 3 sets × 6-8 reps (about 75% 1RM) 85 kg, 3 sets × 6-8 reps (about 75% 1RM)
High reps (3 × 4 min = 12 min)	3a. Half-kneeling single-arm dumbbell overhead press 3b. Half-kneeling single-arm pull-down	22.5 kg, 3 sets × 12-15 reps each side (about 65% 1RM) 45 kg, 3 sets × 12-15 reps each side (about 65% 1RM)
Torso rotation and antirotation (2 × 4 min = 8 min)	4. Torso circuit × 2	4a. Hanging windscreen wipers × 5 reps each side 4b. Landmines 20 kg × 5 reps each side 4c. Paloff press isometric hold 30 kg × 30 sec 4d. Overhead medicine ball helicopter 5 kg × 15 sec

In summary, for lower-level athletes, training programs can be designed with paired agonist–antagonist exercises. With increased training experience, athletes cannot train the key compound lifts this way. Those lifts must be trained by themselves and with longer rest periods. However, training for general strength or muscle size can still continue with agonist–antagonist parings. ES and P training exercises may be performed by themselves, in an agonist–antagonist pairing or in agonist heavy–light pairing.

Upper or Lower Body First?

Whether the upper or lower body is trained first is not important. When dealing with large numbers of athletes and limited training resources (e.g., equipment, space) at one time, programming must be flexible. It may be that half the athletes train the upper body first, and the other half train the lower body first. If time, space and equipment are not issues, train according to priorities.

Workout-Structure Template

What should a single workout program look like? Table 10.11 depicts an exact programme template used for developing upper-body strength and hypertrophy for a single training session. The

MS exercise sets start every 4 minutes, the paired hypertrophy exercises and the four torso exercises also begin on a 4-minute cycle (i.e., both exercises are completed within 4 min). It is a simple, precise template that leaves the athlete with no doubt about what must be done.

Developing a Competitive Training Environment

It is essential that athletes, especially elite athletes, strive to improve their MS, ES and P scores and maintain data on their capabilities in various exercises in these categories. Although regular 1RM testing can occur every 6 to 12 weeks or so, in reality, training should include assessment more often. Training to NME and ME should likely occur in 2 or 3 weeks out of 4. By being regularly exposed to training ME sets, athletes become accustomed to competing with themselves and their training partners, thereby producing an intense training atmosphere.

Circuit Training and Strength Endurance

Circuit training with an emphasis on metabolic conditioning has become popular in some sections of the training community, with ensuing debate about

Table 10.12 Two-Day-Per-Week In-Season Maintenance Programme for Professional Collision-Football Sport Athlete Across 6-Week Wave-Like Cycle

All exercises start on a 4-minute turnaround. Note the progression in exercise, including technically more difficult Olympic weight-lifting exercises and using bands and chains, as well as differences in sets, reps and intensity compared to previous programmes.

DAY 1: MS AND MUSCLE SIZE						
Exercise	Week 1	Week 2	Week 3	Week 4	Week 5	Week 6
1. Bench press	3 × 8 at 70%	8-6-5 at 70%-75%-80%	3-3-3* at 72%-80%-88% chains	8-6-5 at 70%-75%-80%	5-5-5* at 73%-79%-85% bands	3-3-3* at 74%-82%-90% bands
2a. Chin-up	3 × 8 at 70%	8-6-5 at 70%-75%-80%	5-5-5* at 73%-79%-85%	8-6-5 at 70%-75%-80%	5-5-5* at 73%-79%85%	3-3-3* at 74%-82%-90%
2b. Push press	3 × 8 at 70%	8-6-5 at 70%-75%-80%	5-5-5* at 73%-79%-85%	3 × 8 at 70%	8-6-5 at 70%-75%-80%	5-5-5* at 73%-79%-85%
3a. Alternating-leg jump squat	3 × 5 each side at 40%-60%	3 × 4 each side at 40%-60%	3 × 3 each side at 40%-60%	3 × 5 each side at 40%-60%	3 × 4 each side at 40%-60%	3 × 3 each side at 40%-60%
3b. Power shrug jump	3 × 5 at 80% of power clean 1RM	4-4-4 at 80%-85%-90%	3-3-3 at 85%-92%-100%	3 × 5 at 85% of power clean 1RM	4-4-4 at 85%-90%-95%	3-3-3 at 90%-97%-105%
4. Squat	2 × 8 at 60%	8-6 at 60%-67%	6-5 at 67%-75%	8-6 at 63%-70%	6-5 at 70%-78%	5-3* at 75%-85%
DAY 2: ES/POWER						
Exercise	Week 1	Week 2	Week 3	Week 4	Week 5	Week 6
1a. Hang power clean	3 × 5 at 70%	4-4-4 at 70%-75%-80%	3-3-3* at 72%-80%-88%	3 × 5 at 75%	3-3-3* at 72%-80%-88%	2-2-2* at 80%-88%-94%
1b. Split jerk	3 × 5 at 70%	4-4-4 at 70%-75%-80%	3-3-3* at 72%-80%-88%	3 × 5 at 75%	3-3-3* at 72%-80%-88%	2-2-2* at 80%-88%-94%
2a. Box squat with bands (35 kg)	3 × 5 at 55%	3 × 4 at 60%	3 × 3 at 65%	3 × 5 at 58%	3 × 4 at 63%	3 × 3 at 68%
2b. Jump squat	3 × 5 at 35%	3 × 4 at 40%	3 × 3 at 45%	3 × 5 at 40%	3 × 3 at 45%	3 × 2 at 50%
3a. Narrow-grip bench press with bands (20 kg)	3 × 5 at 55%	3 × 4 at 60%	3 × 3 at 65%	3 × 5 at 58%	3 × 4 at 63%	3 × 3 at 68%
3b. Bench throw	3 × 5 at 30%	3 × 4 at 35%	3 × 3 at 40%	3 × 5 at 35%	3 × 4 at 40%	3 × 3 at 45%

*Use maximal effort, do as many reps as possible on the last set and recalculate 1RM from this ME set.

its appropriateness to sport training. It is essential to refer to the athlete or sport needs analysis. Would this type of training be sport relevant and athlete appropriate? In most instances it is not. High-volume training acutely depresses power output; recovery longer for this type of training, especially in stronger athletes because they lift loads of higher volume. In sports where the quality of SE may produce an advantage, it usually relates to absolute SE, which in turn depends on MS. Limit the exposure of athletes to circuit training to where it is sport relevant and athlete appropriate. Do not neglect ME, ES and P training in favour of circuit training just because SE circuit training is popular or difficult!

Nutrition Before, During and After Training in Order to Support Training Aims

The timing of dietary and supplementary input can greatly affect the effects of strength training. Even though a healthy diet is the foundation, some supplements taken around the time of the workout can enhance the response to the workout. An energy drink providing some simple carbohydrates (20-50 g), whey protein or amino acids (10-20 g) and caffeine, creatine and beta-alanine before and during a workout can improve quality and work capacity.

After the workout, another drink containing 20 to 30 grams of simple carbohydrates and 20 to 60 grams of whey protein will aid the anabolic processes. Doses of whey (faster acting) or casein (slower acting) protein at other times during the day may also aid in recovery and muscular growth.

Summary

Every athlete can benefit from strength training. It is important to consider what type of training is sport relevant and athlete specific or appropriate to benefit athletes at different stages of their careers.

CHAPTER 11

Successfully Translating Strength Into Speed

Derek M. Hansen, CSCS, BA, MASc
Simon Fraser University, British Columbia, Canada

Moving faster has been the goal of the human race since humans became bipedal. The fastest human has always held an elevated status in both ancient and modern societies. Until relatively recently it has been a widely held belief that speed was something a person was born with. As we now know, speed can be improved through good planning, coaching and careful repetition. Basic application of workloads, including repeated sprints, jumps, weightlifting and general conditioning efforts, can yield significant improvements in young, developing athletes. However, advanced sprinters and elite athletes require a much more refined approach that involves the integration of a wide variety of training elements organised in a complementary fashion.

This chapter outlines the requirements for preparing an athlete for speed development. In an optimal situation, an athlete would have adequate strength in place to undertake proper sprinting technique. However, the situation is rarely optimal, and deficiencies often need to be addressed. A good coach must be able to assess the abilities of the athletes under his or her charge and then plot out an appropriate course of action. Although many coaches believe that strength must be in place before speed can be developed, the challenge is not so simple. Various abilities must be developed concurrently to take advantage of the limited time available and allow for the natural integration of technical proficiency, coordination and strength.

Ultimately, coaching decisions will be guided by one simple question: Are athletes consistently getting faster? If athletes are not improving or if they are consistently suffering from injury, the coach must reevaluate the approach. Consistent gains in strength, power and general conditioning are always welcome, but if athletes are not getting faster, the coach will have failed in his or her assignment.

Identification of Abilities and Deficiencies

The process of engaging in a comprehensive speed-training program must always begin with an evaluation of the athlete's current physical state, as well as a discussion of training history. Understanding the entire context of the training history will ultimately determine how the coach will proceed with speed training. Making uninformed assumptions on an athlete's training will only result in problems that can sabotage the training process at a later date.

A discussion of training history with the athlete or previous coaches can be useful in determining what has been done in the past and what needs to be done for future training. A review of an athlete's training diary provides a useful means of assessing the workloads, performances and progressions followed by an athlete. If no training diary was kept, conversations with the athlete must suffice in order to accumulate valuable information on which to develop a training plan.

Formal testing can be undertaken to determine current levels of performance. However, care must be taken not to overevaluate the athlete. Although numerous tests are available to evaluate every aspect of performance, not all of these tests may be relevant to work with a particular athlete. Thus, it is important to keep the number of tests to a minimum. It does not matter how strong or explosive athletes are in isolated tests if they are not producing the results in their sport of choice.

When evaluating an athlete for the purpose of determining training requirements for speed development, the key qualities to look for are postural integrity, limb mechanics, general strength, relaxation, acceleration abilities and elastic qualities.

Postural Integrity

Holding optimal posture for starting, acceleration, maximal velocity and even speed endurance is critical for any speed athlete who is looking to maximise performance. Even though many experts claim that special exercise regimens are required to improve posture for speed development, the predominant contribution to posture, in terms of developing appropriate musculature, is from sprinting itself. Sprinting drills can be incorporated into speed workouts to improve awareness of postural requirements, similar to the exercise illustrated in figure 11.1, as well as target specific muscles used during sprinting.

The primary intent of these types of drills is to ingrain the concept of maximal hip height throughout the entire stride cycle. Poor posture typically will result in a lower vertical hip position that does not allow for powerful extension from the hips. The drill shown in figure 11.1 reinforces not only a high-hip position, but also encourages the athlete to create a direct line of force from the shoulders down to the foot at maximal plantar flexion.

Limb Mechanics

The action of the arms and legs must be coordinated in such a way as to maximise force delivery on ground contact. Athletes who do not optimally coordinate the movements of the arms and legs during the cyclical act of sprinting ultimately lose power, limit stride frequency, hamper rhythm and waste energy. As with posture, limb mechanics must be modeled and rehearsed through the application of sprinting drills and careful execution of sprinting mechanics during submaximal efforts. Like any skill, once the movement is mastered at slower velocities, greater effort can be applied to hone the technique over faster repetitions.

General Strength

General strength qualities must be developed throughout an athlete's career to assist in improvements in speed abilities. As with any movement or sport technique, there will be a point of optimal

Figure 11.1 Example of a postural running drill using an overhead medicine ball march.

strength development, as well as a point of diminishing returns. Coaches should always be determining the athlete's optimal window of strength development, without going over the top.

A good example of this concept is in the training of world class shot-putters and the use of the bench press exercise as a general indicator of preparedness. Given that the current world-record holder's (Randy Barnes) best bench press effort was just under 272 kilograms, we could argue that a world-class shot-putter should be in the range of 204 to 272 kilograms for the bench press exercise. This assumption takes into consideration an understanding that the shot put event involves a balanced combination of abilities, including speed, power, strength and technical skill. An overemphasis on strength could easily lead to diminished performance in other important elements. Thus, a goal of 363 kilograms for the bench press would not be realistic since it would require a significantly greater investment in time and energy that could negatively affect speed development and potentially result in a greater risk of injury.

The same concept would apply to 100-metre sprinters for general strength movements such as squatting or deadlifting. How much weight do world-class sprinters need to lift for these movements to improve their performance in the 100 metres? An analysis of the various world-record holders in the event over the past 30 years would reveal a wide array of lifting performances. The loads for these lifts may vary from 125 to 274 kilograms, depending on the athlete. Some top sprinters may not have even used weights in their training regime. Lower-body strength may have been achieved through resisted runs, plyometrics or explosive medicine ball throws. Often, athletes and their coaches find the optimal means of achieving strength given their specific circumstances.

Thus, the general strength requirements for sprinters may vary widely and likely will not play as significant a role in overall performance as those for the shot put athlete. This fact also highlights the importance of specific strength qualities such as speed strength and elastic strength in the training and performance of a high-performance speed athlete. General strength development will likely play a larger role in the training of a developing athlete between the ages of 15 and 20 due to the fact that he or she has not yet developed the foundational strength on which more specific high-performance qualities can be built.

Relaxation

We often associate optimal performance with maximal effort. The athlete who is grimacing and straining to the finish line is often considered the model of success. However, when performing movements that require maximal speed, unbridled maximal effort does not necessarily translate into optimal performance. The concept of relaxation must be ingrained into all aspects of technical execution. If all muscles are tight and contracted, it is much more difficult to initiate a high-velocity movement.

This is true for all movements that require acceleration and technical proficiency, whether the movement is swinging a golf club, hurling a baseball or sprinting. A finely tuned athlete has the ability to not only turn muscles on quickly, but also turn them off quickly, which is important for a high-speed, complex task such as sprinting. Communicating to athletes that the optimal performance does not necessarily come about through the application of maximal exertion can be useful in honing their relaxation abilities.

Wisdom

Performances that require technical excellence, such as maximal speed running, are not necessarily best served by a philosophy of all-out effort. These performances require a combination of force production, skill application and relaxation.

Acceleration Abilities

The ability to accelerate is critical in all sports that require running for locomotion. Given this fact, more attention needs to be placed on training athletes to accelerate smoothly and effectively. Although many training programs focus on reaction time, first-step quickness, agility and maximal velocity, acceleration is the vital quality that must be in place for athletes to succeed in their sport.

Acceleration must be developed throughout the training year. Many coaches believe that an athlete cannot accelerate until the proper strength work is in place. Under this philosophy a significant portion of valuable training time will be lost. Acceleration helps develop the strength, power, coordination and elasticity required for improvement. It is the most specific activity an athlete can do to improve acceleration.

Elastic Qualities

Not only must athletes have great strength and power to produce the forces required for fast acceleration and high velocities, but they must also have the stiffness and elasticity in their muscles and tendons to rebound off the ground at high speeds. It is no different than taking two basketballs, one that is fully inflated and one that is partially inflated, and throwing them down the basketball court, allowing them to bounce the full distance. Experience and science tell us that the fully inflated ball will travel faster and further down the court, whist the partially inflated ball will slowly plop down the court and allow forces of friction to act heavily on its progress.

Human athletes are no different during locomotion. Athletes with a combination of force-development capabilities and greater stiffness in their lower extremities will be able to reach and maintain higher top speeds than athletes who do not have these qualities.

It is important to note that these qualities will not only be part of a subjective evaluation when assessing an athlete's speed potential, but also will form the foundation of the training program. An athlete's improvement will depend greatly on the ability of his or her coach to optimally arrange the training program in a manner that elicits positive adaptations in all these qualities.

Integration of the Speed-Training Elements

Improving speed, particularly for advanced, high-performance athletes, is not just about getting stronger or more powerful in isolation. As with any training program, coaches are trying to improve multiple qualities in athletes in a manner that improves the athletes' overall performance in the sport. If that sport is the 100-metre sprint, the true test of the efficacy of the training program is the athlete's best time in competition, particularly at a championship event such as the Olympics or World Championships.

The selection and integration of work in an overall training program that is directed at making an athlete run faster must be organized in a manner that ensures the athlete receives the optimal contribution from each training element. This is no easy task, as athletes at different stages in their career or different times during the year may require a greater contribution from one element than from another. The job of the coach is to determine which training elements will assume a greater proportion of the overall training load and which elements will play a supportive role in the training program.

Many coaches believe that all training elements should be present in the overall program at all times, albeit at varying volumes. The relative volume of work for each element can vary depending on the emphasis and priority of a given week, month or phase of training. In the case of sprinting efforts, acceleration-based work over shorter distances (e.g., 20 to 30 m) is more compatible with higher volumes of relatively heavy weightlifting. However, the volume of weightlifting must be significantly reduced in the later stages of the programme as speed velocities and volumes, as well as plyometric jump volumes, are increased. Less muscle tension is experienced in low-volume (but mainly high-intensity) lifting periods, allowing for greater expression of high-speed running. A close examination of the training program over time must identify potential conflicts between training elements as well as potential opportunities for enhancing the adaptation potential for key elements, namely speed.

For specific training elements in a speed program, the following characteristics must be recognised when integrating all training elements: sprint training, strength training, power training and general conditioning.

Sprint Training

Athletes can be introduced to sprinting in a gradual, progressive manner that brings in technical concepts whilst also preparing the athlete's body for the stresses of the activity. An example of this concept would be work on acceleration technique over short distances whilst placing a cap on output

Wisdom

The best key performance indicator regarding the success of a training programme is the athlete's performance at a targeted competition. If the athlete does not peak at these events, no one cares about the magnitude of his or her best power clean, vertical jump or bench press.

intensity. Short sprints over 20 metres from a falling start could be performed at a maximal intensity of 85 per cent of the athlete's best time over that distance. An athlete with a best 20-metre time of 2.9 seconds would be expected to run at 3.3 seconds, a profoundly less stressful effort. The intensity, however, is high enough to work on technical aspects of the acceleration whilst gradually exposing the athlete to the stresses of actual sprinting.

The use of a short-to-long approach—which involves perfecting shorter sprint distances in the initial phase of a training program and gradually extending the length of sprints over time—allows athletes to accumulate higher overall volumes of sprinting at a high intensity. Not only does this approach increase an athlete's ability to repeat extraordinary sprint performances throughout the competitive season, broadening the athlete's peak, but it also makes the athlete stronger and more resistant to injury.

The short-to-long approach also proves to be more compatible with a conventional weight-training approach. During acceleration, the quadriceps are more involved in propulsion, and the knee joint experiences greater degrees of flexion on ground contact. This condition is more compatible with the squat, deadlift and Olympic lifting movements from the floor. In the latter stages of speed development, when maximal velocity is being trained and the knee joint is more extended on ground contact, overall weightlifting volume is reduced, and exercises with a reduced range of motion (ROM) can be incorporated.

Figure 11.2 provides an illustration of how weightlifting and sprinting are integrated in a short-to-long approach. Early on, a larger variety of lifting exercises are performed over greater ranges of motion when acceleration is the focus. In the intermediate phase, loads will increase, some exercises will be removed and full Olympic lifting movements can be incorporated because of their ability to provide a greater overall specific stress on the athlete's body in terms of maximal recruitment and velocity of movement.

In the final precompetitive phase, the emphasis is on advancing speed abilities through the use of longer recovery periods between repetitions whilst deemphasising weightlifting. In the weight room, there is a shift towards reduced range of motion with exercises. There can be a greater emphasis on a high-intensity upper-body movement because it allows for adequate stimulation of the central nervous system (CNS) whilst not causing peripheral fatigue on the lower body.[2]

Strength Training

Strength training is not the exclusive domain of the weight-room facility. Jumps, medicine ball throws and body-weight exercises can also effectively improve strength.[3] However, weightlifting becomes attractive in its ability to closely monitor physiological status from workout to workout. Quantifying performance and fatigue is easy because there is instant feedback on how much an athlete is lifting every repetition, set and workout. Combine this with the use of a stopwatch on the track, and we have two great indicators of performance. The complex part of the equation is trying to determine when improvements in the weight room reach a point of diminishing returns and no longer yield added value to speed.

It is best to think of weight training as a general strength training element when integrating it into a speed program. An efficient way to classify weightlifting exercises is to regard them as a means of activating motor units. Francis was a significant proponent of using weights in a general—but strategic—manner for speed athletes. Because no weightlifting movement is specific enough—from a velocity perspective—to provide a useful speed adaptation for sprinters, coaches should not rely on weights for the purpose of speed development for these athletes. However, weight training can be used as a means of stimulating the athlete's CNS whilst, at the same time, targeting various areas of the body (e.g., upper body versus lower body, pulling versus pressing movements).

If we assume that various training activities and exercises have a different impact on the CNS based on the complexity, velocity and intensity of the activity, it becomes much clearer as to how we can arrange and manage our training sessions. Improvements in CNS activation through general weight training—albeit at higher loads, velocities and, in some cases, complexity of movement—can, in theory, facilitate more efficient muscle recruitment when it comes to specific speed training on the track or field. Although this concept has not yet been specifically demonstrated through research, it can provide coaches with a common sense approach to strategically select exercise in an athlete's overall training programme.

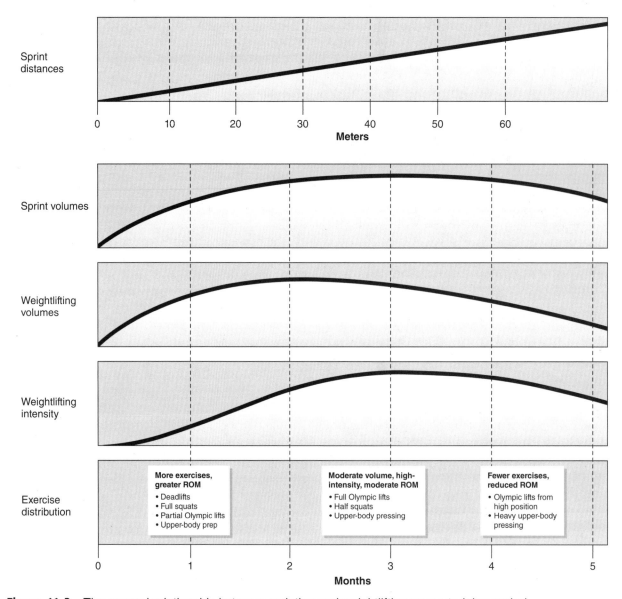

Figure 11.2 The general relationship between sprinting and weightlifting over a training period.

Although Olympic weightlifting movements such as the clean and jerk and snatch provide significant benefits in terms of taxing the central nervous system, an athlete can suffer from too much of a good thing. Athletes who spend too much time and energy on perfecting these lifts may find that their sprinting abilities suffer due to the significant demand placed on all the major muscle groups and the CNS, similar to the impact of maximal effort sprinting.[4]

This notion is supported by the fact that many, if not all, of the fastest sprinters in the world do not demonstrate exceptional abilities in the Olympic weightlifting movements. It has been more common to see sprinters demonstrate impressive feats of strength in what could be deemed less-specific movements such as the squat, deadlift and bench press. These exercises do not reflect many of the sport-specific qualities of sprinting but can involve heavy loads that elicit high levels of muscle recruitment and sufficiently stress the CNS. However, they do not overlap too heavily into the domain of actual sprinting, creating issues of excessive CNS fatigue.

This is not to say that Olympic weightlifting movements cannot be used to develop world-class speed athletes. However, it does mean that coaches must be more strategic in the application of these CNS-intensive and technical exercises. Strength development need not be the same for every athlete. Here are some scenarios in which Olympic weightlifting movements would be more applicable.

Athletes in Colder Climates or Without Ideal Indoor Training Facilities

When athletes cannot accumulate higher volumes of high-speed sprint training, Olympic lifting can be used to work a large proportion of muscular fibre and adequately tax the CNS. This is particularly useful in the early phases of training when short-distance acceleration work is predominant. In the colder regions of the Northern Hemisphere, an Olympic weightlifting regime combined with plyometrics may yield more significant gains than sprinting alone. However, in warmer climates athletes can attain higher volumes of specific sprinting work that can provide the precise central and peripheral adaptations required for improvement.

Athletes Who Begin Olympic Weightlifting at an Early Age

Athletes who have acquired the proper technique for the Olympic lifts in their younger years may be more apt to continue to use these lifts successfully as they mature. Less time and energy is required for teaching and maintaining technique for these athletes. Additionally, appropriate loads for motor-unit recruitment can be achieved more easily and at much less risk for athletes with Olympic weightlifting backgrounds. However, care must still be taken when applying loads to these athletes due to their advanced capabilities, particularly during phases with high volumes of high-velocity sprinting and during in-season tapering periods.

Athletes in Sports That Demand Acceleration Abilities but Not Maximal Velocity or Speed Endurance Capabilities

Team sport athletes who are required to accelerate for shorter distances only (i.e., 10-30 m) may find that Olympic lifting movements are more compatible with the performance requirements in their sport. The repeat acceleration requirements of highly physical sports such as American football and rugby make heavy Olympic lifting movements highly attractive and effective training options. These exercises are also well suited for field-event athletes in track and field, including jumpers, vaulters and throwers, where in most cases a short sprint is followed by an explosive effort. A thorough examination of situational factors will dictate which approach will best serve coach and athlete in the quest to become faster. Some athletes will benefit from heavier strength-training loads than others.

However, coaches must realise that having a love affair with weightlifting can have significant repercussions when an athlete is trying to run faster. The public's fascination with more exercises and infinitely modified versions of perfectly sound exercises has taken the focus off the purpose of strength training, which is to make athletes stronger in a general sense.

Wisdom

When it comes to speed development, weightlifting and other strength-training methods should be treated as a means to an end and not an end in itself. In many ways, the concept of less is more applies to strength training when preparing athletes for speed.

Power Training

For this discussion, it is important to divide power training into explosive power training and elastic power training.

Explosive power training can take the form of explosive jumps, medicine ball throws (figures 11.3 and 11.4), resisted starts and even Olympic lifting exercises. The objective of this work is to improve an athlete's start and early acceleration abilities. Powerful extension at the hip, knee and ankle—commonly referred to as triple extension—is required during starting and accelerating. Introduction of explosive power training in the early portion of the training program is compatible with the maximal strength work carried out in the weight room, as well as the short-distance acceleration work performed in speed workouts, where knee flexion is greater during force application.

The accumulation of sets and repetitions of medicine ball throws, box jumps and Olympic lifting movements in the general and specific preparation phases will ensure that explosive starts and strong acceleration abilities are in place once the precompetitive and competitive phases of training arrive.[4]

Figure 11.3 Medicine ball throws: explosive medicine ball push sequence.

Figure 11.4 Medicine ball throws: explosive medicine ball pull sequence.

The initiation of elastic power training proceeds in a much more gradual fashion in the early stages of the training program. Because elastic training commonly takes the form of successive plyometric jumps, time and care must be taken to ensure athletes are strong enough to handle the landings of these types of jumps. In the early phases of training athletes are getting stronger through concentric activities such as weightlifting and explosive power exercises. Muscles and tendons are being strengthened during this phase, so the stress of landing is minimised throughout the early phases of training.

Any initial multijump training can occur on a soft surface such as grass, cushioning the impact of landings. More forceful elastic work may take the form of hurdle jumps, bounding or hopping over short distances. It is always advisable to begin with lower repetition totals for sets of jumps to take into account the stressful nature of elastic jumps on connective tissue and the CNS. A good starting point is sets of 6 repetitions over 5 sets for a total of 30 total jumps. At a weekly frequency of 2 jumping sessions per week, this would start the athlete at 60 jumps per week. Additional volume could be added at a rate of 20 jumps per week.

In the latter stages of the training program, the volume of elastic work may be increased as the volume of explosive work and overall strength work is decreased. The reduction in overall weightlifting volume can free up the muscles for more dynamic activities such as multijumps and high-velocity sprinting. Although explosive training, maximal weightlifting and acceleration work were complimentary in the earlier phases of the training program, elastic jumps, maximal speed runs and speed endurance training are more compatible for the latter stages as an athlete prepares for competition. Figure 11.5 illustrates the relationship between these two types of power training and the progression of work for a speed athlete.

General Conditioning

Overall fitness in a speed athlete is critical for establishing a foundation of work capacity as well as enhancing recovery and recuperation. Athletes with a well-established circulatory system will warm up more efficiently and stay warmer longer. Thus, a large proportion of the work undertaken by a speed athlete will be comprised of low-intensity, high-volume work arranged in a fashion that complements the high-quality speed, strength and power work that results in the direct adaptations for speed development.[5]

Low-intensity general conditioning work can take several forms for the speed athlete. One of the most common means of improving general conditioning is through the use of low-intensity interval runs, commonly referred to as extensive tempo running. The intent is to train aerobically on a soft surface, such as grass, without creating residual fatigue or muscle soreness that could negatively affect subsequent speed sessions. These low-velocity runs can be interspersed with walking, jogging or body-weight strength circuits to increase the overall low-intensity workload.

Table 11.1 outlines some general volume guidelines for tempo running for various athletes. Athletes with greater work-capacity requirements will have higher running volumes, training as often as 3 times per week over longer interval distances. Alternatively, larger athletes, such as American football linemen, who can weigh well over 300 pounds, may train over only a fraction of the distance covered by a soccer player. Regardless of the distances covered, the intent is to run all repetitions at the same pace from beginning to end.

For athletes who cannot endure high volumes of running for their low-intensity conditioning, many alternatives can be employed to ensure this area of their training program is addressed appropriately. Alternative tempo options may include pool, treadmill or stationary bicycle training.

Pool Training

Athletes can choose one of two options in a swimming pool to work on general conditioning. In the shallow end of the pool, with the water line coming to the height of the chest, athletes can perform running high-knee drills over distances of 10 to 30 metres. In the deep end of the pool, athletes can perform deep-water running with or without the use of a flotation belt.

Treadmill Training

Intervals can be performed on a high-quality treadmill to simulate the low-intensity running work normally carried out on a grass field. When

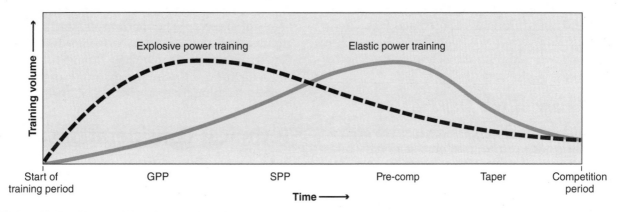

Figure 11.5 Progression of power training over the duration of a speed development program.

Table 11.1 Tempo Running Guidelines for Various Athletes

Athlete type	Typical volume per workout	Typical weekly volume	Sample tempo running workout (metres)
American football, lineman	800-1,200 m	1,600-2,500 m	50 + 50 + 50 + 50 50 + 100+ 100+ 50 50 + 100 + 100 + 50 50 + 50 + 50 + 50 Total = 1,000 m
American football, skill player	1,200-2,000 m	3,000-4,500 m	100 + 100 + 100 + 100 100 + 200 + 100 + 100 100 + 100 + 200 + 100 100 + 100 + 100 + 100 Total = 1,800 m
100 m sprinter	1,800-2,400 m	3,600-7,200 m	100 + 100 + 100 100 + 200 + 100 + 100 100 + 200 + 200 + 100 100 + 100 + 200 + 100 100 + 100 + 100 Total = 2,200 m
400 m sprinter	3,000-4,000 m	9,000-12,000 m	100 + 200 + 200 + 100 100 + 300 + 200 + 100 100 + 300 + 300 + 100 100 + 200 + 300 + 100 100 + 200 + 200 + 100 Total = 3,400 m
Soccer midfielder	3,500-4,500 m	10,000-13,500 m	100 + 200 + 300 200 + 300 + 200 300 + 300 + 300 200 + 300 + 200 300 + 200 + 100 Total = 3,500 m

Note: Athletes typically take a 50-metre walk between reps and a 100-metre walk between sets.

athletes do not have access to a soft running surface, treadmills can provide a well-cushioned surface that results in less impact stress. Repetition durations may be longer than those of regular tempo runs or pool work because the treadmill running does not impose the same cost to the athlete. Thus, durations of 30, 60 and 90 seconds can be used effectively. Athletes can integrate rest intervals by straddling the belt and standing on the treadmill platform.

Stationary Bicycle Training

Similar to the treadmill example, intervals of 30, 60 and 90 seconds can be used on a stationary bike. Rest intervals can be performed seated on the bike at a lower velocity and resistance; work intervals can be performed from a standing position at higher velocities and resistance settings.

Medicine ball circuits, incorporating a variety of low-velocity passes, throws and abdominal work, are also an effective way of achieving overall work-capacity goals. In most cases, these types of circuits complement the tempo running but should not be relied upon as a substitute for tempo runs or any of the acceptable alternatives. Medicine ball circuits can be implemented between sets of tempo runs or carried out immediately after a full tempo run session. For a thorough exploration of the topic of cross-training, refer to chapter 17.

Technical Considerations

Although planning and programming for speed is a critical stage in athlete preparation, ongoing work on the biomechanical execution of the sprinting motion is just as important for the long-term development of the speed athlete. A combination of drills and well-guided sprinting repetitions are typically required to refine running technique. The speed coach is constantly refining, tweaking and reinforcing technique. The successful coach will be able to determine the proper sequence and volume of drills and runs, along with the most appropriate verbal cues, required to improve technique for a particular athlete.[6]

It is difficult to convey a proper teaching sequence for sprinting since each athlete may present unique challenges. Some athletes respond to conventional cues immediately; other athletes require a more drawn-out approach that breaks down the mechanical components to a greater degree. Here are some fundamental guidelines for the instruction and application of running mechanics as applied in drills, starts, acceleration, maximal velocity and deceleration. (For more on deceleration, see chapter 13.)

Drills

Running drills are primarily intended to serve as simplified or broken-down versions of specific movement patterns used in actual running. Drills can be used to emphasise proper posture and limb movements and can be performed whilst sitting, standing, skipping or running. The intent of the drill is to improve on an aspect of the running motion that can be incorporated into the full motion.

The early introduction of drills into the training program is advantageous in that it avoids the stiffness and fatigue associated with the higher volumes and intensities of training encountered deeper into the program. Once key technical elements are introduced and consistently rehearsed, it becomes much easier for athletes to retain these skills after higher-speed running workouts are introduced.

Some of the most commonly used sprint drills are the Mach drills introduced to the track and field world by former Polish national sprint coach Gerard Mach.[7] The Mach drills are set up to act as both active and reactive drills: The drills can be used to introduce technical concepts and improve strength (active involvement) but can also be used to correct flaws and weaknesses (reactive involvement).

The A drills are particularly effective because they involve appropriate knee lift and hip extension. These drills are organised in marching, skipping and running versions. The marching A is a good drill for beginners to emphasise the path of the limbs and to introduce the concept of tall posture. As with all drills, it is important to initiate the learning sequence in a slow, deliberate manner to ensure that athletes learn the proper limb movements and posture before moving on to higher-velocity iterations of the drill.

As illustrated in figure 11.6, the elbows are bent, with the hands coming to the front side of the body up to a height even with the athlete's line of sight. The opposite knee rises to a level equal to the height of the hip. It is important that the athlete stays on the balls of the feet to maintain a high-hip position. The athlete should transition smoothly from step to step, with a slight rotation occurring between the shoulder and hips as the front hand moves towards, but not across, the centerline of the body. Each step should land only a few inches in front of the previous step to avoid a long step that results in a drop in hip height.

The skipping A drill, illustrated in figure 11.7, emphasises the same body posture and limb paths as its marching counterpart, but it encourages higher velocities and force generation from limb movements to effect a dynamic skipping rhythm. A strong upward arm and leg movement by opposing limbs is combined with a strong downward arm and leg movement by the other limbs. The result is a snapping movement that pops the body upward on each foot contact.

The running A drill builds on the limb and postural mechanics of the marching and skipping drills but adds the element of limb velocity and running rhythm. The athlete, as illustrated in figure 11.8, cycles the legs up and down vigorously to create significant downward force into the ground. Each ground contact makes use of the elastic properties of the lower legs and feet, including bouncing on every stride. The arms swing similarly in range to the marching and skipping A drills but are moving at a much higher frequency, matching the legs on every stride. Athletes should be able to complete at least 30 strides of the running A drill over a 10-metre distance.

Even though it is difficult to impart the proper movement mechanics of these drills on the written page and via photo sequences, all of the A drills have commonalities in terms of overall posture and limb mechanics. These common traits are also found in effective sprinting technique.

Figure 11.6 Marching A drill sequence.

Figure 11.7 Skipping A drill sequence.

Figure 11.8 Running A drill sequence.

Starts and Acceleration Mechanics

Teaching athletes the proper mechanics for starting and accelerating is critical for the advancement of their overall speed abilities.[6] Because effective starting often requires good maximal strength and power capabilities, it is often premature to train young athletes in advanced start techniques.

Wisdom

As with many sport movements, how the movement is started will often determine how successful the successive stages of that movement are. Sprinting is no different.

This is why one of the first start techniques to teach athletes is a falling start. The falling start from a low, staggered-stance position allows the athlete to use the momentum from the falling motion to unload the starting movement, requiring less strength to attain a good acceleration position from the first stride. The low-hip position requires that the athlete extend at the hip in a relatively powerful manner. However, the energy required to execute the falling start is still much less than that needed for other deeper static positions such as a three- or four-point start.

As illustrated in figure 11.9, the athlete falls to an angle that is optimal for acceleration. As the athlete reaches a point in the falling motion, just beyond the tipping point, when the athlete feels him- or herself accelerating toward the ground, the athlete must initiate movement with the lead hand (i.e., the hand on the same side as the front foot). A strong initial arm action will not only cue the legs to fire explosively, but it will also help to extend the body into the correct posture out of the start. Athletes with less vigorous or nonexistent arm drive at the start will find that their posture is much more rounded and less rigid, resulting in a poor drive angle out of the start.

Figure 11.9 Falling start from low, two-point stance.

Another approach to improving start and acceleration posture is to have the athlete start from the ground in a flat push-up position as illustrated in figure 11.10. Rather than the athlete falling gradually towards the ground to establish acceleration posture, the athlete starts on the ground and drives up to the correct acceleration position. The push-up start approach works well for beginner athletes because it intuitively places them in an effective acceleration position with few to no cues or instructions.

The push-up start is also valuable during a strength-building phase because it develops explosive upper-body strength on the push-up and requires greater leg strength to drive the athlete out of a low position. For this reason, push-up starts are used often during the initial speed-training phase in a short-to-long speed program. For athletes who do not have a powerful push-up, coaches can segment the push-up start into three phases: The athlete pushes up and pauses, the athlete steps with one leg and then, on the coach's command, the athlete goes. The segmented push-up start, as illustrated in figure 11.11, is an intermediate exercise that can be used before the full push-up start.

Maximal Velocity Mechanics

Although 100-metre sprinters may be the only athletes to reach maximal velocity capabilities consistently, all running athletes should understand the posture and mechanics required to attain and maintain maximal or near-maximal sprinting speed. Football, soccer and rugby players may have to demonstrate maximal velocity abilities on open-field runs over distances of 30 to 50 metres.

As an athlete transitions out of the acceleration phase of a sprint effort, the shift in posture from a driving acceleration to upright sprinting will necessitate an up-and-down action from both the legs and the arms. As maximal force is generated from the highest point in the stride down towards the ground, it is important to emphasise the need for both a high-hip and high-knee position during maximal velocity sprinting. In order to accomplish this leg positioning, athletes must achieve front-side dominant stride mechanics. Additionally, the arms must also demonstrate a strong front-side presence to match the forces produced by the lower body.[8]

Figure 11.10 Push-up start sequence.

Figure 11.11 Segmented push-up start sequence.

From a close examination of figure 11.12, it is apparent that the athlete's foot recovers high and tight to the buttocks and hamstrings, setting up a high-knee position on the front side of the stride cycle. Because the athlete's leg is hinged at the hip, the downward sweep of the leg also produces horizontal propulsion on its way down to the ground. However, the athlete is not reaching in front of his or her body to paw at the ground. The athlete is only focusing on producing significant downward force. This effort is matched by the action of the upper limbs with the athlete's hand travelling well in front of the face and then downward toward the hip.

Loading and Progression of Work

In order for speed training to be successful, it must be applied progressively with gradual loading occurring from week to week. Assuming appropriate recovery times are observed, this approach allows an athlete to adapt and improve without undue risk of injury. Training programs tend to follow one of three approaches when attempting to improve an athlete's sprinting ability: short-to-long, long-to-short or concurrent training.

The Short-to-Long Approach

In the short-to-long approach, athletes initiate the program with shorter acceleration distances and gradually sprint over incrementally longer distances. The intensity of all sprints is 95 to 100 per cent of maximal intensity, with full recoveries after each sprint. The intent is to build up the athlete's adaptive abilities for high-intensity acceleration in an effort to attain maximal speeds. The accumulation of high-intensity acceleration volume not only enhances the athlete's ability to accelerate, but it also strengthens both the CNS and the peripheral muscular system to handle the repeated demands of sprinting throughout a competitive phase. Thus, a short-to-long approach is desirable for team sports that require numerous short sprints throughout the contest duration.

Figure 11.12 Upright sprinting mechanics at maximal velocity.

Team sport athletes who employ the short-to-long approach start with relatively short distances of 5 to 10 metres in distance, working on reaction time, starting strength and explosive power. Running drills are incorporated to help establish proper posture and limb movement patterns from the outset. As the training program progresses, athletes cover distances of 20 to 40 metres since most team sport athletes will almost never need to sprint further.

The starts used by team sport athletes include a combination of hard and soft starts. Hard starts include all starts that require more strength and power, such as push-up starts and three-point starts, and are more suitable for shorter distances of 10 to 20 metres. Soft starts, such as falling starts, are employed when more energy must be applied over a longer sprint distance in training.[4]

Figure 11.13 outlines the progression of work over a 12 to 16 week period, identifying the relative proportions of work over tasks and areas. Table 11.2 outlines sample training sessions in a short-to-long approach for team sport athletes, identifying optimal recovery times between repetitions and sets.

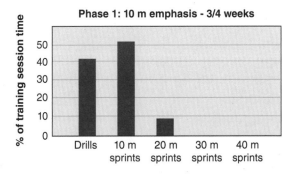

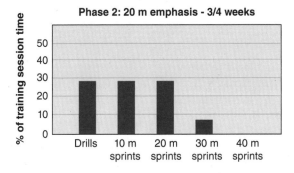

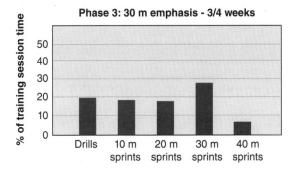

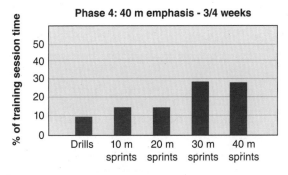

Figure 11.13 A 12-to-16 week, short-to-long sprint progression for team sports.

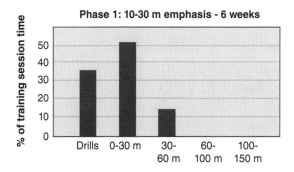

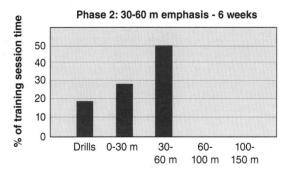

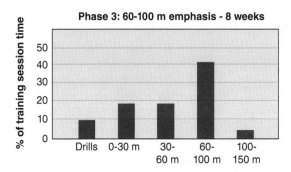

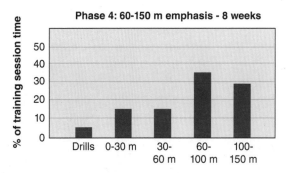

Figure 11.14 Thirty-week short-to-long sprint progression for the 100 metres.

Figure 11.14 illustrates the distribution of work for a 100-metre sprinter using a short-to-long approach. The emphasis on drills is still apparent for the 100-metre sprinter, but less time is spent than for the team sport athlete. In most cases, team sport athletes need relatively more time invested in refining running mechanics and ingraining the concept of relaxation. Athletes

Table 11.2 Sample Short-to-Long Speed Workouts for Team Sport Athletes

Phase	Sample workout
1 10 m emphasis	• Arm mechanics drills from seated position • 4 × 15 m marching A • 4 × 15 m skipping A • 5 × 10 m running A • 5 × 10 m from push-up start, 1 min rep recovery, 3 min set recovery • 5 × 10 m from supine starts, 1 min rep recovery, 3 min set recovery • 4 × 15 m from 3-point starts, 1 min rep recovery, 3 min set recovery • 4 × 10 m acceleration plus 10 m maintain, falling start, 1 min rep recovery • Total speed volume = 240 m
2 20 m emphasis	• 4 × 20 m skipping A • 4 × 15 m running A • Arm reaction drills on start commands • 4 × 10 m from push-up start, 1 min rep recovery, 3 min set recovery • 4 × 10 m from medicine ball push-up start, 1 min rep recovery, 3 min set recovery • 4 × 20 m from push-up start, 2 min rep recovery, 3.5 min set recovery • 4 × 20 m from three-point start, 2 min rep recovery, 3.5 min set recovery • 3 × 20 m acceleration plus 10 m maintain, falling start, 2 min rep recovery • Total speed volume = 330 m
3 30 m emphasis	• 4 × 20 m skipping A • 4 × 20 m running A • Arm reaction drills on start commands • 4 × 10 m from push-up start, 1 min rep recovery, 3 min set recovery • 4 × 20 m from 3-point start, 2 min rep recovery, 3.5 min set recovery • 3 × 30 m from falling start, 3 min rep recovery, 4.5 min set recovery • 3 × 30 m from three-point start, 3 min rep recovery, 4.5 min set recovery • 3 × 30 m acceleration plus 10 m maintain, falling start, 3.5 min rep recovery • Total speed volume = 420 m
4 40 m emphasis	• 4 × 20 m skipping A • 4 × 10 m running A • 4 × 10 m from push-up start, 1 min rep recovery, 3 min set recovery • 4 × 20 m from 3-point start, 2 min rep recovery, 3.5 min set recovery • 3 × 30 m from falling start, 3 min rep recovery, 4.5 min set recovery • 3 × 40 m from three-point start, 3.5 min rep recovery, 5 min set recovery • 3 × 40 m from falling start, 4 min rep recovery • Total speed volume = 450 m

with a background in formal sprint training typically have already invested significant amounts of time on technical drills.

Table 11.3 provides more specific details on the types of runs and recoveries employed for a 100-metre athlete using a short-to-long approach. The first two phases of training focus on distances between 10 and 60 metres, with an emphasis on acceleration and the attainment of a high maximal velocity. Once the athlete enters phase 3 of the training program, distances greater than 60 metres are incorporated into the program, and the athlete moves beyond the alactic anaerobic system into the lactic anaerobic system with greater recovery times required. It is not out of the question for athletes to take 100 seconds of rest for every 1 second expended during a sprint effort. For elite-level sprinters, this is the magnitude of recovery

Table 11.3 Sample Short-to-Long Speed Workouts for 100-Metre Sprint Athletes

Phase	Day 1	Day 2	Day 3
1 0-30 m emphasis	Sprints on grass • 4 × 10 m push-up start • 4 × 20 m falling start • 4 × 20 m push-up start • 4 × 30 m falling start • Total = 320 m	Hill sprints • 4 × 20 m push-up start • 4 × 30 m falling start • 4 × 30 m falling start • Total = 320 m	Sprints on track • 4 × 20 m medicine ball start • 4 × 20 m push-up start • 4 × 30 m falling start • 4 × 30 m plus 20 m maintain • Total = 480 m
2 30-60 m emphasis	Sprints on track • 3 × 30 m falling start • 4 × 30 m block start • 3 × 50 m falling start • 3 × 60 m falling start • Total = 540 m	Sprints on track • 4 × 30 m falling start • 4 × 30 m block start • 4 × 30 m block start • 3 × 30 easy plus 20 m (flying 20s) • Total = 510 m	Sprints on track • 4 × 30 m falling start • 4 × 30 m block start • 3 × (20F plus 20E plus 20F) • 3 × (20E plus 20F plus 20E) • Total = 600 m
3 60-100 m emphasis	Sprints on track • 4 × 30 m falling start • 3 × 30 m block start • 3 × 40 m block start • 4 × 60 m falling start • Total = 570 m	Sprints on track • 4 × 30 m falling start • 3 × 60 m • 2 × 80 m • 1 × 100 m • Total = 560 m	Sprints on track • 4 × 30 m falling start • 4 × 30 m block start • 2 × (20F plus 20E plus 20F) • 2 × (20E plus 20F plus 20E) • 1 × 80 m • Total = 560 m
4 60-150 m emphasis	Sprints on track • 4 × 30 m falling start • 4 × 40 m block start • 2 × (3 × 60 m) falling start • Total = 640 m	Sprints on track • 4 × 30 m falling start • 1 × 80 m, 12 min recovery • 1 × 100 m, 15 min recovery • 1 × 120 m, 20 min recovery • 1 × 150 m • Total = 570 m	Sprints on track • 4 × 30 m falling start • 4 × 40 m block start • 3 × (20E plus 20F plus 20E) • 1 × 80 m • 1 × 100 m • Total = 640 m

*Note: Recovery times will be no less than 1 or 2 minutes per 10 metres of sprint distance covered.

required in training to ensure each sprint repetition is of the highest quality possible.

The Long-to-Short Approach

In a long-to-short approach, athletes run distances longer than they would in competition and then gradually decrease the sprinting distance over time, increasing the velocities of the runs through the progression. The intent is to gradually approach the competition distance and desired velocity as the athlete works from a general preparatory phase to a competitive phase. Because lower velocities are applied in the early stages of a long-to-short program, recovery times can be shortened significantly between repetitions and sets.

The Concurrent Approach

A concurrent approach combines aspects of both short-to-long and long-to-short training to arrive at a training program tailored to the needs of the athlete and the constraints of a particular training location. The concurrent approach works well for athletes who require greater development of both the alactic and lactic anaerobic energy systems for competition distances between 100 and 400 metres. Longer sprints also have the effect of teaching athletes to relax through the effort and manage their energy over a given distance. Table 11.4 incorporates aspects of the other short-to-long programs described in this chapter with the addition of a day of training that progresses from 400-metre runs down to distances in the range of 200 metres.

Table 11.4 Concurrent Speed Workouts for 200-Metre Sprint Athletes

Phase	Day 1: short-to-long	Day 2: short-to-long	Day 3: long-to-short
1	Sprints on grass • 4 × 10 m push-up start • 4 × 20 m falling start • 4 × 20 m push-up start • 4 × 30 m falling start • Total = 320 m	Hill sprints • 4 × 20 m push-up start • 4 × 30 m falling start • 4 × 30 m falling start • Total = 320 m	Sprints on grass • 4 × 30 m falling start • 4 × 400 m at 80% with 8 min breaks • Total = 1,720 m
2	Sprints on track • 3 × 30 m falling start • 4 × 30 m block start • 3 × 50 m falling start • 3 × 60 m falling start • Total = 540 m	Sprints on track • 4 × 30 m falling start • 4 × 30 m block start • 4 × 30 m block start • 3 × 30 easy plus 20 m (flying 20s) • Total = 510 m	Sprints on track • 4 × 30 m falling start • 350m at 85%, 12 min break • 300m at 90%, 15 min break • 250m at 90% • Total = 1020 m
3	Sprints on track • 4 × 30 m falling start • 3 × 30 m block start • 3 × 40 m block start • 4 × 60 m falling start • Total = 570m	Sprints on track • 4 × 30 m falling start • 3 × 60 m • 2 × 80 m • 1 × 100 m • Total = 560 m	Sprints on track • 4 × 30 m falling start • 4 × 30 m falling start • 300m at 95%, 18 min break • 250m at 95%, 20 min break • 220m at 95% • Total = 600 m
4	Sprints on track • 4 × 30 m falling start • 4 × 40 m block start • 2 × (3 × 60 m) falling start • Total = 640 m	Sprints on track • 4 × 30 m falling start • 1 × 80 m, 12 min recovery • 1 × 100 m, 15 min recovery • 1 × 120 m, 20 min recovery • 1 × 150 m • Total = 570 m	Sprints on track • 4 × 30 m falling start • 220 m at 100%, 25-30 min break • 180 m at 100% • Total = 640 m

*Note: Recovery times will be no less than 1 or 2 minutes per 10 metres of sprint distance covered.

Developing Acceleration in All Sports

Faye Downey
High Performance Manager,
Red Bull Extreme Athletes and Newcastle United

Through my work in individual, team, Olympic and extreme sports, I have seen as many similarities as differences in developing acceleration.

I am a big believer in training for capacity, training athletes to enhance their physical abilities to do what they need to become as fast as possible. In terms of acceleration, I look to develop high vertical and horizontal forces, especially in the first couple steps.

Exercises and drills that increase stiffness within the system, develop powerful hip motion and minimise energy leaks in the trunk are critical. This is consistent whether training track sprinters or multidirectional field-sport athletes. In sports in which acceleration is essential, I prioritise the training of force generation and attenuation capacities in such a way that energy is not leaked through poor technique or faulty biomechanics.

The process for developing these qualities depends on the sport and the technical and musculoskeletal competencies of the athlete. Where possible, I prioritise drills such as cleans, jerks, weighted step-ups, squats, hack squats and single-leg squats. For injury resilience, it's also critical to include drills such as Nordic hamstring curls and stiff-legged deadlifts.

Also I like to include heavy sled work in the programme to develop starting strength and force application. This can be coupled with short (5 metre) hill work.

My work with triple jumpers over the years has heavily influenced me in programming for all sports. Particularly I look to bouncing drills to effectively condition the tendons of the lower limbs, which are vital for both performance and protection against injury.

Of course, training track athletes is different than training field-sport athletes. My philosophy with footballers, for example, is that building capacity is key. If able to apply more force, they will accelerate quicker. This is paramount. We also look to increase the stiffness within their feet, ankles and lower legs to ensure the players take full advantage of the elastic nature of their muscles and tendons.

Then we look at basic technique drills aimed at foot placement, getting the feet to point in the direction where we want them to run. This is carried over into agility drills as well. We want our athletes to be powerful through their hips as though they were going to knee something.

Often in field sports, players do not accelerate from a standing start, so in training I have them accelerate from a rolling start. This allows them to build up momentum and is similar to what is seen in football and rugby.

From an injury prevention standpoint, we don't want players exposed to violent accelerations and high-velocity running for the first time in a game. This is when injuries occur, because athletes haven't built up their durability or capacity to withstand the forces. As such, all players are exposed to high speeds during the preseason. We continue this training in-season as well, but only one very fast session per week, usually on Tuesday if we are running a Saturday-to-Saturday schedule. Usually this training is done in a small group setting of five or six players at a time, focusing on distances up to 40 metres.

In the past, I have programmed in a fast but short session on Friday or even Saturday morning to achieve a potentiation effect, preparing players for the match. This is something we will work up to with Newcastle, but at the moment, the players need to be gradually exposed.

Faye Downey has a master's degree in sports science from Loughborough University and has developed conditioning programmes for Olympic, World Championship, European, and Commonwealth athletes. She was on the coaching team for England RFU during the 2007 and 2011 Rugby World Cups. Currently she is high performance manager for Red Bull Extreme athletes and for Newcastle United.

Summary

Ensuring that athletes reach their speed potential requires careful management of all training elements. If the development of greater speed is the ultimate goal, all training elements must serve as a means to that end. Even though circumstances may determine the optimal ordering of elements or choice of approach, an integrated, organised approach that identifies strengths, deficiencies and opportunities for improvement is always superior to a haphazard approach of ongoing loading, useless training gadgets and endless fatigue.

Strength professionals often claim that athletes can never be strong enough; however, it is the job of a speed coach to determine when strength work yields positive contributions towards speed development and when it reaches a point of diminishing returns. As with many aspects of athletic development, every coach will have a formula for success. The right combination of coaching experience, keen observation and common sense will ensure that athletes stay healthy and consistently improve.

CHAPTER 12

Optimising Training for Jumping and Landing

Jeremy Sheppard, PhD
Hurley Surfing Australia High Performance Centre and Edith Cowan University

The jump-and-land sequence is a critical athletic quality for many sports. Sports such as volleyball have a high volume of jumping as a feature of the game, with the sequence performed hundreds of times in a match[1] and its performance as an established performance criteria.[1-3] For other sports (e.g., track and field jumps), jumping is the event itself, and as such jumping *is* the performance outcome (i.e., height or distance). Even though jumping may occur less frequently in some sports, its performance may have a considerable impact upon the outcome. For example, in rugby, an athlete may jump to contest a ball from a high kick relatively few times in a match, yet the result (i.e., whether the offensive or defensive player catches the ball) may determine the outcome of the game. Equally, the ability to jump and land without decay in efficiency over the course of a match is vital in sports such as tennis and badminton.

This chapter describes the key physical and technical qualities that lead to superior jump-and-land performance. In order to optimise the application of the information, however, the chapter should be viewed and interpreted in concert with other chapters since many concepts are interdependent. For example, appropriate assessment (chapter 1) is required to enhance the application of the information in this chapter. Optimal flexibility (chapter 5), movement efficiency (chapter 3) and high levels of strength (chapter 10) are also major considerations in the development of jumping and landing ability. In this chapter, these considerations are discussed only in the context of jumping and landing; refer to other chapters

in this book for in-depth information on these important considerations.

For the purposes of this chapter, the term *jump-and-land* will refer to the entire sequence of force production, take-off and force absorption (figure 12.1, *a-c*).

A vertical jump sequence can include jumps off and onto various surfaces, including turf (e.g., football codes), courts (e.g., basketball), sand (e.g., beach volleyball, long jump), mats (e.g., gymnastics) and water (e.g., surfing). The term *jump* (and jumping) refers broadly to all manifestations in sport, whether performed from an initial stationary position (e.g., Rugby Union lineout, volleyball block), whilst running (e.g., basketball lay-up), from a short approach (e.g., volleyball spike) or from one or both legs. Although the primary focus of this chapter is on considerations for the vertical jump, the testing and training concepts have direct relevance to horizontal jumping tasks. It is important to appreciate that the performance achieved in horizontal jumping involves a considerable vertical displacement and heavily depends on vertical force–time characteristics.[4, 5]

Trainable Properties

In order to improve the outcome of jumping and landing performance, understanding its component parts first will allow strategic coaching of the areas the athlete may be weakest in. The following section outlines considerations for the major trainable components that contribute to improved jumping performance.

Figure 12.1 Vertical jump sequence: (*a*) flexion (force production); (*b*) take-off; (*c*) landing (force absorption)

Maximal Strength and Power

Coaches often refer to power movements, and the vertical jump certainly fits this definition.[6,7] Considering that power is the product of force and velocity, it is helpful to view power generation as being underpinned by the ability to apply high force and achieve high velocity. Although these particular factors are often discussed independently, they are in fact *interdependent* qualities that must be understood to effectively improve power to the greatest degree.

Heavy Strength Training

It is sometimes mistakenly asserted that unloaded jumping (i.e., jumping with only the athlete's body weight) does not require maximal strength characteristics, and therefore maximal strength training is of little benefit to improve jumping ability. This may be due to the fact that peak forces in the vertical jump, compared to maximal force capability, are relatively low in the vertical jump so the need for a high-force capability is not inherently observable in the task itself. However, this last assertion does not make sense: Maximal force capabilities, and maximal strength-training methods, have well-known associations with jumping ability.[2, 7-12] This is an easily explained concept. To increase displacement, athletes must take off with a higher velocity, which is gained through an increase in impulse. To increase this impulse, the athlete must apply more force in the same time, or apply the same force as previously in less time, to have the desired improvement. The outcome is directly related to how quickly the athlete applies this force (rate of force development). Training maximal strength develops the athlete's ability to apply higher forces and, as such, improves his or her capacity for a high rate of force development.

Assuming equal body weight and other factors (e.g., technique), if a stronger athlete applies force at the same *relative* rate as that of a weaker athlete, it will in fact be a higher rate since the stronger athlete has a higher total capability. More force will be applied in the given time and at greater acceleration, thereby generating more impulse and a superior vertical jump.

Wisdom

In the case of jumping performance, strength gain can be viewed as an underpinning and foundational component that all other training needs depend on.

Although detailed strength-training information is provided elsewhere (chapter 10), it should be noted that squat and heavy-pull training is of particular importance for the jumping athlete.[7, 8, 13, 14] Training methods aimed at developing general competency and maximal strength in movements such as the back squat (figure 12.2), front squat (figure 12.3), snatch squat (figure 12.4), single-leg squat (figure 12.5), deadlift (figure 12.6) and Romanian-style deadlift (figure 12.7) are important general-development exercises to include for strength.

Although there may exist a theoretical ceiling, or perhaps even a trade-off between gaining strength and improving jumping ability, this is not something to be overly concerned with when the coach focuses on the development of relative strength (i.e., strength as it relates to body mass). If the primary aim is to develop relative maximal strength, and employ mass-gaining methods and dietary habits only when desirable for total relative strength improvements, this theoretical ceiling, or theoretical trade-off between further strength

Figure 12.2 Back squat.

Figure 12.3 Front squat.

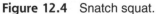

Figure 12.4 Snatch squat.

Figure 12.5 Single-leg squat.

Figure 12.6 Deadlift.

Figure 12.7 Romanian-style deadlift.

gains and jumping performance, is unlikely to be discovered! Although the law of diminishing returns certainly applies to strength training and its effect on improving vertical jumping, for most athletes in high-volume jumping and landing sports (e.g., volleyball, basketball), this point would be reached only by a small number of athletes. Put simply, no evidence exists to suggest that strength gains diminish jumping performance, yet overwhelming support exists for the point that maximal strength and power is associated with jumping ability, and that increasing maximal strength yields improvement in power and jumping performance.[2, 15-22]

Wisdom

With athletes who are required to jump, emphasise year-round development of maximal relative strength for greatest effect on maintaining and improving jumping ability.

Olympic Lifting

Olympic lifting is a vital aspect of training for the jumping athlete. Olympic lifts, and their derivatives and training drills, offer a means to train speed and strength. Their effect is produced by using a range of loads from relatively light (preparatory lifts and accessory-lift variations) to moderately heavy (near-maximal and maximal lifts in snatch and clean) to provide resistance to large ranges of the triple extension movement (hip-knee-ankle) that is transferable to jump performance.[2, 8, 16, 20, 23] This range of motion (ROM), which involves a large sum of motor units, results in high power totals; it could be considered the most important suite of exercises, in addition to maximal strength training, to use for improving jumping performance.

Wisdom

Every athlete training to improve jumping ability should include Olympic lifting in the training approach.

Coaches working with jumping athletes should integrate an appropriate teaching progression for these lifts into the training of developing athletes to ensure that when physically mature, these athletes will have the opportunity to safely and effectively use Olympic lifting as a means to train speed qualities (lighter loads and accessory Olympic lifts) and maximal power (moderate and near-maximal loads), and heavy loaded-power movements (maximal Olympic lifting loads). Table 12.1 presents an example of a long-term teaching progression used in volleyball to progress athletes to competence in the snatch (figure 12.8) and clean (figure 12.9) and several derivatives that can be used in training.

Table 12.1 Olympic Lifting Teaching and Training Progression for Developing Volleyball Players (14 and 15 Years Old)

Target to be achieved before progressing to next exercise and stage is in italics. End-stage (i.e., 16 years old) target expectations are shown in parenthesis.

Snatch	Clean
Snatch squat *50% body mass* (80%-100% body mass)	Front squat *75% body mass* (100% body mass)
Snatch balance *50% body mass* (70%-80% body mass)	
Snatch from hang *50% body mass* (65%-75% body mass)	Clean from hang *65% body mass* (80%-90% body mass)
Snatch *60% body mass* (80%-90% body mass)	Clean *80% body mass* (100%-110% body mass)
Power snatch (70% body mass)	Power clean (90% body mass)

Olympic lifts should be viewed as an outstanding means to safely develop high levels of eccentric strength and control in a way that is entirely relevant to landings. The catch phase of the two Olympic lifts and their derivatives demand a controlled deceleration of the athlete's body mass and the external load in the lift. If taught properly, this is one of few training modalities that can provide such a specific, relevant benefit.

Loaded Jumping

Loaded jumping, primarily through the use of jump squats (i.e., with a countermovement) and squat jumps (i.e., with an extended pause of 2 to 4 seconds between eccentric and concentric action) using extra load has been used to assess performance[24-27] and to train jumping ability in many contexts with excellent outcomes.[18, 28-32]

Figure 12.8 Snatch: *(a)* starting position; *(b)* lift bar to hip height; *(c)* press overhead.

Figure 12.9 Clean: *(a)* starting position; *(b)* lift bar to chin; *(c)* squat deeply; *(d)* stand.

Although some coaches believe that performing loaded jumps is somehow safer or more appropriate in a Smith machine compared to free weights, this is not correct;[25, 33] the use of barbells, weight vests, or other means that allows for unrestricted jumping action is recommended.

Loaded jumping offers the coach a range of loads from which to target the force–velocity spectrum, allowing for the emphasis to be placed on low- (5%-30% of mass in addition to body mass), moderate- (30%-70% of body mass) or heavy- (70%-125% of body mass) load power training. These loads can be selected for the specific aspects they target. For example, heavy-load jump squats are useful for developing heavy-load ballistic strength, which tends to allow for greater power generation with the heavy loads used in training, as well as with some transfer to lighter loads.[18] In contrast, moderate loads elicit high average power outputs, potentially leading to exceptional lower-body power improvements.[24, 29, 31, 32]

Considering that jump squats offer less motor-unit involvement compared to typical strength and Olympic lifting movements, jump squats should be understood as a special exercise used to target low and unloaded conditions[18] and are therefore useful

Table 12.2 Five-Week Lower-Body Strength and Power Sequence Incorporating Jump Squat Training Progression Using Varying Barbell Loads for an Elite Volleyball Player (205.5 cm, 101 kg)

Session 1	Week 1	Week 2	Week 3	Week 4	Week 5
Jump squat Snatch Back squat Single-leg squat	4 × 5 (50 kg) 6 × 3 (60-70 kg) 9 × 5/4/3* (110/115/120, 115/120/125, 120/125/130 kg) 3 × 12 (101 kg)	4 × 3 (60 kg) 7 × 3 (60-70 kg) 9 × 4/3/2* (115/120/125, 120/125/130, 125/130/135 kg) 3 × 10 (111 kg)	5 × 3 (65 kg) 7 × 2 (65-75 kg) 9 × 3/2/1* (120/125/130, 125/130/135, 130/135/140 kg) 4 × 8 (116 kg)	6 × 4 (30 kg) 6 × 2 (65-75 kg) None 4 × 6 (121 kg)	6 × 3 (15 kg) 4 × 2 (70-77.5 kg) 6 × 3 (130-135 kg) None
Session 2	**Week 1**	**Week 2**	**Week 3**	**Week 4**	**Week 5**
Jump squat Clean Front squat Romanian-style deadlift	4 × 4 (60 kg) 6 × 3 (60-70 kg) 6 × 7 (80-85 kg) 3 × 10 (90 kg)	5 × 3 (70 kg) 7 × 3 (60-70 kg) 6 × 6 (82.5-87.5 kg) 4 × 8 (100 kg)	6 × 2 (80 kg) 7 × 2 (65-75 kg) 7 × 5 (85-90 kg) 4 × 6 (110 kg)	6 × 4 (40 kg) 6 × 2 (65-75 kg) None None	6 × 3 (20 kg) 4 × 2 (70-77.5 kg) 4 × 7 (82.5-87.5 kg) 3 × 7 (95 kg)

*For the back squat, the athlete performs a total of 9 sets in groups of 3. Sets 1, 4, and 7 have the highest reps but a lower weight; sets 3, 6, and 9 have the fewest reps but a higher weight. In week 1, for example, the athlete performs 5 reps at 110 kg in set 1, 4 reps at 115 kg in set 2, and 3 reps at 120 kg in set 3, then repeats this pattern two more times with the specified weights.

to peak athletes in vertical jump performance. Table 12.2 provides an example progression where moderate (25%-75% of the athlete's mass) barbell loads in the jump squat are used initially and then reduced to relatively light-load jump squats (>25% of the athlete's mass). This loading progression in the jump squat often results in excellent improvements in jumping performance.

Stretch-Shortening Cycle and Plyometric Training

The stretch-shortening cycle (SSC), where muscle undergoes an initial lengthening before shortening, is an important contributor to potentiating muscular force and power output when compared to movements that do not involve a countermovement or preparatory movement (e.g., run-up).[34-41] Positive work done by the previously stretched and loaded muscle can be accounted for by a combination of neurogenic and myogenic factors.[41-43] In SSC-based movements, the eccentric force, reflex stimuli and elastic contribution is greater than normal due to the eccentric (stretch) load; this is magnified further with accentuated eccentric SSC activities such as depth jumps and overloaded eccentrics.[34, 42, 44-48]

Plyometric training, which emphasises SSC abilities, should be included in a training program aimed at maximising jumping ability. This is an accepted and regular practice in physical conditioning. However, many programs emphasising SSC activity use too many exercises, or drills, with too many repetitions per set.[49] Athletes have a limited opportunity to acquire skill in each exercise. Performing numerous plyometric exercises in training (in addition to sport-skill training) may present more of a skill-acquisition chaotic stress than the desired SSC load: The athlete is spending the majority of the training program learning the new movements, thereby getting only a modest SSC training benefit. Until the athlete can do the exercise with high aptitude, it is unlikely to be effective. As such, coaches should use only plyometric exercises that offer a direct, profound and defensible benefit to the athlete's jumping ability.

Furthermore, the aim of the plyometric exercises should be to target a relevant quality, not necessarily mimic the sport movement. The coach must bear in mind that mimicking the sport movements is an overly simplistic approach to being sport specific; doing so can often interfere with the skill already being performed in the sport training, which may of course be already occurring in the sport at a high volume.

For example, in elite volleyball players, a countermovement-style jump (e.g., block jump, jump set and spike jump) may be performed 1,000 to 4,000 times per week simply through practice and matches. Strength and conditioning coaches and medical practitioners must carefully consider the utility and purpose of any additional jump training and favour targeting a specific physical quality, not simply replicating the movements already being performed in the skill-training sessions of the sport itself.

Some programs take the approach of more is better in relation to exercise variety in plyometric training, including as many as 10 exercises, 2 to 4 sets each, and 6 to 10 repetitions each. Programmes that combine strength training with a few specific plyometric exercises are likely much more effective.[48] Plyometric exercises should be performed with far less exercise variety (1 or 2 exercises per session), and fewer repetitions (1 to 5). Avoiding interset fatigue is imperative to the performance of the movement, and a high intensity is paramount to effectiveness.[50]

Total volume is difficult to prescribe en masse and must be considered in light of the athlete's physical literacy and robustness as well as the other stressors in current training. The coach should carefully consider the athlete's physical preparedness for the exercise, fatigue state from other training and athletic competence to perform the movement safely and effectively. Selecting only the most relevant and specific exercises for the athlete, and applying specific loading conditions, is likely a far superior approach to using plyometrics rather than doing a large number of exercises in hopes that something works.

Depth jumps (also called drop jumps), where the athlete drops from a height before jumping as high as possible, is one of the most effective plyometric exercises for improving vertical jump[45, 48, 51-55] and can be modified to include a horizontal hop or bound from the drop. This exercise presents a unique overload of the eccentric action preceding the concentric vertical propulsive movement, with unique preactivity characteristics[56] and novel training adaptations in neuromuscular characteristics.[48, 56, 57]

The primary purpose of using the depth jump is to increase the stretch load of the eccentric action, as the drop provides an additional (i.e., accentuated) eccentric load through the increase in acceleration and velocity resulting from the drop. Depth jumps can be performed from varying heights to achieve specific loading conditions; they can also be performed with modifications in technique.[45, 48, 51, 52] For example, a bounce depth jump (figure 12.10) can be performed where the athlete drops from a height with the intention to spend as little time on the ground as possible. This instruction results in relatively low joint displacements and a rapid cycle of eccentric-transition-concentric muscular action (i.e., short amortisation phase).[53] This drill, as well as a tuck jump (figure 12.11), forces the athlete to arrest

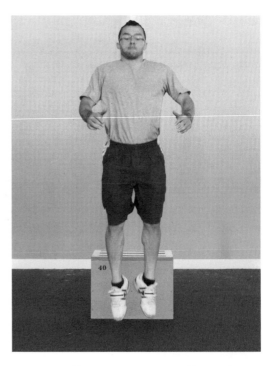

Figure 12.10 Bounce depth jump. The athlete drops from the prescribed height (generally 10-40 cm) and aims to rapidly get off the ground and jump. To ensure the athlete understands the desired outcome, coaching cues such as 'bounce like a ball off the floor' are effective to ensure a short contact time and relatively low joint compliance in the landing.

his or her landing at a faster than normal rate and emphasises a short contact. For this reason, these drills are favoured by many coaches because they have a clear purpose: to develop the fast transition that likely has considerable performance benefits, even for jumps that have a relatively slower eccentric-transition-concentric muscular action.[48]

The bounce depth jump is not the only worthwhile way to use a depth jump, however. The primary purpose of most vertical jump tasks is to jump as high as possible. Performing depth jumps with the intention of jumping as high as possible yields excellent results, even for jump tasks that are apparently grossly dissimilar.[45, 48, 53] This can be easily explained. A depth jump in which the athlete aims to jump as high as possible will result in the athlete performing this task with a high impulse, a higher eccentric velocity,[53] which is effective in developing superior jumping ability even under normal conditions.[58] These accentuated eccentric conditions result in greater neurogenic and myogenic contributions (i.e., overload) and is an

Figure 12.11 Tuck jump. The athlete performs repeated jumps in place whilst driving the knees into a tuck position and extends rapidly downward to the floor whilst descending, emphasising a short contact and explosive jump action.

effective method for developing impulse in jumping, under high stretch-load conditions.[34, 36, 38, 51, 52, 56]

The drop height chosen is a major consideration for programming depth jumps. In addition to assessment of landing technique and general athletic competency, it is best to conduct a stretch-load tolerance assessment to help determine the appropriate training height for each athlete. Table 12.3 provides an example of results for three volleyball athletes, all with the same countermovement jump score, on an incremental stretch-load tolerance-testing session. After a countermovement jump test, the drop height of each depth jump was increased by 10 centimetres progressively, with the athletes having several trials to jump as high as possible from each height. The results demonstrate the athlete with the lowest stretch-load tolerance (player A), the highest stretch-load tolerance (player B) and what is typical of this population (player C). In all three cases, an optimum height can be determined—a specific box height for each athlete elicited a single best jump result. However, it's likely best to include a range of heights in training plans to challenge aspects of the force–velocity spectrum in this exercise; it may also be appropriate to include training types such as depth jumps for maximal height and minimal contact. Table 12.4 provides a sample plyometric program with depth

Table 12.3 Countermovement Vertical Jump (CMVJ) Height and Depth Jump Scores From 20- to 60-Centimetre Drop Heights for Three National Team Volleyball Players

Other plyometrics	Drop height 20 cm	Drop height 30 cm	Drop height 40 cm	Drop height 50 cm	Drop height 60 cm
CMVJ					
Player A	320 cm	318 cm	308 cm	300 cm	294 cm
Player B	324 cm	326 cm	328 cm	330 cm	329 cm
Player C	323 cm	326 cm	323 cm	320 cm	317 cm

Table 12.4 Sample Session for a Depth Jump Training Program for Three Volleyball Players Based on Test Results Presented in Table 12.3

Player A	Tuck jumps 8 × 3	Fast contact 4 × 3	Max height 10 × 2	Altitude landings 6 × 2		
Player B	Single-leg tuck jumps 4 × 3		Fast contact 4 × 3	Fast contact × 3	Max height 8 × 2	Max height 6 × 2
Player C	Assisted jumps, 10% body mass 4 × 5	Fast contact 4 × 3	Max height 8 × 2	Max height 6 × 2	Altitude landings 6 × 2	

jumps for an elite volleyball player, conducted after warm-up and before a strength-training session.

The eccentric phase of jumping can be further accentuated through the use of additional mass in the countermovement of a vertical jump: The athlete releases the load at the bottom position and jumps without load (figure 12.12) or performs a loaded jump squat with additional eccentric load using barbell releasers. Compared to normal countermovement jumps, this method provides for higher jump heights and superior power output, likely due to the enhanced contractile state of the muscles at the initiation of the propulsive phase of the jump.[42] When compared to regular countermovement jumps, jumps with additional eccentric load of 20 to 40 per cent of the athlete's mass provide for a superior improvement in vertical jump scores.[47]

Assisted jumping, in which the athlete's mass is mechanically reduced, may be a unique over-speed method to enhance jumping performance. Coaches can use a harness and bungee system or have the athlete hold on to a powerlifting resistance strap. The reduced load allows for a greater-than-normal concentric velocity and, as a result, a higher jump height. For athletes who have a reasonable strength-training background, and in conjunction with a strength-training program, this may provide a novel stimulus and lead to improved performances.[59]

Leanness

Although most of the coach's focus on improving jumping ability is spent on training methods, excess body fat is clearly deleterious to jump performance. Additional body fat is additional mass. It is not mass that may assist in propulsion, as additional muscle may, so it detracts from jump performance and increases the load that must be absorbed on landing. This is not to say that *skinny*, low-mass athletes are desirable, but that *leanness* (i.e., healthy, low-body-fat level) is a highly desirable trait for athletes wanting to maximise jumping ability.

If a competitive athlete has too much body fat, diet and lifestyle must be addressed. These factors are adaptable and, in large part, are responsible for the problem. It is far too common for strength and conditioning coaches and sport science practitioners to remedy the body-fat problem by prescribing additional conditioning training to increase energy expenditure. Training for sport

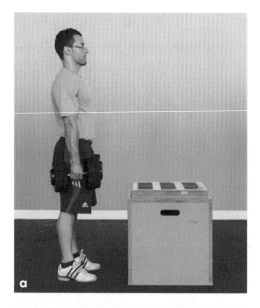

Figure 12.12 Release jumps.

at the elite level involves careful, specific consideration for the volume and intensity required to meet physical requirements, and the total volume of training is generally high. With this in mind, it makes no sense to simply load additional junk training into a program to enable and promote the athlete's current inappropriate eating and lifestyle.

If an athlete is not training enough, then he or she can train more; however, if the athlete is training appropriately for the sport but has too much body fat, the critical aspects of food volume, content and type, timing and distribution, as well as factors such as sleep and stress, must become the priority. It is not appropriate to attempt to remedy the body-fat problem with increased training volume without addressing the nutrition and lifestyle factors that underpin that problem.

Table 12.5 demonstrates the positive impact in jump squat and strength performance that can be achieved when an athlete reduces excess fat mass (as demonstrated by a lower sum of a seven-site skinfold test). The primary focus in the period between observations was to improve the athlete's understanding of the role of diet and lifestyle on body-fat levels and, most importantly, to implement change in these factors and hold the athlete accountable for the results and the goals that were set. The resulting reduction in extra fat tissue increased leanness, reflected by an increase in the athlete's lean mass index (LMI).[60] The benefits to strength and power performance are easily observable and explained by the reduction in additional, noncontributing mass (i.e., excess body fat) during the movements (e.g., jump squat, clean, squat), resulting in better strength and power

performance. In the case of the increases in clean and squat barbell loads, it could be reasoned that some of the fat mass lost was simply placed on the bar in the form of additional plates, allowing a greater expression of strength! Considering that athletes with too much body fat take longer to recover from training generally, it could also be speculated that the now-leaner athlete was also simply in a better position to respond to training.

Planning Training

Integrating training methods into a progressive plan is often referred to as an art because mere scientific understanding of training adaptation is inadequate for the coach or athlete to make all of the necessary multifactorial decisions. Consideration, and therefore an in-depth understanding, must be given to the long-term needs of the athlete, the demands of the sport, other influences on the physical and emotional state of the athlete and the athletic competency of each member of a training group. Importantly, day-to-day variations and decisions of training plans are made in response to up-to-date feedback and observations, so training planning is no small task. Effective training planning relies on the practitioner being a competent scientist and an outstanding coach. If this were not the case, elite athletes could upload test results into a website and receive effective training programs generated solely on data, but this is not wholly effective at the elite level. Nevertheless, the following section provides general concepts that can help the practitioner frame the training approach when considering the objective of improving jump and landing ability.

Classification of Training Exercises

When working with elite sportpeople, practitioners need to quantify total load from training but also identify each specific type of exercise and its effect. Categorising exercises into one of three broad categories—general, special and specific—allows the practitioner to determine the relative approach to each training type deemed appropriate for that athlete at that time.

General exercises can be defined as those that improve broad, performance-relevant components of the jump. These include aspects such as maximal strength, rate-of-force development and maximal power. *Special methods* include those that target highly specific aspects relevant

Table 12.5 Changes in Body Mass

Based on the sum of seven-site skinfold testing, lean mass index (LMI), jump squat displacement and 1RM clean and squat over three months in an elite sprint cyclist (BMX racing) after dietary and lifestyle intervention.

Test measure	Initial testing	Follow-up
Body mass (kg)	84 kg	76 kg
Sum of seven-site skinfold testing (mm)	88 mm	42 mm
Lean mass index (LMI)	1.05	1.81
1RM clean	110 kg	120 kg
1RM squat	190 kg	205 kg

LMI is derived from the formula body mass (kg) / sum of seven-site skinfold testing (mm).

Jumping and Landing Training for Alpine Ski Racers

Bill Knowles
Reconditioning and Athletic Development Specialist

Downhill skiing is a highly-skilled sport in which technical and tactical abilities typically take priority over physical dominance. The speeds achieved and sustained and the highly-unpredictable terrain covered require incredible coordination, balance and reactive endurance.

Unlike most sports, in skiing athletes try to keep both feet on the ground (snow) as much as possible. When the feet do move, they move in unison rather than independently, not dissimilar to the tires on a car. Neither leg has a forceful extension movement, but each limb builds up tremendous force that needs to be transferred from one side to the other (pendulum) at significant speed. The coordination of power in this process is linked through the entire kinetic chain. Regardless of how strong the athlete is, the timing to apply this movement is more valuable than the force he or she possesses.

Adolescent ski racers provide a great opportunity to enhance jumping and landing performance and also mitigate injury risk. These athletes have a higher learning potential in terms of optimal movement patterns than their established adult counterparts and are more at risk both intrinsically and extrinsically. Adolescents are rarely exposed to competent performance training specialists who understand the nuisances of power development and force reduction strategies.

The technical aspects of triple extension (jumping) and triple flexion (landing) can be greatly influenced with quality coaching and exposure. These movements have a high dynamic correspondence to all events in the sport and also, if performed poorly, carry a significant injury risk. Therefore they are the primary movements to focus on in skiing athletic development programmes.

Injury Prevention

Adolescent skiers need to focus on *coordinated fast-movement training*. I purposely avoid the use of the word *powerful* to ensure that movement quality is the focus for the athlete rather than the development of physiological or mechanical characteristics. I also have found that emphasising coordinated and explosive movement off-snow allows for a consistency in approach and terminology used by both the skier and coach, something that aids in the skill transfer from the gym to the snow.

Optimal acceleration and deceleration strategies, essentially landing mechanics, are crucial in preventing injuries in this population. Athletes are required to stabilise significant forces at very high angular velocities in events that last several minutes. The reported risk of intra-articular knee-joint injury remains high in skiing, whilst the long-term cost of subtle inaccuracies in joint kinematics in accelerating degenerative changes would seem intertwined.

Training Priorities

Movement competency is an essential priority in jump and land training. In the sagittal plane, I coach the athlete to generate sufficient system tension and muscular force to dampen vertical force and therefore prevent passive collapse on contact with the ground. In the frontal plane, I expect to see good control of knee mechanics, thereby minimising aberrant stress to intra-articular structures.

Fast coordinative movements in the frontal plane account for a significant proportion of training. These movements often have a slightly forward direction (thus diagonal) as this is more reflective of the action in ski racing.

Training Drill Examples

- Maximum lateral jump. Leave from two feet and land on two feet in a balanced position.

- Forward jump over a low hurdle into a maximum lateral jump.

- Forward jump to a 40 centimetre box. Slightly touch the box unweighted and drop to the ground. Follow with a maximum lateral jump.

- Rebound plyometrics. After a maximum lateral jump to the right, immediately link the movement into a maximum jump to the left and stick the landing.

to jump performance, such as jumping power, SSC function, and targeted motions and postures related to the movement performed in the sport itself. *Specific jump methods* refer to those that are the same as in the sport itself. For example, a basketball player may practise rebound jumping, or a volleyball player may perform spike jumps up to a jump-and-reach apparatus. Table 12.6 shows a sample delineation among general, special and specific methods.

Training Emphasis

Through assessment and profiling of the athlete (chapter 1), and with consideration of the time available in the training period, coaches can determine the relative emphasis on each of the training types. During the general preparation phase, specific methods are often not undertaken at all in strength and conditioning training—*but* considerably high volumes of specific jumps are achieved through the athlete's sport practice. Within the general preparation phase, general strength methods are used to precede a maximal strength emphasis, and only a low number of special methods are

used at this time (e.g., altitude landings, low-height depth jumps). From this foundation of generalised training for strength and power, more specific methods can be added during subsequent stages to augment jumping ability.

In addition to quantifying the type of exercise, practitioners also plan for and quantify the nature of the exercise selected. Classifying training types as plyometric efforts, ballistic strength, maximal strength or general strength or repeated effort (table 12.7) allows a clear determination of the training emphasis by calculating the total sets, total reps and the volume load of each category, as well as the total for the training program. The volume load is calculated simply as this:

$$\text{volume load} = \text{sets} \times \text{reps} \times \text{mass}$$

For example, the plyometric volume load for 4 sets of 10 repetitions of bounding for a 75-kilogram athlete is $4 \times 10 \times 75 = 3,000$, whereas the maximal strength volume load for 6 sets of 3 repetitions of the back squat with 120 kilograms is $6 \times 3 \times 120 = 2,160$. Figure 12.13 shows the volume load for a mesocycle of strength and conditioning training for a junior volleyball player

Table 12.6 Exercises for Volleyball, Basketball and Long Jump Delineated Into General, Special and Specific Categories

Sport	General	Special	Specific
Volleyball	Squat Snatch Single-leg squat	Depth jump Loaded jump squat	Block jump Jump set Spike jump
Basketball	Squat Clean and jerk Power clean	Box hop Tuck jump	Rebounding Dunking Lay-up
Long jump	Squat Barbell step-up	Hurdle hop Bound Short run-up Wind-assisted long run-up	Long jumps

Table 12.7 Exercises Used by Jumping Athletes Categorised as Plyometric, Ballistic Strength, Maximal Strength, General Strength or Repeated Effort

Plyometric	Ballistic strength	Maximal strength	General strength or repeated effort
Depth jump Hop/bound Tuck jump Skip Hurdle hop Accentuate eccentric jumps	Snatch Clean Olympic lift variations Loaded jump squat	Squat and variations Deadlift Front squat Romanian-style deadlift	Squat and variations Lunge variations Step-up Reverse hyperextension Single-leg squat Calf raise

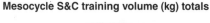

Mesocycle S&C training volume (kg) totals

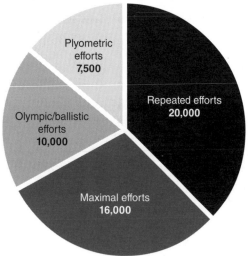

Plyometric efforts 7,500

Repeated efforts 20,000

Olympic/ballistic efforts 10,000

Maximal efforts 16,000

Figure 12.13 Volume load for a mesocycle of strength and conditioning training for a junior volleyball player.

Wisdom

Planning and quantifying training load and type of load, using a volume–load method or similar approach, is essential to ensuring that the coach is effectively addressing the range of qualities relevant to jumping. The outcome of this effort allows for greater individualisation of training to address each athlete's needs more specifically.

Training Delivery

Once the theoretical background is in place and the programme to develop both jumping and landing training has been planned, it's now time to actually deliver the training. There is no doubt that the first two pieces lead into the third, but what separates a good coach from a great coach is his or her ability to effectively implement a programme that produces measurable *performance* gains in the athletes under the coach's tutelage, not just improvements in the general trainable qualities. Higher-level athletes require an understanding of the interplay of physical qualities, training load and the athletes' response to the load, technique and other relevant factors.

Jumping-Technique Training

To jump effectively, a proper summation of forces must take place. The athlete must perform contact (e.g., long jump or countermovement) with an efficient body position and ideal mechanical position (i.e., joint angles) to enable efficient use of elastic energy. Coaches are encouraged to coach this technique, particularly the effective summation of triple extension through the hip, knee, and ankle, and the arm swing. Especially for double-leg jumps, for example, the torso position can contribute to effective jump technique through extension of the torso at the hip; however, excessive flexion is unlikely to be effective. Therefore, inclination of the torso should be viewed as a matter of optimisation for the athlete's individual physicality and body size.

For all technical aspects, there is no perfect technique. Success depends on the athlete's training background, technical experience, body size and inherent qualities. However, when initially teaching athletes to jump more effectively, coaches emphasise the correct techniques for squat (for double-leg take-offs) and single-leg squat (for single-leg take-offs). It is best to view both of these exercises as balance and technique exercises. An athlete who cannot perform these exercises perfectly, with efficiency throughout the movement, is not efficiently able to extend through the appropriate sequence in a balanced manner and therefore is leaking power in the jumping task.

Landing-Technique Training

Teaching and training landing technique as part of an effective jump-training program is a critical component for the practitioner to consider. It is most sensible to prioritise landing technique *before* concentrating on other aspects of jump training.

Wisdom

It would be unsafe to learn to fly an airplane if there was no one to land it. So, too, must the athlete learn to absorb landing forces safely and with effective technique before extensive jump-training occurs.

The primary aim of a safe, effective landing is to do so with modest peak forces and with mechanics that are within a safe range and motion on the involved joints. These two factors are interdependent. Inefficient joint movement (e.g., valgus motion of the knees from poor hip control; figure 12.14) will result not only in hazardous stresses in the knee, but also in higher peak forces due to the reduction in the attenuation of force offered by the knee.[61-63]

Figure 12.14 Valgus knee motion on landing.

Coaches should aim to develop effective biomotor abilities with a particular emphasis on control, motion and strength in their athletes from the earliest age possible to ensure that proper structural strength, stability, range and movement develop.[64, 65] Table 12.8 provides a sample progression plan for the development of landing competencies for both one and two legs in young volleyball players.

A simple means for developing and evaluating landing technique is to use altitude landings. This drill, in which the athlete drops from a box onto the ground and observes the landing, is ideal for developing good technique; the drill also increases the specific eccentric strength required for efficient landings. When coaching these landings, consider the form that the athlete is able to maintain through the kinetic chain. Observing from the front (figure 12.15a) and side (figure 12.15b) allows the coach to ensure the integrity of the athlete's landing and to determine whether the amount of compression through the ankle, knee and hip are appropriate for the drop height. If the athlete's compression appears too great, and the athlete cannot alter this technique with feedback such as to stiffen the spring, it may be that the athlete is not appropriately strong enough to train at the selected drop height (i.e., the box is too high for that athlete at this time).

Too little flexion in the landing generally means that a high peak force is being transferred through the body, resulting in high peak-compression forces at the joints. The athlete should be encouraged to land more quietly. At times, weaker athletes, or those who have not developed a technique that blends the appropriate amount of compliance with cognitively regulated stiffness, land with an initial abrupt landing force and then fail and fall during absorption. This is a signal that the athlete's strength or technique is not adequate for the particular height being used. If the athlete is recovering from ankle or knee injury, such a landing indicates the athlete remains at risk for further injury. Of particular importance, a combination of an abrupt landing (i.e., poor absorption through the hip, knee and ankle) and a valgus movement of the knee during landing is associated with knee-injury risk. Any movement patterns the coach observes that exhibit these traits should be corrected through training.

Table 12.8 Technical Movement Competencies and Progression for Foundation Volleyball Players (12 and 13 Years Old) and Developing Volleyball Players (13-15 Years Old) to Promote Safe, Effective Landing From Jumps

Control strength	Force absorption	Single-leg force absorption
Bilateral squat		
Walking lunge	Vertical hop and stick	
Single-leg squat	Horizontal hop and stick (long jump)	Single-leg hop and stick
	5 × tuck jump (stick last repetition)	Single-leg horizontal hop and stick
	Altitude landing and stick (drop from box) 5 × horizontal hop	5 × single-leg tuck jump (stick last repetition) Single-leg altitude landing (drop from box)
		Single-leg 5 × horizontal hop

Figure 12.15 Altitude landing (*a*) from the front; (*b*) from the side.

Wisdom

The aim of the landing is to develop quiet, controlled landings with effective absorption and body alignment.

Figure 12.16 shows vertical force traces for two professional surfing athletes of similar body

mass performing altitude landings from a 0.50-metre box. One athlete is able to provide enough absorption, primarily through ankle, knee and hip flexion, to keep the peak forces much lower than the other athlete. From this analysis, it is easy to determine that the athlete with the high peak forces should not use such a high drop height. However, even without the use of a force

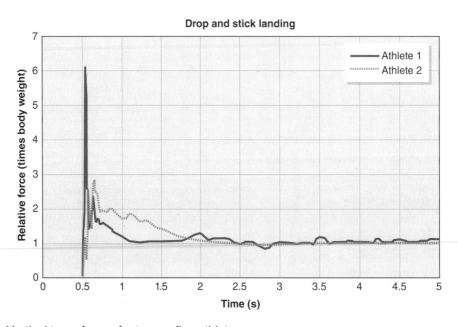

Figure 12.16 Vertical trace forces for two surfing athletes.

trace, this can be determined by the sound of the landing. In this case, the athlete with the high peak landing forces landed with a loud sound from the initial abrupt contact, followed by an observable inefficient compression movement pattern characterised by a failing of muscular control. Although the knees did not fail inward and exhibit a valgus pattern, this drop height was not appropriate for this athlete's strength level at the time of the training.

A program involving altitude landings can incorporate both single- and double-leg landings. Including single-leg landings is important because many landings occur on a single leg. For example, although the run-up jump in volleyball (i.e., spike jump) involves a double-leg take-off, in the majority of cases there will be a single-leg landing: The athlete has to adjust position in the air to strike the ball, altering body position and thereby landing first with one foot, then the other. This is similar for a receiver in American football, where an adjustment in the air to catch the ball or contact by the opponent forces a single-leg landing. Such a landing is not ideal in terms of reducing peak forces acting on the body, but it cannot be eliminated since it is an inherent part of the sport.

Training programmes should include both single- and double-leg landing progressions in order to develop athlete techniques and eccentric strength so that athletes are prepared for the uncontrolled, unpredictable nature of sport.

Table 12.9 provides some highlights from an altitude-landing program of an elite volleyball player for the 4-year period preceding his first Olympic games.

Table 12.9 Altitude-Landing Training Progression to Develop Landing Technique and Eccentric Strength for an Elite Male Volleyball Player

This program is taken from a 4-year period of a single athlete's training.

Athlete's age (yrs)	Bilateral landings	Unilateral landings
16	5 × 3 at 0.40 m 4 × 2 at 0.50 m	4 × 4 at 0.20 m
17	4 × 3 at 0.50 m 4 × 2 at 0.60 m	4 × 4 at 0.30 m
18	4 × 3 at 0.50 m 3 × 2 at 0.75 m	5 × 4 at 0.30 m
19*	3 × 3 at 0.50 m 3 × 2 at 0.75 m	3 × 4 at 0.30 m

*Olympic year. Lower volume was used due to shortened preparatory period.

Summary

Jumping performance is multifactorial and is influenced, both positively and negatively, by considerations such as range and mobility, movement competency and landing efficiency, strength and power levels, anthropometric factors and the athlete's training state. The foundation of jumping performance is relative power, which is underpinned by strength. An athlete's strength is a consideration in program design at all times. From a basis of sufficient relative strength developed through major traditional movements, Olympic lifting, loaded power exercises and special stretch-shortening cycle exercises can be incorporated to yield far greater results than if those methods were performed in isolation.

CHAPTER 13

Increasing Agility

Sophia Nimphius, PhD, ASCC, CSCS*D
Edith Cowan University, Australia

In most sports, changes of speed or rapid and decisive changes of direction result in a break, a score or a defensive stop that can change the momentum of a game or match. Agility is a unique physical attribute that requires multiple types of strength but also requires cognitive abilities such as reaction time and decision making. This chapter breaks down the critical components of agility into their constituent parts, both physical (change of direction ability) and cognitive (reaction time and decision making). Each section describes the physical, technical and even some tactical aspects that are required or need to be considered for developing well-rounded and effective agility in athletes. Specifically, this chapter helps coaches understand, measure and implement immediate coaching strategies and cues to enhance agility. Further, the chapter delves into long-term development planning of agility work through appropriate program design to improve these often underdeveloped aspects of athletic performance.

What Is Agility?

The ability to change initial direction to a predetermined location and space on the field or court is known as *change-of-direction speed* (CODS). However, it is the perceptual–cognitive ability to react to a stimulus such as a defender or the bounce of a ball in addition to the physical ability to change direction that provides a true definition of agility.[1]

In a majority of sports, athletes do not have the time or open space to reach top speed in competition. The constant necessity in sport to react to another player or situation on the field or court often requires athletes to decelerate and then reaccelerate in another direction as rapidly as possible whilst maintaining or regaining as much momentum as possible. This readjustment of the athlete's momentum and can occur during either an offensive or a defensive task.

Recent research has shown that an athlete's lower-body response time may differ depending on whether the athlete's stimulus-response requirement (tactical situation) is offensive (move in the opposite direction) or defensive (move in the same direction).[2-4] The exact reason for these varying response times during an offensive task (termed *incompatible stimulus*) versus defensive task (termed *compatible stimulus*) is not known. However, the processing strategy, which can vary by gender or tactical situation, can influence the length of time it takes an athlete to respond to the situation.[3, 5] It is speculated that the response to an offensive situation requires information to move across the hemispheres of the brain whereas the response to a defensive situation allows the processing to occur within one side of the brain.[3] Therefore, much like training both the left and right side of the body, one should train in scenarios that require processing both within and across the hemispheres of the brain. When developing drills to enhance agility performance, it is wise to

Wisdom

Change-of-direction speed (CODS) is a preplanned action of altering direction of travel whereas agility takes into account both the physical change of direction and includes perceptual and decision-making domains. The way an athlete changes direction when he or she can preplan movement is different from how the athlete changes direction in reaction to a stimulus.

ensure the drills address moving in the opposite direction (offensive) in response to signal or cue. It is quite common for instructions to be 'Move in the direction I point' without a subsequent drill involving the instructions 'Move in the direction opposite from where I point'. If we want an athlete to improve offensive agility, that athlete needs to practise offensive agility. If we want the athlete to improve defensive agility, he or she needs to practise defensive agility.

With the knowledge that the brain processes offensive and defensive responses differently, we must consider the tactical situations that occur and train not only the *physical pathways* of neuromuscular contraction but also these *perceptual–cognitive pathways*. Agility is a multifaceted physical as well as cognitive attribute that varies as tactical situations change.

Training each quality that underpins agility performance in a systematic and logical manner is important during the athlete-development process. To do this, coaches need to be aware of all factors that underpin agility in order to choose the most effective test to assess agility performance. Many coaches and athletes overlook the applied biomechanics that support the performance of a change-of-direction and agility manoeuvre, but they can be explained in simple but effective terms.

Understanding the Plant Phase

Understanding the magnitude and direction of ground-reaction forces applied during the plant phase (figure 13.1) when changing direction gives insight into the complex physical requirements needed. The plant phase involves forces that decelerate, change direction and reaccelerate in less than two-tenths of a second. The situation—preplanned change of direction versus change of direction in reaction to a situation or stimulus—can modify the kinetics involved during the plant or change-of-direction step.

Based on the understanding of kinetics (forces and joint moments) as well as kinematics (joint angles and joint velocities), a coach can create a well-planned and logical progression of specific drills to gradually increase intensity and specificity from both a physical and a cognitive perspective and apply them to a properly periodised agility program. Various drills performed in close conjunction with specific coaching cues can be used to continually enhance overall agility performance in athletes.

Figure 13.1 Plant phase.

Components of Agility

As shown in figure 13.2, agility is a physical fitness component that requires development in a multitude of areas. Coaches and athletes need a multifaceted approach to ensure adequate development in each area. Enhancement of agility performance likely will lag behind enhancement of certain physical attributes that underpin agility. The delay between increased physical capacity and ability to actualise this increase into improved performance is termed *lag time*.[6, 7] For this reason, coaches should trust their plan and convey the reality of lag time to the athlete whilst being aware of adaptation rates for muscle, tendon, ligament and bone that underlie performance changes. Proper progression into more advanced drills should be prescribed with the understanding that muscle may adapt faster than tendon, ligament and bone just as strength may increase faster than it can transfer into improved speed, or in this case, into CODS.

The concept of lag time, or the length of time it takes for an athlete to learn to use his or her newfound strength or power, is important to consider when trying to determine the transfer of training effect from one underlying physical attribute to a fitness component.

To better show the complexity and interwoven nature of the components of agility outlined in

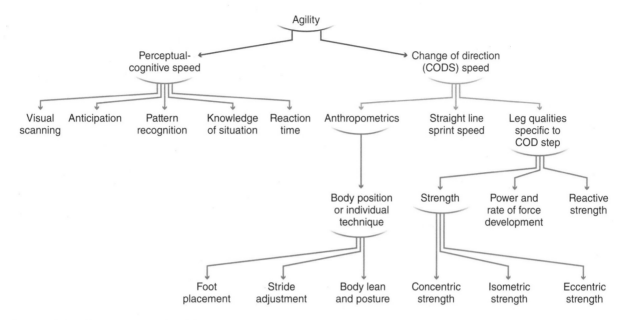

Figure 13.2 Components of agility.

Adapted from W.B. Young, R. James, and I. Montgomery, 2002. "Is muscle power related to running speed with changes of direction?" *Journal of Sports Medicine and Physical Fitness* 42(3): 282-288; and J.M. Sheppard and W.B. Young, 2006, "Agility literature review: Classifications, training and testing," *Journal of Sports Sciences* 24(9): 919-932.

figure 13.2, the diagram has been divided into two parts: factors associated with the cognitive component and factors associated with the physical component of agility performance (CODS). A model of agility has been presented in previous research;[8] however, the theoretical model of agility presented in figure 13.2 has been modified to include more specific aspects of the physical attributes required for agility.

An emphasis has been made on providing a more stepwise progression in the hierarchy of the model. For example, anthropometry of an athlete is something that cannot be immediately modified (mass distribution) or never modified (limb lengths) but will dictate the technique or body position that is most advantageous. There is no one perfect technique because athletes will adopt particular amounts of body-lean, foot-placement and stride-adjustment strategies that work within these constraints. There are, however, general suggestions for appropriate body positions that can enhance CODS, which are discussed later in this chapter.

In addition to hierarchical changes, this model acknowledges strength can be expressed and therefore measured during muscular actions. The force capacity of a muscle is commonly represented on the force–velocity curve of muscle as shown in

figure 13.3. Depending on the inherent characteristics of the athlete (genetics), training age, training background and mesocycle of training, an athlete will have unique levels of eccentric, isometric and concentric strength.

Each type of strength is used during a change of direction as the athlete brakes or decelerates (eccentric), transitions (isometric) and then accelerates in the new direction (concentric). It is not necessarily the case that an athlete who has exceptional concentric strength also has the highest eccentric strength or the combination of the two as displayed in reactive strength. Thus, any one or multiple types of strength may be the limiting factor in an athlete. The limiting factor of agility performance could therefore be masked if only one measure of strength is assessed. Of particular interest (but difficult to measure) is eccentric strength because this determines the athlete's ability to brake rapidly. Eccentric strength is particularly required or challenged when changing direction with a high-entry velocity into a cut or during extreme change-of-direction angles that require substantial eccentric load to be absorbed at the joints.

On the other side of the agility model are the perceptual–cognitive requirements that make agility such a unique physical fitness component. In

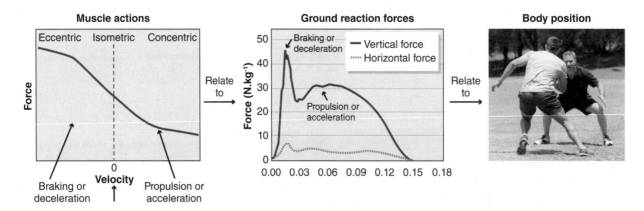

Figure 13.3 Relationship among muscle actions, phases of ground-reaction forces during a change of direction and subsequent body positions.

the model (figure 13.2), there are several areas that combine to allow a faster cognitive processing time that can ultimately enhance agility performance and, for some athletes, compensate for physical deficits, allowing them to still excel in situations that require agility. Improvements in response time must be translated into game-specific or task-specific situations for response time to improve overall agility performance, much like strength must be translated into specific change-of-direction movements to manifest into agility improvements. Therefore, the components of perceptual–cognitive speed—visual scanning, anticipation, pattern recognition and knowledge of situation—represent task- or game-specific perceptual and cognitive abilities thought to improve agility performance.

Wisdom

Agility performance is uniquely underpinned by a multitude of physical and perceptual–cognitive attributes. An athlete and coach who understand the strengths and weaknesses of these underpinning factors will be able to find the largest window of opportunity to enhance agility performance.

Testing Change of Direction and Agility

Although agility is clearly an important physical fitness component, choosing an appropriate, meaningful test can be more difficult. Coaches need to choose a test that considers the physical

CODS aspect and the perceptual–cognitive aspects of agility performance because both have been shown to differentiate between levels of play within a sport.[9]

The original reactive agility test (RAT) allows athletes to not only perform a change of direction rapidly to display CODS, but also to respond to a stimulus on a screen. The athlete is required to assess the position of the image of an athlete on the screen and then change direction to the appropriate side.[9] Since this original RAT, several researchers have used protocols with a variety of stimulus methods that have included (but are not limited to) video projections and human stimuli. The human stimulus has been shown to be reliable during a RAT.[2] The setup of the RAT used to assess the reliability of the human stimulus is shown in figure 13.4. Coaches and athletes are able to set up this testing without additional technological requirements.

In the sample agility test, when the athlete crosses the start timing-gate line, the stimulus will move. The athlete changes direction either to the left or right in response to the direction the stimulus moves. A high-speed camera is used to assess the decision-making time from when the stimulus initiates movement until the athlete initiates movement towards the intended direction.

Appropriate CODS test can provide a large amount of information, but not all CODS tests are equal. A classification method of various CODS and agility tests is shown in table 13.1.

Although there are several direction changes in these tests, in most sports, it is a single, decisive

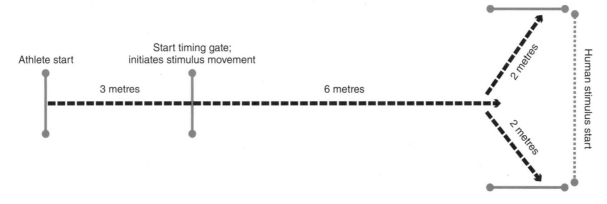

Figure 13.4 Example agility test with a human stimulus.

Table 13.1 Sample Classifications of CODS and Agility Tests

Change-of-direction speed (CODS) tests	Manoeuvrability	Reactive agility test (RAT)
Traditional 5-0-5 (high-velocity CODS)	T-test	RAT in response to an arrow or light
Modified 5-0-5 (low-velocity CODS)	Illinois agility test	RAT in response to a video
Pro-agility (low- and high-velocity CODS)	L-run	RAT in response to a human stimulus
10 m shuttle (moderate- to high-velocity CODS)	AFL agility test	
	Three-cone agility test	

change of direction that is required for a point, a break or a change in game momentum or positional advantage. Therefore, the tests have been split into three categories:

1. CODS tests that require either one or two high- or low-velocity entry changes of direction;

2. CODS tests that require three or more changes of direction with more curves than sharp changes of direction and therefore measure one's manoeuvrability; and,

3. Reactive agility tests that require a change of direction in response to some type of stimulus.

4. Examples of these tests are shown in figures 13.4 and 13.5.

To test a physical quality that contributes to agility, the test must be demanding enough that it can differentiate between performers. However, a test that encompasses many physical qualities makes it virtually impossible to differentiate which physical quality used during the test actually improved or limited the performance.

Although straight-line sprint speed is part of CODS and agility performance, it is important to minimise the amount of straight-line sprinting required in a test to ensure the time that represents CODS is a function of the athlete's actual ability to change direction, not run straight. For this reason, there are no shuttle tests shown in table 13.1 that require multiple passes, except for the 10-metre shuttle, which requires only one 180-degree change of direction after a 10-metre entry followed by a 10-metre exit.

Understanding the impact of the CODS test choice may explain why previous research has shown both significant and nonsignificant relationships existing between various measures of strength and the ability to change direction.[8, 10] Change-of-direction tests such as the 5-0-5, modified 5-0-5 or L-run show only moderate correlations between each other in the same athletes,[11] clearly demonstrating that these tests, although all apparently measures of change-of-direction performance, are actually measuring a variety of physical or performance qualities.

A better understanding of underpinning factors has been drawn from longitudinal training studies. For example, studies show a moderate-to-large relationship in transfer of training for

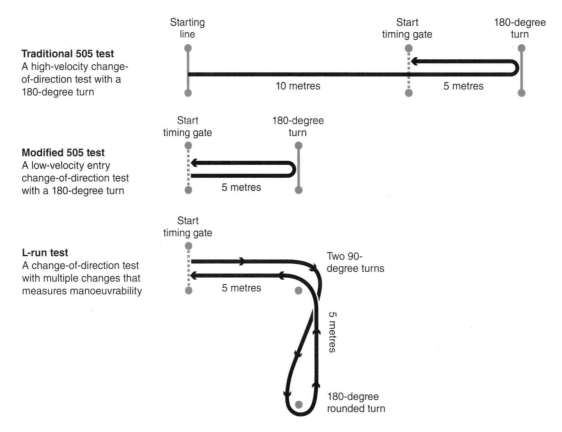

Figure 13.5 Comparison of high-velocity, low-velocity and manoeuvrability CODS tests.

both absolute 1RM squat strength to 5-0-5 CODS dominant side and nondominant side times (0.7 to 1.18) and relative 1RM squat strength (0.95 to 1.62).[12] Therefore, particularly in young or developing athletes, strength is a major determining factor for change-of-direction ability,[13] particularly when performing high-velocity entry CODS tests with physically demanding changes of direction, such as a 180-degree turn.

Therefore, it is recommended that an agility-testing battery include both a CODS test and a RAT. Since a majority of RAT tests require only a 45-degree change of direction, a more physically demanding CODS should be performed. These CODS tests may be a low-velocity turn, such as the modified 5-0-5; a high-velocity turn, such as the traditional 5-0-5; or a test such as the pro-agility, which requires both a low-speed and high-speed change of direction (table 13.1). Further, if the sport requires subtle changes of direction at high speed, a measure of manoeuvrability such as the L-run or the three-cone agility test will measure the last part of the agility and CODS jigsaw.

A comparison of physical fitness measurements of two American football quarterbacks can be seen in table 13.2 and figure 13.6. The radar plot in figure 13.6 produces an easy-to-understand visual showing the areas each athlete excels in or has room for improvement in compared to the position mean. The results are presented as standardised scores, which allows for comparison across many units of measurement. Later in this chapter these results will be used to show how the two athletes' long-term development may be planned using their test results.

Programming to Enhance Agility

A well-constructed testing battery, although seemingly extensive, can provide information on all components that underpin agility performance. Used in conjunction with strength, power and speed testing, it will provide for an effective training programme to improve agility performance and overall athletic performance.

Table 13.2 Comparison of the Physical Fitness Test Results of Two American Football Quarterbacks

Test	Athlete A	Athlete B	Position mean
Relative squat 1RM (relative to body weight)	1.53	1.98	1.81
Relative power clean 1RM (relative to body weight)	1.09	1.19	1.19
Countermovement jump (CMJ)	72 cm	66 cm	71 cm
Depth jump (DJ) from 40 cm	65 cm	70 cm	73 cm
L-run	6.99 sec	7.17 sec	6.95 sec
Pro-agility, 10 m split	2.19 sec	2.19 sec	2.23 sec
Pro-agility, flying 10 m split	2.31 sec	2.17 sec	2.16 sec
Reactive agility test (RAT; reaction time)	25 ms	75 ms	50 ms

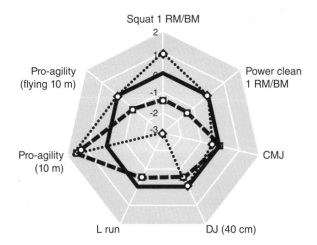

Figure 13.6 Radar plot comparing athlete strengths and weaknesses as a standardised Z-score with a focus on CODS results. Athlete A is represented by the dashed line and athlete B by the dotted line. The solid line represents zero as a standardised score.

Effective Force Application and Body Position During Change-of-Direction and Agility Manoeuvres

Having the physical capacity to produce force is critical when an athlete wants to decelerate, accelerate or change direction. This concept is not original and is drawn from Newton's second law of motion, which states that acceleration of a mass is directly proportional to the force that is applied or is more simply written as the equation $F = ma$. An athlete's ability to apply force effectively and efficiently will give rise to enhanced acceleration, deceleration and overall ability to change direction. The relationship between force application, measured as ground-reaction forces, muscular actions and subsequent deceleration, change of direction and reacceleration has been previously discussed and is shown in figure 13.3.

Key for the development of force production ability is that exercises performed in a vertical plane, such as the squat, power clean and snatch, are related to activities that result in horizontal movement, such as sprinting and CODS. An athlete's ability to decelerate, change direction or reaccelerate will be limited by how much force he or she can rapidly drive into the ground.

To produce a change of direction, the athlete must ensure that the angle at which he or she pushes into the ground does not compromise the ability to produce force to overcome gravity. If the athlete does brake or push off too aggressively during a change of direction, he or she may exceed the friction force and therefore slip. Too much emphasis on the pawing action related to horizontal force instead of pushing or driving into the ground will remove the emphasis from the important factor for movement—overcoming gravity.

Wisdom

The coaching cue 'Push the ground away from you' conveys the important concept that the athlete must drive hard into the ground to move rapidly.

The idea that vertical-strength exercises may not translate into horizontal movement may have not considered the body position adopted for decelerating into a change of direction followed by a subsequent reacceleration. To complete these movements, an athlete should keep the centre of mass low but the trunk slightly upright before deciding the intended direction, followed by a slight rearward total body lean (to decelerate) or a slight forward total body lean (to reaccelerate). This change of body position allows for use of the musculature associated with triple extension to effectively produce maximal force to complete the task required. Specifically, the low body position allows for hip and knee extension to contribute to a rapid change in speed and direction. The muscles responsible for this triple extension do not work exclusively when vertical. Instead, it is the position of the athlete that dictates if this triple extension can be used as the prime movers during deceleration, change of direction and the subsequent acceleration into the new direction.

When a foundation of strength, power, explosive strength and eccentric strength are in place, an athlete can fine-tune body positioning to maximise his or her ability to use these physical capacities effectively to improve CODS and agility performance.

When an athlete has developed the physical underpinnings described in the theoretical model in figure 13.2, then the athlete will be able to learn to use these physical attributes effectively and efficiently, putting the body in the position that within the athlete's anthropometrics allows for optimal force application during a change of direction. The concept of building a strength base before doing extensive work on a skilled performance is not novel. It is the idea that you can't build a perfect structure on top of a foundation that will collapse under weight.

Each joint will be limited by its ability to tolerate a load, and if any joint collapses, including the trunk, hip, knee or ankle, under the load (or compression felt when changing direction), it will result in what can be termed *force leakage*. Just as an athlete would not add weight to the bar during a squat when form breaks, adding complexity or additional velocity to a change-of-direction drill when form breaks in slower or less-complex drills is the equivalent. Agility drills inherently will be more cognitively and physically demanding. Research has shown that adding a defender or reacting to a stimulus during an agility test will increase the ground-reaction forces and joint moments.[14, 15]

It is difficult to describe a perfect agility technique because each sport may have situational or tactical differences due to rules, implements or playing surface. However, there are some basic recommendations for body position that should

remain constant despite these differences. The anthropometry of an athlete will dictate the specific joint angles to maximise agility performance. The ability to decelerate, change direction and reaccelerate from a basic body position should be an athletic skill that may be transferable across sports, positions or situations. However, the perceptual–cognitive component of agility may be more specific and therefore not as transferable as the physical capacity of changing direction. Research on lateral shuffling provides insight into these potentially transferable factors that result in faster CODS:[16]

- Lower centre of mass (figure 13.7)
- Greater hip-extension velocity
- Lower hip-abduction velocity

Before reacting to a stimulus, an athlete tends to have more upright trunk entry and exit positions to allow for a more balanced position. Small considerations about task-specific, position-specific and situation-specific requirements during change of direction explains why more holistic physical development for even the most demanding change of direction is recommended and why one particular technique cannot be strictly enforced.

Figure 13.7 Low centre of mass base position.

A body position that places the centre of mass low and closer to the direction of intended travel allows for optimal production of hip-extension velocity through the use of triple extension. This is the characteristic body position for effective and efficient change of direction. When defending or performing any agility (reaction to a stimulus) drill, an athlete needs to adopt a more upright and balanced posture upon a CODS entry that will modify the subsequent body position at exit. It is therefore vital to consider all factors when giving body-position coaching advice to an athlete.

Coaching Cues, Suggestions and Drill Progression for Agility Development

Knowledge of effective body position for force application will transfer to the athlete only through effective coaching, the use of cues, and visual or kinaesthetic feedback. Motor-learning research has shown that externally focused attention enhances CODS more than internally focused attention.[17] Externally focused attention occurs when an athlete targets attention on the interaction with the environment (such as 'push the ground away'); internally focused attention involves attention on body parts or movements themselves.[18] Drawing a relationship between training in the weight room and application on the field will assist the transfer of training by helping athletes learn to use their new strength and power even during technically demanding skills, decreasing the lag time between turning improved physical attributes into technical proficiency.

These coaching tips may be useful to enhance the actualisation phase of training:

- Identify the verbal coaching cues that elicit immediately visible changes to the athlete's body position or CODS.

- Use cross-cues or those that are often provided in the weight room but have equal application in the field: 'Give me extension like a leap frog'; 'Finish your drive'; 'Push through the ground as hard and fast as possible'; and 'Catch and push through the floor', which is reference to an athlete catching a clean and driving hard out of the bottom to finish the lift just as an athlete would decelerate the body (catching his or her weight),

followed by driving the body out of a turn or change of direction.

- Use visual cues whilst working on agility, such as pointing towards the belly button to ensure the athlete is focusing on keeping the centre of mass balanced before an agility drill so he or she can quickly react in any direction.

- Use kinaesthetic cues to increase body awareness, such as having athletes learn the edge of their base of support and how far they can put their centre of mass outside the base of support by using leaning drills. These drills require the athlete to stand on both feet and lean in each direction as far as possible before taking a step to regain balance.

Training perceptual–cognitive speed, or aspects of decision making, visual scanning, anticipation, knowledge of the situation or reaction time, can also benefit from appropriate coaching cues or deliberate practice.[19, 20] Suggestions such as focusing on the shoulder, trunk, and hip regions of the stimulus, in this case using a video of an attacking player followed by approximately 15 minutes of reactive agility training in response to video clips for 3 weeks, significantly improved perception and response time in the agility test.[20] General coaching suggestions or cues related to perceptual–cognitive speed during agility development are as follows:

- Give verbal cues such as 'focus on the body' to help the athlete zone into the hips and shoulders to provide anticipatory cues during agility drills.

- Provide athletes with several scenarios during each agility drill to ensure they learn to identify several patterns of movement. Include drills that allow athletes to respond in either defensive or offensive scenarios. Help athletes improve the perceptual–cognitive ability by learning to recognise a variety of movement patterns.[4, 11, 20-22]

- Incorporate scenarios that have no direct movement restrictions on the stimulus but challenge the athletes either temporally or spatially by defining the distance they have to move before reacting to the stimulus (temporal restriction) or defining the distance they can move laterally in response to the stimulus (spatial restriction).

Putting It All Together

When developing agility in athletes, the process should remain consistent with the knowledge of the logical, systematic progression of training physical attributes to build a physically and technically strong athlete. The drill progression classification scheme in table 13.3 allows coaches to classify any drills based on movement pattern, velocity and cognitive requirement. The amount of time spent on each drill or in each progression should be individualised based on the athlete's level (maturational and skill) and strength.

Beginning athletes or those without a fundamental strength base should remain in beginner-level complexity acceleration, deceleration and change-of-direction drills before moving into highly complex or cognitively demanding

Wisdom

Improve transfer of training by establishing the relationship between weight-room gains and on-field performance. Choose coaching cues that help athletes identify the correlation between producing force through triple extension and effective and efficient body position during both types of training sessions.

agility drills. This approach helps develop an athlete in a sound manner before increasing the physical or cognitive requirements that will undermine initial technical development if the athlete is unprepared, physically or mentally, for the demands of the drill. An example of how a weight-room training progression may relate to a field-training progression with a focus on attributes required for agility is shown in table 13.4.

Table 13.3 Classification of Change-of-Direction and Agility Drill Progression

Beginner	Intermediate	Advanced
Change-of-direction drills • Movement patterns that are confined to forward, backward and side-shuffling movements • Change of direction at a lower entry velocity (<5 m of entry distance) • Manoeuvrability drills or those that require more bends than sharp changes of direction (some will require an intermediate classification due to some sharper changes of direction)	Change-of-direction drills • Movement patterns of basic drills plus changing direction at various angles • Change of direction at moderate entry velocity (approximately 10 m entry distance) • Agility drills • Moderate entry velocity and response to single stimulus that will display limited movement options	Change-of-direction drills • Combine high-velocity sprinting and >90° directional change • Agility drills • Large degrees of spatial and temporal uncertainty with a stimulus that has unlimited movement options (often practised by small-sided games)

Table 13.4 Comparison of Youth (or Beginner) and Elite (or Advanced) Athlete Focus for Agility Development

Physical capacity	Youth weight room	Youth field work	Elite weight room	Elite field work
Strength	Body-weight exercises	Body awareness such as leaning drills	Back squat, front squat, overhead squat, pulls, deadlift	Resisted work
Explosive strength or concentric power	Concentric jumps to a box	Acceleration drills	Olympic lifts, loaded jump squats	Accelerations: sled, assisted
Load absorption or eccentric strength	Drop landings from a low height	Deceleration drills with a footwork focus and from a low velocity	Drop landings and receiving strength, catch phase in Olympic lifts	Decelerations: high velocity, various angles
Reactive strength	N/A	Sport	Complex training	Plyometrics
Multidirectional and asymmetrical strength	Lunges and unilateral strength exercises	Lateral movements, drop steps	Lunges, landmine (nino) work, asymmetrical carries	Agility drills

Using Test Results for Programming Agility Development

When programming with an emphasis on agility development, the well-rounded battery of physical capacity, agility and CODS tests previously discussed will allow coaches to chart strengths and weaknesses to help target areas for agility development. Test results of the two American football quarterbacks presented in table 13.2 and figure 13.6 have been listed in terms of their strengths and weaknesses in table 13.5 to support planning of agility drills. Similar to how a coach might prepare a progression of agility development for young athletes,[13] a coach should develop a progression based on any athlete's individual performance or performance levels. By targeting the athlete's weaknesses with more dedicated training time, this larger window for adaptation will likely have a greater impact and therefore a higher performance return.

As shown in figure 13.8, a variation in the amount of time spent performing drills associated with either agility, high-velocity change of direction or low-velocity change of direction and manoeuvrability has been suggested to allow for a targeted agility programme to be written. The initial graph separates the time allotted to purely CODS or agility drills. The subsequent graph allows for separation of the CODS drills into the two primary areas of high-velocity and high-braking requirements or low-velocity and manoeuvrability requirements. Many of the specific drills associated with agility development can be incorporated into the dynamic warm-up. However, depending on the age and experience of the athlete or mesocycle of training, a specific agility-development block can also be planned.

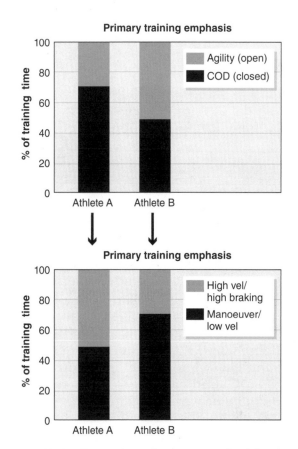

Figure 13.8 Comparison of percentage of training time devoted to training CODS and agility drills.

Frequency of Agility Training

As little as 15 minutes per day of dedicated agility training over 3 weeks can result in significant improvements in agility performance;[20] therefore, it is possible to program agility development with particular peaks related to important points in a season. As shown in figure 13.9, an annual plan can be developed that follows a progression allowing for gradual development of CODS in conjunction

Table 13.5 Comparison Chart of Strengths and Weaknesses of Two Athletes for Agility Programming

STRENGTHS		WEAKNESSES	
Athlete A	**Athlete B**	**Athlete A**	**Athlete B**
Unloaded explosiveness	Loaded conditions	Loaded movement	Unloaded movement
Manoeuvrability	Yielding strength	Eccentric strength, yielding strength	*Manoeuvrability*
Low-velocity COD	Overall strength	Underpinned by weak base strength	*Cognitive speed*
Cognitive speed	*High velocity COD*	*High-velocity COD*	

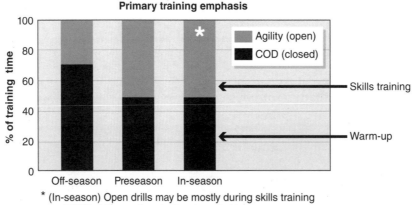

Primary training emphasis

* (In-season) Open drills may be mostly during skills training
and COD drills can then be incorporated in warm-up.

Figure 13.9 Sample annual progression of CODS and agility focus by per cent time distribution.

with agility that becomes more sport relevant as an athlete enters in-season competition.

Agility can be improved with small periods of dedicated training. A majority of the agility training time can be incorporated into skills training (e.g., small-sided games, game-specific agility drills) or in the warm-up. Using the warm-up to address physical fitness components such as agility and speed works well. These components are best performed before fatigue to allow the athlete to learn the most efficient neuromuscular activation methods for rapid movement. Performing CODS drills when fatigued has been shown to relate to changes in kinematics and could explain the increased potential for injury risk when changing direction whilst fatigued.[23]

Wisdom

Red-line drills, or drills performed at the end of training, that are classified as advanced agility or CODS drills should be used sparingly or only with highly trained athletes when part of a planned overreaching phase.

The final stage of writing a periodised agility program is taking the plan for the particular meso-cycle and writing the drills, sets and repetitions that will be performed each day of the mesocycle. Example training blocks for the American football quarterbacks A and B (see tables 13.2 and 13.5,

figure 13.6) are shown in tables 13.6 and 13.7. These blocks can be performed for 3 or 4 weeks, twice per week, based on training requirements and time allotted. The types of drills and percentage of training time within each type of CODS and agility drill are modified in accordance with the proposed focus on areas that are most limited for each athlete (figure 13.8).

Each of these in-season programs lasts 10 to 15 minutes when the athlete takes approximately 45 seconds between repetitions unless noted. These athletes would both be considered advanced due to their strength and power levels as well as years of experience; therefore, their drills even in their weaker areas are composed of mostly intermediate- and advanced-level drills. Even these athletes could regress to using more beginner drills when starting the warm-up or during the off-season as they fine-tune body position and technique in conjunction with improvements in physical capacity. Overall, the ability to test, evaluate and write a logical progression allows for continual gains in agility performance of any level athlete.

Using testing results to inform a program written with an understanding of appropriate progressions for CODS and agility drills will allow an athlete to positively adapt to the loads these drills impose. Additionally, a well-planned agility program allows for the building of skills as perceptual–cognitive and physical demands of drills are increased.

Table 13.6 Sample Drill Block for Athlete A Based on Testing Results

Drill and instruction	Classification	Purpose	Repetitions (with 45 sec rest)	% of training time
Back to receiver drill Red jersey and blue jersey. On whistle turn, identify then scramble to correct side cone.	Advanced (agility)	Cognitive speed (scanning and reaction time) with rapid COD	4	~30%
Figure 8 extended Five cones requiring quick rounding footwork forward and backward for an extended figure-8 pattern.	Intermediate (CODS manoeuvrability)	Forward and backward high-velocity turning (not cutting)	4	~30%
X-pattern multiskill run High-speed forward running and back pedalling combining inside and outside foot plants.	Advanced (CODS: high-velocity and multiple angles)	High-velocity braking and CODS	3 each direction	~40%

Table 13.7 Sample Drill Block for Athlete B Based on Testing Results

Drill and instruction	Classification	Purpose	Repetitions (with 45 sec rest unless noted)	% of training time
Reactive step 45° cuts in response to human stimulus Drill requires only a single step	Intermediate to advanced (agility)	Cognitive speed (decision making and reaction time); initial step reaction	8 (10 second rest)	~20%
Mirror drill Within 2 × 2 m square	Advanced (agility)	Cognitive speed (anticipation and reaction time) with rapid but low velocity COD	4	~30%
Figure-8 extended Five cones requiring quick rounding footwork forward and backward for an extended figure-8 pattern.	Intermediate (CODS manoeuvrability)	Forward and backward high-velocity turning (not cutting)	4	~30%
Three-cone COD drill	Beginner (CODS: low velocity and manoeuvrability)	Low-velocity braking and CODS with subsequent manoeuvrability around cones	3	~20%

Summary

The development and enhancement of CODS and agility require a multifaceted approach. A correct test or series of tests should be chosen to identify athletes' current capacity and the results used to inform the training focus. Physical and perceptual–cognitive development must be targeted in a periodised manner to ensure continued improvement in agility. Within training sessions for CODS and agility, coaches can provide cues that elicit positive changes in either body position or performance. Effective coaching cues and feedback are critical for maximising the ability to use changes in physical capacity to produce measurable changes in CODS or agility performance.

CHAPTER 14

Generating Anaerobic Power

David Martin, PhD
Cycling Australia

Quick, explosive movements, rapid accelerations and intense bursts of speed are not only exciting to watch but are often important for overall performance outcomes. These movements are primarily fuelled by energy provided by anaerobic metabolism. As a result, the topics of assessing and developing anaerobic power and capacity have remained popular among coaches and sport scientists for the last 50 years.

Sport is both diverse and complex, making universal truths difficult. However, one thing that is clear is that the maximal exercise intensity that can be maintained decreases as exercise duration increases. For all-out or maximal efforts that last less than 1 minute it has been suggested that more than half of the total energy required is produced anaerobically.[1] Published sport science research addressing anaerobic fitness generally focuses on the following four areas:

1. Testing methodology and definitions
2. Characteristics of world-class athletes
3. Demands of competition
4. Training to improve power and capacity

Although the scientific literature will be referenced throughout this chapter, concepts are introduced that are based on experiences working with world-class athletes at the Australian Institute of Sport (AIS).

This chapter covers a lot of ground and therefore will sacrifice intricate detail associated with each topic covered. For those interested in learning more about anaerobic power and work capacity there are many excellent scientific review papers that extensively discuss relevant themes and historical debates and discoveries.[1-3]

By the end of the chapter, the reader should have an understanding of anaerobic power testing and how those testing results are interpreted. Additionally, the reader should also have a much greater appreciation of the approaches that can be used to enhance this metabolic system.

Anaerobic Fitness: Topics of Interest

When it comes to high-intensity anaerobic fitness, many variables interact to create unique physical demands, including

- muscle groups (isolated muscles versus groups of muscles),
- type of muscle contraction (concentric, isometric, eccentric),
- velocity of contractions (slow versus fast or transitions from slow to fast),
- number of contractions (less than five to more than 50),
- recovery duration between efforts (short or long) and
- environmental conditions (heat and hypoxia).

Each sport has its unique demands. Just because an athlete can perform weighted squats in the gym does not ensure that he or she will be able to perform numerous repeat jumps at 99 per cent of maximal jump height when playing basketball for an hour. Transferability of fitness often occurs, but numerous research studies have confirmed that athletes tend to become best at what they do most, assuming the training incorporates concepts of deliberate practice. Thus, specificity of training should not to be ignored, especially when it comes to developing anaerobic fitness.

This does not mean that preparatory training is not important. When it comes to high-intensity training, a long jumper will obviously do more than perform numerous maximal jumps throughout the preseason. Because of the risk of injury and also because of possible physiological limitations, it can be beneficial to incorporate general training progressions before turning to sport-specific conditioning exercises that mimic the demands of competition. A training program that ignores the specificity of the competitive event likely will promote many adaptations that do not necessarily translate into improvements in performance. This point is discussed in more detail in chapters 18 and 19.

Wisdom

The take-home message for coaches and trainers attempting to improve anaerobic fitness is to ensure that training sessions are specific to the demands of competition.

Before discussing interventions that can be used to improve anaerobic fitness, it is worthwhile to review definitions. The terminology used in this area of sport science can be diverse and sometimes confusing.

Anaerobic power is the maximal rate of work that can be accomplished. Typically, it is measured in watts (W) or reflected as a peak-movement speed. Anaerobic power depends on muscle mass involved in the activity, neuromuscular recruitment and the ratio of power to body mass that influences acceleration to obtain maximal running, swimming or cycling speed. Peak power generated over 1 second indicates anaerobic power.

Anaerobic capacity is the maximal amount of high-intensity work that can be performed. Typically, it is quantified in units of work such as kilojoules (kJ). Work tends to depend on the total amount of high-energy phosphates stored within skeletal muscle and the ability to resist the metabolic waste products produced during high-intensity exercise. The amount of work accumulated over 30 seconds indicates capacity.

Anaerobic power refers to the maximal rate of energy flux or the maximal mechanical power produced during high-intensity exercise. On the other hand, anaerobic capacity refers to the total amount of high-intensity work fuelled by oxygen-independent energy-yielding systems. Although often linked, anaerobic power and capacity can be independent fitness traits. For example, a cyclist could improve his or her 30-second average power (capacity) without improving 1-second power.

Assessing Anaerobic Power and Anaerobic Capacity

Two approaches have emerged when it comes to quantifying high-intensity fitness. The first involves quantifying mechanical work or movement speed produced over a defined time period, usually less than 1 minute. Common examples of tests for quantifying anaerobic power include a vertical jump height, standing long jump distance, 10-metre sprint run time and maximal power during a 6-second cycling sprint. For those who want to quantify anaerobic capacity, the maximal effort needs to be longer, and the unit of measure changes from power (W) to work (kJ).

One of the most popular tests for anaerobic capacity is the 30-second Wingate cycle test. For sprint running athletes, 100- to 400-metre sprints can reveal anaerobic capacity as maximal exercise from 10 to 60 seconds generally allows anaerobic energy reserves to be nearly depleted. Skiers have been known to use a 60-second box jump test, and combat athletes have incorporated 30-second punching tests during which hand speed and force of impact are recorded. These tests illustrate the importance of testing anaerobic fitness using exercise modalities that mimic the demands of the sport.

The second approach for quantifying anaerobic fitness requires expensive laboratory equipment and also requires some assumptions to be made. Anaerobic energy expenditure can be estimated if the oxygen uptake–power output relationship is quantified during submaximal exercise. This relationship can then be used to estimate how much oxygen uptake would be required for any type of high-intensity exercise assuming the task was 100 per cent aerobic in nature. In cycling, the accumulated oxygen deficit (AOD) is calculated by subtracting the actual amount of oxygen consumed during a high-intensity exercise task from the amount of oxygen consumed assuming the task was performed entirely aerobically. By measuring the actual oxygen uptake and estimating the required oxygen uptake for the high-intensity effort it is possible to quantify the accumulated oxygen deficit. During a maximal high-intensity effort this measurement can become a useful index of anaerobic fitness.

Figure 14.1 presents an example of an exercise task that is performed for 2 minutes at an exercise intensity that equals the power output that elicits the maximal oxygen consumption. The lower, shaded area reflects the aerobic contribution to the effort, and the upper area reflects the anaerobic contribution to the effort. In this example it appears that anaerobic energy-yielding systems contribute approximately one-third of the total energy required for the effort.

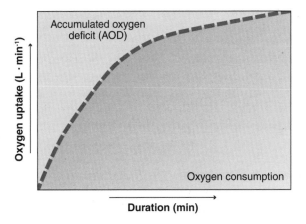

Figure 14.1 Exercise intensity equals the power output that elicits the maximal oxygen consumption for an exercise performed for 2 minutes.

Not only is exercise modality important when assessing anaerobic fitness, but test duration specificity should also be considered. In a group of Australian elite track cyclists, researchers observed that the sprint cyclists achieved their highest AOD, an index of anaerobic capacity, during short sprints (70 sec) that were similar to their events. The pursuit cyclists had their highest AOD measurements during longer efforts (300 sec) that were closer to the duration of their cycling event.[4]

Wisdom

There are numerous ways to assess the anaerobic energy system, both in the field and in laboratory settings. Each has its advantages and disadvantages, but if assessments are to yield valid information that will give a true indication of competitive performance, they should be both modality and duration specific.

Combining Testing and Training

Coaches often ask, 'How often should I test the anaerobic fitness of my athletes?' Many variables need to be considered before an appropriate answer to this question can be established. But one development that has the chance of reforming practice is the concept of making high-precision measurements during normal high-intensity training sessions.

Now that portable light gates, transponder-based timing systems, instrumented gym equipment and instrumented cycling power cranks are more accessible, it is possible to combine training and testing sessions. As long as athletes are sufficiently motivated, and testing and training conditions are relatively similar, a nice progression of adaptations to high-intensity training can be documented. Thus, with the right equipment, the sport-specific high-intensity fitness of athletes can be documented quite frequently during training sessions.

Recent advances in technology have improved the ability to measure contraction velocity and displacement during most major exercises performed it the gym. Devices such as GymAware (www.kinetic.com.au) and Tendo Units (www.tendosports.com) use calibrated encoders and custom software to rapidly and accurately evaluate many aspects of resistance training that previously could be measured only by scientists with expensive equipment in the laboratory. Measurements of acceleration, power, velocity, displacement, force and work completed can all be estimated for each contraction during a training set and then be stored in a manner that allows comparisons to be performed quickly. As a result of this technology a new level of accuracy is available for monitoring the effects of high-intensity training.

Traditionally, the intensity and duration of a training set has been quantified by recording the mass of the barbell and the number of contractions performed. New technology allows subtle variations in lifting velocity and total displacement to be recorded and analysed. With this advancement the terms *power* and *work* take on specific meanings.

For field-based team sport players as well as road cyclists who engage in numerous high-intensity sprints throughout a competition, a structured training session can allow the coach to evaluate both the anaerobic power and the resistance to fatigue associated with repeat sprints. Cycling coaches and scientists at AIS have created a session in which road cyclists engage in a series of progressively longer sprints on the road using a slight uphill grade (2%-4%). Sprints last for 6, 15, 30, and 60 seconds and are performed with a long, complete recovery of 5 to 10 minutes between efforts. Cyclists then perform a series of sprints on the same incline for each duration of effort previously tested, but this time with limited recovery (e.g., 60 sec). Results from this type of testing enable coaches to see the maximal power that can be produced for a relevant time period and also reveal the cyclist's resistance to fatigue.

Figure 14.2 presents a schematic of possible test results. The dotted line is essentially the fatigue-free maximal power–duration relationship. The dots represent test results from a cyclist before training, and the triangles reflect the results after 6 weeks of structured high-intensity intervals focusing on repeat sprints. In this example the maximal power for any given duration has not changed; only the resistance to fatigue has improved. Team sport athletes are often discouraged when they fail to improve their maximal 10-second sprint despite weeks of high-intensity sprint training. It is often the case that the training improved resistance to fatigue but not maximal power.

Sometimes it is difficult to attribute improvements in performance after training solely to enhancements in anaerobic metabolism. This is because energy provision is a continuum, not a discrete, stepwise process, and it is difficult to distinguish between improvements in anaerobic and aerobic fitness. We must not forget that improvements in movement efficiency and technique can contribute to improvements in test scores.

Understanding Improvements

The coach or trainer needs to understand the scientific literature investigating the best way to improve anaerobic fitness to appreciate the type of fitness adaptations that have occurred (i.e., aerobic, anaerobic, technical) with training. With this appreciation, it can be possible to predict how long adaptations will last.

It may be the case that aerobic contributions to short, high-intensity efforts lasting 30 to 60 seconds can be maintained for weeks, whereas anaerobic adaptations are more difficult to maintain. Additionally, there is preliminary evidence from the laboratory at AIS suggesting that recovery from high-intensity exercise is negatively affected when the aerobic contribution to the task is experimentally compromised.[5] This was determined by engaging elite cyclists into two groups during an experimental 4-week altitude-training camp. One group was allowed to experience normal altitude-induced gains in red blood cells and haemoglobin mass. However, the other group had their altitude-induced increase in haemoglobin mass blocked by having blood removed. After the altitude exposure both groups had a similar increase in their maximal 4-minute power output. However, the aerobic contribution to this effort was greater in the group with the altitude-induced increase in haemoglobin. Interestingly, after a brief recovery, the group with the additional haemoglobin mass performed better in a task measuring ride time until exhaustion, suggesting that recovery was enhanced in this group. This discussion highlights why it could be useful for the coach and sport scientist to understand whether changes to high-intensity exercise are primarily due to aerobic or anaerobic adaptations.

Limitations to Anaerobic Power and Capacity

We often wonder why an athlete cannot jump higher, sprint faster or produce more power for a maximal sprint over 1 to 3 seconds. The limitations to anaerobic power and capacity have now been evaluated in many sports, but clear, simple answers to these important questions remain elusive, primarily because it is often difficult to establish what part of the anaerobic fitness system is failing.

Many researchers have attempted to examine what limits anaerobic power and capacity; this

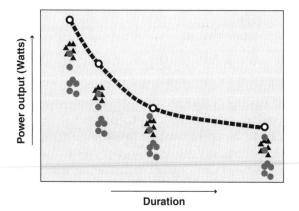

Figure 14.2 Sample test results demonstrating the effect of a 6-week training block on peak power values in sprint cycling.

area of research extends into the complex area of fatigue.[6] Although the precise mechanisms responsible for failure during types of high-intensity exercise are still debated, it is now widely accepted that in many cases, motivation is strongly linked to short-duration maximal physical efforts.

Although a simple dichotomy has been established in the scientific literature whereby some argue for peripheral limitations (e.g., lactic acid accumulation) and others argue for central limitations (e.g., motivation), the most likely truth is that both central and peripheral limitations can influence anaerobic performance. It is often taught that anaerobic power is strongly related to functional muscle mass and fibre-type composition. Additionally, research has confirmed that neuromuscular activation, which is strongly influenced by motivation and emotion, is important for maximal power production.

When it comes to capacity of anaerobic efforts, the prevailing paradigm assumes that waste products of anaerobic metabolism build up to concentrations that both directly impair muscular contractions and activate type III and IV afferent nerve fibres that lead to undesirable sensations (e.g., pain) and a decrease in central-motor drive.

Imagine a Formula 1 racing driver is asked to record the fastest lap possible on the Monaco race track. There are two reasons why the driver doesn't go faster: the car or the driver. Similarly, athletes who are attempting to perform a short, high-intensity effort generally will be limited by the brain's ability to recruit the appropriate muscle mass or because the muscle mass recruited can't do the job. If an athlete is centrally limited, a little bit of motivation (e.g., placebo effects) can result in big improvements. However, if the athlete is peripherally limited, training may be required to change structural elements of the muscle mass and fibre composition.

This simple, practical approach to what is typically a complicated problem is not meant to trivialise the interactions between physiological and biochemical systems that contribute to developing anaerobic power. Instead, this review of mechanisms is meant to raise awareness, and from a practical perspective, make the coach and athlete think about what is holding back performance. It may be the case that for many well-trained anaerobic athletes, central drive, which could be tied into emotional state, is often one of the primary limitations for performance.[6]

Wisdom

Limitations in anaerobic fitness can be linked to muscle mass and composition, motivation, neuromuscular recruitment, removal or buffering of metabolic waste products, resiliency to central feedback and efficiency of high-intensity movement patterns.

One of the great challenges for coaches and sport scientists is to identify techniques that allow an athlete's limitations to be identified. Establishing why an athlete is unable to produce required anaerobic power or capacity can be one of the first steps to designing an efficient, strategic training programme.

Training Anaerobic Power and Capacity

When it comes to anaerobic fitness, many coaches buy in to the popular saying, 'No pain, no gain!' However, although athletes may need to tolerate some discomfort whilst seeking to improve anaerobic fitness, research findings support a more methodical approach to preparing athletes for short, high-intensity exercise. Whereas some old-school coaches may be content to load athletes up until they crack, contemporary training progressions tend to be far more thoughtful in nature and are organised into sequential themes that support one another. Although short, intense anaerobic training methods have great potential for inducing desired fitness, the cautionary note is that this type of training can also result in injury and heavy fatigue and have a negative effect on motivation.

Importance of Experiencing Failure

For high-intensity training, it doesn't matter whether a coach is prescribing interval training or exercises on the field or repetitions in the weight room. A fundamental question is whether the exercise should be performed to failure. In other words, is the athlete compromising potential adaptations if he or she stops short of a maximal effort? Surprisingly, this simple and potentially important question has not received much attention from the scientific community. Based on the available evidence, it has been concluded that we still do not know![7]

It appears that some of the advantages of training to failure include maximal recruitment of skeletal-muscle motor units, which could provide greater magnitude for adaptations and a possible stimulus for a favourable endocrine state (i.e., growth-promoting hormones). However, the disadvantage of training until failure includes negative sensations (i.e., failure) and risk of injury and overtraining if this type of training is programmed frequently.

One study that supports the concept of pushing athletes to repetition failure was conducted using junior elite basketball and soccer players at AIS. In this study, the athletes who were prescribed an exercise session (bench press) that elicited repetition failure demonstrated greater improvements in this exercise over a 6-week training period, tested using a 6RM assessment.[8] More research is required in this interesting area, and it is likely the best approach will depend on the fitness of the athletes and the overall periodisation and structure of training. Training until failure may be more appropriate after a 3- to 6-week block in which the athlete experiences a higher volume of exercise without failure. For this type of training, the target intensity can be prescribed for multiple repetitions without reaching failure.

Use of Exercise Duration to Grade Intensity

Although exercise intensity often is described as exercise heart rate, running speed, cycling power or mass of weight lifted, it is also the case that duration or number of repetitions can reflect exercise intensity. For instance, if a cyclist exercises at a power output that he or she can sustain for only 60 seconds (i.e., 1,000 W), then it is possible to divide the duration of the effort into thirds. The first 20 seconds at 1,000 watts will force muscles to produce relevant force, but the overall perception of effort will be far less than extreme. The second 20 seconds (20-40 sec) at the same power output will start to be perceived as difficult, but the effort will be relatively easy to recover from. In contrast, the final 20 seconds (40-60 sec) at 1,000 watts will required a maximal effort and result in system failure. If the athlete attempts to complete a maximal 1-minute effort at 1,000 watts, sensations will be uncomfortable, and the effort will result in prolonged fatigue, making subsequent efforts difficult if not impossible.

This example highlights how exercise duration can be used to grade the intensity of short, high-intensity exercise. As mentioned earlier, one approach to periodising high-intensity training is first to focus on building up the volume of high-quality exercise without experiencing failure and then move into training sessions that incorporate exercise until exhaustion. This type of training progression could minimise risk of injury and allow motivation to remain high. If the high-intensity sessions occur only two or three times per week, it is unlikely that excessive fatigue or overtraining will occur.

Take the maximal, short-duration anaerobic effort, establish the maximal power that can be sustained over the full duration of the effort and divide the duration of the effort into thirds. The first third allows the body to experience sport-specific fatigue with minor sensations of discomfort. These are great opportunities for working on technique and efficiency. The second third of the effort is difficult but still possible to recover from within a relatively short time, so it provides great opportunities for increasing the volume of relevant exercise intensity. The final third of the effort should be used sparingly since completion of the effort is associated with system failure and exhaustion. However, these efforts are great for pacing and learning how to extend range.

Periodisation of High-Intensity Training

Similar to the many paths that can be taken to reach the top of a mountain—some long, some short, some risky, some safe—there are also many approaches to improving anaerobic fitness. As mentioned earlier, before constructing a training program that will improve an athlete's anaerobic fitness, it can be useful to understand the physiology underpinning anaerobic fitness as well as the athlete's limitations.

If the underpinning attributes that support anaerobic fitness include adequate muscle mass, desirable muscle composition (i.e., fibre type), neuromuscular recruitment, efficiency of movement and resistance to metabolic waste products and peripheral feedback, then rationale exists for designing a training program based on scientific principles.

Another way to categorise a training emphasis includes focusing on peripheral and central limitations. Traditional approaches to anaerobic fitness involve a heavy emphasis on building up the peripheral structural elements first and then transitioning into a lower-volume but much higher-intensity program as the athlete nears important competition.

An alternative approach for promoting anaerobic fitness begins with a focus on improving power development and then training to resist fatigue and encourage anaerobic capacity by extending the number of repetitive contractions at high intensity. Finally, the athlete should not ignore attempts to improve movement velocity for a given amount of power produced.

Figure 14.3 provides a flow chart that connects three fundamental questions:

1. Does the athlete have sufficient muscle mass to produce required power?

2. Does the athlete demonstrate ideal resistance to fatigue for a series of sport-relevant intervals?

3. Does the athlete move at required velocities for the amount of power produced?

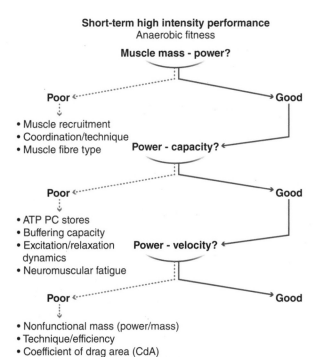

Figure 14.3 Flow chart for determining anaerobic fitness based on three fundamental questions.

Training to Improve Muscle Mass

Training to improve functional muscle mass tends to focus on resistance exercises that have similar relevant movement patterns. For instance, a rower would incorporate chest pull exercises, whereas a sprint cyclist would perform heavily loaded squats to promote improvements in lower-body muscle mass.

A summary of scientific research indicates that the stimulus for improving muscle mass involves a combination of intensity and number of repetitions. Thus, heavy weights lifted for fewer than 5 repetitions appear to have plenty of intensity but not sufficient duration, whereas lifting lighter weights for 20 repetitions or more may allow for a large number of repetitions per training session but not the sufficient intensity to promote hypertrophy.

More recently, there has been quite a bit of attention focusing on the unique role that eccentric exercise can play at remodelling and stimulating development of functional muscle mass. Not only does eccentric exercise help promote gain in muscle mass, but additional benefits may include remodelling of the extracellular matrix (i.e., connective tissue) and preferential stimulus to fast-twitch muscle fibres.[9]

A difficult challenge often faced is increasing lean mass whilst at the same time encouraging losses in fat mass. One approach that appears promising involves a daily diet that is consistently energy deficient but also includes ingestion of dairy protein before, during and after rigorous exercise. One of the most popular approaches for increasing dairy protein for the athlete engaged in heavy training used by some Olympic power athletes is the ingestion of a large glass of chocolate milk after a strenuous workout.

Building Resistance to Fatigue

The next problem to solve is determining whether levels of resistance to fatigue are adequate. This can be thought of as the ability to perform a powerful movement repetitively with limited recovery. As an example, imagine twin soccer players who both can run a 10-metre sprint in exactly the same amount of time. However, when required to complete 10 repeat sprints with only 20 seconds of recovery, one of the twins completes all sprints within 5 per cent of his or her maximal speed whilst the other twin finishes the final sprints at a velocity more than

10 per cent slower than his or her fastest speed. This would be a vivid example of two athletes who are equally fast and powerful but different in resistance to fatigue.

A unique aspect of skeletal-muscle fatigue that could be highly relevant for those interested in anaerobic fitness has recently been introduced—it involves speed of contractions.[10] The number of contractions performed in succession may have a unique and independent effect on fatigue regardless of how much work is done per contraction. On a bike an athlete can perform 20 maximal pedal strokes, and at the end his or her power output will be the same percentage of the maximum regardless whether a big gear (more work per pedal stroke) or a small gear (less work per pedal stroke) was used. For the sport of cycling, these data suggest that sprinters should adopt larger gear ratios during competition to enable more work to be done per contraction. Interestingly, over the past 10 years there has been a dramatic increase in the gear ratio adopted by world-class sprint cyclists during competition.[11]

Overspeed Training

The progression from sport-relevant contractions that are lightly loaded (allowing for rapid movements) to similar contractions that are heavily loaded makes for some interesting progressive overload options when the importance of contraction number for fatigue is considered. The overspeed, lightly loaded contractions will target both the excitation and relaxation aspects of the muscle contraction. In the case of cycling, rapid contractions can be performed using maximal sprints with short crank arms on a bicycle ergometer. The result of the short crank arms (e.g., 120 mm versus standard 170 mm) are extremely high cadences (greater than 250 rpm) that will heavily use the intracellular calcium cycling mechanisms involved with turning on (exciting) and turning off (relaxing) the muscle.

Although overspeed training sessions have been used by many elite coaches in many sports, scientific evidence is just beginning to reveal the possible mechanisms involved. This finding provides rationale for incorporating high-velocity contractions into training programs in hopes of improving resistance to fatigue for prolonged all-out efforts. For other sports that involve running it is interesting to speculate on ways to increase

stride rate (e.g., downhill or unloaded running) in a way that doesn't dramatically increase risk of injury. For sports that use the upper body, such as cross-country skiing, rowing and kayaking, it is relatively easy to undergear ergometers or to use modified equipment (e.g., small paddle blades) to allow sport-specific movement patterns to occur at a high rate.

It would be relatively easy during standard interval sets (e.g., Tabata intervals[12]) to provide a greater overload during training by actually decreasing resistance and increasing contraction frequency versus the traditional progression of increasing the resistance and decreasing the contraction frequency. Conversely, when increasing resistance, it could be desirable to remain focused on contraction frequency as an important criterion variable.

Research is required to document the time frame required for calcium cycling and neuromuscular adaptations to plateau to overspeed training. However, based on other physiological responses to high-intensity training, it is likely that 2 to 4 weeks of training two to four times per week has the chance to induce desired changes.

Wisdom

The coach and athlete looking for options on breaking a plateau in performance should think about adding in a bit of variety and experimenting with overspeed training.

Of the many types of training that can be used to favourably remodel the fibre-type composition of skeletal muscle, three contemporary approaches are receiving a fair amount of attention by practitioners and sport scientists:

1. Plyometrics
2. Multiple short, rapid accelerations
3. Single-limb training.

Plyometrics involve the use of the stretch-shortening reflex to enable forceful dynamic contractions. Research supports the use of these types of training sessions to improve the ability of the muscle to produce power.[13]

Multiple accelerations allow athletes to experience a natural progression from slow contractions to nearly maximal contractions as the athletes progress from a standing start to maximal running speed. In addition to running, maximal accelerations can be performed in many sports, such as swimming, rowing, kayaking and cycling.

Single-limb training is one of the more novel training types that can be used to improve fatigue resistance. Single-limb training is especially well suited for cycling since it is possible to replicate the pedalling action with only one leg. In this case the entire blood volume and neural drive are directed towards only one leg, typically enabling the athlete to overload the skeletal muscle to a greater extent. Preliminary data indicate promising adaptations after single-leg cycle training.[14] Another option made popular with real-time power feedback during gym-training sessions is a focus on maximal power development during each repetition (i.e., a combination of lifting speed and mass).

One of the great advantages of inducing novel training methods is that athletes remain motivated for training and enjoy rapid improvements in training drills as they commit to new exercise routines. As long as there is an element of specificity, the overall adaptations that result from some of these novel training methods should support the desired gains in performance.

Once the athlete has the desired muscle mass to produce the required power output, and the power producing capabilities are sufficiently resistant to fatigue, the relationship between movement velocity and power output needs to be considered. This biomechanics theme will not be discussed in detail here. However, it is important to recognise that just because an athlete is powerful on a laboratory ergometer does not mean he or she will move quickly when rowing, paddling or cycling in the field. By knowing the limitation to short, high-intensity performance, the coach can target training in a way that nurtures an athlete's strengths and improves his or her weaknesses.

New Perspectives on Training to Improve Anaerobic Fitness

It appears that the limitations to maximal high-intensity exercise are peak power–producing capability and the intensity of exercise associated with maximal aerobic capacity. With this in mind, we can design an innovative training program for a 400-metre runner or a 200-metre swimmer focused purely on short (under 10 sec), high-intensity training designed to improve maximal speed combined with high-intensity aerobic intervals (4-10 min efforts) targeting aerobic fitness. In this case, athletes would not engage in the uncomfortable exercise intensity associated with their event (30-60 sec). Essentially, there would be no lactate tolerance intervals prescribed. For those who are strong advocates of interval sets that produce large accumulations of blood lactate and stress intracellular and extracellular buffering capacity, this new format for training would appear strange.

One of the possible advantages of training above and below the exercise intensity used for maximal efforts of 30 to 120 seconds is that training sessions are less psychologically traumatising. Training sessions are still arduous and maximal, but the uncomfortable all-out efforts that last for 30 to 60 seconds and are sometimes associated with extreme nausea are no longer included. By making training sessions more tolerable it may be possible for athletes to engage in relevant intensity more frequently and essentially focus on improving the range of fitness, saving the all-out, 1-minute effort for competition.

Nutritional Supplements and Anaerobic Fitness

The two major peripheral limitations to high-intensity anaerobic exercise are likely energy supply (total pool of adenosine triphosphate [ATP] and creatine phosphate) and ability to buffer waste products of anaerobic metabolism (i.e., the accumulation of H+), which interferes with muscle contraction and production of energy via anaerobic metabolic pathways. Manufacturers of nutrient supplements have been quick to exploit research documenting that creatine loading can improve the content of high-energy phosphates in skeletal muscle[15, 16] and other studies confirming that numerous buffering agents (i.e., sodium bicarbonate, citrate, phosphate) can be used to improve anaerobic capacity and thus performance during high-intensity exercise.[17]

Multiple studies have been published in reputable scientific journals that have confirmed loading with creatine monohydrate (about 20 g/day for 5-10 days) can help athletes engage in high-intensity repeat sprints.[16] Similarly, there are now numerous well-controlled studies that document the benefits of sodium bicarbonate consumed 1 to 2 hours before short, high-intensity exercise (30-300 sec) at a dose of 0.3 grams/kilogram of body mass.[17] More recently, beta-alanine has been shown to act as a nutrient aid to improve intracellular buffering capacity and in many cases maximal performances lasting 60 to 240 seconds, most likely by contributing to an enrichment of muscle carnosine content, which maintains the acid–base balance within skeletal muscle.[18,19]

In addition to supplements that target energy stores and buffering capacity, there is also rationale supporting the high-intensity performance-enhancing effects of the stimulant caffeine, highlighting the importance of motivation and maximal effort when athletes give a maximal effort. A caffeine dose of as little as 2 milligrams/kilogram of body mass has been shown to help improve repeat sprint capabilities in some studies.[20] It may be the case that caffeine is more helpful for well-trained athletes than for active participants who likely suffer from other limitations to performance. It should also be noted that caffeine could have some short-term side effects, such as anxiety and muscular shakes, particularly for those unaccustomed to it. Therefore, it is recommended that caffeine be trialled in training before it is adopted as a competition strategy.

A Cautionary Note

For the incredibly trained and committed athlete it remains to be established how much supplements actually help since tightly controlled studies using this population of athletes is difficult to conduct. It could be the case that for the untrained athlete the use of supplements often has a greater impact on performance because the supplementation makes up for many of the metabolic limitations that are not appropriately adapted to training.

Also important to consider is the powerful effect of the placebo, also known as the belief effect. When it comes to supplements, especially those that are used for high-intensity exercise associated with pain and hopelessness (i.e., wanting to give up), supplements can become powerful agents for inducing hope and motivation. In some cases, the belief effect can be so powerful that it may be more important to believe in a product that does not actually have a proven mechanism of action than to not believe in a supplement that is known to work.

Performance gains due to supplements are typically in the order of magnitude of 1 to 3 per cent, whereas 4 to 8 weeks of training can be associated with performance gains that exceed 5 per cent. The tendency for many athletes is to go for the quick-and-easy solution to improving performance (i.e., supplements) versus the more arduous training required to produce long-lasting physiological adaptations, which requires far more commitment.

Figure 14.4 presents four scenarios that can occur when discussing supplementation with an athlete based on low and high experimental evidence that the supplement works and low and high belief effects from the athlete's perspective. Although it would be nice if all nutritional supplements used by athletes were backed up with scientific evidence and strong belief effects, the athlete will often have a strong belief in a supplement that does not have much evidence supporting its use. In contrast, for some supplements there is strong evidence of efficacy, but the athlete does not believe in the supplement. These scenarios can be extremely frustrating for the coach, but it is always important to recognise how powerful belief effects are in sport. An athlete who does not believe in the process of supplementation can actually block the potential positive effects of a supplement. The experienced coach will develop management strategies for each condition that can emerge and tend to yield to the athlete's strong beliefs.

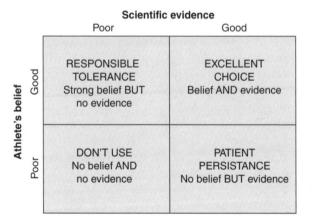

Figure 14.4 Categories of supplements based on scientific evidence and athlete belief.

Altitude Training for the Anaerobic Athlete

Sprint track cyclists from the AIS have documented positive physiological adaptations during a highly structured altitude camp as well as outstanding performance at an important competition 3 weeks after such a camp.[21] The exact adaptations underpinning these performance gains are yet to be fully established, but there is some evidence that altitude training can promote improvements in the buffering capacity in skeletal muscles.

Another unexpected potential benefit of altitude training is the observation that athletes who embark on a unique altitude training program start to be more consistent with other important peripheral aspects of training, including diet, sleep, supplements and recovery, because they want to maximise the benefits of altitude training. For athletes who think this way, altitude training is acting as motivation, helping the athletes adopt a desired behaviour.

We should not forget the impact of motivation when it comes to high-intensity training. Supervision of, and encouragement in, training sessions enhances competitiveness and encourages greater performances. High-intensity training requires exceptional motivation for every repetition and interval. The coach who understands the importance of motivation will recognise that the structure of a high-intensity training session must combine the physical loading with positive social dynamics if the athletes are to optimally respond to the training session.

Summary

Anaerobic fitness is important for performance in many sports; the testing and training methodology used to assess and improve anaerobic fitness is complex and rapidly improving. Numerous scientific studies are revealing many interesting aspects of anaerobic fitness, including the relationship between muscle mass and power production, the relationship between power production and resistance to fatigue and the relationship between power production and movement velocity. When it comes to training anaerobic fitness, the ability to progress through a logical sequence of training blocks, each with a unique emphasis, is critical. Because adaptations to short, high-intensity exercise can be rapid, and excessive loads of high-intensity exercise can lead to injury, illness, heavy fatigue and loss of motivation, it is important to monitor the athlete's health and performance ability closely during training cycles that target anaerobic fitness. Finally, great conditioning coaches recognise how important it is for the athlete to remain motivated for training and to believe in the coach and the training methodology. For this reason, programs with variety that incorporate appropriate ergogenic aids and a healthy lifestyle get the best results.

Acknowledgements

The topics covered and opinions expressed in this chapter are the direct result of many discussions I have had with outstanding sport scientists working within the department of physiology at the Australian Institute of Sport lead by professor Chris Gore. I would particularly like to recognise Dr. Jim Martin from the University of Utah and track sprint cycling specialists Dr. Scott Gardner, Dr. Tammie Ebert and Nicholas Flyger, who have not only been amazing PhD students but also have substantially shaped my thoughts and opinions when it comes to anaerobic fitness. Also, it is important to thank the committed and knowledgeable Australian cycling coaches and cyclists I have the opportunity to work with who are always looking for that winning edge.

CHAPTER 15

Establishing Endurance for Repeated Performance

Darcy Norman
German National Football Team and EXOS (formerly Athletes' Performance), United States

This is not a typical chapter on physiologic adaptations and improvement of $\dot{V}O_2$max or anaerobic threshold. On the contrary, these adaptations form but small components of this chapter because topics on this kind of endurance have been well documented and are found elsewhere in this volume. Instead, this chapter takes a holistic view, and the concepts contained within apply to any sport, not just those conventionally thought of as endurance sports. This chapter aims to lift the veil of traditional thinking and shine a spotlight on the science of establishing muscular endurance platforms both for performance and rehabilitation.

We can look at the development of the human life cycle and its relationship to long-term athletic development to provide perspective. We should look at building and rebuilding athletes in the same way humans have developed over time: building stability on mobility,[1] strengthening the movement and then adding the ability to endure it for the goal of the activity. In the quest for repeated performance, most people make the mistake of looking first at the development of the metabolic or cardiovascular system and less at the strength and movement efficiency that got them there in the first place.

Research on this topic is difficult because so many variables need to interact in order to allow an athlete to develop the ability to endure multiple repetitions of a particular task or movement. Accordingly, what is discussed in this chapter are concepts and checklists, similar to a pilot's preflight manifesto, to ensure the coach or practitioner is covering all the components necessary for establishing endurance for repeated performance for athletes.

Defining Endurance

As it relates to this chapter, the definition of endurance is not its relationship to the cardiovascular system but more literal: having the ability to endure, enduring something by having the ability to perform something more than once. For many, the concept of endurance has to do with a person's cardiovascular ability, how far he or she can run, swim or cycle, and not necessarily how many times he or she can lift a weight. However, the literal meaning of endurance holds equally true for a power lifter, who may have to lift a weight only a few times in competition to find his or her maximum, as it does a marathon runner, who has to take approximately 90 steps (reps) per minute for 124 minutes with no rest between each step. The same concept of having the capacity to minimise decay in force production and withstand hardship or stress through competition exists for both athletes. At their core, both athletes have the goal of being as efficient as possible in order to produce more successful work. Efficiency can mean something different to each athlete, and it is important to make sure there is a complete understanding of the physiological qualities and requirements to provide this endurance platform.

The common denominator in all circumstances is power and power endurance, the mechanical work athletes have to do in the given time allotted or required to be successful. In the powerlifting example, to win the meet the athlete has to create bar speed or momentum to move the weight to complete the lift. In the running example, the runner has to move his or her body and generate and maintain enough power over the given distance to be the first across the line. In both examples the concepts are the same.

Wisdom

Endurance is the ability to endure work. Cardiovascular capacity is merely the means by which we fuel this ability to sustain the work over time.

What is work? Broadly speaking, there are two types of work (stress): positive work and negative work. The goal is to increase the positive side of the ledger and reduce the negative stress in the equation, so we are not training with the brakes on. In our organisation, we use the phrase work + rest = success.[2] Although this chapter deals more with the work side of the equation, rest and recovery (discussed in depth in chapter 24) are integral parts of the formula for repeated performance capacity; they need to be carefully considered if we are truly serious about developing endurance platforms.

Work can be further divided into physiologic and training components. The physiological components can be sectioned into mechanical work qualities and the metabolic (cardiovascular) response to that work. Mechanical work can be broken down further into muscular (strength), neurological and structural qualities. Athletic performances are judged on the mechanical work that the individual displays. Road cyclists get awarded prizes for being first over the line (a display of mechanical work), not for their $\dot{V}O_2$max (their metabolic work). Aerobic capacity is merely the ends to the means.

Once we understand the mechanical work demands placed on athletes as well as their ability to produce them in training or competition, we can develop a clear understanding of the metabolic underpinnings of such displays. We then can alter programming through various combinations of training modalities to improve the metabolic qualities necessary for providing fuel for the mechanical work (discussed in detail in chapter 19).

The metabolic capacities chosen as the focus are determined by the needs of the athlete with reference to the requirements of the sport and areas of relative weaknesses. It is somewhat of a jigsaw puzzle, though, as all the metabolic responses to work are interrelated. Just as a nutritionist prescribes a combination of protein, fat, carbohydrate, vitamins and minerals for an athlete with a particular goal to feed the athlete for success, all athletes need all components but in various ratios (quantities) to maximise performance and be successful. These metabolic relationships lead to the proper response to mechanical work necessary for a particular sport. Thinking in these terms gives a clearer and less-cluttered high-level view of how we can start to train athletes.

Mechanical Muscular Strength Qualities

Strength qualities are part of the foundation for any movement, athletic activity or sport, whether the activity is intermittent or continuous. Not having strength training in the programme is a disservice to the team and athletes and can significantly affect the athlete's ability to sustain high level, injury-free performance.

In certain sports, strength training is overlooked as a quality that will enhance endurance performance.[3] For some, strength training is not perceived as directly affecting success in the sport. Culturally, this view can come from a coach who didn't weight-train as an athlete but was successful and now thinks the athletes he or she coaches don't need to weight-train to be successful. Sometimes, the athlete may not wish to undertake strength training for aesthetic reasons or on the mistaken belief that strength work will make him or her big and slow.

When strength training and its direct benefits are not seen as the primary focus, that type of training often gets left out of the program. For example, endurance sports traditionally train for long periods at relatively low intensities or loads, and skills training tends to bias the technical aspects of the activity. In either case, the complete or partial omission of strength training from a programme is a lost opportunity to improve the athlete's performance.

We should approach programming with the thoughts of the book *The Power of Less*.[4] The paradigm shift I am advocating can be summarised this way: What is the minimal amount of work needed for the maximal benefit? If coaches and athletes start looking at things through this lens, they would find more time to commit to other training components such as strength or plyometric training.

Common Errors in Strength Training for Endurance Sports

When training for endurance sports, athletes often fall into the trap of completing only a high number of repetitions at low load of a particular exercise. Most likely this is because many coaches and athletes believe that since sports such as running and cycling are endurance sports, the athlete has to do endurance-based repetitions whilst working on strengthening to match the specificity of the sport (e.g., 3 × 20 at 30%-50% 1RM). Indeed, many textbooks and position statements state this is only way to improve endurance.

The fact is, endurance sports are witness to so many repetitions (e.g., 90 rpms for 1 hour equals 5,400 reps) that the best and only manner to improve muscular endurance to cope with these volumes is the training within the sport itself. Clearly, doing 3 sets of 25 repetitions of a low-resistance squat will do nothing from either a volume or an intensity point of view. Not only does the programming itself not transfer, but it also promotes a limited strength quality (depending on the per cent maximal weight lifted for those reps) and adds extra work to the athlete with no direct benefit to the remaining filler hours of peddling, running, swimming, skiing, rowing and so on that can only be established through the sport itself. Time is wasted and is better spent training properly or recovering.

Case for Maximal Strength Development

When strength programming and prescription are done well, there is significant benefit to the athlete. To understand this reasoning we have to work backward from the ultimate goal of improved power output or, more importantly, preservation of high power outputs throughout the course of an event. It has been proven that strength is the basis for expressing power.[5]

We also know that in any sport related to time, power (work divided by time) is critical. To develop power, we have two options. First, we can increase the athlete's ability to do more work in the same time, or second, we can make the athlete more efficient at movement so he or she is able to do the same amount of work in less time. In one case we are working on the force side of the equation, and in the other we are working on the time efficiency side.

We know that poor maximal strength is the biggest limiter to power output.[6, 7] When we look at sports such as cycling, running and soccer that have more metabolic stress, and where the athlete has to deal with the clock and his or her body, then *relative* maximal strength becomes more the limiting factor. In either case, there needs to be some kind of emphasis on power and maximal strength development so that the metabolic logistics of the sport will improve the necessary skill efficiency for transferring the maximal strength qualities to benefit the athlete.

The endurance athlete can benefit greatly from strength training with a direct emphasis on maximal strength or relative maximal strength.[8] There are two main benefits to this type of training. The most obvious is that with increased maximal strength, the athlete has to produce less relative force per repetition of the skill, which then creates a decreased energy demand. The second is that focusing on maximal strength development helps enhance neural durability and motor recruitment, making the whole system more resilient.

As the maximal strength of an athlete improves, it shifts the overall demand on the metabolic system. During the activity, the athlete will have less demand on the muscular system for the same amount of work, enabling the athlete to perform the level of work longer and producing indirect improved muscular endurance. Essentially, the same work demands are less costly.

Tendon and Muscle Interactions That Reduce the Metabolic Cost of Movement

Although we used to think of tendons as passive attachments of muscle to bone, their structure affords them the ability to store and release energy. Efficient use of tendons reduces the metabolic cost of movement. Tendons are not contractile, however, and so rely on the muscle to generate the force to overcome inertia. Without having good relative maximal strength, the muscle is unable to maintain the contraction needed to maximise the elastic properties of the tendon.

Through a process known as dynamic isometric strength (DIS), the strength of the contraction of the muscle accumulates energy in the tendon, ready to be multiplied and released. This acts in much the same way that a rubber band stores energy and then snaps back. This capability minimises the metabolic cost of the muscular contraction, which reduces oxygen demand and allows more oxygen to remain in the bank to help the athlete endure more repetitions, put more power into each repetition and maintain greater economy of motion. These are all goals of the endurance athlete.

If the athlete is insufficiently strong, the contraction of the muscle will not be strong enough to stretch the tendon and use the elastic properties, resulting in less power in the movement, more work on the muscle, decreased economy and a greater amount of metabolic work or stress for the same or less mechanical load. Developing the strength part of the performance puzzle is key to establishing endurance for repeated performance.

Strength and Tendon Health in Endurance Athletes

The advantages of being strong are clear from a performance; the same is true from the perspective of managing injury risks. We know that the rates of tendon pain are high in endurance sports and that muscular strength is a key player in those rates.[9] Lack of muscular strength can reduce the efficiency of the elastic and energy-sparing tendon, increasing the metabolically costly work of the muscle and effectively forcing the athlete to spend more energy. This is particularly of concern in sports such as cycling and swimming where ground-contact times are limited and athletes do not develop DIS or the stiffness within the tendons; as a result these athletes are more susceptible to tendon injuries.[10, 11]

Having these athletes spend a fraction of their training schedule doing progressive plyometric training will positively affect performance and support the long-term benefit of maintaining an active lifestyle many years after the athletes have retired from competitive sport. Cycling is a great example. In professional cycling it is common for track cyclists to have a strength and power emphasis in gym training because of the direct relationship to performance on the track. Those cyclists will often make the transition from track to road cycling and either become the team's sprinters, lead-out riders or one-day winners; they tend to be durable.[12] Riders who have grown up in road cycling without ground-based training tend to be less durable, have trouble generating high power outputs on their bikes and become susceptible to long-term injuries even outside their sport.

Fear Campaigning and Strength Work

Coaches and athletes often limit their time in the weight room due to their preconceived notion that lifting heavier weight will lead to increased muscle hypertrophy, decreasing the power-to-weight ratio and making the athletes slower. They do not realise the benefits that will make athletes more durable and efficient in their sport with less stress to the system. If an athlete were to follow the appropriate maximal strength prescriptions, strength gains could be realised without significant increases in muscle size. Strength gains are often due to neural factors such as improved motor-unit recruitment efficiency, something that does not add mass to the body.

Appropriate programming enhances relative muscular strength. Because there is such a need to develop the metabolic system in endurance athletes, the body will naturally metabolise the muscle that is not needed to perform the demands of the task.[13] So by increasing the maximal strength of the athlete in conjunction with improving the metabolic adaption needed for the sport, any lean body mass the athlete adds will be of 100 per cent use.

Inappropriate programming, on the other hand, can add mass to an athlete without significant strength advances. We have seen this many times: Professional athletes actually train themselves out of a position on the team by employing socially promoted programming such as what one would see in bodybuilding. However, it has been well documented with U.S. National Football League (NFL) combine athletes that when programming is done correctly, athletes can put on in excess of 4 kilograms of lean body mass (LBM) and at the same time develop the appropriate strength and power qualities to decrease 40-metre sprint times by one-tenth to two-tenths of a second.[12]

Another fallacy that prohibits endurance-based athletes from participating in strength training is the belief that strength comes naturally as a consequence of technical training. A common example of this is in soccer where many coaches believe that to become better soccer players, athletes just need to spend more time with the ball and play. In reality, though, when a little more time is spent improving strength and movement efficiency, athletes have more tools to express abilities technically. This predicament can be solved through paying more attention to more cohesive, long-term development of the athletes in his or her career, club or organisation.

It can also be resolved by carefully planning and integrating the various training components within the structure of the sport practice.

Strength work, when programmed appropriately and factored in as part of a long-term athletic development plan, makes the athlete more efficient, increases his or her capacity to endure and make him or her more resilient against injury.

Neurological Component of Mechanical Work

The training necessary for improving maximal or relative maximal strength has more benefit to the power output than the strength quality itself. Physiological components of this type of training are the coordination and efficiency of contraction of the inter- and intramuscular components.[14]

The intramuscular adaptation that occurs from strength training refers to

- recruitment of the number of fibres called to action to generate force,

- the rate coding (discharge coding) of the motor neurons, and

- synchronisation, which is how well the nervous system manages to fire the muscle fibres in concert within the muscle.

The more efficient the recruitment, coding and synchronisation, the higher levels of force the athlete is able to generate efficiently, and the more the athlete is able to moderate effort for the specific activity or skill.[15]

The second component is the intermuscular part of movement. This is the coordination and efficiency of the simultaneous sequence of contractions of multiple muscles to complete basic to complex movements.[15] This is where muscular strength and skill begin to overlap. The more skill and precision needed in a movement, the more important the role of muscular strength becomes. As the coordination and efficiency of the movement improves, muscular strength increases the skill threshold (the point at which the intensity of the activity affects the skill quality) of the movement, making the athlete more efficient and improving overall muscular endurance. This end result has a significant benefit to the complex movements, such as triple flexion and triple extension, needed in sports.

In order for an athlete to perform complex movements such as running, all the muscles need to coordinate these actions to fire at the optimal moment to have a summative effect maximising the athlete's effort. Intermuscular coordination will not necessarily affect the force generated by a single muscle, but it will greatly affect the force generated in a complex movement. The more muscles involved and more complex the task, the more the athlete needs intermuscular coordination to be successful.

Two examples provide context. First is the example of using an exercise called resisted walking or running (figure 15.1). This method is just as effective when rehabilitating an athlete from a lower-extremity injury as it is for improving acceleration and absolute-speed mechanics. This activity is excellent for activating and engaging the posterior chain of muscles; reinforcing the appropriate biomechanics of walking and running; and emphasising the coordination of triple extension, triple flexion and spinal stabilisation.[16] This type of exercise prescription is for sports such as running, cycling or soccer where instability and neural fatigue play a role over time in the long-term movement quality of an athlete.

In this protocol we attach a resistance to the athlete's waist and have him or her pull a sled. The same can be done by pushing a sled, but it is good to reinforce the normal gait pattern along with the arm swing. As the athlete attempts to start walking, the nervous system quickly realises what it must do to coordinate all the pieces effectively to get the sled moving. If the coordination sequence

Figure 15.1 Resisted walking.

of the one leg pushing into triple extension and the other into triple flexion doesn't happen optimally, the athlete will stall out on the extension leg, losing balance and stumbling to the side. It typically takes 10 to 12 steps for the athlete's brain to put into practice the whole-body intermuscular coordination to establish the stability and coordination necessary for taking successful steps.

Once the athlete has the pattern, we start to add resistance to change the demand of the activity. The first adaptation for improved strength is for the athlete to purposely initiate the movement in an efficient manner. As this improves, the athlete walks for progressively longer periods up to 60 minutes, depending on the type of athlete. Increasing the strength of the movement pattern leads to improved muscular endurance in the skills needed to accomplish the activity; it also improves the aerobic metabolic adaptation needed to maintain that quality. As the athlete progresses to acceleration and absolute-speed mechanics, the weight is reduced, which increases the velocity of the movement.

In the second example we use stability-limiting lifts to improve intermuscular efficiency of the muscles and the relative maximal strength of the athlete. A stability-limiting lift is a movement pattern that is completed with some form of resistance: The athlete will be able to lift only as much weight as he or she can stabilise against maintaining balance and quality pattern. A simple example is a single-leg squat.[16] During the 1990s and into the new millennium practitioners realised that athletes could back squat in excess of 450 pounds, but if they were asked to single-leg squat their body weight, they were unable to complete the range of motion (ROM) of 1 repetition with a quality pattern. The athletes had underlying strength, demonstrated by the amount of weight lifted on a more stable platform, but they could not express this strength once the platform demanded more balance and intermuscular coordination from the whole system. Some athletes almost used the weight they lifted to counterbalance the compensations they made. Once the platform becomes more unstable, compensating behaviors become harder to hide.

This concept can be taken into more functional patterns specific to the skill of the sport. For example, the single-leg squat is effective for any pushing sport that relies on using the lower extremities (e.g., running, soccer or cycling). One effective exercise for our cyclists was an alternating dumbbell press with both feet elevated in the air (figure 15.2). The

Figure 15.2 Alternating dumbbell press with feet elevated.

athlete needs to have the overall mobility to get into the starting position. Once the athlete establishes the starting position, he or she lowers one arm, making a dumbbell-benching motion, then returns to the start position and repeats on the other side. If the athlete is unable to stabilise through counterrotation of the trunk whilst keeping his or her hips in a neutral position similar to what is done when torqueing on the bike during climbs, sprints and accelerations, the athlete will lose balance.

The alternating dumbbell press starts with weights that the rider can manage safely. As intermuscular coordination improves, the weight the athlete is able to manage and the speed at which he or she is able to move the weight improves significantly. It is this relative overloading of the system that creates a quicker, more efficient contraction of the necessary muscles to react to the movement.

Wisdom

There are many secondary benefits to stability-limited lifting. If the athlete is concerned about increasing lean body mass, in the beginning this method limits the amount of weight and the number of repetitions, so the adaptation is more neuromuscular than it is hypertrophic. Once the athlete has maximised the neuromuscular benefit, he or she will have bought into the process and will feel the benefits of this type of training.

Another concern inexperienced athletes often have with lifting weights is the potential for delayed-onset muscle soreness (DOMS) that can occur from lifting heavier weights. The weight the athlete starts with will be minimal in comparison to that used traditional primary lifting movements, and the exercises will distribute the effort over the system rather than focusing on the load to a specific muscle group. This approach can be a great way to get buy-in from the athlete whilst still getting something accomplished.

Stability-limiting lifting is for the beginner but can also be used for the more experienced lifting athlete. It is a method that can be used to train secondary lifts or as a way to unload the athlete within an undulating program. Even for the experienced lifting athletes the amount of weight they can lift with stability-limiting lifts will be considerably less than with their primary lifts.

This type of training starts to affect the athlete's movement efficiency, improving endurance for repeated performances. As discussed earlier, one of the ways to improve power output is to be able to do the same amount of work in less time, essentially making the athlete more efficient and powerful. A certain amount of stability is needed for the duration of the event in order for the body to generate the power needed to propel itself from point A to point B. For most athletes the stability anchor point tends to be the trunk. It is important to pick movements that have close movement relationships to the sport and that are also stability-limiting lifts. These neurological components in conjunction with strength qualities and the structural components of the athlete make up all the mechanical-work attributes needed.

Stability-limiting lifts improve intermuscular coordination, which translates into greater movement efficiency. This is an unconventional, yet highly effective way of improving muscular endurance because it pulls up the anchors of poor, metabolically expensive movement patterns.

Structural Qualities That Determine the Efficiency of Mechanical Work

The body's ability to endure repeated efforts also depends on the quality and efficiency of movement through the muscles and joints and their relative interplay.[1] The biggest issue is ensuring good mobility and stability. If joint motion and stability are compromised, this will lead to altered mechanics,[17] creating more stress in the system and producing acute and chronic issues, sometimes ending athletes' careers and definitely limiting world-class performances. Many examples exist of how the structural-movement quality of the athlete in conjunction with the chronicity of the training ends up having a long-term effect creating imbalance in the athlete, resulting in injury.[18] If the athlete lacks the strength qualities along with the inter- and intramuscular neurologic components of movement, altered joint mechanics and stress, leading to acute and chronic injuries, can result.

The more we can ensure the athlete is strengthening and grooving the correct path, the better the opportunity the athlete will have for using the correct motor pattern and sequence of joints to move his or her body. This is no different than the attention a sport skill is given when honing it for optimal efficiency. These issues are discussed in greater detail in chapters 3 and 7. The fact that concepts of efficiency and endurance are discussed in relation to other capabilities goes a long way to proving the point that all of these issues are critical in athletic performance and injury rehabilitation.

As a summary, consider the metaphor of an umbrella and its function. A person with a large surface-area umbrella of protection made of mobility, stability and strength is able to move freely under that umbrella without getting wet. If that umbrella is small, however, the person will have fewer movement options and smaller breadth of movement before losing protection and getting wet or injured. By extension, it is not only about the total load of what the athlete is doing but also what that athlete is able to do in that given time. Once the structure of the umbrella is built to protect the athlete, the metabolic system needs to be developed to help support the demand of the mechanical load. An athlete with this strong, durable umbrella can spend as much time out in the rain as he or she likes, enjoying the activity without getting wet. This is a much more holistic approach to improving the endurance platform than simply improving cardiovascular responses to repeated repetitions.

Metabolic Response to Mechanical Work

We have established that the athlete first needs the strength, skill, movement efficiency and elasticity to complete the repetitions of an activity with the highest quality and intensity possible. Once this has been achieved, the athlete can start adding volume to get the central and peripheral adaptations necessary for enduring the intensity and volume needed to be successful at the sport. It has been shown that a combination of poor movement quality in conjunction with poor metabolic capacity increases the risk of injury.[19] As discussed previously, maximal or relative maximal strength as well as the appropriate neurological and structural components are needed to be able to complete 1 repetition with the highest quality. This approach is similar to Roger Bannister's philosophy of breaking the 4-minute mile: He first wanted to run the 100 metres as fast as he could, then repeat it two, three, and four times until he was at a mile.

Unfortunately, in sports that have any kind of endurance requirement, training frequently starts in the opposite direction: The volume gets ramped up without the athlete having a solid base or platform to build the house. The athlete starts running and has to try to develop the necessary strength and neurologic and structural qualities to continue to perform. The ones who do are able to sustain and move on; the ones who do not typically are either slower or become injured and quit.

The cardiovascular system is paramount to the success of the athlete's ability to perform metabolic work as a response and to allow the necessary mechanical work to take place. Think of the metabolic working system as the gas and engine of the race car and the mechanical working system as the frame, springs, electrical system and tires. In motor sports there are fuels for different activities; the human system is the same. We are familiar with the aerobic, anaerobic lactic and alactic systems, but we will not delve into them here. Instead, we will focus on the big picture of developing a good metabolic system and the integration of that system to the mechanical system for an athlete.

An athlete who has to do something quick and responsive will use the alactic anaerobic system, but the aerobic system keeps the athlete going.[20-23] Similarly if we have to link multiple quick, responsive actions together, we do it at a pace that it is sustainable. If, at any point the athlete starts to break down mechanically and the metabolic system cannot replenish the systems necessary for maintaining the movement demand, compensation occurs, and the risk of breakdown increases. It is up to the coach, trainer or practitioner to find the right balance of training, using the various energy systems, for that athlete to be successful in the particular sport (see chapter 19).

Wisdom

It is a mistake to think of the aerobic, lactic anaerobic and alactic anaerobic systems as operating at separate levels. Rather, the metabolic system works in a continuous but overlapping manner with all three methods of energy provision at once, irrespective of the volume and intensity of the activity. The more an activity is repeated, the more the aerobic system is working.

In the endurance world of running, cycling and swimming, the trend in the 1970s and 1980s with the introduction of heart rate technology was to do more long, slow training to develop the aerobic engine. One anecdotal example was triathlete Mark Allen's story of how he improved his threshold pace from running a mile in 8.5 minutes to, I think, 5.5 minutes in one year by doing more aerobic work. What is often overlooked in the story was that Allen said he would always run, cycle and swim as fast as he could. For him, developing the aerobic quality was paramount to his success and longevity in the sport because he already had the speed component. The problem was that many coaches and trainers thought, *Oh, we just have to do more long, slow distance training, and we will win the Ironman*, and that is what endurance training has become.

Eventually, this philosophy was shown to be flawed in more elite levels of sport. Athletes realise that in order to be fast, they also have to be fast in training. However, in order to train successfully, the athlete needs to have the foundational strength and neurologic and structural systems so that movement quality is maintained irrespective of the duress—speed, volume, resistance—placed on it.

This is why interval training, if done correctly, is so beneficial. The athlete runs at a purposeful pace for a duration he or she can sustain for success, takes a break and completes the desired number of repetitions until technical or volume thresholds are breeched. The system then adapts, and the athlete either increases the duration of the purposeful run or decreases the amount of rest between intervals. This has been documented to be one of the best ways to improve $\dot{V}O_2$max and the anaerobic threshold of the athlete, the peripheral adaptation in the muscular and nervous system and the central adaptation in increased stroke volume and skill mastery.[24] These benefits are best achieved when the skill movement quality is able to meet the training demands.

Many trainers and coaches in start-and-stop sports believe they have to train more in the anaerobic systems to improve that metabolic quality within in the sport. It is possible to get so focused on repeated sprinting and intervals that athletes do not develop the aerobic engine to sustain that kind of training. For example, a soccer player may have the ability to endure one, two or three difficult interval-based training sessions but doesn't have the aerobic endurance platform necessary for enduring this type of training and repeated games over a season. This is when injuries begin to mount, and performance suffers.

A good rule of thumb is that an athlete in a long, slow sport such as long-distance running needs more speed work to be successful. An athlete in a start-and-stop sport probably needs more long, slow work without the extra impact, such as cycling, to build the engine to be better able to sustain the intensity and repetitiveness of the sport.

Summary

I hope this chapter has given you a different perspective on what it means to establish endurance for repeated performance for a team or athlete. You should be able to understand and appreciate the types of work and have a checklist of the necessary components for an athlete to effectively execute the foundation of mechanical work regardless of the sport. None of this is new and is addressed in books on periodisation and programming; however, I see these aspects overlooked time and time again. Look at programming and periodisation through a variety of lenses and in many contexts to make sure you have a holistic approach along the continuum of human performance.

I would also encourage you to continuously review how we have developed as humans and review the natural development as it relates to training athletes. At birth we had a basic level of strength (mechanical) and a basic level of cardiovascular ability (metabolic), and we were probably the most mobile we would ever be. Our neurologic system developed to coordinate the pieces of human movement so we could stand, balance, step and walk. In that process we also developed the strength qualities to make standing, balancing, stepping and walking happen with more purpose, efficiency and quickness. Coupled with these efforts to improve our efforts to move for life, we also needed frequent rest. As we developed and the demand to move more increased, only then did our metabolic system respond appropriately to the demands we placed on it. But without a strong foundation of mobility, stability and subsequently strength, the potential of our metabolic system could not be developed.

This metaphor of human development is used to remind us to look at the development of athletes, regardless of the culture, history or misconceptions of the sport. Our ability to enhance endurance platforms will improve when we understand the true limitations to movement efficiency and can integrate the metabolic components of work with the mechanical stresses placed on the body.

CHAPTER 16

Boosting Aerobic Capacity

Grégory Dupont, PhD
LOSC Lille and University of Lille, France

Endurance is an important factor for success in many activities such as athletic events, cycling and rowing, but it is also an essential quality in team sports such as the various football codes, hockey, basketball and handball. Endurance helps maintain a high level of intensity as long as possible and helps delay the effects of fatigue that may contribute to deterioration in technical skill. It is one thing to be able to execute a skill in the first minute of a match but another one entirely to be able to perform it in the final minute when fatigued. This ability is highly contingent on aerobic fitness.

Aerobic fitness is also involved in the ability to recover from high-intensity activities, especially when the sprints are numerous, long and alternated with brief recovery periods, a feature of most field-based sports. From a practical point of view, a high level of aerobic fitness is reported as an asset in counteracting fatigue in sports involving sprint repetitions or high-intensity intermittent exercises.

Aerobic fitness is so important that frequent evaluation is needed in order to help in the selection of athletes and to check the effects of the training program. For this reason, the first part of this chapter defines the terms associated with the concept of aerobic fitness, while the second part presents the protocol used to assess it. The third part of the chapter focuses on the training methods currently known to improve aerobic fitness, including some specific strategies such as altitude and hypoxic training and strength training. The final section discusses the detraining effect, a phenomenon that can occur after a prolonged period of rest after injury or inactivity.

What Is Aerobic Fitness?

Many terms are used when discussing aerobic fitness, including aerobic capacity, $\dot{V}O_2$max, energetic cost and endurance. It is important to understand the definitions in order to use the right terms. For example, the expression *aerobic capacity* is inaccurate because it refers to the total amount of oxygen consumption during a lifetime and therefore cannot be estimated until someone dies.

A more relevant variable is the amount of oxygen that the body uses per minute, termed *oxygen consumption*. At rest, our oxygen consumption is about $0.3\,L \cdot min^{-1}$ but is proportional to the intensity of the contractions being performed. In elite athletes, it can surpass 20 times the resting values at maximal level of exertion. *Maximal oxygen consumption* ($\dot{V}O_2$max) represents the maximum rate at which oxygen can be consumed by a human at sea level. The absolute $\dot{V}O_2$max is expressed in litres of oxygen consumed per minute ($L \cdot min^{-1}$) and represents 2 to 7 L min⁻¹. However, as more energy is required to move a heavier body, the absolute value can be divided by the body mass and represents the relative or specific $\dot{V}O_2$max, which is expressed in millilitres of oxygen consumed per kilogram of body mass per minute ($mL \cdot kg^{-1} \cdot min^{-1}$). So, a rugby player of 100 kilograms and a soccer player of 70 kilograms who have a common absolute $\dot{V}O_2$max of $5\,L \cdot min^{-1}$ will get a relative $\dot{V}O_2$max of 50 (5,000 mL 100 kg⁻¹) and 71.4 mL kg⁻¹ · min⁻¹ (5,000 mL · 70 kg⁻¹), respectively. With this better relative $\dot{V}O_2$max, the performance in endurance events will be higher in the soccer player.

The $\dot{V}O_2$max is normally obtained during a maximal incremental exercise test during some constant work-rate exercises near $\dot{V}O_2$max and involving more than about one-third of the total muscle mass. Figure 16.1 presents an example of the pulmonary $\dot{V}O_2$ responses to a running incremental field test where, after 2 minutes of rest, the initial speed was set at 10 km · h⁻¹ and then was increased by 1 km · h⁻¹ every 2 minutes. The highest point of the graph (seen at 59 mL · kg⁻¹ · min⁻¹) represents this individual's $\dot{V}O_2$max.

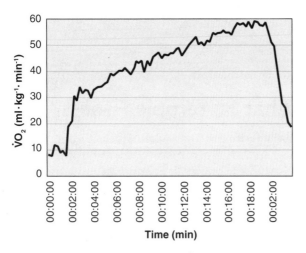

Figure 16.1 An example of the $\dot{V}O_2$ response during an incremental field test.

Maximal oxygen consumption ($\dot{V}O_2$max) has long been used as a determinant of performance in long- and middle-distance events. However, when the range of $\dot{V}O_2$max is narrow, the correlation between $\dot{V}O_2$max and performance is relatively poor. For example, an athlete with a $\dot{V}O_2$max of 75 mL · kg⁻¹ · min⁻¹ will have a superior performance than a person with a $\dot{V}O_2$max of 45 mL · kg⁻¹ · min⁻¹. However, athlete A who has a $\dot{V}O_2$max of 70 mL · kg⁻¹ · min⁻¹ may perform better than athlete B who has a $\dot{V}O_2$max of 75 mL · kg⁻¹ · min⁻¹. In these conditions where the values of $\dot{V}O_2$max are close, additional components of aerobic performance are required to estimate performance, such as the net energy cost of running and endurance and psychological factors.

The *energy cost* is calculated from the measured steady-state $\dot{V}O_2$ above resting divided by the running speed and is expressed in mLO₂ · kg⁻¹ · km⁻¹.[1] Lower energy cost is an advantage for endurance performance because it reduces the energy metabolism (characterised by a lower percentage of the $\dot{V}O_2$max) for any particular exercise intensity. Strength training, discussed later, can help reduce the energy cost.

Endurance corresponds to the maximal fraction of $\dot{V}O_2$max that can be sustained throughout the duration of effort.[2] This endurance has been associated with a combination of several factors, such as proportion of type I muscle fibres, the capacity to store large amounts of glycogen and the capacity to efficiently dissipate heat, but not with $\dot{V}O_2$max.[3] It means that individuals with the same $\dot{V}O_2$max can have durations in which they maintain a given intensity. So, in our previous example, it means that athlete A, who has the lowest $\dot{V}O_2$max, will compensate by lower energy cost or by a higher level of endurance. Therefore, performance depending on aerobic metabolism is mainly associated with $\dot{V}O_2$max, then with endurance and finally with energy cost.

Wisdom

Contrary to popular belief, the term *aerobic capacity* is not the same as endurance. Aerobic capacity refers to the total oxygen consumed during a lifetime, while endurance reflects the time an athlete is able to maintain exercise at a certain level of intensity.

Assessing the Aerobic Engine

While $\dot{V}O_2$max assessment requires some expensive laboratory-specific instruments to analyse the respiratory gas of a subject, it is possible to assess the aerobic fitness and also to estimate $\dot{V}O_2$max from field tests. The assessment of aerobic fitness from field tests presents some practical interest for coaches. A large group can be assessed at the same time, there is no cost and the material requirements are minimal, only requiring a field, a whistle and some cones or markers.

MAS test

One of the most common tests used for running activity is the maximal aerobic speed (MAS) test.[4] This test includes both $\dot{V}O_2$max and economy dimensions and is related to performance from 1,500 to 3,000 metres.[5] It is useful to discriminate a population, to prescribe training intensities (see next section) and to analyse the effects of a training program.

The initial speed is set between 8 and 12 km · h⁻¹, according to the initial level of the participant. For example, for sedentary people it is better to start at the lowest speed (8 km · h⁻¹); high-elite athletes should start at 12 km · h⁻¹. The speed is then increased by 1 km · h⁻¹ every 2 minutes until the participants cannot maintain the speed. The last speed sustained for at least 2 minutes is considered the speed associated with $\dot{V}O_2$max, also called *maximal aerobic speed* (MAS). This speed at the last completed stage is increased by 0.5 km · h^{-1} if the subject is able to run a half stage. From the MAS, it is easy to estimate $\dot{V}O_2$max (expressed in mL · kg^{-1} · min^{-1}) since it corresponds to $3.5 \times$ MAS (expressed in km · h^{-1}).[6]

Yo-Yo Test

For team sports, the yo-yo intermittent recovery test[7] is frequently used to evaluate an athlete's ability to repeatedly perform intense exercise and his or her potential to recover from intense exercise. It consists of repeated 2×20-metre runs back and forth between the starting, turning and finishing lines at a progressively increased speed controlled by audio bleeps from a computer.[7] Between each run, the athlete has a 10-second active rest period, consisting of 2×5 metres of jogging. This test version is characterised by four runs at 10 to 13 km · h^{-1} (0-160 m) and another seven at 13.5 to 14 km · h^{-1} (160-440 m). Thereafter, the test continues with stepwise 0.5 km · h^{-1} speed increments after every eight runs until exhaustion. The test ends when the subject fails to reach the finishing line in time on two occasions. The outcome of interest in this test is the distance covered, which is efficient to class a population or to analyse the effects of a training program. It is also possible to individualise the training intensity from the peak speed reached during the test.

Two levels of the yo-yo test have been proposed. Level 1 is more focused on the aerobic system, while level 2 involves a large contribution from the anaerobic system. The level 2 test is shorter and aims at evaluating a trained person's ability to perform a repeated intense exercise session with a high anaerobic energy contribution. Although the estimate of $\dot{V}O_2$max from the yo-yo intermittent recovery test results is not particularly accurate, this test is reliable and valid as a significant relationship was found between performance in the test and the high-intensity running distance covered during a soccer match.[8-10]

Aerobic Endurance

Aerobic endurance represents the ability to sustain a high percentage of $\dot{V}O_2$max for a long period.[2] It is one of the parameters of performance in long-distance events and is independent of $\dot{V}O_2$max. Several models, such as critical speed, have been proposed to estimate endurance.

If you have no time to implement a field test and you have to implement a training program, use the critical speed concept. It is easy to use. You need just two maximal performances over 3 minutes on two distances to calculate critical speed and anaerobic distance capacity. The *critical speed* concept is the threshold intensity above which exercise of sufficient duration leads to attainment of $\dot{V}O_2$max.[11] For continuous runs, the range of critical speed is generally between 70 and 90 per cent of MAS. In a training program aiming to improve $\dot{V}O_2$max, the intensity should be higher than this speed.

Theoretically, critical speed can be sustained without fatigue; in practice, however, exhaustion occurs after about 30 to 60 minutes of exercise at this intensity, based on the endurance level of the athlete. The second parameter, the anaerobic distance capacity, is a measure of the amount of distance performed at the expense of the complete use of anaerobic stores.

When an athlete has poor anaerobic distance capacity, training should focus on the improvement of this quality. So, critical speed is a simple and easy concept to use to determine the strength and the weaknesses of an athlete, as well as a way to identify which quality to develop.

Case Example

Let's say an athlete runs 1,500 metres in 4 minutes and 10 seconds (250 seconds) and 3,000 metres in 9 minutes and 10 seconds (550 seconds). From this, it is simple to calculate critical speed and anaerobic distance capacity. The slope of the linear distance–time relationship (figure 16.2) represents the critical speed and is calculated as

$$(3{,}000 - 1{,}500) / (550 - 250) = 5 \text{ m} \cdot \text{s}^{-1} \ (19.3 \text{ km} \cdot \text{h}^{-1})$$

The y-intercept of the linear distance–time relationship represents the anaerobic distance capacity (ADC):

$$1{,}500 = 5 (250) + ADC$$

which can be rearranged as

$$ADC = 1{,}500 - 1{,}250$$
$$ADC = 250 \text{ m}$$

These calculations are interesting to estimate performances (time) of an athlete over several distances, to determine training intensities and therefore to better design training sessions. To estimate performance over 2,000 metres, calculate

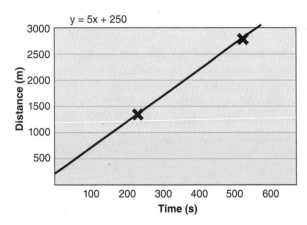

Figure 16.2 An example of the linear relationship between distance and time for an athlete.

the time on this distance (CS means critical speed; ADC means anaerobic distance capacity):

distance = CS (time) + ADC

2,000 m = 5 × (time) + 250 m

2 000 − 250 = 5 × (time)

(1,750) / 5 = time

350 sec = time

So the time for 2,000 metres will be close to 350 seconds, or 5 minutes and 50 seconds.

These calculations also help analyse the effects of training. Training aimed at increasing aerobic endurance will have the tendency to shift the slope of the relationship between distance and time, that is, the critical speed (case A, figure 16.3). Training based on anaerobic-type exercises will have the tendency to change or shift at the origin of this relationship, that is, the anaerobic capacity distance (case B, figure 16.4).

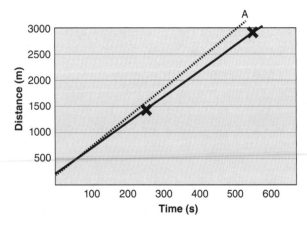

Figure 16.3 Effects of a training program based on aerobic endurance exercises (case A).

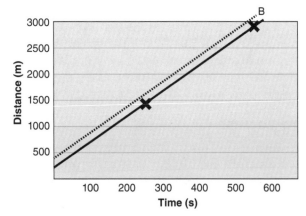

Figure 16.4 Effects of a training program based on anaerobic exercises (case B).

Developing Aerobic Fitness

Although there is a certain genetic ceiling, the method of training aerobic fitness also influences the magnitude of its improvement. Several factors should be taken into account to establish a training program:

• *Initial level*. When the population is sedentary with a low initial level, the training program will produce a bigger improvement, and the majority of the exercises will be effective. The choices of the training program components are more complex for the elite athlete and are more critical to competition success. The lower the starting point, the greater the improvement from any intervention; for the elite athlete, however, the incremental gains in aerobic fitness are smaller, and therefore we have to be much more strategic in our programme design.

• *Frequency*. Although the optimal dose–response relationship for improving aerobic performance is difficult to establish, a minimum of 2 sessions per week is recommended for sedentary people, but at least 3 sessions are required when the initial level is above 50 mL · kg^{-1} · min^{-1}.

• *Intensity*. This is the most important variable to manipulate since all the other variables depend on the intensity. Whilst in the past we have thought that a minimum intensity of 55 to 65 per cent of the maximal heart rate was sufficient, the weight of research now tells us that the maximal gains in aerobic power are elicited by exercise intensities ranging from 90 to 100 per cent of $\dot{V}O_2$max.

• *Duration*. This variable is related to the duration both of the individual sessions and of the program itself. Maximal gains seem to be obtained with exercise sessions of 35 to 45 minutes.

- *Specificity.* Training is specific to the type of activity that an athlete usually performs. For example, after 10 weeks of training focused on the improvements of aerobic power in swimming, the gain in $\dot{V}O_2$max was about 11 per cent in swimming against 1.5 per cent in running. So the triathlete should train specifically in the three activities by swimming, cycling and running.

- *Mechanisms.* Improving $\dot{V}O_2$max requires performing exercises that allow the individual to attain and maintain a high percentage of $\dot{V}O_2$max (higher than 90 per cent of $\dot{V}O_2$max) for the longest time possible. Improvements in $\dot{V}O_2$max are attributed to both central adaptations (characterised by a greater maximal cardiac output) and peripheral adaptations (characterised by a bigger arterial–venous oxygen difference).[12]

Wisdom

Continuous exercising at low intensity (about 65 per cent of $\dot{V}O_2$max) lasting 30 to 60 minutes induces central adaptations. High-intensity training, characterised by intensities close or above $\dot{V}O_2$max performed with an intermittent mode, induces peripheral adaptations.

Continuous and Intermittent Exercises

For continuous exercise, it is vital to define the intensity and the duration. Although continuous exercise seems to be more effective in improving aerobic endurance, it also increases $\dot{V}O_2$max. During continuous exercises, the $\dot{V}O_2$max is attained when the intensity is included between the critical speed and 110 to 120 per cent of the MAS and when this intensity is maintained until exhaustion.[13]

Slow-continuous training, also called high-volume sessions, is performed at less than 75 per cent of MAS or under critical speed over a long duration and is often used during the restart of training to prepare the body for more intense exercises. This type of exercise is relatively easy and is also performed to expend a large amount of energy and, consequently, to lose fat mass.

Fast-continuous training is performed at intensities over 75 per cent of MAS, or above critical

speed, and allows the improvement of endurance and $\dot{V}O_2$max. When the intensity is between 75 and 85 per cent of MAS, the sessions are performed in one set. On the contrary, when the intensity is 85 to 90 per cent of $\dot{V}O_2$max, the sessions can be performed in several sets. This model forms the border between intermittent and continuous training.

Intermittent training consists of alternating periods of high-intensity exercise with periods of active or passive recovery. The introduction of recovery periods between periods of intense exercise allows participants to maintain the exercise intensity longer than when the exercise is performed continuously until exhaustion. Intermittent exercises are characterised by the combination of many variables, including the period of exercise and its intensity and the type and duration of recovery. Consequently, one of the difficulties for the coach in the design of intermittent training is to determine the combination of these variables to allow the achievement of the desired objective. Table 16.1 presents the objectives of the types of intermittent training sessions.

Wisdom

Well-designed intermittent exercise is more effective than continuous exercise to optimise the time spent at a high percentage of $\dot{V}O_2$max.

Most studies investigating intermittent exercise have not found a correlation between the time to exhaustion of continuous exercises and those of intermittent exercises. Therefore ,the qualities required to maintain an intermittent exercise are probably different from those required to maintain a continuous exercise. Because the specificity of intermittent exercises involves periods of recovery between efforts, the performance during intermittent exercise probably depends on the quantity and quality of the recovery.

When the intensity of short-short intermittent exercises is higher than the MAS, the $\dot{V}O_2$max and the anaerobic capacity can be improved. In a study involving high-level soccer players performing two 2 sessions per week during 10 weeks (the first session consisted of 12-15 × 40 m sprints alternated with 30 sec of passive recovery; the second session consisted of 2 sets of 12-15 runs at 120% of MAS alternated with 15 sec passive recovery), MAS and

High Intensity Interval Training

Mike Favre
*Director of Strength and Conditioning,
University of Michigan*

I direct the strength and conditioning philosophy and delivery to 28 different sports at the University of Michigan. Every sport is characterised by the fact their results are often determined by a single or cumulative total of high-intensity effort.

We don't have to look far to see these game-defining moments. Think of a sprint down the wing in soccer or field hockey, a sudden flurry of dynamic efforts in the combat sports or a short sprint to reach a ball in softball or tennis. Even in endurance sports such as middle- or long-distance running or swimming, it is still a race to be the fastest.

We have a saying, 'You play how you train, so you should train how you play.' With this in mind, our energy system development philosophy across all sports relies heavily on high-intensity interval training (HIIT) as this form of training matches most closely the heart and respiratory rate demands seen in competition.

In reality, we work with athletes on strength and conditioning three times per week. With such a time restriction, we need to ensure we get the most bang for our buck so at all times, we emphasise the quality and intensity of effort.

We use HIIT extensively because the rest intervals seen in the duty cycle are short enough to ensure the work demand is great, but long enough to replenish energy stores so that the intensity of the next effort does not decay to the point of being a waste of time.

By maintaining this approach, we ensure there are no garbage efforts from the athlete. What's the point of training slow when winning is done fast? Athletes get enough slow repetitions of effort in technical practice so when they're with me I make them earn it!

This philosophy on quality and intensity extends further than the running track. We see it in the weight room, on the Spin bikes and in the swimming pool. One of my sayings is, 'Don't run the speed out of athletes and don't lift the power out of them.' Essentially this means we should not fatigue the athlete by asking him or her to complete long, slow training sessions.

We use a variety of modalities for HIIT from spin bikes to resisted swimming, from cross trainers to resistance circuits. Whichever technique is used, the emphasis is on high-quality effort. The work:rest intervals depend on the sport but some examples can be seen in the table.

We look to slide in at least some HIIT into every training programme. Athletes need to train with the intensity to meet or surpass the demands of competition. If an athlete is unable to cope with the training, he or she is unlikely to be able to cope with competition demands and either performance would suffer or injury would result. Either way, essentially the athlete would be selected out of the programme.

In terms of periodising HIIT, we gradually introduce athletes to it. The intensity required to really gain from HIIT can be foreign to young athletes, so a graduated exposure is begun and may last several weeks. Depending on the sport and the time of the season, we look to programme one or two heavy HIIT weeks followed by a deload week. This deload week is a reduction in volume but not in intensity.

Generally speaking, we look to programme on a day on, day off schedule, but given the high levels of neuromuscular fatigue that HIIT can induce, in-season we plan sessions at the beginning of the week to give athletes a few days to freshen up before competition on the weekend.

Mike Favre was the 2011 NSCA College Strength and Conditioning Coach of the Year. At the University of Michigan, he oversees 28 varsity teams and more than 600 student-athletes. He is on several committees with the NSCA and is a certification assessor and member of the editorial panel for the United Kingdom Strength and Conditioning Association

Sample Training Protocols for Five Sports

Sport	Training method	Protocol
Sprint swimming (female)	Stair sprints, resisted bike sprints	1x stair sprint (17-18 sec.), 1 min. rest. Repeat 4x then 4 min. rest. Repeat cycle 1x.
Field hockey	Repeated sprints	One 30m sprint every 20 sec., 4-6 reps. 1-3 sets. Rest 1-2 min. between sets.
Basketball (female)	Repeated sprints ('quarters'). Down and back (D&B; full-court sprint, change directions and sprint back). Work:rest intervals range from 1:1 (in example) for elite to 1:3 for introduction.	1 set of 1x D&B in 12 sec., 12 sec. rest; 2x D&B in 24 sec., 24 sec. rest; 3x D&B in 36 sec., 36 sec. rest; 2x D&B in 24 sec., 24 sec. rest; 1x D&B in 12 sec., 12 sec. rest. 2 min. rest between sets. Repeat up to 4x.
Wrestling	Sprints (running or bike), resistance training circuits, wrestling	20 sec. on, 10 sec. off, repeat for 2-3 min. followed by 1 min. rest. Repeat cycle 2-3 times (match replication).
Volleyball	Sprints (running or bike), resistance training circuits	10-20 sec. on, 20-40 sec. rest. Repeat for 6-10 min.

Table 16.1 Classification and Objectives for Intermittent Sessions

	Exercise phase	Recovery phase	Number of repetitions	Number of sets	Effects
Long-long	3-10 min 90%-100% MAS	2-3 min AR	3-5	1	↑ Endurance ↑ $\dot{V}O_2$max
Moderate-moderate	30 sec-2 min 100%-110% MAS	30 sec-3 min AR	5-2	1-3	↑ $\dot{V}O_2$max
Short-short	10-20 sec 110% MAS to sprint	10-20 sec AR or PR	10-16	3-5	↑ $\dot{V}O_2$max ↑ Anaerobic capacity

MAS: maximal aerobic speed; AR: active recovery; PR: passive recovery

sprint speed were significantly improved using intermittent exercises (+1.2 km · h^{-1} for the MAS and +1 km · h^{-1} for the sprint speed over 40 m).[14]

Training based on repeated sprints is also effective to improve aerobic performance and $\dot{V}O_2$max and anaerobic performance. For example, 6 sessions of sprint interval training (4-7 reps of 30 sec of all-out cycling with 4 min of recovery) over 2 weeks were sufficient to improve $\dot{V}O_2$max, time trial performance and maximal activity of various enzymes involved in both glycolytic and oxidative energy provision.[15]

High-intensity training of short duration should be favoured when the time available is limited since it leads to performance improvements. It also reduces the training volume and consequently the risk of overtraining.[16] These results can be effective in team sports, where improvement is required in anaerobic and aerobic performance.

Aerobic Training in Team Sports

Two types of training are regularly used in training sessions in team sports: generic training and specific aerobic training. Generic training corresponds to a training modality where players run a distance at a given intensity. For example, Helgerud and colleagues[17] trained soccer players twice a week for 8 weeks, using a 4 × 4-minute running interval training at 90 to 95 per cent of maximal heart rate alternated with 3 minutes of active recovery. After this training, $\dot{V}O_2$max, the distance covered during a match and the number of sprints improved by 11, 20, and 50 per cent, respectively. The advantage of this generic training is that the variables of distance and time can easily be controlled. This training is also easy to structure and to implement: all that is needed are two markers to define the distance and a stopwatch to set the time the players have to run. One disadvantage of this method is linked to the players' motivation: In general they dislike these sessions because they prefer to run with a ball. Another limit of this training is that it is based on the hypothesis that fatigue in team sports is linked to running activities. However, other factors, such as concentration and muscle damage, are also involved in fatigue.[18]

Specific aerobic training corresponds to a training modality where players do specific exercises with a ball, such as in a small-sided game (SSG). It is possible to attain sufficient intensity using SSGs. The exercise intensity in an SSG can be manipulated with

- pitch dimensions (the intensity will be higher on a large pitch than on a small pitch);

- number of players (the intensity will be higher with 3 versus 3 compared to 6 versus 6);

- rules of play (the intensity will be higher with player-to-player marking);

- use of a goalkeeper (it increases the intensity during 3 versus 3 but decreases the intensity in 6 versus 6); and

- motivation (coach encouragement will increase the intensity).

The advantages of this training method are that it is popular for players of all ages and standards, it ensures the activation of muscle groups as they are engaged during matches and it includes technical and tactical skills. In some conditions muscular activation can exceed match levels. The limits are that these games are less structured than traditional fitness training methods and that the intensity of play can differ among players. The use of SSGs in a preseason training programme is discussed in chapter 21.

Strength Training and Aerobic Fitness

Strength training can improve running economy and consequently aerobic performance. Explosive strength training also is effective for improving running economy. A training programme of 9 weeks based on various sprints (20-100 m) and jumping, leg press and knee extensor–flexor exercises with low loads but high or maximal movement velocities was effective in improving running economy in elite male cross-country runners.[19] The improvements in running economy induced by plyometric training can be linked to the muscles' ability to generate power by exaggerating the stretch-shortening cycle and the increase of the stiffness of the muscle–tendon system, which allows the body to store and use elastic energy more effectively.[20]

Wisdom

When using both strength and endurance training, be aware of the concurrent training effect. Interference would be maximised when athletes use high-intensity interval training and 8-to-12 repetitions maximum (RM) multiple-set resistance-training program. Interference is covered in detail in chapter 20.

Hypoxic Training to Develop Aerobic Fitness

Hypoxic methods consist of using altitude or specific equipment that lowers the oxygen partial pressure of the air breathed. It has been well established that performance in endurance events is impaired at altitude; the higher the elevation, the greater this performance decrement. Conversely, altitude training also can promote increased anaerobic fitness and may enhance sprint capacity. The factors involved in the decrement of $\dot{V}O_2$max at altitude are the decrease of maximal heart rate and stroke volume, which reduce the cardiac output, as well as a reduction of haemoglobin saturation. Although the intensity of training is reduced in altitude, exposure to altitude for a few weeks induces some specific adaptations. It stimulates the renal release of erythropoietin (EPO), which may increase erythrocyte (red blood cell) production and haemoglobin content while decreasing muscle mass.

In some cases, athletes use these hypoxic methods to prepare for a competition or match at altitude. Although aerobic performance decreases with altitude, altitude acclimatisation improves performance at altitude. This acclimatisation phase lasts 7 to 10 days and includes only light-intensity exercises. Conversely, when a training camp is planned at altitude to improve aerobic performance at sea level, the duration of the exposure should be longer than 2 to 3 weeks.

In some other cases, hypoxic methods are used to improve aerobic fitness. Several methods have been proposed to optimise the advantages of exposure at altitude and to reduce the limitations. The purpose of these methods is to improve performance either at sea level or altitude. There are strategies that can be used when it comes to altitude training: live high, train high; live high, train low; or intermittent hypoxic exposure.[21]

Live High, Train High

This is the most traditional form of hypoxic training and consists of a training camp based at altitude where athletes live and train. The training period should last at least 3 weeks, including 7 to 10 days for the acclimatisation phase. Several beneficial effects of this method have been reported on endurance performance and muscle-buffering capacity; however, this method is still debated because there is rarely a control period at sea level, the training intensity is reduced at altitude and often a high inter-individual variability in training responses is seen.

Live High, Train Low

This method was implemented to reduce the side effects—such as decrease in training intensity, muscle mass loss and fatigue—of the first approach but keep the beneficial effects of altitude on physiological functions. In addition, the technical development of new devices made it possible to use artificial altitude without travelling. Results of this method show bigger improvement in endurance performance, $\dot{V}O_2$max and running economy in elite endurance athletes than with sea-level training. The most appropriate altitude for living high has been proposed as 2,200 to 2,500 metres to provide an optimal stimulation of EPO, while the most effective duration at altitude appears to be 3 to 4 weeks.

Intermittent Hypoxic Exposure and Intermittent Hypoxic Training

Intermittent hypoxic exposure or training lasts from seconds to hours and is repeated over several days to weeks. Although intermittent hypoxic *exposure* is generally accepted as ineffective for performance enhancement, intermittent hypoxic *training* seems more beneficial on aerobic performance. This method does not seem to have an effect on erythrocyte production. Consequently, in order to obtain a greater improvement in aerobic performance, athletes could combine both intermittent hypoxic exposure and intermittent hypoxic training. However, the optimal combination in terms of intensity, altitude and duration remains to be identified.

Many factors can influence the enhancements in physiological status induced by an altitude camp. In order to justify the expense, coaches should consider the stated physical objectives of the camp and whether these aims will be achieved after such a short (usually 10-14 days) exposure to altitude. Certainly, it appears that a camp should be held for greater than 2 weeks in order for it to be sufficiently long enough to improve longer-term aerobic qualities in comparison with a similar camp at sea level.

Detraining

A reduction in training load often is planned by coaches during the days before competition in order to improve performance. This strategy, called the taper, aims to have the athlete reach peak performance by reducing accumulated fatigue while retaining or further improving physical fitness (see chapter 22 for a more detailed discussion). Tapering, however, should not be confused with detraining. Detraining is defined as the partial or complete loss of training-induced anatomical, physiological and performance adaptations as a consequence of training reduction or cessation.[22] This happens when athletes are injured or occurs during the off-season when no training is planned.

When training stops, endurance performance declines quickly, and the magnitude of this decrement depends on several factors such as the level of athletes and the duration of the break. The magnitude of the decline in $\dot{V}O_2$max depends on the athlete's level of fitness. After an inactive period of 4 weeks (e.g., off season), the decline is about 5 per cent for moderately trained subjects and can reach 15 per cent for highly trained athletes although running economy is not affected.[23]

The initial part of the detraining-induced reduction in $\dot{V}O_2$max (within a few weeks) is mainly due to a reduced blood volume of 5 to 12 per cent.[22] As a consequence, submaximal and maximal heart rate increase slightly while stroke volume is more markedly decreased. Thus, the first part of this decrement in $\dot{V}O_2$max is mainly due to central factors. In these conditions, when the athlete restarts, long, continuous exercises at low intensity, inducing central adaptations, are recommended.

When the inactivity period lasts longer (e.g., end of a career, injury), other mechanisms such as peripheral factors are involved. In these conditions, both long, continuous exercises at low intensity, inducing central adaptations, and high-intensity training, inducing peripheral adaptations, could be successfully implemented.

Performing alternative training modes may delay the detraining effect. Thus, injured athletes should carefully consider cross-training (e.g., biking, swimming, using a hand bike or electrical stimulation, strength training) to maintain fitness and strength. It would help them to come back more quickly as well as avoid a recurrent or other injury.

Summary

Aerobic exercise training is an important factor in many sports. It improves performance in training and in competition. With a high level of aerobic fitness, athletes are able to train harder and longer and recover more quickly between sets. In order to develop this quality, begin by assessing aerobic fitness to establish benchmarks and individualise training intensities. In team sports, this enables us to split the training group into two or three groups, rather than just manage the squad as a homogenous mass.

Once the testing has been completed, the next step is to select a combination of variables to use to design the training program. Some coaches prefer to work by cycles, which means they plan the same exercises for a certain period. This method can be boring and not really effective. Another method deals with periodisation and changes and seems more effective. For this method the coach sets an objective and proposes several forms of exercises that will enable the athlete to reach the defined objective. For example, to improve $\dot{V}O_2$max, repeated sprints can alternate with short recovery periods, high-intensity intermittent exercises (long to short) and high-intensity continuous exercises during the training week.

Improving aerobic fitness is not just about numbers of repetitions, though. Hypoxic training methods can be used preseason to improve $\dot{V}O_2$max and endurance or during the season to prepare for competition at altitude. Strength training also is effective in augmenting aerobic fitness, although care must be taken when programming to ensure that this concurrent training does not lead to an interference effect.

Finally, we know that a reduction in training loads due to injury or holidays reduces aerobic fitness, and the fitter the person, the steeper the decline. A strategic approach to training programming in this instance is required and will aid the athlete in returning to competition and avoiding injury.

CHAPTER 17

Optimising Effective Cross-Training Methods

Anthony Rice, PhD
Rowing Australia and Australian Institute of Sport

Chris Spinks
Geelong Football Club, Australia

Cross-training (CT) for optimising athletic performance has been widely used in both elite professional and amateur sports for more than three decades to improve athletic performance as well as a means of conditioning injured athletes who may not be able to participate in regular training. Its use has been implemented in strictly controlled and prescriptive methods to more informal general practices.

But what is CT, and what is the rationale behind it? How do we select CT activities, and how do we strategically employ CT so that it is not just entertainment? This chapter addresses all these questions and provides coaches with a solid understanding of how to implement CT into an athlete's periodised plan. As every athlete, sport and personal circumstance is unique, we will not give you a recipe to follow but rather provide a firm understanding of the principles that should be considered. Specifically, this chapter provides guidance on how to

- fit targeted CT into a weekly schedule,
- reduce the risk of overuse injuries based on poorly selected activities,
- measure the effectiveness of the CT program, and
- better understand the manipulation of training stimuli to better achieve desired outcomes.

Defining Cross-Training

For this chapter CT does not refer to any basic circuit training. Instead, it is defined as (1) participating in an alternative training mode exclusive to the one normally used (i.e., not task or sport specific) or (2) combining an alternative training mode with task-specific training.[1] Regardless of the type of CT employed, the main purpose is to gain a training adaptation that leads to an improvement in sport-specific performance greater than sport-specific training alone.

For a sport such as rowing, CT refers to any training that is not undertaken in a rowing shell on water. Hence, running, cycling, swimming and field sports are all considered CT modalities. Interestingly, stationary rowing on an ergometer is considered CT since it is an 'alternative training mode with task-specific training'.[1]

Although we commonly think of CT in terms of aerobic conditioning, it is not uncommon to see activities based on strength training also used as stimuli to improve athletic development. CT is also often confused or used interchangeably with circuit training, which primarily refers to a combination of high-intensity aerobic exercise and resistance training. In this chapter, we accept that strength and circuit training can form essential elements of athletic development, and we will cover some of this in detail; however, the body of this chapter focuses on physiological adaptations produced by cardiovascular-based activities.

CT has been used in some form or another with high-performance sports for decades. Research into its effects began in the early 1970s with a focus on the central and cardiovascular changes and on the peripheral and cellular changes in muscle.[2, 3] Since the introduction of the triathlon and the subsequent explosion of its popularity, the benefits of CT have gained wider attention in the literature as triathletes strove to improve their performance in swim events through run training or improve run performance through cycling training.

Elite triathletes quickly realised that they could not dedicate themselves to full-time training in each discipline without incurring significant risk of injury. As such, their training is based on the premise that certain benefits of training in one specific modality transfer to some degree to one of the other two modalities. The benefits from CT are attributed to variability, change in training stimulus and optimal arousal from the introduction of novel tasks or activities. The important questions for high-performance triathletes are how much time should they devote to improving their weakest discipline, and how much of this training will benefit the other two disciplines. This leads to examining the theory behind transfer of adaptation or specificity of training adaptation.

Theory of Adaptation or Transferability

Consistent endurance training promotes a number of physiological adaptations that enable the body to better cope with the demands placed on it. This type of training can elicit central and peripheral adaptations. Central adaptations refer to an improvement in oxygen transport to the muscles (secondary to enlarged overall heart dimensions, increased blood volume and increased muscle capillarisation). Peripheral adaptations refer to an enhancement of the muscles' capacity to use this oxygen (due to increased mitochondrial density, aerobic enzyme concentrations and increased type I muscle-fibre proportions).

Interestingly, the relative contributions of central adaptation and peripheral adaptation to the improvement in exercise tolerance and capacity remain controversial and may well be different based on age as well as short-term and long-term training history.

How well these adaptations transfer between exercise modes has largely been attributed to the central mechanisms; it is believed these are pathways that are used in all endurance pursuits involving large muscle mass. In contrast, it was originally understood that local adaptations in the actual muscles used for specific endurance modalities are not transferrable unless the exercise mode operates the muscles with similar characteristics (e.g., force, range of motion, duty cycle).

CT for elite endurance athletes relies on the basic premise that training adaptations, both central and peripheral in nature, do transfer across exercise modes. This may well be the case for less-fit individuals who have the capacity for general improvement, but the evidence in highly trained to elite endurance athletes is less prevalent.

The type of CT exercise in competitive athletes is crucial to the transferability of the adaptation. When dissimilar modes of exercise are employed (e.g., arm-cranking CT for a competitive cyclist) the benefit to the competitive athlete may be more relevant during a period of injury when the athlete may be unable to train with any real specificity. In contrast, CT in a similar mode (e.g., running for a competitive cyclist, cycling for a competitive runner) appears to have positive results for trained athletes as shown by the result that 5 weeks of run training alone demonstrated similar improvements in $\dot{V}O_{2peak}$ and 5,000-metre run performance compared with 5 weeks of run and cycle training combined.[4]

Wisdom

Highly-trained individuals will profit more from similar-mode cross-training, but the higher the aerobic capacity of the athlete, the smaller the relative improvement. For athletes who are injured, have low training compliance or are in their off season, cross-training using dissimilar modes is effective.

Benefits of Cross-Training

We know that CT can improve performance via one or a combination of physiological, biomechanical and psychological factors. Specifically, when combined with sport training, it has been shown to improve performance by positively affecting numerous performance outcomes, including reducing the risk of injury, aiding in rehabilitation, improving endurance fitness and energy efficiency, increasing motivation, helping recovery and improving deficiencies.

Injury-Risk Reduction

Commonly, elite endurance athletes train more than 20 hours per week in their discipline. When this load is combined with strength, conditioning and flexibility sessions, this value can exceed 30 hours per week. This volume of training is necessary for stimulating the adaptation required to improve competition performance, but it can also give rise to overuse injuries. Based on the premise that training consistency (i.e., more than 95 per cent of prescribed training is completed) is a strong indicator to improved competition performance, then any training modality that assists with this goal is extremely valuable to include in a training program.

Supplementing sport-specific training with CT enables athletes to continue to train the central mechanisms involved with endurance performance whilst resting the muscles that may be fatigued and require recovery from sport-specific training. For sports that involve a high degree of on-foot load (i.e., running, triathlon, team field sports) increasing the CT load and decreasing the sport-specific training load whilst still maintaining total training load may well prove the difference between maximising training consistency or risking chronic overuse injuries, such as Achilles tendinopathy.

For competitive athletes whose sport is based on running (e.g., field sports, court sports, athletics) or is highly repetitive in nature (e.g., cycling, swimming, rowing) a period of exposure during the off season dedicated to CT can help reduce the strain placed on repetitively used muscle groups and provide the athlete with the opportunity to improve muscular symmetry by activating opposing muscle groups or using muscles through another range of motion (ROM) or movement. Similar benefits are presented to running-based athletes who can reduce the load stress experienced through ground-reaction forces applied whilst competing.

Injury Rehabilitation

CT can be useful when an injured athlete is transitioning back to the main form of training. The specific aim of the CT program in this instance would be to maintain (or attenuate the decline in) specific fitness without exacerbating the injury or prolonging the recovery time needed to return to full training load. CT enables the athlete to maintain some cardiovascular and strength (power) training consistency whilst providing the injury sufficient time to heal.

Acute soft-tissue and joint injuries are common in team sports that involves physical contact. In these instances injuries may result in muscle atrophy (i.e., number and size of motor units) and a neural inhibition (i.e., swelling, pain or structural damage) that may prevent correct motor patterning and activation. CT in the form of specific strength training serves as a great tool for trainers since it is possible, with a well-designed rehabilitation program, to minimise the reduction in muscular function via specific contractile force or velocity and coordination exercises.

Wisdom

Cross-training can be the injured athlete's rescue plan. It can help maintain cardiovascular fitness and, when used in conjunction with a well-designed rehabilitation program, can minimise the reduction in muscular strength.

Improved Endurance Fitness and Energy Efficiency

The sole aim of training for the competitive endurance athlete is to improve competition performance. This can be achieved in numerous ways, but one of the most common is to increase training volume (time or distance). This strategy will not always be associated with improved performance, especially as the athlete approaches his or her true peak; however, in the early and middle stages of the competition pathway increased training volume can have positive effects.

Training specificity is a key to improved performance, but if an athlete is to increase training volume, it will be nearly impossible to keep the entire training program sport specific. This is where the inclusion of CT in an athlete's program can assist without necessarily increasing the risk of injury or excessive fatigue. Importantly, when incorporating similar-mode CT into the program, adaptations will reach into both the central and peripheral pathways, leading to greater efficiency and an overall increased training effect.

For athletes (i.e., team sport athletes) who undertake high-force strength training, training modalities should not be limited to the weight room. The use of high-intensity or high-resistance efforts within a CT session can have similar effects. Sprint efforts whilst running uphill, short bursts with high resistance on the bike (or any stationary CT apparatus) can produce a similar demand on the muscles to produce high force; specific adaptations to high-force training include improved efficiency at lower intensities.

Wisdom

Although cross-training can be beneficial, it may lack the specificity of angle, motor control or speed of movement that can be replicated by strength-based exercises. A balanced program is the key!

Increased Motivation

The long, sometimes lonely, hours of training that an elite endurance athlete completes can often lead to staleness, especially if periods of competition are sparse. During long training blocks, athletes who undertake only sport-specific training often find themselves not achieving the maximal benefit from every session because their intent to train with the required intensity is intrinsically linked to and reflected in their motivation. Motivation is difficult to maintain with monotonous training. Incorporating CT modalities into some sessions of high training stress can assist the elite athlete in applying the required intensity for the session and making the greatest gains possible. It is possible in some instances that these sessions may also enable the athlete with low motivation to rediscover the desire to train with the right intent.

Motivation for intense sport-specific training sometimes may be difficult to harness during the off season or during a noncompetition period. Including CT during these times can help the elite athlete maintain training consistency by allowing the athlete to reduce the monotony of training, improve a deficiency (e.g., base aerobic capacity),

manage an ongoing injury or recover from an earlier postseason surgery.

During the off season, when optimal performance is not the primary goal, training benefits can be gained through the introduction of novel tasks in the form of CT. These can vary from structured sessions with specific physiological outcomes to more enjoyment-focused activities (e.g., playing tennis for fun). Doing so can relieve some of the monotony of training experienced by the athlete, thereby increasing motivation to train when the task-specific activities return.

Effective Recovery

Training forces the body to adapt so that it is better equipped to cope with the demands that are placed on it. In this sense, training is the stress, but the adaptation to this stress takes place during the recovery period. Recovery is discussed in greater detail in chapter 24.

Recovery strategies fall into two broad categories: active and passive (including outright rest). The latter is extremely beneficial, for it enables the body and mind to recover at the quickest rate. However, at key times within specific training cycles, combining outright rest with active recovery in the form of both similar and dissimilar modes of CT may be the direction to take. The subsequent adaptation can be enhanced by increasing blood flow to the exercised muscles, thereby delivering valuable nutrients directly to the tissue, as well as removing residual waste metabolites associated with previous exercise.

Deficiency Improvement

The competitive phase of training can leave little time for anything other than the delivery of optimal performances. CT during the off season can help improve a specific physiological deficiency without compromising the goals of this phase, which include (but are not limited to) athlete regeneration, rest and recuperation.

Common Uses in Olympic Sports

Olympic endurance sports differ in the volume and frequency to which CT is employed in their elite programs. In Australia, the winter climate does not dictate off-season CT nearly as much as it does in northern Europe and North America. Table 17.1

Table 17.1 Use of Cross-Training in Olympic Endurance Sports

Sport	Does sport use cross-training (yes or no)?	CROSS-TRAINING MODALITIES EXPRESSED AS A % OF TOTAL CROSS-TRAINING VOLUME UNDERTAKEN							
		Stationary rowing	Running	Cycling (all forms)	Swimming	Team activities	Cross-country skiing	Arm cranking	Other
Rowing	Yes	30	20	40	3	5	Much greater predominance in Northern Hemisphere	2	
Road cycling	Yes			80					20
Endurance track cycling	Yes			70					30
Mountain biking	Yes			70					30
Middle- to long-distance running	No								
Swimming	No								
Flatwater canoeing or kayaking	Yes		30	65	5				
Triathlon	No								
Race walking	No								

outlines some key summer and winter Olympic endurance sports and the degree to which they use CT as part of their regular training. Table 17.2 captures the main reasons why the chosen sport uses CT a part of its routine training program.

Fundamental Considerations When Including Cross-Training in a Programme

As is the case with any periodised approach to training, a poorly constructed, nonspecific (in rationale or modality) and inadequately monitored CT program can lead to a negative impact on an athlete. In extreme cases it may even lead to injury. This section covers the important factors to consider when programming for CT.

The most commonly used principles of exercise prescription apply to CT as they do to any other form of sport training. It is imperative when designing a CT session that these principles are properly considered: mode, frequency, duration and intensity.[5] There is a wealth of literature on use of these principles in effective exercise prescription, yet it is common for coaches, sport scientists and other practitioners to skip these steps, especially when it comes to CT. Far too often CT is seen as nonspecific, low-risk, low-impact training that, as long as athletes feels as though they have worked hard, the desired outcome has been achieved. Athletes who are often prescribed CT sessions are those who are returning from injury, have a training restriction, or are in their off-season or noncompetitive phase of training where a level of detraining may have occurred; as a result, these athletes are possibly at the highest risk when it comes to a poorly constructed session.

Mode

In planning for CT, it is important to choose a mode of activity that allows the specific energy system to be stressed in the manner required. As outlined earlier, CT activities that require the use of large muscle mass and multiple joints will allow for a greater chance of transference. Careful consideration must also be given when selecting the most appropriate mode for athletes who are

Table 17.2 Reasons Olympic Endurance Sports Use Cross-Training

Sport	Central transfer (maintain or improve O₂ transport pathways)	Peripheral transfer (O₂ utilisation pathways)	Strain and monotony reduction	Injury rehabilitation or prevention	Development of efficiency, non-specific strength or power	Increased training volume without increasing risk of overuse or chronic injury	Rejuvenated or enhanced motivation	Seasonal application (inability do sport-specific training)
Rowing	√√√	×	√	√√√	√	√√√	√	√√√
Road cycling	√	√	√	√	×	×	√√√	×
Endurance track cycling	√	√	√	√	×	×	√√√	×
Mountain biking	√	√	√	√	×	×	√√√	×
Middle- to long-distance running								
Swimming								
Flatwater canoeing or kayaking	√√	√	√√	√√	×	√√√	√√	√
Triathlon								
Race walking								
Cross-country skiing								

injured or are returning from injury so as not to interfere with the recovery process. In this stage of planning a close collaboration with medical staff familiar with the injury is key.

Frequency

The frequency or number of sessions that an athlete completes in a day, week, month or training cycle can have significant impact on whether the training goals and objectives are met. A balance must be kept between achieving CT goals without affecting the athlete's specific sport activities.

The phase of training the athlete is in may influence the time available for CT. In competition-phase team training, individual skills sessions, strategy meetings and recovery from competition can reduce the number of sessions available to the athlete, although during this phase the goals may reflect the time available. An injured athlete may begin a rehabilitation program with a high frequency of CT sessions spread across a number of modalities (similar and dissimilar) in order to maximise the training effect but minimise the risk of non-sport-specific overuse injuries. As time progresses the aim of the program would be to integrate the athlete back towards full-time sport-specific programs, which would be indicated by a reduced number of sessions, especially those of a dissimilar CT type.

Duration

The duration or time allocated to each session is influenced by session intensity, mode (apparatus, similar or dissimilar modes) and training goal. Sessions that are more intense and aim to improve anaerobic metabolism, speed and power are typically shorter in total duration (20-40 min) with shorter, high-intensity efforts interspersed with active recovery periods. Sessions aimed towards improving aerobic metabolism are likely to be longer (45-120 min) with a focus on periods of more moderate intensity. The key is to determine the needs of the athlete and programme accordingly. This approach is discussed in more detail in chapter 1 and throughout part II of this book.

Intensity

The intensity of each CT session not only must be matched to the session goals, but also to the athlete's specific capabilities. Often, intensity is dictated by the duration of the intended session. Only with the correct intensity can the opportunity for CT transference be maximised. For example, an athlete in the general preparation phase of training may be required to complete a higher number (frequency) of sessions, and as a result, the intensity would be based on improving aerobic power using intensities of 70 to 90 per cent of maximal oxygen consumption.

Determining Intensity in Cross-Training Sessions

A simple method for determining the appropriate level of intensity for athletes who are using a variety of CT apparatuses and modalities is to conduct basic progressive intensity tests on each apparatus to be used at or near the start of the training phase. Since elite athletes have little difficulty determining what is an easy effort and what is a maximal effort, determining the intensities in between these end points can be valuable. Using the apparatus the athlete will use to complete most of his or her training helps with specificity and familiarisation. If the coach or athlete plans to use a wide variety of equipment concurrently, this process may pose a time pressure; however, these testing or baseline sessions can be used as sessions in themselves, thereby maximising time.

To run a test, start the athlete at a low intensity and progressively increase the work intensity at set intervals (2-4 min) until the athlete is at maximal effort and cannot continue in the test. As the athlete progresses through each step, ask the athlete to provide a rating of perceived exertion (RPE) for each level just before completing the time for that level and record the response.[6] In the early stages the athlete will be able to give a verbal answer, but as the athlete reaches the higher intensities, it will be handy to have the RPE scale on a card so the athlete can point to the answer (remember the simple talk test for intensity). These are not scientific tests, but rather simple and practical means of setting intensity for work periods whilst cross-training.

The practitioner then has the flexibility to prescribe sessions through two means—RPE or work intensity (e.g., gear, level, power output, cadence)—since both have been collected during the test. In practical terms, if an athlete is experienced on the apparatus, has a history of CT and understands the differences in set-work intensities, then prescribing via RPE can be effective. For athletes who lack these attributes, use the work intensity data to reduce the variability of an athlete who is inexperienced with perceptions of intensity.

It is important to note that when using RPE scales to set training intensity, an athlete's experience in using these scales will determine how accurately the athlete achieves the desired intensity. The athlete's RPE can be affected by other factors, such as previous exertion (fatigue), familiarity with the training apparatus and understanding of the session demand. However, the use of RPE scales can be extremely beneficial for measuring and prescribing cross-training activities without the use of expensive or limited access to monitoring technology.

Case Studies

Examples of how we integrate the theory of CT into practice in sport populations are demonstrated in the case studies that follow.

Periodisation of Cross-Training Into a Rowing Training Plan

For many Olympic endurance sports, CT forms a moderate-to-large part of routine training volume. One of the real advantages of using CT this way is that it is easy to manipulate the overload of the training program simply by adding or subtracting

CT sessions or alternatively by varying the intensity of specific sessions. In Australian high-performance rowing, CT forms a large component of the base preparation phase of each season (domestic is October to December; international is April to June).

The main aim of the base phase is to increase training volume and ultimately improve basic aerobic fitness traits that will enable the rower to have a solid foundation on which to produce higher-intensity efforts at a later time with good repeatability. As the preparation approaches the two major peaks of the year (national team selection in March and World Championships in August), the frequency of CT sessions is typically reduced. Interestingly, the sessions that remain in the program are often split between low-intensity volume-type sessions and mid- to high-intensity

interval-type sessions. The real advantage of using CT in rowing (especially in the precompetition and taper phases) is that each session (or lack thereof, as it may be in some cases) can be 100 per cent tailored to the individual athlete's needs as opposed to on-water sessions in crew boats where each rower must attempt to work at similar levels and undertake every session.

As shown in table 17.1, CT use in Olympic endurance sports spans a broad spectrum with rowing having one of the highest percentages of training time applied through CT and triathlon showing little to none. For the sport of rowing, CT incorporates all aspects of load, frequency, intensity and duration.

Table 17.3 outlines a typical training week for an elite rower in the general preparation phase of the domestic season. In Australia, this weekly

Table 17.3 Sample Training Programme During General-Preparation Phase for an Elite Rower

Weekly goals: Continue to establish training routine, 90%-95% session compliance, update online training logs daily with metabolic and perception data

	Mon.	Tues.	Wed.	Thurs.	Fri.	Sat.	Sun.
Notes	Leave for boat sheds at 6:30 a.m.	Leave for boat sheds at 6:30 a.m.	Leave for boat sheds at 6:45 a.m.		Leave for boat sheds at 6:30 a.m.		Leave for boat sheds at 8:00 a.m.
Session 1	Ride to and from training (60 min)	Ride to and from training (60 min)	Row 3 × 21 min pieces (7', 7', 7') at SR22, SR28, SR24	Off	Ride to and from training (60 min)	Off	Cycle to and from training (60 min)
Session 2	Row 20 km at SR 18-20	Row 2 × 2000 m at SR20 and SR24		Off	Row 20 km at SR 18-20	Off	Row 20 km with 36 min (8', 7', 6', 5', 4', 3', 2', 1') at SR 20, 22, 24, 26, 24, 26, 28, 30
Session 3		WattBike: aerobic threshold for 90 min at 70%-75% HRmax	Strength and conditioning	Rowing ergometer: anaerobic threshold for 3 × 15 min at 80%-83% peak power	Strength and conditioning	Ride 90 min or run 45 min at 70%-80% HRmax	Ride 150 min hills and flats at 70%-90% HRmax
Session 4	Strength and conditioning	Flexibility	Hydrotherapy	Row 12 km on water at 75% HRmax	Hydrotherapy		

Total training time: 23.3 hours

Total on-water distance: 150 km

Endurance cross-training time: 10.5 hours (45%)

SR: stroke rate; HRmax: maximal heart rate

program would be implemented during the months of October and November. During that period the major training outcomes focus on improved training capacity, greater than 95 per cent compliance to the prescribed training plan, increased metabolic efficiency at intensities between 70 and 90 per cent of maximal capabilities and ultimately improved rowing performance over 15 to 30 minutes. Training load is supplemented with CT sessions of stationary rowing and cycle ergometer as well as running to make up over 45 per cent of total training time.

Some of the CT sessions are simple bicycle commuting to and from training; typically, these are done at low intensity (less than 70% maximal heart rate). In contrast, some of the stationary cycle and rowing ergometer sessions can be among the most intense sessions of the week (e.g., Thursday's session 3 on the stationary rowing ergometer). For the elite rower CT forms a large aspect of the weekly training load. CT enables the rower to increase or maintain high-training volume without the associated drawback of continual on-water rowing (e.g., chronic overuse injuries, blistered hands and overall body tightness due to the inability to move out of the rowing seat during the training session).

Table 17.4 summarises how multimodality CT can form a large component of a rehabilitation or fitness-maintenance program for an injured rower. One of the increasingly common injuries in elite rowers over the last decade is rib stress fractures. The causes are not well understood, but the outcomes are clear: minimal to no rowing for 5 to 21 days depending on the severity. In these cases the medical and coaching team look to CT as the only mechanism by which the rehabilitating athlete can maintain some degree of current fitness capacity and training consistency whilst importantly reducing the stress and demotivation that often accompany injury. In this example it is quite noticeable how CT (i.e., stationary rowing ergometer and stationary bicycle) forms a large part of the initial rehabilitation program. As the athlete progresses to a greater number of on-water sessions with varying volume and intensity, the number and severity of CT sessions, especially stationary bicycle sessions, are reduced.

Periodisation of Cross-Training Into a Team Sport Athlete's Training Plan

The considerations for team sport athletes do not differ from those for athletes in individual sports.

Rather, it is the rationale behind the CT and how it can be factored into a team sport athlete's training demands that differs. This section focuses on the important factors that need to be considered when including CT into a team sport from the perspectives of general periodisation and injury rehabilitation.

Table 17.5 shows how CT is periodised into the general program of the team sport athlete. It has its highest use during the preseason phase of preparation, although there remains a significant amount of CT done throughout the entire training year.

Tables 17.6 and 17.7 divide the preseason phase of the training year into greater detail, outlining how CT modality, frequency, intensity and duration shift as the required training becomes more focused on game-specific loads.

Periodisation of Cross Training Into an Injured Team Sport Athlete's Training Plan

An athlete who has a lower-limb injury that prevents him or her from running due to associated impact stress can continue to improve the cardiovascular system with the use of non-weight-bearing activities such as cycling, swimming, rowing ergometer training and strength training. It is possible for an injured athlete's CT program to use similar if not the same parameters designed for the regular weight-bearing or specific-activity training. In the example provided in table 17.8 the running planned for the noninjured athlete can be transferred to the athlete's CT program when he or she is not capable of completing the session as prescribed.

The challenge with the example in table 17.8 is choosing an appropriate intensity on the bike to elicit the desired training effect. In this case it has been determined that the bike session needs to have an increased level of intensity, which can be achieved in many ways. In this example the passive rest used in the run session is replaced in the bike session with moderate-intensity cycling.

A period of transition occurs when an injured athlete returns to the chosen activity or sport and is still limited in the amount of specific training that can be completed. The factors contributing to limited training exposure can be many and varied based on the athlete's medical or injury status. It is important to understand the mechanisms and justification underpinning the athlete's return to full-training status, and a strong collaboration is

Table 17.4 Rib Stress-Fracture Rehabilitation Program

Notes:
- Perform thorough warm-up and stretching before rowing.
- Do not progress to next level if morning symptoms are worse.
- Build volume prior to increasing rate or intensity.
- Review with physiotherapist every 2 or 3 days. Obtain medical reviews as indicated by doctor.

	ON-WATER ROWING SESSIONS				ENDURANCE CROSS-TRAINING SESSIONS				
	Daily sessions	Distance (km)	Handle pressure (light; moderate; firm)	Stroke rate (s/min)	Stationary rowing ergometer	Stationary cycle ergometer	Strength and conditioning or abdominal endurance program	Comments	Treatment
Day 1	0				2 × 20 min at 75% HRmax		Gym		
Day 2	0					Intense interval: 4 × 10 min at 400 W			Doctor review
Day 3	1	6		<18					
Day 4	Rest								
Weekly total	1	6			1	1	1		
Day 5	1	8	Moderate	<22	2 × 20 min at 300 W		Gym		Physiotherapist or doctor review
Day 6	1	6	Moderate	Technical and exercises only		4 × 10 min at 330 W	Abdominal endurance program		Massage
Day 7	1	14	Moderate to firm	<24	2 × 20 min at 300 W				Physiotherapy
Day 8	0					2 × 15 min at 380 W/420 W	Gym		Optional massage
Day 9	1	12	Moderate to firm	<28			Abdominal endurance program		Physiotherapy
Day 10	1	10	Firm	<32	1 × 30 min at 290 W	4 × 10 min at 330 W		Shorter efforts but faster and more intense (lots of recovery)	
Day 11	Rest								
Weekly total	5	50			3	3	2		

	ON-WATER ROWING SESSIONS				ENDURANCE CROSS-TRAINING SESSIONS				
Day 12	1	16	Moderate to firm	<28			Abdominal endurance program		Physiotherapist or doctor review
Day 13	2	2 15	1. Race: moderate to hard 2. Light	1. 30-36 2. <22				Race to full capabilities	Massage or physiotherapy
Day 14	0				2 × 20 min at 320 W	45 min < 75% HRmax			Massage
Day 15	2	15	1. Moderate 2. Light	1. <24 2. 18-22					Physiotherapy
Day 16	1	12	Firm	30-36				Race to full capabilities	
Day 17	0								
Day 18	1	14	Firm	30-36				Race to full capabilities	
Weekly total	7	57				1			
Day 19	0						Gym	Full training begins	Physiotherapist or doctor review
Day 20	1	20	Light to moderate	22-24	1 × 40 min at 290W		Abdominal endurance program	Depending on pain	Physiotherapy
Day 21	0								Massage
Day 22	2	30	1. Moderate to hard 2. Light	1. <28 2. 18 to 24	2 × 25 min at 325 W		Gym		Physiotherapy
Day 23	0					90 min at <75% HRmax	Abdominal endurance program		Massage
Day 24	2	30	1. Hard 2. Light to moderate	1. <30 2. 22-28			Abdominal endurance program		
Day 25	0								
Weekly total	5	80			2	1			

Table 17.5 Impact of Training Phase on Cross-Training Programmes

Injury, nonselection, limited competition, playing time and specific conditioning goals can impact all variables.

	Mode	Frequency (days per week)	Duration	Intensity
Off-season	Varied (e.g., bike, swim, row, run)	2 or 3	30-90 min	2 × moderate 1 or 2 × moderate or low
Preseason, general preparation	As above	3-5	45-120 min	2 × moderate 1 or 2 × high or moderate 1 or 2 × moderate or low
Preseason, specific preparation	As above	3 or 4	45-90 min	1 or 2 × high 1 or 2 × high or moderate
In-season or competition	As above	2 or 3	45-60 min	1 or 2 × high or moderate 1 or 2 × moderate

Table 17.6 Sample Preseason Routine, General Preparation Phase

Notes:
- The objective of this phase of training is to improve an athlete's general physical condition. Therefore exposure to a broad range of activities can be extremely beneficial.
- The training intensity, work-to-rest ratio and mode should match the type of physiological adaptation required for this phase. (In this sample the athlete could focus on improving aerobic power.)
- The CT content is relatively high (3+ hours).
- Strength and power have been given a higher priority by being placed prior to team-skills training. (Strength training is a form of CT.)

	Sun.	Mon.	Tues.	Wed.	Thurs.	Fri.	Sat.
A.M.	Rest	Strength and power session	Cross-training (60 min)	Strength and power session	Cross-training (60 min)	Team-skills session	Aerobic conditioning (specific)
P.M.	Rest	Team-skills session	Active recovery	Team-skills session	Active recovery	Strength and power session	Cross-training (60-90 min)

Table 17.7 Sample Preseason Routine, Specific Preparation Phase

Notes:
- The objective of this phase of training is to focus on sport-specific performance as the team gets closer to competition.
- Cross-training content is scheduled slightly differently to reflect the importance of team training. The time allocated to CT has also been reduced slightly.
- Team-skills sessions are now scheduled before strength and power sessions, again reflecting the shift in focus.
- The training intensity, work-to-rest ratio, and mode should match the type of physiological adaptation required for this phase. (In this sample, the athlete could focus on improving aerobic power.)

	Sun.	Mon.	Tues.	Wed.	Thurs.	Fri.	Sat.
A.M.	Rest	Team-skills session	Individual technical skills session	Team game—style session	Individual techni-cal-skills session	Team-skills session	Team game—style session
P.M.	Rest	Strength and power session	Cross-training (45 min)	Strength and power session	Cross-training (45 min)	Strength and power session	Cross-training (45-60 min)

Table 17.8 Cross-Training for an Injured Team Sport Athlete

Run session	Cross-training (cycle ergometer)
Warm-up: non-specific CV running, mobility exercises *Session*: maximal aerobic speed (MAS) run sets; 5 min work period of 15 sec at 110% MAS, 15 sec at 60% MAS. *Repeats*: 5 repeats *Recovery*: 4 min between sets (passive rest) *Cool-down*: active mobility and flexibility exercises, water-based mobility exercises	*Warm-up*: varying speed cycling (low to moderate), mobility exercises off the bike *Session*: 5 min work period of 15 sec at 110% MAS, 15 sec at 60% MAS. *Repeats*: 5 repeats *Recovery*: 4 min moderate-intensity cycling between sets *Cool-down*: 5 min decreasing intensity cycling, active mobility and flexibility exercises off the bike, water-based mobility exercises

required between the medical practitioner and those responsible for designing the athlete's training plan. It is only with this level of understanding that an appropriate plan can be put in place.

CT can be used to supplement training loads so that the athlete continues to progress not only in terms of returning from injury but also in terms of cardiovascular fitness. This is a critical phase as it can assist in shortening the time before an athlete has an adequate level of fitness to return to full-training status and ultimately competition.

Periodisation of Cross-Training in a Team Sport Athlete Returning From Injury

An athlete who has missed an extended period of training due to a ligament strain in the knee has started to be integrated back into team training. Due to the nature of the injury and the athlete's limited exposure to high-intensity activities such

as high-speed running and agility, the athlete can participate in only a portion of team activities. In this example, the athlete completes a range of controlled, specific tasks that relate to individual rehabilitation goals. However, it is determined that the cardiovascular load (or stress) that the athlete has been exposed to is not sufficient to elicit the desired training effect. This athlete then completes an additional CT portion (e.g., bike, stationary rower or swimming). Table 17.9 shows what this session would look like in a training plan.

In the example in table 17.9, the training completed by the injured athlete is deemed to be insufficient for the progression of cardiovascular fitness. The injured athlete is removed from drill 5 (match practice) because it is deemed that his or her injury status and the level of intensity (and unpredictability) of this drill would place the athlete at greater risk of reinjury. However, in order to supplement the high cardiovascular stress that this drill would have otherwise provided, a CT session has been designed and is conducted concurrently.

Table 17.9 Sample Session Integrating Cross-Training Into a Team-Training Session

Notes:
- In this example the athlete is capable of completing a mixture of team drills (drills 1-3, 6) as well as progressive rehabilitation-specific exercises (drills 4 and 5).
- The athlete's participation must be closely monitored to determine the appropriateness of each drill. Even the best planned drills can and will change.
- A quick assessment of training demands will help determine the efficacy of the CT session. Has the session outcome changed from the planned outcome?

Team session	Injured athlete's session
Warm-up: nonspecific CV running, mobility exercises, progressive speed run-throughs, dynamic skill warm-up drills	*Warm-up*: nonspecific CV running, mobility exercises, progressive speed run-throughs, dynamic skill warm-up drills
Session: team tactical and technical session (40 min) Drill 1 (5 min): static skill practice (kicking) Drill 2 (10 min): team ball movement (tactical) Drill 3 (5 min): small-group, set-play structure Drill 4 (5 min): tackle technique Drill 5 (10 min): match practice Drill 6 (5 min): goal kicking	*Session*: integrate to team training, progress open and closed agility drills, top-up CV fitness with cross-training Drill 1 (5 min): static skill practice (kicking) Drill 2 (10 min): team ball movement (tactical) Drill 3 (5 min): small-group, set-play structure Drill 4: (5 min) modified, controlled agility Drill 5: (10 min) modified, continue controlled agility, game-specific repeat-effort drills Drill 6 (5 min): goal kicking
Cool-down: active mobility and flexibility exercises, water-based mobility exercises	*Cross-training* (30 min): row, ski, or bike ergometer, pyramid 15 sec on/15 sec easy; 30 sec on/30 sec easy; 45 sec on/45 sec easy; 60 sec on/60 sec easy; then back down again (10 min). Complete for each modality. On = RPE of 7; easy = RPE of 4.
	Cool-down: active mobility and flexibility exercises, water-based mobility exercises

Summary

Depending on the sport and athlete-specific requirements CT can contribute in varying degrees to the overall training load. The reasons for adding CT into a training plan include

- supplementing an increase in training volume without increasing the risk of injury;

- enabling continuation of training whilst rehabilitating from a separate injury;

- maintaining sport-specific motivation or possibly remotivating the stale athlete;

- improving overall fitness through increased efficiency; and

- enhancing recovery from high-stress sport-specific training.

When programming CT into a plan, the governing factors are the same as with any other well-constructed training plan: Identify the goals or aims for the athlete and plan to introduce CT progressively through manipulations of mode, frequency, intensity and duration. Whether included as a major focus of a training plan or to help focus the athlete on key sport-specific sessions, CT can make a real difference to the performance outcomes of any athlete.

PART

III

Delivering Performance

Zuma Press/Icon SMI

CHAPTER 18

Planning a Performance Programme

Benjamin Rosenblatt, ASCC
Senior Strength and Conditioning Coach, English Institute of Sport,
England and Great Britain Hockey

Athletes can be viewed as self-organising and adaptive in nature. Therefore, the purpose of training is to exploit their adaptive capacity to improve their ability to self-organise and achieve their goals. Monotonous training (i.e., training with little variation) can lead to an exhaustion response in the form of increased risk of injury and illness. Since an athlete may be at a different stage of the stress–response cycle on any given day, the periodic, planned fluctuations in training volume and intensity are a vital consideration when attempting to manipulate the stress response for positive adaptations. Periodisation is simply the strategic planning and monitoring of training in order to facilitate the right adaptations at the right time to lead to competitive success.

The aim of this chapter is to use real-world examples to illustrate strategies that have been used to design effective training programmes for successful athletes. Every training programme should be written with the end in mind. The strategy used should be the one that best fits the constraints of the sport and the objectives of the athlete. The first section of the chapter addresses the nature of adaptation, the second discusses how to construct a programme, the third illustrates how training programmes are structured and the fourth demonstrates strategies that can be used to achieve the desired goals.

General Adaptation Syndrome

Exploiting the adaptive capacity of the human body (first described by Selye in 1950 as the general adaptation syndrome[1]) is the central component to designing an effective training programme. The acute cell-signalling, hormonal and immune responses that lead to protein synthesis and functional adaptations are highly specific to the training stress imposed on the athlete.[2] If a training session has sufficient volume and intensity to cause overload, it is followed by acute fatigue (alarm). In time this is followed by a supercompensation (resistance) response, which is a positive adaptation. The summation of several training sessions and subsequent adaptation is the central tenet to cyclical loading.[3,4] The summation of several training sessions over time will also have a greater fatigue and subsequent supercompensation response.

If the appropriate stresses are added together with appropriate recovery time, an adaptive response will take place that will leave the organism in a better-prepared state than previously. This supercompensation response or positive adaptation is due to the mobilisation of energy resources and hormonal responses. This is why fitness gains are found with consistent, long-term training. As with the acute response, if the overall volume, intensity, frequency and type of stress are too great and recovery is not sufficient, a chronic maladaptive or exhaustive state will result. In sports, this is demonstrated by illness, susceptibility to injury or overtraining, which has symptoms similar to chronic fatigue syndrome.[5,6]

Designing a Training Plan

The purpose of a training plan is to exploit the adaptive capacities of the athlete to increase the probability of achieving a sport objective. In order to write a training plan and determine which method of periodisation should be used, the following steps should be taken (figure 18.1).

• *Sport profile.* It is vital to have a thorough and detailed understanding of the demands of the sport and the key performance indicators. An excellent example of a performance model for sprint cycling has been detailed by Martin and colleagues.[7] Constraints to consider are the competition calendar and locations, opponents, tactical demands, style of play, what is required to win and physical characteristics that underpin performance.

• *Athlete profile.* Once the competitive demands and key performance indicators of the sport are understood, it is vital to determine what physical characteristics an athlete has and his or her strengths and weaknesses. This information will help determined what qualities support performance and what qualities are limiting performance. This process is described in more detail in chapters 1 and 2.

• *Objectives.* With knowledge of the competitive calendar, the demands of the sport and the needs of the athlete, it is possible to determine clear objectives for the athlete's physical development. Objectives must be specific, accountable and time based. What precisely does the athlete need to achieve, and when does he or she need to achieve it?

• *Training plan.* Once we know what the athlete needs to do and when it needs to be done, training opportunities within the competitive calendar will start to emerge. The decision can then be made on volume and intensity of types of training based on

knowledge of periodisation strategies (discussed later) and the time frame of adaptations for physical qualities.

• *Monitoring.* In order to make informed decisions regarding the effectiveness of the chosen training strategy, the training completed and the individual response must be monitored. This step is detailed further in chapter 6. Information gained from monitoring can lead to real-time adjustments training strategies.

A large body of evidence suggests that general adaptation syndrome can be applied to training for sport performance.[8] Whilst training is aimed at exploiting the adaptive capacity of the athlete, muscle injury and upper respiratory tract infections (URTI) are both examples of an athlete responding negatively to the total amount of stress placed on the system.

Positive, specific chronic adaptations can be facilitated by providing a specific overload stress, which facilitates an alarm response. It is possible to manipulate several variables to promote an overload and gain an adaptation rather than exhaustion. Whilst the idea of ever-increasing training loads may be attractive to coaches, failure to vary the elements of a training plan is known to result in significantly increased risk of muscle injury[9] and respiratory infections.[10] We cannot, therefore, simply ask the athlete to do more and more with impunity. The aim when designing programmes is to manipulate several training variables to gain a positive response to training load, rather than a negative one. The variables that can be manipulated include volume and intensity, frequency, overload and recovery.

Volume and Intensity

Training volume is the amount of training completed; training intensity refers to how strenuous training is. Typically, training volume is quantified in total amount of work done (time or distance) and training intensity is work done in relation to a known maximum (percentage of max). The acute volume and intensity of training must be sufficient enough to cause an acute stress response. This is known as overload.

The overall volume and intensity of training over a specified period must be sufficient to

Sport profile ⟩⟶ Athlete profile ⟩⟶ Objectives ⟩⟶ Training plan ⟩⟶ Monitoring

Figure 18.1 A schematic of the training planning process.

facilitate long-term adaptations. A positive stress response to training is an athlete being able to tolerate greater volumes of work and greater volumes of higher-intensity work. However, excessive training volumes and intensity over time has been shown to cause an exhaustion response, which leads to overtraining or injury.[6] It is important to quantify both the volume and intensity of training an athlete is completing in order to determine the magnitude of the training stress.

Frequency

The training frequency is how often a training stress is applied and is typically quantified in number of sessions. As with volume and intensity, training stress must be applied frequently enough to overload the athlete and initiate an alarm response, but not too frequently that an exhaustion response is triggered.

Overload

The overload principle suggests that training must be of sufficient volume, intensity and frequency to stimulate a stress response.

Recovery

Recovery is the time course of the alarm phase. If successive training stresses are applied in the alarm phase, secondary alarm phases will be triggered that could lead to exhaustion rather than adaptation.

Manipulating Training Variables to Structure Training Programmes

Several strategies exist for manipulating training volume and intensity to facilitate overload, encourage recovery and adaptation and provide variation. These are detailed in table 18.1 and illustrated in figure 18.2, *a-e*. Ultimately, each strategy has its merits, but these are simply tools to facilitate the adaptive response. The strategy used should be determined by the objective for each phase of the training units discussed in the next section. Planning the volumes and intensities of work and monitoring the responses to training (both acute and chronic) is the only way to determine how an individual athlete or team has responded to the strategy employed. Having monitoring plans facilitates making more informed decisions in the future.

Case Study: Elite Ski-Cross Athlete Returning From Injury

A high-performance ski-cross athlete was returning from injury in order to compete at a qualification tournament for the Winter Olympic Games. She was using the rating of perceived exertion–based training impulse (RPE-based TRIMP) system to record training load in order to monitor and modulate total training stress (see chapter 6). Figure 18.3 shows how a week of high training stress was accumulated on weeks 1, 4 and 7. (Figure 18.4 shows the athlete's daily training load.) She returned to skiing in week 5; in week 8 she had a reaction in her knee and was unable to complete the planned training load. Although the total training load was only slightly higher than her previous high-load weeks (figure 18.3), the strain of training was much greater on this week, indicating little variation in training. The athlete was able to race at the qualifying tournament. However, one cannot help but wonder if the training stress had been planned more effectively (less total stress and greater intersession variation), she may not have had the reaction in her knee and may have entered the competition in a better-prepared

Table 18.1 Strategies Used to Manipulate the Volume and Intensity of Training

Name	Strategy
Classical	Reciprocal change of overall volume and intensity
Wave	Similar fluctuations in volume and intensity of work
Incremental	Gradual increase in volume and intensity of work
Varying volume	Maintenance of high training intensity with oscillating volume
Varying intensity	Maintenance of high training volume with oscillating intensity
Reactive	Manipulation of daily training volume and intensity based on how the athlete and coach feel

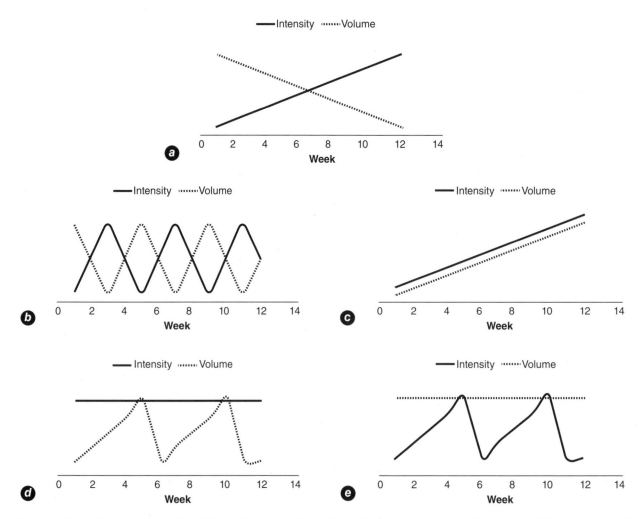

Figure 18.2 Manipulation of training volume and intensity using a (a) classical, (b) wave, (c) incremental, (d) varying volume, or (e) varying intensity strategy.

state. This example highlights the value in varying training load between sessions in order to prevent overreaching and facilitate performance gains.

Definition of Training Units

A training plan is divided into several units, each with a specific objective. The training units are hierarchical in nature. *Macrocycles* generally are periods of a year and consist of several blocks called *mesocycles*. Each mesocycle aims at achieving certain objectives and is made up of several *microcycles* (figure 18.5). A microcycle generally lasts 5 to 14 training days, and the volume and intensity of work is manipulated for each microcycle to prevent over- or underreaching. Several training days make up a microcycle. The volume

and intensity of work are manipulated on a daily basis to ensure an athlete is not over- or underreaching. Several training sessions can make up a training day with competing or complimentary objectives.

Strategies for Manipulating Training Units to Achieve Desired Goals

Several strategies have been defined in order to optimise training adaptations and are described in table 18.2. The purpose of this section is to review some evidence for each strategy and to demonstrate when they have been successful.

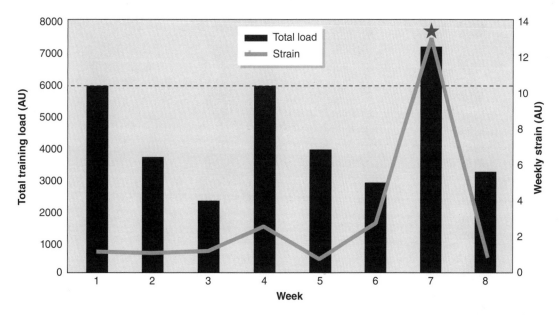

Figure 18.3 Total weekly training load and training strain accumulated by a high-performance ski-cross athlete before an Olympic qualification tournament. The star indicates the week when her knee had an adverse reaction. The straight black line indicates a potential limit to total training stress for this athlete.

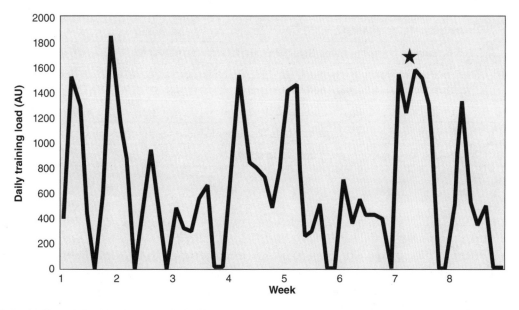

Figure 18.4 Daily training load accumulated by a high-performance ski-cross athlete before an Olympic qualification tournament. The star indicates the week her knee had an adverse reaction.

Linear Strategy

This training strategy involves the sequential development of one physical quality after another, each becoming more specific to the sport performance. An example for a sprinter would be to develop general fitness and strength in the first mesocycle; specific strength, power and speed endurance in the next mesocycle; and speed in the last mesocycle before competition. Evidence for a linear approach to training certainly exists in strength training, where it has been demonstrated that stronger athletes have greater capacities to adapt to power training than do weaker athletes.[11]

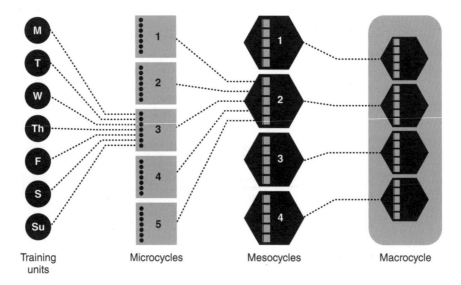

Figure 18.5 Training fits into microcycles, which fit into mesocycles, which make up the macrocycle.

Table 18.2 Common Names and Descriptions of Strategies to Manipulate Training Units

Name	Strategy
Linear	Periodic sequencing of one physical quality after another: hypertrophy, strength, power
Concurrent	Training several competing qualities such as endurance and strength during one mesocycle
Conjugate	Training several complimentary physical qualities such as power and strength during one period
Concentrated	Short periods of high training stress aimed at improving an individual physical quality, for example, a 2-week mesocycle to develop aerobic capacity
Block	Sequential blocks of concentrated mesocycles
Taper	Rapid reduction in either volume or intensity of work to facilitate supercompensation before competition
Competition	Preparation for sequential competitions in short succession

This would suggest that an athlete who needed to improve maximal power capabilities should progress in a linear fashion by developing hypertrophy, maximal strength and finally power. The advantage of this strategy is that there is an obvious progression of physical development. The disadvantage is that the linear progression does not always match the physical development requirements of all athletes.

Case study. In figure 18.6, the total volume and average intensity of strength training during three mesocycles have been displayed for an elite soccer goalkeeper with no previous history of strength training. The training period was undertaken at the start of preseason (July) and ended during the season (October). After this training phase the goalkeeper continued to lift once per week to maintain strength. Each mesocycle was 4 weeks long, and the exercises (hang clean, back squat and step-up) were kept the same for the entire training period. The first mesocycle was aimed at hypertrophy and tolerance to strength training. The second was designed to maintain a relatively high volume but increase the intensity of training in order for the goalkeeper to be able to tolerate the high intensities of the maximal strength mesocycle. The outcome of the training was that despite an intensive preseason and the playing demands of the season, the goalkeeper was able to increase countermovement jump (CMJ) height by 4 centimetres. Since goalkeeping performance can be limited by jump height, this was a meaningful change in physical performance, which in turn led to improvements in technical performance.

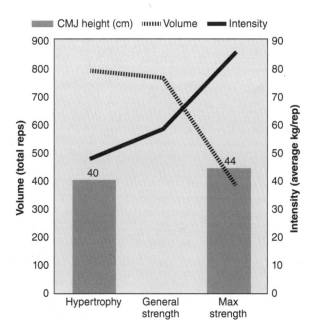

Figure 18.6 Example of a linear strength training programme that increased countermovement jump (CMJ) height of a Premier League goalkeeper by 10 per cent. The total volume and average intensity for each mesocycle are displayed as well as the CMJ height at the beginning and the end of the training phase.

Concurrent Strategy

Many sports require the development of several physical qualities for performance. However, the development of some physical qualities may come at the expense of others due to fatigue caused by one form of training or competing cell-signalling pathways.[12] However, rather than conceptualising physical qualities as competing, it may be more appropriate to consider training stress as a whole. Over a mesocycle it may be possible to undulate the volume and intensity of strength and endurance work to maintain a constant total training stress, but leave energy resources for training and adaptation to both forms of training (see chapter 20).

A concurrent strategy may be appropriate for maintenance or small longitudinal gains in several fitness qualities over a long season (e.g., in professional rugby or football) or for a developing athlete. This strategy may not be appropriate for a well-trained athlete who is attempting to make considerable gains in a specific physical quality. The advantages and disadvantages of concurrent training are discussed in greater detail in chapter 20.

Case study. An elite judo fighter ruptured her ACL 6 months before a selection tournament

for the Olympic Games. Before her injury, her fighting style was to wear down opponents and win towards the end of the contest. After her injury, high-intensity aerobic fitness was of paramount importance to her performance. Because she had ruptured her ACL, lower-limb strength and muscle–tendon stiffness (particularly of the medial hamstrings) were limiting her capacity to return to full judo training. The constraints of her plan were that she had to accumulate 2 months of progressive judo training before competition, and she could not undertake meaningful training within the first 2 weeks postsurgery. Her training aims were to develop high-intensity aerobic fitness (measured by a repeated-effort test on the rowing machine) and lower-limb strength (measured by single-leg squats to failure, hip bridge time to failure, single-leg heel raises to failure and maximal hopping distance) to improve lower-limb function concurrently within a 12-week period before the planned start of judo training.

Three strength-training sessions and 5 fitness sessions, including 2 long interval sessions (3-6 × 3-6 min work, 3-6 min rest), 2 short interval sessions (3 or 4 × 20-40 sec work, 10-20 sec rest) and one anaerobic session (3-6 × 40 sec work, 4 min rest) were undertaken per week.

There was an undulating decrease in strength- and fitness-training volume throughout the period to facilitate greater training intensity (figure 18.7). By the end of the training period she was able to achieve a 10 per cent fatigue index on the repeated rowing test (a high-level score is considered under 20 per cent), make vast improvements in muscular conditioning (figure 18.8) and in muscular power (figure 18.9). These results demonstrated that a concurrent training strategy can be effective at improving markers of strength and aerobic fitness during the rehabilitation of an elite athlete.

Conjugate Strategy

Advanced and elite athletes are capable of training at much greater intensities than subelite and developmental athletes. The amount of training stress they can accumulate with a maximal intensity session is high. A linear approach to training this could lead to issues since it may require elite athletes to accumulate high levels of training-specific stress several times within a microcycle. To counter this issue, the conjugate method of periodisation was developed by Verkoshansky.[13]

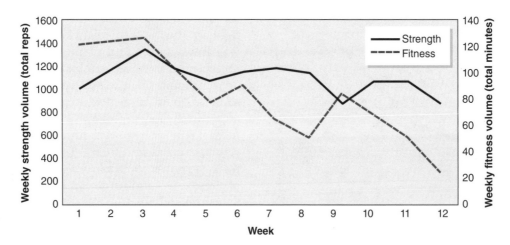

Figure 18.7 Total weekly volume of strength and fitness training during a concurrent training period aimed at improving strength and fitness of an elite judo fighter.

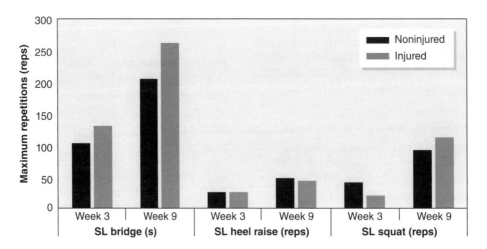

Figure 18.8 Changes in muscular conditioning from weeks 3 to 9 of the concurrent training period.

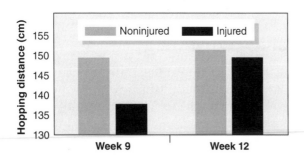

Figure 18.9 Change in maximum single-leg hopping distance from weeks 9 to 12 of the concurrent training period.

The conjugate method involves training several physical qualities within one microcycle but maximising intensity in only one of those physical qualities per mesocycle. For example, maximal strength, speed strength and strength speed are all required to maximise long jump performance. If strength training is undertaken three times per week, one session would involve all three strength qualities; one would be emphasised and the other two would be submaximal each week.

The emphasis in week 1 might be on maximal strength; in week 2 it might be strength speed and in week 3 it might be speed strength. Repeating these mesocycles would facilitate the longer-term development of all three strength qualities without inducing unnecessary fatigue. This approach is most famously used by powerlifters at the Westside Barbell powerlifting club in the United States but is also successfully employed by rugby clubs in season and jumpers.

The advantage of a conjugate training strategy is that it is possible to develop several physical attributes during one training period. However, the athlete must be of sufficient physical development in order to achieve the required levels of training intensity.

Concentrated Strategy

There is growing evidence for the efficacy of concentrated loading at improving various parameters of fitness. Ronnestad, Hansen and Ellefsen[14] demonstrated greater gains in endurance parameters of well-trained cyclists when five of eight planned high-intensity aerobic training sessions were placed in the first week of a 4-week mesocycle compared to spreading these training sessions evenly throughout the mesocycle. The Bulgarian weightlifting team also employed periods of concentrated loading to great success. It is reported that they lifted maximally several times per day in short, concentrated mesocycles.[4]

The clear advantage of a concentrated loading strategy is that large gains in physical development are made in short spaces of time. However, training volume and intensity is high and potentially monotonous; therefore, this is a short-term strategy to be used with highly developed and specialised athletes.

Case study. A Premier League football team had a 6-week preseason. It was decided that all training would be undertaken using small-sided games and football drills with an emphasis on achieving certain durations in heart rate zones. The coaching team did not plan for any matches within the first 3 weeks of training. Instead, the coaches opted for a 3-week period of concentrated loading of conditioning-orientated football training followed by a 3-week period involving more tactical work and match play. A maximal aerobic running-speed assessment was undertaken during week 1 and at the end of week 3 to determine if the training stress was sufficient to improve aerobic capacity. Training load was calculated using a bespoke system.

Figure 18.10 shows how the training strain and load for weeks 1 to 3 were much greater than in weeks 4 to 6. Forty-seven per cent of the total training load for the 6-week period was concentrated into weeks 2 and 3. There was a 10 per cent increase (effect size of 2.03) in the maximal aerobic running speed of the team from 4.42 +0.27 m/s to 4.85 +0.13 m/s. This indicated that the concentrated loading of football-specific training was an effective strategy for increasing aerobic running performance in a Premier League football team.

Block Strategy

This approach was first developed to navigate around the challenges of athletes having to peak several times in a season.[15] The block strategy involves planning sequential blocks of concentrated mesocycles. As each block accumulates high

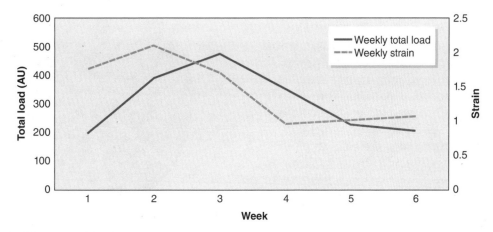

Figure 18.10 Weekly total training load and training strain over a 6-week period of preseason in a Premier League football team. The load is concentrated into the first 3 weeks of training.

levels of fatigue, the delayed effects of training are exploited with a performance peak at the end of the third block.

Essentially, the blocks are three mesocycles: accumulation, transmutation and realisation. The accumulation block aims to develop physical qualities, such as maximal strength and endurance, with long-term residual training effects. The transmutation block involves concentrated loading of sport-specific fitness qualities. The final realisation block involves a large reduction in training stress and an emphasis on training to model performance. This strategy involves heavy periods of fatigue, and due to concentrated periods of high training volumes and intensities, it may be useful for athletes who have major competitions on a monthly or bimonthly basis, such as those in boxing, kayaking, bobsleighing and rowing.

Case study. A developmental 500-metre female sprint kayaker was aiming to maximise performance for the last regatta of the year so she could step up to the national team. She was already strong and had naturally high levels of aerobic fitness but was detrained. She was limited by her technical execution especially at higher stroke rates. She had 9 weeks before competition.

The accumulation block was 3 weeks long and was aimed at improving aerobic capacity and technical execution at high and low stroke rates. Training was divided into strength maintenance (2 times a week), aerobic development (5 times a week cross-training), technical paddles at low stroke rates (4 times a week) and technical paddles at high stroke rates (3 times a week).

The transmutation block lasted 4 weeks and was aimed at transferring her aerobic fitness and technical execution into race-specific speed and speed endurance. This block of training involved strength maintenance and power (2 times a week), aerobic maintenance (1 time a week cross-training), technical paddles at low stoke rates (3 times a week), speed endurance (5 times a week) and speed training (3 times a week).

The final realisation block aimed at improving race strategy and reducing training volume to facilitate adaptations. This block involved power maintenance (2 times a week), aerobic maintenance (1 time a week), technical paddles at low stroke rates (3 times a week) and race modelling sessions (3 times a week). This strategy facilitated a personal best performance at the regatta by 7 seconds and resulted in selection to the national team (see figure 18.11, *a-c*).

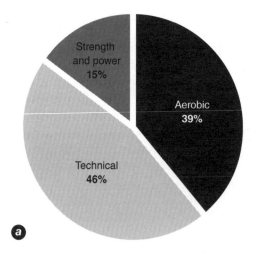

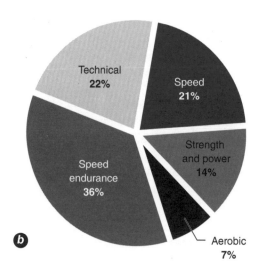

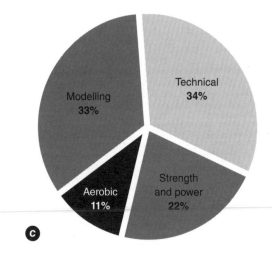

Figure 18.11 Distribution of training in the (*a*) accumulation, (*b*) transmutation and (*c*) realisation blocks of training for the developmental sprint kayaker.

Tapering Strategy

Tapering is the rapid reduction in either volume or intensity of work to facilitate supercompensation before competition. Tapering can occur with a microcycle (e.g., with a team preparing for weekly competition) or can be a dedicated mesocycle (e.g., for a swimmer preparing for a world championships). Current thinking favours a drastic reduction in volume but maintenance of intensity when close to competition. As with all other responses to loading, responses to unloading are highly individual in nature[16] and should be characterised to determine the optimal response for each athlete. This concept is explored in more detail in chapter 22.

Competition Strategy

One of the most challenging aspects of periodisation is the manipulation of training stress to optimise fitness adaptations without accumulating excessive fatigue during the competition phase. In elite-level professional football and rugby, teams have to play once or twice per week every week for several months. An effective periodisation strategy is one that gives the individual players enough training stress of the right type at the right time to maximise performance without causing too much fatigue. This phase of training is commonly characterised by low training volumes with physical qualities maintained but rarely developed.

Kelly and Coutts[17] have outlined a strategy they used in the Australian professional Rugby League. Their model factors in the level of competition, the time between matches and the location of the match to determine a match-difficulty rating. When the match-difficulty rating is plotted week by week, it is possible to determine how much training load should be accumulated each week and to identify opportunities for fitness gains and recovery.

On a smaller scale, figure 18.12 displays the football-specific training load of a Premier League team before a match on Saturday. Over 60 per cent of the total training stress was accumulated at the start of the week with a recovery day in the middle and the remaining 40 per cent of training

stress towards the end of the week. The last 2 days before the match tended to be devoted to more tactical aspects whilst the start of the week was orientated towards maintenance of fitness through small-sided games.

A competition strategy is vital for performance. Being able to maintain and develop physical qualities for competition without accumulating undesirable fatigue is a fine balance and one that should be explored in much further detail with the athletes involved.

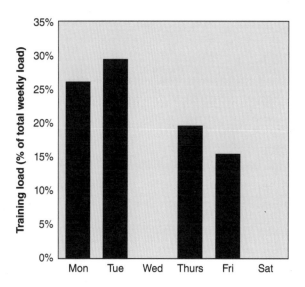

Figure 18.12 Training load distribution for a Premier League football team over a microcycle with competition on Saturday.

Summary

Periodisation is essentially the manipulation of training stress to produce a desired outcome. Several strategies can be employed to achieve this objective, each with its own merits. The decision-making process should be based on the demands of the sport and the needs of the athlete. The training plan should be monitored to ensure it is effective and to learn more about how the athletes adapt to stress. When writing training plans, consider what each athlete needs, when he or she needs it and, only then, what is the best way of training to meet those needs.

CHAPTER 19

Designing Energy-Specific Programmes

Joel Jamieson
8 Weeks Out

Energy-system development is essential to every area of athletic performance, and yet any discussion on such principles needs to begin with the recognition that the body's energy pathways were not designed with this goal in mind. The body does not care how fast an athlete can run a 40-yard dash any more than it wants to be pushed to run 26.2 miles in the shortest time possible.

Instead, all the pieces of the energy-system puzzle, in their elegant complexity and beauty, have one fundamental purpose: support life rather fuel performance. By providing the constant, unending supply of energy that every cell in the body needs to function, energy systems are at the heart of every aspect of the biological drive to maintain life.

It is this biological drive to produce energy and survive that makes it possible to reach the limits of human performance through specific training. Only with a true understanding of this simple truth can effective programmes be designed and athletic performance enhanced as a result.

The purpose of this chapter is to explore the concept of energy-system development within the greater context of athletic performance and program design. More specifically, this chapter provides an overview of the role of energy systems along with key principles that every coach should understand when designing the yearly training program.

Energy Systems and Athletic Performance

It is not an overstatement to say that success in every sport fundamentally relies on the body's ability to produce energy. This is because, in many ways, athletic performance represents the limits that the human body is capable of being pushed to, and each cell must function at its peak if an athlete is going to perform at his or her best. Although usually only the working muscles or heart are discussed when the topic of energy systems comes up, many tissues in the human body require far more energy to function properly during athletic events than at rest.

The brain itself, for example, has a massive job to perform during athletic events. Coordinating the intricate and rapid firing of hundreds of muscles within milliseconds takes a tremendously large amount of energy. Research has even shown that due to the high energy demands of exhaustive exercise, the brain can respond by increasing the amount of glycogen it stores locally to make it better equipped to meet such needs.[1]

In other words, supercompensation and changes in energy production are not confined just to the working muscles or the cardiovascular system. Such changes take place throughout the body in response to exercise because energy production and usage is literally a matter of life or death.

Wisdom

The brain is incredibly important when it comes to energy systems. Not only does it coordinate motor control and power output, but it also regulates blood flow, hormone levels and a variety of cellular functions that support energy production and expenditure. Energy systems are about much more than just muscles and the cardiovascular system. The brain reigns supreme.

Without a constant supply of energy, the body cannot survive, which is what makes exercise such a powerful stimulus. Exercise challenges the body's energy-producing machinery in ways that ultimately lead to improved function. This is a prime example of the nature of the body's adaptive mechanisms at their finest.

When challenged appropriately, the changes in energy-system function stimulated by training lead to increased athletic performance and success. However, when the stimulus is inappropriate to the demands of a particular sport or individual athlete, the results can be disastrous, and performance can suffer. Having a thorough understanding of the specific energy requirements of a given sport as well as the physiological demands resulting from a given training program are two important prerequisites to effective coaching.

At the most basic level, the biggest differentiators in athletic performance are technical skill level, speed of skill execution and the effectiveness of strategy and tactics used. The best athletes are more skilled, have a higher level of power output and use more effective strategies than less-successful athletes. These three factors are largely what separate the world-record holders from everyone else.

Within this context of athletic performance, energy systems play the biggest role in determining the level of power output an athlete is capable of. This power output is ultimately the limiting factor that determines the speed at which an athlete is able to execute skills; all things being equal, when skills are executed faster, performance is greater.

Consider the speed of a professional soccer game compared to that of a game played between two high school teams, or the velocity generated by a professional baseball player's bat swing compared to that of a little leaguer, for example. Even in endurance sports, those with the best times are those who are able to move their limbs the fastest for the longest amount of time without slowing down.

There is no doubt that at higher levels of performance, skills are executed not only with a higher level of technical precision, but also with greater speed, which requires increased energy production. As a result, energy production is intimately linked with performance on all levels, and it provides the foundation for an athlete to effectively use his or her skills. After all, a biomechanically perfect baseball swing won't do much good if it's performed too slowly to hit the ball.

Components of Energy Production

Energy systems must be adaptable in order to produce the amount of energy necessary for meeting whatever demands may be placed on the body. Consider, for example, the vast differences in the power output and overall demands placed on the body between sprinting 100 metres in under 10 seconds and running 26.2 miles in 2 hours. Such performances represent not just opposite ends of the athletic spectrum, but also are testament to the inherently adaptable and versatile nature of the body's energy production systems. Each sport represents a specific environment to the body and thus a unique challenge that it must solve in order to produce the required energy necessary for keeping every cell functioning at the highest levels.

Within this challenge, the demands placed on the energy systems by sports can be broken down into three components: rate, duration and the work-to-recovery ratio. These are the defining features that make up each sport's unique environment and are explored through this chapter.

Wisdom

Understanding the interplay between the three types of demands placed on the body's energy systems—rate, duration and work-to-recovery ratio—is essential in order to effectively design and deliver training programmes.

Rate of Energy Production

Although the word *power* is often thrown around casually in the field of strength and conditioning, its definition within the realm of physics as the rate of change in energy is an appropriate one when it comes to energy systems. The rate of energy supply needed at any time is always dictated by the level of power output required and amount of force that must be produced by the body.

Take the explosive sport of weightlifting, for example. Extremely high rates of power must be generated to lift the barbell over the athlete's head within the blink of an eye. This means the muscles have to produce a high level of force in an incredibly short time. To achieve this, the body's energy systems must produce the necessary energy at an unbelievably quick rate. If energy is not supplied fast enough, the highest levels of force and power cannot be achieved, and the athlete's skills will not be able to be performed at maximal speeds.

Sports that require the highest rates of energy production are always inherently anaerobically dominant because only the anaerobic energy system is capable of producing energy fast enough to meet such requirements. More can be learned about this in chapter 14. Sports such as weightlifting, powerlifting, shot put, discus, high jump and hammer throw all fall into this category because of their high energy-production requirements. In this case, a higher rate of energy production means higher levels of force and power and thus improved performance.

Wisdom

Athletes in the sport of Olympic weightlifting produce tremendously high rates of power output. Peak power can reach over 4,000 watts during the snatch. Generating that much power requires a tremendously high rate of energy production.

Duration of Energy Production

On the other end of the spectrum are sports defined not by a high rate of energy production, but rather by the requirement for prolonged durations of energy production. Endurance events such as marathons, triathlons and distance cycling demand the body produce energy for extended periods of time. This provides a much different stress and a unique challenge for the body's energy-producing machinery.

Instead of having to produce energy at the highest rate possible, the body must become extremely efficient and economical so that homeostasis can be maintained despite hours of mechanical work performed as the athlete runs, bikes or swims across great distances. The more economical the body becomes, the longer it will be able to produce a higher level of energy, and the faster an athlete will be able to cover a given distance. This is true because such improvements in the economy of energy production mean that power output can be maintained longer, and thus fatigue will be minimised throughout the event.

The majority of energy produced during endurance sports comes from the aerobic energy system. It is largely improvements in aerobic function that take place through the course of training that allow for improved economy of energy production and thus greater performance in such long-duration sports.[2] Given the nature of endurance sports, the importance of energy-system programming is generally well understood and is a primary focus in the year-round training schedule of such athletes. This concept is discussed in greater detail in chapter 15.

Work-to-Recovery Ratio

Aside from the rate of energy production and its duration, the third component that makes up a given sport's energy-system landscape is the ratio between work and recovery. In pure endurance sports, there is little to no recovery. In sports where the highest levels of strength and power are displayed, the work is typically extremely short, while the recovery is exceedingly long by comparison. Consider the short time it takes to get the barbell overhead in a snatch compared to the several minutes of recovery often taken between lifts in the sport of weightlifting, for example.

Given the clarity and general uniformity of work-to-recovery ratios for sports at both ends of the strength–endurance continuum, the energy demands and profiles of such sports are typically well understood. In mixed sports, those with repetitive explosive bursts of strength and power followed by periods of recovery, is where the precise length of work and recovery periods can have the largest impact on the energy requirements of the sport and on the most appropriate programming.

In general, research has shown that the shorter the recovery periods and the longer the work periods, the more aerobic in nature an activity becomes as the duration increases.[3] Conversely, sports with shorter periods of work and longer periods of recovery in between rely on a greater contribution from anaerobic energy production.[4] This relationship makes it clear that there is always a distinct and unyielding trade-off between the amount of strength and power produced and the ability to maintain it.

When viewed within the context of energy systems and sport performance, this trade-off can best be seen by looking at the differences in power output and duration across a wide range of individual and team sports (figure 19.1). Virtually every sport falls somewhere within this spectrum of maximal power and greatest durations.

It is essential to understand the energy demands imposed by a sport in order to develop training programmes that are appropriately specific to develop the body and brain's ability to function at an optimal level whilst minimising fatigue.

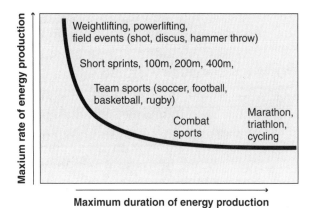

Figure 19.1 Energy-systems profile.

Effective Energy-System Programming

In order to develop effective energy-systems training programs, the first place to start is by understanding the unique energy demands of the sport that an athlete is training for. Where these demands fall between rate and endurance will ultimately dictate the specific challenge that the body must overcome in order to perform at the highest levels and thus dictate the direction the training needs to take.

To improve performance, athletes in sports that require a high rate of energy production will need to focus their training on challenging the body to do exactly that. Athletes in sports that require the body to produce energy for long durations must challenge the body to become efficient in the way that it produces and uses energy so that it's better equipped for the task. Athletes in mixed sports must train to achieve the right balance between rate and duration by training whichever is necessary based on the unique profile of their sport and their individual needs.

Once the precise demands of the sport and the individual needs of the athlete have been determined, programming starts with an understanding that improving energy production is a continual process. Each portion of the yearly developmental training program (figure 19.2) should be considered within the greater context of the role of energy systems in performance discussed earlier. Just as there is a progression used in training to develop skills, the progression principle must be applied to energy-system development as well.

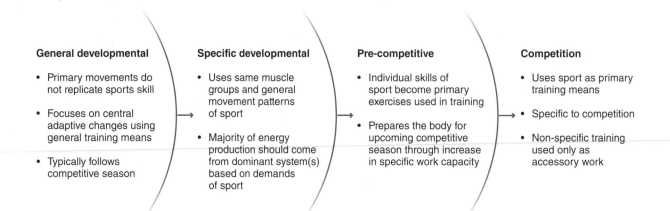

Figure 19.2 Energy-system programming overview.

Throughout the training year, pieces of the energy-system puzzle must be put together so that each piece builds on the progress made in previous phases. Within this framework, an annual training program can be broken down into four phases, each with a specific emphasis in how the energy systems are trained. These four phases progress from general to specific over the course of the year; each phase works together to progressively prepare the body to achieve the highest levels of performance during the competitive season.

Just as a combat athlete must first learn the basics of striking, wrestling and submission grappling before learning to put them together to be a well-rounded mixed martial artist, the components of energy systems need to be trained in a specific sequence so that the body ultimately increases its ability to produce energy, and performance is improved.

General Preparatory Phase

Within the general-to-specific spectrum of energy-system development, the most general period of training can best be termed the *general preparatory phase* (GPP). This is an appropriate description precisely because of the nature of training done during this phase. It should be both general and performed with the goal of preparing the body for the more specific energy-system training to come in the later phases.

This general preparatory phase typically takes place several months from the competitive season; because it primarily includes movements that are not specific to the athlete's sport, it can be especially beneficial in the period immediately after a long, gruelling season. At this point, the body has likely had a great deal of repetitive stress placed on it as a result of the high volume of skill training and competition inherent within any season. Moving to a more general period of energy-system development and overall training not only allows the body to take a break from the repetitive movements of the athlete's chosen sport, but it also begins the process of building the foundation of energy production for the next season.

Goals of the General Preparatory Phase

The primary goal of the GPP is to develop the components of energy-system function necessary for supporting a higher level of energy production and athletic performance. This is a similar process to the common practice of breaking down complex skills into simpler components to be worked on at the individual level so that the pieces are stronger when put back together.

A mixed martial artist, for example, may spend hours working on improving highly technical aspects of throwing a single punch or a combination of punches. Once technique has improved, the next goal is to integrate this new level of skill into the broader range of punches, kicks, knees and elbows involved in the sport. In much the same way, in order to improve the body's ability to produce the energy necessary for performing at a higher level, components of energy-system function must be targeted during the GPP as well.

Programming Guidelines in the General Preparatory Period

Programming during this phase should focus on the use of general training exercises that do not replicate in part or in whole specific movements from an athlete's sport. Although the same muscle groups may be used, there should be no effort to match the movement patterns, velocities or levels of force and power of the competitive skills. In the same context, the rate, duration and pattern of work-to-recovery ratios of the training should not mimic those of the competitive sport. Instead, training should take place across a wider range of the power–endurance spectrum, and more specific energy-system development should be saved for later phases of development.

During this phase, aerobic-dominant sports should focus on the central aspects of aerobic energy production: the development of the cardiovascular system's ability to deliver oxygen. This topic is covered in greater detail in chapter 16. An increase in this ability will serve to support later development of changes in endurance and sustained power output that involve specific muscles.

Anaerobic-dominant sports should focus on the more central aspects of anaerobic power output related to central nervous system function as well as overall strength and muscle size. These qualities provide the cornerstone for an increase in the rate of energy production and muscular power output that will be the focus of later training phases.

For mixed sports, the emphasis during the GPP should primarily depend on the needs of the athlete. An athlete lacking endurance will benefit the most by focusing on general development in this area, while an athlete with sufficient endurance who needs to improve power output should instead focus in increasing strength, power and overall rate of energy production.

Wisdom

Mixed sports require the right balance of rate and duration of energy production. It is especially important in such sports that all phases of training be focused in the appropriate area of development, given each athlete's need.

An example of the difference emphases of a GPP according to the energy demands of the sport can be seen in table 19.1.

Table 19.1 Emphases of the General Preparatory Period for a Basketball Player and a Combat Athlete

Basketball player	Combat athlete
General strength-training exercises: total body strength and power lifts 2 or 3 days per week, 40-60 min	Low- to moderate-intensity aerobic work: jogging, jumping rope, swimming, etc. 3 days per week, 40-60 min
Low-intensity bounding and track work: 1 or 2 days per week, 20-30 min	General strength-training exercises: 2 days per week, 40-60 min

Specific Preparatory Phase

The *specific preparatory phase* (SPP) of energy-system development should build on the general development from the previous phase and progress towards the use of more specific exercises and movement patterns. These exercises and patterns do not need to replicate the entirety of the competitive skills, but they should primarily use the same muscle groups within the same ranges of motion (ROM) as various components of the athletic skills.

This phase of training should take place several months from competition and only after the preceding period of general preparatory work. After the break from the high volume of repetitive movements inherent in any competitive season, there is a need to gradually reintroduce the same general movement and muscular work back into the training program.

Goals of the Specific Preparatory Phase

This phase serves as the bridge between the general phases of energy-system development and the more specific phases to come as an athlete begins to near the competitive season. It is in these later phases when the primary training means and exercises transition to those specific to the competitive sport. It's essential to prepare these muscles and supporting tissues, and indeed the entire body itself, with the necessary developmental work.

Also, due to the specific nature of energy production, in terms of how the body adapts to the given rate, duration, work-to-recovery ratio and muscles used in a given sport, the working muscles themselves are always of prime importance as related to performance and must be trained accordingly. In this phase, the working muscles will begin to become the emphasis of energy-system training; the goal of this phase is to increase their overall energy-production ability within the general context of the demands of the sport.

Programming Guidelines in the Specific Preparatory Phase

The emphasis in this phase is centered on improving the functional energy-production potential within the working muscles themselves, so exercise selection during this phase is of primary importance. The exercises and training means chosen must use the same muscles and movement patterns inherent in the skills of the athlete's sport.

This does not mean that exact skills need to be precisely replicated, however, only that components and movements within these skills are also in the training exercises. A runner does not need to perform only running exercises during this phase, for example. However, exercises and movements that emphasise the hip flexion component of running, performed in an upright posture, would be preferable because of the biomechanical similarities to aspects of the running motion.

Selecting exercises that are biomechanically similar to the skills of the sport, both in ROM and in patterns of resistance, ensures that the same general muscle groups will be trained, and thus the necessary adaptive response will take place in these working muscles.

Although the exact muscle-recruitment patterns depend on the level of force, power output and duration, it is not necessary in the SPP to perform all exercises and movements with the precise speeds and durations of the competition skills. As long as the same muscle groups are used and the majority of the energy being produced is coming from the dominant system or systems of the sport, this will lead to the desired training effect.

If the goal is to improve performance in an anaerobic-dominant sport, for example, the exercises should be performed in a manner that demands that the majority of energy is coming from anaerobic metabolism. If they are performed at forces and speeds that are too low, and the aerobic energy system provides the majority of energy, the desired adaptive responses will not be triggered, and the body will not be adequately prepared for the next training phase. For mixed sports, each training session can have a specific emphasis, but this should be done in accordance with the principles of minimising interference as discussed in chapter 20.

Table 19.2 shows how the training emphasis in the SPP differs from that of the GPP for the two sports.

Table 19.2 Emphases of the Specific Preparatory Period for a Basketball Player and a Combat Athlete

Basketball player	Combat athlete
Specific strength training: jumping exercises and explosive lifts, 2 or 3 days per week, 40-60 min	High-intensity sprints and medicine ball throws and drills: 5-10 sec work, 30-40 sec rest periods, 2 or 3 days per week, 30-40 min
Moderate-intensity plyometrics: 1 or 2 days per week, 20-30 min	Specific strength-training exercises: 2 days per week, 20-30 min

Precompetitive Phase

Just as the name implies, the *precompetitive phase* of energy-system development is the period of training that precedes the beginning of the competitive season. Most often, this period begins a month or two before the start of a preseason training camp. This is where the work done in the two preceding preparatory phases begins to have an impact on performance as the skills of the sport begin to become the primary training means.

Goals of the Precompetitive Phase

This transition towards predominantly specific training marks the period whereby all the components developed previously are brought together to improve performance. If the goal was to improve the rate of energy production and power output, for example, the precompetitive phase is where the specific skills of the sport will begin to be performed with a higher level of speed and power.

If the goal was an increase in endurance, on the other hand, then this phase should mark a noticeable improvement in the ability to maintain a given level of power output for an increased duration. These increases are what ultimately serve as the foundation for the improved performance to come in competition. The precompetitive phase is where the increased potential for energy production is realised within the greater context of the specific demands of the sport.

The work done in the precompetitive phase becomes increasingly specific to both the skills and the energy-system demands of the sport. This phase serves to bridge the gap between the more general training done previously and the training that will take place throughout the competitive season to come.

Programming Guidelines in the Precompetitive Phase

The most notable change in this phase compared to the last one is that the selected training exercises should now be primarily composed of highly specific movements and skills of the sport. All nonspecific exercises and training methods should be considered accessory work as the competition movements take their place.

A soccer player, for example, may replace general running and sprints with technical ball-handling drills done at high speed. A mixed martial artist may begin to use technical drills, such as hitting the pads or heavy bag for conditioning work, instead of jumping rope or other less specific training means. In either case, the central principle is that the skills of the sport rather than the more general means used previously are now used for the purposes of energy-system development.

In training, the work completed should replicate the work-to-recovery ratios and duration of the skills used in the sport. This ensures that the profile of energy production closely matches the demands of the sport so that the training effect is maximised and performance improved.

A mixed martial artist will want to make sure that his or her punches, kicks, knees and elbows are thrown at the same speed and power as they are in a fight. An American football lineman may do sled drills for 5 or 6 seconds at a time, the same length as an average play. The nature of each sport will ultimately dictate whether just a few skills or a wide range of skills can be used for energy-system training purposes.

Sports on each end of the power–endurance spectrum typically have far less variety in their skills than those in between. Olympic weightlifters, powerlifters, marathoners, and triathletes all have a much narrower range of skills than a soccer player, mixed martial artist or basketball player, for example. In either case, however, the skills of the sport can almost always be broken down into components, and these components can be used as a training means in this phase.

This level of specific work sets the stage for the final phase to come, where all the skills are brought together within the context of the competitive sport. If the training has followed the template laid out in the previous phases, energy production will have been greatly improved, and the body will be better physically prepared to perform at the highest levels.

Table 19.3 details programming in the precompetitive phase in comparison to the training programmes shown in tables 19.1 and 19.2.

Table 19.3 Emphases of the Precompetitive Phase for a Basketball Player and a Combat Athlete

Basketball player	Combat athlete
Basketball practice: moderate-intensity technical drills and game-simulated scrimmage; short, intensive interval conditioning	Combat-specific drills and training: 5-10 sec work, 5-10 sec rest periods; anaerobic threshold, 5 min rounds; 3 or 4 days per week, 60 min or more
Specific strength-training exercise: 2 days per week, 30 min	Specific strength-training exercises: 2 days per week, 20 min

Competitive Phase

Athletes and coaches may not consider the importance of energy-system development until just before or at the start of the competition phase. This approach fails to consider the complex nature of energy production and its true role in performance as discussed previously and throughout other chapters. Depending on the sport, the highest levels of performance can be achieved only through either a tremendously high rate of energy production, as is necessary in anaerobic sports, or the ability to sustain a given level of energy production for long durations without fatigue, the hallmark of aerobic-dominant sports. Mixed sports require some combination of both rate and duration, and this is where balancing the two demands is essential to performance.

Goals of the Competitive Phase

By the time the competitive season has begun, the primary goal shifts from trying to increase the body's ability to produce energy to working towards ensuring the energy that's produced is channelled effectively into the skills of the sport. Throughout each of the previous three phases, the training exercises and methods should have gradually shifted towards being more specific to the demands of the sport; in this final phase, the sport itself becomes the primary means. This progression ensures that the body is able to use the increased energy-production potential that was developed in the preceding phases and that an increase in performance is ultimately realised.

Programming Guidelines in the Competitive Phase

The programming guidelines for the competitive phase depend in large part on the specifics of a sport's competitive season. The underlying principle as it relates to energy-system development and performance is that the sport itself should serve as the primary training means throughout its duration.

Making the mistake of using too much general work in this phase most often serves only to increase fatigue and take away from the quality of skills training. Focusing instead on specific energy-system training through the use of the sport itself is the most effective way to ensure the body is able to fully use the increased potential for energy production developed throughout the previous phases of training.

There are a variety of ways to use the sport itself as the primary means of energy-system development, ranging from competition simulation to slightly more or less intense variations of it. A soccer team can choose to play 11 versus 11, use small-sided games or run tactical-training periods that are specific to game scenarios. A mixed martial artist can spar for 3 to 5 rounds with a minute rest in between as in an actual fight, or he or she can have a fresh opponent rotate in each round and be forced to fight at a higher intensity. In either case, the overall profile of energy production in terms of its rate, duration and work-to-recovery ratio is highly specific to the competition itself. This is what ensures that the training will have the desired transfer into a heightened level of performance.

Depending on the length and nature of the competitive season—how long it lasts, how many competitions there are, how frequent they are and the overall demands of the sport—the amount of time spent in skill work, tactics and strategy and energy-system development will likely change from one week to the next. Typically, more time is spent early in the season on improving fundamental skills and getting in shape to use them. Then, work in the areas of specific tactics and strategies begins to increase as the season progresses while fitness levels are maintained rather than improved.

Wisdom

During the competitive phase, nonspecific exercises, methods and training means should be used only for accessory work, restoration or injury prevention and treatment, not for the purpose of energy-system development.

The biggest challenge is to find the right balance between these areas so that both fitness and skill levels reach their peak without an accumulation of fatigue, which can have a negative impact on performance and increase the risk of injury. Such organisational and planning decisions are ultimately up to the judgement of the coaching staff.

If performance is to be maximised, however, the underlying principle throughout the competitive season should be to ensure that energy-system development work is entirely specific to the demands of the competition itself. When this principle is adhered to and intelligent energy-system programming is paired with effective skill development, the result will be the highest level of performance possible.

Summary

Effective energy-system programs are developed through a solid understanding of the energy demands of the sport combined with a well-thought-out and organised plan that spans the entire training year. Performance at the highest level in any sport is a true test of the body's ability to produce energy. Pushing the body to its limits requires far more than a few weeks of extra running or preseason conditioning training.

Instead, an effective yearly training program should be developed with the greater context of the importance of energy production in mind. Muscular force and power do not exist in isolation. How much weight can be lifted in the weight room cannot transfer to the field of play unless the body has the ability to produce the energy necessary for sustaining it.

A successful strategy to improve performance requires the planned progression from general to specific training means and exercises so that the pieces of the energy-system puzzle are developed in the right order. Each phase of training should develop a component of energy production while preparing the body for the more specific work to follow. This is how greater levels of strength, power and endurance are developed in a meaningful way that will ultimately translate into improved performance when it counts.

CHAPTER 20

Minimising the Interference Effect

Glenn Stewart

West Coast Eagles Football Club, Australia

Many team-based sports require physical capacities that emphasise endurance, strength and power. In particular, team sports that require high-intensity intermittent running and have game activities demanding explosive, maximal effort and actions such as tackling, jumping, blocking and other forms of body contact, needs training units that develop both aerobic capacity and strength and power simultaneously throughout periodised training blocks.

In Australia three popular team-based field sports are Australian football (AF), Rugby Union (RU) and Rugby League (RL). Using global positioning system (GPS) technology and digital video analysis systems, the activity profiles of players in these sports can be determined to better understand the physiological demands of the game. This approach allows for the tailoring of training units following the principle of training specificity.

AF midfielders can cover up to 15 kilometres throughout the course of a game lasting 120 minutes.[1] Of that, up to 4 kilometres is high-intensity running, consisting of over 90 intense efforts.[2] In addition to this physiological load, players in general lay up to seven tackles and are involved in some 15 or more contests to gain possession of the ball that require some degree of body contact.[3]

In RU, players travel distances of up to 7 kilometres during a game, and 11 per cent of this running time is spent in high-intensity running. Forwards are involved in 1,200 body impacts.[4] Tackling is seen as a discrimination of success in RU, with successful teams making more than 110 tackles.[5]

In RL matches, players can travel more than 6 kilometres during the course of the game, with 17 per cent of their time spent in high-intensity, power-related activities.[6] Statistics from games show some players making more than 50 tackles, accompanied by other high-intensity game actions.[7]

In world football (soccer [SO]), players can run an average 10.8 kilometres with ranges between 9 and 14 kilometres.[8] This total distance is interspersed with up to 24 highly intense sprints and over 20 headers and tackles.[8]

It is obvious from game data collected in sports such as these that the athletes require a high capacity for aerobic metabolism plus the ability to generate significant forces statically and dynamically in a game to produce high running velocities and frequent accelerations. These athletes need to absorb and transmit actions engaging body contact of several g-forces.[4]

Concurrent training may be defined as the specific training of endurance and strength capacities in 'immediate succession or with up to 24 hours of recovery separating the two exercise modes.'[9] In the development of athletic potential in all sports, training units are constructed and periodised to train the functional components critical to sport success. Training time is a finite commodity; therefore, fitness professionals train multiple capacities in blocks to maximise the response to this training stimulus. When concurrently training both the capacities of endurance and strength, interference may occur when the development of one capacity hinders the development of the other capacity compared to training either capacity independently and in isolation.[9]

Research in the Interference Effect

The first significant observation of the interference effect was noted by Hickson in 1980.[10] In a study on recreational athletes, he assessed the development of strength and endurance through three distinct training protocols: a group that trained strength only, a group that trained endurance only, and a group that trained strength and endurance concurrently. Over a 10-week training block, the strength-only group improved strength and the endurance-only group improved aerobic capacity—but the concurrent group had only minimal improvement in strength whilst endurance improved as per the endurance-only group (figure 20.1). This prompted Hickson to conclude that muscular changes induced through strength training are opposed to the changes induced through endurance training, and that muscle may not be capable of adapting to training from both training regimens.

Since Hickson's initial work, considerable research has been directed towards validating the interference effect and gaining a greater understanding of the impact that concurrent training may have on the development of strength and endurance. It is beyond the scope of this chapter to detail all the research conducted in this area, but

it is relevant to highlight aspects of that research to obtain a clearer understanding of the weight of evidence that will allow strength and conditioning professionals to approach the possible issue of concurrent training with confidence of the key principles involved.

Studies in concurrent training follow similar experimental design parameters. In general, research assesses the outcomes of training in three distinct groups within the same study: a group that undertakes aerobic-only training, a group that undertakes strength-only training and a third group that undertakes some variation of both aerobic and strength training. Variations within research occur with the type of aerobic training (continuous versus interval), its intensity (with some authors observing that interference occurs only at intensities close to $\dot{V}O_2$max) and the type of strength training (circuit versus high-intensity versus high-volume training). Research can then vary between the type of cohorts (untrained versus trained) and the order of concurrent training (strength or endurance trained first).

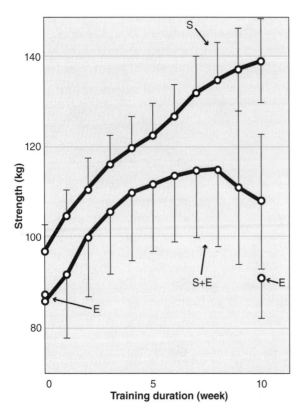

Figure 20.1 Strength changes in response to the three types of training. Measurements were made on a weekly basis in the strength (S) and strength and endurance (S + E) groups. The endurance (E) group was tested before and after 10 weeks of training.

With kind permission from Springer Science + Business Media: *European Journal of Applied Physiology*, "Interference of strength development by simultaneously training for strength and endurance," 45(2), 1980, p. 259, R.C. Hickson, fig. 1, © Springer-Verlag 1980.

Wisdom

Because the literature seems to vary in its recommendations, conclusions drawn can be validly applied to a group of athletes only if the experimental design used in the study matches the athlete population and training protocols.

Interference Effect in Untrained People

Research on untrained individuals shows the greatest degree of contradiction in outcomes and in the significance of the interference effect. A number of researchers[11-13] found no evidence of the interference effect with gains of similar magnitude in both strength and endurance in those undertaking concurrent training. However, other researchers found evidence of an interference effect with gains in strength being significantly limited in those training endurance and strength concurrently.[14-16]

With research on untrained subjects failing to demonstrate conclusively that concurrent training creates an interference effect, the weight of evidence suggests the following:

- The interference effect may be minimal with untrained subjects. Therefore, in those individuals, it is possible to train strength and endurance concurrently, with improvements in both capacities being realised.

- The frequency of training sessions has an influence on the degree of interference, if any. Low-frequency training (2 days/wk) shows minimal interference and thus is best recommended for untrained individuals looking for gains in both capacities.

Interference Effect in Trained Athletes

Research on the effects of concurrent training on elite and trained individuals is more weighted towards demonstrating an interference effect.[17-19] It would appear that in well-trained individuals, concurrent training interferes with the development of strength and power.

- Concurrent training affects the rate of force development or power more significantly than absolute strength.
- Large volumes of endurance training, in terms of intensity and of frequency, have the greatest impact on strength development in concurrent training.
- Endurance is only minimally affected by the introduction of concurrent strength training.

Mechanisms Behind the Interference Effect

Research into the possible mechanisms producing the interference effect has been limited. A number of potential reasons have been suggested, including energy balance, overreaching, disrupted muscle-fibre hypertrophy, enzyme activation, motor unit recruitment and acute residual fatigue.

Energy Balance

Endurance training, particularly with high loads, creates a negative energy balance.[19] This in turn minimises hypertrophy when strength training is done at the same time. During periods of negative energy balance, muscle protein synthesis is reduced. Strength training alone has a limited energy cost when compared to concurrent training, and this is a more ideal environment for muscle hypertrophy.

An extension of the negative–energy balance theory is the alteration to hormonal balance, creating either catabolic or anabolic states.[20] Strength training has been shown to alter the ratio of the hormones testosterone and cortisol to an anabolic state, and endurance training enhances a catabolic state, thus limiting strength development.[21]

Overreaching

In the majority of studies in concurrent training, the groups training both strength and endurance had higher training workloads than the groups training either one. In the research highlighted previously in the chapter, the concurrent training groups combined the strength and endurance training sessions, effectively doubling the training volume of the single-focus training groups. Therefore, it is possible that the workload crossed an optimal threshold and overreaching occurred. This may have resulted in impaired testing results and consequently indicated an interference effect.

Disrupted Muscle-Fibre Hypertrophy

Strength training has been shown to increase the diameter of type I, IIa and IIc muscle fibres.[18] Endurance training, however, reduces the diameter of type I and IIc fibres, thereby creating interference when concurrent training occurs.[18] If both strength and endurance training are conducted at the same time, possibly only type IIa fibres will develop, thereby limiting overall muscle hypertrophy when compared to results from strength-only training.

Enzyme Activation

When an athlete undertakes endurance training, an enzyme known as adenosine monophosphate-activated protein kinase (AMPK) is activated.[22] This enzyme increases the oxidation of fat and the uptake of sugar, thus improving aerobic energy production. Another enzyme, mTORC1 (target of rapamycin complex 1) is activated after resistance training; it regulates protein synthesis, resulting in increased muscle hypertrophy and, consequently, strength.[23] An issue for concurrent training programmes is that AMPK can block the activation of mTORC1, so when endurance training is undertaken the AMPK produced inhibits the activation of mTORC1, thus limiting protein synthesis and muscle hypertrophy.[24] The two enzymes are counterproductive.

Motor-Unit Recruitment

Motor-unit recruitment patterns may alter during concurrent training.[25] Early research showed that the neural pathways for rapid force development in activities such as the vertical jump are dampened through endurance training.[26] If fibre types are recruited preferentially in a different order in endurance and strength training, then concurrent training may affect the efficient organisation of this recruitment.

Acute Residual Fatigue

Some studies have shown that concurrent training impaired only the development of strength in the lower body, not the upper body, when endurance was undertaken as either cycling or running.[17] Researchers have not concluded the exact reasons for this other than a localised accumulation of metabolites or possible muscle damage in that area, particularly in the case of running, where eccentric loads are larger than in cycling. This possibility suggests this impairment was a consequence of increased localised fatigue[17, 27] and not necessarily a systemic issue.

The interference effect is maximised when athletes use high-intensity interval training and an 8-to-12 repetitions maximum (RM) multiple-set resistance-training program. When applied separately, these two modalities of training lead to peripheral adaptations; when applied concurrently, they have competing physiological demands, which renders them incompatible. Under these conditions, there would be a limited change in skeletal muscle cross-sectional area or a reduced hypertrophy of individual muscle fibres.[14] The trick seems to be to avoid scheduling high-intensity endurance work alongside high-volume, high-frequency strength work.

Strategies to Minimise the Interference Effect

Through the skilful manipulation of training variables, it is possible to reduce the interference effect of concurrent training. It has been proposed that when high-intensity interval training is combined with high-load resistance training (lower than 5RM), there is less interference because the training stimulus in strength would

be focused on the neural system and not on the metabolic demands on the muscle. As a result, the metabolic demands on skeletal muscle are not competing.

Equally, continuous aerobic training at low intensity (lower than 80 per cent of $\dot{V}O_2max$) should not interfere with the improvement of strength indices whatever the load. This is because continuous aerobic training at low intensity involves central adaptations mediated by cardiac output and should not impair neural adaptation or muscle hypertrophy.

This method used to predict the training zones that may or may not result in an interference effect is shown in figure 20.2.

When 2 sessions per week of combined strength and high-intensity endurance exercise are performed, a 3-day break between sessions is sufficient to avoid the interference effect.[28] This is of particular relevance to team sports where time between weekly matches needs to be used wisely. If we assume that the match itself counts as a high-intensity endurance session, this finding may provide us with an understanding of when during the week after a match it is best to conduct in-season strength sessions.

There are other issues to consider when planning programmes to minimise the interference effect.

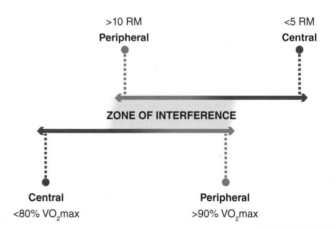

Figure 20.2 Model to predict the training protocols that would minimise or maximise the interference effect.

With kind permission from Springer Science + Business Media: *Sports Medicine*, "A proposed model for examining the interference phenomenon between concurrent aerobic and strength training," 30(6), 2000, p. 390, D. Docherty and B. Sporer, fig. 3, © Adis International Limited. All rights reserved.

Train Strength and Endurance at the Same End of the Fitness Continuum

The interference effect appears more significant when endurance training is based on longer, more continuous running protocols at high intensities (greater than 80 per cent $\dot{V}O_2$max). When strength training is being undertaken after a high-intensity protocol, low-volume concurrent aerobic workouts should be similarly structured: higher-intensity interval sets with increased velocities and reduced recovery times. By attempting to keep both training protocols at a similar end of the fitness continuum, there may be a likely innervation (stimulation) of similar-fibre types and a similar focus of specificity.[18]

Prioritising Training Goals

When trained athletes are participating in sports with competing elements of strength and endurance, the strength and conditioning coach must undertake a detailed profile analysis of each athlete and create individual performance plans that first prioritise those areas that need improvement and, second, those strengths that need to be maintained. Once the plan has been constructed, then priority should be given to the capacity in most need of improvement. Training volume will then be directed in appropriate areas. This approach will minimise the potential of interference of concurrent training by potentially reducing the volume (and hence the effect) of one training entity (strength or endurance) over the other.

Other than the impact of the volume of training of one capacity over the other, some research has shown that by prioritising the athlete's training goals, the primary physical capacity can be trained first in a rested state, and other training sessions added to the plan around it.[20]

Sequencing or Training Order

In addition to prioritising goals, there is some argument for sequencing training so that strength and power workouts are conducted before conditioning—if not immediately before, then on the day before conditioning training.[29] This reduces the potential of neural and metabolic fatigue from conditioning training interfering with the demands of a resistance-training session. When conditioning is conducted before strength training, then the duration between should be at least 24 hours to enable full recovery.

A contradictory view exists, however.[24] Based on the enzymes AMPK and mTORC1, it is suggested that endurance training occur first and strength training last. If endurance training is performed first and strength training later in the day, the AMPK produced as a consequence of the endurance activity is switched off quickly once recovery from that training has occurred and will not interfere with the strength training. The mTORC1 produced from the strength training will remain high for the remainder of the day and night, thus assisting in the promotion of muscle hypertrophy. It will not be limited by the production of AMPK until the endurance session the next day. This theory, however, has yet to be tested rigorously in a controlled experimental setting

Wave (Block) Periodisation

Using the approach of a wave, or undulating, periodisation model, it is possible to concurrently train strength and endurance but with an alternating emphasis and focus on blocks of volume and intensity.

Using Baker's 2007 research on periodisation,[30] a coach could construct a block of training where the emphasis is on developing strength or power whilst maintaining endurance. The volume and intensity of resistance training is high with three 3 or four 4 sessions per week. Endurance training is in maintenance mode, with lower volumes, and is trained 1 or 2 times per week. During the next block of training, the emphasis changes to developing endurance and maintaining strength. This process of alternating emphasis over a complete training period reduces a number of factors contributing to the interference effect. The timing and duration of the training block is left to the skill of the strength and conditioning professional based on training objectives and the overall periodised training plan.

Conditioned Athletes

In order to minimise the possible diminished development of capacities resulting from concurrent training, athletes should be in a well-conditioned state before beginning a block of concurrent training.[29] Athletes with higher levels of strength, power and endurance initially showed fewer negative effects of concurrent training than the athletes with poor training history and little exposure to concurrent training. Therefore, if concurrent training is necessary in mixed-capacity team sports, then athletes should be trained regularly in concurrent training, improve their overall conditioning before concurrent training and follow a well-periodised plan. Doing so will minimise the interference of any effects from concurrent training.

Case Study

This example from an Australian Rules football club illustrates an approach to addressing the potential interference effect from concurrent training undertaken by an elite footballer.

The player is a second-year footballer who needs to increase mass and size to become more effective at winning the football in contested situations. His position on the team is on the wing, which in Australian football requires a high level of aerobic capacity to fulfil the role's demands in this team's style of play.

The player already has a high $\dot{V}O_2max$ (table 20.1) but still requires aerobic training to maintain and, if possible, improve his running capacity. The strength and conditioning coach faces the dilemma of increasing mass and size on a player where this has been identified as a critical area for his development whilst continuing to improve the player's aerobic fitness, which is essential for the position he plays.

The following notes outline the modifications and adjustments to the player's periodised plan to focus on developing hypertrophy and strength and to minimise the interference effect. The team follows a classic periodised plan using an undulating model[30] (table 20.2). The team undertakes 3 strength sessions and 3 conditioning sessions per week for most weeks (table 20.3). The player has a varied weekly program (table 20.4) where

conditioning sessions are reduced to 1 per week and strength sessions increased to 4 per week in some weeks.

Week 1: Player and team undertake 2 aerobic and 2 strength sessions per week as part of the initial adaptation process before starting preseason training. (Refer to table 20.2.)

Weeks 2, 3, 5, and 6: The player's conditioning sessions are reduced to 1 per week whilst weights are increased to 3 and 4 sessions per week with hypertrophy as the main focus.

Weeks 4, 8, 12, 15, and 20: Speed sessions for the player are the same as for the team: 2 sessions per week. Speed is not considered to interfere with strength development and may compliment the program in the weight room.[18]

Weeks 7, 11, 13, 14, 18, and 19: Short-interval training is not reduced significantly for the player as with his other conditioning sessions because it lies at the same end of the training continuum as strength training.[18]

Weeks 9, 10, 18, 19, 20, and 21: The player's focus is hypertrophy and strength, not power. During the power phase, aerobic conditioning becomes significant as strength training is minimised. Weights have been reduced to 1 session per week, and conditioning sessions have been increased in number.

Weeks 16 and 17: Conditioning is again reduced for the player, and intermediate intervals (II) are the primary running focus. Weights are increased to 4 sessions per week when the block of maximal strength training is reintroduced.

Weeks 18, 19, 20, and 21: This is a tapering phase. The player's power cycle in weights is reduced from 2 to 1 session per week, and conditioning sessions are gradually reduced in number to assist tapering.

Table 20.1 Player Characteristics for an Australian Rules Football Player

	Height (cm)	Weight (kg)	$\dot{V}O_2max$ (ml kg^{-1} min^{-1})	1RM bench press (kg)	3RM leg press (kg)
Current	183	80.5	62.9	89.5	305
Planned	183	86.0	63.0	105	410

Table 20.2 Periodised Training Plan Following an Undulating Model

Months	I				II				III				IV					V			
Weeks	1	2	3	4	5	6	7	8	9	10	11	12	13	14	15	16	17	18	19	20	21
Training phase	General preparation								Specific preparation									Precompetition			
Strength	AA				Hypertrophy				Power		Hyper-trophy		Maximal strength					Conversion to power			
Strength	AA				Hypertrophy		Maximal strength		Power				Maximal strength					Power			
Team sessions/week	2	3	3	3	3	3	3	3	3	3	3	3	3	3	3	3	3	2	2	2	1
Player sessions/week	2	3	3	4	4	4	3	4	1	1	3	4	3	3	4	4	4	2	2	1	1
Endurance	Aerobic capacity								Repeat sprint ability						Speed						
	AE	II		SP	II		SI	SP	II		SI	SP	SI		SP	II		SI		SP	
Team sessions/week	2	3	3	2	3	3	3	2	3	3	3	2	3	3	2	3	3	3	2	2	1
Player sessions/week	2	1	1	2	1	1	2	2	3	3	2	2	2	2	2	2	2	3	2	2	1
Speed	Technique (sprint and agility)								Speed				Specific speed and agility								
Total player sessions/week	4	4	4	6	5	5	5	6	4	4	5	6	5	5	6	6	6	5	4	3	2

AA: anatomical adaptation; AE: aerobic endurance; II: intermediate intervals; SI: short intervals; SP: speed

275

Table 20.3 Weekly Team Schedule

	Day	1	2	3	4	5	6	7
TEAM	**A.M.**	Skills	Strength	Skills or conditioning	Recovery	Skills or conditioning	Skills	Recovery
	P.M.	Conditioning	Individual skills	Strength	Off	Strength	Off	Off

Table 20.4 Weekly Player Schedule

	Day	1	2	3	4	5	6	7
PLAYER	**A.M.**	Skills	Conditioning	Skills	Recovery	Skills	Skills or strength	Recovery
	P.M	Strength	Individual skills	Strength	Off	Strength	Off	Off

Summary

Although research on the interference effect from concurrent training is not absolutely conclusive, enough evidence suggests that combining strength and endurance training in the same training period dampens the development of one or the other when compared to training either one in isolation. We are still unsure of the definitive causes although a number of potential mechanisms, including hormonal, neural and morphological factors, appear to be involved.

Developing athletes can make significant improvements in strength and endurance when training both concurrently. However, as training volume increases in the high-performance athlete over the long term, concurrent training can lead to attenuated development of either strength or endurance, and research indicates strength is affected most.

Overcoming the interference effect involves careful planning, timing, sequencing and prioritising training blocks for those sports where multiple physiological capacities are deemed necessary for success.

CHAPTER 21

Optimising Preseason Training in Team Sports

Darren Burgess, PhD
Liverpool Football Club, Merseyside, UK

The success of a season in elite team sports is largely contingent on the planning and successful delivery of a world-class preseason. This period is crucial for both physical and mental preparation for the forthcoming season. A fitness coach must be able to integrate coaching demands and philosophy from tactical and physical perspectives whilst ensuring training loads remain optimal for performance and injury prevention.

Primarily, the preseason presents an opportunity for the fitness staff to provide an appropriate conditioning overload for the team. This should be the principal aim regardless of the length of the preseason. The conditioning should be specific to the game and allow players to experience training sessions at least as demanding (and ideally more so) than the game. However, the preseason should not be dominated by conditioning exercises only; it should aim to allow appropriate integration of fitness and tactical training.

The preseason should overload the players sufficiently and specifically. Essentially, the players should feel that the in-season games place *less* stress on their bodies than the preseason conditioning. In order to prevent soft-tissue injuries, a key aim should be building muscle and tendon resilience so that the in-season demands are comfortably met.

This chapter provides a practical guide to preparing and delivering such a preseason program for team sports. It details aspects of program design and implementation and provides an overview of how preseason training can be evaluated.

Aims of the Preseason

It is important to understand the objectives of the preseason training programme. The specific training aims of a preseason in team sports include injury prevention, strength and power development, conditioning development and tactical training.

Injury Prevention

Most team sports involve large numbers of high-risk movement, such as accelerations, decelerations, jumping, landing, changes of direction, tackling and sprinting. A player's ability to repeatedly execute these movements at game-specific speeds requires optimal combinations of speed, strength, power, agility, flexibility and endurance. For this reason, successful injury prevention practices should be initiated during the preseason and continued throughout the season. Of course, some injuries remain impossible to prevent. For instance, in contact sports the position and actions of the opponent can rarely be predicted, and therefore contact-related injuries such as shoulder or knee damage as a result of tackles are not covered here.

An integrated preseason screening process should take place at the beginning of the preseason. The purpose of this process is to identify any muscular imbalance or weakness, joint laxity or movement deficiencies. The sport science and sports medicine staff should agree on the tools to be used for this process; a movement assessment as well as clinical screening (medically based assessment) are recommended. Additional screening such as blood profiling or isokinetic dynamometry can provide detailed profiling information that can influence injury-prevention programming. Physiological and strength assessments can also assist in preventing injuries. For instance, if a soccer player has poor aerobic endurance (perhaps identified by a yo-yo test),[1] he or she may be susceptible to fatigue-related soft-tissue injuries during a game.

Injury prevention should not be thought of as existing only as dedicated sessions or isolated drills. Applying suitable strength-, conditioning- and skill-session loads to team sport players during preseason can prevent overtraining whilst ensuring enough demand is placed on the players to prepare them for the in-season period. For example, if the preseason program is too demanding, players are likely to be injured during preseason or, at the very least, fatigued when the season begins. If the preseason program is too light, the in-season games will present a demanding stimulus that the players are unfamiliar with, and injuries or fatigue-affected performance will be the likely result. This last scenario is quite common as fitness staff ensure players get through the preseason unscathed rather than protecting players from game demands by overloading these demands during preseason.

Wisdom

Perhaps the most influential form of injury prevention occurs as a result of appropriate load management.

High-Speed Running in Preseason

One common intervention is to restrict the volume and intensity of preseason high-speed running (HSR), defined here as running over 20 kilometres per hour. Quite often this restriction occurs due to the inherent injury risk associated with this type of running,[2] particularly early in preseason training. The conundrum facing the fitness coach is that performing appropriate, regular HSR loads during the preseason actually provides possible protection against speed-related soft-tissue injuries through frequent exposure. However, there is an injury risk associated with these sessions if they are too frequent, too intense or inappropriately periodised.

In order to minimise injury risk, these sessions need to be introduced relatively gradually into the preseason. For instance, if the preseason is 6 weeks long, then HSR should be introduced within the second week. This schedule enables the fitness coach to prescribe enough volume to ensure players are able to perform appropriately in practice games, which would presumably follow shortly thereafter. Conversely, during a 14-week preseason period, the fitness coach might limit exposure to this type of running until week 3 or 4 of preseason.

Once HSR has been introduced, it needs to be periodised appropriately into the preseason program. This periodisation depends strongly on the high-speed demands of the sport. For example, Rugby League players need to be conditioned to run at extremely high speeds once each week (during matches) for at least a 26-week in-season period. Training between games during this period might place additional high-speed demands on players. Therefore, in preseason the total weekly high-speed demands (training plus game) need to be catered for. Ideally, this should involve identifying an individual's in-season high-speed demands and then programming for this during the preseason period.

Practically, there should be at least one day of rest between HSR exposures during the preseason period. This is particularly important when maximal speed running is prescribed. There is no problem with training on consecutive days; however, the sessions in-between high-speed sessions (either skill-based or running) should involve minimal HSR.

Wisdom

High-speed running should be integrated gradually in the preseason period. Coaches should ensure at least 1 day between high-speed running exposures during preseason.

Targeted Injury-Prevention Sessions

One injury prevention technique that should be used during preseason is regular prehabilitation sessions. These sessions typically consist of various proprioception, balance, activation, dynamic flexibility and strength exercises and have been shown to reduce injuries in team sport athletes.[9]

Ideally, these sessions should be included before the team warm-up so the more technical prehabilitation exercises can be performed without interrupting the flow of the warm-up. Some prehabilitation exercises such as landing techniques can be incorporated into the more dynamic aspects of team warm-ups. Coaches should ensure variety in the exercises used and the frequency of these sessions since player compliance can be an issue throughout the season. These exercises also need to be considered when evaluating total team load.

Practically, pretraining prehabilitation sessions can consist of a variety of approaches. One way is to have a circuit-style session of approximately 15 minutes where groups of players navigate their way through the circuit stations. This approach means each player is exposed to similar exercises, and these stations can be tailored to suit team focus areas perhaps identified by screening. A second method may be to individualise prehabilitation sessions by providing each player with his or her own prehabilitation workout. This is a far more precise method but also requires greater staff supervision and may not be suitable for a larger-squad sports.

Preventing contact injuries is far more problematic. The most effective way to do this for contact sports is to integrate controlled contact as the preseason progresses. Once full-contact training has begun, limiting the volume of contact training should be a priority for the conditioning staff. This is because the more often a player is exposed to high-impact contact training, the greater the risk of injury as a result. Of course, some exposure is essential for players to be hardened to this type of training.

The guidelines for integrating contact training into the preseason program are similar to the HSR guidelines outlined earlier. As with HSR, contact sessions involve significant injury risk and therefore need to be carefully planned during preseason. Most team sports involving heavy contact (e.g., the various football codes, ice hockey, lacrosse) have extended preseason periods lasting 12 to 18 weeks. This allows for a slow integration of contact sessions into preseason training and ample time to ensure sufficient recovery between contact sessions.

Practically, contact should be introduced in stages through the use of equipment such as tackle bags and tackle suits as well as techniques such as on-knees tackling, grappling only and sand-based tackling. Once players have progressed through the contact stages (e.g., tackle suits, on knees, sand, grappling, full contact), the dilemma for the fitness coach then becomes how often to allow for full-contact sessions within each weekly cycle. This depends on many factors, such as coaching philosophy and profile of playing list; however, a general guideline of no more than two full-contact sessions per week should be adhered to.

Wisdom

Injury prevention is multifaceted and involves an integrated screening process, training-load modification, prehabilitation sessions and the gradual introduction of high-risk activities such as high-speed running and tackling.

Strength and Power Development in Preseason

Developing appropriate levels of strength and power (collectively referred to as *strength* in this section) for optimal performance during the season remains a core goal of the preseason period. Similar to conditioning training (discussed later), strength training is well suited to the preseason. This period represents the ideal opportunity to appropriately load muscles and tendons, allowing them to adapt and ensure readiness for the forthcoming season, which is critical from performance and injury-prevention perspectives.

Broadly speaking, qualities such as hypertrophy, strength, power and muscular endurance need to be periodised into a preseason strength program. The process by which this periodisation of strength occurs depends on many factors:

- Sport played: Sports such as the various football codes or water polo require a significant degree of hypertrophy compared to sports such as field hockey or volleyball.
- Position: Certain positions require more hypertrophy or power than others (e.g., a centre back compared to a winger in soccer).
- Player history: Injury history as well as age and training age should influence the strength approach taken for each athlete.
- Strength-training history: Experienced players require less time to reach maximal strength levels than do inexperienced players.

- Coaching philosophy: The team's coach or manager may have a preferred style of play that requires a specific strength focus. If the coach of a rugby team, for example, wants the players to dominate the opposition at tackling and contested play, more time would need to be spent on developing strength for these purposes.

- Playing list: The strength profile of the team should be evaluated and this profile matched up with the coaching philosophy. If a discrepancy between desired playing style and list capabilities exists, then discussion between coaches and fitness staff should assist in developing training priorities.

Once these factors have been considered and individual player and team goals have been established, the design of the preseason strength program becomes paramount. The time available to dedicate to strength training depends on the importance placed on strength by the coaching and fitness staff. Generally speaking, at least 3 exposures per week are recommended during preseason training periods. Player training age and strength history can influence these guidelines as previously suggested.

Historically, the progression of strength training throughout the preseason for most team sports has been to start with hypertrophy training and progress to a strength focus before beginning specific power training as the season approaches. This rather simplistic model fails to consider the initial development of sport-specific movement patterns by the player.

A more appropriate model for team sport strength development is to begin preseason training with a general preparatory phase (GPP). Within this phase, aspects of hypertrophy, movement preparation, technique establishment, imbalance correction and general strength can all be emphasised according to individual and team requirements. Once this phase is complete, progression can be made toward strength and power training as the season approaches (figure 21.1).

The duration of each phase depends on the time available for training as well as the team physical status at the beginning of the preseason. For a professional English Premier League soccer team, for example, the preseason period lasts only 6 weeks and typically includes friendly games after only 7 to 10 days. This presents large logistical issues for strength development. The solution in this scenario might be to use the entire 6-week period as an individual GPP and have players train according to their individual requirements. On the other hand, in Australian football (AF), the preseason period lasts approximately 16 weeks. In this sport, a GPP might last 6 to 8 weeks with the remaining time split between strength and power phases. Of course, experienced players with significant training history would not need such an extended GPP phase and might have their programs adjusted accordingly. Alternatively, these players may have specific muscular weaknesses or movement imbalances that can be addressed during this period.

Exercise selection, volume and intensity of lifts and periodisation models to achieve each aspect of strength has been the object of much research,[3-5] and caution should always be applied when prescribing or interpreting generic rules for strength development. Perhaps the most appropriate guideline for practitioners to follow when it comes to

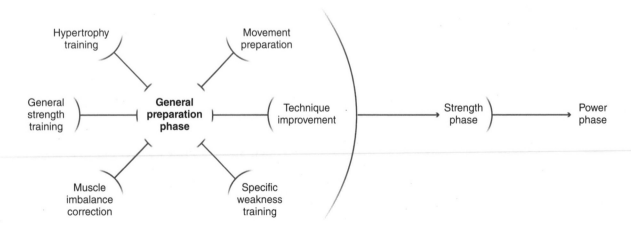

Figure 21.1 Alternate strength model for preseason preparation.

strength training is for the player to lift as close to 100 per cent 1RM as possible. Alternatively, for power training, the player should perform the movement as fast as possible with the weight moved being the maximal amount the player can lift at this specific speed. Further specific prescription details of strength development can be found in chapter 10.

Wisdom

Strength periodisation for team sports should be based on a needs analysis of each individual with specific focus on movement proficiencies, correction of imbalances and strength. In general, strength training during preseason should occur at least 3 times per week, although any plan should to be based on the needs of the individual.

Conditioning Development in Preseason

Conditioning programming (in this section the term *conditioning* will be broadly used to describe endurance, repeat speed, speed and agility training) in preseason should prepare the players for the conditioning requirements of a single match and for the demands of multiple matches over an extended period.

The volume and intensity of conditioning training depends on factors that also influence strength development:

- Sport played: Sports such as field hockey and soccer may require a higher degree of focus on endurance than cricket or basketball.

- Position: In netball, for example, the centre position is required to perform a substantially higher work-to-recovery ratio (W:R) than the goal defence and therefore requires different levels of conditioning.

- Player history: Injury history as well as age should influence the conditioning approach taken. For instance, younger players straight out of junior ranks should not be exposed to typical adult training loads because this will likely present a dramatic increase from previous training experience. Players with significant injury history will need an adjusted program, emphasising reconditioning of the previously injured area.

- Conditioning background: Similar to strength, experienced players require less time to reach maximal endurance and repeat speed levels than do inexperienced players.

- Coaching philosophy: If, for example, the technical coach wants the players to dominate the opposition in the domains of running and uncontested possession, more time might need to be spent on developing appropriate conditioning for these purposes.

Conditioning for aerobic endurance in team sport scenarios has been the subject of considerable research.[6-8] The dilemma facing conditioning coaches is how best to combine the aspects of speed, agility, repeat speed and endurance as well as the need for tactical sessions into a single preseason program. This balance is particularly relevant for sports involving limited preseason periods, such as most professional soccer leagues, single tournament preparation (Olympics, World Cups, etc.) and the National Basketball Association (NBA) basketball. One solution is to combine all aspects of conditioning as well as tactical influences in small-sided games (SSG). This method will be covered in more detail later in this chapter.

Conditioning training needs to be specific to the demands of the sport, but this does not necessarily mean the game should simply be replicated in training across the preseason. The W:R, distance travelled, number of accelerations, number of skill executions and so on should all be factored into the preseason conditioning programmes. For example, if the W:R of high-speed running in a team sport match is estimated at 1:3, the fitness coach may want to overload this ratio at the start of preseason training to 1:1 and progress throughout the preseason to a more specific 1:3. There are two benefits to this approach. First, it allows the body to be exposed to an overload of match demands initially. Second, and specifically with respect to high-speed running, it will force players to reduce running speeds and therefore the risk of injury at the start of preseason because they will not be able to sustain high speeds at 1:1. As the preseason progresses, the W:R might increase to 1:1.5, 1:2 and so on up to match-specific running speeds and W:R.

The careful planning of conditioning training should allow the fitness coach to combine the principals of overload, specificity, regeneration and individualisation for all aspects of preseason conditioning. The experience of the fitness coach and knowledge of individual players are paramount. The ability to identify players who are not coping with workloads via testing and fitness coach observation will also help this process work effectively. Monitoring the training response is covered in greater detail in chapter 6.

Tactical Training

The preseason presents the ideal opportunity to implement a team style of play through dedicated team tactical sessions and player education. During the season, game preparation and recovery demands limit a coach's ability to dedicate time to technical and tactical training. These time limitations are often diminished in preseason, presenting the coaching staff with a greater chance of spending time on team tactics.

Tactical sessions should be incorporated from the beginning of the preseason to ensure maximal exposure throughout this important learning period. Incorporating tactical sessions into total training loads needs to be deliberate and periodised. There are some tactical sessions (e.g., walk-throughs) that require little prior physical preparation. However, players need to be physically prepared before beginning full-field, restriction-free tactical sessions. This preparation should include systematic progressions of agility, accelerations, decelerations and speed. The difficulty faced by the fitness coach involves increasing tolerance of, and proficiency in, all these variables at the beginning of preseason whilst ensuring training and conditioning volumes remain high.

Initially, this can be achieved by increasing field dimensions or reducing player numbers in tactical drills (i.e., using SSG). These adjustments generally lead to reduced agility and greater physical demands. Increasing field dimensions will lead to players having to cover more distance in the game or drill prescribed. The increased space provided by larger fields will also lead to less interaction with opposition players and therefore less demand for changes of direction and less risk of physical contact with another player. This important restriction should be imposed on players in the initial stages of preseason because tendons and muscles should not be exposed to sharp changes of direction without a suitable progression period. As preseason progresses, according to the fitness coach's periodisation of training loads, fields can be reduced in size or training numbers increased

until players are conditioned to be involved in unrestricted tactical sessions. These adjustments should occur only as progressions inside the theme of overloading in-season match demands in preseason programming.

The aim of this type of SSG training is to create specific training games and drills that exceed match physical demands whilst also improving skills and decision making in players. As mentioned, initially the aerobic demands of the sport should be exceeded. As the preseason progresses, the speed, acceleration and deceleration requirements should be addressed, which is when smaller field dimensions and or larger numbers of players are used.

For instance, in preseason soccer preparation the fitness coach may prescribe SSG to combine skills and physical overload. Initially, this should involve larger field dimensions or smaller player numbers (e.g., 6 versus 6 on a full pitch or 3 versus 3 on a half pitch) in order to overload the conditioning element as well as the skill involvement. As the preseason progresses, the field dimensions should be reduced or player numbers increased (e.g., 6 versus 6 on half pitch or 11 versus 11 on full pitch) so that conditioning overload is reduced, and players become more exposed to match-specific demands.

When using these exercises it is important that the fitness coach is able to monitor each session closely and make sure each individual is exposed to the prescribed training load. Highly skilled players can often perform exceptionally well in SSG without large physical exertion, which is not possible in traditional running sessions where a fitness coach is able to judge time and distance progressions quite easily. However, the benefits associated with SSG training (e.g., skill practice, enjoyment, decision making) should make this form of training a crucial component of the preseason program for team sports.

Blending Physical and Technical Training

Integrating technical training into fitness sessions can be a useful technique for a fitness coach, particularly in preseason. Some skill-dominant sports such as soccer and basketball have limited preseason periods and therefore often require the fitness coach, in conjunction with the coaching staff, to make adjustments to technical sessions to achieve physical goals.

The most popular form of integrating technical and physical training is through the use of SSG. Much research has evaluated the physical benefits of SSG[10, 11] in a variety of sports. In general, the research suggests that SSG work can elevate heart rate values to game levels but is limited in its ability to generate high-speed running levels equivalent to actual game demands in most team sports. To overcome this limitation supplementary high-speed running may be added, perhaps at regular intervals during SSG.

These games can be adjusted to suit the majority of preseason needs. At the start of preseason when endurance training may be the priority, the field can be enlarged, player numbers can be reduced or time can be extended. Making the field bigger (per player) may be the best option at this stage as agility demands are reduced in this type of game. This is important at the start of preseason when the fitness coach should be looking to limit sharp directional changes. As mentioned previously, the use of SSG within a preseason period should be monitored closely to ensure all physical demands are met.

During preseason periods when high-speed running might be a physical priority, one option is to combine this type of running with more isolated technical exercises. In soccer this might involve adding sprints to existing passing and shooting drills. In basketball this could be achieved by adding a jump shot after a set number of court sprints. Importantly, these drills can be useful only with effective communication between coaching and fitness staff so that both technical and physical goals can be achieved.

Defining Preseason Success

The success of a preseason is often difficult to define. The role of fitness and medical staff within this setting is to enhance physical performance and prevent injuries. The emphasis placed on each of these goals could arguably be divided evenly; however certain situations may dictate that one takes preference over the other. For instance, if a coach or manager feels the team is sufficiently skilled and experienced to be a serious premiership or title contender, then the coach may instruct the fitness staff to emphasise injury prevention over an expanded conditioning program. Conversely, if a coach feels that extra conditioning may compensate for some technical or tactical shortfalls, then the instruction to fitness staff might be to increase conditioning components, even though doing so may come with an accepted increased injury risk.

With these two goals in mind, establishing the success of a preseason program for team sports falls under two categories: injury rate reduction and physical performance enhancement.

Injury Rate Reduction

Maintaining reliable and valid injury statistics will enable the fitness staff to keep accurate track of injuries and evaluate the success of the program. These statistics can include the number of new injuries occurring (injury incidence), duration of time unavailable because of each injury (injury prevalence), percentage of players available for training and matches and comparison of these figures to those of previous years or opposition clubs (where available).

The injury trends of most interest to fitness staff are those that relate to injuries that may be preventable via prudent programming and injury-prevention training. These injuries are predominantly musculotendinous (i.e., soft-tissue injuries) although some injuries of the ankle and knee joints could also arguably be classified as preventable. Ankle and knee injuries have been substantially investigated, and prevention methods have been outlined.[12-14] Therefore, monitoring and intervening on injury trends of these body parts should form part of any team sport preseason evaluation. Of course, these are general guidelines, and each injury should be treated individually with causes and preventability determined by fitness and medical staff.

These statistics (as well as measures such as percentage of total training completed by the team) should be recorded for both the preseason and in-season periods. Preseason statistics should serve to influence training immediately (if trends are emerging) as well as in subsequent preseason periods. For instance, if an alarming trend for hamstring injuries is identified, the fitness staff should investigate why this might be occurring and look to address this trend immediately. In-season statistics should influence both preseason and in-season training. For example, if a disproportionately high number of calf injuries occurs during the season, preseason methods should be revisited to ensure the source of these injuries is detected and the problem rectified in future preseasons.

Preseason Training, National Football League (NFL) Style

Tom Myslinsk
*Head Strength and Conditioning Coach,
Jacksonville Jaguars, United States*

We in the NFL face significant challenges in terms of physically preparing our athletes. Our sport is so technically and tactically demanding that the emphasis unquestionably lies here, despite the fact that the game is getting more physically taxing every year. There is a trade-off between time spent learning the technical system and time spent improving physical capacities. You could say it's a battle of installation versus adaptation. To a large extent we rely on the athletic qualities inherent to the player and the player's professionalism in maintaining and developing capacities during his time away from the club.

The head coach and general manager set the direction of the squad. As the head strength coach, my priorities are to learn the offensive and defensive strategies they want to employ. This enables me to shape our programme accordingly. For example, if our emphasis is on repetitive, quick plays, I prioritise a thread of repeated speed. If, however, we plan to play with a more physical emphasis, I may concentrate a bit more on time in the weight room. Essentially, our coaching team's strategy will determine the energy system we aim to emphasise in training.

The annual training calendar goes something like this: After the conclusion of the season, the players can take almost 15 weeks away from the organisation. We get them back in April for 9 weeks. During this time, attendance is recommended but not required. Weeks are broken down into three distinct phases:

1. Phase 1 lasts for 2 weeks and is spent strictly with the strength and conditioning staff, our physiotherapists and myself.

2. During phase 2, which lasts for 4 weeks, the technical and tactical teaching is initiated with position coaches, although competition on the field is kept to a minimum.

3. Phase 3, the final 3 weeks, is a time better known as organised team activities (OTAs), during which the emphasis is on competitive technical and tactical training. OTAs are unpadded, offseason practices;

they allow us to organise training drills with a specific emphasis on positional demands (e.g., running distance, sprint volume, acceleration, deceleration) without the concern of contact injuries that can accumulate during full-contact training. This phase leads into the preseason and concludes with a 3-day, mandatory veteran minicamp.

During the first two phases, athletes engage in physical training 4 days per week. Once OTAs begin, it's 3 times per week.

At the conclusion of this block, players go away again for 6 weeks. Before their departure, players are given a periodised training plan to prepare them for the preseason. The sprinting volumes prescribed are determined through position-specific global positioning system (GPS) data gathered during OTAs.

After their offseason break, players report back for 6 weeks of preseason training, typically starting late in the third week of July. This period begins 15 days before the first preseason game, so all coaches have a 2-week window in which to prepare the athlete to play in the first preseason match. The first 2 days are devoted to screening and testing, the results of which enable us to advise the coaches on physical limitations and training-load modifications based on the physical robustness of each individual. We start preseason with about 90 athletes, and that number is whittled down to 53 at the conclusion. In some years, a majority of this starting number will be familiar to us, but in other years there may be a large turnover, and as a result we need to get to know 30 to 40 new players.

Given the fact that the league is getting more physically demanding, we emphasise hypertrophy, maximal strength and power output as much as possible, and we work around the fact that daily practice can consume up to 2.5 hours. We rarely have many opportunities to develop some of the more complex integrated athletic skills such as agility because the time we have with players is so brief. Therefore, we rely somewhat on the innate capabilities of

Tom Myslinski is strength and conditioning coordinator for the Jacksonville Jaguars of the National Football League (NFL). He played nine seasons as an offensive lineman in the NFL and spent three seasons as strength and conditioning coach for the Cleveland Browns. He is certified by the NSCA and serves on the Coaching Performance Committee and Human Performance Centre Committee. He has a master's degree is exercise physiology from the University of Pittsburgh.

the athletes selected and their time spent practicing the game to develop their skills. When time permits, we will integrate specific and nonspecific change-of-direction skills into training.

We periodise energy-system development by following a Charlie Francis–style high-low, vertically integrated approach (see chapter 11). This allows us to concurrently train all motor abilities whilst varying the volume and intensity. In developing speed and stamina, we use a short-to-long programme rather than a traditional long-to-short programme, so athletes are consistently developing their capabilities and adapting to the gradual increase in intensity over time. This is extremely important because as the preseason progresses, the volume and intensity of technical training are elevated, especially when competition is present.

We play four or five preseason matches during the month of August. This, to a large extent, dictates the structure of the training week. The initial session of the week will be largely focused on recovery. Depending on our training block, we will prioritise hypertrophy or maximal strength; as we are getting closer to the next game, we will emphasise optimising the athlete's state of readiness through whatever methods necessary.

The biggest challenge in the NFL is individualising training programmes for 90 players. We break down the team into various subgroups for needs analysis: offense or defense, position, role and player needs. Then we work backward, building the athlete and customising his abilities according to the demands that will be required of him in the position he plays.

Initial testing ranges from biomechanical to biochemical. Biomechanical tests can be broken down further into movement screens and performance screens. The results of these tests lead us to more precise screens in order to further pinpoint an athlete's asymmetries or weaknesses. We use the functional movement screen (FMS) as our initial movement screen and a variety of performance tests such as unilateral vertical hopping for power output and horizontal movements for distance and landing mechanics.

Biochemical testing is quite new to the NFL. We have regularly been tracking each athlete's testosterone, omega-3 status, creatine kinase, vitamin D, folate, homocysteine and thyroid labs. We firmly believe we must construct the athlete from the inside out and develop what is under the hood. This takes time and patient teaching, reinforcement and lifestyle changes for most athletes.

Once the results are in, supplementation recommendations are based off each athlete's nutritional habits and labs. We like to say that if you are not testing, you are just guessing. In the NFL, we are not allowed to distribute supplements to athletes. We can only recommend and advise they use NSF's Certified for Sport supplements. We rely on our athletes to be proactive and professional in their approach to health and wellness.

In the weight room, the strength programme and training methods are the developed based on the results of the athlete's performance tests, movement screens, injury history and positional needs. Unfortunately, due to the lack of development time, sometimes we must strip the programme down to the absolute basics: squats, versions of the Olympic pull, posterior chain, bench press and pull-ups. Additionally, we devote a reasonable amount of time on developing adequate levels of stability and mobility of the neck, hip and shoulder girdle. We've discovered that the more we know, the less we tend to do. We would rather our athletes be very good at very little rather than just average at a lot.

American professional football is a physically demanding sport. In fact, I often say to our players that the first day of preseason training is the best they will feel until the end of the season! We aim to equip each player with the skills, knowledge and wisdom to understand what being a professional athlete means, especially in looking after his biggest asset: his body.

Physical-Performance Enhancement

Establishing whether physical-performance capacity has been improved is often difficult in team sports. The success of the team is important; however, this success does not always correlate to greater physical capacity. In soccer, for example, research suggests more successful teams demonstrate less physical output during matches than do less successful teams.[15, 16] Anecdotally, this is probably because teams that are more successful maintain possession and are more effective in their tactical positioning in both attack and defence and therefore do not need to run as much.

Late-game success or failure is one common measure of a successful preseason conditioning program, particularly in early season matches. However, this measure can be flawed. For example, if a basketball team overturns a 20-point deficit in the final quarter, it is often assumed that they are fitter than their opponents. However, in the first three quarters, this team may have been comprehensively outworked by its opposition; therefore, when all four quarters are evaluated, rather than just the fourth quarter, the team that won had a lighter physical output.

Physical assessment can determine whether preseason conditioning methods have been successful. The type of assessment chosen is critical and should attempt to reflect the demands of the sport rather than be used simply to collect information. The risk associated with performing an assessment as well as the value the assessment adds to team selection or success should also be considered. In a 6-week European soccer preseason, for example, the conditioning coach should ask whether scheduling 2 or 3 assessment sessions is the most prudent use of the limited time available. In this instance, a submaximal assessment might be useful.

In this type of assessment a standard, submaximal work rate is prescribed, and the players have their heart rate responses to this workload evaluated. Additionally, the speed of heart rate recovery (HRR) from this set workload can also be measured. HRR has been shown to represent fitness levels in numerous sports using this type of assessment.[17, 18] Submaximal assessment places little demand on the players and therefore can be used quite frequently throughout preseason to evaluate the physical progress of the players.

Wisdom

Submaximal heart rate assessment (HRR) protocols might offer a reliable, valid method of assessing players' aerobic fitness levels during the preseason. This type of assessment places little demand on players and therefore can be repeated quite regularly during this period.

Methods to Ensure a Successful Preseason

A successful preseason, as defined by the parameters described, is the aim of all fitness coaches. The methods by which success occurs are affected by many factors, such as the type of sport, coaching characteristics and duration of preseason. However, there are a number of options that a fitness coach can use to—at the very least—prevent an unsuccessful preseason.

Effective Programming

Effective preseason programming of physical qualities has previously been mentioned in this chapter as well as elsewhere in this book. Fitness coaches should ensure that the program is appropriate for the level and is individualised where appropriate.

Broadly speaking, an undulating periodisation model should be employed during preseason, with the number of steps dependant on the preseason duration. Ideally, 3 weeks of gradually increased training load should be followed by a week of reduced load. This deloading week should consist of a training volume that is reduced at least 25 per cent from the previous week. However, if, for example, a preseason period consists of 6 weeks, then 2 weeks of gradually increased load followed by a week of reduced load should be employed. Flexibility in programming is required.

Consistent with the strength model outlined in figure 21.1, the programming of all aspects of conditioning should be individualised. This may mean separating players into various groups based on training age, position, injury or other variables. Young players, in particular, may need to have a separate conditioning model, which may involve reduced volume or more emphasis on movement-pattern development early in the preseason program.

Effective Monitoring

Monitoring players effectively during periods of intense training, such a typical preseason, is a crucial component of a successful program. The ability to identify when a team or individual player requires an alteration in the programme can mean the difference between a well-conditioned player and an overtrained player. As mentioned previously, preseason loads should be estimated based on overloading in-season game demands. Once this plan has been established, detailed monitoring of these loads is a critical component of ensuring a successful preseason.

A fitness coach has many tools to monitor players and many of these are outlined in great detail elsewhere in this book. Generally, a fitness coach should be aware of the external load placed on a player over the preseason as well as the internal cost of this load on the player.

The external load of a field session is predominantly assessed objectively using equipment such as GPS devices. Gym sessions are assessed objectively using a combination of sets, repetitions and weight lifted expressed as actual weight (e.g., kg, lb) or as a percentage of a player's one-repetition maximum (1RM). Other examples of external assessment include duration of session and fitness coach rating of session difficulty.

The internal cost of a session is most commonly determined using heart rate assessment or player rating of perceived exertion (RPE). Both values provide a fitness coach with a cost of the session to the individual player and team.

Prudent use of these (and other similar) session-monitoring techniques permits fitness coaches to assess each session with respect to the original session goals. Crucially, these tools can also then be used to adjust future sessions in accordance with programme aims. For example, suppose the aim of the session was for the team to train at a load that equated to 700 training-load units (session RPE × session time) or run 1,200 high-speed distance metres throughout a skill session. At the conclusion of the session, if these targets were not met, the fitness coach has the option of adding any missing distance or training-load units to the next session. Without these monitoring techniques, making such adjustments would not be possible.

Arguably more important than the monitoring of individual sessions on the success of preseason is the ability to monitor the accumulative effect of training on the player and team. This long-term approach to preseason monitoring should provide the fitness coach with the ability not only to assess the effects of training periods on each player, but also to assess the team readiness for the in-season program. The tools used for this type of monitoring can include heart rate variability, blood profiling and regular fitness assessments in addition to the tools used to monitor individual sessions.

Along with effective programming, the ability to monitor players and sessions is paramount to a successful preseason. The monitoring should provide the fitness coach with the information that can then be used to adjust the program accordingly. The use of monitoring is discussed in greater detail in chapter 6.

Wisdom

Monitoring both external work or output as well as the internal cost of the training session and preseason allows coaches to make necessary alterations as required.

Development of Desirable Team Behaviours

The preseason should be used by coaching and fitness staff to develop the behaviours they want the team to display throughout the season. Behaviours such as resilience under pressure, team harmony, and mental toughness can all, to varying degrees, be trained. During the season these behaviours can significantly influence team success; however, the pressure of games as well as training limitations during the season make it difficult to establish these behaviours once the season has started.

Practically, these behaviours can be developed through numerous techniques. For example, fitness staff can alter training times for an early (or late) start to sessions to evaluate how players react to being placed outside their comfort zone. Deliberate incorrect decisions during practice matches, alternate training activities (e.g., strongman) and military-style team camps may also provide opportunities for fitness staff to influence team behaviours in preseason.

The use of team bonding, mental toughness or even fitness-based camps is a strategy generally used in extended preseason periods, such as those required for the various football codes around the world. These camps can certainly provide a break from the typical daily training routine and challenge players both physically and mentally. Other potential benefits include extended periods of time with players to discuss team tactics, goals and behaviours, allowing new teammates to get to know each other, as well as the benefits of allowing coaches to assess how players react to difficult circumstances. The timing of these camps needs to be carefully considered. The camps need to be scheduled sufficiently far enough into preseason to ensure that players have a large enough training base to cope with the camp's physical demands yet not too close to the in-season period so the camp does not interfere with technical preparation.

However, care must be taken when applying these techniques too frequently. Although some individuals and teams respond well to this type of training, others may not. Critically analysing team (and player) needs is crucial in determining whether this type of approach is required. For example, if a coach is determined to implement a new game plan, spending a week at a military camp during an 8-week preseason might be superfluous to this team's needs.

The successes as well as the physical impacts of these types of camps are also difficult to assess. Training loads during these camps are often dangerously high and are the result of novel tasks; unless sufficient postcamp recovery time is implemented, the accumulated fatigue from the camp will almost certainly affect subsequent training sessions.

Wisdom

The use of military-style camps during preseason can be an effective way of strengthening team bonds and seeing how players react under physical and mental stress; however, they come with inherent risks of injury and excessive fatigue. Coaches need to be careful about using camps and ensure that their use will contribute significantly to the success of the preseason.

Alternate Training Modalities

Use of alternate training methods, if programmed effectively, can add significant and much-needed variety to lengthy preseason programs. In this context the term *alternate* applies to variations to normal running-, skill- or gym-based methodologies and can range from swimming training to yoga.

Often, fitness coaches will provide team sport players with regular reduced-impact training modalities throughout the preseason. These sessions (e.g. biking, swimming, use of a crosstrainer) serve to maintain aerobic and anaerobic fitness levels; reduce impact (load) through the knee, ankle and hip joints; and add variety to training. Care must be taken in the prescription of these sessions because they might not always be the most appropriate form of variety in training. For instance, in a shortened preseason such as in European soccer, every session is critical; it may be that performing additional skill sessions might be a more effective use of limited time. Additionally,

certain modalities might not be suitable for all players. For instance, the additional hip and spinal joint flexion often associated with bike riding might place taller players at a greater level of discomfort and possibly even increase injury risk. In this case other modalities, such as reduced-gravity treadmills or water running, might offer a more appropriate form of training variety.

The transfer of fitness benefits from some non-weight-bearing modalities to running is questionable;[19] therefore, the transfer of benefits to team sport success is even less certain. When considering these training options, the fitness coach should perform a cost–benefit analysis. Are the benefits of using these training modalities sufficient to outweigh the potential injury costs? This is a difficult analysis to make, and the fitness coach can do so only through experience and, in particular, from knowledge of individual player training thresholds. A more detailed discussion of this topic can be found in chapter 17.

Altitude training has often been used in the preseason to develop more efficient aerobic pathways in players. The timing of this training becomes paramount if the benefits of altitude are to be fully realised. For example, most team sport altitude camps occur many months before to the start of the season. Even though this may have some benefit in preparing players for the rigours of preseason training as well as some benefits associated with team bonding, any specific aerobic improvements as a result of altitude training would disappear by the time the season starts. If, however, a club has access to hypoxic facilities, then the benefits of an initial altitude camp may be extended via regular use of hypoxic training.

Other training options such as yoga and Pilates should be included regularly in any preseason training program. Players requiring this type of training should be identified through the preseason screening process, and prescription should be based on individual requirements rather than following a blanket approach for the whole team.

Effective Tapering in Preseason

A comprehensive guide to tapering can be found in chapter 22. A preseason taper, just before in-season play, should be carefully planned. The coach or manager and the fitness coach should evaluate the importance of the initial in-season matches, which should dictate the size and duration of the prior taper period employed. For example, in Australian football (AF) the preseason period can be up to 16 weeks, and therefore a significant 2-week taper is suggested. This is, of course, assuming the fitness coach wants the team to be at peak fitness for the first month or so of matches.

The risk associated with this strategy occurs later in the season when the tapering team may not be able to maintain preseason fitness levels compared with a team that continues to train during the initial month of the season in order to attempt to maintain fitness levels for the entire season. Both of these strategies require careful planning and significant input from coaching staff.

The philosophy remains the same in sports with a substantially shorter preseason; however, the duration of the taper should be altered. For instance, in a 6-week preseason, the taper period might last only 1 week. In this case, it is almost impossible to provide players with a comprehensive loading and tapering period during this limited preseason time. Therefore, the fitness of each player and perhaps the team as a whole would have to be evaluated during the season and additional sessions prescribed as necessary.

Summary

An effective preseason program can establish the framework for team sport success during the season. The training loads prescribed during the preseason need to be sufficient to place players under greater stress than in-season demands in order to maximise physical performance and prevent injury. Careful integration of strength, conditioning and tactical training, along with appropriate use of various monitoring techniques, will enable the fitness coach to provide team coaches with a group of players in the best possible physical condition for in-season play.

CHAPTER 22

Peaking for Competition in Individual Sports

G. Gregory Haff, PhD, CSCS*D, FNSCA, AWF-3, ASCC, ASCA-2
Centre for Exercise and Sport Science Research,
Edith Cowan University, Joondalup, Western Australia

The ability to perform at the highest level when it matters most during the competitive calendar is a critical aspect of athletic performance. Elevation of performance is often referred to as *peaking* because the athlete's overall performance capacity is elevated to its highest level.[1] Traditionally, a peak is achieved via a reduction in overall training loads at key predetermined times dictated by the competitive calendar contained in the athlete's annual training plan. This reduction in training load is often termed a *taper* and is considered to be a significant aspect underlying the physical preparation of athletes.[1, 2]

The overall success of a taper is predicated on how effectively it is integrated into the competitive period of the annual training plan. Additionally, the degree of performance elevation is dictated by the amount and quality of training that occurs during the preparatory and competitive periods of training. Based on this premise, the foundation of a true peak is therefore established during the preparatory and competition periods of training when the athlete builds a physical, tactical and technical training base.[1, 3] If this foundation is not established, the athlete's ability to peak will be incrementally reduced, and performance optimisation will not likely occur because the athlete has not established the necessary physiological adaptations.[4]

The ability to truly peak an athlete is a complex process that is affected by a multitude of factors, including the training volume, frequency and intensity.[1, 5, 6] The interaction of these training factors is typically manipulated in a taper in order to affect overall performance capacity. However, although tapers are widely used by coaches and athletes from a variety of sports to gain a competitive advantage,[7-15] there are varying opinions about the overall structure to be employed for the optimal taper. Therefore, in order to maximise the performance gains achieved during a taper, we need to understand the basic physiological responses to training and the scientific evidence on how to integrate, sequence and structure loading and unloading periods into the annual training plan in order to create an optimal taper.

Understanding Tapering

The scientific literature uses numerous definitions to describe the modifications to an athlete's training plan during the days leading into a major competitive event.[16-21] Typically, this time frame is marked by a reduction in the overall workload encountered in training as the athlete moves closer to the targeted competitive event.[18] This reduction in overall training load is what we typically call a taper.[1,16,18,22] It is, however, better to define tapering more comprehensively as 'a progressive, non-linear reduction of the training load during a variable period of time, in an attempt to reduce the physiological and psychological stress of daily training and optimise performance.'[23] This definition is preferable as it includes some indications about the actual design elements that are specific to an effectively implemented taper.[18]

Physiological Premise

Key premises underpin the ability to peak an athlete: the optimisation of fitness, the time involved in fatigue dissipation and their collective relationship to *preparedness*.

The *fitness–fatigue relationship*[24, 25] (figure 22.1) provides a general explanation for how fitness and fatigue interact to affect an athlete's preparedness or overall readiness for competition. The fitness–fatigue paradigm is based on the concept that the athlete's preparedness is in a constant state of variability and is directly affected by changes in the level of fitness or fatigue induced by the training stimulus, be it a single training session or the overall training structure.[3, 26, 27]

Based on this relationship, it is clear that preparedness is optimised as a result of training that maximises the athlete's overall fitness whilst minimising the overall development of fatigue.[28] However, when training workloads are high, preparedness is typically lower as a result of accumulated fatigue induced by the training stimulus masking the increase in preparedness.

The *delayed training effects* paradigm[4, 25] examines the relationship between the *supercompensation* of performance, the elevation of preparedness and the magnitude of the training stress undertaken by the athlete (figure 22.2).[1]

Wisdom

If adequate rest, recovery, or reductions in training load are implemented, fatigue will be dissipated, resulting in an elevated preparedness. If these reductions in training stimuli are continued for too long, there will also be a reduction in fitness, resulting in a state of *involution*, or detraining, which will negatively affect the athlete's overall preparedness.

If the magnitude of the training stress is large or is undertaken for a long time, the amount of fatigue generated is magnified as is the increase in the level of fitness.[1, 3, 29] Additionally, the greater the accumulated fatigue, or overall training load encountered, the longer the time frame needed to dissipate fatigue and stimulate a concomitant elevation in preparedness or performance. Conversely, if the training workload is relatively small, the level of accumulated fatigue is less, and the rate at which this fatigue is dissipated is markedly faster. However, lower training workloads result in smaller fitness adaptations and lower elevations in overall preparedness.[25] Based on these relationships we can see that the effectiveness of the taper is, to a large extent, determined by the training that precedes it. We cannot expect a taper to elevate performance when performance is linked to poor

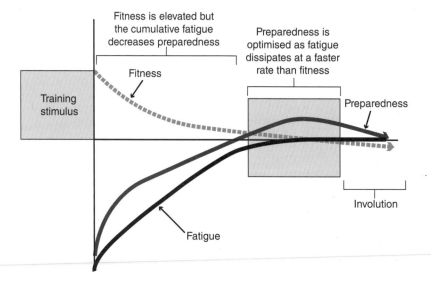

Figure 22.1 Fitness–fatigue paradigm.

Reprinted, by permission, from G.G. Haff and E.E. Haff, 2012, Training integration and periodization. In *NSCA's guide to program design*, edited by J.R. Hoffman for the National Strength and Conditioning Association (Champaign, IL: Human Kinetics), 219. Adapted from M.H. Stone, M.E. Stone, and W.A. Sands, 2007, *Principles and practice of resistance training* (Champaign, IL: Human Kinetics), 376, and L.Z.F. Chiu and J.L. Barnes, 2003, "The fitness-fatigue model revisited: Implications for planning short- and long-term training," *NSCA Journal* 25(6): 42-51.

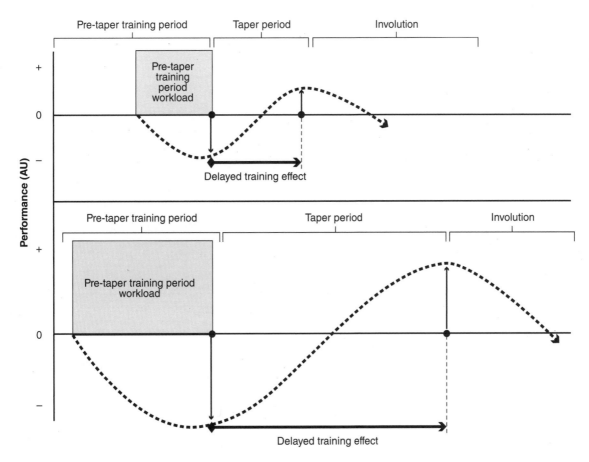

Figure 22.2 Delayed training effects and tapers.

preparation. Equally, it is folly to think that a short tapering period will be able to fully freshen up an athlete who has just been through a massive training block.

Conceptually, the ultimate goal of the taper is to reduce the accumulated fatigue that develops in response to the overall training load undertaken by the athlete whilst retaining as many of the fitness characteristics stimulated by the training plan as possible.[1]

Generally, fitness is considered a slow-changing component of athletic preparedness and is relatively stable over several minutes, hours or days, depending on the acquired level of fitness established in response to the training interventions.[1] On the other hand, fatigue is a highly variable and rapidly changing component of preparedness because it is affected by physiological and psychological stressors.[3, 27] By decreasing training loads, accumulated fatigue (rapidly changing) can be swiftly decreased whilst overall fitness (slowly changing) is maintained.

Although the basic concept of a taper is rather simple, the implementation of a taper is a more complex undertaking where numerous training and recovery-based factors must be understood. For example, if the taper is extended for too long a duration, fitness will begin to decline because of a lack of a training stimulus being present. In reality when this occurs, a state of involution (i.e., detraining) will occur, and overall preparedness will be significantly affected (figures 22.3 and 22.4).[23]

Ultimately, the level of preparedness is a result of a compromise between the extent of the training load reduction and the duration of this reduction.[22] For example, if the training load preceding a taper is high, a greater reduction of training load over a longer duration would be required to effectively reduce the accumulated fatigue and elevate overall preparedness for competition.[22, 30] Conversely, if the training stress is relatively low, the taper would not need to be undertaken for a long duration or require a larger reduction in

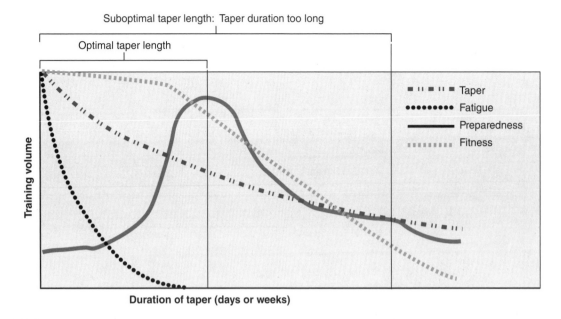

Figure 22.3 Relationship between fatigue, fitness, preparedness and taper length.

Reprinted, by permission, from T.O. Bompa and G.G. Haff, 2009, *Periodization: Theory and methodology of training,* 5th ed. (Champaign, IL: Human Kinetics), 189.

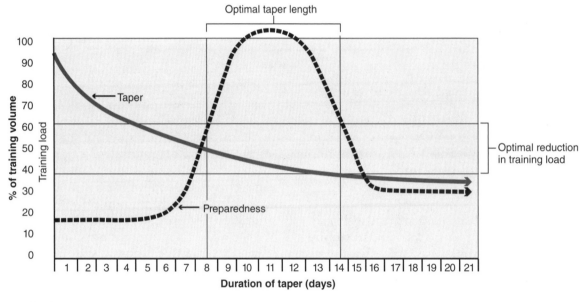

Figure 22.4 Relationship between preparedness and a taper.

Reprinted, by permission, from T.O. Bompa and G.G. Haff, 2009, *Periodization: Theory and methodology of training,* 5th ed. (Champaign, IL: Human Kinetics), 190. Adapted from L. Bosquet, L. Leger, and P. Legros, 2002, "Methods to determine aerobic endurance," *Sports Medicine* 32(11): 675-700.

workload.[1] Overall, it appears many integrating factors converge to dictate an athlete's overall preparedness. In order to effectively elevate this preparedness for competition, the effects of the taper need to be considered from a multilateral perspective rather than being focused solely on reducing training loads.

Primary Aim of a Taper

The ultimate target of any taper is to optimise the athlete's preparedness at a specific time, allowing for a greater potential for competitive success. This goal is accomplished through a complex balancing act in which cumulative physiological and psychological fatigue developed in response to the training process is reduced whilst sport-specific fitness is maintained or slightly elevated.[18, 31]

Ultimately, the tapering process allows the athlete to recover from the previous periods of training, allowing for overall performance capacity to increase.[18, 22, 31] The ability of the taper to increase overall performance is strongly supported by scientific research in which the reduction of fatigue results in an increase in physical performance capacity, [12] improvements in psychological perceptions of effort, enhanced mood status and a reduction in overall sense of fatigue (table 22.1).[18, 32, 33]

Key to the effectiveness of a taper is the realisation that the physiological adaptations to the training program have already occurred before the initiation of the taper;[18] they are simply revealed when the reduction of training load results in a dissipation of accumulated fatigue.[25]

Advantages of Tapering

In high-level sport, small elevations in performance can have a significant impact on performance outcomes and can differentiate between winning and losing. For example, across the swimming events in the 2000 Sydney Olympics there was only a 1.62 per cent difference between the gold medal and fourth place and a 2.02 per cent difference between third and eighth place.[34] Similarly, in the 2004 Athens Olympics there was a 1.96 per cent difference (women = 2.2%; men = 1.73%) between first and third in weightlifting.[1]

When looking at the variability in weightlifting performance, McGuigan and Kane[35] report that the within-athlete variation in performance is around 2.5 per cent (95% confidence interval = 2.2%-2.9%) and that as little as a 1.2 per cent increase in total weight lifted can significantly enhance performance results. Similarly, at the 2012 London Olympic Games, the variation in performance between

Table 22.1 Primary Aims of a Taper

Responses to reduced training stress	Potential effect of a taper
Global responses	Reduction in cumulative fatigue Increase in performance capacity Slight increase in fitness
Hormonal responses	Increase in testosterone (T) Decrease in cortisol (C) Increase in T/C ratio
Hematological responses	Increase in red blood cell volume Increase in hematocrit Increase in hemoglobin Increase in haptoglobin Increase in reticulocytes
Muscular adaptations	Increase in myosin heavy chain IIa fibre diameter Increase in myosin heavy chain IIa force output Increase in myosin heavy chain IIa power output
Biochemical response	Decrease in blood creatine kinase
Psychological responses	Decrease in perception of effort Decrease in global mood disturbance Decrease in perception of fatigue Increase in vigor Increase in sleep quality

Sources: I. Mujika, 2009, *Tapering and peaking for optimal performance* (Champaign, IL: Human Kinetics) and N. Luden, E. Hayes, A. Galpin, et al., 2010, "Myocellular basis for tapering in competitive distance runners," *Journal of Applied Physiology* 108(6): 1501-1509.

first and third was 2.3 per cent (95% confidence interval =1.7%-3.7%) across all weight classes; as little as a 1.1 per cent increase in performance would be expected to enhance performance results. Additionally, Hopkins[36] suggests that elite track athletes can significantly alter their competitive placing with a 0.3 to 0.5 per cent increase in performance, whilst elite field athletes (i.e., throwers) can improve placing with improvements of 0.9 to 1.5 per cent.

After the employment of a well-crafted tapering strategy, it is reasonable to expect competitive performance enhancements of equal or greater magnitude to these variances. Research into tapering strategies has revealed that significant improvements in competitive performance (0.5%-11.0%) and muscular strength and power (8%-25%) in runners, triathletes, cyclists and swimmers can occur when properly implementing a taper before a competitive event (figure 22.5).[9, 13, 15, 18, 37-42]

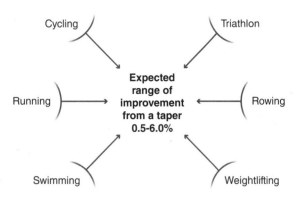

Figure 22.5 Expected improvement in performance from a taper.

Based on data from I. Mujika and S. Padilla, 2003, "Scientific bases for precompetition tapering strategies," *Medicine & Science in Sports & Exercise* 35(7): 1182-1187.

As a general rule, a pre-event taper typically results in about a 3 per cent (0.5%-6.0%) increase in competitive performance.[18, 37] For example, swimming performance was elevated by 2.2 per cent with the implementation of a 3-week taper leading into the 2000 Sydney Olympic Games.[34] Interestingly, the elevation in performance stimulated by this 3-week taper is similar to the differences between first and fourth place (1.62%) and third and eighth place (2.02%) across the swimming events.[16, 34]

If a taper is employed to elevate muscular strength, a 2 to 8 per cent increase in performance

is typically expected,[1] which is greater than the 1.1 per cent increase needed to alter performance results in the sport of weightlifting.[35] When examining the effects of a taper on bench press and back squat performance, Izquierdo and colleagues[43] report a 2.0 per cent increase in maximal strength; Coutts and colleagues[44] report a 7.2 per cent increase in 3RM back squat performance and a 5.2 per cent increase in bench press performance. Similarly, Gibala and colleagues[45] report a 3 to 8 per cent increase in maximal isometric and dynamic force-generating capacity when a taper is employed.

If these results are taken collectively, it is clear that a properly constructed taper can produce increases in performance.[5] The overall effectiveness of the planned taper is related to many factors, including the type of taper selected.[18] In general one can expect to see a 3.0 per cent increase in performance in response to a taper. This magnitude of performance increase can differentiate between first and third place at the Olympic Games.

Wisdom

If we get the tapering strategy right, we maximise our chances of achieving competitive success. Another way of looking at it, though, is that if we get it wrong, our odds of victory begin to lengthen.

Variables to Consider During a Taper

Many tapering strategies can be used as part of an annual training plan in order to peak the athlete for a specific competition. Regardless of the strategy employed, the main premise is based on reducing training workloads and dissipating fatigue.

The reduction of training load during the critical time before competition can be accomplished through alterations in volume, frequency or intensity. Regardless of which training variable is altered, the overall success of the taper is affected by the training that comes before the taper,[22] the overall duration of the taper[20] and the type of taper that is used.[16, 18] If the taper is not structured appropriately, a reduction in athlete preparedness can occur in response to too short a taper, in which cumulative fatigue masks preparedness, or an extended taper, in which involution occurs from a reduced training stimulus.[23] Either scenario will compromise the main goal of optimising competitive performance. Therefore, we need to understand how the type and duration of the tapering plan influence the effectiveness of the strategy.

Type of Taper

There are several types of tapers that have been proposed in the literature for individual sport events.[16, 18] Globally, these tapering strategies can be considered to be either *nonprogressive* or *progressive*. A nonprogressive, or stepwise taper, is accomplished with the implementation of a standardised reduction in training workloads; a *progressive taper* is marked by a systematic, progressive reduction in training workload (figure 22.6).

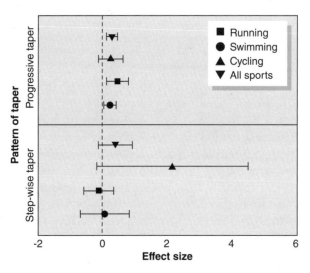

Figure 22.6 Effect sizes for taper-induced performance gains.

Adapted from L. Bosquet, J. Montpetit, D. Arvisais, and I. Mujika, 2007, "Effects of tapering on performance: A meta-analysis," *Medicine & Science in Sports & Exercise* 39(8): 1358-1365.

A hallmark of a nonprogressive taper is a sudden reduction in training load, which could result in a greater loss of fitness and preparedness during the course of the taper.[46] Generally, this strategy appear to result in enhancements to both physiological and performance adaptations that are typically gained from training.[18, 39, 47-52] However, when compared to slow or fast progressive tapers, the stepwise taper produces significantly lower enhancements in performance.[15, 16, 46] For example, performance has been reported to increase by only 1.2 to 1.5 per cent in response to a stepwise taper;

a progressive taper resulted in a 4.0 to 5.0 per cent increase in performance.[18] This trend is also seen in traditional endurance sports such as running and swimming.[31]

Contradicting this information is a finding in the sport of cycling that has demonstrated a greater performance gain in response to a stepwise taper. However, Mujika[31] suggests that because of the small sample of data analyzed to create these effect sizes, more research is warranted. Taken collectively, though, the general tapering recommendation is to employ a progressive tapering strategy in order to peak an athlete for a specified competitive event.[16, 18, 22]

Given the progressive tapering strategy, the next thing to consider is how to best structure this progressive taper. With all progressive tapers, the training load is generally reduced in either a linear or exponential fashion.[1] A *linear* taper incorporates a systematic reduction in training load applied linearly across a predetermined time frame (figure 22.7).[18] Conversely, an *exponential taper* can contain either a slow or fast reduction in training loads. However, there are several methods of employing a progressive taper that can be considered depending upon the individual athlete's needs. For example, Bosquet and colleagues[5] suggest that there are two major subdivisions of the progressive taper including the linear and exponential tapering strategy.

Typically, the training loads contained in a linear taper are higher than those seen in the exponential taper.[18] During a slow exponential taper, the training loads are generally higher than in a fast exponential taper and are reduced at a much slower rate.

When comparing these tapering strategies, the fast exponential taper results in significantly greater performance gains (3.9%-4.1%) when compared to the linear or the slow exponential taper.[15, 18, 46]

Wisdom

Many factors, including the training load of the period before the implementation of the taper and the time frame allotted for the tapering strategy, influence the overall effectiveness of the taper. As a general rule it is recommended that a fast exponential taper be used when reducing the training workload before a competitive event.

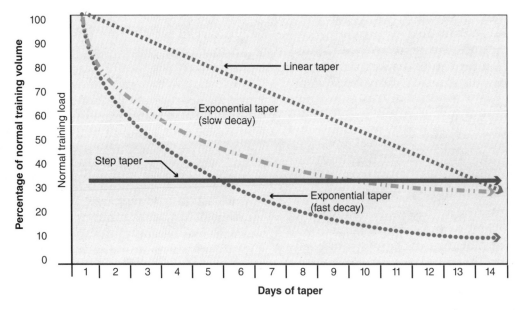

Figure 22.7 Common types of tapers.

Reprinted, by permission, from T.O. Bompa and G.G. Haff, 2009, *Periodization: Theory and methodology of training*, 5th ed. (Champaign, IL: Human Kinetics), 193. Adapted from I. Mujika and S. Padilla, 2003, "Scientific bases for precompetition tapering strategies," *Medicine & Science in Sports & Exercise* 35(7): 1182-1187.

Training Volume

The volume of training the athlete undertakes is an important factor affecting the training load. Of specific interest is the question of how best to manipulate this volume during the tapering period. The two options available are to reduce the *duration* of each training session or reduce the *frequency* of training. The optimal choice is to reduce the volume of training during each training session; this has been shown to exert a greater performance-improving effect when compared to reducing the frequency of training during the taper.[16]

When attempting to create a pre-event taper by reducing training volume, one key factor to consider is the overall training load (i.e., training volume and intensity) that occurred in the periods *before* the taper. These earlier training loads will dictate the amount of reduction in training volume required and the duration required for the taper.[22] The interplay between the preceding training workload and the taper is a large part of the reason why there are variable recommendations for volume reductions during the tapering period.[16, 18] Based on the literature, tapers generally involve a 50 to 90 per cent reduction in training volume in sports such as swimming,[21, 53-56] running,[13, 17, 42, 49-51, 57] cycling,[39, 40, 58, 59] triathlon[15, 46, 60] and strength training.[43, 45]

In a recent meta-analysis on tapers it is evident that a 41 to 60 per cent reduction in training volume during a progressive taper results in the greatest positive impact on performance.[16] However, since there is an interrelationship with the overall training load before the implementation of a taper, there could be situations where the volume of training may need to be reduced by 60 to 90 per cent of pretaper loads.[18, 22] Additionally, a short-duration taper may be warranted if the overall training volume is reduced by a larger amount.[30]

If a large amount of training volume is removed during the taper, the longer the taper, the greater the chances of decreasing fitness. This outcome ultimately could reduce the athlete's overall preparedness and competitive capacity. Overall, though, somewhere between a 60 to 90 per cent reduction in training volume seems to be the most effective strategy to employ.

Training Frequency

Another popular method for creating a taper is to reduce the frequency of training, which effectively reduces the overall volume of training the athlete must undertake. There is some scientific evidence to support this practice: Reducing training frequency by 50 per cent has been shown to result in elevations in performance.[53, 61] Conversely, there is scientific evidence that reducing training frequency for 2 to 4 weeks during a taper only results in the maintenance of training-induced adaptations and performance capacities. [14, 18, 19, 39, 49, 50, 51, 57, 59]

From an examination of the tapering practices of endurance athletes, it is apparent that a high frequency of training results in a supercompensation of performance in highly trained runners; moderate frequency-tapering strategies do not simulate the same response.[17] In their meta-analysis Bosquet and colleagues[16] reported that reducing the frequency of training during a taper does not result in improvements in performance. It is likely that highly trained athletes need a greater frequency of training in order to maintain technical proficiency.[18] Conversely, moderately trained individuals can maintain the physiological adaptations stimulated by pretaper training with 30 to 50 per cent reductions in training frequency during pre-event tapers.[18]

Overall, it is clear that training frequency should be maintained at a level greater than or equal to 80 per cent of pretaper training frequency. This level helps maintain physiological adaptations, preserve technical proficiency and optimise competitive performance.[16, 18]

Training Intensity

Another potential tool for developing a taper is to manipulate the training intensity encountered during the taper.[1, 5] When training volumes and frequency are reduced during a taper, training intensity is a key influence on the athlete's ability to maintain the training residuals stimulated before the taper.[16, 19, 42, 48] For example, when lower training intensities ($<70\%\dot{V}O_2max$) are employed during a taper for endurance athletes, there tends to be a decrease in or maintenance of performance.[51, 57] Conversely, if higher training intensities (greater than $90\%\dot{V}O_2max$) are included in the taper, performance tends to supercompensate.[42] Similarly, when higher intensities are included during a taper for strength and power athletes, significant increases in strength are noted.[43, 45]

Wisdom

Maintaining training intensity throughout the tapering period is critical.

Taper Duration

One of the hardest things to do when constructing a taper is to determine the duration required to optimise performance.[18] The magnitude of fatigue established in the pretaper training will dictate the time frame required to dissipate fatigue and elevate preparedness.[22] The ability to dissipate fatigue, maintain fitness and elevate preparedness will be affected by the volume of training workload reduction and the tapering strategy employed across the taper. Therefore, duration of the taper will largely be affected by how rapidly fatigue is reduced or how much the volume of training is decreased. For example, if a large reduction in training volume is employed during the taper, then a shorter taper should be used.[22, 30] Conversely, if more gradual reductions in training volume are employed, then the taper can be undertaken for a longer duration.

Physiological, psychological and, more importantly, performance improvements have generally been associated with tapers lasting between 1 and 4 weeks with the optimal time between 8 and 14 days.[16] This time frame seems adequate for dissipating accumulated fatigue and avoiding the negative effects of a reduced training workload on fitness and performance capacity that can occur when a taper lasts too long.[16, 30]

Although an 8 to 14 day taper appears to be the most effective duration, the tapering process is highly individualised.[16, 18] There are differences in physiological and psychological responses to reductions in training workloads,[12, 16, 34] and so tapering strategies should be individualised for each athlete.

A key to personalising tapers is to practice various tapering strategies when preparing for less important competitions in order to gauge how each athlete responds to specific reductions in training loads. Additionally, the use of methods of monitoring training loads and alterations in athlete preparedness is critical in sorting out how each athlete responds to various tapering strategies.

A second key to consider with tapering is that tapering cannot be scheduled for every competitive event in the annual training plan. When structuring an overall competitive calendar, the main competitive target, such as the National Championships, Commonwealth Games, World Championships or Olympics, would warrant a full taper. Other minor competitions would be contested under a small degree of fatigue. If tapering strategies are used too frequently, there will be a loss of time in the annual plan dedicated to preparation because of the frequent reductions in training workloads that are required during tapering periods. Strategically, short reductions in training loads that are not true tapers should be employed before minor competitions.

Summary

Using tapering strategies is a major part of preparing athletes for competitive events. Conceptually, the main goal of a taper is to elevate athletic performance capacity at appropriate times through reducing accumulated fatigue, maintaining or elevating fitness and optimising the athletes' preparedness for competition (table 22.2).

When a taper is appropriately applied, an approximately 3 per cent increase in performance can be expected. This increase appears to make a significant difference in competitive results (figure 22.5).

Based on the scientific literature, it appears that during a taper the training load should be reduced by about 41 to 60 per cent in most instances. Larger

reductions in workload (60%-90%) may be warranted if the pretaper training load is high, and greater levels of fatigue must be accounted for.

When reducing the training load, maintain training frequency at greater than or equal to 80 per cent of pretaper values. It also is essential that some intensity is maintained during tapering periods because this has been shown to result in greater performance gains.

Finally, a taper should last approximately 8 to 14 days. Extending the taper too long can result in involution (i.e., detraining) effects, which negatively affect the athlete's preparedness and overall fitness (figure 22.4).

Although these points are important considerations, tapering strategies are highly individualised. It does not matter how old or what sex the athlete is, or the individual sport contested. The tapering plan must be structured based on the athlete's needs, which are dictated by the pretaper training workloads encountered. Regardless of the athlete, appropriately structured tapers can significantly increase the athlete's competitive success and should be considered an important part of the athlete's training.

Table 22.2 Tapering Recommendations

General guidelines
1. Create individualised progressive nonlinear taper model.
2. Reduce training volume by 41%-60% of pretaper training volumes. If a greater amount of fatigue needs to be dissipated because of larger workloads in the pretaper training period, a 60%-90% reduction can be used.
3. Use moderate to high training intensities during the taper period in order to help avoid involution (detraining) effects.
4. Maintain training frequency at ≥80% of pretaper training frequencies.
5. Plan tapers to last between 1 and 4 weeks, with 8-14 days as the period most commonly used.

Adapted from T.O. Bompa and G.G. Haff, 2009, *Periodization: Theory and methodology of training*, 5th ed. (Champaign, IL: Human Kinetics), 191.

CHAPTER 23

Maintaining an In-Season Conditioning Edge

Stuart Yule
Glasgow Warriors, Scotland

Individuals or teams with superior levels of strength, speed or endurance dominate sports at every level. Competitive seasons are long and arduous, and the difference between success and failure is often a fine line. Therefore, the physical preparation and maintenance of athletes in sport today is at the forefront of improving performance and considered integral to achieving success. As such, there are significant investments into resources (e.g., practitioners, equipment, facilities) to ensure athletes are as optimally prepared as possible throughout the competitive seasons.

Typically, annual training mesocycles are broken up into preseason, competitive season and postseason periods. The in-season is defined as the period in which an athlete or team compete over several months within a tournament or league-based format; this period is the focus of this chapter. Specifically, the chapter discusses a strength and conditioning philosophy and approach to programming that enables athletes or teams to maintain the conditioning edge throughout the season.

The in-season presents some unique challenges to the strength and conditioning coach. It is important that the coach identify the challenges but ultimately seek where the opportunities are present to maintain the conditioning edge in athletes. The dominant focus during the season is the sport itself. As such, the physical development of an athlete often is neglected at the expense of technical and tactical training. Other potential challenges that the strength and conditioning coach may face are athletes with reduced motivation levels due to a long season or long-term, increased travel time to competitions. In most cases the biggest challenge is

attempting to maintain conditioning qualities with limited time to perform strength and conditioning training and accumulating fatigue levels.

The 10 Critical In-Season Training Philosophies

An in-season conditioning-edge training process has specific aims. A discussion of those aims helps frame the content of the chapter and puts the philosophies and principles that are discussed into context. Let's start with a statement of intent:

> *'Our team is consistently able to maximise their physical development and realise their physical potential in the sporting arena, throughout the whole of the season.'*

This statement of intent is focused on what a team or individual can achieve and control and is not concerned with the uncontrollable: what the opposition is doing.

The statement of intent is supported by the 10 key philosophies that underpin the training process.

Training Philosophy 1: Efficiency in the Training Process

Strength and conditioning training and tactical and technical training both provide physiological stimuli. In-season the strength and conditioning coach may have limited time to solely address all the physical needs of an athlete. Therefore, it is important that this coach works closely with the head coach to ensure planned physical stimuli are achieved through tactical and technical training. This coordination will help ensure that unplanned training stimuli are not replicated in both environments. For example, a football coach may want to implement a series of drills twice a week involving multiple changes of direction at high speeds. The strength and conditioning coach will need to identify which individuals achieve the desired stimuli through these drills and how much speed work they still need to gain a conditioning edge.

In many team sports, team-training sessions provide each player with a training load depending on the drills; however, a player may miss part of a tactical and technical training session. Therefore, the strength and conditioning coach should be aware of the individuals who have limited physical exposure and ensure they are provided with supplementary training to address the physical stimuli that were not achieved. For example, the player pulled from rugby contact should do some repeat high-intensity running or some metabolic resistance exercise for the desired volume and intensity.

Training Philosophy 2: Keep It Simple

An athlete's physical condition during the competitive season depends on many variables that often subtly interact to form a complex performance system. This interaction has been highlighted in Training Philosophy 1 as an opportunity for the strength and conditioning coach to be able to realise specific conditioning objectives through tactical and technical training. The ability to manage and understand this as well as integrate strength and conditioning training into the programme that doesn't just merely add fatigue but enhances performance can be an intricate process to grasp. However, a complex performance system does not require complicated training programmes or systems to succeed. Training programmes should remain simple. There should be no ambiguity as to what the strength and conditioning programme is attempting to achieve. It should have a clear, directed focus towards an area of improvement. For example, for athletes to achieve stronger lower bodies, a programme would include a progressive squatting prescription at intensities between 75 and 100 per cent 1RM; for athletes to improve speed, they must have opportunities to sprint at or close to top speed as part of weekly training.

Wisdom

Before implementing a strength and conditioning programme, the coach should always ask what the goal of the programme is and confirm the content is targeted towards achieving that goal.

To ensure the training programme remains simple and effective, it is vital for the practitioner to know how to coach the content of the prescribed programme. Reading a book indicating that power cleans will improve explosive strength and then trying to implement that exercise in a programme will be counterproductive if the practitioner does not know how to coach the lift. Being confident and comfortable coaching the various drills and lifts will help the coach make the programme easier to follow. A simple process will also be easy to monitor, thus ensuring the coach can review the effectiveness of the training objectively and quickly introduce adjustments to influence performance.

Training Philosophy 3: Strength Is the Foundation

An athlete's strength qualities provide the physical attributes needed to execute dynamic movement and skills. Strength development is a critical component of in-season training programmes. The physical nature of the sport will determine the extent to which strength is needed and the type of strength qualities required. For example, a prop forward in rugby requires high maximal-strength qualities, and a basketball player requires explosive-speed strength qualities. As has been discussed, appropriate tactical and technical training and competition can provide stimuli that enable the athlete to realise the specific strength qualities required in the sport. The role of the coach is to ensure the player has the capacity and the potential to realise these specific strength qualities in tactical and technical training and the competitive environment. This is achieved in-season through the development and consolidation of maximal and explosive strength qualities throughout the entire season. The volume and intensity of the strength dosage and the exercise selection depend on many factors, including the training history of the athlete; competition schedule; involvement in the team; injury history; and the type, volume and intensity of the tactical and technical training during the week or training block.

The in-season strength pyramid (figure 23.1) illustrates the levels at which strength is developed and realised. Each level provides a foundation from which additional strength qualities can be built.

Each level of the pyramid provides a strength quality directed towards sport performance. Technical and skill training provide the specific strength and power qualities. Meanwhile, the sport itself provides the ability to repeat specific efforts under the pressure of competition.

Training Philosophy 4: Continual Improvement, Not Maintenance

A fundamental principle to abide by is the need to *improve* strength qualities during the season, not simply maintain them. Typically, seasonal sports adopt a philosophy of developing strength during the preseason and then maintaining it during the season. However, following the concept of a strength-maintenance programme will result in a net reduction in strength potential. By definition strength maintenance means that strength will stay the same; there will be no improvement. During the season, fatigue and stress accumulate. Both these factors

undoubtedly have a negative impact on an athlete's strength potential. Therefore, as the season rolls on, if the athlete does not improve his or her strength level, there will be a summative *loss* in strength potential. This is the *strength-maintenance paradox*. Assuming these components are given unit values, the paradox may be expressed as follows:

Strength realization = strength potential – stress impact

Let's consider a case study. At the start of the season (September), a professional rugby player has the following attributes:

Strength potential = 100%

Stress impact = –10%

Strength realization = 90%

At midseason (January), when the goal for in-season training is strength maintenance only, the athlete shows these attributes:

Strength potential = 100% (no improvement)

Stress (fatigue levels) impact = –30%

Strength realization = 70%

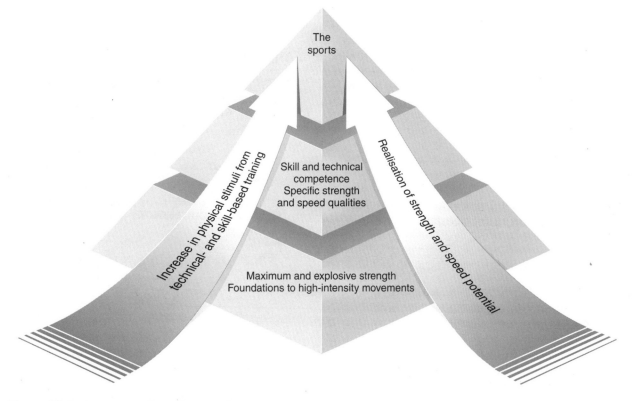

Figure 23.1 In-season strength pyramid.

The net result of a training process where strength potential has been maintained is that the strength that can be accessed has, in fact, declined.

Wisdom

To maintain an in-season edge it is vital that strength potential is continually built so that accessible strength is not eroded.

To follow this example, the aim would be—at the very least—to maintain realizable strength at 90 per cent. If we assume the negative effect of fatigue remains at −30 per cent, we actually need to improve strength levels from 90 per cent to 120 per cent (increase them by 20% from the start of the season). In other words, we need to sprint in order to stand still!

Training Philosophy 5: Sharpening the Edge

The philosophy of the in-season strength programme is to improve. Emphasising this is important at two levels. As we have just seen, it is important from a physical perspective, but it is also critical from a mental perspective. Maintaining an in-season conditioning edge is the outcome that will result from both the well-designed training processes and the level of athlete intent to achieve the desired outcomes. Intent will be heightened when the aim of the programme is to improve. This, in turn, heightens the effect of the training programme. The two components of achieving the edge are interdependent for achieving a successful outcome.

The edge = effective programming
+ athlete intent to improve

Discipline, directed mental effort and consistent focus are the intent behaviors that will underpin the training process.

Discipline

Athlete discipline includes areas such as lifestyle and nutrition. Using an example of an athlete who trains for 3 hours on a given day during the season, assume the training session that day provided the desired adaptive response due to effective programming, coaching and athlete intent. The athlete now has 21 hours remaining to make decisions about the extent to which there will be positive adaptation to the training. Misguided or poor recovery, nutrition and sleep will do nothing but blunt the adaptation aimed for. Therefore, we need to understand what the player is doing between training sessions and use our influence appropriately.

Directed Mental Effort

Every exercise and training session should have a specific goal (e.g., maximal strength, maximal power, speed, technique under fatigue). Meeting the session goal requires maximal intent by the athlete to achieve the desired physical response. In the gym every load should be executed with perfect form, and there should be an intent to accelerate the bar as quickly as possible on the upward concentric portion of the lift, regardless of the load. This intent will ensure the optimal development of maximal and explosive strength qualities. In addition this intent will develop the mental skills required to apply force in a dynamic manner.[2]

As has been previously described, the sport itself and the tactical and technical training provide specific speed and strength stimuli. To this end, maximal intent should be displayed by athletes when performing speed- or power-based drills or techniques. This will ensure speed and strength qualities are maintained and additional sessions do not need to be prescribed, allowing for optimal recovery time.

Consistent Focus

Competitive seasons can be long. The athlete must keep a determined focus on the goal to ensure the desired progress is made through the season. Several factors, such as injury, training monotony, failure or nonselection, can result in an athlete losing focus, which will in turn reduce the directed mental effort into training.

To reduce the potential of these variables affecting the conditioning edge, we must ensure that the following exist:

- The athlete has a physical goal.
- The athlete has a programme specific to the athlete and his or her goals.
- The athlete is provided regular, understandable feedback on progress.
- The athlete and the staff engage in regular communication regarding his or her training.
- The athlete feels a sense of achievement every week, whether competing or not.

- The athlete understands the training process and training expectations.
- The athlete's training has variation in type, volume and intensity.

The intent behaviors are vital during the in-season. The role of the strength and conditioning coach is to *positively* influence the athlete to maximise the training effect. This is done through coaching and creating a positive training environment.

Wisdom

Ensure an athlete is displaying the intent to improve at all times. If he or she is not, identify the factors that may be limiting the athlete.

Training Philosophy 6: Train in Threshold-Strength Zones Below Maximal Levels

Strength training with maximal loads and intensities for sustained periods of time will result in the athlete burning out and potentially overtraining. Inevitably, the critical exercises are high load and demanding. Even without the added stress of concurrent training and competitive demands, training close to 100 per cent is not a sensible option for anyone aiming at improving strength qualities. This does not mean that the athlete will not be able to improve during the in-season; rather, it means that the majority of the strength-training volume for critical exercises is at a submaximal load.

By adopting a prescriptive system for critical exercises, the athlete receives loadings, sets and repetitions based on an approximate 1RM or estimated 1RM (table 23.1). This allows the strength and conditioning coach to have an element of control based on the bigger picture of other training loads. The prescription should not be the sole determinant of dictating a load, however. This prescriptive system is a framework for the coach to build a progressive plan. Coupled with coaching, this plan will determine the actual loadings achieved on any given day.

Training Philosophy 7: Coach the Athlete

Each athlete on any given day will have a training window in which to respond to a given training load. Training can be too light and not provide enough of an adaptive response to improve, or training can be too hard and could result in injury or overtraining or affect other training variables. The window is presented in figure 23.2.

The prescription has been set based on external and other training variables remaining in status quo. There will have been careful consideration of these variables when planning the strength programme, hence the rationale for submaximal loading prescriptions. However, on the positive side, on any day the athlete could be feeling extremely good, weights are flying up in the gym or a technique has clicked. The prescription, therefore, could be limiting an athlete's progression based on a particular load being potentially too light. The coach must make decisions based on observations and the performance process. In this situation the coach may advise the athlete to go beyond the prescriptive loads, repetitions and sets to achieve new personal bests.

On the other hand, the accumulation of stressors may have had an unplanned adverse effect on the athlete, making it necessary to reduce planned loadings to ensure the athlete remains in or returns to an optimal training window. In some instances, however, the observed or reported fatigue is planned; in this case, the expected load should be maintained if desired adaptations are to take place. The coach should be able to distinguish

Table 23.1 Guide to Critical Exercise-Strength Prescription Training Zones

Relative intensity	Approximate % of 1RM	Sets × reps	Training block
Light	50-60	3-5 × 5	Deload week
Moderate	70-80	8-3 × 3-6	Preparatory
Medium heavy	80-85	5-3 × 3-5	Intensification
Heavy	85-95	2-5 × 3-1	Realization

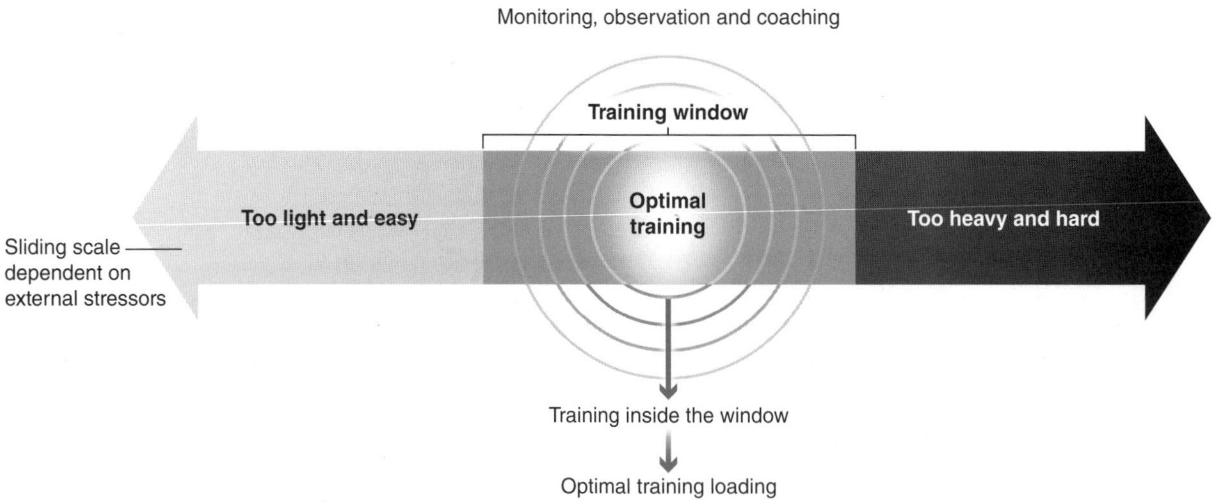

Monitoring, observation and coaching

Training window

Optimal training

Too light and easy

Too heavy and hard

Sliding scale dependent on external stressors

Training inside the window

Optimal training loading

Figure 23.2 The training window.

when a reduction, maintenance or increase in the prescribed load is the appropriate course of action.

When deviating from the prescribed load, the strength and conditioning coach could follow the guidelines presented in table 23.2.

These examples of reducing or increasing loadings to stay in the training window are important in season. The physical and mental demands in season are tremendous and varied; therefore, for the athlete to retain an edge, the coach needs to be coaching and observing at all times. In most instances, the coach will have no qualms about reducing load, nor will athletes if they are feeling slightly fatigued. However, there is a real coaching skill and art in increasing the load or adding another set onto what was prescribed if it is felt to be appropriate for the athlete's development.

Training Philosophy 8: Variation

Variation is an important training principle that ensures the continual development of the athlete. The manipulation of load, sets and repetitions in

conjunction with a variation (i.e., assistance or accessory exercise selection) ensures the athlete is provided with a continual stress for adaptation.

Another key reason for varying exercises is to reduce the potential for boredom and to keep the athlete motivated. The strength and conditioning programme for a motivated athlete is seen as integral to the performance process, but it is an ends, not a means.

Wisdom

It is compulsory that the athlete remains challenged and does not become stale from a monotonous strength-training programme.

Ensure Light- and Heavy-Loading Days

To ensure maintenance of the conditioning edge throughout the competitive season, weekly training consistency is vital. To facilitate an athlete's ability to be consistent in training, the athlete must have the opportunity to attain appropriate training stimuli and then have time to recover and adapt.

Table 23.2 Indicators to Increase or Decrease Load

Increase load	Decrease load
Athlete did not compete at the weekend, which was not planned. Athlete moves warm-up weights well and reports that weights feel lighter than normal. Athlete performs prescribed loads easily.	Athlete seems to have reduced coordination in multijoint movements. Athlete takes longer than usual to warm up. Athlete reports excessive joint or muscular pain. Athlete has had a significant period of training and a good training history; therefore, a reduced load for a day will do no long-term harm.

By planning heavier and lighter days into a training week, the athlete has this opportunity to progress. This manipulation in loading is vital as part of a macro recovery process. An athlete who has no opportunity to recuperate regularly from the stress of competition and training will burn out quickly. An athlete also can mentally prepare and sustain mental efforts over the season. This mental aspect is vital as was described earlier regarding the importance of intent. Determining whether the athlete will be able to and should perform a heavy planned training load is based on a triangulation of factors:

1. Strength and conditioning training, tactical and technical training and competition loadings in the previous weeks. The two types of training should be planned; however, the extent to which competition takes its toll on the athlete needs to be monitored and reviewed.
2. Consideration of any objective monitoring markers (discussed in chapter 6).
3. Coaching intuition. An experienced strength and conditioning coach should understand the athlete's physical and mental responses to training and competition. He or she should therefore be in the best position, along with the athlete, to determine the athlete's ability to execute planned heavy-loading training sessions.

Ensure Light and Heavy Neuromuscular Days Based on Exercise Selection

Aligned to the principle of having lighter and heavier days is the concept of manipulating exercise selection based on inherent loadings. The critical exercises that have been described typically involve high force and power outputs. They involve a significant amount of muscle mass, and the physical cost after performing these exercises tends to be high. Isolation exercises, some lower-level trunk exercises and exercises that involve lying on a bench, such as bench press, will have less of a cost than a heavy back squat or deadlift session. This is important when considering the sequence and prioritisation of training and the desired relative loading of training sessions during a weekly plan.

It is important to include reduced neuromuscular-fatigue sessions in the week. They will allow progression of a strength quality and also provide an anabolic endocrine response, both positive components of maintaining the conditioning edge.

Training Philosophy 9: Create Training in Blocks Incorporating Deload Weeks

There are three primary reasons why it is important to give identity to training periods and split the training process into blocks:

1. Block scheduling provides the opportunity to prioritise training and allow the athlete to retain or progress and adapt in the desired physical areas.
2. Each block can be more accurately monitored and reviewed, and interventions can be implemented for subsequent blocks. This allows athletes to focus and refocus through a long season.
3. A deload period allows for mental and physical recuperation and adaptation before embarking on the next block.

Training Philosophy 10: Aim to Increase Strength Potential Not Peak

After a true peak there will be a reduction in performance. If an athlete has to compete every week, and every competition is equal, then peaking could be detrimental to maintaining the in-season conditioning edge. There can be manipulation of training loads to facilitate the process of feeling fresh going into priority fixtures. The strategy is to increase the base adaptive level of the athlete.

As a result, what used to be heavy for an athlete is now light. Therefore, on any given day, regardless of levels of fatigue the athlete is operating at a higher level. Increasing the physical potential of an athlete will give the athlete the capacity to continue to improve technical ability with increasing intensities and under increasing levels of fatigue.

Training System

Based on these philosophies, the next stage of the process is to create a training system that aims to achieve an in-season conditioning edge whilst providing the coach with a consistent and measureable process.

Priming

Nicholas Gill
*Head Strength and Conditioning Coach,
New Zealand All Blacks*

Priming is a training strategy we sometimes employ either on the day of or the day before a match. With our players, all of whom are well-trained elite athletes, the objective is to produce an acute performance enhancement, although the exact nature of this effect varies according to the type of stimulus we apply.

Priming differs from a warm-up in that a warm-up traditionally takes place less than an hour before competition. Although a warm-up does have substantial priming effects, it is aimed at thermogenesis and practice of technical skills. When we refer to a priming session, we are talking about a session in a window between 5 and 30 hours out from the match. The timing of this session depends on the effect we are hoping to have.

For some players, our aim may be to produce an acute hormonal or neuromuscular boost (short-term emphasis); for others the primer may simply represent an opportunity to add another lifting session to the week, thereby contributing to longer-term athletic development aims.

Once we have decided on the broader goal of the primer, we then decide on the narrative of the session: Will it have a velocity emphasis, a strength emphasis or a skill emphasis (or some combination of the three!)? Which end of the force-velocity curve do we focus on, or what are the priorities for each athlete to transfer to an enhancement of performance? We decide all this by understanding the needs of the athlete both in terms of his profile and the demands placed on him in a match. The exercises we use may include those shown in the table.

Although the content of a session may differ depending on the needs of the athlete, what is consistent within all our priming sessions is that they are low volume and high intensity. Generally speaking, they will last 15 to 35 minutes and comprise low-volume, high-quality repetitions with long recovery times. The emphasis is always on the intensity of the movement (whether that is resistance or speed), and there is a directive that the programme has a feel-good factor about it. We cannot have the players finishing the session feeling tired or heavy as this will have negative physical and psychological effects.

Even though our playing group are all experienced athletes, priming does potentially have a role for novice athletes as well; however, the emphasis really is on the longer-term benefits of adding another adaptive stimulus rather than on any acute hormonal or neuromuscular alterations.

I should note that there is limited research in high-performance athletes regarding priming. Although there is an ever-expanding body of literature on the association between hormonal concentration, postactivation potentiation and the like, the aim of these sessions is likely to be different for each athlete.

We do not perform these sessions all the time. We tend to periodise them with a clear plan of when they will or will not be used. The key determinant in this decision-making process is the athlete himself, as it is only he who really understands how the sessions make him feel and whether there are diminishing marginal returns from repeated primers.

Given that neuromuscular and hormonal profiles are highly variable between individuals (and even fluctuate within individuals), it makes sense, then, that priming sessions need to be bespoke. There will normally need to be a period of trial and error to determine the best strategy for each player with both physical and psychological outcome measures needed. This is certainly *not* a variable to be experimenting with on the eve of a World Cup final!

Possible Exercises for Priming Session

Strength emphasis	Speed emphasis	Skill emphasis
Squat	Dynamic squat (e.g., assisted-band squat)	Sprint drills, jump-land mechanics
Heavy pull (snatch grip pull or chin-up)	Jump squat, plyometrics, resisted or assisted movements	Heavy-ball passing and throwing
Bench press	Sprints, agility, evasion drills	Unit- or position-specific drills using accommodating resistance or assistance to prime specific muscles in exact skill

Nicholas Gill is the head strength and conditioning coach for the World Champion New Zealand All Blacks, arguably the world's most successful sporting team. He is an internationally renowned coach who also has supervised eight PhD candidates to completion and peer reviewed 55 journal publications. He is a senior research fellow at Auckland University of Technology, New Zealand.

Strength-Training Model

The strength-training model (figure 23.3) illustrates how interactions between the strength-training modalities are directed towards maintaining the in-season edge.

The exercise classifications from the strength-training model are critical exercises, assistance exercises and technical accessory exercises.

Critical Exercises

These exercises are the spine of the strength-training programme. They provide the undisputed maximal and explosive strength stimuli that the programme is attempting to attain. The strength qualities developed will provide the base from which speed and power qualities can be enhanced. Some examples of critical exercises are these:

- Squat
- Deadlift
- Olympic lift
- Dynamic overhead lift
- Bench press or overhead press
- Heavy row (e.g., bent-over row or weighted chin)

Mastery of these exercises is integral to the development of high levels of strength and power. Loads can be progressed or manipulated to achieve a desired response. For example, a heavy relative loading in squats will provide a maximal strength stimulus, and a light load used in a jump squat will provide a greater power stimulus. Variation of these exercises during in-season training is typically through the manipulation of loads, sets and repetitions. These manipulations are used to achieve desired force, speed or power outputs or to ensure the recovery process is managed.

The following points need to be considered when aiming to maximise the in-season conditioning edge using critical exercises:

- Select an exercise the athlete can perform competently under load. For example, if a player cannot back squat due to loading issues through the spine, allow the athlete to front squat or trap bar deadlift.
- Make sure the relative loading is high enough to achieve a strength stimulus.
- Plan for the volume to be less than in the preseason.
- Plan in-season blocks where the athlete can perform higher volumes of critical exercises.
- Provide the relatively higher volume of critical exercises at the beginning of the week rather than at the end of the week. This will ensure the strength session can be maximised and that it does not add to fatigue at the end of the week close to competition. (This recommendation is for a sport in which the competition or match is towards the end of the week.)

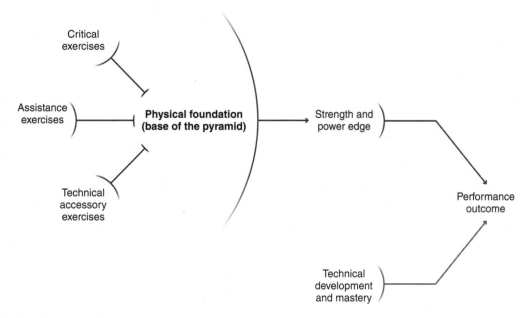

Figure 23.3 Strength-training model.

- Select the relative intensity based on the exercise, physical goal of the athlete and the requirements of the sport. For example, a light power clean will not provide a maximal power stimulus; power cleans need to be loaded to at least 70 per cent of 1RM to achieve an appropriate stimulus. On the other hand, light loading on a jump squat will provide closer to peak power than will a heavy squat. However, this load will not provide a maximal strength stimulus.

- Limit lower-body exercises to 5 reps or fewer if the sport involves a lot of time performing on-feet activities.

- Make sure there is consistency in the selection of a critical exercise each week to ensure a continual development programme is in place. For example, if back squats are chosen to develop lower-body strength, back squats should remain in the programme for at least three training blocks. Variation of exercise and muscular action can be integrated through the appropriate selection of assistance exercises.

- Do not use the critical exercises to mimic the sport. For example, in rowing do not perform hundreds of repetitions in season to mimic the endurance effect of rowing. Use the sport for the specific endurance requirements, and use the critical exercises to increase the intensity at which the athlete can operate.

Assistance Exercises

Assistance exercises have four key roles during in-season strength training. First, they support the critical exercises (table 23.3). For example, if bench press was chosen as a critical exercise, then narrow-grip bench press could be selected as an assistance exercise. Any exercise can be an assistance exercise. There merely has to be a sound rational for what it is assisting.

Second, assistance exercises provides variation to the training programme. Based on their supporting role, there is scope to vary the assistance-exercise selection to continue to stimulate the muscle group and movements being targeted.

Third, assistance exercises can be used to produce a positive hormonal response.[1] This anabolic response from strength training is crucial to establishing a conditioning edge and can be used as part of the planning strategy. Hormonal monitoring is expensive and may be inaccessible

Table 23.3 Sample Critical Exercises and Corresponding Assistance Exercises

Critical exercise	Assistance exercises
Back squat	Lunge and variations Step-up Bulgarian squat Front squat
Deadlift	RDL Hypers Partial deadlift Bent-over row Pull-ups
Dynamic overhead push press or jerk	Military press Dumbbell press and variations Weighted dips Isolated shoulder Isolated triceps Bench press and variations
Olympic lifts and variations	Pull Deadlift Deadlift assistance

for many teams. Therefore, it is important to take a principle-based approach that the inclusion of strength training has positive hormonal responses at medium to high intensities and medium volumes. The inclusion of the critical exercises alone will result in a hormonal response; however, the volume of these exercises may be low, and their inclusion may be limited at certain times of the competition week. After a game or on a technical training day, the inclusion of high-load critical exercises may add too much neuromuscular fatigue. However, some assistance-based training exercises such as dumbbell bench press or seated press can be included. These exercises have reduced neural load but will still create a positive hormonal response.

During the season, assistance exercises should not become the absolute focus; however, the coach needs to be aware of how relative intensities and volumes affect an athlete's performance. The volumes should be prescribed at medium levels and performance and fatigue levels monitored to ensure positive adaptations.

Fourth, the inclusion of lighter assistance exercises for higher repetitions will provide musculotendinous conditioning and local muscular endurance. This is important in maintaining strong joints and muscles and increasing robustness in the injury prevention process.

Technical Accessory Exercises

Every sport has unique musculoskeletal and biogenetical demands. The demands placed on these systems increase the need to boost the work-capacity requirements of these areas. For example, a wrestler requires high levels of neck strength, and a sprinter requires high levels of hamstring strength and function. In-season restrictions in strength and conditioning training loads can potentially result in limited stimuli being achieved around critical musculoskeletal areas. Technical accessory exercises are implemented to maintain a work capacity around critical musculoskeletal regions: neck exercises for wrestlers, judo and rugby players; hamstring and calf exercises for sprinters or high-speed athletes. It is important to understand the intricate performance, technical and loading demands of the sport to ensure exercise selection and prescription add value to the performance process.

In all cases, the dominant strength qualities that need to be developed will dictate the organisation and prioritisation of the exercise groups highlighted. Depending on the goal of the strength-training programme, all exercises can be classified as assistance or technical accessory. Few, however, can be classified as critical exercises because the relatively high loading and intensity of these exercises limits the type of exercise that can be performed.

Olympic Lifts

Olympic lifts are a popular exercise for the development of explosive strength. They are technical lifts that require a lot of hours of dedication to master. When executed well and with appropriate load they are extremely useful exercises to have as part of the explosive strength development tool kit; when performed with an inappropriate load or ineffective technique, the adaptive response will not be as desired or planned. However, this should not discourage the athlete or strength and conditioning coach from using them as exercises; rather, the strength and conditioning coach needs to be alert to any performance issues and reclassify where the Olympic lift fits as part of the strength-training programme. It may be that it is included as an assistance exercise for pulling, grip or posterior-chain development.

The physical returns from Olympic lifts far outweigh the costs if they are programmed and performed appropriately, but they should be included only if they can be coached competently.

Olympic lifts present a mental challenge to the athlete. During the competitive season physical and mental demands are high. It may be determined that the inclusion of an Olympic lift is one step too far for an athlete. However, this lift should be considered a viable option for inclusion when part of the development and maintenance of a conditioning edge is the continued development of the mental attributes required to stay ahead of competitors.

In-Season Strength-Training Methodology

The in-season strength programme needs to remains simple. The following sections give examples of how to arrange the in-season strength-training programme to ensure fitness advancement throughout the season. The programme is a three-block system, with each block lasting 4 weeks. These blocks are arranged as follows:

Block 1: Prepare

Block 2: Advance

Block 3: Conquer

After the completion of block 3, the athlete returns to block 1. The volume begins to be scaled down through the three training blocks, and the intensity is increased. The rationale for returning to block 1 is that the intensity needs to be reduced after 3 months, allowing for recuperation and some time to prepare to make further gains later on in the season.

The relative-intensity loadings will vary each week depending on priority competition, but it is assumed that there are weekly fixtures. The weekly relative-loading pattern follows either pattern shown in table 23.4.

A principle-based approach applied to variations of relative strength-training loads within a 4-week block (tables 23.5 and 23.6).

The use of effective tactical and technical training has been discussed as a means to elicit specific speed and power qualities. Table 23.7 uses tennis as an example to outline session variation in relative intensity, which ensures that strength and conditioning and tactical and technical sessions are maximised to produce a conditioning edge.

Table 23.4 Relative Intensity Loading Pattern

PATTERN A			
Week 1	**Week 2**	**Week 3**	**Week 4**
Moderate	Moderately heavy	Heavy	Deload
PATTERN B			
Week 1	**Week 2**	**Week 3**	**Week 4**
Moderately heavy	Moderate	Heavy	Deload

Table 23.5 Relative Daily Strength Loadings, Pattern A: Saturday to Saturday

	Mon.	**Tues.**	**Wed.**	**Thurs.**	**Fri.**	**Sat.**	**Sun.**
Event			Recovery			Competition	Recovery
Relative intensity	Moderate	Heavy		Moderate to moderately heavy			
Relative volume	Moderate	Moderate		Low			
Session type	Assistance	Critical Accessory Assistance		Critical Accessory			

Table 23.6 Relative Daily Strength Loadings, Pattern A: Friday to Friday

	Mon.	**Tues.**	**Wed.**	**Thurs.**	**Fri.**	**Sat.**	**Sun.**
Event		Recovery	Recovery		Competition	Recovery	
Relative intensity	Heavy		Moderate to moderately heavy				Moderate
Relative volume	Moderate		Low				Moderate
Session type	Critical Accessory Assistance		Critical Accessory				Assistance

Table 23.7 Session Relative-Intensity Variation

	Mon.	**Tues.**	**Wed.**	**Thurs.**	**Fri.**	**Sat.**	**Sun.**
Tactical and technical training: speed and power, relative intensity	Low	Moderate	High	Recovery	Low	Competition	
Strength and conditioning training: relative intensity	High	Recovery	Low	Recovery	Medium-high	Recovery	

By ensuring there is planned speed and power stimuli from both kinds of training, the athlete will be able to maximise each session and will not be in danger of overtraining.

Content of the Programme

Based on these loading-pattern models and on the three-block system, table 23.8 shows an example of a programme that applies the principles outlined previously. This example could be applied to a rugby player.

There are identified critical exercises: back squat, clean and dynamic overhead. There are accessory exercises to support technical demands, including those for hamstrings, shoulders and neck, trunk rotation and pulling and grip strength.

The example in table 23.8 illustrates the exercise selection and session construction for a programme. The strength and conditioning coach must examine the sport in question to determine and prioritise the selection of exercises related to the strength requirements of the sport.

Let's use hockey to further illustrate the selection of in-season strength exercises. Hockey requires a player to be in flexed postures for prolonged periods and involves multiple repetitions of lunging, sprinting and changing direction. Strong legs and a level of robustness around the hip and lower back are prerequisites. Based on this brief description, the following exercises are options to consider for the in-season programme:

Critical exercises

Back squat: Provides lower-body strength qualities required to sprint and maintain strong trunk posture in a flexed position.

Power snatch: Explosive exercise that helps develop speed strength qualities. Promotes thoracic extension strength through pulling movement and in overhead position.

Single-arm row: Coordinates upper-back strength with trunk control to provide base and for prolonged flexed position.

Assistance exercises

Pull-up

Deadlift

Pressing movement (various)

Table 23.8 Sample In-Season Training Sessions

	Exercise classification	Block 1: Prepare	Block 2: Advance	Block 3: Conquer
Session 1	Critical	Back squat Push press	Clean Back squat Jerk	Clean Back squat Jerk behind neck
	Assistance	Step-up		
	Accessory	Hamstring and eccentric trunk series	Hamstring and eccentric trunk series	Hamstring and eccentric trunk series
Session 2	Critical			
	Assistance	Incline bench press Weighted pull-up	Narrow-grip bench press Bent-over row Lunge	Bench press Single-arm row Bulgarian split squat
	Accessory	Shoulder and neck series	Shoulder and neck series	Shoulder and neck series
Session 3	Critical			
	Assistance	Back squat (reduce load from session 1) Military press	Back squat (bands) Single-arm dumbbell press	Single-arm dumbbell push press
	Accessory	Single-arm row Rotational-trunk series	Weighted chin Rotational-trunk series	Bent-over row Rotational-trunk series

Accessory exercises

Lunge (multidirectional)

Step-up

Split squat

Stiff-leg deadlift

Trunk rotation

These exercises will ensure the hockey player retains and develops lower-body and upper-back strength. Additionally, the assistance exercises can be varied to achieve progression in the critical exercises or reduced in volume to allow dissipation of fatigue. Finally, the accessory exercises can be used to condition and enhance specific technical limitations and movements. As with the assistance exercises, the volume of these accessory exercises needs to match the demands and quality of similar movements in tactical and technical training and in games. If a player demonstrates poor technical-movement patterns, it is important that these accessory movements remain as part of an in-season strength and conditioning programme. If, however, the athlete is technically competent and performs a high volume of lunge and change-of-direction activities well, the suggested

approach would be to keep the volume of accessory work low but increased in planned heavy-load weeks and reduced significantly during deload or weeks of high technical-training volume.

Prescription for Strength Sets and Repetitions

The prescription in table 23.9 applies to critical exercise and any other maximal strength–based exercise. These exercises can be selected from any of the classifications, but the sole aim of this prescription is improving maximal strength. Figure 23.4 charts the volume and intensity in training blocks 1, 2 and 3.

The example programme and the graph in figure 23.4 show that the majority of volume is less than 90 per cent. Figure 23.4 shows that through each block there is an increase in exercise intensity and a reduction in volume.

There are opportunities for the athlete to push to new levels each week and in each training block. This principle was introduced earlier in the chapter in the discussion of the optimal training window. The framework is in place from which an athlete can be motivated to progress, and the strength and

Table 23.9 Sample Strength-Exercise Prescription

	BLOCK 1: PREPARE		BLOCK 2: ADVANCE		BLOCK 3: CONQUER	
Week	Lower body	Upper body	Lower body	Upper body	Lower body	Upper body
1	60% × 5 65% × 5 75% × 5 × 3	60% × 5 65% × 5 75% × 5 × 2 75% × AMRAP*	65% × 3 75% × 3 80% × 3 × 2, then 2 or more sets of 2 >85%	65% × 3 70% × 3 75% × 3 80% × 3 × 2 80% × AMRAP	65% × 3 75% × 3 80% × 3 85% × 2 × 2, then 2 or more sets of 1 >87%	70% × 3 75% × 3 80% × 3 85% × 2 × 2 85% × AMRAP
2	60% × 5 65% × 5 75% × 5 80% × 5 × 3	60% × 5 65% × 5 75% × 5 80% × 5 × 2 80% × AMRAP	70% × 3 80% × 3 85% × 3 × 2, then 2 or more sets of 2 >87%	65% × 3 70% × 3 75% × 3 80% × 3 85% × 3 × 2 85% × AMRAP	65% × 3 75% × 3 80% × 3 85% × 2 87% × 2 × 2, then 2 or more sets of 1 >90%	70% × 3 80% × 3 85% × 3 90% × 2 × 2 90% × AMRAP
3	67% × 5 72% × 5 78% × 5 83% × 5 × 3	67% × 5 72% × 5 78% × 3 83% × 2 Work up to 5RM	77% × 3 82% × 3 87% × 3, then 2 or more sets of 2 >90%	70% × 3 75% × 3 80% × 1 85% × 1 Work up to 3RM	80% × 3 85% × 2 87% × 2 90% × 2 × 2, then 2 or more sets of 1 >93%	70% × 3 80% × 3 85% × 3 90% × 2 Work up to 1RM
4	60% × 5 × 3	65% × 5 × 3	60% × 5 × 3	65% × 5 × 3	60% × 5 × 3	65% × 5 × 3

*AMRAP: As many reps as possible.

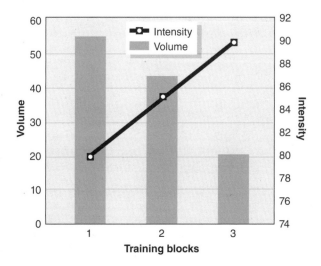

Figure 23.4 Volume and intensity through training blocks 1, 2 and 3.

conditioning coach can continue to guide from training observations.

The AMRAP (as many repetitions as possible) sets for the upper body in the first two weeks of the training block motivate the athlete to push the limits but with a load-controlled intensity. The athlete should not go to failure. There is no need to go to failure at this intensity range to make strength gains. In addition, going to failure could compromise technique and increase the potential for injury.

Every third week in all three blocks the athlete has an opportunity to be challenged by upper-body exercises to reach new levels for a prescribed repetition range. For lower-body exercises, the volume is less than for upper-body work. This difference accommodates for the volume of running or other on-feet activities the athlete may be undertaking. Opportunities to progress lower-body strength occur in blocks 2 and 3. A minimum prescription has been given to progress lower-body strength. However, the nature of the prescription then allows the athlete to push the intensity further if

it's required, if the athlete is directed to or if the athlete feels particularly good that day.

Other Prescription Guidelines

Exercise selection will determine the load, sets and repetitions. (See table 23.10 for guidelines.) The same general principles should be applied as the example given for maximal strength—increasing intensity and reducing volume through the training blocks. Any change in exercise technique due to load or repetition prescription needs to be addressed immediately and the appropriate alterations made.

In-Season Speed and Plyometric Training

Speed has a far greater direct link with running-based technical and skills-based training than do weight-room exercises. The type of speed qualities depends on the sport, the situation and the decision-making processes the athlete has to make in the field of play. Within the season, the primary analysis process the coach must undertake concerns determining the type of speed and plyometric training the athlete requires.

The foundations of speed and acceleration often are neglected in the technical arena; the speed of action often is practiced secondarily to the movement patterning involved in the technique or skill. The strength and conditioning coach needs to work closely with the sport coach to ensure the skill is practised as a whole or that there is an integrated plan developed by which speed and acceleration potential is developed concurrently whilst technical components are addressed by the sport coach.

Due to the amount of time spent on the feet performing tactical and technical training and competition in sports that require speed and power, the

Table 23.10 Exercise-Prescription Guide

	BLOCK 1		BLOCK 2		BLOCK 3	
	Sets × reps	Load	Sets × reps	Load	Sets × reps	Load
Explosive strength	3-7 × 3-5	Moderate	3-6 × 1-3	Moderate to heavy	3-8 × 1 or 2	Moderate to heavy
Assistance	3-5 × 8-15	Moderate	3-5 × 8-12	Moderate	3 × 5, 6, 10	Moderate
Technical accessory	3-5 × 8-15	Moderate	3-5 × 8-12	Moderate	3 × 5, 6, 10	Moderate

volume of speed and plyometric exercise should remain low. The amount of time allocated to strength and conditioning in a competitive week is low, so training needs to be prioritised effectively.

In the block-based approach, speed and plyometric training and exercises can be integrated into the previously described strength-training system. The example in table 23.11 illustrates a speed and plyometric integrated approach for a player of a field- or court-based sport (e.g. hockey, football, tennis) who has a significant volume of speed- and agility-based tactical and technical training.

In-Season Conditioning

The last physical variable to consider in the maintenance of in-season fitness is the athlete's conditioning. A competitive match provides a significant specific metabolic stimulus. In many instances, this stimulus once a week will be enough to maintain a level of conditioning. However, in order to improve, training must be performed in the subsequent week (table 23.12), predominantly in season, to tactically learn and progress to the next competitive event. Several factors need to be considered to ensure the optimal

conditioning dose is prescribed in subsequent weeks postcompetition:

- The competition may not have elicited a significant metabolic stimulus due to tactics or weather.
- The athlete may have had limited game time due to injury or being used as a replacement.
- The competition may have been extremely hard, surpassing workloads experienced.
- If the athlete has not competed, this may be an opportunity to increase the volume in speed or strength work based on presented physical limitations.

If athletes are playing at a high level and training consistently and regularly in the week, in most cases these athletes will be performing the appropriate amount of conditioning. An athlete who is not competing and is training only once or twice a week is likely not achieving the appropriate metabolic stimuli to maintain a conditioning edge. This athlete either needs to replace or top-up reduced playing time with sport-related fitness (SRF) or maximise the recovery opportunity to progress at other physical variables that are limiting.

Table 23.11 Sample In-Season Session Content Integrating Speed and Plyometrics

	Exercise classification	Block 1: Preparation	Block 2: Intensification	Block 3: Realization
Session 1	Critical	Back squat Push press Resisted accelerations and sprints	Back squat Jerk Accelerations and sprints	Back squat Jerk behind neck Resisted to unresisted accelerations and sprints
	Assistance	Step-up		
	Accessory	Hamstring and eccentric trunk series	Hamstring and eccentric trunk series	Hamstring and eccentric trunk series
Session 2	Critical			
	Assistance	Incline bench press Weighted pull-up	Narrow-grip bench press Bent-over row Lunge (variations)	Bench press Single-arm row Bulgarian split squat
	Accessory	Shoulder and neck series	Shoulder and neck series	Shoulder and neck series
Session 3	Critical	Box jump	Hurdle jump complex with squats	Drop jump complex with squats
	Assistance	Back squat (decrease load from session 1) Military press	Back squat Single-arm dumbbell press	Back squat Single-arm dumbbell push press
	Accessory	Single-arm row Rotational-trunk series	Weighted chin-up Rotational-trunk series	Bent-over row Rotational-trunk series

Table 23.12 Metabolic Loading Pattern in the Week

	Mon.	Tues.	Wed.	Thurs.	Fri.	Sat.	Sun.
Relative metabolic workload	Tactical and technical recovery: low	Tactical and technical: moderate	Tactical and technical: moderately high	Recovery: low	Tactical and technical: moderately low	Game: high	Recovery: low
Planned rating of perceived exertion (RPE) (1-10)	3	4	7	2	3 or 4	9 or 10	2
Volume	Moderate	Moderately high	Moderate	Low	Low	High	Low

Competing in the sport will provide a conditioning effect across several variables:

- Skills whilst fatigued
- Decision making whilst fatigued
- Repeat sprints of random work: rest intervals specific to scenario
- Specific speed qualities such as acceleration, deceleration and speed adjustments

The most effective way to top-up fitness is to perform conditioning through sport-related activities, which is often accomplished in team sports through small-sided games (SSG). Even when there are only 1 or 2 players, the coach can devise SRF drills that mimic the specific energy and neuromuscular demands involved in the game.

The volume of a top-up conditioning session should be low since the athlete will still have to be involved in other tactical and technical training. If the athlete is not involved on the competition day, this is the ideal time to perform SRF because the athlete will have the same recovery time as the rest of the team. If tactical and technical training provides some of the sport-related neuromuscular demands, top-ups can be performed purely for the energy system on a bike or rowing machine.

The development and maintenance of in-season conditioning is vital to ensure the athlete can perform the sport-related competition at the desired intensities. Just as important is the athlete's ability to recover from the competition and have the work capacity to perform training in the following week. In turn, increasing speed and strength qualities throughout the season and continuing tactical and technical development will increase the athlete's efficiency and effectiveness. This increased efficiency will allow the athlete to impose a conditioning edge on opponents and demonstrate consistent and improving performances.

Wisdom

Continuous improvement is one of the philosophies of the training process. Therefore, athletes must have a capacity to endure training and competition. This capacity is developed throughout the in-season through competition and the subsequent tactical and technical training and top-up sessions.

Summary

The principles of the interdependent training process framework are these:

- The technical model drives the direction of the strength and conditioning programme.
- There is a planned distribution of physical loading between strength and conditioning and technical training, which is manipulated depending on the goal.
- The strength and conditioning intervention either supports or potentiates the technical process, or it facilitates the recovery process.

To maintain an in-season conditioning edge, there has to be optimal, planned interactions between strength and conditioning training and sport training. Interaction helps ensure training is prioritised on performance goals, there is no duplication of training stimuli, the athlete's training loads are optimised and the athlete achieves the performance goals.

Mismanagement of the performance process and blind prescription of training with no regard for technical training can be catastrophic. Physical, technical and mental qualities will be affected adversely, and no strength and power edge will be observed.

Finally, maintaining an in-season conditioning edge is hard work. The athlete must have a relentless daily pursuit of excellence in his or her training, nutrition, recovery and lifestyle. The athlete's understanding of and ability to drive and own the training process should be evident throughout the season. Athletes who gain an in-season conditioning edge are not dependent on those around them but are independent and will continuously challenge themselves to improve.

CHAPTER 24

Recovering Effectively in High-Performance Sports

Christian J. Cook
UK Sport

Liam P. Kilduff
Exercise and Medicine Research Centre, Swansea University, Wales

Marc R. Jones
Scarlets Rugby, Wales

Elite athletes are in a cyclic state of adaptation and recovery from the stressors associated with training and competition. However, as athletes seek to optimise performance, sufficient recovery is sometimes overlooked as a way of increasing overload, intensity and volume. In addition to large training volumes, athletes may have to perform repeated high-intensity competition within several days and with limited recovery.

In its simplest terms, recovery is marked by the athlete's return to resting function and physical performance. Therefore, an imbalance between exercise and recovery can result in a fatigued state and a reduction in physical performance marked by either a decrease in force production or the perception that production of that same force feels more effortful. Clearly, recovering effectively is one of the most critical determinants of sport success.

Physiological stress results in a complex, multisystem response that involves the neuromuscular, endocrine and autonomic nervous systems. In an attempt to optimise recovery after training and competition, it is common practice to employ one or more postexercise recovery strategies.

The primary aim of this chapter is to examine the rationale for employing the most common postexercise recovery strategies. To understand how certain strategies may enhance recovery, we explore the characteristics of fatigue and recovery before presenting the rationale and evidence for using recovery strategies. We also discuss the potential contraindications to using recovery strategies. Finally, we introduce and explore the interaction between psychological and physiological recovery and the exciting prospects for athlete management that this new area opens up.

Physiological Characteristics of Fatigue and Recovery

In order to fully understand the dynamics between fatigue and recovery, it's important to get a clear understanding of the physiological characteristics of both fatigue and recovery.

Exercise-Induced Muscle Damage

Recovery may be determined by the extent of exercise-induced muscle damage (EIMD) experienced during exercise and the subsequent inflammation process. The mechanisms of EIMD may be mechanical, metabolic or oxidative, with the extent and relative contributions determined by the nature and volume of exercise. Initial damage to the muscle cell structure creates an inflammatory process and impairs the muscle's ability to contract effectively.

The extent of EIMD and its effect on subsequent performance is more pronounced in people who are not used to a given exercise stimulus, either the type of exercise or the volume. These people are more susceptible to experiencing delayed-onset muscle soreness (DOMS).[1] Although we believe that the repeated-bout effect (RBE) means that DOMS is somewhat protective, and there is more resistance to subsequent damage and soreness when the exercise session is repeated, we often still see the presence of EIMD or fatigue several days after competition even in elite athletes who have been exposed to these stresses multiple times previously.[2, 3]

EIMD produces the characteristic pain and tenderness within the muscle, decrease in muscular strength and power and increase in muscular stiffness, which reduces joint range of motion (ROM) and attenuated stretch reflex during stretch-shortening cycle (SSC) types of activities.[4]

Subjectively, DOMS is most often reported 24 to 48 hours postexercise, which may be explained by increased inflammation and secondary muscle damage. It has been widely demonstrated that the functional expression of power and strength are compromised for several days after exercise.[3, 4]

Strong correlations between functional recovery and blood markers of muscle damage (e.g., creatine kinase [CK]) indicate that these patterns of recovery partly depend on the extent of EIMD.[4] A loss in muscle function may result in compensatory neuromuscular alterations (e.g., altered kinematics, increased ground-contact times, reduced movement velocity).[4]

Potentially, EIMD may make an athlete work at a much higher intensity to maintain performance or cause unaccustomed strain on the compensating muscles, joints, ligaments and tendons, increasing the risk of injury. EIMD may impair oxygen kinetics and glycogen repletion, both of which can impair performance, especially in endurance and intermittent sports that rely on these metabolic outputs.[5, 6] The perception of these functional impairments has further implications for subsequent skill acquisition and injury susceptibility.[7]

Although EIMD and the ensuing inflammatory response may be responsible for an acute reduction in muscle function, this process appears to be necessary for the subsequent repair and adaptive remodelling of muscle tissue to also improve muscular function (figure 24.1).

Despite initiating events that elicit further muscle damage,[8] certain cells (e.g., macrophages) also secrete factors that enable repair and provide a structure for satellite cells to begin the formation of new myofibres, thus facilitating regeneration.[8]

Wisdom

Muscle damage is not always associated with classic DOMS or even obvious pain. It can restrict muscular function for 24 to 48 hours, and it means the athlete needs more effort to achieve the same outcome. It may be an important trigger for adaptation but comes at a metabolic cost.

Impact on the Autonomic Nervous System

Physical exercise causes an increase in sympathetic (fight or flight) activity, resulting in higher heart rates. The time needed to restore a pre-exercise autonomic nervous system (ANS) level has been shown to depend on exercise intensity and duration. High-intensity exercise reduces the autonomic activity for longer than does submaximal exercise; research suggests that EIMD and the subsequent inflammatory response may temporarily attenuate parasympathetic (rest and digest) reactivation.[9]

This is relevant because greater parasympathetic activity is usually associated with a better recovery state and readiness to perform. Therefore

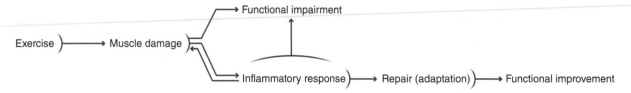

Figure 24.1 Summary of the adaptation process initiated by training.

ANS regulation is important in facilitating recovery, and parasympathetic reactivation is a useful indicator in monitoring the recovery status in elite athletes. This forms the basis of heart rate variability monitoring, which is discussed in more detail in chapter 6.

Hormones in Relation to Fatigue and Recovery

Hormones are chemical messengers, traditionally thought to facilitate protein synthesis and degradation after exercise. Two hormones in particular—testosterone and cortisol—have been researched in relation to fatigue and recovery.

Testosterone

Testosterone is a steroid hormone, anabolic (building) in nature, important in facilitating muscle hypertrophy and increasing muscle glycogen synthesis. It has more complex training roles outside of direct hypertrophy, however, with a direct role in regulating adaptive physiology and physical performance itself.[10] Testosterone is linked to muscular function and the cognitive processes that control movement. In individuals with relatively high strength levels, free testosterone is a strong individual predictor of the expression of strength and power qualities.[11] Furthermore, testosterone is important as a stress biomarker, and the testosterone responses to a challenge can provide information on dominance. Winning in sport competition is often accompanied by elevated testosterone concentrations relative to losing.[12]

Cortisol

Cortisol is catabolic (redistributive) in nature, increasing protein degradation in muscle and connective tissue and causing reductions in muscle protein synthesis, allowing energy to be redistributed. Hormones can be disrupted for several days after either competition or increases in training volume, with cortisol suggested to be most sensitive to change.[3, 13]

Hormones may help in the muscle restoration process, but an even more important role may be psychological. If a win or even a good performance is perceived as such, it results in a better psychological mood state and may influence recovery time.

Suppression of the Immune System

When athletes are engaged in heavy training or competition over a season, they may experience a chronically depressed immune function.[14] Individuals engaged in heavy training or competition programmes, particularly those involved in endurance events, appear to be more susceptible than normal to upper respiratory tract infection (URTI).[14]

Recovery demands will be different for sports. Recovery is a psychological as well as a physiological issue. Poor recovery results in either a reduction of muscular function or a greater effort required to produce the same function, which leads to accumulated debt. This accumulated debt leads to other vulnerabilities, including immune-function suppression.

Recovering Immediately After Training or Competition

The following section outlines the possible recovery modalities that could be used by practitioners immediately after training or competition (see tables 24.1 and 24.2).

Cold-Water Immersion (CWI)

The main rationale for immersing body parts in cold water is based on the effects of hydrostatic pressure and the cooling of body tissue.[15] When external pressure is applied to the body by immersion in water, removal of exudates (plasma) and inflammatory cells is enhanced, which may improve nutrient delivery to cells, enhance metabolic waste removal, improve contractile function and reduce secondary muscle damage.

Similarly, a reduction in skin temperature may also reduce the extent of inflammation, help reduce the perception of pain and aid in the recovery of muscular contractile function.[1, 15]

The orientation of the body, or body parts, in water is an important consideration. For a person immersed standing to the superior aspect of the iliac crest, the foot immersed at a depth of 1 metre has 981Pa extra pressure acting on it, whereas the hip (0.1 metre below the surface) has only an extra 98.1Pa.[15] Therefore, to maximise the effects of hydrostatic pressure, standing when immersed in water is recommended.

Overall, the literature findings examining CWI as a recovery tool are inconclusive. Some studies demonstrate no additional benefit when compared to passive recovery on the outcomes of pain, swelling and performance 24, 48 and 72 hours after unaccustomed eccentric loading.[16] However, Howatson and van Someren[17] stated that the temperatures used in these studies (5 ± 1°C) were too cold, possibly eliciting the hunting reaction. This phenomenon occurs when tissue temperature falls below 18°C, and there is periodic vasodilation and warming of the tissue, which may eliminate any potential benefits of CWI.

A meta-analysis of 14 studies by Leeder and colleagues[18] also found that CWI had little effect on recovery of strength (isometric and isokinetic knee extension or elbow flexion), but this approach was effective in improving the recovery rate of muscular power postexercise during more functional SSC activities. Furthermore, Halson[19] found that CWI had a greater effect on weight-bearing activity compared to a non-weight-bearing activity, which is more representative of the actual performance tests likely to be undertaken by elite athletes. Indeed, previous research has found that SSC-type activities are more sensitive to contractile failure after EIMD than concentric-only activities.[4] These data highlight some of the difficulties in determining the efficacy of recovery strategies (see tables 24.1 and 24.2) due to variation in

Table 24.1 Recovery Strategies Applied to Elite Athletes

Method	Sample protocols
Cold water immersion (CWI)	10°C-15°C, 1-15 min Single or multiple immersions (e.g., 2 x 5 min with 2 min seated rest at room temperature between immersions) Immerse part of body trained (i.e., lower body, immerse to anterior superior iliac spine; whole body, immerse to neck) Greater hydrostatic pressure to lower limbs when standing
Contrast water therapy (baths or showers)	1 or 2 min cold (8°C-15°C), 1 to 2 min hot (38°C-42°C) x 1-4 sets Minimal time between baths or showers Immerse part of body trained (i.e., lower body, immerse to anterior superior iliac spine; whole body, immerse to neck) Greater hydrostatic pressure to lower limbs when standing Alternate to finish on cold for more aggressive recovery; finish on hot for relaxation
Compression garments	Minimum 12 hr Apply to appropriate limbs Custom-fitted garments may have greatest effect
Whole-body cryotherapy (WBC)	Dependent on design of the chamber, e.g., two-stage chamber consists of one or two vestibules where the temperature -60°C (~30 sec) and a main chamber in which the temperature is maintained within the range -110°C to -160°C (1-3 min) Individual required to slow walk in chamber and remain in eye and voice contact with operators outside the cryochamber
Active recovery	Continuous 8-25 min e.g. light jogging (multidirectional, dynamic stretching), cycling (e.g. 80 to 100 rpm), cross-trainer Intensity ~65% $\dot{V}O_2$max Intervals e.g. 3 or 4 min moderate to fast, 3 to 4 min slow x 2 to 4 sets e.g. cycling (>100 rpm, 80-90 rpm) Intensity session average ~65% $\dot{V}O_2$max Tempo running: e.g., 6-12 x 12-15 sec at 70%-75% max speed (60-90 sec rest between reps) Pool recovery (continuous, intervals or combination): e.g., ~25 min consisting of low- intensity swimming, shallow water walking, jogging, stretching, games Intensity session average ~65% $\dot{V}O_2$max
Electrostimulation	Minimum 3 hr Applied to posterior aspect of both knees Pulse adjusted to width that is tolerable and produces visible dorsiflexion and plantarflexion
Occlusion	2 x 3 min each leg; 220 mm/Hg Supine position, cuff positioned around the proximal portion of the lower leg Opposite leg acts as recovery time between ischemic doses

Table 24.2 When Recovery Strategies May be Applied to Elite Athletes

Nutrition and hydration strategies should be sought from the athlete's nutritionist for all situations. It is assumed that athlete sleep is adequate.

Situation	Example strategy options
Post-exercise (>24 hr between exercise sessions)	Use one strategy alone or multiple strategies together (may be repeated hourly or next day): • Active recovery • Occlusion • Cold-eater immersion (CWI), contrast water therapy (CWT) or cryotherapy • Compression garments* • Electrostimulation
Postexercise (<24 hr between exercise sessions)	Use one strategy alone or multiple strategies together (may be repeated hourly or next day): • Active recovery • Occlusion • Compression garments* • Electrostimulation
During periods of development or adaptation	No applied recovery strategies

*Duration may be modulated according to intensity, soreness, or proximity of subsequent exercise.

study methodologies. Despite not showing evidence of enhanced function, data exist to show that 5 minutes of CWI may accelerate parasympathetic recovery 5 minutes[20] and 12 hours postintervention.[21]

CWI has some recovery benefits; however, these are not particularly temperature dependent insofar as cold tap water appears as efficacious as ice baths. As with all recovery modalities, though, care should be taken not to overadminister, as spurious use could potentially interfere with adaptive processes.

Hot and Contrast Water Therapy

Unlike CWI, hot water immersion (HWI) is thought to increase tissue temperature and local blood flow and enhance muscular elasticity, leading to local vasodilation, an increase in metabolite production and a reduction in muscle spasms.[22] In response to HWI, increases in blood flow and lymphatic function have the net effect of improving metabolism, nutrient delivery and waste removal from the cells.[15] However, increasing the permeability of these vessels may increase the inflammatory response by facilitating the influx of exudates and inflammatory cells into the interstitial space.[15]

Alternating time spent in hot and cold water, also known as contrast water therapy (CWT), can reduce oedema and enhance recovery. This method combines the properties of CWI and HWI to alternate the vasoconstrictor and vasodilator response of blood vessels to temperature changes.[2] Vaile, Gill

and Blazevich[23] demonstrated that CWT (8°C-10°C, 60 sec; 40°C-42°C, 120 sec × 5 sets) enhanced recovery compared to passive recovery (15 min seated) after an eccentric resistance exercise session (5 × 10 eccentric leg press). Data collected immediately, 24, 48 and 72 hours after recovery showed restored jump squat peak power and serum CK levels at 48 hours after CWT as opposed to passive recovery. CWT may also enhance parasympathetic reactivation after 60 minutes of high-intensity cycling,[24] which may help augment the recovery process.

Wisdom

Both HWI and CWT may potentially be contraindicated in hard-contact sports and theoretically may increase bruising. Whether this occurs or not is unknown; however, given current evidence that cold water immersion on its own is equally effective to CWT or HWI, our recommendation for contact sports is to be conservative.

Compression Garments

Compression garments are becoming increasingly widespread as a recovery aid within sports and exercise. Typically, these garments are elastic, body-moulded suits with an engineered compression gradient that can be worn as an upper-, lower- or full-body piece. Compression garments are proposed to enhance muscular recovery by exerting pressure on the covered limbs to improve blood flow and reduce inflammation, possibly via mechanisms similar to hydrostatic pressure from water immersion.

Although garments are commercially available in varying sizes, it has been questioned whether these products can exert enough pressure to be effective for each individual due to widespread differences in leg dimensions and tissue structure within a population.[25] Nevertheless, some studies have reported beneficial effects in terms of reducing EIMD and perceived muscular soreness and restoring exercise performance.[26] The use of compression garments (and other recovery strategies) may further create a positive placebo effect on an athlete's perception of muscular soreness and functional recovery. Although compression garments may constitute a small component of the overall recovery strategy, they should not form the central plank of it.

Whole-Body Cryotherapy (WBC)

Whole-body cryotherapy (WBC) has been predominantly applied and researched within clinical settings for inflammatory conditions such as swelling and acute, localised pain. However, WBC may also be a means of accelerating postexercise recovery.

Research has shown health benefits after exposure to very cold air (e.g. –110°C).[27] A single exposure has been shown to alter hormonal profiles in men[28] and increase antioxidant defence system activity.[29] Furthermore, data exists to suggest repeated exposures may enhance motor performance[30] and anaerobic capacity[31] and increase levels of white blood cells[32] and antiinflammatory cytokines (e.g., IL-10) whilst decreasing proinflammatory cytokines (IL-2, Il-8).[33]

However, limited research has been performed after exercise using WBC, largely due to the expense and limited availability of cryochamber facilities, which consequently explains why WBC is used by few athletes at present. Mechanisms for enhanced recovery are likely to be related to vasoconstriction and a reduction in nervous activity.

After a single simulated trial race, WBC (3 min at –110°C) was shown to restrict the inflammatory response compared to that of a passive recovery group.[27] Levels of C-reactive protein (CRP) significantly increased in both groups 24 hours postexercise; however, levels in the WBC groups

returned to pre-exercise 48 hours post whilst CRP levels in the passive group remained elevated at 96 hours. It may also be beneficial to enhance the recovery of muscular strength and perceived pain after competition.[34]

Research also suggests that a week of daily WBC sessions after training reduced markers of muscle damage and proinflammatory cytokines compared to a passive recovery group in an international Rugby Union team.[33]

Active Recovery

Performing low-intensity exercise after intense exercise may enhance recovery by inducing a pumping effect. Repetitive mechanical squeezing by the muscles during contraction and relaxation may increase blood flow and improve ROM, which may increase the translocation and removal of markers of inflammation and metabolites, such as lactate, from the muscle.[2]

Active recovery is commonly used when several hours separate exercise sessions. Anaerobic exercise increases lactic acid concentration within the working muscle, leading to fatigue and a reduction in force or power output. Therefore, the ability to remove lactate and H^+ from the muscle after exercise is important where time between sessions is limited and an improved oxygen supply may enhance clearance. Even though it seems that continuous moderate-intensity exercise is more effective than passive recovery, a combination of high intensity (65%$\dot{V}O_2$max) and low intensity (35%$\dot{V}O_2$max) is no more beneficial than a recovery of low intensity (35%$\dot{V}O_2$max).[35] As little as 20 minutes of low-intensity active recovery produced better recovery outcomes several days later.[2] Given the ease of such application, incorporating this simple procedure into recovery menus is recommended.

Active recovery may be performed in various ways; however, performing an active-recovery session immersed in water may provide the added effects of buoyancy, hydrostatic pressure and parasympathetic reactivation, which may enhance recovery. Furthermore, activities such as deep-water running and water aerobics are convenient methods of recovery due to the non-weight-bearing nature of activity, thus avoiding exacerbation of soft-tissue injury whilst providing active recovery.

Recovering Effectively in High-Performance Sports

Electrostimulation

Electrostimulation may be an effective treatment in enhancing recovery after exercise despite little research on its effectiveness having been done. In this treatment, electrodes are positioned on the posterior aspect of the knee to stimulate the lower limb musculature and enhance blood flow. Beaven and colleagues[36] showed that when wearing the electrodes with compression garments, rugby players perceived improved recovery after training compared to wearing compression garments alone. Furthermore, the combination of methods was shown to be more effective in attenuating increases in CK after competition compared to compression garments alone.[36] Electrostimulation in isolation has recently been shown to enhance recovery of function 24 hours after a simulated team circuit to an extent similar to a CWT treatment.[37]

Occlusion

Brief, repeated periods of occlusion followed by reperfusion have previously been shown to mitigate the injurious effects of prolonged ischemia in cardiac muscles as well as attenuate other cellular damage.

Recent research suggests that occlusion may enhance recovery after a high-intensity exercise protocol. After 2 sets of 3-minute lower-limb occlusions of each leg at 220 mmHg, various markers of power displayed improved recovery 24 hours after exercise when compared to a condition when 15 mmHg compression was applied.[38] Although the mechanisms are unclear, the authors propose that the cycles of ischemia and reperfusion may enhance blood flow, thereby increasing muscular oxygenation, vasodilation, and oxygen delivery.

Sleep

Sleep is a basic requirement for human health due to its physiological and psychological restorative effects. During sleep, the highest concentrations of growth hormones, which play a significant anabolic role in skeletal-muscle growth, are observed. Sleep is a vital component of an athlete's recovery and preparation. It may be the single most efficacious recovery strategy after exercise in elite athletes.[19] Despite this, athletes often suffer from sleep deprivation, especially after evening competition.[39]

Sleep should be stressed as contributing an important role in muscular recovery.

The regenerative effects of sleep are not limited to muscular function, however. Sleep is also an important regulator of central nervous system and cognitive functions. Simply lengthening the total hours slept each night had a marked effect on athletic performance in basketball players.[40]

Sleep deprivation reduces anabolic hormone and increases catabolic hormone concentrations. It also inhibits restoration by increasing inflammation and sympathetic nervous system activity, leading to impairments in strength and power production, muscle glycogen repletion and cognitive function. Sleep deprivation can result in a loss of high-level sport skill and a decrease in voluntarily chosen workload, both of which may be viewed as important recovery features.[41, 42]

Following a shortened night's sleep, however, cognitive and motor performance has been shown to be enhanced by a short nap,[43] which has important implications for the athlete struggling to sleep due to a variety of reasons (e.g., anxiety about performing, young children at home, travelling).

Wisdom

Educate athletes to make the bedroom the sleep room. The bedroom should be used only to sleep in, not also to study in or watch TV. The room should be kept dark (e.g., blackout blinds), quiet (or with white noise) and at a comfortable temperature.

Nutrition and Hydration

Dietary antioxidants have been proposed to enhance recovery by reducing the extent of inflammation and secondary muscle damage. The supplementation of polyphenols in preparation for and recovery from training and competition is becoming more prevalent, but their efficacy as antioxidants depends on the specific foods they are sourced from.[44] Some of the highest antioxidant and antiinflammatory properties have been identified in tart cherries.[45] Consumption of approximately 45 cherries per day has been shown to reduce circulating concentrations of inflammatory markers in healthy men and women; however, supplementation of tart cherry juice is a more efficient and economical alternative.

After a period of supplementation, tart cherry juice has been shown to reduce the extent of muscle damage, improve recovery of function and alleviate the sensation of pain after a session of eccentric elbow-flexion contractions.[45] Furthermore, a period of supplementation has been shown to increase total antioxidative capacity and enhance recovery after a marathon run.[46]

Nonsteroidal antiinflammatory drugs (NSAIDs) such as ibuprofen and aspirin are common ergogenic means proposed to reduce EIMD in sports.[47] Ibuprofen (2,400 mg) taken before and after eccentric arm exercise has been shown to reduce CK appearance in the blood, indicating reduced muscle damage.[48]

Various nutritional strategies are available to maintain immune function and avoid infection, including probiotics, colostrum, herbals (e.g., echinacea, ginseng, kaloba), glutamine and zinc lozenges; however, there is no strong evidence to suggest that any of these are of added benefit in preventing exercise-induced immune depression.[14]

Maintaining hydration status is also important for performance and recovery. The use of rehydration strategies after exercise should be considered for providing a favourable hormonal environment for adaptation and facilitating preparation for the next session. For example, based on research by Shirreffs and colleagues,[49] it is easy to calculate the required fluid volume to rehydrate by weighing the athlete pre- and postexercise. Required fluid intake should be (pre-exercise weight – postexercise weight) × 1.5. Consideration should be given to electrolyte content of postexercise beverages and nutrition, which may be prescribed according to individual needs.

Soft-Tissue and Manual Therapies

Massage, foam rolling, acupuncture and other manipulations (e.g., osteopath, chiropractic) may all have recovery benefits, and these are anecdotally reported. Individuality in recovery is an important feature, and people do respond differently when it comes to healing-hand modalities. There may be a large psychological component to these interventions that should not be underestimated as a potent recovery strategy.

Psychological Recovery Postexercise

In addition to physiological recovery, psychological recovery should be an integral component for consideration.

Fatigue after training and competition may be associated with changes in behaviour,[50] reduced motivation, disturbed mood and increased perceived soreness.[51] If insufficient recovery occurs, symptoms may be observable and detected before the athlete reaches a condition of overtraining. To detect the onset of these symptoms, monitoring psychometric variables has been suggested as an efficient means of monitoring both overtraining and recovery.[52]

The psychological symptoms of overtraining may include depressed mood, general apathy, decreased self-esteem, emotional instability, impaired performance, restlessness, irritability and disturbed sleep.

Relationship Between Psychological and Physiological Parameters

Physiological functions may be somewhat determined by the psychological response to a stressor. The psychological perception of benefit appears both additive and subtractive to any measured physiological change.[53] For example, watching video clips can change male testosterone concentration and influence subsequent exercise performance in both nonathletes and athletes.[54, 55] Athlete testosterone levels increased after the athletes viewed aggressive training clips; this correlated to an improvement in subsequent 3RM squat (r = 0.85, p < 0.001) when compared to a control condition when no video was shown.[55]

Research has shown that viewing footage showing player success with positive coaching feedback increased testosterone and lowered cortisol responses compared with viewing footage of player failure and negative coaching feedback in Rugby Union.[56] Furthermore, these changes in hormone response were associated with better key performance indicators during competition.[56]

Strategies to Enhance Psychological Recovery in Sport

Perceptions of—and the emotions associated with—stress, including feelings of depression and anger, negatively affected wound healing through psychoneuroimmunological pathways.[57] The physiological responses of elite athletes may exhibit a degree of plasticity that can be influenced by prior exposure to stressful events or perceptions of those events.[56] The use of relatively simple psychological recovery interventions, with specific relevance to that event, may modify the free hormonal state of the athlete, which in turn may influence subsequent recovery and performance. For example, the postgame presentation of player-specific video footage appears to influence the free hormonal state of rugby players and their game performance several days later.[56] This is a clear indication of the multidimensional nature of recovery and how the process can be attacked down many avenues and affected by many members of the coaching and performance-support team.

A recent paper by Cook and Beaven[53] suggests that psychological perception and physiological change summate (or, more importantly, can act in opposition) in terms of recovery outcome. Their study using elite rugby players found that the degree of body temperature normalisation after exercise and a cool immersion predicted recovery outcomes but was confounded by the psychological perception of the treatment: If temperature declined, but players reported not enjoying the procedure, recovery was less than predicted by the temperature change itself. This opens up an exciting avenue around psychological recovery and its influence on physical expression.

Wisdom

Stress on an athlete is the sum total of his or her life, not just what occurs in training and competition. This understanding needs recognition and accounting for. Psychological and physiological components interweave, and this quality is an essential point of attack for recovery.

Impact of Recovery Strategies on Training Adaptation

The following section outlines the physiological rationale that questions the use of certain recovery modalities during periods of adaptation. These modalities need to be considered due to their potential to interfere with the adaptation process.

Multiple Periods of Activity Performed Within One or on Consecutive Days

Repeated exercise performance in the heat may be improved when a short period of CWI is applied between exercise sessions.[58] However, when multiple competitive sessions are performed on the same day, evidence exists to suggest that the use of cold-water immersion after one session may impair performance in the next.[59]

Tissue cooling stimulates inhibitory cells that regulate the impulse of pain perception to the central nervous system. However, tissue cooling may also decrease the rate of transmission along neurons by decreasing the production of vital neurotransmitters such as acetylcholine. Reduction in neural transmission would therefore decrease muscular contractile speed and force generating ability, which may inhibit subsequent performance.[15] A decrease in heart rate after CWI may also decrease cardiac output and arterial blood pressure, thus decreasing blood flow to the prime-mover muscles, which may also impair performance.

Enhanced parasympathetic activity after CWI[20] may inhibit cardio-acceleration from exercise onset, compromising the attainment of peak heart rate and possibly reducing cardiac output and oxygen delivery. This process may increase blood lactate accumulation and oxygen deficit.[59]

Potential Attenuation of Adaptation After Exercise

Reducing the extent of EIMD and thus inflammation by means of postexercise recovery strategies may have important implications for training adaptations. For example, Yamane and collegues[60] explained that the myofibre microdamages and cellular and humoral events induced by endurance and strength training are preconditions not only for repair processes, such as myofibre regeneration, but also for the adaptive processes leading to improved muscular performance. In particular, they noted satellite cell proliferation and recruitment as the basis of myofibre hypertrophy and increased capillary supply. By reducing the extent of muscle damage postexercise, the stimulation and proliferation of satellite cells are reduced; this interferes with the regenerative processes and 'thus retard[s] rather than support[s] the desired improvement of muscular performance'.[60]

Although equivocal evidence exists, literature does exist to support the hypothesis that attenuating the inflammatory process associated with muscle damage (using a variety of recovery strategies) may inhibit the stimulus for adaptive physiology.[60] To assist in the development of best practices for both recovery and training, further research is needed with particular attention to elite athletes under normal training and in particular with measurement in competitive conditions.

Implementing a Recovery Programme in the National Basketball Association (NBA)

Mark Simpson
Applied Sports Scientist,
Oklahoma City Thunder

The physical, mental and emotional demands placed on NBA players are extraordinarily high, but at the same time, the ability to implement optimal recovery strategies is highly compromised. This presents significant challenges since the potential for injury, burnout and underperformance is high.

The challenges faced by NBA players include the following:

- Fixture load. Many teams play more than 90 games in a season. Often, games are played on consecutive days, and teams may have four games in a week.

- Travel. During the regular season, most teams have close to 70 flights, many of which take off between the hours of 11:00 p.m. and 2:00 a.m. When on the road, players have limited access to recovery facilities and equipment.

- Nutrition. Good food choices on the road can be limited, and the lure of convenience food can be strong.

- Outside demands. Players are in high demand by the media and sponsors, and social pressures to go out at night constantly compete with best-practice recovery programmes.

The first place to start when designing recovery programmes in this environment is to base strategies on an understanding of the physical loads each player encounters. We consider both acute loadings (over the last 2 or 3 days) as well as the cumulative loads to that point in a season. We also consider the summation of the types of loading, from the weight room, to the practice court, to games. We developed a bespoke system to track these overall loads. One part of this system involves the use of an inertial measurement unit (accelerometer) to track mechanical loads on the court.

I've found that one of the frequently cited drawbacks of cold-water immersion (CWI)—that CWI attenuates the adaptive response—is not as applicable during an NBA season when the players are well trained. Accordingly, we implement a CWI strategy that involves 10 to 15 minutes in a cold plunge set at 50 degrees F (10°C).

It's important to be pragmatic when choosing the interventions to implement. Sustainability and manageability are high on my priority list. We've found that the more complicated the strategy is, the less well performed it is. As such, we favour a programme that involves few modalities and requiring limited staff input and technology: sleep, nutrition, CWI and contrast-therapy interventions. Incorporating soft-tissue therapy and electrostimulation for all players after all games, for instance, would be unsustainable for many NBA programmes.

Given all the constraints in the NBA, it is simply not possible to implement the kind of all-round strategy that might be found in an individual physiological sport, such as what was present when I worked with the British cycling team. A pragmatic approach is to ensure that the aspects with the biggest impact are prioritised. My experience, consistent with the overwhelming evidence, is that sleep and nutrition are the two most critical elements of the recovery process. Therefore, much of our energy is directed towards these two areas. Both these types of recovery are similar: Players need to receive ongoing tailored education to help inform their daily decisions. Also, it is wise to facilitate good practice by doing such things as providing good food and liaising with hotels regarding the location, size and temperature of player rooms. As an example, we will ensure player rooms are in quiet locations, not on the roadside or near elevators or doors.

It's important to have a bespoke strategy for each player. Just as athletes benefit from an individualised training programme, they also benefit from an individualised recovery programme. I find out what the player's

Mark Simpson is the applied sport scientist for the Oklahoma City Thunder in the National Basketball Association (NBA). He was lead strength and conditioning coach for the northwest region of the English Institute of Sport (EIS) and head of strength and conditioning for the British Cycling Team. He has worked with Olympic gold medalists and world record holders, including Sir Chris Hoy, Victoria Pendleton, and Sir Bradley Wiggins. He also has consulted extensively on sport science and strength and conditioning with teams in the English Premier League and England's rugby and cricket teams.

specific recovery preferences are by talking to him and observing him. An example of an area in which there are varying preferences is with CWI, mainly varying tolerance of cold. For a player with a low tolerance to cold water, it is worthwhile considering a substitute modality, such as a cold compression device. Furthermore, I continually engage the player and provide positive reinforcement when the opportunity presents, which leads to a greater level of compliance.

It's important for us that our recovery strategy is a holistic one, taking into account physical loading stress and off-court demands. Travel, media and lifestyle demands can be high in the NBA. To this end, our strategy considers the fact that many aspects of psychological and physiological recovery are intertwined. The length and intensity of an NBA season can often cause players to experience emotional and mental fatigue. Facilitating opportunities for players to mentally switch off and recuperate is key. In some instances, this might be by allowing them to do things that might otherwise be contraindicated, such as watching movies on late-night flights. A positive mood state also can be affected simply by the way you interact with players during practices and lifting sessions and after games. This is when a practitioner must draw on his or her interpersonal skills and emotional intelligence

The sample recovery process between two road games explained here illustrates the standard recovery players experience. Further modalities can be introduced as required, based on player circumstances. This is the process after the game ends:

- Immediate hydration with carbohydrate-electrolyte solution (fluid consumption remains a priority throughout the rest of the evening)
- CWI strategy or cold compression device within 10 minutes
- Compression tights worn
- Postgame meal
- Physical and psychological rest and relaxation on coach and then plane (both environments dimly lit, quiet and temperature regulated)
- Further meal and nutrition on plane
- Personal sleep hygiene routine immediately on hotel arrival (may include eye masks and ear plugs)
- At least 8 hours in bed
- Early-morning recovery questionnaire
- Breakfast
- Light early-morning practice in the form of a team shoot-around, followed by assisted lower-body passive stretching
- Lunch
- Structured mid-afternoon nap
- Game build-up begins

During periods of adaptation, it may be appropriate for the use of recovery strategies to be limited to hydration and nutritional strategies with an emphasis on good general management practices, including adequate sleep and rest.

Strategy Adaptation

It is possible that the positive effects of a postexercise recovery strategy could be blunted if the strategies employed are not varied. For example, it has been demonstrated that people can become cold acclimated if subjected to daily CWI even though adaptations are reversed after 2 weeks with no immersions.[61] Therefore, varying cold-water strategies and using them periodically with other strategies in an attempt to accelerate recovery is a suggested approach. However, further research in a variety of settings is required before we can be categorically certain regarding the periodisation of recovery strategies.

Individual Variation

Practitioners should be wary of individualised responses to a stressor. Research shows an individualised nature of recovery after contact sports, suggesting that recovery and subsequent training should be individually prescribed.[51] Effective monitoring procedures should be established to determine expected recovery patterns—and how these may vary according to performance—and to identify athletes who may require altered recovery or training provision.

The variable response to postexercise strategies should also be considered. The interactions between psychological and physiological recovery as described previously would suggest a rationale for the application of recovery strategies aimed at enhancing physiological functions that are perceived to reduce pain, soreness and fatigue. It would also be pertinent for practitioners to monitor individual responses to the recovery strategies that seek to enhance psychological recovery.

Summary

Despite the mechanisms underlying each method remaining unclear, evidence exists to suggest that various strategies used postexercise may attenuate the extent of fatigue and enhance recovery. Furthermore, we are now beginning to appreciate that physiological and psychological recovery may be intertwined. An individual's perception of a stressor may also have a great influence on subsequent physiological recovery and readiness to train or compete.

Various recovery strategies have been discussed in the chapter; however, at present no gold-standard recovery strategy or combinations of strategies exist.

When identifying the best recovery protocols to use, consider the practicalities of using each method. For example, the use of water-immersion techniques may not be practical when a group of 20 athletes are changing within a confined space with limited wet-floor space. Instead, strategies such as active recovery, compression garments, occlusion and electrostimulation could be used in combination or alone, with support of good nutritional and lifestyle choices. Modification of strategies may also be necessary according to the situation (e.g., facilities, athlete number, logistics, travel). Be alert to the potential means of enhancing recovery and be both proactive and reactive in their provision.

After certain sessions and periods during the season, consideration should be given to whether certain recovery strategies or indeed any strategies should be implemented. Strategies that seek to reduce muscle damage and inflammation may attenuate adaptation to a training stimulus. Therefore, the application of certain recovery strategies may depend on the training or competition phase the athlete is in. Furthermore, some recovery strategies may induce short-term impairment to subsequent performance. The nature of exercise and recovery, and subsequent rationale for using a particular strategy, should be considered before implementing a recovery strategy.

Effective monitoring and evaluation procedures should be established to determine the expected recovery patterns after exercise and recovery responses across athletes to exercise and postexercise recovery strategies (subjective and objective). This kind of monitoring and evaluation may then enable postexercise recovery strategies to be individualised.

This chapter has discussed the use of strategies to enhance recovery for subsequent exercise. However, it should be recognised that strategies are only part of the recovery process. The importance of good lifestyle and nutrition choices and a well-managed training load should not be undervalued when facilitating athlete recovery.

From the evidence provided, we propose that managing the elite athlete in terms of recovery requires knowledge of what is needed during the season, the athlete's development and his or her overall lifestyle and how to balance these realities against continuing to enhance gains relative to this period of training or competition.

References

Chapter 1

1. Hill, A. 1927. *Muscular Movement in Man: The Factors Governing Speed and Recovery From Fatigue*. New York: McGraw-Hill.
2. Hopkins, W. 2012. Retrieved from http://sportsci.org/resource/stats/xrely.xls.
3. Hopkins, W.G., S.W. Marshall, A.M. Batterham, and J. Hanin. 2009. Progressive statistics for studies in sports medicine and exercise science. *Medicine and Science in Sports and Exercise,* 41(1): 3-13.
4. Hopkins, W. 2012. Retrieved from http://sportsci.org/resource/stats/xvalid.xls.
5. Hopkins, W. 2004. How to interpret changes in an athletic performance test. *Sportscience,* 88: 1-7.
6. Gentles, J.A. 2012. Reducing injuries is not enough: It also helps to win. *Medicine and Science in Sports and Exercise,* 44(5): S599.
7. Hopkins, W., J. Hawley, and L. Burke. 1999. Design and analysis of research on sport performance enhancement. *Medicine and Science in Sports and Exercise,* 31(3): 472-485.
8. Pettitt, R. 2010. The standard difference score: A new statistic for evaluating strength and conditioning programs. *Journal of Strength and Conditioning Research,* 24(1): 287-291.
9. Buchheit, M., A. Mendez-Villanueva, G. Delhomel, M. Brughelli, and S. Ahmaidi. 2010. Improving repeated sprint ability in young elite soccer players: Repeated shuttle sprints vs. explosive strength training. *Journal of Strength and Conditioning Research,* 24(10): 2715-2722.
10. Chelly, M.S., S. Hermassi, and R.J. Shephard. 2010. Relationships between power and strength of the upper and lower limb muscles and throwing velocity in male handball players. *Journal of Strength and Conditioning Research,* 24(6): 1480-1487.
11. Sheppard, J.M., and W. Young. 2006. Agility literature review: Classifications, training and testing. *Journal of Sport Sciences,* 24(9): 919-932.
12. Jullien, H., C. Bisch, N. Largouet, C. Manouvrier, C.J. Carling, and V. Amiard. 2008. Does a short period of lower limb strength training improve performance in field-based tests of running and agility in young professional soccer players? *Journal of Strength and Conditioning Research,* 22(2): 404-411.
13. Szymanski, D., J.M. Szymanski, R.L. Schade, T.J. Bradford, J.S. McIntyre, C. DeRenne, and N.H. Madsen. 2010. The relation between anthropometric and physiological variables and bat velocity of high-school baseball players before and after 12 weeks of training. *Journal of Strength and Conditioning Research,* 24(11): 2933-2943.
14. Young, W., and D.A. Rath. 2011. Enhancing foot velocity in football kicking: The role of strength training. *Journal of Strength and Conditioning Research,* 25(2): 561-566.
15. McEvoy, K.P., and R.U. Newton. 1998. Baseball throwing speed and base running speed: The effects of ballistic resistance training. *Journal of Strength and Conditioning Research,* 12(4): 216-221.
16. Olsen, P.D., and W.G. Hopkins. 2003. The effect of attempted ballistic training on the force and speed of movements. *Journal of Strength and Conditioning Research,* 17(2): 291-298.
17. Stone, M.H., K. Sanborn, H.S. O'Bryant, M. Hartman, M.E. Stone, C. Proulx, B. Ward, and J. Hruby. 2003. Maximum strength-power-performance relationships in collegiate throwers. *Journal of Strength and Conditioning Research,* 17(4): 739-745.
18. Baker, D., and R.U. Newton. 2006. Adaptations in upper-body maximal strength and power output resulting from long-term resistance training in experienced strength-power athletes. *Journal of Strength and Conditioning Research,* 20(3): 541-546.
19. Hoffman, J., N.A. Ratamess, and J. Kang. 2011. Performance changes during a college playing career in NCAA division III football athletes. *Journal of Strength and Conditioning Research,* 25(9): 2351-2357.
20. Gabbett, T.J., J. Kelly, and T. Pezet. 2007. Relationship between physical fitness and playing ability in rugby league players. *Journal of Strength and Conditioning Research,* 21(4): 1126-1133.
21. Sawyer, D.T., J. Z. Ostarello, E.A. Suess, and M. Dempsey, M. 2002. Relationship between football playing ability and selected performance measures. *Journal of Strength and Conditioning Research,* 16(4): 611-616.
22. Kuzmits, F., and A.J. Adams. 2008. The NFL combine: Does it predict performance in the National Football League? *Journal of Strength and Conditioning Research,* 22(6): 1721-1727.
23. Leary, B.K., J. Statler, B. Hopkins, R. Fitzwater, T. Kesling, J. Lyon, B. Phillips, R.W. Bryner, P. Cormie, and G.G. Haff. 2012. The relationship between isometric force-time curve characteristics and

club head speed in recreational golfers. *Journal of Strength and Conditioning Research,* 26(10): 2685-2697.

24. Kinugasa, T., E. Cerin, and S. Hooper. 2004. Single-subject research designs and data analyses for assessing elite athletes' conditioning. *Sports Medicine,* 34(15): 1035-1050.

25. Zatsiorsky, V., and W.J. Kraemer. 2006. *Science and Practice of Strength Training.* 2nd ed. Champaign: Human Kinetics.

Chapter 2

1. Beunen, G.P., and R.M. Malina. 2008. Growth and biologic maturation: Relevance to athletic performance. In H. Hebestreit and O. Bar-Or (eds.), *The Child and Adolescent Athlete* (pp. 3-17). Oxford: Blackwell.

2. Malina, R.M., C. Bouchard, and O. Bar-Or. 2004. *Growth, Maturation, and Physical Activity.* Champaign: Human Kinetics.

3. Viru, A., J. Loko, M. Harro, A. Volver, L. Laaneaots, and M. Viru. 1999. Critical periods in the development of performance capacity during childhood and adolescence. *European Journal of Physical Education,* 4(1): 75-119.

4. Kraemer, W.J., A.C. Fry, P.N. Frykman, B. Conroy, and J. Hoffman. 1989. Resistance training and youth. *Pediatric Exercise Science,* 1(4): 336-350.

5. Rogol, A.D., P.A. Clark, and J.N. Roemmich. 2000. Growth and pubertal development in children and adolescents: Effects of diet and physical activity. *American Journal of Clinical Nutrition,* 72(2): S521-S528.

6. Philippaerts, R.M., R. Vaeyens, M. Janssens, B. Van Renterghem, D. Matthys, R. Craen, J. Bourgois, J. Vrijens, G.P. Beunen, and R.M. Malina. 2006. The relationship between peak height velocity and physical performance in youth soccer players. *Journal of Sports Sciences,* 24(3): 221-230.

7. Kaneshia, H., T. Abe, and T. Fukunaga. 2003. Growth trends of dynamic strength in adolescent boys: A 2-year follow-up survey. *Journal of Sports Medicine and Physical Fitness,* 43(4): 459-464.

8. Naughton, G., L. Farpour, J. Carlson, M. Bradney, and E. Van Praagh. 2000. Physiological issues surrounding the performance of adolescent athletes. *Sports Medicine,* 30(5): 309-325.

9. Beunen, G.P. 1997. Muscular strength development in children and adolescents. In K. Froberg, O. Lammert, H.S. Hansen and C.J.R. Blimkie (eds.), *Children and Exercise XVIII: Exercise and Fitness: Benefits and Risks* (pp. 193-207). Odense: Odense University Press.

10. Baxter-Jones, A.D.G., J.C. Eisenmann, and L.B. Sherar. 2005. Controlling for maturation in pediatric exercise science. *Pediatric Exercise Science,* 17(1): 18-30.

11. Mirwald, R.L., A.D.G. Baxter-Jones, D.A. Bailey, and G.P. Beunen. 2002. An assessment of maturity from anthropometric measurements. *Medicine and Science in Sports and Exercise,* 34(4): 689-694.

12. Lloyd, R.S., and J.L. Oliver. 2012. The Youth Physical Development model: A new approach to long-term athletic development. *Strength and Conditioning Journal,* 34(3): 37-43.

13. Balyi, I., and A. Hamilton. 2004. *Long-Term Athlete Development: Trainability in Childhood and Adolescence: Windows of Opportunity: Optimal Trainability.* Victoria: National Coaching Institute British Columbia & Advanced Training and Performance.

14. Ford, P.A., M.B.A. De Ste Croix, R. Lloyd, R. Meyers, M. Moosavi, J. Oliver, K. Till, and C.A. Williams. 2011. Critical review of the Long-Term Athlete Development model: Physiological evidence and application. *Journal of Sports Sciences,* 29(4): 389-402.

15. Lubans, D.R., P.J. Morgan, D.P. Cliff, L.M. Barnett, and A.D. Okely. 2010. Fundamental movement skills in children and adolescents. *Sports Medicine,* 40(12): 1019-1035.

16. Auvinen, J.P., T.H. Tammelin, S.P. Taimela, P.J. Zitting, P.O. Mutanen, and J.I. Karppinen. 2008. Musculoskeletal pains in relation to different sport and exercise activities in youth. *Medicine and Science in Sports and Exercise,* 40(11): 1890-1900.

17. Moody, J., F. Naclerio, P. Green, and R.S. Lloyd. 2013. Motor skill development in youths. In R.S. Lloyd and J.L. Oliver (eds.), *Strength and Conditioning for Young Athletes: Science and Application* (pp. 49-65). Oxon: Routledge.

18. Lloyd, R.S., J.L. Oliver, R.W. Meyers, J. Moody, and M.H. Stone. 2012. Long-term athletic development and its application to youth weightlifting. *Strength and Conditioning Journal,* 34(4): 55-66.

19. Lloyd, R.S., J.L. Oliver, R.W. Meyers, P. Read, I. Jeffreys, and S. Nimphius. 2013. The natural development and trainability of agility during childhood. *Strength and Conditioning Journal,* 35(3): 2-11.

20. Oliver, J.L., R.S. Lloyd, and M. Rumpf. 2013. The natural development and trainability of sprint ability during childhood. *Strength and Conditioning Journal,* 35(3): 42-48.

21. Lloyd, R.S., J.L. Oliver, and R.W. Meyers. 2011. The natural development and trainability of plyometric ability during childhood. *Strength and Conditioning Journal,* 33(2): 23-32.

22. Lloyd, R.S., A.D. Faigenbaum, G.D. Myer, M.H. Stone, J.L. Oliver, I. Jeffreys, J. Moody, C. Brewer, and K. Pierce. 2012. UKSCA position statement: Youth resistance training. *Professional Strength and Conditioning Journal,* 26: 26-39.

23. Faigenbaum, A.D., W.J. Kraemer, C.J. Blimkie, I. Jeffreys, L.J. Micheli, M. Nitka, and T.W. Rowland. 2009. Youth resistance training: Updated position statement paper from the National Strength and Conditioning Association. *Journal of Strength and Conditioning Research*, 15: 459-465.

24. Behringer, M., A. vom Heede, M. Matthews, and J. Mester. 2011. Effects of strength training on motor performance skills in children and adolescents: A meta-analysis. *Pediatric Exercise Science*, 23(2): 186-206.

25. Baker, D. 2013. 10-year changes in upper body strength and power in elite professional rugby league players: The effect of training age, stage, and content. *Journal of Strength and Conditioning Research*, 27(2): 285-292.

26. Faigenbaum, A.D., A. Farell, M. Fabiano, T. Radler, F. Naclerio, N.A. Ratamess, J. Kang, and G.D. Myer. 2011. Effects of integrative neuromuscular training on fitness performance in children. *Pediatric Exercise Science*, 23(4): 573-584.

27. Kaneshia, H., K. Funato, S. Kuno, T. Fukunaga, and S. Katsuta. 2003. Growth trend of the quadriceps femoris muscle in junior Olympic weight lifters: An 18-month follow-up survey. *European Journal of Applied Physiology*, 89(3): 238-242.

28. Myer, G.D., K.R. Ford, J.P. Palumbo, and T.E. Hewett. 2005. Neuromuscular training improves performance and lower extremity biomechanics in female athletes. *Journal of Strength and Conditioning Research*, 19(1): 51-60.

29. Valovich-McLeod, T.C., L.C. Decoster, K.J. Loud, L.J. Micheli, J.T. Parker, M.A. Sandrey, and C. White. 2011. National Athletic Trainers' Association position statement: Prevention of pediatric overuse injuries. *Journal of Athletic Training*, 46(2): 206-220.

30. Pierce, K.C., R. Byrd, and M.H. Stone. 1999. Youth weightlifting: Is it safe? *Weightlifting USA*, 17(4): 5.

31. Besier, T.F., D.G. Lloyd, J.L. Cochrane, and T.R. Ackland. 2001. External loading of the knee joint during running and cutting manoeuvres. *Medicine and Science in Sports and Exercise*, 33(7): 1168-1175.

32. Weyand, P.G., D.B. Sternlight, M.J. Bellizzi, and S. Wright. 2000. Faster top running speeds are achieved with greater ground forces not more rapid leg movements. *Journal of Applied Physiology*, 89(5): 1991-1999.

33. Rumpf, M.C., J.B. Cronin, S.D. Pinder, J. Oliver, and M.G. Hughes. 2012. Effect of different training methods on running sprint times in male youth. *Pediatric Exercise Science*, 24(2): 170-186.

34. Casey, B.J., J.N. Giedd, and K.M. Thomas. 2000. Structural and functional brain development and its relation to cognitive development. *Biological Psychology*, 54(1-3): 241-257.

35. Casey, B.J., N. Tottenham, C. Liston, and S. Durston. 2005. Imaging the developing brain: What have we learned about cognitive development? *Trends in Cognitive Sciences*, 9(3): 104-110.

36. Clark, E., J. Tobias, L. Murray, and C. Boreham. 2011. Children with low muscle strength are at increased risk of fracture with exposure to exercise. *Journal of Musculoskeletal and Neuronal Interactions*, 11(2): 196-202.

37. McManus, A.M., C.H. Cheng, M.P. Leung, T.C. Yung, and D.J. Mafarlane. 2005. Improving aerobic power in primary school boys: A comparison of continuous and interval training. *International Journal of Sports Medicine*, 26(9): 781-786.

38. Malina, R.M. 2007. Growth, maturation and development: Applications to young athletes and in particular to divers. In R.M. Malina and J. L. Gabriel, *USA Diving Coach Development Reference Manual* (pp. 3-29). Indianapolis: USA Diving.

39. Sands, W.A. 2002. Physiology. In W.A. Sands, D.J. Caine, and J. Borms, *Scientific Aspects of Women's Gymnastics* (pp. 128-61). Basel: Karger.

40. Matos, N.F., R.F. Winsley, and C.A. Williams. 2011. Prevalence of non-functional overreaching/overtraining in young English athletes. *Medicine and Science in Sports and Exercise*, 43(7): 1287-1294.

41. Malina, R.M. 2010. Early sport specialization: Roots, effectiveness, risks. *Current Sports Medicine Reports*, 9(6): 364-371.

Chapter 3

1. Roberts, T.J. 2002. The integrated function of muscles and tendons during locomotion. *Comparative Biochemistry and Physiology. Part A:Molecular and Integrative Physiology*, 133: 1087-1099.

2. Engebretsen, A.H., G. Myklebust, I. Holme, L. Engebretsen, and R. Bahr. 2008. Prevention of injuries among male soccer players: A prospective, randomized intervention study targeting players with previous injuries or reduced function. *American Journal of Sports Medicine*, 36: 1052-1060.

3. Bosch, F., and R. Klomp. 2005. *Running: Biomechanics and Exercise Physiology in Practice*, Edinburgh: Elsevier.

4. Bonacci, J., P.U. Saunders, A. Hicks, T. Rantalainen, B.G. Vicenzino, and W. Spratford. 2013. Running in a minimalist and lightweight shoe is not the same as running barefoot: A biomechanical study. *British Journal of Sports Medicine*, 47: 387-392.

5. Macwilliams, B.A., T. Choi, M.K. Perezous, E.Y. Chao, and E.G. McFarland. 1998. Characteristic ground-reaction forces in baseball pitching. *American Journal of Sports Medicine*, 26: 66-71.

Chapter 4

1. Mottram, S., and M. Comerford. 2008. A new perspective on risk assessment. *Physical Therapy in Sport*, 9(1): 40-51.

2. Panjabi, M.M. 2003. Clinical spinal instability and low back pain. *Journal of Electromyography and Kinesiology*, 13(4): 371-379.

3. Hides, J.A., M.J. Stokes, M. Saide, G.A. Jull, and D.H. Cooper. 1994. Evidence of lumbar multifidus muscle wasting ipsilateral to symptoms in patients with acute/subacute low back pain. *Spine*, 19(2): 165-172.

4. Dangaria, T.R., and O. Naesh. 1998. Changes in cross-sectional area of psoas major muscle in unilateral sciatica caused by disc herniation. *Spine*, 23(8): 928-931.

5. O'Sullivan, P.B., K.M. Grahamslaw, M. Kendell, S.C. Lapenskie, N.E. Moller, and K.V. Richards. 2002. The effect of different standing and sitting postures on trunk muscle activity in a pain-free population. *Spine*, 27(11): 1238-1244.

6. Mitchell, T., P.B. O'Sullivan, A.F. Burnett, L. Straker, and A. Smith. 2008. Regional differences in lumbar spinal posture and the influence of low back pain. *BMC Musculoskeletal Disorders*, 9: 152.

7. Wilke, H., P. Neef, B. Hinz, H. Seidel, and L. Claes. 2001. Intradiscal pressure together with anthropometric data: A data set for the validation of models. *Clinical Biomechanics*, 16(Suppl 1): S111-S1126.

8. Threlkeld, A.J. 1992. The effects of manual therapy on connective tissue. *Physical Therapy*, 72(12): 893-902.

9. Vleeming, A., M.D. Schuenke, A.T. Masi, J.E. Carreiro, L. Danneels, and F.H. Willard. 2012. The sacroiliac joint: An overview of its anatomy, function and potential clinical implications. *Journal of Anatomy*, 221(6): 537-567.

10. Hodges, P.W., and C.A. Richardson. 1996. Inefficient muscular stabilization of the lumbar spine associated with low back pain: A motor control evaluation of transversus abdominis. *Spine*, 21(22): 2640-2650.

11. O'Sullivan, P.B., D.J. Beales, J.A. Beetham, J. Cripps, F. Graf, I.B. Lin, B. Tucker, and A. Avery. 2002. Altered motor control strategies in subjects with sacroiliac joint pain during the active straight-leg-raise test. *Spine*, 27(1): E1-E8.

12. Barker, K.L., D.R. Shamley, and D. Jackson. 2004. Changes in the cross-sectional area of multifidus and psoas in patients with unilateral back pain: The relationship to pain and disability. *Spine*, 29(22): E515-E519.

13. Gubler, D., A.F. Mannion, P. Schenk, M. Gorelick, D. Helbling, H. Gerber, V. Toma, and H. Sprott. 2010. Ultrasound tissue Doppler imaging reveals no delay in abdominal muscle feed-forward activity during rapid arm movements in patients with chronic low back pain. *Spine*, 35(16): 1506-1513.

14. Mannion, A.F., F. Caporaso, N. Pulkovski, and H. Sprott. 2012. Spine stabilisation exercises in the treatment of chronic low back pain: A good clinical outcome is not associated with improved abdominal muscle function. *European Spine Journal*, 21(7): 1301-1310.

15. Allison, G.T., S.L. Morris, and B. Lay. 2008. Feed-forward responses of transversus abdominis are directionally specific and act asymmetrically: Implications for core stability theories. *Journal of Orthopaedic and Sports Physical Therapy*, 38(5): 228-237.

16. Hodges, P., W. van den Hoorn, A. Dawson, and J. Cholewicki. 2009. Changes in the mechanical properties of the trunk in low back pain may be associated with recurrence. *Journal of Biomechanics*, 42(1): 61-66.

17. McGregor, A.H., L. Anderton, and W.M. Gedroyc. 2002. The trunk muscles of elite oarsmen. *British Journal of Sports Medicine*, 36(3): 214-217.

18. Niemelainen, R., M.M. Briand, and M.C. Battie. 2011. Substantial asymmetry in paraspinal muscle cross-sectional area in healthy adults questions its value as a marker of low back pain and pathology. *Spine*, 36(25): 2152-2157.

19. Grenier, S.G., and S.M. McGill. 2007. Quantification of lumbar stability by using 2 different abdominal activation strategies. *Archives of Physical Medicine and Rehabilitation*, 88(1): 54-62.

20. Cholewicki, J., K. Juluru, and S.M. McGill. 1999. Intra-abdominal pressure mechanism for stabilizing the lumbar spine. *Journal of Biomechanics*, 32(1): 13-17.

21. Bergmark, A. 1989. Stability of the lumbar spine. A study in mechanical engineering. *Acta Orthopaedica Scandinavica*, 230(Suppl): 1-54.

22. Blazevich, A.J., N.D. Gill, R. Bronks, R.U. Newton. 2003. Training-specific muscle architecture adaptation after 5-wk training in athletes. *Medicine and Science in Sports and Exercise*, 35(12): 2013-2022.

23. McGill, S. 2007. *Low back disorders: Evidenced-based prevention and rehabilitation, second edition*. Champaign: Human Kinetics.

24. Hamlyn, N., D.G. Behm, and W.B. Young. 2007. Trunk muscle activation during dynamic weight-training exercises and isometric instability activities. *Journal of Strength and Conditioning Research*, 21(4): 1108-1112.

25. McGill, S.M., A. McDermott, and C.M. Fenwick. 2009. Comparison of different strongman events: Trunk muscle activation and lumbar spine motion, load, and stiffness. *Journal of Strength and Conditioning Research*, 23(4): 1148-1161.

Chapter 5

1. Jaggers, J.R., A.M. Swank, K.L. Frost, and C.D. Lee. 2008. The acute effects of dynamic and ballistic stretching on vertical jump height, force, and power. *Journal of Strength and Conditioning Research*, 22(6): 1844-1849.

2. Kay, A.D., and A.J. Blazevich. 2012. Effect of acute static stretch on maximal muscle performance: A systematic review. *Medicine and Science in Sports and Exercise*, 44(1): 154-164.

3. McMillian, D.J., J.H. Moore, B.S. Hatler, and C. Taylor. 2006. Dynamic vs. static-stretching warm up: The effect on power and agility performance. *Journal of Strength and Conditioning Research*, 20(3): 492-499.

4. Young, W.B. 2007. The use of static stretching in warm-up for training and competition. *International Journal of Sports Physiology and Performance*, 2(2): 212-216.

5. Stecco, C., A. Porzionato, V. Macchi, C. Tiengo, A. Parenti, R. Aldegheri, V. Delmas, R. De Caro. 2006. Histological characteristics of the deep fascia of the upper limb. *Italian Journal of Anatomy and Embryology*, 111(2): 105-10.

6. Findley, T. 2009. Fascia research II: Second International Fascia Research Congress. *International Journal of Therapeutic Massage & Bodywork*, 2(3): 4-9.

7. Grinnell, F. 2008. Fibroblast mechanics in three-dimensional collagen matrices. *Journal of Bodywork and Movement Therapies*, 12(3): 191-193.

8. Kubo, K., H. Kanehisa, Y. Kawakami, and T. Fukunaga. 2001. Influence of static stretching on viscoelastic properties of human tendon structures in vivo. *Journal of Applied Physiology*, 90(2): 520-527.

9. Day, J.A., L. Copetti, and G. Rucli. 2012. From clinical experience to a model for the human fascial system. *Journal of Bodywork and Movement Therapies*, 16(3): 372-380.

10. Gracovetsky, S. 2008. Is the lumbodorsal fascia necessary? *Journal of Bodywork and Movement Therapies*, 12(3): 194-197.

11. Ingraham, S.J. 2003. The role of flexibility in injury prevention and athletic performance: Have we stretched the truth? *Minnesota Medicine*, 86(5): 58-61.

12. Shrier, I. 2004. Does stretching improve performance? A systematic and critical review of the literature. *Clinical Journal of Sport Medicine*, 14(5): 267-273.

13. Pagaduan, J.C., H. Pojskić, E. Užičanin, and F. Babajić. 2012. Effect of various warm-up protocols on jump performance in college football players. *Journal of Human Kinetics*, 35: 127-132.

14. Simic, L., N. Sarabon, and G. Markovic. 2012. Does pre-exercise static stretching inhibit maximal muscular performance? A meta-analytical review. *Scandinavian Journal of Medicine and Science in Sports*, 23(2): 131-148.

15. Taylor, J.M., M. Weston, and M.D. Portas. 2013. The effect of a short, practical warm-up protocol on repeated sprint performance. *Journal of Strength and Conditioning Research*, 27(7): 2034-2038.

16. Thacker, S.B., J. Gilchrist, D.F. Stroup, and C.D. Kimsey. 2004. The impact of stretching on sports injury risk: A systematic review of the literature. *Medicine and Science in Sports and Exercise*, 36(3): 371-378.

17. Weldon, S.M., and R.H. Hill. 2003. The efficacy of stretching for prevention of exercise-related injury: A systematic review of the literature. *Manual Therapy*, 8(3), 141-150.

18. Wilk, K.E., L.C. Macrina, G.S. Fleisig, R. Porterfield, C.D. Simpson, P. Harker, N. Paparesta, and J.R. Andrews. 2011. Correlation of glenohumeral internal rotation deficit and total rotational motion to shoulder injuries in professional baseball pitchers. *American Journal of Sports Medicine*, 39(2): 329-335.

19. Cibulka, M.T., and J. Threlkeld-Watkins. 2005. Patellofemoral pain and asymmetrical hip rotation. *Physical Therapy*, 85(11): 1201-1207.

20. Vad, V.B., A. Gebeh, D. Dines, D. Altchek, and B. Norris. 2003. Hip and shoulder internal rotation range of motion deficits in professional tennis players. *Journal of Science and Medicine in Sport*, 6(1): 71-75.

21. Chorba, R.S., D.J. Chorba, L.E. Bouillon, C.A. Overmyer, and J.A. Landis. 2010. Use of a functional movement screening tool to determine injury risk in female collegiate athletes. *North American Journal of Sports Physical Therapy*, 5(2): 47-54.

22. Kiesel, K., P.J. Plisky, and M.L. Voight. 2007. Can serious injury in professional football be predicted by a preseason functional movement screen? *North American Journal of Sports Physical Therapy*, 2(3): 147-158.

23. Minick, K.I., K.B. Kiesel, L. Burton, A. Taylor, P. Plisky, and R.J. Butler. 2010. Interrater reliability of the functional movement screen. *Journal of Strength and Conditioning Research*, 24(2): 479-486.

24. Shultz, R., K. Mooney, S. Anderson, B. Marcello, D. Garza, G.O. Matheson, and T. Besier. 2011. Functional movement screen: Inter-rater and subject reliability. *British Journal of Sports Medicine*, 45(4): 374-374.

Chapter 6

1. Matveyev, L. 1981. *Fundamentals of Sports Training.* Moscow: Progress.

2. Selye, H. 1956. *The Stress of Life.* London: Longmans Green.

3. Harre, D. 1982. *Principles of Sports Training: Introduction to the Theory and Methods of Training*. Berlin: Sportverlag.

4. Halson, S.L., and A.E. Jeukendrup. 2004. Does overtraining exist? An analysis of overreaching and overtraining research. *Sports Medicine,* 34(14): 967-981.

5. Meeusen, R., M. Duclos, C. Foster, A. Fry, M. Gleeson, D. Nieman, J. Raglin, G. Rietjens, J. Steinacker, and A. Urhausen. (2013). Prevention, diagnosis, and treatment of the overtraining syndrome: Joint consensus statement of the European College of Sport Science and the American College of Sports Medicine. *Medicine and Science in Sports and Exercise,* 45(1): 186-205.

6. Brink, M.S., C. Visscher, S. Arends, J. Zwerver, W.J. Post, and K.A.P.M. Lemmink. 2010. Monitoring stress and recovery: New insights for the prevention of injuries and illnesses in elite youth soccer players. *British Journal of Sports Medicine,* 44(11): 809-815.

7. Gabbett, T.J. 2010. The development and application of an injury prediction model for noncontact, soft-tissue injuries in elite collision sport athletes. *Journal of Strength and Conditioning Research,* 24(10): 2593.

8. Viru, A., and M. Viru. 2000. Nature of training effects. In J. Garret, W.E. Kirkendall, and D.T. Kirkendall (eds.), *Exercise and Sport Science* (pp. 67-95). Philadelphia: Lippincott Williams and Wilkins..

9. Åstrand, P.O., and K. Rodahl. 1986. *Textbook of Work Physiology*. New York: McGraw Hill.

10. Morton, R.H., J.R. Fitz-Clarke, and E.W. Banister. 1990. Modeling human performance in running. *Journal of Applied Physiology,* 69(3): 1171-1177.

11. Foster, C., L.L. Hector, R. Welsh, M. Schrager, M.A. Green, and A.C. Snyder. 1995. Effects of specific versus cross-training on running performance. *European Journal of Applied Physiology,* 70(4): 367-372.

12. Lucía, A., J. Hoyos, A. Santalla, C. Earnest, and J.L. Chicharro. 2003. Tour de France versus Vuelta a Espana: Which is harder? *Medicine and Science in Sports and Exercise,* 35(5): 872-878.

13. Borg, G. 1982. Psychophysical bases of perceived exertion. *Medicine and Science in Sports and Exercise,* 14(5): 377-381.

14. Borg, G. 1970. Perceived exertion as an indicator of somatic stress. *Scandinavian Journal of Rehabilitation Medicine,* 2(2): 92-98.

15. Borg, G., and H. Dahlstrom. 1962. The reliability and validity of a physical work test. *Acta Physiologica Scandinavica,* 55: 353-361.

16. Borg, E., and L. Kaijser. 2006. A comparison between three rating scales for perceived exertion and two different work tests. *Scandinavian Journal of Medicine and Science in Sports,* 16(1): 57-69.

17. Noble, B.J., G.A. Borg, I. Jacobs, R. Ceci, and P. Kaiser. 1983. A category-ratio perceived exertion scale: Relationship to blood and muscle lactates and heart rate. *Medicine and Science in Sports and Exercise,* 15(6): 523-528.

18. Foster, C., J.A. Florhaug, J. Franklin, L. Gottschall, L.A. Hrovatin, S. Parker, P. Doleshal, and C. Dodge. 2001. A new approach to monitoring exercise training. *Journal of Strength and Conditioning Research,* 15(1): 109-115.

19. Foster, C., and M. Lehmann. 1997. Overtraining syndrome. In N. Gnuten (ed.), *Running Injuries* (pp. 173-188). Philadelphia: W.B. Saunders..

20. Foster, C. 1998. Monitoring training in athletes with reference to overtraining syndrome. *Medicine and Science in Sports and Exercise,* 30(7): 1164-1168.

21. Rogalski, B., B. Dawson, J. Heasman, and T.J. Gabbett. 2013. Training and game loads and injury risk in elite Australian footballers. *Journal of Science and Medicine in Sport.* doi:10.1016/j.jsams.2012.12.004 [epub ahead of print]

22. Impellizzeri, F.M., E. Rampinini, A.J. Coutts, A. Sassi, and S.M. Marcora. 2004. Use of RPE-based training load in soccer. *Medicine and Science in Sports and Exercise,* 36(6): 1042-1047.

23. Lovell, T.W.J., A.C. Sirotic, F.M. Impellizzeri, and A.J. Coutts. 2013. Factors affecting perception of effort (session rating of perceived exertion) during rugby league training. *International Journal of Sports Physiology and Performance,* 8(1): 62-69.

24. Halson, S.L., M.W. Bridge, R. Meeusen, B. Busschaert, M. Gleeson, D.A. Jones, and A.E. Jeukendrup. 2002. Time course of performance changes and fatigue markers during intensified training in cyclists. *Journal of Applied Physiology,* 93(3): 947-956.

25. Hooper, S.L., L.T. Mackinnon, and A. Howard. 1999. Physiological and psychometric variables for monitoring recovery during tapering for major competition. *Medicine and Science in Sports and Exercise,* 31(8): 1205-1210.

26. Kellmann, M., and K.W. Kallus. 1993. The Recovery-Stress-Questionnaire: A potential tool to predict performance in sports. In J. R. Nitsch and R. Seiler (eds.), *Movement and Sport: Psychological Foundations and Effects* (pp. 242-247). Augustin: Academia Sankt..

27. Morgan, W.P., D.R. Brown, J.S. Raglin, P.J. O'Connor, and K.A. Ellickson. 1987. Psychological monitoring of overtraining and staleness. *British Journal of Sports Medicine,* 21(3): 107-114.

28. Lane, A.M., P.C. Terry, M.J. Stevens, S. Barney, and S.L. Dinsdale. 2004. Mood responses to athletic performance in extreme environments. [Review].

Journal of Sports Sciences, 22(10): 886-897; discussion 897.

29. McNair, D.M., M. Lorr, and L.F. Droppleman. 1971. *EITS Profile for Mood States.* San Diego: Educational and Industrial Testing Service.

30. Morgan, W.P., P.J. O'Connor, K.A. Ellickson, and P.W. Bradley. 1988. Personality structure, mood states, and performance in elite male distance runners. *International Journal of Sports Psychology,* 19(4): 247-263.

31. Filaire, E., B. Legrand, K. Bret, M. Sagnol, J.M. Cottet-Emard, and J.M. Pequignot. 2002. Psychobiologic responses to 4 days of increased training and recovery in cyclists. *International Journal of Sports Medicine,* 23(8): 588-594.

32. Morgan, W.P., D.L. Costill, M.G. Flynn, J.S. Raglin, and P.J. O'Connor. 1988. Mood disturbance following increased training in swimmers. *Medicine and Science in Sports and Exercise,* 20(4): 408-414.

33. Rushall, B.S. 1990. A tool for measuring stress tolerance in elite athletes. *Journal of Applied Sport Psychology,* 2(1): 51-66.

34. McClean, B.D., A.J. Coutts, V. Kelly, M.R. McGuigan, and S. Cormack. 2010. Neuromuscular, endocrine and perceptual fatigue responses during different length between-match microcycles in professional rugby league players. *International Journal of Sports Physiology and Performance,* 5: 367-383.

35. Montgomery, P.G., and W.G. Hopkins. 2013. The effects of game and training loads on perceptual responses of muscle soreness in Australian Football. *International Journal of Sports Physiology and Performance,* 8(3): 312-318.

36. Fowles, J.R. 2006. Technical issues in quantifying low-frequency fatigue in athletes. *International Journal of Sports Physiology and Performance,* 1: 169-171.

37. Jones, D.A. 1996. High-and low-frequency fatigue revisited. *Acta Physiologica Scandinavica,* 156(3): 265-270.

38. Lattier, G., G.Y. Millet, A. Martin, and V. Martin. 2004. Fatigue and recovery after high-intensity exercise part I: Neuromuscular fatigue. *International Journal of Sports Medicine,* 25(6): 450-456.

39. Martin, V., G.Y. Millet, A. Martin, G. Deley, and G. Lattier. 2004. Assessment of low-frequency fatigue with two methods of electrical stimulation. *Journal of Applied Physiology,* 97(5): 1923-1929.

40. Welsh, T.T., J.A. Alemany, S.J. Montain, P.N. Frykman, A.P. Tuckow, A.J. Young, and B.C. Nindl. 2008. Effects of intensified military field training on jumping performance. *International Journal of Sports Medicine,* 29(1): 45-52.

41. Cormack, S.J., R.U. Newton, M.R. McGuigan, and P. Cormie. 2008. Neuromuscular and endocrine responses of elite players during an Australian Rules Football season. *International Journal of Sports Physiology and Performance,* 3(4): 439-453.

42. Cormack, S.J., M.G. Mooney, W. Morgan, and M.R. McGuigan. 2013. Influence of neuromuscular fatigue on accelerometer load in elite Australian Football players. *International Journal of Sports Physiology and Performance,* 8(4): 373-378.

43. Mooney, M.G., S. Cormack, B.J. O'Brien, W.M. Morgan, and M. McGuigan. 2013. Impact of neuromuscular fatigue on match exercise intensity and performance in elite Australian football. *Journal of Strength and Conditioning Research,* 27(1): 166-173.

44. Buchheit, M., S. Racinais, J.C. Bilsborough, P.C. Bourdon, S.C. Voss, J. Hocking, J. Cordy, A. Mendez-Villanueva, and A.J. Coutts. 2013. Monitoring fitness, fatigue and running performance during a pre-season training camp in elite football players. *Journal of Science and Medicine in Sport.* doi:10.1016/j.jsams.2012.12.003 [epub ahead of print]

45. Lamberts, R.P., J. Swart, B. Capostagno, T.D. Noakes, and M.I. Lambert. 2010. Heart rate recovery as a guide to monitor fatigue and predict changes in performance parameters. *Scandinavian Journal of Medicine and Science in Sports,* 20(3): 449-457.

46. Schmikli, S., M. Brink, W. de Vries, and F. Backx. 2011. Can we detect non-functional overreaching in young elite soccer players and middle-long distance runners using field performance tests? *British Journal of Sports Medicine,* 45(8): 631-636.

47. Uusitalo, A., A. Uusitalo, and H. Rusko. 2000. Heart rate and blood pressure variability during heavy training and overtraining in the female athlete. *International Journal of Sports Medicine,* 21(01): 45-53.

48. Hooper, S.L., L.T. Mackinnon, A.W. Bachmann, A. Howard, and D. Gordon. 1995. Markers for monitoring overtraining and recovery. *Medicine and Science in Sports and Exercise,* 27(1): 106-112.

49. Borresen, J., and M.I. Lambert. 2008. Autonomic control of heart rate during and after exercise: Measurements and implications for monitoring training status. *Sports Medicine,* 38(8): 633-646.

50. Buchheit, M., G.P. Millet, A. Parisy, S. Pourchez, P.B. Laursen, and S.I.D. Ahmaidi. 2008. Supramaximal training and postexercise parasympathetic reactivation in adolescents. *Medicine and Science in Sports and Exercise,* 40(2): 362-371.

51. Mujika, I., and S. Padilla. 2001. Cardiorespiratory and metabolic characteristics of detraining in humans. *Medicine and Science in Sports and Exercise,* 33(3): 413.

52. Lamberts, R.P., K. Lemmink, J.J. Durandt, and M.I. Lambert. 2004. Variation in heart rate during submaximal exercise: Implications for monitoring training. *Journal of Strength and Conditioning Research,* 18(3): 641-645.

53. Pichot, V., T. Busso, F. Roche, M. Garet, G. Costes, D. Duverney, J.R. Lacour, J.C. Barthélémy. 2002. Autonomic adaptations to intensive and overload training periods: A laboratory study. *Medicine and Science in Sports and Exercise,* 34(10): 1660-1666.

54. Adlercreutz, H., M. Harkonen, K. Kuoppasalmi, H. Naveri, I. Huhtaniemi, H. Tikkanen, K. Remes, A. Dessypris, and J. Karvonen. 1986. Effect of training on plasma anabolic and catabolic steroid hormones and their response during physical exercise. *International Journal of Sports Medicine,* 7(Suppl 1): 27-28.

55. Hakkinen, K., A. Pakarinen, M. Alen, H. Kauhanen, and P.V. Komi. 1987. Relationships between training volume, physical performance capacity, and serum hormone concentrations during prolonged training in elite weight lifters. *International Journal of Sports Medicine,* 8(Suppl 1): 61-65.

56. Kirwan, J.P., D.L. Costill, J.B. Houmard, J.B. Mitchell, M.G. Flynn, and W.J. Fink. 1990. Changes in selected blood measures during repeated days of intense training and carbohydrate control. *International Journal of Sports Medicine,* 11: 362-366.

57. Stone, M.H., R.E. Keith, J.T. Kearney, S.J. Fleck, G.D. Wilson, and N.T. Triplett. 1991. Overtraining: A review of the signs, symptoms and possible causes. *Journal of Applied Sport Science Research,* 5(1): 35-50.

58. Stray-Gundersen, J., T. Videman, and P.G. Snell. 1986. Changes in selected objective parameters during overtraining. *Medicine and Science in Sports and Exercise,* 18: S54-55.

59. Cook, N.J., A. Ng, G.F. Read, B. Harris, and D. Riad-Fahmy. 1987. Salivary cortisol for monitoring adrenal activity during marathon runs. *Hormone Research,* 25(1): 18-23.

60. Port, K. 1991. Serum and saliva cortisol responses and blood lactate accumulation during incremental exercise testing. *International Journal of Sports Medicine,* 12(5): 490-494.

61. Vining, R.F., R.A. McGinley, and R.G. Symons. 1983. Hormones in saliva: Mode of entry and consequent implications for clinical interpretation. *Clinical Chemistry,* 29(10): 1752-1756.

62. Cormack, S.J., R.U. Newton, and M.R. McGuigan. 2008. Neuromuscular and endocrine responses of elite players to an Australian rules football match. *International Journal of Sports Physiology and Performance,* 3(3): 359-374.

63. Elloumi, M., F. Maso, O. Michaux, A. Robert, and G. Lac. 2003. Behaviour of saliva cortisol [C], testosterone [T] and the T/C ratio during a rugby match and during the post-competition recovery days. *European Journal of Applied Physiology,* 90(1-2): 23-28.

64. Haneishi, K., A.C. Fry, C.A. Moore, B.K. Schilling, Y. Li, and M.D. Fry. 2007. Cortisol and stress responses during a game and practice in female collegiate soccer players. *Journal of Strength and Conditioning Research,* 21(2): 583-588.

65. Griggs, R.C., W. Kingston, R.F. Jozefowicz, B.E. Herr, G. Forbes, and D. Halliday. 1989. Effect of testosterone on muscle mass and muscle protein synthesis. *Journal of Applied Physiology,* 66(1): 498-503.

66. Crewther, B., J. Cronin, J. Keogh, and C. Cook. 2008. The salivary testosterone and cortisol response to three loading schemes. *Journal of Strength and Conditioning Research,* 22(1): 250-255.

67. Cumming, D.C., G.D. Wheeler, and E.M. McColl. 1989. The effects of exercise on reproductive function in men. *Sports Medicine,* 7(1): 1-17.

68. Kraemer, R.R., R.J. Durand, E.O. Acevedo, L.G. Johnson, L.B. Synovitz, G.R. Kraemer, T. Gimpel, and V.D. Castracane. 2003. Effects of high-intensity exercise on leptin and testosterone concentrations in well-trained males. *Endocrine,* 21(3): 261-265.

69. Sutton, J.R., M.J. Coleman, J. Casey, and L. Lazarus. 1973. Androgen responses during physical exercise. *British Medical Journal,* 1(5852): 520-522.

70. Filaire, E., X. Bernain, M. Sagnol, and G. Lac. 2001. Preliminary results on mood state, salivary testosterone:cortisol ratio and team performance in a professional soccer team. *European Journal of Applied Physiology,* 86(2): 179-184.

71. Urhausen, A., H. Gabriel, and W. Kindermann. 1995. Blood hormones as markers of training stress and overtraining. *Sports Medicine,* 20(4): 251-276.

72. Parry-Billings, M., R. Budgett, Y. Koutedakis, E. Blomstrand, S. Brooks, C. Williams, P.C. Calder, S. Pilling, R. Baigrie, and E.A. Newsholme. 1992. Plasma amino acid concentrations in the overtraining syndrome: Possible effects on the immune system. *Medicine and Science in Sports and Exercise,* 24(12): 1353-1358.

73. Rowbottom, D.G., D. Keast, and A.R. Morton. 1996. The emerging role of glutamine as an indicator of exercise stress and overtraining. *Sports Medicine,* 21(2): 80-97.

74. Smith, D.J., and S.R. Norris. 2000. Changes in glutamine and glutamate concentrations for tracking training tolerance. *Medicine and Science in Sports and Exercise,* 32(3): 684-689.

75. Coutts, A.J., P. Reaburn , T.J. Piva, and G.J. Rowsell. 2007. Monitoring for overreaching in rugby league players. *European Journal of Applied Physiology,* 99(3): 313-324.

76. Halson, S.L., G. Lancaster, A.E. Jeukendrup, and M. Gleeson. 2003. Immunological responses to overreaching in cyclists. *Medicine and Science in Sports and Exercise,* 35(4): 854-861.

77. Gleeson, M., and N.P. Walsh. 2012. The BASES Expert Statement on Exercise, Immunity, and Infection. *Journal of Sports Sciences,* 30(3): 321-324.

78. Mackinnon, L.T. 1997. Immunity in athletes. [Review]. *International Journal of Sports Medicine,* 18(Suppl 1): S62-S68.

79. Hopkins, W.G., S.W. Marshall, A.M. Batterham, and J. Hanin. 2009. Progressive statistics for studies in sports medicine and exercise science. *Medicine and Science in Sports and Exercise,* 41(1): 3-13.

80. Pettit, R.W. 2010. The standard difference score: A new statistic for evaluating strength and conditioning programs. *Journal of Strength and Conditioning Research,* 24(1): 287-291.

Chapter 7

1. Orchard, J., T.M. Best, and G.M. Verrall. 2005. Return to play following muscle strains. *Clinical Journal of Sport Medicine,* 15(6): 436-441.

2. Blackburn, T.A., and J.A. Guido. 2000. Rehabilitation after ligamentous and labral surgery of the shoulder: Guiding concepts. *Journal of Athletic Training,* 35(3): 373-381.

3. Riemann, B.L., and S.M. Lephart. 2002. The sensorimotor system, part I: The physiologic basis of functional joint stability. *Journal of Athletic Training,* 37: 71-79.

4. Hertel, J. 2006. Overview of the etiology of chronic ankle instability. Third International Ankle Symposium, Dublin.

5. Cook, C.J., and C.M. Beaven. 2013. Individual perception of recovery is related to subsequent sprint performance. *British Journal of Sports Medicine,* 47(11): 705-709.

6. Walker, N., J. Thatcher, and D. Lavallee. 2010. A preliminary development of the Re-Injury Anxiety Inventory (RIAI). *Physical Therapy in Sport,* 11: 23-29.

Chapter 8

1. Rochelle, R., E. Michael, and V. Skubic. 1957. Effect of warm-up on softball throw for distance. *Research Quarterly,* 28: 357-363.

2. Karpovich, P.V. 1965. *Physiology of Muscle Activity.* Philadelphia: Saunders.

3. Fradkin, A.J., T.R. Zazryn, and J.M. Smoliga. 2010. Effects of warming up on physical performance: A systematic review with meta-analysis. *Journal of Strength and Conditioning Research,* 24(1): 140-148.

4. Hedrick, A. 1992. Physiological responses to warm-up. *National Strength and Conditioning Association Journal,* 14(5): 25-27.

5. Shellock, F.G. 1986. Physiological, psychological, and injury prevention aspects of warm-up. *National Strength and Conditioning Association Journal,* 8(5): 24-27.

6. Bonci, A.S., and S. Oswald. 1993. Barrier trigger points and muscle performance. *National Strength and Conditioning Association Journal,* 15(6): 39-42.

7. Robertson, M. 2008. *Self-Myofascial Release: Purpose, Methods and Techniques.* Retrieved from http://www.RobertsonTrainingSystems.com.

8. McGill, S. 2004. *Ultimate Back Fitness and Performance.* Waterloo: Wabuno.

9. Duhigg, C. 2012. *The Power of Habit.* New York: Random House.

10. Lebon, F., C. Collet, and A. Guillot. 2010. Benefits of motor imagery training on muscle strength. *Journal of Strength and Conditioning Research,* 24: 1680-1687.

11. Cook, C.J., and B.T. Crewther. 2012. Changes in salivary testosterone concentrations and subsequent voluntary squat performance following the presentation of short video clips. *Hormones and Behavior,* 61: 17-22.

12. Carre, J.M., and S.K. Putman. 2010. Watching a previous victory produces an increase in testosterone among elite hockey players. *Psychoneuroendocrinology,* 35: 475-479.

13. Klinesmith, J., T. Kasser, and F.T. McAndrew. 2006. Guns, testosterone, and aggression: An experimental test of a meditational hypothesis. *Psychological Science,* 17: 568-571.

14. Cressy, E. 2008. *The Truth About Unstable Surface Training.* [Ebook]. Retrieved from http://www.cresseyperformance.com.

15. Bird, S.P., and W. Stuart. 2012. Integrating balance and postural stability exercises into the functional warm-up for youth athletes. *Strength and Conditioning Journal,* 34(3): 73-79.

16. Jordan, M.J., S.R. Norris, D.J. Smith, and W. Herzog. 2005. Vibration training: An overview of the area, training consequences, and future considerations. *Journal of Strength and Conditioning Research,* 19(2): 459-466.

17. Mester, J., P. Spitzenfeil, J. Schwarzer, and F. Seifriz. 1999. Biological reaction to vibration: Implication for sport. *Journal of Science and Medicine in Sport,* 2: 211-226.

18. Cook, G. 2010. *Movement: Functional Movement Systems.* Aptos: On Target.

19. Staley, C. 2000. Warming-up to a great workout: A five stage event! *T-Nation.* Retrieved from http://www.t-nation.com.

20. Young, W.B., and D.G. Behm. 2002. Should static stretching be used during a warm-up for strength and power activities? *Strength and Conditioning Journal,* 24(6): 33-37.

21. Thacker, S.B., J. Gilchrist, D.F. Stroup, and C.D. Kimsey, Jr. 2004. The impact of stretching on sports injury risk: A systematic review of the literature. *Medicine and Science in Sports and Exercise,* 36(3): 371-378.

22. Church, J.B., M.S. Wiggins, M. Moode, and R. Crist. 2001. Effect of warm-up and flexibility treatments

on vertical jump performance. *Journal of Strength and Conditioning Research*, 15(3): 332-336.

23. DeRenne, C., K.W. Ho, R.K. Hetzler, and D.X. Chai. 1992. Effects of warm-up with various weighted implements on baseball bat swing velocity. *Journal of Strength and Conditioning Research*, 6(4): 214-218.

24. Gullich, A.C., and D. Schmidtbeicher. 1996. MVC-induced short-term potentiation of explosive force. *New Studies in Athletics*, 11: 67-81.

25. Elam, R. 1986. Optimum performance: Warm-up and athletic performance: A physiological analysis. *National Strength and Conditioning Association Journal*, 8(2): 30-33.

26. Fredrick, A., and C. Fredrick. 2006. *Stretch to Win*. Champaign: Human Kinetics.

27. Myer, T. 2009. *Anatomy Trains*. 2nd ed. Edinburgh: Churchill Livingston.

28. Tsatsouline, P. 2001. *Relax Into Stretch*. St. Paul: Advanced Fitness Solutions and Dragon Door Publications.

Chapter 9

1. Schmidt, R.A., and T. Lee. 2008. *Motor Control and Learning*. 4th ed. Champaign: Human Kinetics.

2. Kelso, J.A.S. 1995. *Dynamic Patterns: The Self-Organization of Brain and Behavior*. Cambridge: MIT Press.

3. Latash, M.L. 2008. *Synergies*. Oxford: Oxford University Press.

4. Goodale, M.A., and A.D. Milner. 1992. Separate visual pathways for perception and action. *Trends in Neuroscience*, 15(1): 20-25.

5. Carey, D.P. 2010. Two visual streams: Neuropsychological evidence. In D. Elliott and M. Khan (eds.), *Vision and Goal-Directed Movement* (pp. 265-277). Champaign: Human Kinetics.

6. Wulf, G. 2008. *Attention and Motor Skill Learning*. Champaign: Human Kinetics.

7. Bosch, F., and R. Klomp. 2005 *Running: Biomechanics and Exercise Physiology Applied in Practice*. Edinburgh: Churchill Livingston.

8. Sayers, M. 2000. Running techniques for field sports players. *Sports Coach*, 23(1): 26-27.

Chapter 10

1. Lawton, T.W., J.B. Cronin, and M.R. McGuigan. 2011. Strength testing and training of rowers: A review. *Sports Medicine*, 41(5): 413-432.

2. Sheppard, J.M, P. McNamara, M. Osborne, M. Andrews, T. Oliveira-Borges, P. Walshe, and D.W. Chapman. 2012. Association between anthropometry and upper-body strength qualities with sprint paddling performance in competitive wave surfers. *Journal of Strength and Conditioning Research*, 26(12): 3345-3348.

3. Baker, D., and S. Nance. 1999. The relationship between running speed and measures of strength and power in professional rugby league players. *Journal of Strength and Conditioning Research*, 13(3):230-235.

4. Baker, D. 1996. Improving vertical jump performance through general, special and specific strength training: A brief review. *Journal of Strength and Conditioning Research*, 10(2):131-136.

5. Baker, D., G. Wilson, and R. Carlyon. 1994. Generality versus specificity: A comparison of dynamic and isometric measures of strength and speed-strength. *European Journal of Applied Physiology and Occupational Physiology*, 68: 350-355.

6. Moritani, T. 1992. Time course of adaptations during strength and power training. In P.V Komi (ed.), *Strength and Power in Sport* (pp. 266-278). Oxford: Blackwell Science.

7. Moritani, T. 1993. Neuromuscular adaptations during the acquisition of muscle strength, power and motor tasks. *Journal of Biomechanics*, 26(Suppl 1): 95-107.

8. Cormie, P., M.R. McGuigan, and R.U. Newton. 2011. Developing maximal neuromuscular power: Part 2 training considerations for improving maximal power production. *Sports Medicine*, 41(2):125-146.

9. Jaric, S., R. Ropert, M. Kukolj, and D.B. Ilic. 1995. Role of agonist and antagonist muscle strength in rapid movement performances. *European Journal of Applied Physiology and Occupational Physiology*, 71:464-468.

10. Baker, D. 2007. Progressing the difficulty of bodyweight exercises for child and youth resistance training. [DVD]. Beenleigh: Australian Strength and Conditioning Association.

11. Hakkinen, K., A. Pakarinen, M. Alen, H. Kauhanen, and P. Komi. 1998. Neuromuscular and hormonal adaptations in athletes to strength training in two years. *Journal of Applied Physiology*, 65(6): 2406-2412.

12. Baker, D.G. 2013. 10-year changes in upper body strength and power in elite professional rugby league players: The effect of training age, stage and content. *Journal of Strength and Conditioning Research*, 27(2): 285-292.

13. Anderson, C.E., G.A. Sforzo, and J.A. Sigg. 2008. The effects of combining elastic and free weight resistance on strength and power in athletes. *Journal of Strength and Conditioning Research*, 22(2): 567-574.

14. Wallace, B.J., J.B. Winchester, and M.R. McGuigan. 2006. Effects of elastic bands on force and power characteristics during the back squat exercise. *Journal of Strength and Conditioning Research*, 20(2): 268-272.

15. Baker, D., and R.U. Newton. 2009. Effect of kinetically altering a repetition via the use of chain resistance. *Journal of Strength and Conditioning Research*, 23(7):1941-1946.

16. Baker, D., and R.U. Newton. 2006. Methods to increase the effectiveness of maximal power training for the upper body. *Strength Conditioning Journal,* 27(6): 24-32.

Chapter 11

1. Francis, C., and P. Patterson. 1992. *The Charlie Francis Training System.* Ottawa: TBLI.
2. Francis, C., and J. Coplon. 1999. *Speed Trap: Inside the Biggest Scandal in Olympic History.* Toronto: Lester and Orpen Dennys.
3. Schmolinsky, G. 1978. *Track and Field: Athletics Training in the G.D.R. (East Germany).* Berlin: Sportverlag.
4. Vermeil, A. 2010. Speed: The ultimate weapon. Conference Presentation, Vancouver.
5. McFarlane, B. 2000. *The Science of Hurdling and Speed.* Ottawa: Athletics Canada.
6. Mann, R. 2007. *The Mechanics of Sprinting and Hurdling.* [Course materials]. Las Vegas.
7. Mach, G. 1988. *Sprints & Hurdles.* Vanier: Canadian Track and Field Association.
8. Mann, R.V. 1985. Biomechanical analysis of the elite sprinter and hurdler. In N.K. Butts, T.T. Gushiken, and B. Zarins (eds.), *The Elite Athlete* (pp. 43-80). Jamaica: Spectrum.

Chapter 12

1. Sheppard, J.M., T. Gabbett, and L.C. Stanganelli. 2009. An analysis of playing positions in elite men's volleyball: Considerations for competition demands and physiological characteristics. *Journal of Strength and Conditioning Research,* 23: 1858-1866.
2. Sheppard, J.M., D. Chapman, C. Gough, M.R. McGuigan, and R.U. Newton. 2009. Twelve month training induced changes in elite international volleyball players. *Journal of Strength and Conditioning Research,* 23: 2096-2101.
3. Sheppard, J.M., T.J. Gabbett, K.L. Taylor, J. Dorman, A.J. Lebedew, and R. Borgeaud. 2007. Development of a repeated-effort test for elite men's volleyball. *International Journal of Sports Physiology and Performance,* 2: 292-304.
4. McClay, I., J. Robinson, T. Andriacchi, E. Frederick, T. Gross, and P. Martin. 1994. A profile of ground reaction forces in professional basketball. *Journal of Applied Biomechanics,* 10: 222-236.
5. Weyand, P.G., D.B. Sternlight, M.J. Bellizzi, and S. Wright. 2000. Faster top running speeds are achieved with greater ground forces not more rapid leg movements. *Journal of Applied Physiology,* 89: 1991-1999.
6. Sheppard, J.M., S. Cormack, K.L. Taylor, M.R. McGuigan, and R.U. Newton. 2008. Assessing the force-velocity characteristics of well-trained athletes: The incremental load power profile. *Journal of Strength and Conditioning Research,* 22: 1320-1326.
7. Sheppard, J.M., J. Cronin, T.J. Gabbett, M.R. McGuigan, N. Extebarria, and R.U. Newton. 2007. Relative importance of strength and power qualities to jump performance in elite male volleyball players. *Journal of Strength and Conditioning Research,* 22: 758-765.
8. Carlock, J.M., S.L. Smith, M.J. Hartman, R.T. Morris, D.A. Ciroslan, K.C. Pierce, R.U. Newton, E.A. Harman, W.A. Sands, and M.H. Stone. 2004. The relationship between vertical jump power estimates and weightlifting ability: A field test approach. *Journal of Strength and Conditioning Research,* 18: 534-539.
9. Haff, G.G., M. Stone, H.S. O'Bryant, E. Harman, C. Dinan, R. Johnson, and K. Han. 1997. Force-time dependant characteristics of dynamic and isometric muscle actions. *Journal of Strength and Conditioning Research,* 11: 269-272.
10. Kawamori, N., S.J. Rossi, B.D. Justice, E.E. Haff, E.E. Pistilli, H.S. O'Bryant, M.H. Stone, and G.G. Haff. 2006. Peak force and rate of force development during isometric and dynamic mid-thigh clean pull performed at various intensities. *Journal of Strength and Conditioning Research.* 20: 483-491.
11. Kraska, J.M., M.W. Ramsey, G.G. Haff, N. Fethke, W.A. Sands, M.E. Stone, and M.H. Stone. 2009. Relationship between strength characteristics and unweighted and weighted vertical jump height. *International Journal of Sports Physiology and Performance,* 4: 461-473.
12. Stone, M.H., H.S. O'Bryant, L. McCoy, R. Coglianese, M. Lehmkuhl, and B. Schilling. 2003. Power and maximum strength relationships during performance of dynamic and static weighted jumps. *Journal of Strength and Conditioning Research,* 17: 140-147.
13. Bobbert, M.F., and A.J. Van Soest. 1994. Effects of muscle strengthening on vertical jump height: A simulation study. *Medicine and Science in Sports and Exercise,* 26: 1012-1020.
14. Sands, W.A., S.L. Smith, D.M.R. Kivi, J.R. McNeal, J.C. Dorman, M.H. Stone, and P. Cormie. 2005. Anthropometric and physical abilities profiles: US national skeleton team. *Sports Biomechanics,* 4:197-214.
15. Fry, A.C., W.J. Kraemer, C.A. Weseman, B.P Contory, S.E. Gordon, J.R. Hoffman, and C.M. Maresh. 1991. The effects of an off-season strength and conditioning program on starters and non-starters in women's intercollegiate volleyball. *Journal of Applied Sports Science Research,* 5: 174-181.
16. Garhammer, J., and R. Gregor. 1992. Propulsion forces as a function of intensity for weightlifting and vertical jumping. *Journal of Applied Sport Science Research,* 6: 129-134.

17. Marques, M.C., R. Van den Tillar, J.D. Vescovi, and J.J. Gonzalez-Badillo. 2008. Changes in strength and power performance in elite senior female professional volleyball players during the in-season: A case study. *Journal of Strength and Conditioning Research,* 22: 1147-1155.

18. McBride, J.M., T.N. Triplett-McBride, A. Davie, and R.U. Newton. 2002. The effect of heavy- vs. light-load jump squats on the development of strength, power, and speed. *Journal of Strength and Conditioning Research,* 16: 75-82.

19. Riggs, M., and J.M. Sheppard. 2009. The relative importance of strength and power qualities to vertical jump height of elite beach volleyball players during the countermovement and squat jump. *Journal of Human Sport and Exercise,* 4: 221-236.

20. Sheppard, J.M., and R.U. Newton. 2012. Long-term training adaptations in elite male volleyball players. *Journal of Strength and Conditioning Research,* 26(8): 2180-2184.

21. Weiss, L.W., G.E. Relyea, C.D. Ashley, and R.C. Propst. 1997. Using velocity-spectrum squats and body-composition to predict standing vertical jump ability. *Journal of Strength and Conditioning Research,* 11: 14-20.

22. Young, W., G. Wilson, and C. Byrne. 1991. Relationship between strength qualities and performance in standing and run-up vertical jumps. *Journal of Sports Medicine and Physical Fitness,* 39: 285-293.

23. Hedrick, A. 2008. An evaluation of the weightlifting movements for the volleyball athlete. *Performance Conditioning Volleyball,* 14: 3-12.

24. Dugan, E.L., T.L.A. Doyle, B. Humphries, C.J. Hasson, and R.U. Newton. 2004. Determining the optimal load for jump squats: A review of methods and calculations. *Journal of Strength and Conditioning Research,* 18: 668-674.

25. Sheppard, J.M., T.L. Doyle, and K.L. Taylor. 2008. A methodological and performance comparison of Smith-machine and free weight jump squats. *Journal of Australian Strength and Conditioning,* 16: 5-9.

26. Sheppard, J.M., S. Cormack, K.L. Taylor, M.R. McGuigan, and R.U. Newton. 2008. Assessing the force-velocity characteristics of the leg extensors in well-trained athletes: The incremental load power profile. *Journal of Strength and Conditioning Research,* 22: 1320-1326.

27. Cormie, P., M.R. McGuigan, and R.U. Newton. 2010. Changes in the eccentric phase contribute to improved stretch-shorten cycle performance after training. *Medicine and Science in Sports and Exercise,* 42: 1731-1744.

28. Alemany, J.A., C.E. Pandorf, S.J. Montain, J.W. Castellani, A.P. Tuckow, and B.C. Nindl. 2005. Reliability assessment of ballistic jump squats and bench throws. *Journal of Strength and Conditioning Research,* 19: 33-38.

29. Baker, D., S. Nance, and M. Moore. 2001. The load that maximizes the average mechanical power output during jump squats in power-trained athletes. *Journal of Strength and Conditioning Research,* 15: 92-97.

30. Baker, D., and R.U. Newton. 2007. Change in power output across a high-repetition set of bench throws and jump squats in highly trained athletes. *Journal of Strength and Conditioning Research,* 21: 1007-1011.

31. Newton, R.U., W.J. Kraemer, and K. Hakkinen. 1999. Effects of ballistic training on preseason preparation of elite volleyball players. *Medicine and Science in Sports and Exercise,* 31: 323-330.

32. Newton, R.U., R.A. Rogers, J.S. Volek, K. Hakkinen, and W.J. Kraemer. 2006. Four weeks of optimal load ballistic resistance training at the end of season attenuates declining jump performance of women volleyball players. *Journal of Strength and Conditioning Research,* 20: 955-961.

33. Doyle, T.L.A., J.M. Sheppard, and A. Sachlikidis. 2008. Smith machine jump squats versus free weight jump squats: Which is safer? Paper presented at the Second World Congress on Sports Injury Prevention, Tromso, Norway. In *Second World Congress on Sports Injury Prevention.* Tromso, Norway: British Journal of Sports Medicine.

34. Avela, J., P.M. Santos, and P.V. Komi. 1996. Effects of differently induced stretch loads on neuromuscular control in drop jump exercise. *European Journal of Applied Physiology and Occupational Physiology,* 72: 553-562.

35. Bobbert, M.F., K.G.M. Gerritsen, M.C.A. Litjens, and A.J. Van Soest. 1996. Why is countermovement jump height greater than squat jump height? *Medicine and Science in Sports and Exercise,* 28: 1402-1412.

36. Bosco, C., and P.V. Komi. 1981. Prestretch potentiation of human skeletal muscle during ballistic movement. *Acta Physiologica Scandanavica,* 111: 135-140.

37. Giovanni, A., A. Cavagna, B. Dusman, and R. Margaria. 1968. Positive work done by a previously stretched muscle. *Journal of Applied Physiology,* 24: 21-32.

38. Komi, P.V., and C. Bosco. 1978. Utilization of stored elastic energy in leg extensor muscles by men and women. *Medicine and Science in Sports and Exercise,* 10: 261-265.

39. Steben, R.E., and A.H. Steben. 1981. The validity of the stretch-shortening cycle in selected jumping events. *Journal of Sports Medicine,* 21: 28-37.

40. Van Ingen Schenau, G.J., M.F. Bobbert, and A. De Haan. 1997. Does elastic energy enhance work and efficiency in the stretch-shortening cycle? *Journal of Applied Biomechanics,* 13: 389-415.

41. Walshe, A.D., G.J. Wilson, and G.J. Ettema. 1998. Stretch-shorten cycle compared with isometric

preload: Contributions to enhanced muscular performance. *Journal of Applied Physiology,* 84: 97-106.

42. Sheppard, J.M., M. McGuigan, and R.U. Newton. 2007. The effect of accentuated eccentric load on vertical jump kinetics kinematics in elite male athletes. *International Journal of Sports Science and Coaching,* 2: 267-273.

43. Sheppard, J.M., and K.Y. Young. 2010. Using additional eccentric loads to increase concentric performance in the bench throw. *Journal of Strength and Conditioning Research,* 24: 2853-2856.

44. Enoka, R. 2000. *Neuromechanics of Human Movement.* Champaign: Human Kinetics.

45. Bobbert, M.F. 1990. Drop jumping as a training method for jumping ability. *Sports Medicine,* 9: 7-22.

46. Sheppard, J.M., A. Giorgi, and S. Hobson. 2008. Jump squats with additional eccentric load. *Journal of Australian Strength and Conditioning,* 16: 25.

47. Sheppard, J.M., S. Hobson, D. Chapman, K.L. Taylor, M. McGuigan, and R.U. Newton. 2008. The effect of training with accentuated eccentric load counter-movement jumps on strength and power characteristics of high-performance volleyball players. *International Journal of Sports Science and Coaching,* 3: 355-363.

48. Sheppard, J.M., M.R. McGuigan, and R.U. Newton. 2008. The effects of depth-jumping on vertical jump performance of elite volleyball players: An examination of the transfer of increased stretch-load tolerance to spike jump performance. *Journal of Australian Strength and Conditioning,* 16: 3-10.

49. Baechle, T.R. 1994. *Essentials of Strength and Conditioning.* Champaign: Human Kinetics.

50. Villarreal, E.S., E. Kellis, W.J. Kraemer, and M. Izquierdo. 2009. Determining variables of plyometric training for improving vertical jump height performance: A meta-analysis. *Journal of Strength and Conditioning Research,* 23: 495-506.

51. Bobbert, M.F., P.A. Huijing, and G. Jan Van Ingen Schenau. 1987. Drop jumping. I. The influence of jumping technique on the biomechanics of jumping. *Medicine and Science in Sports and Exercise,* 19: 332-338.

52. Bobbert, M.F., P.A. Huijing, and G. Jan Van Ingen Schenau. 1987. Drop jumping. II. The influence of jumping technique on the biomechanics of jumping. *Medicine and Science in Sports and Exercise.* 19: 339-346.

53. Bobbert, M.F., M. Mackay, D. Schinkelshoek, P.A. Huijing, and G.J. Van Ingen Schenau. 1986. Biomechanical analysis of drop and countermovement jumps. *European Journal of Applied Physiology,* 54: 566-573.

54. Clutch, D., and M. Wilton. 1983. The effect of depth jumps and weight training on leg strength and vertical jump. 54: 5-10.

55. Schmidtbleicher, D., A. Gollhofer, and U. Frick. 1987. Effects of a stretch-shortening typed training on the performance capability and innervation characteristics of leg extensor muscles. In *Biomechanics X1-A.* Amsterdam: Free University Press.

56. Horita, T., P.V. Komi, C. Nicol, and H. Kryolainen. 2002. Interaction between pre-landing activities and stiffness regulation of the knee joint musculoskeletal system in the drop jump: Implications to performance. *European Journal of Applied Physiology.* 88: 76-84.

57. Walshe, A.D., and G. Wilson. 1997. The influence of musculoskeletal stiffness on drop jump performance. *Canadian Journal of Applied Physiology,* 22: 117-132.

58. Toumi, H., T.M. Best, A. Martin, S.F. Guyer, and G. Poumarat. 2004. Effects of eccentric phase velocity of plyometric training on vertical jump. *International Journal of Sports Medicine,* 25: 391-398.

59. Sheppard, J.M., A. Dingley, I. Janssen, W. Spratford, D. Chapman, and R.U. Newton. 2011. The effect of assisted jumping on vertical jump height in high-performance volleyball players. *Journal of Science and Medicine in Sport,* 14: 85-89.

60. Slater, G.J., G.M. Duthie, D.B. Pyne, and W.G. Hopkins. 2006. Validation of a skinfold based index for tracking proportional changes in lean mass. *British Journal of Sports Medicine,* 40: 208-213.

61. Doan, B.K., R.U. Newton, J.L. Marsit, T.N. Triplett-McBride, P.L. Koziris, A.C. Fry, and W.J. Kraemer. 2002. Effects of increased eccentric loading on bench press 1RM. *Journal of Strength and Conditioning Research,* 16: 9-13.

62. Dufek, J.S., and S. Zhang. 1996. Landing models for volleyball players: A longitudinal evaluation. *Journal of Sports Medicine and Physical Fitness,* 36: 35-42.

63. Ford, K.R., G.D. Myer, and T.E. Hewett. 2003. Valgus knee motion during landing in high school female and male basketball players. *Medicine and Science in Sports and Exercise,* 35: 1745-1750.

64. Barber-Westin, S.D., S.T. Smith, T. Campbell, and F.R. Noyes. 2010. The drop-jump video screening test: Retention of improvement in neuromuscular control in female volleyball players. *Journal of Strength and Conditioning Research,* 24: 3055-3062.

65. Myer, G.D., K.R. Ford, S.G. McClean, and T.E. Hewett. 2005. The effects of plyometric versus dynamic stabilization and balance training on lower extremity biomechanics. *American Journal of Sports Medicine,* 34: 445-455.

Chapter 13

1. Sheppard, J.M., and W. Young. 2006. Agility literature review: Classifications, training and testing. *Journal of Sports Sciences,* 24(9): 919-932.

2. Spiteri, T., J.L. Cochrane, and S. Nimphius. 2012. Human stimulus reliability during an offensive and defensive agility protocol. *Journal of Australian Strength and Conditioning*, 20(4): 14-21.

3. Spiteri, T., J.L. Cochrane, and S. Nimphius. 2013. The evaluation of a new lower-body reaction time test. *Journal of Strength and Conditioning Research*, 27(1): 174-180.

4. Spiteri, T., S. Nimphius, and J.L. Cochrane. 2012. Comparison of running times during reactive offensive and defensive agility protocols. *Journal of Australian Strength and Conditioning*, 20(Suppl 1): 73-78.

5. Adam, J.J. 1999. Gender differences in choice reaction time: Evidence for differential strategies. *Ergonomics*, 42(2): 327-335.

6. Nimphius, S. 2010. Lag time: The effect of a two week cessation from resistance training on force, velocity and power in elite softball players. *Journal of Strength and Conditioning Research*, 24(Suppl 1): 1.

7. Stone, M.H., H.S. O'Bryant, L. McCoy, R. Coglianese, M. Lehmkuhl, and B. Schilling. 2003. Power and maximum strength relationships during performance of dynamic and static weighted jumps. *Journal of Strength and Conditioning Research*, 17(1): 140-147.

8. Young, W.B., R. James, and I. Montgomery. 2002. Is muscle power related to running speed with changes of direction? *Journal of Sports Medicine and Physical Fitness*, 42(3): 282-288.

9. Farrow, D., W. Young, and L. Bruce. 2005. The development of a test of reactive agility for netball: A new methodology. *Journal of Science and Medicine in Sport*, 8(1): 52.

10. Nimphius, S., M.R. McGuigan, and R.U. Newton. 2010. Relationship between strength, power, speed, and change of direction performance of female softball players. *Journal of Strength and Conditioning Research*, 24(4): 885-895.

11. Gabbett, T.J., J.N. Kelly, and J.M. Sheppard. 2008. Speed, change of direction speed, and reactive agility of rugby league players. *Journal of Strength and Conditioning Research*, 22(1): 174-181.

12. Nimphius, S., M.R. McGuigan, and R.U. Newton. 2012. Changes in muscle architecture and performance during a competitive season in female softball players. *Journal of Strength and Conditioning Research*, 26(10): 2655-2666.

13. Lloyd, R.S., P. Read, J.L. Oliver, R.W. Meyers, S. Nimphius, and I. Jeffreys. 2013. Considerations for the development of agility during childhood and adolescence. *Strength and Conditioning Journal*. Doi:10.1519/SSC.1510b1013e31827ab31808c [epub ahead of print]

14. Besier, T.F., D.G. Lloyd, T.R. Ackland, and J.L. Cochrane. 2001. Anticipatory effects on knee joint loading during running and cutting maneuvers. *Medicine and Science in Sports and Exercise*, 33(7): 1176-1181.

15. McLean, S.G., S.W. Lipfert, and A.J. Van Den Bogert. 2004. Effect of gender and defensive opponent on the biomechanics of sidestep cutting. *Medicine and Science in Sports and Exercise*, 36(6): 1008-1016.

16. Shimokochi, Y., D. Ide, M. Kokubu, and T. Nakaoji. 2013. Relationships among performance of lateral cutting maneuver from lateral sliding and hip extension and abduction motions, ground reaction force, and body center of mass height. *Journal of Strength and Conditioning Research*, 27(7): 1851-1860.

17. Porter, J.M., R.P. Nolan, E.J. Ostrowski, and G. Wulf. 2010. Directing attention externally enhances agility performance: A qualitative and quantitative analysis of the efficacy of using verbal instructions to focus attention. *Frontiers in Psychology*, 1: 216.

18. Wulf, G., M. Höß, and W. Prinz. 1998. Instructions for motor learning: Differential effects of internal versus external focus of attention. *Journal of Motor Behavior*, 30(2): 169-179.

19. Gabbett, T., M. Rubinoff, L. Thorburn, and D. Farrow. 2007. Testing and training anticipation skills in softball fielders. *International Journal of Sports Science and Coaching*, 2(1): 15-24.

20. Serpell, B.G., W.B. Young, and M. Ford. 2011. Are the perceptual and decision-making components of agility trainable? A preliminary investigation. *Journal of Strength and Conditioning Research*, 25(5): 1240-1248.

21. Sheppard, J.M., W.B. Young, T.L. Doyle, T.A. Sheppard, and R.U. Newton. 2006. An evaluation of a new test of reactive agility and its relationship to sprint speed and change of direction speed. *Journal of Science and Medicine in Sport*, 9(4): 342-349.

22. Young, W., D. Farrow, D. Pyne, W. McGregor, and T. Handke. 2011. Validity and reliability of agility tests in junior Australian football players. *Journal of Strength and Conditioning Research*, 25(12): 3399-3403.

23. Greig, M. 2009. The influence of soccer-specific activity on the kinematics of an agility sprint. *European Journal of Sport Science*, 9(1): 23-33.

Chapter 14

1. Gastin, P.B. 2001. Energy system interaction and relative contribution during maximal exercise. *Sports Medicine*, 31(10): 725-741.

2. Bangsbo, J. 1996. Oxygen deficit: A measure of the anaerobic energy production during intense exercise? *Canadian Journal of Applied Physiology*, 21(5): 350-363.

3. Bundle, M.W., and P.G. Weyand. 2012. Sprint exercise performance: Does metabolic power matter? *Exercise and Sport Sciences Reviews*, 40(3): 174-182.

4. Craig, N.P., K.I. Norton, R.A. Conyers, S.M. Woolford, P.C. Bourdon, T. Stanef, and C.B. Walsh. 1995. Influence of test duration and event specificity on maximal accumulated oxygen deficit of high performance track cyclists. *International Journal of Sports Medicine*, 16(8): 534-540.

5. Garvican, L.A., T. Pottgiesser, D.T. Martin, Y.O. Schumacher, M. Barras, and C.J. Gore. 2011. The contribution of haemoglobin mass to increases in cycling performance induced by simulated LHTL. *European Journal of Applied Physiology*, 111(6): 1089-1101.

6. Marino, F.E., M. Gard, and E.J. Drinkwater. 2011. The limits to exercise performance and the future of fatigue research. *British Journal of Sports Medicine*, 45(1): 65-67.

7. Willardson, J.M. 2007. The application of training to failure in periodized multiple-set resistance exercise programs. *Journal of Strength and Conditioning Research*, 21(2): 628-631.

8. Drinkwater, E.J., T.W. Lawton, R.P. Lindsell, D.B. Pyne, P.H. Hunt, and M.J. McKenna. 2005. Training leading to repetition failure enhances bench press strength gains in elite junior athletes. *Journal of Strength and Conditioning Research*, 19(2): 382-388.

9. Schoenfeld, B.J. 2012. Does exercise-induced muscle damage play a role in skeletal muscle hypertrophy? *Journal of Strength and Conditioning Research*, 26(5): 1441-1453.

10. Tomas, A., E.Z. Ross, and J.C. Martin. 2010. Fatigue during maximal sprint cycling: Unique role of cumulative contraction cycles. *Medicine and Science in Sports and Exercise*, 42(7): 1364-1369.

11. N. Flyger. 2013. Personal communication.

12. Tabata, I., K. Nishimura, M. Kouzaki, Y. Hirai, F. Ogita, M. Miyachi, and K. Yamamoto. 1996. Effects of moderate-intensity endurance and high-intensity intermittent training on anaerobic capacity and VO_2max. *Medicine and Science in Sports and Exercise*, 28(10): 1327-1330.

13. Markovic, G., and P. Mikulic. 2010. Neuromusculoskeletal and performance adaptations to lower-extremity plyometric training. *Sports Medicine*, 40(10): 859-895.

14. Abbiss, C.R., L.G. Karagounis, P.B. Laursen, J.J. Peiffer, D.T. Martin, J.A. Hawley, and J.C. Martin. 2011. Single-leg cycle training is superior to double-leg cycling in improving the oxidative potential and metabolic profile of trained skeletal muscle. *Journal of Applied Physiology*, 110(5): 1248-1255.

15. Hultman, E., K. Soderlund, J.A. Timmons, G. Cederblad, and P.L. Greenhaff. 1996. Muscle creatine loading in men. [Clinical trial]. *Journal of Applied Physiology*, 81(1): 232-237.

16. Zuniga, J.M., T.J. Housh, C.L. Camic, C.R. Hendrix, M. Mielke, G.O. Johnson, and R.J. Schmidt. 2012. The effects of creatine monohydrate loading on anaerobic performance and one-repetition maximum strength. *Journal of Strength and Conditioning Research*, 26(6): 1651-1656.

17. Horswill, C.A. 1995. Effects of bicarbonate, citrate, and phosphate loading on performance. *International Journal of Sport Nutrition*, 5(Suppl): S111-S119.

18. Harris, R.C., and C. Sale. 2012. Beta-alanine supplementation in high-intensity exercise. *Medicine and Sport Science*, 59: 1-17.

19. Hobson, R.M., B. Saunders, G. Ball, R.C. Harris, and C. Sale. 2012. Effects of beta-alanine supplementation on exercise performance: A meta-analysis. *Amino Acids*, 43(1): 25-37.

20. Davis, J.K., and J.M. Green. 2009. Caffeine and anaerobic performance: Ergogenic value and mechanisms of action. *Sports Medicine*, 39(10): 813-832.

21. Ebert, T.R. April 2012. Personal communication.

Chapter 15

1. Cook, G. 2011. *Movement: Functional Movement Systems: Screening, Assessment, Corrective Strategies*. West Sussex: Lotus Pub.

2. Verstegen, M., and P. Williams. 2005. *The Core Performance: The Revolutionary Workout Program to Transform Your Body & Your Life*. Emmaus: Rodale Books.

3. Quatman, C.E., C.C. Quatman, and T.E. Hewett. 2009. Prediction and prevention of musculoskeletal injury: A paradigm shift in methodology. *British Journal of Sports Medicine*, 43(14): 1100-1107.

4. Babuata, L. 2009. *The Power of Less: The Fine Art of Limiting Yourself to the Essential . . . in Business and in Life*. New York: Hyperion.

5. Cormie, P., M.R. McGuigan, and R.U. Newton. 2010. Adaptations in athletic performance after ballistic power versus strength training. *Medicine and Science in Sports and Exercise*, 42(8): 1582-1598.

6. Cormie, P., M.R. McGuigan, and R.U. Newton. 2011. Developing maximal neuromuscular power part 2: Training considerations for improving maximal power production. *Sports Medicine*, 41(2): 125-146.

7. Cormie, P., M.R. McGuigan, and R.U. Newton. 2011. Developing maximal neuromuscular power part 1: Biological basis of maximal power production. *Sports Medicine*, 41(1): 17-38.

8. Yamamoto, L.M., J.F. Klau, D.J. Casa, W.J. Kraemer, L.E. Armstrong, and C.M. Maresh. 2010. The effects of resistance training on road cycling performance among highly trained cyclists: A systematic review. *Journal of Strength and Conditioning Research*, 24(2): 560-566.

9. Bosch, F., and R. Klomp. 2005. *Running: Biomechanics and Exercise Physiology Applied in Practice*. Maarssen: Elsevier.

10. Bailey, A.J., S.P. Robins, and G. Balian. 1974. Biological significance of the intermolecular crosslinks of collagen. *Nature,* 251(5471): 105-109.

11. Enoka, R. 1988. *Neuromuscular Basis of Kinesiology.* Champaign: Human Kinetics.

12. Winkelman, N. 2012. NFL Combine Training Results. Interview, D. Norman, interviewer.

13. Davids, K., and D. Araujo. 2010. The concept of 'Organismic Asymmetry' in sport science. *Journal of Science and Medicine in Sport,* 13(6): 633-640.

14. Moritani, T. 1993. Neuromuscular adaptations during the acquisition of muscle strength, power and motor tasks. *Journal of Biomechanics,* 26(Suppl 1): 95-107.

15. Zatsiorsky, V. 1995. *Science and Practice of Strength Training.* Champaign: Human Kinetics.

16. Willson, J.D., C.P. Dougherty, M.L. Ireland, and I.M. Davis. 2005. Core stability and its relationship to lower extremity function and injury. *Journal of the American Academy of Orthopaedic Surgeons,* 13(5): 316-325.

17. Saharmann, S. 2001. *Movement: Functional Movement Systems: Screening, Assessment, Corrective Strategies.* New York: Mosby.

18. Page, P., C. Frank, and R. Lardner. 2009. *Assessment and Treatment of Muscle Imbalance: The Janda Approach.* Champaign: Human Kinetics.

19. Lisman, P., F.G. O'Conner, P.A. Deuster, and J.J. Knapik. 2013. Functional movement screen and aerobic fitness predict injuries in military training. *Medicine and Science in Sports and Exercise,* 45(4): 636-643.

20. Bundle, M.W., R.W. Hoyt, and P.G. Weyand. 2003. High-speed running performance: A new approach to assessment and prediction. *Journal of Applied Physiology,* 95(5): 1955-1962.

21. Hamilton, A.L., M.E. Neville, S. Brooks, and C. Williams. 1991. Physiological responses to maximal intermittent exercise: Differences between endurance-trained runners and games players. *Journal of Sports Sciences,* 9(4): 371-382.

22. Spencer, M., D. Bishop, B. Dawson, and C. Goodman. 2005. Physiological and metabolic responses of repeated-sprint activities: Specific to field-based team sports. *Sports Medicine,* 35(12): 1025-1044.

23. Storen, O., S. Bratland-Sanda, M. Haave, and J. Helgerud. 2012. Improved VO$_2$max and time trial performance with more high aerobic intensity interval training and reduced training volume: A case study on an elite national cyclist. *Journal of Strength and Conditioning Research,* 26(10): 2705-2711.

24. Noakes, T. 2002. *The Lore of Running.* Champaign: Human Kinetics.

Chapter 16

1. Brueckner, J.C., G. Atchou, C. Capelli, A. Duvallet, D. Barrault, E. Jousselin, M. Rieu, and P.E. di Prampero. 1991. The energy cost of running increases with the distance covered. *European Journal of Applied Physiology,* 62(6): 385-389.

2. Péronnet, F., and G. Thibault. 1987. Physiological analysis of running performance: Revision of the hyperbolic model. *Journal of Physiology,* 82(1): 52-60.

3. Bosquet, L., L. Léger, and P. Legros. 2002. Methods to determine aerobic endurance. *Sports Medicine,* 32(11): 675-700.

4. Léger, L., and R. Boucher. 1980. An indirect continuous running multistage field test: The Université de Montréal track test. *Canadian Journal of Applied Physiology,* 5(2): 77-84.

5. Lacour, J.R., S. Padilla-Magunacelaya, J.C. Barthélémy, and D. Dormois. 1990. The energetics of middle-distance running. *European Journal of Applied Physiology and Occupational Physiology,* 60(1): 38-43.

6. Léger, L., and D. Mercier. 1984. Gross energy cost of horizontal treadmill and track running. *Sports Medicine,* 1(4): 270-277.

7. Bangsbo, J. 1994. *Fitness Training in Football: A Scientific Approach.* Bagsvaerd: HO and Storm.

8. Bangsbo, J., F.M. Iaia, and P. Krustrup. 2008. The yo-yo intermittent recovery test: A useful tool for evaluation of physical performance in intermittent sports. *Sports Medicine,* 38(1): 37-51.

9. Krustrup, P., M. Mohr, T. Amstrup, T. Rysgaard, J. Johansen, A. Steensberg, A. Pedersen, and J. Bangsbo. 2003. The yo-yo intermittent recovery test: Physiological response, reliability, and validity. *Medicine and Science in Sports and Exercise,* 35(4), 697-705.

10. Krustrup, P., M. Mohr, H. Ellingsgaard, and J. Bangsbo. 2005. Physical demands during an elite female soccer game: Importance of training status. *Medicine and Science in Sports and Exercise,* 37(7): 1242-1248.

11. Hill, D.W., and C.S. Ferguson. 1999. A physiological description of critical velocity. *European Journal of Applied Physiology and Occupational Physiology,* 79(3): 290-293.

12. Murias, J.M., J.M. Kowalchuk, and D.H. Paterson. 2010. Time course and mechanisms of adaptations in cardiorespiratory fitness with endurance training in older and young men. *Journal of Applied Physiology,* 108(3): 621-627.

13. Billat, V.L., N. Blondel, and S. Berthoin. 1999. Determination of the velocity associated with the longest time to exhaustion at maximal oxygen uptake. *European Journal of Applied Physiology,* 80(2): 159-161.

14. Dupont, G., K. Akakpo, and S. Berthoin. 2004. The effect of in-season, high-intensity interval training in soccer players. *Journal of Strength and Conditioning Research,* 18(3): 584-589.

15. Burgomaster, K.A., G.J. Heigenhauser, and M.J. Gibala. 2006. Effect of short-term sprint interval

training on human skeletal muscle carbohydrate metabolism during exercise and time-trial performance. *Journal of Applied Physiology*, 100(6): 2041-2047.

16. Bangsbo, J., T.P. Gunnarsson, J. Wendell, L. Nybo, and M. Thomassen. 2009. Reduced volume and increased training intensity elevate muscle Na+-K+ pump alpha2-subunit expression as well as short- and long-term work capacity in humans. *Journal of Applied Physiology*, 107(6): 1771-1780.

17. Helgerud, J., L.C. Engen, U. Wisloff, and J. Hoff. 2001. Aerobic endurance training improves soccer performance. *Medicine and Science in Sports and Exercise*, 33(11): 1925-1931.

18. Nédélec, M., A. McCall, C. Carling, F. Legall, S. Berthoin, and G. Dupont. 2012. Recovery in soccer part I: Post-match fatigue and time course of recovery. *Sports Medicine*, 42(12): 997-1015.

19. Paavolainen, L., K. Häkkinen, I. Hämäläinen, A. Nummela, and H. Rusko. 1999. Explosive-strength training improves 5-km running time by improving running economy and muscle power. *Journal of Applied Physiology*, 86(5): 1527-1533.

20. Saunders, P.U., D.B. Pyne, R.D. Telford, and J.A. Hawley. 2004. Factors affecting running economy in trained distance runners. *Sports Medicine*, 34(7): 465-485.

21. Millet, G.P., B. Roels, L. Schmitt, X. Woorons, and J.P. Richalet. 2010. Combining hypoxic methods for peak performance. *Sports Medicine*, 40(1): 1-25.

22. Mujika, I., and S. Padilla. 2000. Detraining: Loss of training-induced physiological and performance adaptations part I: Short-term insufficient training stimulus. *Sports Medicine*, 30(2): 79-87.

23. Houmard, J.A., T. Hortobágyi, R.A. Johns, N.J. Bruno, C.C. Nute, M.H. Shinebarger, and J.W. Welborn. 1992. Effect of short-term training cessation on performance measures in distance runners. *International Journal of Sports Medicine*, 13(8): 572-576.

Chapter 17

1. Loy, S.F., J.J. Hoffmann, and G.J. Holland. 1995. Benefits and practical use of cross-training in sports. *Sports Medicine*, 19(1): 1-8.

2. Clausen, J.P., K. Klausen, B. Rasmussen, and J. Trap-Jensen. 1973. Central and peripheral circulatory changes after training of the arms or legs. *American Journal of Physiology*, 225(3): 675-682.

3. Pechar, G.S., W.D. McArdle, F.I. Katch, J.R. Magel, and J. DeLuca. 1974. Specificity of cardiorespiratory adaptation to bicycle and treadmill training. *Journal of Applied Physiology*, 36(6): 753-756.

4. Mutton, D.L., S.F. Loy, D.M. Rogers, G.J. Holland, W.J. Vincent, and M. Heng. 1993. Effect of run vs. combined cycle/run training on VO₂max and

running performance. *Medicine and Science in Sports and Exercise*, 25(12): 1393-1397.

5. Beachle, T., and R. Earle. 2008. *Essentials of Strength Training and Conditioning*. 3rd ed. Champaign: Human Kinetics.

6. Borg, G. 1970. Perceived exertion as an indicator of somatic stress. *Scandinavian Journal of Rehabilitation Medicine*, 2(2): 92-98.

Chapter 18

1. Selye, H. 1950. *The Physiology and Pathology of Exposure to Stress*. Montreal: Medical Publisher.

2. Spiering, B.A., J. Kraemer, J.M. Anderson, L.E. Armstrong, B.C. Nindl, J.S. Volek, and C.M. Maresh. 2008. Resistance exercise biology: Manipulation of resistance exercise programme variables determines the responses of cellular and molecular signalling pathways. *Sports Medicine*, 38(7): 527-540.

3. Matveyev, L.P. 1964. *Fundamentals of Sports Training*. Moscow: Progress.

4. Zatsiorsky, V.M. 1995. *Science and Practice of Strength Training*. Champaign: Human Kinetics.

5. Shepard, R. J. 2001. Chronic fatigue syndrome: An update. *Sports Medicine*, 31(3): 167-194.

6. Foster, R.G., and T. Roenneberg. 2008. Human responses to the geophysical daily, annual and lunar cycles. *Current Biology*, 18 (17): R784-R794.

7. Martin, J.C., A.S. Gardner, M. Barras, and D.T. Martin. 2006. Modelling sprint cycling using field-driven parameters and forward integration. *Medicine and Science in Sports and Exercise*, 38(3): 592-597.

8. Viru, A. 1995. *Adaptation in Sports Training*. Boca Raton: CRC Press.

9. Gabbett, T.J., and D.G Jenkins. 2011. Relationship between training load and injury in professional rugby league players. *Journal of Science and Medicine in Sports*, 14(3): 204-209.

10. Novas, A.M., D.G. Rowbottom, and D.G. Jenkins. 2003. Tennis, incidence of URTI and salivary IgA. *International Journal of Sports Medicine*, 24(3): 223-229.

11. Cormie, P., M.R. McGuigan, and R.U. Newton. 2010. Influence of strength on magnitude and mechanisms of adaptation to power training. *Medicine and Science in Sports and Exercise*, 42(8): 1566-1581.

12. Baar, K. 2009. The signalling underlying FITness. *Applied Physiology Nutrition Metabolism*, 34(3): 411-419.

13. Verkoshansky, Y.V. 1985. *Programming and Organisation of Training Process*. Moscow: FiS.

14. Ronnestad, B.R., J. Hansen, and S. Ellefsen. 2012. Block periodization of high intensity aerobic intervals provides superior training effects in trained cyclists. *Scandinavian Journal of Medicine and Science in Sports*. Doi:10.1111/j.1600-0838.2012.01485.x [epub ahead of print]

15. Issurin, V.B. 2010. New horizons for the methodology and physiology of training periodization. *Sports Medicine,* 40(3): 189-206.

16. Mujika, I. 1998. The influence of training characteristics and tapering on the adaptation in highly trained individuals: A review. *International Journal of Sports Medicine,* 19(7): 439-446.

17. Kelly, V.G., and A.J. Coutts. 2007. Planning and monitoring training load during the competition phase in team sports. *Strength and Conditioning Journal,* 29(4): 32-37.

Chapter 19

1. Matsui, T., T. Ishikawa, H. Ito, M. Okamoto, K. Inoue, M.C. Lee, T. Fujikawa, Y. Ichitani, K. Kawanaka, and H. Sova. 2012. Brain glycogen supercompensation following exhaustive exercise. *Journal of Physiology,* 590 (Pt 3): 607-616.

2. Ingham, S.A, H. Carter, G.P. Whyte, and J.H. Doust. 2008. Physiological and performance effects of low- versus mixed-intensity rowing training. *Medicine and Science in Sports and Exercise,* 40(3): 579-584.

3. Bogdanis, G.C., M.E. Nevill, L.H. Boobis, and H.K. Lakomy. 1996. Contribution of phosphocreatine and aerobic metabolism to energy supply during repeated sprint exercise. *Journal of Applied Physiology,* 80: 876-884.

4. Gaitanos, G.C., C. Williams, L.H. Boobis, and S. Brooks. 1993. Human muscle metabolism during intermittent maximal exercise. *Journal of Applied Physiology,* 75(2): 712-719.

Chapter 20

1. Wisbey, B., D. Pyne, and B. Rattray. 2011. Quantifying changes in AFL player game demands using GPS tracking: 2011 season. *AFL Research Board Report.* Melbourne: Australian Football League.

2. Aughey, R. 2011. Increased high intensity activity in elite Australian football finals matches. *International Journal of Sports Physiology and Performance,* 6: 367-379.

3. Champion Data. 2012. Official Statistics Provider to Australian Football League. Melbourne, Australia.

4. Cunniffe, B., W. Proctor, J. Baker, and B. Davies. 2009. An evaluation of the physiological demands of elite rugby union using global positioning system tracking software. *Journal of Strength and Conditioning Research,* 23(4): 1195-1203.

5. Vaz, L., M. Van Rooyen, and J. Sampaio. 2010. Rugby game-related statistics that discriminate between winning and losing teams in IRB and Super twelve close games. *Journal of Sports Science and Medicine,* 9: 51-55.

6. King, T., D. Jenkins, and T. Gabbett. 2009. A time-motion analysis of professional rugby league match play. *Journal of Sports Sciences,* 27(3): 213-219.

7. Sports Data. 2012. NRL Statistics. Sydney.

8. Bangsbo, J. 1994. *Fitness Training in Football: A Scientific Approach.* [English ed.]. Bagsvaerd: HO and Storm.

9. Reed, J.P., B.K. Schilling, and Z. Murlasits. 2013. Acute neuromuscular and metabolic responses to concurrent endurance and resistance exercise. *Journal of Strength and Conditioning Research,* 27(3): 793-801.

10. Hickson R. 1980. Interference of strength development by simultaneously training for strength and endurance. *European Journal of Applied Physiology,* 45: 255-263.

11. McCarthy, J., J. Agre, B. Graf, M. Pozniak, and A. Vailas. 1995. Compatibility of adaptive response with combing strength and endurance training. *Medicine and Science in Sports and Exercise,* 27(3): 429-436.

12. Gravelle, B., and B. Blessing. 2000. Physiological adaption of women concurrently training for strength and endurance training. *Journal of Strength and Conditioning Research,* 14(1): 5-13.

13. McCarthy, J., M. Pozniak, and C. Agre. 2002. Neuromuscular adaptations to concurrent strength and endurance training. *Medicine and Science in Sports and Exercise,* 34: 511-519.

14. Bell, G., D. Syrotuik, T. Martin, R. Burnham, and H. Quinney. 2000. Effect of concurrent strength and endurance training on skeletal muscle properties and hormone concentrations in humans. *Journal of Applied Physiology,* 81: 418-427.

15. Hakkinen, K., M. Alen, W. Kraemer, E. Gorostiaga, M. Izquierdo, H. Rusko, J. Mikkola, A. Hakkinen, H. Valkeinen, E. Kaarkainen, S. Romu, V. Erola, J. Ahtiainen, and L. Paavolainen. 2003. Neuromuscular adaptations during concurrent strength and endurance training versus strength training. *European Journal of Applied Physiology,* 89: 42-52.

16. Chtara, M., A. Chaouachi, G. Levin, M. Chaouachi, K. Chamari, M. Amri, and P. Laursen. 2008. Effect of concurrent endurance and circuit resistance training sequence on muscular strength and power development. *Journal of Strength and Conditioning Research,* 22(4): 1037-1045.

17. Hennessey, L., and A. Watson. 1994. The interference effects of training for strength and endurance simultaneously. *Journal of Strength and Conditioning Research,* 8(1): 12-19.

18. Rhea, M., J. Oliverson, G. Marshall, M. Peterson, J. Kenn, and F. Ayllon. 2008. Noncompatibility of power and endurance training among college

baseball players. *Journal of Strength and Conditioning Research*, 22(1): 230-234.

19. Ronnestad, B., and E. Hansen. 2012. High volume of endurance training impairs adaptations to 12 weeks of strength training in well-trained endurance athletes. *European Journal of Applied Physiology*, 112: 1457-1466.

20. Leverett, M., and P. Abernethy. 1999. Acute effects of high intensity endurance exercise on subsequent resistance activity. *Journal of Strength and Conditioning Research*, 13(1): 47-51.

21. Kraemer, W., J. Patton, S. Gordon, E. Harman, M. Deschenes, K. Reynolds, R. Newton, N. Triplett, and J. Dziados. 1995. Compatibility of high-intensity strength and endurance training on hormonal and skeletal muscle adaptations. *Journal of Applied Physiology*, 78: 976-989.

22. Terada, S., K. Kawanaka, M. Goto, T. Shimokawa, and I. Tabata. 2005. Effects of high-intensity intermittent swimming on PGC-1a protein expression in rat skeletal muscle. *Acta Physiologica Scandinavica*, 184(1): 59-65.

23. Terzis, G., G. Georgiadis, G. Stratkos, I. Vogiatzis, S. Kavouras, P. Manta, H. Mascher, and E. Blomstrand. 2008. Resistance exercise-induced increase muscle mass correlates with p70S6 kinase phosphorylation in human subjects. *European Journal of Applied Physiology*, 102: 145-152.

24. Baar, K. 2008. Beyond genes: Maximising strength and endurance. *Peak Performance Journal*, 263: 8-11.

25. Chromiak, J., and D. Mulvaney. 1990. A review: The effects of combined strength and endurance training on strength development. *Journal of Applied Sports Science Research*, 4: 55-60.

26. Ono, M., M. Myashita, and T. Asami. 1976. Inhibitory effects of long distance running training on the vertical jump and other performances among aged males. In P.V. Komi (ed.), *Biomechanics v-b* (pp. 94-100). Baltimore: University Park Press..

27. Wilson, J., P. Marin, M. Rhea, S. Wilson, J. Loenneke, and J. Anderson. 2012. Concurrent training: A meta-analysis examining interference of aerobic and resistance exercises. *Journal of Strength and Conditioning Research*, 26(8): 2293-2307.

28. Silva, R.F., E.L. Cadore, G. Kothe, M. Guedes, C.L. Alberton, S.S. Pinto, R.S. Pinto, G. Trindade, and L.F.M. Kruel. 2012. Concurrent training with different aerobic exercises. *International Journal of Sports Medicine*, 33(8): 627-634.

29. Baker, D. 2001. The effects of an in-season of concurrent training on maintenance of maximal strength and power in professional and college-aged rugby league football players. *Journal of Strength and Conditioning Research*, 15(2): 172-177.

30. Baker, D. 2007. Cycle length variations in periodised strength/power training. *Journal of Strength and Conditioning Research*, 29(4): 10-17.

Chapter 21

1. Bangsbo, J., F.M. Iaia, and P. Krustrup. 2008. The yo-yo intermittent recovery test: A useful tool for evaluation of physical performance in intermittent sports. *Sports Medicine*, 38(1): 37-51.

2. Gabbett, T.J., and S. Ullah. 2012. Relationship between running loads and soft-tissue injury in elite team sport athletes. *Journal of Strength and Conditioning Research*. 26(4): 953-960.

3. Simao, R., B.F. de Salles, T. Figueiredo, I. Dias, and J.M. Willardson. 2012. Exercise order in resistance training. *Sports Medicine*, 42(3): 251-265.

4. Uchida, M.C., B.T. Crewther, C. Ugrinowitsch, R.F.P. Bacurau, A.S. Moriscot, and M.S. Aoki. 2009. Hormonal responses to different resistance exercise schemes of similar total volume. *Journal of Strength and Conditioning Research*, 23(7): 2003-2008.

5. Prestes, J., A.B. Frollini, C. de Lima, F.F. Donatto, D. Foschini, R. de Cássia Marqueti, A. Figueira Jr., and S.J. Fleck. 2009. Comparison between linear and daily undulating periodized resistance training to increase strength. *Journal of Strength and Conditioning Research*, 23(9): 2437-2442.

6. Astorino, T.A., R.P. Allen, D.W. Roberson, and M. Jurancich. 2012. Effect of high-intensity interval training on cardiovascular function, $\dot{V}O_2$max, and muscular force. *Journal of Strength and Conditioning Research*, 26(1): 138-145.

7. Berthoin, S., F. Mantéca, M. Gerbeaux, and G. Lensel-Corbeil. 1995. Effect of a 12-week training programme on Maximal Aerobic Speed (MAS) and running time to exhaustion at 100% of MAS for students aged 14 to 17 years. *Journal of Sports Medicine and Physical Fitness*, 35(4): 251-256.

8. Impellizzeri, F.M., S.M. Marcora, C. Castagna, T. Reilly, A. Sassi, F.M. Iaia, and E. Rampinini. 2006. Physiological and performance effects of generic versus specific aerobic training in soccer players. *International Journal of Sports Medicine*, 27(6): 483-492.

9. Kirkendall, D.T., and J. Dvorak. 2010. Effective injury prevention in soccer. *Physician and Sportsmedicine*, 38(1): 147-157.

10. Gabbett, T.J., B. Abernethy, and D.G. Jenkins. 2012. Influence of field size on the physiological and skill demands of small-sided games in junior and senior rugby league players. *Journal of Strength and Conditioning Research*, 26(2): 487-491.

11. Hill-Haas, S.V., B. Dawson, F.M. Impellizzeri, and A.J. Coutts. 2011. Physiology of small-sided games training in football: A systematic review. *Sports Medicine*, 41(3): 199-220.

12. Steffen, K., G. Myklebust, O.E. Olsen, I. Holme, and R. Bahr. 2008. Preventing injuries in female youth football: A cluster-randomized controlled trial.

Scandinavian Journal of Medicine and Science in Sports, 18(5): 605-614.

13. Zebis, M.K., L.L. Andersen, J. Bencke, M. Kjaer, and P. Aagaard. 2009. Identification of athletes at future risk of anterior cruciate ligament ruptures by neuromuscular screening. *American Journal of Sports Medicine,* 37(10): 1967-1973.

14. Quinn, K., P. Parker, R. de Bie, B. Rowe, and H. Handoll. 2000. Interventions for preventing ankle ligament injuries. *Cochrane Database of Systematic Reviews,* 2, CD000018.

15. Castellano, J., A. Blanco-Villasenor, and D. Alvarez. 2011. Contextual variables and time-motion analysis in soccer. *International Journal of Sports Medicine,* 32(6): 415-421.

16. Rampinini, E., F.M. Impellizzeri, C. Castagna, A.J. Coutts, and U. Wisloff. 2009. Technical performance during soccer matches of the Italian Serie A league: Effect of fatigue and competitive level. *Journal of Science and Medicine in Sport,* 12(1): 227-233.

17. Lamberts, R.P., J. Swart, B. Capostagno, T.D. Noakes, and M.I. Lambert. 2010. Heart rate recovery as a guide to monitor fatigue and predict changes in performance parameters. *Scandinavian Journal of Medicine and Science in Sports,* 20(3): 449-457.

18. Bradley, P.S., M. Mohr, M. Bendiksen, M.B. Randers, M. Flindt, C. Barnes, P. Hood, A. Gomez, J.L. Andersen, M. Di Mascio, J. Bangsbo, and P. Krustrup. 2011. Sub-maximal and maximal yo-yo intermittent endurance test level 2: Heart rate response, reproducibility and application to elite soccer. *European Journal of Applied Physiology and Occupational Physiology,* 111(6): 969-978.

19. Roecker, K., H. Striegel, H.H. Dickhuth. 2003. Heart-rate recommendations: Transfer between running and cycling exercise? *International Journal of Sports Medicine,* 24(3): 173-178.

Chapter 22

1. Bompa, T.O., and G.G. Haff. 2009. *Periodization: Theory and Methodology of Training.* 5th ed. Champaign: Human Kinetics.

2. Pyne, D.B., I. Mujika, and T. Reilly. 2009. Peaking for optimal performance: Research limitations and future directions. *Journal of Sports Sciences,* 27(3): 195-202.

3. Zatsiorsky, V.M., and W.J. Kraemer. 2006. *Science and Practice of Strength Training.* 2nd ed. Champaign: Human Kinetics.

4. Mujika, I. 2010. Intense training: The key to optimal performance before and during the taper. *Scandinavian Journal of Medicine and Science in Sports,* 20(Suppl 2): 24-31.

5. Bosquet, L., J. Montpetit, D. Arvisais, and I. Mujika. 2007. Effects of tapering on performance: A meta-analysis. *Medicine and Science in Sports and Exercise,* 39(8): 1358-1365.

6. Wenger, H.A., and G.J. Bell. 1986. The interactions of intensity, frequency and duration of exercise training in altering cardiorespiratory fitness. *Sports Medicine,* 3(5): 346-356.

7. Flynn, M.G., F.X. Pizza, J.B. Boone Jr., F.F. Andres, T.A. Michaud, and J.R. Rodriguez-Zayas. 1994. Indices of training stress during competitive running and swimming seasons. *International Journal of Sports Medicine,* 15(1): 21-26.

8. Houmard, J.A. 1996. Tapering for the competitive cyclist. *Performance Conditioning for Cyclists,* 2(7): 1-8.

9. Houmard, J.A., and R.A. Johns. 1994. Effects of taper on swim performance: Practical implications. *Sports Medicine,* 17(4): 224-232.

10. Houmard, J.A., B.K. Scott, C.L. Justice, and T.C. Chenier. 1994. The effects of taper on performance in distance runners. *Medicine and Science in Sports and Exercise,* 26(5): 624-631.

11. Mujika, I. 1998. The influence of training characteristics and tapering on the adaptation in highly trained individuals: A review. *International Journal of Sports Medicine,* 19(7): 439-446.

12. Mujika, I., T. Busso, L. Lacoste, F. Barale, A. Geyssant, and J.C. Chatard. 1996. Modeled responses to training and taper in competitive swimmers. *Medicine and Science in Sports and Exercise,* 28(2): 251-258.

13. Mujika, I., A. Goya, S. Padilla, A. Grijalba, E. Gorostiaga, and J. Ibanez. 2000. Physiological responses to a 6-d taper in middle-distance runners: Influence of training intensity and volume. *Medicine and Science in Sports and Exercise,* 32(2): 511-517.

14. Neufer, P.D. 1989. The effect of detraining and reduced training on the physiological adaptations to aerobic exercise training. *Sports Medicine,* 8(5): 302-320.

15. Zarkadas, P.C., J.B. Carter, and E.W. Banister. 1995. Modelling the effect of taper on performance, maximal oxygen uptake, and the anaerobic threshold in endurance triathletes. *Advances in Experimental Medicine and Biology,* 393: 179-186.

16. Bosquet, L., L. Leger, and P. Legros. 2002. Methods to determine aerobic endurance. *Sports Medicine,* 32(11): 675-700.

17. Mujika, I., A. Goya, E. Ruiz, A. Grijalba, J. Santisteban, and S. Padilla. 2002. Physiological and performance responses to a 6-day taper in middle-distance runners: Influence of training frequency. *International Journal of Sports Medicine,* 23(5): 367-373.

18. Mujika, I., and A. Padilla. 2003. Scientific bases for precompetition tapering strategies. *Medicine and Science in Sports and Exercise,* 35(7): 1182-1187.

19. Mujika, I., S. Padilla, D. Pyne, and T. Busso. 2004. Physiological changes associated with the pre-event taper in athletes. *Sports Medicine,* 34(13): 891-927.

20. Smith, D.J. 2003. A framework for understanding the training process leading to elite performance. *Sports Medicine,* 33(15): 1103-1126.

21. Trappe, S., D. Costill, and R. Thomas. 2000. Effect of swim taper on whole muscle and single muscle fiber contractile properties. *Medicine and Science in Sports and Exercise,* 32(12): 48-56.

22. Thomas, L., T. Busso. 2005. A theoretical study of taper characteristics to optimize performance. *Medicine and Science in Sports and Exercise,* 37(9): 1615-1621.

23. Mujika, I., and S. Padilla. 2000. Detraining: Loss of training-induced physiological and performance adaptations part I: Short term insufficient training stimulus. *Sports Medicine,* 30(2): 79-87.

24. Busso T. 2003. Variable dose-response relationship between exercise training and performance. *Medicine and Science in Sports and Exercise,* 35(7): 1188-1195.

25. Stone, M.H., M.E. Stone, and W.A. Sands. 2007. *Principles and Practice of Resistance Training.* Champaign: Human Kinetics.

26. Busso, T., K. Häkkinen, A. Pakarinen, H. Kauhanen, P.V. Komi, and J.R. Lacour. 1992. Hormonal adaptations and modeled responses in elite weightlifters during 6 weeks of training. *European Journal of Applied Physiology,* 64(4): 381-386.

27. Zatsiorsky, V.M. 1995. *Science and Practice of Strength Training.* Champaign: Human Kinetics.

28. Plisk, S.S., and M.H. Stone. 2003. Periodization strategies. *Strength and Conditioning,* 25(6): 19-37.

29. Viru, A. 1995. *Adaptations in Sports Training.* Boca Raton: CRC Press.

30. Kubukeli, Z.N., T.D. Noakes, and S.C. Dennis. 2002. Training techniques to improve endurance exercise performances. *Sports Medicine,* 32(8): 489-509.

31. Mujika, I. 2009. *Tapering and Peaking for Optimal Performance.* Champaign: Human Kinetics.

32. Hooper, S.L., L.T. Mackinnon, and A. Howard. 1999. Physiological and psychometric variables for monitoring recovery during tapering for major competition. *Medicine and Science in Sports and Exercise,* 31(8): 1205-1210.

33. Raglin, J.S., D.M. Koceja, J.M. Stager, and C.A. Harms. 1996. Mood, neuromuscular function, and performance during training in female swimmers. *Medicine and Science in Sports and Exercise,* 28(3): 372-377.

34. Mujika, I., S. Padilla, and D. Pyne. 2002. Swimming performance changes during the final 3 weeks of training leading to the Sydney 2000 Olympic Games. *International Journal of Sports Medicine,* 23(8): 582-587.

35. McGuigan, M.R., and M.K. Kane. 2004. Reliability of performance of elite Olympic weightlifters. *Journal of Strength and Conditioning Research,* 18(3): 650-653.

36. Hopkins, W.G. 2005. Competitive performance of elite track and field athletes: Variability and smallest worthwhile enhancements. *Sportscience,* 9: 17-20.

37. Chtourou, H., A. Chaouachi, T. Driss, M. Dogui, D.G. Behm, K. Chamari, and N. Souissi. 2012. The effect of training at the same time of day and tapering period on the diurnal variation of short exercise performances. *Journal of Strength and Conditioning Research,* 26(3): 697-708.

38. Hellard, P., M. Avalos, G. Millet, L. Lacoste, F. Barale, and J.C. Chatard. 2005. Modeling the residual effects and threshold saturation of training: A case study of Olympic swimmers. *Journal of Strength and Conditioning Research,* 19(1): 67-75.

39. Martin, D.T., J.C. Scifres, S.D. Zimmerman, and J.G. Wilkinson. 1994. Effects of interval training and a taper on cycling performance and isokinetic leg strength. *International Journal of Sports Medicine,* 15(8): 485-491.

40. Neary, J.P., T.P. Martin, and H.A. Quinney. 2003. Effects of taper on endurance cycling capacity and single muscle fiber properties. *Medicine and Science in Sports and Exercise,* 35(11): 1875-1881.

41. Papoti, M., L.E. Martins, S.A. Cunha, A.M. Zagatto, and C.A. Gobatto. 2007. Effects of taper on swimming force and swimmer performance after an experimental ten-week training program. *Journal of Strength and Conditioning Research,* 21(2): 538-542.

42. Shepley, B., J.D. MacDougall, N. Cipriano, J.R. Sutton, M.A. Tarnopolsky, and G. Coates. 1992. Physiological effects of tapering in highly trained athletes. *Journal of Applied Physiology,* 72(2): 706-711.

43. Izquierdo, M., J. Ibanez, J.J. Gonzalez-Badillo, N.A. Ratamess, W.J. Kraemer, K. Häkkinen, H. Bonnabau, C. Granados, D.N. French, and E.M. Gorostiaga. 2007. Detraining and tapering effects on hormonal responses and strength performance. *Journal of Strength and Conditioning Research,* 21(3): 768-775.

44. Coutts, A., P. Reaburn, T.J. Piva, and A. Murphy. 2007. Changes in selected biochemical, muscular strength, power, and endurance measures during deliberate overreaching and tapering in rugby league players. *International Journal of Sports Medicine,* 28(2): 116-124.

45. Gibala, M.J., J.D. MacDougall, and D.G. Sale. 1994. The effects of tapering on strength performance in trained athletes. *International Journal of Sports Medicine,* 15(8): 492-497.

46. Banister, E.W., J.B. Carter, and P.C. Zarkadas. 1999. Training theory and taper: Validation in triathlon athletes. *European Journal of Applied Physiology and Occupational Physiology,* 79(2): 182-191.

47. Graves, J.E., M.L. Pollock, D. Foster, S.H. Leggett, D.M. Carpenter, R. Vuoso, and A. Jones. 1990. Effect of training frequency and specificity on isometric lumbar extension strength. *Spine,* 15(6): 504-509.

48. Hickson, R.C., C. Foster, M.L. Pollock, T.M. Galassi, and S. Rich. 1985. Reduced training intensities and loss of aerobic power, endurance, and cardiac growth. *Journal of Applied Physiology*, 58(2): 492-499.

49. Houmard, J.A., D.L. Costill, J.B. Mitchell, S.H. Park, W.J. Fink, and J.M. Burns. 1990. Testosterone, cortisol, and creatine kinase levels in male distance runners during reduced training. *International Journal of Sports Medicine*, 11(1): 41-45.

50. Houmard, J.A., D.L. Costill, J.B. Mitchell, S.H. Park, R.C. Hickner, and J.N. Roemmich. 1990. Reduced training maintains performance in distance runners. *International Journal of Sports Medicine*, 11(1): 46-52.

51. Houmard, J.A., J.P. Kirwan, M.G. Flynn, and J.B. Mitchell. 1989. Effects of reduced training on submaximal and maximal running responses. *International Journal of Sports Medicine*, 10(1): 30-33.

52. Neufer, P.D., D.L. Costill, R.A. Fielding, M.G. Flynn, and J.P. Kirwan. 1987. Effect of reduced training on muscular strength and endurance in competitive swimmers. *Medicine and Science in Sports and Exercise*, 19(5): 486-490.

53. Johns, R.A., J.A. Houmard, R.W. Kobe, T. Hortobágyi, N.J. Bruno, J.M. Wells, and M.H. Shinebarger. 1992. Effects of taper on swim power, stroke distance, and performance. *Medicine and Science in Sports and Exercise*, 24(10): 1141-1146.

54. Mujika, I., J.C. Chatard, and A. Geyssant. 1996. Effects of training and taper on blood leucocyte populations in competitive swimmers: Relationships with cortisol and performance. *International Journal of Sports Medicine*, 17(3): 213-217.

55. Mujika, I., J.C. Chatard, S. Padilla, C.Y. Guezennec, and A. Geyssant. 1996. Hormonal responses to training and its tapering off in competitive swimmers: Relationships with performance. *European Journal of Applied Physiology and Occupational Physiology*, 74(4): 361-366.

56. Mujika, I., S. Padilla, A. Geyssant, and J.C. Chatard. 1998. Hematological responses to training and taper in competitive swimmers: Relationships with performance. *Archives of Physiology and Biochemistry*, 105(4): 379-385.

57. McConell, G.K., D.L. Costill, J.J. Widrick, M.S. Hickey, H. Tanaka, and P.B. Gastin. 1993. Reduced training volume and intensity maintain aerobic capacity but not performance in distance runners. *International Journal of Sports Medicine*, 14(1): 33-37.

58. Neary, J.P., Y.N. Bhambhani, and D.C. McKenzie. 2003. Effects of different stepwise reduction taper protocols on cycling performance. *Canadian Journal of Applied Physiology*, 28(4): 576-587.

59. Rietjens, G.J., H.A. Keizer, H. Kuipers, and W.H. Saris. 2001. A reduction in training volume and intensity for 21 days does not impair performance in cyclists. *British Journal of Sports Medicine*, 35(6): 431-434.

60. Neary, J.P., T.P. Martin, D.C. Reid, R. Burnham, and H.A. Quinney. 1992. The effects of a reduced exercise duration taper programme on performance and muscle enzymes of endurance cyclists. *European Journal of Applied Physiology and Occupational Physiology*, 65(1): 30-36.

61. Hickson, R.C., and M.A. Rosenkoetter. 1981. Reduced training frequencies and maintenance of increased aerobic power. *Medicine and Science in Sports and Exercise*, 13(1): 13-16.

Chapter 23

1. Crewther, B., J. Cronin, J. Keogh, and C. Cook. 2008. The salivary testosterone and cortisol response to three loading schemes. *Journal of Strength and Conditioning Research*, 22: 250-255.

2. Ives, J.C. and G.A. Shelley. Psychophysics in functional strength and power training: Review and implementation framework. *Journal of Strength and Conditioning Research*, 17(1): 177-186.

Chapter 24

1. Cheung, K., P. Hume, and L. Maxwell. 2003. Delayed onset muscle soreness: Treatment strategies and performance factors. *Sports Medicine*, 33: 145-164.

2. Gill, N.D., C.M. Beaven, and C. Cook. 2006. Effectiveness of post-match recovery strategies in rugby players. *British Journal of Sports Medicine*, 40: 260-263.

3. Cormack, S.J., R.U. Newton, and M.R. McGuigan. 2008. Neuromuscular and endocrine responses of elite players to an Australian rules football match. *International Joural of Sports Physiology*, 3: 359-374.

4. Horita, T. 2000. Stiffness regulation during stretch-shortening cycle exercise. [PhD thesis]. University of Jyvaskyla, Jyvaskyla.

5. Davies, R.C., R.G. Eston, D.C. Poole, A.V. Rowlands, F. DiMenna, D.P. Wilkerson, C. Twist, and A.M. Jones. 2008. Effect of eccentric exercise-induced muscle damage on the dynamics of muscle oxygenation and pulmonary oxygen uptake. *Journal of Applied Physiology*, 105: 1413-1421.

6. O'Reilly, K.P., M.J. Warhol, R.A. Fielding, W.R. Frontera, C.N. Meredith, and W.J. Evans. 1987. Eccentric exercise-induced muscle damage impairs muscle glycogen repletion. *Journal of Applied Physiology*, 63: 252-256.

7. Saxton, J.M., P.M. Clarkson, R. James, M. Miles, M. Westerfer, S. Clark, and A.E. Donnelly. 1995. Neuromuscular dysfunction following eccentric exercise. *Medicine and Science in Sports and Exercise*, 27: 1185-1193.

8. Jarvinen, T.A., T.L. Jarvinen, M. Kaariainen, H. Kalimo, and M. Jarvinen. 2005. Muscle injuries:

Biology and treatment. *American Journal of Sports Medicine,* 33: 745-764.

9. Jae, S.Y., K.S. Heffernan, S.H. Park, S.H. Jung, E.S. Yoon, E.J. Kim, E.S. Ahn, and B. Fernhall. 2010. Does an acute inflammatory response temporarily attenuate parasympathetic reactivation? *Clinical Autonomic Research,* 20: 229-233.

10. Crewther, B.T. and C.J. Cook. 2012. The effects of different pre-game motivational interventions on athlete free hormonal state and subseqent performance in professional rugby union matches. *Physiology and Behavior,* 106: 683-688.

11. Crewther, B.T., L.P. Kilduff, C.J. Cook, D.J. Cunningham, P. Bunce, R.M. Bracken, and C.M. Gaviglio. 2012. Relationships between salivary free testosterone and the expression of force and power in elite athletes. *Journal of Sports Medicine and Physical Fitness,* 52: 221-227.

12. Fry, A.C., B.K. Schilling, S.J. Fleck, and W.J. Kraemer. 2011. Relationships between competitive wrestling success and neuroendocrine responses. *Journal of Strength and Conditioning Research,* 25: 40-45.

13. Passerlegue, P., and G. Lac. 1999. Saliva cortisol, testosterone and T/C variations during a wrestling competition and during the post-competitive recovery period. *International Journal of Sports Medicine,* 20: 109-113.

14. Gleeson, M. 2007. Immune function in sport and exercise. *Journal of Applied Physiology* 103: 693-699.

15. Wilcock, I.M., J.B. Cronin, and W.A. Hing. 2006. Physiological response to water immersion: A method for sport recovery? *Sports Medicine,* 36: 747-765.

16. Paddon-Jones, D.J., and B.M. Quigley. 1997. Effect of cryotherapy on muscle soreness and strength following eccentric exercise. *International Journal of Sports Medicine,* 18: 588-593.

17. Howatson, G., and K.A. van Someren. 2008. The prevention and treatment of exercise-induced muscle damage. *Sports Medicine,* 38: 483-503.

18. Leeder, J., C. Gissane, K. van Someren, W. Gregson, and G. Howatson. 2011. Cold water immersion and recovery from strenuous exercise: A meta-analysis. *British Journal of Sports Medicne,* 46: 233-240.

19. Halson, S.L. 2008. Nutrition, sleep and recovery. *European Journal of Sport Science,* 8(2): 119-126.

20. Buchheit, M., J.J. Peiffer, C.R. Abbiss, and P.B. Laursen. 2009. Effect of cold water immersion on post-exercise parasympatheric reactivation. *American Journal of Physiology: Heart and Circulatory Physiology,* 296: H421-H427.

21. Al Haddad, H., J. Parouty, and M. Buchheit. 2012. Effect of daily cold water immersion on heart rate variability and subjective ratings of well-being in highly trained swimmers. *International Journal of Sports Physiology and Performance,* 7: 33-38.

22. Cochrane, D. 2004. Alternating hot and cold water immersion for athlete recovery: A review. *Physical Therapy in Sport,* 5: 26-32.

23. Vaile, J.M., N.D. Gill, and A.J. Blazevich. 2007. The effect of contrast water therapy on symptoms of delayed onset muscle soreness. *Journal of Strength and Conditioning Research,* 21: 697-702.

24. Stanley, J., M. Buchheit, and J.M. Peake. 2012. The effect of post-exercise hydrotherapy on subsequent exercise performance and heart rate variability. *European Journal of Applied Physiology,* 112: 951-961.

25. Davies, V., K.G. Thompson, and S.M. Cooper. 2009. The effects of compression garments on recovery. *Journal of Strength and Conditioning Research,* 23: 1786-1794.

26. Jakeman, J.R., C. Byrne, and R.G. Eston. 2010. Lower limb compression garment improves recovery from exercise-induced muscle damage in young, active females. *European Journal of Applied Physiology,* 109: 1137-1144.

27. Pournot, H., F. Bieuzen, J. Louis, R. Mounier, J.R. Fillard, E. Barbiche, and C. Hausswirth. 2011. Time-course of changes in inflammatroy response after whole-body cryotherapy multi exposures following severe exercise. *PLoS One,* 6: e22748.

28. Zagrobelny, Z., B. Halawa, C. Niedzielski, and A. Wawrowska. 1993. The influence of a single whole body cryostimulation on selected hemodynamic indices and hormone concentrations in the serum of healthy individuals. *Polski tygodnik lekarski,* 48: 303-305.

29. Wozniak, A., B. Wozniak, G. Drewa, C. Mila-Kierzenkowska, and A. Rakowski. 2007. The effect of whole-body cryostimulation on the pro-oxidant-antioxidant balans in blood of elite kayakers after training. *European Journal of Applied Physiology,* 101: 533-537.

30. Luczak, J., and J. Michalik. 2006. Wplyw skrajnie niskich temperatur na wybrane cechy motoryczne czlowieka. *Fizjoterapia polska,* 3: 206-201.

31. Chwalbinska-Moneta, J. 2003. Influence of whole-body cryotherapy on results of selected exercse response. *Sport wyczynowy,* 5-6: 461-462.

32. Lubkowska, A. 2010. Cryotherapy: Physiological considerations and applications to physical therapy. In J. Bettany-Saltikov and B. Paz-Lourido (eds.), *Physical Therapy Perspectives in the 21st Century: Challenges and Possibilites* (pp. 155-176).

33. Banfi, G., G. Melegati, A. Barassi, G. Dogliotti, G.M. d'Eril, B. Dugue, and M.M. Corsi. 2009. Effects of whole-body cryotherapy on serum mediators of inflammation andserum muscle enzymes in athletes. *Journal of Thermal Biology,* 34: 55-59.

34. Hausswirth, C., J. Louis, F. Bieuzen, H. Pournot, J. Fournier, J.R. Fillard, and J. Brisswalter. 2011. Effects of whole-body cryotherapy vs. far-infared

vs. passive modalities on recovery from exercise-induced muscle damage in highly-trained runners. *PLoS One*, 6: e27749.

35. Dodd, S., S.K. Powers, T. Callender, and E. Brooks. 1984. Blood lactate disappearance at various intensities of recovery exercise. *Journal of Applied Physiology*, 57: 1462-1465.

36. Beaven, C.M., C. Cook, D. Gray, P. Downes, I. Murphy, S. Drawer, J.R. Ingram, L.P. Kilduff, and N. Gill. 2013. Electrostimulation's enhancement of recovery during a rugby preseason. *Interntational Journal of Sports Physiology and Performance,* 8(1): 92-98.

37. Finberg, M., R. Braham, C. Goodman, P. Gregory, and P. Peeling. 2013. Effects of electrostimulation therapy on recovery from acute team sport activity. *Int Journal of Sports Physiology and Performance*, 8(3): 293-299.

38. Beaven, C.M., C.J. Cook, L. Kilduff, S. Drawer, and N. Gill. 2012. Intermittent lower-limb occlusion enhances recovery after strenuous exercise. *Applied Physiology, Nutriton, and Metabolism,* 37(6): 1132-1139.

39. Leeder, J., M. Glaister, K. Pizzoferro, J. Dawson, and C. Pedlar. 2012. Sleep duration and quality in elite athletes measured using wristwatch actigraphy. *Journal of Sports Sciences,* 30: 541-545.

40. Mah, C.D., K.E. Mah, E.J. Kezirian, and W.C. Dement. 2011. The effects of sleep extension on the athletic performance of collegiate basketball players. *Sleep,* 34: 943-950.

41. Cook, C.J., C.M. Beaven, L.P. Kilduff, and S. Drawer. 2012. Acute caffeine ingestion's increase of voluntarily chosen resistance-training load after limited sleep. *International Journal of Sport Nutrition and Exercise Metabolism,* 22: 157-164.

42. Cook, C.J., B.T. Crewther, L.P. Kilduff, S. Drawer, and C.M. Gaviglio. 2011. Skill execution and sleep deprivation: Effects of acute caffeine or creatine supplementation: A randomised placebo-controlled trial. *Journal of the International Society of Sports Nutrition,* 8: 2.

43. Waterhouse, J., G. Atkinson, B. Edwards, and T. Reilly. 2007. The role of a short post-lunch nap in improving cognitive, motor and sprint performance in participants with partial sleep deprivation. *Journal of Sports Sciences,* 25: 1557-1566.

44. Bravo, L. 1998. Polyphenols: Chemistry, dierary sources, metabolism, and nutritional significance. *Nutritional Reviews,* 56: 317-333.

45. Connolly, D.A., M.P. McHugh, O.I. Padilla-Zakour, L. Carlson, and S.P. Sayers. 2006. Efficacy of a tart cherry juice blend in preventing the symptoms of muscle damage. *British Journal of Sports Medicine,* 40: 679-683.

46. Howatson, G., M.P. McHugh, J.A. Hill, J. Brouner, A.P. Jewell, K.A. van Someren, R.E. Shave, and S.A. Howatson. 2010. Influence of tart cherry juice on indices of recovery following marathon running. *Scandinavian Journal of Medicine and Science in Sports,* 20: 843-850.

47. Howatson, G., S. Goodall, and K.A. van Someren. 2009. The influence of cold water immersions on adaptation following a single bout of damaging exercise. *European Journal of Applied Physiology,* 105: 615-621.

48. Pizza, F.X., D. Cavender, A. Stockard, H. Baylies, and A. Beighle. 1999. Anti-inflammatory doses of ibuprofen: Effect on neutrophils and exericse-induced muscle injury. *International Journal of Sports Medicine,* 20: 98-102.

49. Shirreffs, S.M., A.J. Taylor, J.B. Leiper, and R.J. Maughan. 1996. Post-exercise rehydration in man: Effects of volume consumed and drink sodium content. *Medicine and Science in Sports and Exercise,* 28: 1260-1271.

50. Gonzalez-Bono, E., A. Salvador, M.A. Serrano, and J. Ricarte. 1999. Testosterone, cortisol, and mood in a sports team competition. *Hormones and Behavior,* 35: 55-62.

51. West, D.J., C. Finn, D.J. Cunningham, D.A. Shearer, M.R. Jones, B. Harrington, B.T. Crewther, C.J. Cook, and L.P. Kilduff. 2013. The neuromuscular function, hormonal, and mood responses to a professional rugby union match. *Journal of Strength and Conditioning Research.* [epub ahead of print]

52. Foster, C. 1998. Monitoring training in athletes with reference to overtraining syndrome. *Medicine and Science in Sports and Exercise,* 30: 1164-1168.

53. Cook, C.J., and C.M. Beaven. 2013. Individual perception of recovery is related to subsequent sprint performance. *British Journal of Sports Medicine,* 47(11): 705-709.

54. Hellhammer, D.H., W. Hubert, and T. Schurmeyer. 1985. Changes in saliva testosterone after psychological stimulation in men. *Psychoneuroendocrinology,* 10: 77-81.

55. Cook, C.J., and B.T. Crewther. 2012. Changes in salivary testosterone concentrations and subsequent voluntary squat performance following the presentation of short video clips. *Hormones and Behavior,* 61: 17-22.

56. Crewther, B.T., and C.J. Cook. 2012. Effects of different post-match recovery interventions on subsequent athlete hormonal state and game performance. *Physiology and Behavior,* 106: 471-475.

57. Kiecolt-Glaser, J.K., G.G. Page, P.T. Marucha, R.C. MacCallum, and R. Glaser. 1998. Psychological influences on surgical recovery: Perspectives from psychoneuroimmunology. *American Psychologist,* 53: 1209-1218.

58. Peiffer, J.J., C.R. Abbiss, G. Watson, K. Nosaka, and P.B. Laursen. 2010. Effect of a 5-min cold-water

immersion recovery on exercise performance in the heat. *British Journal of Sports Medicine,* 44: 461-465.

59. Parouty, J., H. Al Haddad, M. Quod, P.M. Lepretre, S. Ahmaidi, and M. Buchheit. 2010. Effect of cold water immersion on 100m sprint performance in well trained swimmers. *European Journal of Applied Physiology,* 109: 483-490.

60. Yamane, M., H. Teruya, M. Nakano, R. Ogai, N. Ohnishi, and M. Kosaka. 2006. Post-exercise leg and forearm flexor muscle cooling in humans attenuates endurance and resistance training effects on muscle performance and on circulatory adaptation. *European Journal of Applied Physiology,* 96: 572-580.

61. Jansky, L., H. Janakova, B. Ulicny, P. Sranek, V. Hosek, J. Heller, and J. Parizkova. 1996. Changes in thermal homeostasis in humans due to repeated cold water immersions. *Pflugers Archiv,* 432(3): 368-372.

Index

Note: The italicized *f* and *t* following page numbers refer to figures and tables, respectively.

About the Editors

David Joyce is one of the first people in the world to lecture on and hold postgraduate master's degrees encompassing both sports science and sports medicine. He has trained, rehabilitated, and maintained multiple World and Olympic Champions, along with more than 100 national champions and 300 national representatives. The first athletic performance coach in history to work with Team China after having worked with another national Olympic team, Joyce is currently head of athletic performance at Western Force, the most traveled team in world sport, in the toughest club rugby competition in the world spanning Australia, New Zealand and South Africa. He lives in Western Australia.

Daniel Lewindon is uniquely qualified with postgraduate master's degrees in both sports science and sports medicine. He has more than 10 years' experience working full-time in elite sport, and is currently a physiotherapist for the England Rugby Team, a post he has held for more than four years. Working as part of a world leading Performance Team to ensure the health and performance of England's best rugby players, Lewindon is also a consultant physiotherapist for Red Bull extreme sports athletes. He lives in Market Harborough, UK.

About the Contributors

Mark Verstegen is one of the world's most innovative human performance experts. Verstegen pioneered the concept of integrated performance training and brought that system to top athletes, teams and sports organizations; the United States military; and companies such as Intel, Walgreens, LinkedIn, and Sheraton Hotels and Resorts. As the founder and president of EXOS, formerly Athletes' Performance and Core Performance, Verstegen leads more than 500 employees at performance centers in Arizona, California, Florida, and Texas, as well as supplying international support to top athletes and organizations. Verstegen and EXOS consult for high-performance companies including adidas, EAS, SKLZ, Keiser, and Axon Sports, helping with product and program inspiration, development, and testing, as well as consumer marketing. Verstegen serves as the director of performance for the NFL Players Association, where he focuses on player safety and welfare. He's regularly interviewed for training insight for publications and is a sought-after industry speaker who regularly presents at the leading conferences in the field. Verstegen is the author of six books, including *Every Day Is Game Day* (2014) and *Core Performance*. His widely acclaimed performance system is also available online through TeamEXOS.com.

Mike McGuigan is professor of strength and conditioning in the Sports Performance Research Institute New Zealand at Auckland University of Technology. He is associate editor-in-chief and section editor on resistance and strength training for the *Journal of Sports Science and Medicine,* senior associate editor for the *Journal of Strength and Conditioning Research,* associate editor for the *Journal of Australian Strength and Conditioning,* and an editorial board member for the *International Journal of Sports Physiology and Performance.* His research areas primarily are in strength and power development and the assessment and monitoring of training in high-performance athletes.

Rhodri S. Lloyd is senior lecturer at Cardiff Metropolitan University, Wales. He is a qualified physical education teacher and accredited strength and conditioning coach with the UK Strength and Conditioning Association (UKSCA) and the National Strength and Conditioning Association (NSCA). His research interests surround the impact of growth and maturation on long-term athletic development and

the neuromuscular mechanisms underpinning resistance training adaptations in youth. He has published extensively on athletic training for youth and co-edited the textbook *Strength and Conditioning for Young Athletes: Science and Application*. He was lead author for the 2014 International Consensus on youth resistance training and lead author for the UK (UKSCA) position statement on youth resistance training. He is a board director and paediatric lead for the UKSCA and is an executive council member for the NSCA Youth Training Special Interest Group. He has consulted on the long-term athletic development pathways of professional sports organisations including the Irish Rugby Football Union and the Lawn Tennis Association.

Jon L. Oliver is senior lecturer in exercise physiology at Cardiff Metropolitan University, Wales. He is at the fore of challenging existing and developing new models of youth athlete development. This has been supported by extensive experimental research examining the natural development and trainability of fitness during childhood and adolescence. His research extends beyond performance to consider potential injury risks and the wellbeing of youth athletes. He has collaborated with international governing bodies on research and worked in elite youth soccer, rugby union, martial arts, golf and athletics. He recently co-edited the textbook *Strength and Conditioning for Young Athletes: Science and Application*.

Craig Ranson is senior lecturer in sport and exercise medicine at Cardiff Metropolitan University and a sport physiotherapist with the Wales Rugby Team. His previous posts include chief physiotherapist with UK Athletics and national lead physiotherapist to the England and Wales Cricket Board. He consults with a variety of sport organisations including the International Cricket Council and the Sports Medicine Department of the University of the West Indies.

Andy Barr is director of conditioning with the New York Knicks of the National Basketball Association (NBA). After earning a physiotherapy degree at the University of Salford, in 2001 he joined Bolton as the first team physiotherapist. While at Bolton, Barr earned qualifications in Pilates and strength and conditioning and a master's degree in sports science and injury. In 2006 he became the head of sport science and medicine at Southampton. He returned to Bolton in 2007 as the head of the physiotherapy team. In 2009 he became the injury prevention specialist and then head physiotherapist for Manchester City. After Manchester City, he joined the New York Knicks where he has established himself as a leader in sport injury prevention and performance enhancement, specialising in movement screening, performance training, injury treatment and rehabilitation and performance monitoring. He consults with many professional sport teams and athletes and runs an innovative sport injury prevention and performance course called The Way To Move For Sport.

Sue Falsone is head athletic trainer and physical therapist for the LA Dodgers in Major League Baseball (MLB). Not only is Sue the first female head athletic trainer in MLB history, she is the first female head trainer in any of America's four biggest leagues (MLB, NFL, NBA, and NHL). She also is director of performance physical therapy for EXOS (formerly Athletes' Performance). She holds a master's degree in human movement science, specialising in sports medicine and lectures internationally on core stability and flexibility for athletic performance.

Aaron J. Coutts is professor in sport and exercise science at the University of Technology, Sydney (UTS). His research focuses around developing methods for quantifying training, managing fatigue and recovery and improving performance in team-sport athletes. He has published more than 100 scientific  articles and has been an invited speaker to many conferences. He is an accredited sport scientist with the Exercise and Sport Science Australia (ESSA) and is a consultant to several professional football clubs. He is a member of the International Advisory Board for NIKE SPARQ. Aaron is associate editor for the *International Journal of Sports Physiology and Performance* and an editorial board member for the *Journal of Science and Medicine in Sport*.

Stuart Cormack is senior lecturer in the school of Exercise Science at Australian Catholic University. He spent 14 years working in the Australian Football League including eight years as the fitness coach at the West Coast Eagles highlighted by appearing in two Grand Finals and  winning the 2006 AFL Premiership. He spent four years as strength and conditioning coach at the Australian Institute of Sport, where he worked with many elite athletes in preparation for the 2000 Sydney Olympics. He received his PhD from Edith Cowan University and is actively involved in applied sports science research. He is a Level 3 strength and conditioning coach and a Life Member of the Australian Strength and Conditioning Association. He has published in scientific journals, co-authored several book chapters and regularly presents at sports science and coaching conferences in addition to consulting with organisations including the International Cricket Council and Paris Saint-Germain Football Club. He is interested in all areas of athletic preparation with a particular focus on monitoring training load and fatigue in elite athletes and the impact of training load and fatigue on performance.

Rett Larson is project manager for EXOS (formerly Athletes' Performance) in China. He worked with many Chinese Olympic teams before moving to Shanghai to train elite athletes for the National Games. He was with Velocity Sports Performance for 10 years and became the  director of coaching at their headquarters in Newport Beach, CA. While at Velocity, he held various coaching and support positions and worked with many elite and professional athletes. He received his master's degree in exercise physiology from the University of North Carolina at Chapel Hill. While at UNC, he was an assistant strength coach with the football team and did his master's thesis on the effect of a weight-vested plyometric program on the vertical jump of elite athletes. Aside from coaching, he has been one of the primary fitness writers for *Volleyball Magazine* for the last 10 years.

Frans Bosch teaches at Fontys University for Applied Science, mainly in the fields of anatomy, biomechanics, strength training and motor learning. He earned a degree in physical education in 1977 and was employed as a PE teacher before becoming a self-employed expres-  sive artist and medical illustrator. In 1980 he started to work in athletics, coaching elite sprinters and Olympic high jumpers. For many years, he was the national coach for jumping events. He frequently consults internationally and appears as a conference speaker on training-related subjects. He has worked with the he English Institute of Sport, the Wales National Rugby Team, the British and Irish Lions, and the England Cricket Board. With Ronald Klomp, he wrote *Running, Biomechanics and Exercise Physiology Applied in Practice*, and recently published *Krachttraining en coördinatie, een integratieve benadering (Strength Training and Coordination: An Integrated Approach)* in the Netherlands.

Daniel Baker is president of the Australian Strength and Conditioning Association (ASCA) and has been a member of the National Strength and Conditioning Association (NSCA) since 1987. He is a Level 3 Master Coach of Elite Athlete Strength and Conditioning in the ASCA. He has a PhD in sport and biomedical science and more than 30 international peer-reviewed publications in the field of strength and conditioning. He has presented at international strength and conditioning conferences in Australia, the United States and the United Kingdom. As a strength and conditioning coach, he has trained professional and elite athletes in many sports including rugby league, rugby union, soccer, diving, track and field and powerlifting. He has been strength coach of the Brisbane Broncos Rugby League team since 1995, during which they have won four championships. A former competitive powerlifter, he still enjoys heavy lifting, surfing and relaxing with family and friends.

Derek M. Hansen is a sports performance consultant out of Vancouver, British Columbia, Canada. His areas of expertise include sport speed development, running mechanics, hamstring rehabilitation and electrical muscle stimulation for speed, strength and recovery. He works as the head strength and conditioning coach for Simon Fraser University in Burnaby, BC, the first non-United States university to achieve full membership and compete in the National Collegiate Athletic Association (NCAA). He has worked with numerous national teams competing in both the summer and winter Olympics for both Canada and the United States. A number of the athletes from those teams have achieved podium and world record performances. In the professional sporting world, Derek has worked with athletes and coaches from the NFL, NBA, MLB and NHL.

Jeremy Sheppard has been a strength and conditioning coach since 1993. He is head of strength and conditioning and sport science manager for Surfing Australia, and is senior lecturer in strength and conditioning at Edith Cowan University. He worked as senior strength scientist and coach for Queensland Academy of Sport, Australian Men's Volleyball, Australian Institute of Sport and Canadian Sport Centre. He has worked with professional teams in the NRL, NFL and AFL.

Sophia Nimphius is senior lecturer in the MSc: strength and conditioning at Edith Cowan University. She has been recognized for her research efforts, winning awards from the National Strength and Conditioning Association (NSCA), Australian Strength and Conditioning Association (ASCA) and Exercise and Sports Science Australia (ESSA). She is an elected member of the NSCA Research and Education Committee. She has authored or co-authored more than 30 peer-reviewed articles and conference abstracts and presented at more than 20 national and international conferences. She has been a strength and conditioning coach in the United States and Australia and currently is a consultant in strength and conditioning and biomechanics for several elite and junior athletes in softball, cricket, baseball, ARF, soccer and rugby. She was an NCAA scholarship athlete in both basketball and softball and played in state, national and international competitions in softball.

David Martin is the senior sport physiologist working within the department of physiology at the Australian Institute of Sport in Canberra and is also the national sport science coordinator for Cycling Australia. He provided support for Australian Cycling teams leading up to the 1996, 2000, 2004, 2008 and 2012 Olympic

Games. He received his bachelor of science degree in zoology from the College of Idaho, his master's degree in exercise physiology from Northern Michigan University and his PhD in physiology from the University of Wyoming. He worked as a research assistant at the United States Olympic Training Centre in Colorado Springs, Colorado. His master's research focused on stability of the anaerobic threshold training intensity and his doctoral research focused on better understanding peaking, tapering and overtraining in cyclists. He has more than 80 peer-reviewed publications, eight book chapters and many articles in popular cycling magazines. As an advisor to Olympic coaches and athletes, he is very interested in winning environments and methodology that reveals human potential.

Darcy Norman is director of the performance innovation team at EXOS (formerly Athletes' Performance) where he contributes to the innovations of the Adidas miCoach products. His was a fitness and rehabilitation coach for the German National Men's Soccer team, FC Bayern Munchen, and performance specialist for

HTC Highroad Pro Cycling. He received his physical education and biology degrees with an emphasis in athletic training and pre-med from Washington State University and physical therapy degree from the University of Washington. A licensed physical therapist, certified athletic trainer, and certified strength and conditioning specialist, his manual therapy skills were developed through the eclectic approach of the North American Institute of Manual Therapy (NAIOMT). His knowledge of functional biomechanics, pre- and post-rehabilitation, and testing come from the latest in continuing education and years of developing philosophies from working health-care professionals around the world.

Grégory Dupont is head of sport science for Lille Olympiqué Sporting Club (France). He implemented a research and development department in this club and is still involved in applied research with Lille North of France University. He worked as head of sport science for Glasgow Celtic FC (Scotland) from 2007 to 2009.

He graduated in 2003 with a PhD in sport science and exercise physiology from the University of Lille (France).

Anthony Rice works for the rowing program at the Australian Institute of Sport. He has been to two Olympic Games (Beijing and London) with the Australian rowing team and is currently the national physiology lead and performance science coordinator for the Australian rowing team. He has published

a number of peer-reviewed journal articles on the physiology, training load and performance aspects of elite level rowers. His other interests lie in applied sports technology and respiratory mechanics and energetics during intense exercise. Prior to working for the Australian Institute of Sport, he undertook a postdoctoral placement with professor Jerry Dempsey at the University of Wisconsin, where his studies focused on neural control of breathing during sleep and exercise.

Chris Spinks completed his undergraduate degree in human movement at the University of Technology, Sydney (UTS). He completed his master's by doing research in acceleration training for field-sport athletes. His professional career started at New South Institute of Sport (NSWIS), where he prepared athletes for state

and national events as well Olympic athletes heading to the Athens Games. Following this, he worked in Australian Rules Football with the Port Adelaide Football Club as a strength and conditioning coach. His next post was with the Fremantle Football Club as a senior strength and conditioning coach. He currently holds the position of physical performance manager at the Geelong Football Club.

Benjamin Rosenblatt is senior strength and conditioning coach for Great Britain and England Hockey and the English Institute of Sport. He was the senior rehabilitation scientist at the British Olympic Association's intensive rehabilitation unit and physically prepared athletes and teams for Olympic and

professional success. He is completing his PhD in a biomechanical evaluation of the principles of training. He also has a special interest in periodisation of training programmes for athletic success.

Joel Jamieson is regarded as one of the foremost authorities on strength and conditioning for combat sports. He has more than 10 years of experience working with many of the top fighters from all over the world and has trained more than 30 of the biggest names in MMA, including eight world champions. He served as director

of strength and conditioning for Pride FC, Dream FC and consulted for countless top-level teams and organisations. Joel is the founder of 8 Weeks Out, author of the highly acclaimed book *Ultimate*

MMA Conditioning and creator of the BioForce HRV Training Management System. He is a highly sought-after speaker and a regularly featured contributor to *Fight! Magazine* and *Fighting Fit* (UK).

Glenn Stewart is high performance manager at the West Coast Eagles Football Club in the AFL. He oversees the fitness and medical areas of the club together with initiating research into football-related areas of physiology, injury prevention and rehabilitation. He coaches the playing squad in speed development and assists the

coaching staff in developing programs for improving skill and decision-making. During his career at the Eagles, they have won three Premierships, played in four Grand Finals and participated in 16 finals series. He has a master's degree in physical education from the University of Western Australia. He was a sprints and hurdles coach for the WA Institute of Sport, where he coached athletes to Olympic and Commonwealth Games and the World Cup. As an athlete, he represented Australia in the long jump. He is a co-author of the book *Speed To Win* and author of *Strength and Conditioning for Netball*.

Darren Burgess is high performance manager at Port Adelaide Football Club (AFL). He was head of fitness and conditioning at Liverpool Football Club and head of sports science for Football Federation Australia as well as the Australian soccer team's fitness coach. Previously he worked as head of high performance at Port

Adelaide Football Club (2004 to 2007) and assistant fitness coach with Sydney Swans in the AFL (1997 to 2000), as well as head fitness coach with the Parramatta Power in the Australian National Soccer League (2002 to 2004). He worked as a video analyst with the Australian Olympic soccer team prior to the 2004 Athens Olympics. He completed his PhD in movement analysis of AFL and soccer in 2012. He has published many papers in peer-reviewed journals and is a reviewer for the *Journal of Sports Sciences* and the *Journal of Strength and Conditioning Research*. He also is a Nike Sparq performance expert.

G. Gregory Haff is a senior strength scientist and course coordinator for the Masters of Science in Strength and Conditioning at Edith Cowan University. He is a Level 2 ASCA strength and conditioning coach and a Level 3 Australian Weightlifting Association coach. He was the 2011 NSCA's William J.

Kraemer Sport Scientist of the Year award winner and served as the vice president of the NSCA, assistant editor and chief for the *Journal of Strength and Conditioning* and is senior associate editor for the *Journal of Strength and Conditioning Research*. He is a certified strength and conditioning specialist with distinction, a founding fellow of the NSCA, and an accredited member of the United Kingdom Strength and Conditioning Association. He is a national level weightlifting coach in the United States and has served as an outside scientist with the United States Olympic Training Centre's performance enhancement teams for weightlifting.

Stuart Yule is head strength and conditioning coach at Glasgow Warriors, a professional rugby team, competing in the Rabo Direct Pro12 and the Heineken Cup. He has 13 years' experience in strength and conditioning. He was a lead strength and conditioning coach for the Scottish Institute of Sport,

where he led and coordinated the strength and conditioning delivery for the West of Scotland athletes and sports and the Scottish judo and badminton squads. Stuart continued to work in judo after moving to the English Institute of Sport, where he became the lead strength and conditioning coach leading up to the 2008 Olympic Games. In 2009 Stuart briefly led the strength and conditioning programme for the Great Britain and England women's hockey team before moving to his current role with Glasgow Warriors. He represented Scotland at two Commonwealth Games in the sport of Olympic weightlifting. He has been Scotland's Strongest Man in both u90kg and u105kg categories and was second at Britain's Strongest Man u90kg.

Christian J. Cook obtained a PhD in paediatrics from Auckland School of Medicine. He first worked in medical research before working in both the physiology of stress and in related sport science in America's Cup yachting, international rugby and Olympic sports via UK Sport. He is professor in physiology at Bangor University.

Liam P. Kilduff obtained a PhD from Glasgow University examining the effects of creatine supplementation in health and disease. He has worked for the last 10 years as associate professor in applied sport physiology at Swansea University where his research interests focus on elite athlete preparation strategies. He works with

a number of summer and winter Olympic sports via UK Sport and also sits on the editorial board of two sport science journals.

Marc R. Jones is assistant strength and conditioning coach at the Scarlets regional rugby team in West Wales. He is undertaking a PhD on recovery in Rugby Union under the supervision of Dr Liam Kilduff. He obtained a bachelor of science degree in sport and exercise science at Loughborough University prior

to continuing his education at Swansea University and earning an master's in sport science in 2007. After two years with the Scarlets, he worked at the English Institute of Sport as a physiologist, providing support to the London Wasps before returning to the Scarlets in 2011. His main roles include the physical preparation of the development squad and the management and implementation of sport science provision within the region, which includes all testing and monitoring and several aspects concerning player recovery.

You'll find
other outstanding
sports and fitness resources at

www.HumanKinetics.com

In the U.S. call

1-800-747-4457

Australia 08 8372 0999
Canada 1-800-465-7301
Europe +44 (0) 113 255 5665
New Zealand 0800 222 062

HUMAN KINETICS
The Premier Publisher for Sports & Fitness
P.O. Box 5076 • Champaign, IL 61825-5076 USA